JUNIOR

PEARS

ENCYCLOPAEDIA

FIFTEENTH EDITION

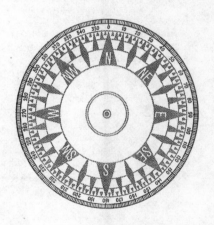

EDITED BY EDWARD BLISHEN

First published 1975

© *Pelham Books Ltd. 1975*

All enquiries to be addressed to
Pelham Books Ltd.,
52 Bedford Square WC1B 3EF

ISBN 0 7207 0843 5

*Printed and bound in Great Britain
by Richard Clay (The Chaucer Press), Ltd., Bungay, Suffolk*

About This Book

'How on earth,' someone asked me not long ago, 'do you set about editing an encyclopaedia?' 'Ah,' I said, eagerly, preparing to give a long, clear, riveting account of the process. 'Ah, well, what I do . . . What I do is—you see . . . hmm.' Then I dried up. What *did* I do? As hard to describe as the experience of being in a boxing ring with an opponent twice your size . . . Late in the autumn I send contributors the loose pages of last year's sections. With them go any letters of complaint or doubt or downright contradiction I've received from readers. ('Aren't you a foot out in the height of the Eiffel Tower?' 'I've personally measured the Simplon Tunnel and I must say . . .') To each contributor I write (poor, suffering fellows—as if they hadn't heard it before): 'We must work within the same space as usual. Not a page extra.' If we hadn't bound ourselves by that cruel rule, the book would now be three times as fat and ten times as expensive. Then come the phone calls and the urgent notes. Can we add a diagram, or an illustration, or alter one? Some international body has decided to change all the units used in science. Someone else has suddenly decided we're not to have a Channel Tunnel, after all. That ship at the top of the list on K8—it's sunk. Revised sections begin to come in, amazingly scribbled over. They go to the printer. They return. Meanwhile, the second and third ships on that list have vanished without a trace in the Arctic Ocean, the Government has resigned, and someone has decided we should use the old measurements in science, after all. I write to the Geography contributor: 'Thank goodness the heights of the waterfalls remain the same every year.' 'I was just going to tell you,' she replies, 'someone's remeasured that one in Outer Mongolia, and it's 100 feet less than they thought it was.'

Somehow it all gets done, and the result is *Junior Pears*. After all these labours, it's as free of error, and as up-to-date, as we can make it. (I'm a little sad, and even a little mad, when someone writes to say we're wrong on some fact or other, and it turns out that he's using the Third Edition.) The chief problem, as it happens, is always that one of space. Knowledge tends to expand: *Junior Pears*, as I've said, tries desperately to remain the same size. It's difficult for an encyclopaedia. Well, think what, strictly, the word means. Literally it means a volume, or set of volumes, that tells you everything about everything. Of course, the days when anyone could do that, if ever they existed, are long since over: but even so, an encyclopaedia can hardly be a slim volume. This, in fact, is a specialised encyclopaedia, for a particular audience. It's for young people, and is intended to provide information on the main topics in which, as we judge, young people are likely to be interested. Partly we hope it will be found a helpful handbook by students: thus the sections on history, geography, and so on. But no young reader is simply a schoolboy, or a schoolgirl, or a student: and though we hope your schooling is so wide-based that sections on sport and ships and railways and music may often have some bearing on what you're studying, still these and other similar sections are there mainly to supply information about out-of-school or out-of-college activities.

But if our basic purpose is to provide information, we've never wanted the book to be merely a bulging collection of facts. We've tried to make it pleasant to read as well as easy to consult: here, for example, are all the main facts about motor cars, but imbedded in a history of the motor-car, and an account of the workings and makings of the motor-car, that form, we hope, more than a dry assemblage of information.[1]

Nevertheless, we've tried to bear in mind that you ought to be able to track down as quickly as possible any single piece of information for which you have some desperate need: therefore each section is arranged so that it yields any particular fact as easily as possible. The list of contents on the title-pages of some sections will be found useful; and other sections, which lend themselves to such treatment, are in dictionary form.

But, of course, a single-volume encyclopaedia is not and could not be a substitute for deeper reading. You can learn from *Junior Pears* that the Gunpowder Plot occurred in 1605 and was a conspiracy to blow up James I and his Parliament; but for further details about James, or the conspirators, or the reasons for their obviously very keen dislike of the King and his supporters, you must look beyond *Junior Pears*. This is one kind of book—aiming to give the gleaming bare bones of information. For the flesh you must look to the other sorts of book to which we provide pointers here and there in our lists of 'Further Reading'.

Now and then, alas, a reader fails to find the bone he is after, or finds something amiss with the bone itself. If this happens to you, write to me about it. Complaints or comments of any kind—addressed to 52 Bedford Square, London, WC1B 3EF—will be taken into account in next year's revision. Behind certain changes in this 14th edition lie the very helpful suggestions made by many readers. On the whole, I'd be glad if you wouldn't ask me to carry out extensive research on some subject or other: I'd have to be twenty men to provide such a service. And now and then I've had the mean suspicion that I was being asked to do someone's homework. ('Please tell me everything about the French Revolution and let me have it, with maps, diagrams and time-charts, by next Monday at the latest.') But simpler inquiries, and certainly any criticism you wish to make, will be most welcome. A book like this ought to be shaped not only by a body of contributors but also by a body of readers, and all of us who are responsible for *Junior Pears* will welcome your collaboration.

---

[1] It may be worth giving our usual warning that this section has been found so useful by some fathers that the true owners of the book have been deprived of it. Keep it in a safe place.

Contents

About this Book . . . . **v**

THE WORLD

   1. Its History . . . . A 1–78

      A Diary of World Events—Index of Battles—
      Kings and Queens of Scotland—Historic Acts
      of Parliament—Explorations and Discoveries—
      British Prime Ministers—Presidents of the U.S.
      —The Royal Line—A Glossary of Political
      Terms—Government in Britain—The Com-
      monwealth—The United Nations.

   2. Its Geography . . . . . B 1–56

      The Earth: Some Facts and Figures—The
      Oceans and Seas: Their Areas and Depths—
      The Continents: Their Areas and Populations
      —The Largest Islands—The Countries of the
      World, by Continents—The Largest Cities—
      The Highest Mountains—Highest and Lowest
      Points in each Continent—Principal Volcanoes
      —Lakes of the World—Principal Rivers of the
      World—Great Waterfalls—Great Ship Canals
      —Principal Languages—Distances by air be-
      tween Main Cities—The Counties of Great
      Britain—Britain's Largest Cities, Highest
      Mountains, Largest Lakes—Important Rivers
      —London Boroughs—London Postal Districts
      —A Dictionary of Geographical Terms—
      Clouds—Other Influences on Weather—Violent
      Kinds of Weather—World Weather Records—
      British Weather Records.

   3. Its Famous People (Actual and Mythical) . C 1–50

      A Dictionary of Famous People—Names in the
      News—A Dictionary of Mythology.

A DICTIONARY OF SCIENCE AND MATHE-
MATICS   .   .   .   . D 1-52
Including Formulae, Conversion Tables, a
List of Elements and Atomic Weights, and
Scientific Laws.

A DICTIONARY OF RADIO AND TELE-
VISION   .   .   .   . E 1-34

A DICTIONARY OF AIRCRAFT, ROCKETS
AND MISSILES (with a section on Astronomy)   F 1-44

MOTOR CARS, MOTORCYCLES, THREE-
WHEELERS, SCOOTERS AND MOPEDS   . G 1-42
History and Development of Cars—How Cars
Work—Racing Cars—Land Speed Records—
Identifying Cars—Group Manufacturers—
History of Motorcycles—How Motorcycles
Work—Motorcycle Sport—Scooters—Mopeds
—Three-wheelers.

RAILWAYS (with a note on loco-spotting)   . H 1-34
A Short History of Railways in Britain—Some
Classic Steam Locomotives—How a Steam
Locomotive Works—Locomotives and Modern-
isation—How a Diesel Locomotive Works—
Electric Locomotives — Coaches — Brakes —
Track—Signalling—Freight Services—Rail-
way Speeds—The Channel Tunnel—Num-
bering and Loco-spotting—Preservation—
Some British Railways Facts and Figures —
World Railways Facts and Figures.

SHIPS   .   .   .   . K 1-18
Sailing-ships — Identifying Ships — Funnel
Markings and House Flags—The International
Code of Signals—Sirens—Distress Signals—
Measures of Wind and Wave—The World's
Biggest Ships—Fastest Atlantic Crossings
Before 1900—The Blue Riband: Record
Atlantic Crossings by Screw Steamers since
1900 — Naval Vessels — The Hovercraft —
Lights at Sea—A Dictionary of Nautical
Terms—Nautical Measures.

641 Arabs capture Alexandria, destroy its famous library.

643 The Arabs defeat armies of the Eastern empire at YARMAK.

669 Arabs unsuccessfully attack Constantinople from sea.

711 Having conquered East and North Africa, Arabs cross into Spain.

720 Spain subdued, the Arabs (with the Moors) invade France.

732 **Charles Martel** drives Arabs out of France.

751 **Pepin,** son of Charles Martel, crowned King of the Franks, founding Carolingian dynasty.

762 Baghdad founded; becomes capital of Arab empire.

768 Pepin dies; his kingdom divided between his sons Charles (later known as **Charlemagne**) and **Carloman**.

771 Carloman dies and Charlemagne takes possession of his lands. From then onwards Charlemagne enlarges his dominions until his power reaches from the Pyrenees to the river Elbe in Germany, and from the Atlantic to the Danube and Tiber.

786 **Haroun-al-Raschid** becomes Caliph at Baghdad; under him Arab empire is at its greatest.

800 Charlemagne crowned in Rome emperor of the Holy Roman Empire.

802 **Egbert** king of Wessex, one of seven Anglo-Saxon kingdoms fighting for supremacy in England. Others are Northumbria, Mercia, Kent, Sussex, Essex and E. Anglia.

809 Haroun-al-Raschid dies; beginning of 200 years of chaos and civil war in Arab empire.

Viking Ship

814 Charlemagne dies.

829 Egbert unites England for first time under one king.

840 Frankish empire is divided between Charlemagne's sons and grandsons, whose quarrels lead to its breaking up.

871 **Alfred the Great** king of Wessex, practically the only part of England not in Danish hands.

878 Alfred defeats Danes, compels them by Treaty of Wedmore to stay in their settlements in N.E. England and become Christians.

900 Alfred dies.

919 **Henry I** king of Germany; completes the separation of the Frankish empire into Germany and France.

987 **Louis V,** last Carolingian king of France, dies, and is succeeded by **Hugh Capet,** first modern French king.

1013 **Sweyn** of Denmark conquers England, is accepted as king.

1015 **Canute,** Sweyn's son, defeats **Edmund Ironside,** son of last Anglo-Saxon king, and divides realm with him.

1016 Edmund dies; Canute becomes sole king.

1042 **Edward the Confessor** returns to England as king from Normandy, where he has been living at the court of the Norman duke. Leaves government to **Earl Godwin,** devotes himself to religion.

1054 Eastern Orthodox Church breaks with Church of Rome.

1065 Westminster Abbey, rebuilt by Edward the Confessor consecrated.

1066 Edward the Confessor dies; **Harold,** son of Earl Godwin, elected king. **William** of Normandy invades England and kills Harold at HASTINGS.

1071 Seljuk Turks, having seized Baghdad, sweep across Asia Minor and take fortress of Niceaea opposite Constantinople.

1075 Turks take Jerusalem and Holy Places.

1086 Domesday Book, a survey of England, completed.

1095 **Pope Urban II** summons Christian nations to First Crusade.

1098 Crusaders take Antioch.

1099 Crusaders take Jerusalem.

1135 England plunged in civil war when **Stephen,** grandson of William the Conqueror, allows himself to be elected king although he had previously recognised **Mathilda,** Henry I's daughter, as heir to throne.

1149 Second Crusade ends in failure.

1153 Stephen acknowledges Mathilda's son as his heir.

1164 **Henry II** tries to bring English clergy into the power of the royal courts and clashes with **Thomas à Becket**, his chancellor and Archbishop of Canterbury, who flees to France.

1170 Becket returns, but the quarrel breaks out afresh, and he is murdered in Canterbury Cathedral.

1174 **Saladin** proclaimed caliph; launches a holy war of all Muslims against Christians.

1187 Saladin recaptures Jerusalem.

1189 Third Crusade, under **Philip Augustus** of France and **Richard I**, fails to retake Jerusalem. Siege of Acre.

1191 Crusaders capture ACRE.

1192 Richard concludes armistice with Saladin.

1202 Fourth Crusade; Constantinople captured.

1206 Mogul empire founded in India.

1215 **King John** is forced at Runnymede to accept Magna Carta, which lays it down that no freeman may be imprisoned or punished except by the law of the land.

1218–21 Fifth Crusade captures Damietta, in Egypt, but loses it again.

1228–29 Sixth Crusade recovers Jerusalem by negotiation.

1264 **Henry III**, whose misrule has caused barons to revolt, is taken prisoner at LEWES by **Simon de Montfort**.

1265 De Montfort summons first Parliament in which towns are represented; is defeated and killed at EVESHAM.

1273 **Rudolf of Hapsburg**, founder of dynasty that is to reign in Austria until 1918, elected Holy Roman Emperor.

1280 **Kublai Khan** emperor of China; encourages trade and teaches religious tolerance. Visited by **Marco Polo**.

1282 **Edward I** completes conquest of Wales.

1291 Acre, last Christian stronghold in Syria, is lost.

1295 Edward I summons Model Parliament, so called because for the first time King, Lords and Commons meet.

1296 Edward I attempts to annex Scotland.

1297 **Sir William Wallace** defeats Edward at STIRLING.

1298 Edward defeats Wallace at FALKIRK.

1301 Edward makes his son Prince of Wales.

1304 Wallace captured and executed, but **Robert Bruce** raises another revolt against Edward.

1306 Robert Bruce crowned king of Scotland.

1309 Papacy falls into French control; residence of the Popes moved to Avignon.

1314 **Edward II** defeated at BANNOCKBURN by Robert Bruce.

1328 Robert Bruce recognised by England as king of Scotland.

1337 Outbreak of 'Hundred Years' War' between England and France. Causes: a conflict of commercial interests and Edward III's claim to French throne.

1340 English defeat French by sea at SLUYS.

1346 **Edward III** defeats French at CRECY.

1347 Edward captures Calais.

1348–49 Black Death, the bubonic plague, reaches England, killing nearly one half of the population, and causing acute shortage of labour and social unrest.

1356 **Edward, the Black Prince,** defeats French at POITIERS.

1369 French renew the war; reconquer province after province.

1372 English fleet destroyed. Impoverished by war, weakened by quarrels between Black Prince and his brother, **John of Gaunt,** England loses all her French possessions except Bordeaux and Calais.

1378 Rival Popes elected in Rome and Avignon.

1381 Heavily taxed, tied to the land as serfs, the peasants revolt under **Wat Tyler.** Tyler is murdered and the rising crushed, but from this time serfdom gradually declines.

1384 Death of **John Wycliffe,** who has attacked abuses in the Church of Rome and ordered a translation of the Bible into English.

1385 Scots invade England; **Richard II** takes Edinburgh.

1388 Scots again invade; are victorious at OTTERBURN.

1397 Richard II executes or banishes leaders of the barons. Among those banished is **Henry, Duke of Hereford, John of Gaunt's** son and heir.

1399 John of Gaunt dies; Richard II confiscates his estates. Henry, Duke of Hereford, returns to England to lead revolt of the nobles. Parliament deposes Richard and accepts Henry as king—the first to speak English (grown out of Norman French and Anglo-Saxon) as his mother-tongue.

1400 Welsh revolt under **Owen Glendower.**

1403 Scots defeated at HOMILDON HILL. Henry IV crushes revolt at SHREWSBURY.

1415 **Henry V** renews war against France, captures HARFLEUR and is victorious at AGINCOURT.

1420 Henry V recognised by French king as his heir; marries French princess.

1422 Henry dies. French refuse to recognise his one-year-old son, **Henry VI**, as king of France; Henry V's brother continues war.

1429 English overcome all French resistance except in ORLEANS; they besiege the town, but are driven off by an army led by **Joan of Arc**.

1431 Joan of Arc, captured by the English, is burned at the stake; but French advance continues.

1445 **Johann Gutenberg**, first European printer, sets up business in Mainz.

1453 The Eastern empire is at an end when Constantinople falls to the Ottoman Turks, who sweep into Greece and across to the Danube.

1455 Disastrous end of Hundred Years' War had made the English government unpopular, and the **Duke of York** (white rose) claims the throne from Henry VI, a Lancastrian (red rose). So begin Wars of the Roses. Yorkists win at ST ALBANS, but are then defeated; York flees to Ireland.

1460 York returns, is victorious at NORTHAMPTON, but is defeated and killed at WAKEFIELD.

1461 Edward, York's son, proclaimed king in London as **Edward IV**. Defeats the Lancastrians at TOWTON; Henry VI is captured and imprisoned.

1464 Lancastrians defeated at HEXHAM.

1470 Yorkist **Earl of Warwick**, the 'Kingmaker', quarrels with Edward IV, frees Henry VI. Edward flees to Flanders.

1471 Edward returns, defeats and kills Warwick at BARNET and routs Lancastrians at TEWKESBURY.

1476 **Caxton** sets up as printer.

1478 Inquisition begins in Spain.

1483 Edward IV succeeded by 12-year-old son, **Edward V**. Richard, Duke of Gloucester, Protector of the Realm, has himself proclaimed king as **Richard III**. Edward V and his brother are murdered in the Tower.

1485 Henry Tudor, Earl of Richmond, lands in England and defeats Richard III at BOSWORTH. As **Henry VII**, he founds the line of Tudors, breaks the power of the nobles and establishes strong central government.

1492 **Ferdinand** of Aragon and **Isabella** of Castile, whose marriage unites Spain for the first time, finally free the country

The *Santa Maria* 1492

from the Moors by capturing GRANADA.

1513 James IV of Scotland invades England, is defeated at FLODDEN.

1517 Martin Luther, founder of Protestantism, nails to church door at Wittenberg his condemnation of many practices of the Church of Rome.

1519 Cortes conquers Mexico.

1520 Luther publicly burns the Papal Bull excommunicating him, and refuses to go back on his teachings. Protestantism spreads; is adopted in Sweden in 1527, in Denmark in 1536. In Switzerland it is established by **Calvin,** whose followers in France, the Huguenots, wage bitter wars with the Catholics between 1562 and 1598. In Scotland the Reformation, as this great movement is called, triumphs by 1560, largely owing to teaching of Calvin's disciple, **John Knox.**

1526 Baber, Moslem warrior king, captures Delhi.

1528 Conquest of Peru.

1529 The Ottoman Sultan, **Suleiman** the Magnificent, having taken Belgrade, the island of Rhodes and Budapest, attempts

The Tower of London

to storm Vienna but is beaten back.

Cardinal Wolsey, Henry VIII's chief minister, fails to persuade the Pope to grant Henry a divorce from **Catherine of Aragon**, and Henry dismisses him.

1533 Archbishop Cranmer dissolves Henry's marriage and crowns **Anne Boleyn** as queen.

1534 Henry VIII, though no Protestant, repudiates authority of the Pope, proclaims himself head of the Church and dissolves the monasteries, confiscating their wealth.

1536 Death of Catherine of Aragon; execution of Anne Boleyn. Henry marries **Jane Seymour**.

1538 Henry VIII excommunicated.

1540 Henry marries **Anne of Cleves**; later in the year marries **Catherine Howard**.

1542 Catherine Howard executed; Henry marries **Catherine Parr**.

1547 Ten-year-old **Edward VI** succeeds Henry VIII.

1549 & 1553 First Prayer Books in English are issued by Cranmer.

1553 Mary, Henry VIII's daughter and a Catholic, becomes Queen. **Lady Jane Grey**, to whom Edward VI had bequeathed the crown to avoid return to Catholicism, is also proclaimed Queen, but is arrested and executed. Cranmer is burnt at the stake and succeeded by a Catholic Archbishop of Canterbury. Supremacy of Pope again acknowledged. Persecution of Protestants marking Mary's reign wins her the nickname of 'Bloody Mary'.

1558 Calais, last French possession still in English hands, falls.

Elizabeth succeeds Mary and repudiates authority of the Pope. To spare England the bitter religious wars with which

Europe is being ravaged, she begins working out a religious compromise, in which the Protestant doctrines of the Church of England are mixed with many Catholic elements in its ritual.

1568 Mary Queen of Scots, Catholic and heir to Elizabeth, forced to flee to England; imprisoned by Elizabeth.

1571 Fleet of the Christian League, led by Spain, defeats Turkish fleet at LEPANTO and destroys Moslem sea power in Mediterranean.

1585 Elizabeth lands English army in Netherlands to support Dutch in their revolt against Spanish rule, and this brings into the open the undeclared war England has been fighting with **Philip of Spain** as a result of trade rivalry and religious differences.

1586 Battle of ZUTPHEN; **Sir Philip Sidney** slain.

1587 Mary Queen of Scots executed.
　　Drake attacks Cadiz.

1588 Philip of Spain sends Great Armada against England; it is destroyed by the English fleet under **Howard of Effingham,** Drake, **Hawkins** and **Frobisher.**

1603 Elizabeth dies; James VI of Scotland becomes king as **James I.** His High Church views displease the Puritans, and the powerful new merchant class is offended by his insistence on the Divine Right of Kings.

1605 Gunpowder Plot, a Catholic conspiracy to blow up James and his Parliament, is discovered.

1609 Holland frees herself from Spain; is soon to be a great power, leading the world in trade, art and science and founding an empire in East and West Indies.

1618 Outbreak of the Thirty Years' War, last attempt of the Catholics to stamp out the Reformation in Europe. The Catholics are at first successful, but the tide turns against them when in 1629 **Gustavus Adolphus** of Sweden comes in on the Protestant side.

1620 Pilgrim Fathers sail from Plymouth in the *Mayflower* to found the first colony in New England.

1628 Parliament refuse to vote **Charles I** any money until he has accepted their Petition of Right, which declares taxation without consent of Parliament and imprisonment without trial illegal.

1629 Charles dissolves Parliament, imprisoning its leaders. He

The *Mayflower* 1620

reigns without parliament for the next eleven years, raising
money by means regarded as illegal, and suppressing all opposition by special royal courts.

1632 Gustavus Adolphus wins the battle of LUTZEN but is slain.

1640 England invaded by Scots; Charles I obliged to recall
Parliament to raise money for the war. The 'Short' Parliament insists on airing its grievances before voting money,
and is dismissed. Charles has to summon new Parliament
immediately, and this (the 'Long' Parliament lasting until
1660) sets out to make personal government by a monarch
impossible.

1641 Irish rebel against English.

1642 Charles I goes to House of Commons to arrest his enemies,
finds them gone. Slips out of London and the Civil War begins. First battle, at EDGEHILL, is indecisive.

1644 Royalists defeated at MARSTON MOOR by **Cromwell.**

1645 Cromwell wins decisive victory at NASEBY.

1646 Charles surrenders to Scots.

1647 The Scots, having made alliance with Parliamentarians,
hand Charles over.

1648 Scots, uneasy about their alliance and encouraged by
Charles, invade England, are defeated by Cromwell at PRESTON.

1648 Thirty Years War ends without victor.

1649 Charles I executed. England, calling itself a Commonwealth, becomes a republic. Cromwell ruthlessly restores English rule in Ireland.

1650 Charles I's son, later **Charles II**, lands in Scotland, is crowned King of Scotland.

1651 Prince Charles invades England, is defeated by Cromwell at WORCESTER, and escapes to the continent.

1652–54 Trade rivalry between English and Dutch leads to war. Cromwell's navy, commanded by admirals like **Robert Blake**, holds its own against the mighty Dutch fleet.

1653 Cromwell becomes Lord Protector.

1655 Cromwell seizes Jamaica from Spain.

1658 Cromwell dies; is succeeded by his son, **Richard Cromwell**.

1659 Richard Cromwell resigns.

1660 **General Monk**, Commonwealth commander in Scotland, occupies London and invites Prince Charles to return as Charles II.

1664 War between Britain and Holland; British capture New Amsterdam and rename it New York.

1665 Great Plague of London.

1666 Great Fire of London.

1667 Dutch fleet sails up the Medway and destroys British squadron. Britain makes peace but keeps New York.

1670 Charles II makes secret Treaty of Dover with **Louis XIV** of France, promising to declare himself a Catholic, restore Catholicism in England and support Louis against the Dutch; in return Louis agrees to help Charles with money and, if necessary, troops.

1672 Charles suspends all laws against Catholics, and joins with France in attacking Holland. The Dutch, under **William of Orange**, hold up the French by piercing the dykes; the Dutch admiral **De Ruyter** puts the Anglo-French fleet out of action in SOUTHWOLD BAY.

1673 Charles II forced to summon Parliament to ask for money; is compelled to accept Test Act excluding all Catholics from office and to end war with Holland.

1678 **Titus Oates** announces 'Popish plot' to restore Catholicism in England. Attempt is made to exclude from the succession Charles's brother, **James**, a Catholic convert.

1681 **William Penn** establishes colony of Pennsylvania as refuge for persecuted Quakers.

1683 Turks make final effort to carry Islam into the heart of Europe; are defeated at VIENNA.

1685 Charles II dies; James, though a Catholic, becomes king as James II. **Monmouth**, illegitimate son of Charles II and a Protestant, tries to seize the throne, but is defeated at SEDGE-MOOR and executed.

1688 **William of Orange**, married to **Mary**, James's Protestant daughter, is invited to come over with an army to save the English constitution and Church. William lands at Torbay, and James II flees to France.

1689 The Crown is accepted by William and Mary after they have agreed to the Bill of Rights, limiting royal power. James II lands in Ireland to lead an Irish rising.

1690 William defeats James and the Irish at the battle of the BOYNE.

1701 Parliament passes the Act of Settlement confining the succession to Protestants.

Louis XIV uses a dispute over the succession to the Spanish throne to resume his plan to make France strongest European power. William forms Britain, Holland and Austria into 'Grand Alliance' to stop him.

1702 William dies; succeeded by **Anne.**

1704 **Marlborough's** victory at BLENHEIM saves Vienna from the French.

1704 **Admiral Rooke** captures Gibraltar.

1706 Marlborough defeats French at RAMILLIES.

1707 Act of Union between England and Scotland.

1708 Marlborough defeats French at OUDENARDE.

1709 Marlborough victorious at MALPLAQUET.

1710 Replacement of Whigs by Tories, who want to end the war, leads to Marlborough's downfall.

1713 War ends. Britain receives Newfoundland and Hudson Bay territory from France; Gibraltar and Minorca from Spain.

1714 Anne dies and Elector of Hanover becomes king as **George I.** He cannot speak English and has no interest in English affairs; his reign helps to make Parliament even more powerful, leads to the modern pattern of government by a cabinet of ministers.

1715 The 'Old Pretender', son of James II, lands in Scotland to find his supporters have already been defeated.

1720 A financial crisis, the 'South Sea Bubble', produced by wild speculation, ruins thousands.

    Sir Robert Walpole becomes first Prime Minister.

1739 Walpole, though anxious to preserve peace, is forced into war with Spain (the 'War of Jenkins' Ear').

1740 Hapsburg emperor, **Charles VI,** dies. The European powers have agreed to accept his daughter, **Maria Theresa,** as his heir; but France, Spain and Prussia ignore the arrangement. Prussia attacks Austria; France invades Germany. Britain and Holland enter this War of the Austrian Succession on Maria Theresa's side.

1743 **George II** defeats French at DETTINGEN—the last time a British king is personally in command in a battle.

1745 French defeat Austro-English army at FONTENOY. **Prince Charles Edward,** the 'Young Pretender', lands in Scotland and wins victory at PRESTONPANS. He invades England, but finds little support; his army returns to Scotland.

1746 The Jacobites (Charles Edward's followers) defeated at CULLODEN; the 'Young Pretender' escapes to the continent.

1748 War of the Austrian Succession ends. Prussia under **Frederick the Great** has emerged as the strongest power in

N. Germany; Britain has proved herself superior at sea over the French, with whom she continues a struggle for supremacy in India and America.

1756 Seven Years' War breaks out. Maria Theresa, helped by France and Russia, seeks to win back Silesia from Frederick of Prussia, who is supported by Britain under the elder **Pitt. The Nawab of Bengal** captures Calcutta; locks 140 British men and women into small military guardroom—the 'Black Hole of Calcutta'—where most suffocate. In America French capture Fort Oswego, main British trading centre on Great Lakes.

1757 **Clive** defeats Nawab of Bengal at PLASSEY.

1758 Fort Oswego recaptured; British take Fort Duquesne, renaming it Pittsburgh in honour of Pitt.

1759 French defeated at MINDEN; in America **General Wolfe** is slain capturing QUEBEC. There are British naval victories at LAGOS and QUIBERON BAY.

1760 French defeated in India, leaving British supreme. George II succeeded by his grandson, **George III,** first Hanoverian king to speak English and to regard himself as king of England rather than Elector of Hanover.

1761 George brings about downfall of Pitt (afterwards Earl of Chatham).

1763 Seven Years' War ends, leaving Britain with her conquests in India and America.

1773 'Boston Tea Party' brings to a head the long quarrel between George III and American colonists. Colonists maintain they should not be taxed without their consent. When Britain imposes tax on tea, a group of colonists, disguised as Indians, board ships in Boston and throw their cargoes into the harbour.

1775 First shots exchanged between colonists and British troops at Lexington. **George Washington** made American Commander-in-Chief.

1776 The 13 American colonies issue Declaration of Independence (July 4).

1777 **General Burgoyne,** marching from Canada to New York, forced to surrender at SARATOGA. France and Spain declare war on Britain.

1781 British army under **General Cornwallis** forced to surrender at YORKTOWN, Virginia.

1783 Britain recognises American independence.

1788 Founding Fathers draw up American constitution.

1789 George Washington first U.S. President. French Revolution breaks out. Faced with bankruptcy, **Louis XVI** is compelled to summon the States-General (French Parliament) for first time since 1614. States-General turns itself into National Assembly, determined to abolish absolute power of king, and proclaims principles of Liberty, Equality, Fraternity. Louis calls in soldiers; people of Paris retaliate by storming Bastille prison (July 14).

1791 Louis XVI flees, but is caught and brought back to Paris.

1792 Austria and Prussia, wishing to restore Louis, make war on France; Louis is deposed and imprisoned, France becoming republic. Extreme revolutionaries (the Jacobins) gain control.

1793 French occupy Austrian Netherlands (now Belgium); Britain joins in war against France with Holland, Spain, Austria and Prussia. Louis XVI is executed; Reign of Terror begins. In Britain the government, afraid that revolutionary ideas will spread, suppresses all societies in favour of reform.

1794 Execution of **Robespierre** ends Reign of Terror.

1795 Prussia has withdrawn from war, Holland been conquered and Spain defeated; only Austria and Britain are left. **Napoleon Bonaparte** becomes French C.-in-C. in Italy, where he rapidly masters the Austrians. Britain takes Cape of Good Hope, formerly Dutch.

1797 Napoleon threatens Vienna; Austria makes peace. **Jarvis** and **Nelson** defeat Spanish fleet at CAPE ST VINCENT; **Duncan** the Dutch fleet at CAMPERDOWN.

1798 Bonaparte eludes a British fleet under Nelson, lands in Egypt and defeats Mameluke Turks in BATTLE OF THE PYRAMIDS. Nelson destroys French fleet anchored in Aboukir Bay, in BATTLE OF THE NILE. Bonaparte advances into Syria, is stopped by **Sir Sidney Smith** at ACRE.

1799 Britain, Turkey, Austria and Russia combine against France. Bonaparte abandons army in Egypt and returns to France, where he makes himself First Consul.

1800 Bonaparte defeats Austrians at MARENGO. Ireland made part of United Kingdom.

1801 Austria sues for peace. Russia has withdrawn from war and, with Denmark, Sweden and Prussia, has taken measures

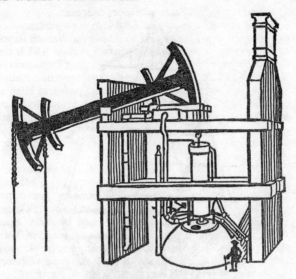

Watt's early Rotative Steam Engine

against Britain for searching neutral ships to ensure that they do not carry cargoes useful to France. Nelson smashes Danish fleet at COPENHAGEN.

1802 Peace returns for a time. Britain restores Cape of Good Hope to Dutch, but keeps Ceylon (formerly Dutch) and Trinidad (formerly Spanish). Bonaparte made First Consul for life.

1803 War between Britain and France renewed, with Spain on France's side. Bonaparte sells Louisiana to the U.S.A.

1804 Bonaparte becomes Emperor Napoleon.

1805 Younger **Pitt** builds alliance against Napoleon with Austria and Russia. Napoleon gathers army at Boulogne to invade England. Nelson defeats French and Spanish fleets at TRAFALGAR. Napoleon defeats Austrians and Russians at AUSTERLITZ. Pitt dies.

1806 Austria again sues for peace; **Francis II** drops title of Holy Roman Emperor, becomes Emperor of Austria. Napoleon crushes Prussia at JENA; is master of Germany.

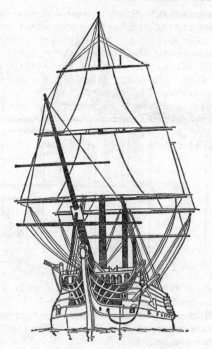

The *Victory*, Nelson's flagship

1807 Napoleon defeats Russians at EYLAU and FRIEDLAND; forms
an alliance with Russia at Tilsit. Britain now his only enemy;
he seeks to ruin her by excluding British goods from Europe.
Britain replies by blockading all countries under Napoleon's
control; forces surrender of the Danish fleet by bombardment
of Copenhagen. Napoleon occupies Portugal, which has
thriving trade with Britain.

1808 Napoleon makes brother Joseph king of Spain. Spain and
Portugal revolt; Peninsular War begins.

1809 Sir Arthur Wellesley (later Duke of Wellington) defeats
French at TALAVERA. Austria re-enters war; is defeated at
WAGRAM and again sues for peace.

1812 Napoleon invades Russia; occupies Moscow after battle of BORODINO, but the Russians burn the city and he is forced to retreat in winter, his 'Grande Armée' being destroyed. Wellington defeats French at SALAMANCA; occupies Madrid.

Dispute arising out of Britain's insistence on searching neutral ships leads to war between Britain and U.S. Britain occupies and burns Washington.

1813 Prussia and Austria drive Napoleon from Germany. Wellington defeats French at VITTORIA; drives them out of Spain.

1814 Britain and America make peace.

Austria, Russia and Prussia invade France, occupy Paris; Wellington marches into S. France. Napoleon abdicates, is banished to Elba. Bourbon dynasty restored.

1815 Napoleon escapes, resumes power, but is defeated at WATERLOO. Banished to St Helena. **Louis XVIII** returns to Paris.

1819 At 'Peterloo Massacre' in Manchester cavalry charge an open-air meeting of supporters of parliamentary reform.

1821 Greeks revolt against Turkish rule. Death of Napoleon.

1822 The poet **Lord Byron** is among many volunteers who go to Greece to help her in her war of independence.

1823 Spain tries to regain her American colonies; Britain recognises their independence, threatens to use British navy to prevent interference from Spain. **President Monroe** of the U.S.A. issues what is known as the 'Monroe Doctrine', saying that any interference by European powers on the American continent would be regarded as unfriendly to the U.S.A.

1827 British, French and Russian fleets destroy the Turkish fleet at NAVARINO, making it impossible for the Turks to put down the Greeks.

1829 Greece becomes independent kingdom.

1830 **Charles X** of France, who has tried to re-establish absolute monarchy, is driven from the throne and replaced by **Louis-Philippe**. Belgians revolt against Dutch rule and become independent. Unrest in Italy and Germany; in Britain the struggle for parliamentary reform becomes intense.

1832 Great Reform Bill is passed (see HISTORIC ACTS OF PARLIAMENT).

1833 Slavery abolished throughout British Empire.

1835–36 Boers undertake their 'Great Trek' to escape from British rule in the Cape; set up republic in Transvaal.

1837 Queen Victoria ascends the throne.

1846 Faced with famine in Ireland, **Sir Robert Peel** repeals Corn Laws (see HISTORIC ACTS OF PARLIAMENT).

1848 Another year of unrest: revolt against Austrian rule by Hungarians, Czechs and Italians; Rome declared a republic; Sicily and Naples rise against their King. All these revolts suppressed. The crown of a unified Germany offered to **Frederick William IV** of Prussia, but as a believer in Divine Right of Kings he refuses because crown is offered by representatives of the people. He is forced to give his own subjects a constitution. Louis-Philippe of France deposed; republic proclaimed. In Britain the Chartists demand the vote for all.

1851 Great Exhibition in London.

Paxton's Crystal Palace, home of the Great Exhibition

1852 Louis-Napoleon makes himself French emperor as Napoleon III.

1853 Britain, seeing her position in India threatened by Russian ambitions, and France, under Napoleon III, who wants to strengthen his power by military triumphs, declare war on Russia. Anglo-French and Turkish force landed in the Crimea to capture Sevastopol. In the battles of BALACLAVA ('The charge of the Light Brigade') and INKERMANN, the Russians fail to drive out allied force. The harsh winter exposes the inefficiency of the British army, especially of its medical services, which **Florence Nightingale** does her best to remedy.

1855 Sardinia, wanting French and British support in the struggle to unite all Italy, joins war against Russia. Russians abandon SEVASTOPOL.

1856 Crimean War ends.

1857 Indian Mutiny breaks out. Delhi seized by rebels, besieged and captured by the British; Lucknow defended by British garrison. Last Mogul emperor is deposed and British Crown takes over administration of India from East India Company.

1859 Sardinia, under **Victor Emmanuel II**, and France declare war on Austria; defeat her at MAGENTA and SOLFERINO. Sardinia receives Lombardy, gives Nice and Savoy to France.

1860 **Garibaldi** overthrows Kingdom of the Two Sicilies (Naples and Sicily), which, with four remaining Italian duchies, are annexed by Sardinia.

Abraham Lincoln elected U.S. President. Eleven southern states, wishing to maintain State rights against the central government, particularly on the issue of Negro slavery, claim the right to break away from the Union. Lincoln denies this right; American Civil War breaks out.

1861 Victor Emmanuel proclaimed first king of a United Italy.

1862 **Bismarck**, foreign minister of Prussia, sets out to unify Germany.

1863 **General Robert E. Lee**, commander of Southern forces in the American Civil War, defeated at GETTYSBURG. Lincoln proclaims abolition of slavery.

1864 **Maximilian of Hapsburg** made emperor of Mexico by Napoleon III. Mexican republicans, under **Juarez**, bitterly oppose him.

1865 General Lee surrenders to **General Grant** at Appomattox Court House and American Civil War is over. Abraham Lincoln assassinated.

1866 U.S.A. insists that French troops be withdrawn from Mexico. Maximilian shot.

In brief seven weeks campaign against Austria, ending in overwhelming victory at SADOWA, Prussia smashes Austria's influence over Germany and insists that Venetia be handed over to Italy.

1867 Canada becomes Dominion.

1869 Suez canal opened.

1870 Napoleon III declares war on Prussia. French army surrounded at METZ and another, with Napoleon in command, surrenders at SEDAN. Napoleon's Empire collapses; is followed by Third Republic.

1871 United Germany proclaimed with king of Prussia as Emperor. France forced to give Alsace-Lorraine to Germany.

1872 Voting becomes secret in Britain.

1875 **Disraeli** wins control of Suez Canal for Britain by buying shares of the Khedive of Egypt. The Khedive's misrule has made Egypt bankrupt, and Britain and France have to pour money into the country to save it from collapse.

1877 Queen Victoria becomes Empress of India. Russia comes to aid of Serbs, Montenegrans, Rumanians and Bulgarians, risen against Turkish rule. Turks defeated; only under threat from Britain and Austria does Russia stop the war.

1878 Bulgaria established as a separate principality under Turkey; Serbia and Montenegro become independent kingdoms; and Bosnia and Herzogovina, both with largely Serbian populations, pass into Austrian hands, thus causing bad blood between Serbia and Austria. Britain receives Cyprus.

1881 At MAJUBA HILL Boers defeat British force trying to occupy Transvaal. Transvaal is recognised as independent republic under British authority.

France occupies Tunis as part of her policy of creating an empire for herself in Africa and Indo-China. Following discovery of the interior of Africa by **Livingstone** and others between 1841 and 1873, 'scramble for Africa' becomes intense.

1882 Britain occupies Egypt and is drawn into the affairs of the Sudan, where **Mohammed Ahmed** has proclaimed himself Mahdi (Messiah) and declared a holy war against Egypt and all non-Moslems.

1884 Germany joins in 'scramble for Africa', acquiring S.W. Africa, Cameroons, Togoland and Tanganyika.

1885 **General Gordon**, sent to evacuate British and Egyptian garrisons in the Sudan, killed in Khartoum by Mahdi's forces.

1886 Royal Niger Company formed to open up interior of Nigeria.

1888 British East Africa Company secures what is now Kenya and takes over Uganda.

William II becomes German emperor.

1890 Cecil Rhodes, founder of Rhodesia, who hopes to see British territory extend from the Cape to Cairo, becomes Prime Minister of Cape Colony.

In Germany William II drops Bismarck as Chancellor; the German drive to 'win a place in the sun' becomes fiercer.

1896 Jameson's raid into the Transvaal in support of the British there, whose lives the Boers are making difficult, is a failure. Rhodes, suspected of backing Jameson, has to resign as Prime Minister of Cape Colony.

Italy, having established herself in Eritrea as part of the 'scramble for Africa', tries to conquer Ethiopia; is defeated at ADOWA.

1898 British General **Kitchener,** having defeated the Mahdi's forces at OMDURMAN and recaptured Khartoum, encounters a French force at Fashoda. The 'Fashoda incident' brings Britain and France close to war; but France, fearing the growing strength of Germany, gives in.

Grievances of British settlers in the Boer republic leads to the Boer War, beginning with a series of British defeats.

1900 Lord Roberts wipes out main Boer forces, but Boer guerilla units continue war.

Failure of the Boxer rising in China (a revolt against European and Japanese interference in Chinese affairs) speeds the collapse of Chinese imperial rule.

1901 Queen Victoria dies.

Australia becomes self-governing dominion.

1902 Boer War ends; Boer republics are annexed by the British Crown.

1904 'Entente Cordiale' ('warm understanding') established between Britain and France.

Russia which, after completion of the Trans-Siberian Railway, has extended her influence into Manchuria and Korea, clashes with Japan, which is trying to secure for herself as much of the decaying Chinese empire as she can. Japan declares war on Russia, and in a series of brilliant land and sea victories crushes Russia's Far Eastern forces.

1905 Russia forced to make peace and evacuate Manchuria.

1906 In Britain Liberals win great electoral victory and embark on sweeping programme of social reform.

1907 New Zealand becomes dominion.

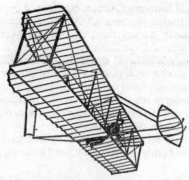

Wright Brothers' biplane 1907–8

Alliance between Britain and France extended to include Russia. There are now two great power blocs in Europe—Germany and Austria on one hand, Britain, France and Russia on the other. Tension increases, and the powers begin an armaments race.

1908 Austria annexes Bosnia and Herzogovina, offending Serbia and Russia, since both provinces have largely Serb (or Slav) populations.

1910 Union of S. Africa formed of Cape of Good Hope, Natal, Orange Free State and Transvaal; becomes a dominion.

1911 In Britain the powers of the House of Lords are sharply cut.

Italy, seeking colonies, makes war on Turkey in order to seize Tripoli.

Germany tries to prevent French penetration of Morocco by sending a warship to Agadir. Backed by Britain, France refuses to give way.

1912–13 Two Balkan wars result in the expulsion of Turkey from Europe.

British government introduces an Irish Home Rule Bill which nearly leads to civil war in Ireland.

Tripoli is yielded to Italy.

1914 Assassination of the heir to the Austrian throne at Sarajevo triggers off First World War.

The Germans sweep through neutral Belgium; are halted only a few miles from Paris. The Allies force the Germans back in the battle of the MARNE; by October the struggle has

settled down into trench warfare. Russians invade East
Prussia, are stopped by **Hindenburg**'s victory at TANNENBERG.

1915 Both sides make costly attempts to break through, without
success.

On the eastern front the Germans push the Russians further
back.

Turkey, fighting on Germany's side, tries to cut the Suez
Canal, but fails. The British fail to open communications
with Russia through the Black Sea by forcing the Dardanelles
and landing troops on the Gallipoli peninsula.

Italy enters the war on the Allied side. Germans announce
that their U-boats will sink all merchant ships in British
waters.

1916 Trench warfare continues; huge losses on both sides.
British and German fleets meet off JUTLAND; the Germans are
so battered that they remain in port for the rest of the war.

Following the sinking of the *Lusitania* with many Americans
on board, the Germans are forced to abandon their unrestricted submarine campaign. The Arabs, aided by **T. E.
Lawrence**, revolt against Turkish rule. In Britain **Lloyd
George** becomes Prime Minister.

1917 Anti-war feeling in Russia leads to overthrow of the Czar;
but the provisional government's attempt to continue the war
enables **Lenin** and the Bolsheviks to seize power.

The Germans renew unrestricted submarine warfare, and in
April the U.S.A. declares war.

British and French troops are sent to Italy after the Germans and Austrians have broken through the Italian front at
CAPORETTO.

General Allenby captures Jerusalem.

1918 Germans launch their final offensive, but fail to break
through. Allies counter-attack under **Marshal Foch** and
force Germans to sue for armistice in November. William II,
the Kaiser, abdicates; Germany becomes republic. Hapsburg
monarchy in Austria comes to an end.

1919 Under peace treaties France regains Alsace-Lorraine; Germany loses the 'Polish Corridor' to the new Polish republic;
Austria and Hungary are separated; Serbia is enlarged and
becomes Yugoslavia; Czechoslovakia is created; the Ottoman
empire is broken up, leaving only Turkey itself, which
becomes a republic; a League of Nations is created, but

its founder, **President Wilson**, fails to persuade his own country, the U.S.A., to become a member; Germany's colonies become League of Nation's mandates; and Germany has limits set on the size of her armed forces.

1921 Ireland, with the exception of Northern Ireland, which remains linked to the U.K., is made a dominion after nearly three years of disturbances.

1922 **Kemal Ataturk** seizes power in Turkey, sets out to modernise his country.

Mussolini becomes head of the Italian government, establishes Fascism.

1924 Lenin, having established Communist rule in Russia despite famine and foreign intervention, dies; **Stalin** emerges as his successor and sets out to make Russia a great industrial power.

In Britain **Ramsay MacDonald** forms the short-lived first Labour government.

1926 General Strike in Britain collapses after six weeks.

1929 World-wide economic crisis causes millions to be thrown out of work in the U.S.A. and Europe. In Germany **Hitler**'s National Socialist ('Nazi') party makes large gains.

1931 In Britain the second Labour government is replaced by a largely conservative National Government.

In Spain the monarchy collapses and a republic is established.

Japan invades China, sets up a puppet regime in Manchuria. China appeals unsuccessfully to the League of Nations, from which Japan resigns.

1933 **Franklin D. Roosevelt** becomes U.S. President and launches his 'New Deal' of social and economic reform to help America out of the Great Depression. Hitler is appointed Chancellor, suppresses all opposition and makes himself dictator of Germany.

1935 Hitler denounces the terms of the Versailles Treaty limiting the size of the German armed forces.

Mussolini invades and conquers Ethiopia, which appeals in vain to the League of Nations. Mussolini leaves the League.

1936 Military rising against the left-wing government in Spain leads to the outbreak of the Spanish Civil War. Germans and Italians fight openly on Franco's side, and the government receives aid from Russia.

1938 Hitler occupies Austria and claims the Sudetenland in Czechoslovakia. Under the Munich Agreement, signed by Britain, France, Germany and Italy, the Sudetenland is given to Germany; the new frontiers of Czechoslovakia are guaranteed.

1939 The Spanish Civil War ends with the surrender of Madrid; Fascist dictatorship established under **General Franco**. Hitler seizes the rest of Czechoslovakia. Mussolini seizes Albania.

Hitler makes a pact with Stalin and invades and crushes Poland, which is divided between Germany and Russia. Britain and France declare war; the Second World War has begun.

Russia makes war on Finland (in order to bring the approaches to Leningrad under her control), but her armies are beaten in the winter campaign.

1940 Russians break through; Finland sues for peace. Hitler occupies Norway and Denmark. In Britain **Chamberlain** is brought down, and **Winston Churchill** forms a coalition government. Sweeping through Holland, Belgium and Luxembourg, Hitler crushes France, which sues for armistice. Free French under **General de Gaulle** continue to fight from Britain. Britain, having extricated her army from France at Dunkirk, fights on alone. Hitler's plan to invade Britain collapses when his air force (the Luftwaffe) fails to win control of the air in the Battle of Britain; but the Luftwaffe continues its effort to smash Britain by 'blitz' bombing.

Italy enters war on German side, attacks Greece. British troops begin the capture of Italian colonies in E. Africa; reconquer Ethiopia.

1941 Hitler conquers Yugoslavia and Greece; in June, attacks Russia. Germans sweep to gates of Moscow and Leningrad, are caught by the winter. German force under **Rommel** arrives to strengthen Italians in N. Africa and becomes a dangerous threat to Egypt, the Suez Canal and Britain's position in the Middle East.

In December Japan attacks the U.S. Pacific Fleet at Pearl Harbor, bringing the U.S.A. into the war, and invades Malaya, Siam, the Philippines, Burma and Indonesia. Hong Kong falls.

1942 In Russia the Germans conquer the Ukraine and penetrate deep into the Caucasus, but winter sets in again, and

American Eagle

a German army of over 300,000 is trapped and wiped out at
STALINGRAD.

In Africa Rommel defeats the British and gets within 60
miles of Alexandria, but in the battle of ALAMEIN **Montgomery** defeats him decisively. An Anglo-American force
under **Eisenhower** takes French N. Africa. Singapore falls,
and by May the Japanese are masters of S.E. Asia, but their
advance in the Central and S.W. Pacific is halted by American
naval and air victories in the CORAL SEA and off MIDWAY.

The Americans begin to roll back the Japanese across the
Pacific, capturing Guadalcanal in 1943, the Gilbert, Marshall
and Mariana Islands in 1943 and 1944, the Philippines in 1944
and Iwo-Jima and Okinawa in 1945.

1943 German forces sent against Eisenhower in Africa, together
with what remains of Rommel's force—altogether over a
quarter of a million men—are forced to surrender.

The Allies invade Italy, but the Germans put up stiff resistance, and the Allied advance becomes a long, bitter push up
the mountainous Italian peninsula, lasting until the end of the
war. Mussolini is deposed and imprisoned; Italy joins the
Allies. With Hitler's help, Mussolini escapes.

1944 Russians push Germans out of Russia and advance into
Europe.

The Western allies, under Eisenhower, land in Normandy
and sweep across France almost to the Rhine. A group of
German officers attempt to assassinate Hitler, without success.

The British foil a Japanese attempt to invade India from
Burma and launch a drive for the reconquest of Burma,
Malaya and Singapore which is completed successfully in
1945.

1945 The Allies cross the Rhine; the Russians invade Germany from the East. Hitler commits suicide as the Russians take Berlin. Germany surrenders. Japan surrenders after atom bombs have been dropped on Hiroshima and Nagasaki.

In Britain the Labour party wins an overwhelming victory and sets out on a programme of social reforms designed to produce the 'welfare state' and to give self-government to non-white colonial peoples.

The United Nations organisation is formed.

1947 India, Pakistan, Burma and Ceylon become independent. **General Marshall,** U.S. Secretary of State, pledges American aid for Europe's recovery provided the European nations unite in a co-operative effort. With help given under this Marshall Plan living standards in nearly the whole of Western Europe rise within three years well above those of before the war. Russia and countries under her control boycott the Plan.

1948 Communists take over government in Czechoslovakia. There is now an 'iron curtain' between east and west. The Russians try to squeeze the Western Allies out of Berlin by cutting road and rail communications. The Allies supply Berlin by airlift until the blockade is lifted.

The state of Israel is proclaimed.

1949 The U.S.A., Canada, Britain, France and eight other W. European countries join together for mutual defence in the North Atlantic Treaty Organisation (NATO). Chinese Nationalists, under **Chiang-Kai-Shek,** are driven from Chinese mainland and take refuge in Formosa; Communist Chinese People's Republic is set up in China.

1950 N. Korea, under communist control, invades S. Korea. United Nations Security Council (from which the Russian delegate happens to be absent) calls upon its members to stop the aggressor; and American, British and other U.N. forces land just in time to save Korea from being overrun. The communists are driven back into N. Korea, but as they near the Chinese frontiers the Chinese intervene to drive the UN forces back into S. Korea.

1951 In Britain the Conservatives under Churchill defeat Labour.

1952 In Egypt **King Farouk** is forced to abdicate by **General Neguib.**

Elizabeth II succeeds her father, **George VI.**

United Nations Building, New York

1953 General Eisenhower becomes first Republican president for twenty years.

Stalin dies; there is a struggle for political power inside Russia.

In Egypt Neguib is replaced by **Nasser**.

Korean War ends.

1954 After seven years of war between French and communists in French Indo-China, an armistice is arranged. At the Geneva Conference, French rule in Indo-China is ended, and Laos, Cambodia and Vietnam become independent; but N. Vietnam is left under communist control.

1955 Heads of government of the U.S.A., Russia, Britain and France hold a 'summit' meeting at Geneva, and tension is temporarily eased.

1956 **Kruschev** denounces Stalin's methods in a speech at the 20th Congress of the Soviet Communist party. His speech causes the downfall of the Stalinist government in Poland; and in Hungary it leads to a popular uprising, put down by Russian tanks.

In Egypt Nasser seizes the Suez Canal. Goaded by the aggressive attitude of the Arabs, who refuse to recognise her, Israel invades Egypt and advances on the Suez Canal. Britain and France demand an immediate cease-fire and, when their demand is disregarded, land at Port Said. Their action is condemned by the United Nations, who order the Anglo-French forces to withdraw. This they do.

1957 Ghana and Malaya become independent.

Russia launches into space the first man-made satellite, Sputnik I.

1958 In France, on the brink of civil war as a result of the disobedience of the Algerian settlers and sections of the army, de Gaulle is returned to power, remodels the constitution, and gives independence within the French community to France's colonies.

1959 Macmillan visits Kruschev in Moscow, and Kruschev becomes the first Soviet head of government to visit the U.S.A.

In Cuba **Fidel Castro** ends the **Batista** regime.

Fidel Castro

1960 Belgian Congo given independence; sinks almost immediately into chaos. U.N. intervenes, but disagreement between the great powers and the African nations hampers its work.

Nigeria becomes independent.

1961 John F. Kennedy, a Democrat and the youngest candidate ever to be elected to the White House, is installed as President of the U.S.A.

Man's first flight into space is made by **Major Yuri Gagarin,** Soviet airman, who circles the earth at 25,000 miles an hour before landing safely in Russia.

South Africa leaves the Commonwealth because of the opposition of the African and Asian Commonwealth countries to her racial policies. Sierra Leone and Tanganyika become independent. Cyprus joins the Commonwealth.

In Algeria extremists among the European settlers and French Army make two attempts to seize power, but President de Gaulle reasserts his authority on both occasions and continues his efforts to reach a settlement with the Algerian Arabs. The extremists form a Secret Army (the O.A.S.) and launch a terrorist campaign in Algeria and France.

World tension mounts when the Communist East German authorities build a wall across Berlin to stop the flow of East German refugees to West Berlin.

Dag Hammarskjoeld, the U.N. Secretary-General, is killed in an air crash in Africa, and is succeeded by a Burmese, **U Thant.**

Britain applies to join the European Common Market.

1962 Colonel John Glenn, American astronaut, successfully circles the earth three times in his Mercury space capsule.

Two Russian astronauts, **Major Nicolaev** and **Colonel Popovich,** are launched into space, the former orbiting the earth for $94\frac{1}{2}$ hours and the second for 71 hours.

France and the Algerian Arabs sign a cease-fire, and Algeria becomes an independent country.

Jamaica and Trinidad become independent. Tanganyika declares itself a republic but stays within the Commonwealth.

The world's first communications satellite, Telstar, is launched.

Three thousand Cardinals and Bishops of the Roman Catholic Church meet in Rome to discuss Church problems and Christian unity under the guidance of **Pope John XXIII.**

The Soviet Union establishes atomic missile bases in Fidel Castro's Cuba, President Kennedy orders Cuba to be blockaded, and the world seems to be on the brink of nuclear war between the United States and the Soviet Union. War is avoided, and tension eases when Kruschev orders the dismantling of the Soviet missile bases.

1963 President de Gaulle objects to Britain's proposed entry into the Common Market, and the negotiations between Britain and the Common Market 'Six' are broken off.

U.N. military forces seize the main towns in Katanga,

President Tshombe's secessionist province in the Congo, thus breaking the power of the biggest of the many separatist governments which have been defying the authority of the Central Congolese Government since independence in 1960.

Valentina Tereshkova, of Russia, becomes first woman in space.

Signing of Test Ban Treaty in Moscow between U.S.A., Russia and Britain marks easing of East-West tension.

Pope John XXIII dies. His successor is **Pope Paul VI.**

New state of Malaysia, comprising Malaya, Singapore, Sarawak and parts of Borneo, is set up despite strong opposition of **President Soekarno** of Indonesia. Kenya and Zanzibar become independent members of Commonwealth.

Harold Macmillan resigns for health reasons and is succeeded by Lord Home who relinquishes his peerage to become **Sir Alec Douglas-Home.**

President Kennedy is assassinated. His Vice-President, **Lyndon B. Johnson,** takes over as 36th President of the United States.

1964 In Zanzibar the Sultan is expelled, a republic set up and Zanzibar unites with Tanganyika to form the new state of Tanzania.

Kruschev falls from power. As Secretary General of the Russian Communist Party he is succeeded by **Brezhnev** and as Chairman of the Soviet Council of Ministers by **Kosygin.**

Labour Party narrowly defeats Conservatives in General Election. Sir Alec Douglas-Home resigns. **Harold Wilson** becomes Prime Minister.

Lyndon B. Johnson, the Democratic candidate, wins a landslide victory in U.S. presidential election over **Senator Barry Goldwater,** the Republican candidate.

1965 Sir Winston Churchill dies and is given a State funeral.

Russian **Colonel Leonov** becomes first man to 'walk' in space, American **Major White** the second.

Fighting breaks out between India and Pakistan over Kashmir. A cease-fire is arranged after three weeks.

The Government of **Mr. Smith** in Rhodesia, a British colony, declares independence without Britain's consent, and is condemned as 'illegal'.

Singapore leaves Malaysia to become independent state within Commonwealth.

1966 Mrs. Gandhi, Nehru's daughter, becomes India's first woman Prime Minister after **Mr. Shastri's** death.

Nigeria's unity is shaken by a series of military coups in which many of the country's leaders are killed. A colonel in his thirties, **Yakubu Gowon,** emerges as Head of State.

President Nkrumah of Ghana is deposed by a military coup while on a visit to China.

The fighting in Vietnam, already some years old, between the Communist Vietcong supported by the North Vietnamese, and the South Vietnamese supported by the Americans, becomes fiercer and casualties mount on both sides.

Mr. Wilson and Labour Party win substantial victory in General Election.

England wins World Cup in football.

Dr. Erhard's Christian Democrat Government in West Germany collapses. Christian Democrats under a new leader, **Herr Kiesinger,** form a coalition government with the main opposition party, the Social Democrats.

1967 Britain applies for membership of the Common Market for the second time but again General de Gaulle says no.

A military junta seizes power in Greece.

Israel routs the armed forces of Egypt, Jordan and Syria in six days but, despite a hurriedly arranged cease-fire, there is no relaxation of tension in the Middle East.

Civil war rages in Nigeria between the Federal Nigerian Government and the breakaway state of Biafra.

Moscow celebrates 50th anniversary of the 1917 October Revolution.

1968 In Czechoslovakia **President Novotny,** a 'Stalinist hard-liner', is ousted by **Alexander Dubcek** and other Communist 'liberals' who introduce political, social and economic reforms. To stop Dubcek's 'liberalisation' movement, the Russians invade and occupy Czechoslovakia and arrest Dubcek and many of his followers, but when they fail to find any Czechoslovak Communist willing to run the country for them they are forced to reinstate Dubcek. Dubcek's powers of government are, however, drastically reduced.

Britain announces her intention to withdraw from all her bases East of Suez by 1971 (with the exception of Hong Kong).

France is brought virtually to a standstill by violent student riots and strikes by more than 8 million workers, and it is several weeks before General de Gaulle restores his authority.

Peace talks begin in Paris to end the Vietnam War.

Dr. Martin Luther King, the American Negro leader, and **Senator Robert Kennedy,** the late President Kennedy's brother, are assassinated.

Three American astronauts, **Frank Borman, Bill Anders** and **Jim Lovell,** become the first men to circle round the moon.

1969 Richard M. Nixon, a Republican and President Eisenhower's Vice-President, is installed as US President. He begins withdrawal of American troops from Vietnam.

Alexander Dubcek is ousted as First Secretary of Czechoslovak Communist Party and replaced by **Dr. Husak.** 'Hardline' Communists tighten their control in Czechoslovakia.

American astronauts **Neil Armstrong** and **Edwin Aldrin** become the first men to walk on the moon.

General de Gaulle, defeated in a referendum on local regional reform, retires from public life. **Georges Pompidou,** a Gaullist, is elected President.

After general elections in West Germany, the Social Democrats become the dominant partners in a coalition government for the first time in the twenty years since the foundation of the West German Federal Republic, with **Willy Brandt** as Chancellor.

Greece withdraws from Council of Europe to avoid being expelled because of the undemocratic and repressive nature of its military regime.

1970 The Nigerian civil war comes to an end with the capitulation of Biafra.

Treaty, limiting spread of nuclear armaments, comes into force after ratification by 43 states, including Britain, the U.S.A. and the Soviet Union, but excluding France and Communist China.

In Britain the Conservatives, led by **Edward Heath,** defeat Labour.

Britain, for the third time, begins negotiations to join the Common Market.

President Nasser of Egypt dies and is succeeded by **Anwar Sadat.**

Serious riots in the Polish ports on the Baltic, sparked off by large increases in food prices, cause down-fall of **Gomulka** and his replacement by **Gierek.**

1971 Commonwealth Prime Ministers meet in Singapore, the first Commonwealth Prime Ministers' Conference ever to be held in Asia.

In East Pakistan, the Awami League, victorious in the previous year's elections, demands first autonomy for the eastern province and then independence as the Republic of Bangladesh. **President Yahya Khan** treats this demand as sedition. The Awami League's leader, **Sheik Mujibur Rahman,** is arrested and flown to West Pakistan. West Pakistani troops are flown to East Pakistan to suppress all support for East Pakistani independence. An estimated number of ten million refugees flood across the border into India. Eventually India intervenes with its armed forces. The war between India and Pakistan is short. In East Pakistan the West Pakistani forces surrender, and Bangladesh is proclaimed. In the West of the Indian sub-continent, a cease-fire is arranged between India and Pakistan. Yahya Khan resigns and hands over the presidency to a West Pakistani politician, **Zulfikar Ali Bhutto.**

Britain reaches agreement on the main points in her negotiations for joining the Common Market, and Parliament votes in favour of the principle of Britain becoming a member.

Communist China replaces Chiang-Kai-Chek's government as the official representative of China in the U.N.

Kurt Waldheim, an Austrian diplomat, is elected fourth Secretary-General of the U.N. in succession to U Thant.

1972 President Bhutto releases Sheik Mujibur Rahman who becomes Prime Minister of Bangladesh.

Pakistan leaves the Commonwealth when some Commonwealth countries recognise Bangladesh as an independent state.

Britain signs a Treaty of Accession to the Common Market. Eire, Denmark and Norway sign similar treaties.

President Nixon visits Peking at the invitation of the Chinese Communist Government, and later Moscow at the invitation of the Soviet Government.

Edward Heath's Conservative Government takes over direct rule of Northern Ireland, suspending the powers of the Northern Irish Government and Parliament.

West German Parliament ratifies treaties of reconciliation between West Germany on the one hand and on the other the Soviet Union, Poland and East Germany.

Conference opens in Helsinki on European Security and Co-operation in order to reduce tension between East and West.

Elizabeth II becomes the first British monarch to visit a Communist country when she pays a State Visit to Yugoslavia.

Faced with deadlock in the West German Parliament, **Willy Brandt** calls for a general election and wins a substantial majority for his Social Democrats and his coalition partners, the Free Democrats (Liberals), over the Christian Democrat Party.

The British Parliament ratifies the Treaty of Accession to the European Economic Community. Both Eire and Denmark vote in plebiscites in favour of joining but Norway votes against doing so.

President Amin of Uganda expels tens of thousands of Asians from his country in pursuit of his policy of 'Africanisation'. Britain receives nearly 30,000 Ugandan Asians.

1973 Britain, together with Eire and Denmark, become full members of the enlarged European Economic Community.

President Nixon is sworn in for his second term of office after his sweeping victory over the Democratic Party's nominee, **Senator George McGovern**, the previous November.

Cease-fire agreement in Vietnamese war is signed between U.S., North Vietnam, South Vietnam and Vietcong.

President Nixon is suspected of being involved in the attempt, during the 1972 Presidential campaign, to break into the headquarters of his political opponents in a building called Watergate, and several of his top assistants resign.

Vice-President **Spiro Agnew**, after pleading guilty to tax evasion, resigns his office, and is replaced by **Gerald Ford**, until then leader of the Republican Party in the House of Representatives.

Dr Henry Kissinger is appointed U.S. Secretary of State, the first non-U.S.-born citizen to be appointed to this office.

Leonid Brezhnev, General Secretary of the Soviet Communist Party, visits the United States and stresses the importance of detente between the super-powers.

The Conference on European Security and Co-operation opens in Geneva; and talks begin in Vienna between East and West on the reduction of forces in Central Europe.

Elections for a new local assembly are held in Northern Ireland; a 12-man executive is created, and the setting-up of a Council of Ireland is agreed.

In Argentina, **Juan Peron** returns to power.

In Chile, **President Allende's** Marxist government is overthrown by a military junta. Allende dies.

In Greece, **President Papadopoulos**, after having deposed **King Constantine** and the monarchy and declared his country a republic, is himself overthrown by a rival military junta.

Egypt and Syria attack Israel on Yom Kippur, the Jewish Day of Atonement, and, after initial successes, are fought to a standstill. The United States and the U.S.S.R. agree, after a visit to Moscow by Dr Kissinger, to bring the fighting to an end to prevent a worldwide conflagration. The Soviet–U.S. agreement is approved by the U.N. Security Council; but before the fighting is stopped, a second cease-fire agreement has to be negotiated. On Dr Kissinger's initiative, a Middle East peace conference convenes in Geneva.

The oil-producing states of Kuwait, Saudi Arabia, Algeria, Abu Dhabi and Libya cut back oil deliveries to countries declared to be pro-Israel. The use of the so-called 'oil weapon' causes an acute energy crisis—particularly in Britain, where it is made worse by the overtime ban imposed by miners and railway drivers.

1974 The British Government announces that the working week for most of British industry has to be cut to three days. The executive of the National Union of Mineworkers asks its members to authorise it to call a national coal strike, and 81% of the miners vote in favour.

The U.S. government convenes a conference of oil-consuming countries in Washington to discuss the world energy crisis.

Edward Heath calls an election on the issue 'Who governs Britain?' Labour wins 301 seats, the Conservative 296, and others (including 14 Liberals) 38. After an attempt to form a Con–Lib coalition, Harold Wilson takes power at the head of a minority Labour Government. The miners accept a settlement of over £100,000,000.

Harold Wilson calls a second election in the autumn and wins a narrow majority over all other parties. The British government presses ahead with re-negotiating the terms of British membership of the European Economic Community.

High oil prices cause the economies of many industrial countries, including Britain, to slow down.

President Nixon is forced to resign because of his involvement in the attempt, during the 1972 Presidential campaign, to break into the headquarters of the Democratic Party in a building called Watergate and in the manoeuvres to cover up the break-in. He becomes the first President in U.S. history to resign his office. He is succeeded as President by Gerald Ford, who nominates **Nelson Rockefeller** as Vice-President. Rockefeller's nomination is approved by Congress.

An uneasy peace is maintained in the Middle East. **Mrs Golda Meir** resigns as Prime Minister of Israel on grounds of age and is succeeded by **Yitzhel Rabin**.

President Makarios is forced to leave Cyprus after a coup organised by Greek Cypriots who support union with Greece (*Enosis*), and are encouraged in their action by the military junta in Athens. The Turks invade Cyprus and occupy the northern part of the island. The Turkish invasion leads to the collapse of military junta in Athens, whose leading members are eventually arrested. **Constantine Karamanlis**, a former Prime Minister living in exile in Paris, is recalled and becomes Prime Minister. He promises Greece a return to democracy. In a plebiscite, organised by Karamanlis, the Greek people vote overwhelmingly in favour of remaining a republic and against the restoration of the monarchy.

President Makarios returns to Cyprus but the Turks continue to occupy the northern part of the island.

In Portugal, 50 years of dictatorship are ended when **Dr Caetano** is ousted. The new government includes Socialists, Communists and members of the so-called Armed Forces Movement, which is headed first by **General Spinola** and later by **General Costa Gomes.** The new government moves rapidly to give Portugal's African colonies—Guinea-Bissau, Mozambique and Angola—their independence.

The approach of independence and African rule in Mozambique and Angola changes the balance of power in southern Africa, and under pressure from **Mr. Vorster**, the South African Prime Minister, Mr. Ian Smith, the Rhodesian leader, releases two black leaders of the banned African Nationalist parties and allows them to fly to Lusaka in Zambia for talks with leaders of other African states. Negotiations between the black and white leaders of Rhodesia are initiated, but soon become bogged down.

President Pompidou of France dies and **Giscard d'Estaing** is elected President in his place.

Emperor Haile Selassie of Ethiopia is deposed by radical elements in his army.

Willy Brandt, West Germany's first Social Democratic Chancellor, resigns when it is revealed that an alleged East German spy has been working in his office. He is succeeded as Chancellor by a fellow Social Democrat, **Helmut Schmidt.**

President Peron of Argentina dies and is succeeded by his wife, **Isabelita.**

The IRA extends its terrorist activities from Northern Ireland to Britain.

1975 Sheik Mujibur Rahman, the Prime Minister of Bangladesh, changes his country's constitution and makes himself President.

Harold Wilson announces that a referendum is to be held in Britain later in the year on whether or not Britain is to stay in the European Economic Community.

The British Government decides to halt work on the Channel Tunnel because of rapidly rising construction costs.

Mrs Margaret Thatcher is elected leader of the Conservative Party, replacing Edward Heath.

Fort Sumter: the beginning of the American Civil War

An Index of Important Battles
mentioned in the Diary of World Events

Acre, 1191
Actium, 31 B.C.
Adowa, 1896
Agincourt, 1415
Alamein, 1942
Austerlitz, 1805
Balaclava, 1853
Bannockburn, 1314
Barnet, 1471
Blenheim, 1704
Borodino, 1812
Bosworth, 1485
Boyne, 1690
Camperdown, 1797
Cannae, 216 B.C.
Cape St Vincent, 1797
Caporetto, 1917
Chalons, 451
Copenhagen, 1801
Coral Sea, 1942
Crecy, 1346
Culloden, 1746
Dettingen, 1743
Drogheda, 1649
Dunbar, 1650
Edgehill, 1642
Evesham, 1265
Eylau, 1807
Falkirk, 1298
Flodden, 1513
Fontenoy, 1745
Friedland, 1807
Gettysburg, 1863
Granada, 1492
Guadalcanal, 1943
Harfleur, 1415

Hastings, 1066
Hexham, 1464
Homildon Hill, 1403
Inkermann, 1853
Iwo-Jima, 1945
Jena, 1806
Jutland, 1916
Kardessia, 637
Lagos, 1759
Lepanto, 1571
Lewes, 1264
Magenta, 1859
Majuba Hill, 1881
Malplaquet, 1709
Marathon, 490 B.C.
Marengo, 1800
Marne, 1914
Marston Moor, 1644
Metz, 1870
Midway, 1942
Minden, 1759
Mylae, 260 B.C.
Naseby, 1645
Navarino, 1827
Nile, 1798
Northampton, 1460
Okinawa, 1945
Omdurman, 1898
Orleans, 1429
Otterburn, 1388
Oudenarde, 1708
Pharsalus, 48 B.C.
Plaetaea, 479 B.C.
Plassey, 1757
Poitiers, 1356
Preston, 1648

Prestonpans, 1745
Pyramids, 1798
Ramillies, 1706
Quebec, 1759
Quiberon Bay, 1759
Salamanca, 1812
Salamis, 480 B.C.
St Albans, 1455
Saratoga, 1777
Sedan, 1870
Sedgemoor, 1685
Sevastopol, 1855
Shrewsbury, 1403
Sluys, 1340
Solferino, 1859
Southwold Bay, 1672
Stalingrad, 1942
Stirling, 1297

Talavera, 1809
Tannenberg, 1914
Tewkesbury, 1471
Thermopylae, 480 B.C.
Towton, 1461
Trafalgar, 1805
Trasimene, 217 B.C.
Vienna, 1529
Vienna, 1683
Vittoria, 1813
Wagram, 1809
Wakefield, 1460
Waterloo, 1815
Worcester, 1651
Yarmak, 643
Yorktown, 1781
Zama, 202 B.C.

List of Kings of Scotland

ALPINES

Kenneth I, 843–60
Donald I, 860–63
Constantine I, 863–77
Aedh, 877–78
Eocha, 878–89
Donald II, 889–900
Constantine II, 900–43
Malcolm I, 943–54
Indulf, 954–62
Duff, 962–67
Colin, 967–71
Kenneth II, 971–95
Constantine III, 995–97
Kenneth III, 997–1005
Malcolm II, 1005–34
Duncan I, 1034–40
Macbeth, 1040–57
Malcolm III, 1057–93
Donald Bane, 6 months in 1093
Duncan II, 6 months in 1094
Donald Bane again, 1094–97
Edgar, 1097–1107
Alexander I, 1107–24
David I, 1124–53
Malcolm IV (The Maiden), 1153–65

William I (The Lion), 1165–1214
Alexander II, 1214–49
Alexander III, 1249–86
Margaret, 1286–90
No king, 1290–92
John Baliol, 1292–96
No king, 1296–1306

BRUCES

Robert I, 1306–29
David II, 1329–71

STUARTS

Robert II, 1371–90
Robert III, 1390–1406
Regent Albany, 1406–19
Regent Murdoch, 1419–24
James I, 1424–37
James II, 1437–60
James III, 1460–88
James IV, 1488–1513
James V, 1513–42
Mary, 1542–67
James VI, 1567–1625

Until 1603 James VI reigned over Scotland only; in 1603 he became King of England and Ireland. From 1603 onwards the kings of Scotland are the same as the kings of England.

Historic Acts of Parliament

Act	Date	What it did
Catholic Emancipation Act	1829	Gave full civic rights to Catholics.
Combination Acts	1799 & 1800	Made trade unions and meetings of men to discuss wages and hours illegal. Repealed, 1824. Trade Unions made legal, 1871.
Conventicle Act	1664	Made it illegal for more than five people to meet for religious worship. An anti-Catholic measure.
Corn Laws	1815	Prohibited import of foreign corn till wheat reached famine prices. Repealed, 1846.
Corporation Act	1661	Required that anyone taking up a municipal office should receive communion according to the rites of the Anglican Church and should declare it unlawful on any grounds to take up arms against the king. An anti-Presbyterian measure.
Education Act	1870	Introduced elementary education for all.
Education Act	1944	Introduced secondary education for all.
Factory Acts	Throughout 19th century	Regulated conditions of work. The Act of 1833 provided for the appointment of factory inspectors; the Act of 1847 limited the working day to 10 hours.
Government, Act	1657	Made Cromwell's rule legal, and enabled him to name his successor.
Habeas Corpus	1679	Made it illegal to hold a man in prison without trial.

Act	*Date*	*What it did*
Heresy, Statute of	1401	Provided that all heretics (people whose beliefs were not those of the Church) were to be imprisoned and, if they refused to give up their heresy, to be burned alive. Repealed, 1548.
Indemnity, Bill of	1660	First measure passed after restoration of Charles II; pardoned all offences committed during the Cromwellian period.
Kilkenny, Statute of	1366	Forbade the mixing of the English in Ireland with the Irish people.
Labourers, Statute of	1349	Passed during the labour shortage that followed the Black Death; bound a labourer to serve under anyone requiring him to do so for wages current two years before the plague began.
Libel Act	1791	Made the decision as to what was libellous a matter for the jury and not the judge.
Mines Act	1842	Prohibited the employment in mines of women, girls and boys under 10.
National Insurance Act	1916	First introduced compulsory national health contributions and a scheme of insurance against unemployment.
Navigation Act	1652	Prohibited the importation in foreign ships of any but products of the countries to which the ships belonged. Aimed at the Dutch.
Old Age Pensions Act	1908	Introduced old age pensions for the first time.
Parliament Acts	1911 & 1949	Limited the powers of the House of Lords.
Poor Laws	1562–1601	Placed on local authorities the responsibility for settling and supporting the poor.
Poyning's Act	1494	Forbade the Parliament of the Pale in Ireland to deal with matters not first approved of by the English King and his Council. Repealed, 1779.
Public Health Act	1848	Set up the first Central Board of Health.

Act	Date	What it did
Reform Bill	1832	Took away the right to elect M.P.s from 56 'rotten boroughs', gave the seats to counties or large towns hitherto unrepresented in Parliament, and gave the vote to £10 householders. Followed by the Act of 1867, which extended the vote to working people in towns; the Act of 1884, which gave the vote to country labourers; and the Acts of 1918 and 1928, which gave the vote to women.
Rights, Bill of	1689	Established the right of the people, through their representatives in Parliament, to depose the King and set on the throne whomever they chose.
Security, Act of	1706	Required the sovereign to swear to support the Presbyterian Church.
Settlement, Act of	1701	Confined the succession to the throne to Protestants and settled it on the House of Hanover.
Six Articles, Act of the	1539	An anti-Protestant measure, establishing the celibacy of the clergy, monastic vows and private masses. Repealed, 1548.
Stamp Act	1765	Imposed a tax on all legal documents issued within the colonies. Repealed, 1766.
Succession, Act of	1534	Required an oath to be taken by all acknowledging that Henry VIII's marriage with Catharine of Aragon was invalid.
Supremacy, Act of	1534	Ordered that the king 'shall be taken, accepted and reputed the only supreme head on earth of the Church of England'.
Test Act	1563	First anti-Catholic Act, exacting from all office-holders an oath of allegiance to Queen Elizabeth and a declaration that the Pope had no authority. A similar act was passed in 1673, and set aside in 1686.

Act	Date	What it did
Toleration Act	1689	Established freedom of worship.
Treaty of Accession to European Communities, Act	1972	It made Britain a full member, as from 1 Jan 1973, of the three European Communities, i.e. the Economic Community, the Coal and Steel Community and of Euratom.
Triennial Bill	1641	Enforced the assembly of the House of Commons every three years.
Uniformity, Act of	1559	Restored the English Prayer Book and enforced its use on the clergy.
Union, Act of	1707	United England and Scotland.
Union with Ireland, Act of	1800	United England and Ireland.
Winchester, Statute of	1285	Bound every man to serve the king in case of invasion or revolt and to pursue felons when the hue and cry was raised against them.

Explorations and Discoveries

Date	Explorer	Nationality	Exploration or Discovery
982	Eric the Red	Viking	Discovered Greenland
c. 1000	Leif Ericsson	Viking	Reached N. America
1255	Nicolo and Maffeo Polo	Venetian	Travelled to Peking
1271–94	Marco Polo	Venetian	Journeyed through China, India and other parts of Asia
14th century	João Zarco, Tristão Vas and others	Portuguese	Discovered Madeira and the Azores
1487–88	Bartholomew Diaz	Portuguese	Rounded Cape of Good Hope
1492	Christopher Columbus	Italian in Spanish service	Discovered San Salvador (now Watling Island), the Bahamas, Cuba and Haiti

Date	Explorer	Nationality	Exploration or Discovery
1493–96	Christopher Columbus	Italian in Spanish service	Discovered Guadeloupe, Montserrat, Antigua, Puerto Rico and Jamaica
1497	John Cabot	Genoese in English service	Discovered Cape Breton Island, Newfoundland and Nova Scotia
1497–1503	Amerigo Vespucci	Florentine	Explored Mexico, part of E. coast of America and S. American coast
1498	Vasco da Gama	Portuguese	Discovered sea-route from Europe to India
1498	Christopher Columbus	Italian in Spanish service	Landed on mainland of S. America
1501–16	Various	Portuguese	Discovered Ceylon, Goa, Malacca, Canton, Japan and E. Indies
1502–4	Christopher Columbus	Italian in Spanish service	Discovered Trinidad
1509	Sebastian Cabot	Genoese in English service	Explored American coast as far as Florida, Brazilian coast and mouth of R. Plate
1519–22	Ferdinand Magellan	Portuguese in Spanish service	First to sail round the world; discovered the Magellan Strait, reached the Philippines and named the Pacific
1534–36	Jacques Cartier	French	Discovered Canada, explored the St Lawrence and named Mount Royal (Montreal)
1539	De Soto	Spanish	Discovered Florida, Georgia and the R. Mississippi
1554	Sir Hugh Willoughby and Richard Chancellor	English	Discovered the White Sea and the ocean route to Russia

Date	Explorer	Nationality	Exploration or Discovery
1557–80	Sir Francis Drake	English	Sailed round the world in the *Golden Hind*
1576	Martin Frobisher	English	Began search for N.W. Passage
	John Davis	English	Discovered Davis Strait between Atlantic and Arctic Oceans
1606	William Janszoon	Dutch	Discovered Australia
1606	Capt. John Smith and a party of colonists	English	Explored Chesapeake Bay, discovered Potomac and Susquehannah
1611	Henry Hudson	English	Sought N.E. and N.W. Passages; discovered Hudson River, Strait and Bay
1642	Abel Tasman	Dutch	Discovered Tasmania, New Zealand, the Tonga and Fiji islands
1700	William Dampier	English	Explored W. Coast of Australia
1728	Vitus Bering	Danish in Russian service	Discovered Bering Strait between Asia and America
1740–44	George, Lord Anson	English	Sailed round the world in the *Centurion*
1767	Capt. Wallis	English	Discovered Tahiti
1768–71	Capt. James Cook	English	Sailed round the world in the *Endeavour*; charted New Zealand coasts and surveyed E. Coast of Australia, naming New South Wales and Botany Bay
1772	Capt. James Cook	English	Discovered Easter Island, New Caledonia and Norfolk Island
1776	Capt. James Cook	English	Discovered several of the Cook (or Hervey) islands. Rediscovered Sandwich (now Hawaiian) islands

Date	Explorer	Nationality	Exploration or Discovery
1776	Mungo Park	Scottish	Explored the course of R. Niger
1831	Sir James Clark Ross and Rear-Admiral Sir John Ross	English	Located the magnetic pole
1839–43	Sir James Clark Ross	English	Discovered Victoria Land, Mounts Erebus and Terror, the Ross ice barrier
1847	Rear-Admiral Sir John Franklin	English	Lost in Arctic Ocean while seeking N.W. Passage
1852–73	David Livingstone	Scottish	Discovered the course of the Zambesi, the Victoria Falls and Lake Nyasa
1856	Capt. John Speke	English	Discovered Lake Tanganyika
1858	Capt. John Speke	English	Discovered Lake Victoria Nyanza
1862	Capt. John Speke and Lt.-Col. J. A. Grant	English	Discovered source of White Nile
1901	Capt. R. F. Scott	English	Discovered King Edward VII Land
1903–6	Capt. Roald Amundsen	Norwegian	First navigation of the N.W. Passage
1908–9	Sir Ernest Shackleton	English	Reached within 100 miles of South Pole
1909	Rear-Admiral Robert Peary	American	Reached North Pole
1911	Capt. Roald Amundsen	Norwegian	First reached South Pole (December 14)
1912	Capt. R. F. Scott	English	Reached South Pole (January 18)
1929	Admiral R. Byrd	American	First flight over South Pole
1957–58	Sir Vivian Fuchs and Sir Edmund Hillary	English and New Zealander	First crossing of the Antarctic Continent

Date	Explorer	Nationality	Exploration or Discovery
1961–62	Major Yuri Gagarin, Major Gherman Titov, Commander Alan Shepard, Capt. Virgil Grissom and Col. John Glenn	Russian and American	First journeys into space
1963	Valentina Tereshkova	Russian	First woman in space
1965	Col. Leonov Major White	Russian and American	First men to 'walk' in space
1968	Frank Borman, Bill Anders, and Jim Lovell	American	First men to circle moon
1969	Neil Armstrong and Edwin Aldrin	American	First men to step on the moon
	Charles Conrad and Alan Bean	American	Second pair to step on the moon

British Prime Ministers

REIGN OF GEORGE I

Sir Robert Walpole (*Whig*)   1721–27

REIGN OF GEORGE II

Sir Robert Walpole (*Whig*)	1727–42
Earl of Wilmington (*Whig*)	1742–43
Henry Pelham (*Whig*)	1743–46
Henry Pelham (*Whig*)	1746–54
Duke of Newcastle (*Whig*)	1754–56
Duke of Devonshire (*Whig*)	1756–57
Duke of Newcastle (*Whig*)	1757–60

REIGN OF GEORGE III

Duke of Newcastle (*Whig*)	1760–62
Earl of Bute (*Tory*)	1762–63
George Grenville (*Whig*)	1763–65
Marquess of Rockingham (*Whig*)	1765–66
Earl of Chatham (*Whig*)	1766–67
Duke of Grafton (*Whig*)	1767–70
Lord North (*Tory*)	1770–82

Marquess of Rockingham (*Whig*)	1782
Earl of Shelburne (*Whig*)	1782–83
Duke of Portland (*Coalition*)	1783
William Pitt (*Tory*)	1783–1801
Henry Addington (*Tory*)	1801–4
William Pitt (*Tory*)	1804–6
Lord Grenville (*Whig*)	1806–7
Duke of Portland (*Tory*)	1807–9
Spencer Perceval (*Tory*)	1809–12
Earl of Liverpool (*Tory*)	1812–20

REIGN OF GEORGE IV

Earl of Liverpool (*Tory*)	1820–27
George Canning (*Tory*)	1827
Viscount Goderich (*Tory*)	1827–28
Duke of Wellington (*Tory*)	1828–30

REIGN OF WILLIAM IV

Earl Grey (*Whig*)	1830–34
Viscount Melbourne (*Whig*)	1834
Sir Robert Peel (*Tory*)	1834–35
Viscount Melbourne (*Whig*)	1835–37

REIGN OF VICTORIA

Viscount Melbourne (*Whig*)	1837–41
Sir Robert Peel (*Tory*)	1841–46
Lord John Russell (*Whig*)	1846–52
Earl of Derby (*Tory*)	1852
Earl of Aberdeen (*Peelite*)	1852–55
Viscount Palmerston (*Liberal*)	1855–58
Earl of Derby (*Conservative*)	1858
Viscount Palmerston (*Liberal*)	1858–65
Earl Russell (*Liberal*)	1865–66
Earl of Derby (*Conservative*)	1866–68
Benjamin Disraeli (*Conservative*)	1868
W. E. Gladstone (*Liberal*)	1868–74
Benjamin Disraeli (*Conservative*)	1874–80
W. E. Gladstone (*Liberal*)	1880–85
Marquess of Salisbury (*Conservative*)	1885–86
W. E. Gladstone (*Liberal*)	1886
Marquess of Salisbury (*Conservative*)	1886–92
W. E. Gladstone (*Liberal*)	1892–94
Earl of Rosebery (*Liberal*)	1894–95
Marquess of Salisbury (*Conservative*)	1895–1902

REIGN OF EDWARD VII

A. J. Balfour (*Conservative*)	1902–5
Sir Henry Campbell-Bannerman (*Liberal*)	1905–8
Herbert H. Asquith (*Liberal*)	1908–10

REIGN OF GEORGE V

H. H. Asquith (*Liberal*)	1910–15
H. H. Asquith (*Coalition*)	1915–16
D. Lloyd George (*Coalition*)	1916–22
A. Bonar Law (*Conservative*)	1922–23
Stanley Baldwin (*Conservative*)	1923–24
J. Ramsay MacDonald (*Labour*)	1924
Stanley Baldwin (*Conservative*)	1924–29
J. Ramsay MacDonald (*Labour*)	1929–31
J. Ramsay MacDonald (*National Government*)	1931–35
Stanley Baldwin (*National Government*)	1935–36

REIGN OF EDWARD VIII

Stanley Baldwin (*National Government*)	1936

REIGN OF GEORGE VI

Stanley Baldwin (*National Government*)	1936–37
Neville Chamberlain (*National Government*)	1937–40
Winston S. Churchill (*Coalition*)	1940–45
Clement R. Attlee (*Labour*)	1945–51
Winston S. Churchill (*Conservative*)	1951–52

REIGN OF ELIZABETH II

Sir Winston S. Churchill (*Conservative*)	1952–55
Sir Anthony Eden (*Conservative*)	1955–57
Harold Macmillan (*Conservative*)	1957–63
Sir Alec Douglas-Home (*Conservative*)	1963–64
Harold Wilson (*Labour*)	1964–70
Edward Heath (*Conservative*)	1970–74
Harold Wilson (*Labour*)	1974–

United States Presidents

George Washington (*Federalist*)	1789–97
John Adams (*Federalist*)	1797–1801
Thomas Jefferson (*Republican*)	1801–9
James Madison (*Republican*)	1809–17
James Monroe (*Republican*)	1817–25
John Quincy Adams (*Republican*)	1825–29
Andrew Jackson (*Democrat*)	1829–37
Martin Van Buren (*Democrat*)	1837–41
William Henry Harrison (*Whig*)	1841
John Tyler (*Whig*)	1841–45
James Knox Polk (*Democrat*)	1845–49
Zachary Taylor (*Whig*)	1849–50
Millard Fillmore (*Whig*)	1850–53
Franklin Pierce (*Democrat*)	1853–57
James Buchanan (*Democrat*)	1857–61
Abraham Lincoln (*Republican*)	1861–65
Andrew Johnson (*Republican*)	1865–69
Ulysses Simpson Grant (*Republican*)	1869–77
Rutherford Birchard Hayes (*Republican*)	1877–81
James Abram Garfield (*Republican*)	1881
Chester Alan Arthur (*Republican*)	1881–85
Grover Cleveland (*Democrat*)	1885–89
Benjamin Harrison (*Republican*)	1889–93
Grover Cleveland (*Democrat*)	1893–97
William McKinley (*Republican*)	1897–1901
Theodore Roosevelt (*Republican*)	1901–9
William Howard Taft (*Republican*)	1909–13
Woodrow Wilson (*Democrat*)	1913–21
Warren Gamaliel Harding (*Republican*)	1921–23
Calvin Coolidge (*Republican*)	1923–29
Herbert C. Hoover (*Republican*)	1929–33
Franklin Delano Roosevelt (*Democrat*)	1933–45
Harry S. Truman (*Democrat*)	1945–53
Dwight D. Eisenhower (*Republican*)	1953–61
John F. Kennedy (*Democrat*)	1961–63
Lyndon B. Johnson (*Democrat*)	1963–69
Richard M. Nixon (*Republican*)	1969–74
Gerald Ford (*Republican*)	1974–

The ENGLISH LINE of SUCCESSION

ALFRED the GREAT 871-901

EDWARD the ELDER 901-924

ATHELSTAN 924-940   EDMUND the ELDER 940-946   EDRED 946-955

EDWY 955-959   EDGAR 959-975

EDWARD the MARTYR 975-978   ETHELRED 978-1016   CANUTE 1016-1035

EDWARD the CONFESSOR 1042-1066   EDMUND IRONSIDE 1016   HAROLD I 1035-1040

Edward   HARDICANUTE 1040-1042

WILLIAM the CONQUEROR 1066-1087   Margaret
m. Matilda of Flanders   m. Malcolm III of Scotland

WILLIAM II 1087-1100. Adela   HENRY I 1101-1135 m. Matilda

STEPHEN 1135-1154   Matilda
m. Geoffrey of Anjou

HENRY II 1154-1189
m. Eleanor of Aquitaine

RICHARD I 1189-1199   JOHN 1199-1216
m. Isabella of Angouleme

HENRY III 1216-1272
m Eleanor of Provence

EDWARD I 1272-1307
m. Eleanor of Castille

EDWARD II 1307-1327
m. Isabella of France

EDWARD III 1327-1377
m. Philippa of Hainault

Edward the Black Prince   John of Gaunt   Edmund of York
m. 1 Blanche of Lancaster 11 Katherine Swynford

RICHARD II 1377-1399   Richard of York
m Anne Mortimer

HENRY IV 1399-1413   John Beaufort
m Mary Bohun

Richard of York
m Cicely Neville

HENRY V 1413-1422
m. Katherine of France   John Beaufort

HENRY VI 1422-1461   Margaret
m. Edmund Tudor

EDWARD IV 1461-1483   RICHARD III
m Elizabeth Woodville   1483-1485

HENRY VII 1485-1509 m Elizabeth   EDWARD V 1483
m. Anne Neville

Margaret
m. James IV of Scotland

HENRY VIII 1509-1547

EDWARD VI
1547-1553

MARY I
1553-1558

ELIZABETH I
1558-1603

James V of Scotland
m. Mary of Guise

Mary Queen of Scots
m. Henry, Lord Darnley

JAMES I of England 1603-1625
m. Anne of Denmark

CHARLES I 1625-1649
m. Henrietta Maria of France

Elizabeth
m. Frederick V Elector Palatine

CHARLES II
1660-1685
m. Katherine of
Braganza

Mary
m. William II
of Orange

JAMES II 1685-1688
m. 1 Anne Hyde 2 Mary of
Modena

Sophia of Hanover
m. Ernest Augustus of Hanover

WILLIAM III m. MARY II
1689-1702   1689-1694

ANNE
1702-1714
m. George of
Denmark

James, the
Old Pretender

Charles, the
Young Pretender

GEORGE I 1714-1727
m. Dorothea of Zell

GEORGE II 1727-1760
m. Caroline of Brandenburg-Anspach

Maria of Brunswick- m. Frederick V m. Louisa

Louisa of Denmark   Frederick of Denmark

Louisa of Hesse Cassel   Charlotte

Christian IX m. Louisa of Hesse-Cassel

William became George I, King of Hellenes

Frederick
m. Augusta of Saxe Gotha

GEORGE III 1760-1820
m. Charlotte of Mecklenburg Strelitz

GEORGE IV
1820-1830
m. Caroline of Brunswick
Wolfenbuttel

WILLIAM IV
1830-1837

Edward
m. Victoria of Saxe-Coburg-Gotha

Adolphus

VICTORIA 1837-1901
m. Albert of Saxe-
Coburg-Gotha

Marie
m. Francis
of Teck

Alice
m. Louis of Hesse

EDWARD VII 1901-1910
m. Alexandra of Denmark

Victoria
m. Louis of Battenburg
(Mountbatten)

GEORGE V m. Mary of Teck
1910-1936

Andrew, Prince of m. Alice
Greece

EDWARD VIII
1936
m. Wallis Simpson

GEORGE VI
1936-1952
m. Elizabeth Bowes-Lyon

Mary Henry George

Philip m. ELIZABETH II
1952

Margaret
m. Antony Armstrong-Jones

Charles Anne Andrew Edward
m. Mark Phillips

David Sarah

A Glossary of Political Terms

Absolutism or Absolute Monarchy A system of government where the hereditary ruler, usually a king, has complete power to decide a country's internal and external policy without having to consult anyone. A good example of an absolute monarch: Louis XIV of France. The French Revolution heralded the end of absolutism, and in the nineteenth century absolute monarchies everywhere gave place to constitutional monarchies or republics.

Amnesty An act granting forgiveness (literally, forgetfulness) to political and other offenders.

Anarchism Anarchists (from the Greek word *anarchia,* non-rule) believe that every form of government is evil. Towards the end of the last century anarchists assassinated Czar Alexander of Russia and other political leaders in order to draw attention to their theories. There was a strong anarchist movement in Spain during the 1930s.

Aristocracy From the Greek, meaning government by the best. It has come to mean the best by birth. The government of Britain can be said to have been aristocratic up to the Great Reform Bill of 1832 in the sense that both Houses of Parliament were virtually controlled by members of the great landed aristocratic families.

Autocracy Absolute rule by one man.

Authoritarian A term denoting a dictatorial system of government.

Autonomy A word of Greek origin meaning 'self-government'.

Balance of Payments The balance between the cost of a country's imports and the receipts for its exports. Britain is said to pass through a balance-of-payments crisis whenever the value of her imports exceeds the value of her exports.

Balance of Power The theory that the strength of one group of powers on the European continent should be equal to the strength of the other group, thus preventing one group from becoming dominant. Britain's foreign policy in Europe before the First World War is often said to have been dictated by the wish to achieve a balance of power between the countries on the continent of Europe and so prevent aggression and war.

Bi-partisan Foreign Policy A foreign policy on which both the government and opposition parties are agreed.

Bourgeoisie French for 'citizen class'. A term used by Marxist socialists to denote manufacturers, merchants and people with a business of their own, as opposed to the 'proletariat', who earn a living only by selling their labour.

Buffer State A small state established or preserved between two greater states to prevent direct clashes between them.

Common Market See special section in this edition.

Communism The theory, as expounded by Marx and Engels, which aims at the creation of a society in which the private ownership of land, factories, banks, trading houses, etc., is abolished, and everyone receives what he needs and works according to his capacity. Communists believe that revolution and the use of force are justified to bring about the creation of such a society.

Constitution Document or set of documents which set out how a country is to be governed. Britain is said to have an 'unwritten constitution' because, although there are many documents, such as the Great Reform Bill of 1832 or the Parliament Act of 1911, which deal with constitutional matters, there is no single document which sets out the constitutional machinery of Britain, and such written documents as the Great Reform Bill make sense only against the background of the unwritten customs and traditions which have grown up in Britain over the centuries. By contrast, countries such as the U.S.A., France and Germany are all said to have 'written constitutions' because there is a single document or set of documents to which one can refer.

Constitutional Monarchy A system of government where the king's political power is limited by the constitution. Usually it means that real power in a country rests with an elected parliament.

Coup d'état A seizure of power and the machinery of government by force.

Democracy From Greek words meaning 'government by the people'. Democracy may be either direct, as practised in some city-states in Ancient Greece where all the adult citizens met in the market-place to discuss and decide on all questions of policy, or indirect, as practised in modern times when the people elect representatives to some kind of parliament. A democracy can be either a monarchy if its head of State is a king or queen as in Britain, or a republic if its head of State is a president as in the U.S.A. and France.

Dictatorship Rule by one man who, in deciding what to do about the internal or external affairs of the country he controls, does not have to consider or consult anyone but himself.

Fascism An authoritarian extreme right-wing nationalist movement which denies the individual all rights in his relations with the state. In Italy Fascism was led by Mussolini, who held power from 1922 to 1943, and there were strong Fascist movements in many other countries between the two world wars. The German version of Fascism was Hitler's National Socialism. Fascism derives from the Latin word *fasces*, the name for the axe encased in a bundle of rods which was carried in procession before the chief magistrates in Ancient Rome as a symbol of their power over the life and liberty of ordinary citizens.

Federation A union of states or provinces under a common central government to which they surrender some but not all their powers of government. A federal form of government is usually found in countries which cover a vast area such as the U.S.A., Canada and Australia, but in Europe Switzerland is a federation, and its component states, called cantons, enjoy a large measure of autonomy.

Free Trade A policy of allowing goods to move freely between countries without imposing tariffs or customs duties. Adam Smith in 1776 set out the classic case for Free Trade in his *Wealth of Nations*. Britain's superiority as a manufacturing country in the Victorian era made her favour Free Trade, but as other countries became industrialised towards the end of the nineteenth century and her superiority vanished, the demand for 'Protection', i.e. tariffs and customs duties to 'protect' goods manufactured in Britain from foreign competition, grew. All countries today are partially 'protected', but many countries, such as Britain and the U.S.A., are working towards making industrial trade as free as possible.

Imperialism In its original sense, the system of government by an emperor. It has come to be used of any policy of political, military or economic expansion carried out at the expense of weaker people. British imperialism saw its heyday in the latter part of the nineteenth century, its leading exponents being Disraeli, Lord Rosebery and Joseph Chamberlain; but since then the tendency within the British Commonwealth has been to give colonial people self-government and independence as soon as and wherever possible.

Industrial Revolution Term applied to the economic developments which between the 1750s and the 1830s transformed Britain from a primarily agricultural to a primarily industrial country.

Isolation A refusal to enter into firm commitments and alliances with other powers.

Laisser-Faire The theory that the state should refrain from all interference in economic affairs. From a phrase coined by eighteenth-century French economists, 'laisser-faire et laisser-passer', 'to let go and pass', i.e. to leave the individual alone and let commodities circulate freely. A reaction against laisser-faire set in in the nineteenth century, inspired by a revulsion against the social conditions created by the Industrial Revolution, and found expression, for example, in the Factory Acts regulating working conditions. The twentieth century has seen an ever-increasing degree of state intervention for social and economic reasons.

Liberalism The body of political and social ideas associated with the Liberal Party in Britain and with similar parties elsewhere. The British Liberal Party, which developed out of the Whig Party in the nineteenth century, stood for parliamentary reform, individual liberty, freedom of speech, of the press and of worship, for laisser-faire, i.e. a minimum of state interference in economic affairs, and for international free trade. Towards the end of the nineteenth century, the Liberal Party modified its views on laisser-faire to ensure minimum living standards for the working class, and, inspired by Lloyd George, the Liberal governments of 1906–14 laid the foundation of what we call today the Welfare State. Since the First World War the influence of the Liberals has declined everywhere, their place as the party of social reform being taken by the Socialists.

Nationalism Term for movements which aim at the strengthening of national feeling and at the unification of a nation or its liberation from foreign rule. Modern nationalism was born in the French Revolution, and under the impact of that event nationalism became a potent factor in European politics in the nineteenth century and helped to bring about the unification of Germany and Italy. In the twentieth century nationalism became a powerful force in Asia and Africa.

National Socialism A German authoritarian extreme right-wing nationalist movement which denied the individual all rights in his relations with the state, personified by Hitler as the Fuehrer ('Leader').

Neutral Term used to describe the condition of a country which in war refrains from taking part in hostilities and maintains a strictly impartial attitude towards the belligerents, and in peace stands aloof from the quarrels of other countries and refuses to enter into military alliances. Example: Switzerland and Sweden.

Neutralist Term which has come into use since the Second World War to describe countries which are unwilling to become involved in the Cold War disputes between the Communist and Western power blocs. Example: India.

Nuclear Test Ban Treaty The agreement signed by the Soviet Union, the U.S.A. and Britain in Moscow in July, 1963, by which the signatories bound themselves not to test nuclear weapons of any sort by exploding them either under water or in the atmosphere, including outer space. The purpose of the Treaty was to stop the further pollution of the world by radio-active debris. The conclusion of the Treaty led to a dramatic lessening of tension (*détente*) between the Western and Communist powers.

Plebiscite A direct vote by the voters of a country or district on a specific question. In the usual election the people vote for or against the government on all the policies for which it stands; in a plebiscite or referendum they vote only on one particular question.

Radical A person seeking political, social or economic reform 'from the root'. Term used to describe the wing of the Liberal party which was most forward in its demands for reform. Radicalism lost much of its popular support with the rise of Socialism in this century.

Reactionary In politics, a person who wants to prevent or undo reforms.

Republic A country where the head of state is a president and not a king.

Responsible Government A country is said to have responsible government where the government is responsible to Parliament for everything it does, and where it must resign if it loses the 'confidence' of Parliament. In this sense Britain has responsible government, but the U.S.A. has not, because there the President, elected by the whole country for a term of four years, continues in office whether he has the approval of Congress (Parliament) or not. Both countries are, of course, democracies, despite this difference in their constitutions.

Socialism The political, social and economic theories which aim at the establishment of a classless society, through the substitution of common for private ownership of the means of production (land, factories), distribution (shops, transport), and exchange (banks). The Communists believe that all means, including revolution, violence and oppression, are justified in the pursuit of their aims. The Socialists in Britain, in Western Europe and in most of the African and Asian countries of the Commonwealth are Social Democrats, i.e. they want to bring about a Socialist Society by democratic means such as elections and through democratic institutions such as Parliament. Some Social Democrats want a '*mixed economy*', i.e. one in which not all the means of production, distribution and exchange pass into public ownership, but a large proportion remains in private hands.

Tory Name given to the forerunner of the present Conservative party. Traditionally the Tories were the party of the squire and the parson, as opposed to the *Whigs*, the forerunners of the Liberals, who, though led by a group of great land-owning families, drew their support mainly from the business classes and Nonconformists.

White House The official residence of the President of the U.S.A. in Washington. It was partially burnt when the British occupied Washington briefly during the 1812–14 war with the U.S.A., and afterwards painted white to hide the scars left by the fire. Hence the name. The term 'The White House' is often used to mean 'the American government', e.g. 'The White House reviews its Far Eastern policy.'

Government in Britain

1. National Affairs

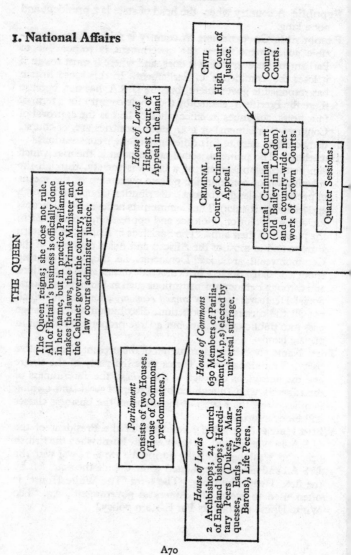

THE QUEEN

The Queen reigns; she does not rule. All of Britain's business is officially done in her name, but in practice Parliament makes the laws, the Prime Minister and the Cabinet govern the country, and the law courts administer justice.

Parliament
Consists of two Houses. (House of Commons predominates.)

House of Commons
630 Members of Parliament (M.p.s) elected by universal suffrage.

House of Lords
2 Archbishops; 24 Church of England bishops; Hereditary Peers (Dukes, Marquesses, Earls, Viscounts, Barons), Life Peers.

House of Lords
Highest Court of Appeal in the land.

CRIMINAL
Court of Criminal Appeal.

CIVIL
High Court of Justice.

County Courts.

Central Criminal Court (Old Bailey in London) and a country-wide network of Crown Courts.

Quarter Sessions.

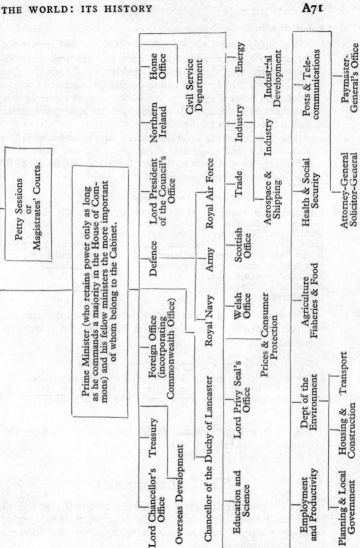

Petty Sessions
or
Magistrates' Courts.

Prime Minister (who retains power only as long as he commands a majority in the House of Commons) and his fellow ministers the more important of whom belong to the Cabinet.

Lord Chancellor's Office

Treasury

Overseas Development

Chancellor of the Duchy of Lancaster

Foreign Office (incorporating Commonwealth Office)

Defence

Lord President of the Council's Office

Northern Ireland

Home Office

Civil Service Department

Industry

Energy

Education and Science

Lord Privy Seal's Office

Prices & Consumer Protection

Royal Navy

Welsh Office

Scottish Office

Army

Royal Air Force

Trade

Industry

Aerospace & Shipping

Industrial Development

Employment and Productivity

Planning & Local Government

Dept of the Environment

Housing & Construction

Transport

Agriculture Fisheries & Food

Health & Social Security

Attorney-General Solicitor-General

Posts & Telecommunications

Paymaster-General's Office

2. Local affairs

The management of local affairs is left to local authorities subject to supervision—largely exercised through financial control—by the central Government in London. The administration of London which became the Greater London Council in place of the London County Council in the 1960's, continues as at present but outside London local government was drastically reorganised in 1974.

The 1,400 existing local authorities in England and Wales (County Councils, County Borough Councils, Municipal Boroughs, Rural Districts, Urban Districts, Parish Councils and Meetings) were replaced by:

6 Metropolitan counties —large conurbations— West Midlands, Mersey-Side, West Yorkshire, South Yorkshire, Tyne and Weare, Greater Manchester—responsible for education and personal social services.	52 new counties responsible for planning, transport, education and personal social services.	some 375 new district authorities responsible for housing, refuse collection, play- and sports-grounds etc.

The existing 430 local authorities in Scotland (counties, counties of cities, town councils and district councils) are to be replaced by:

8 regional authorities responsible for major planning, transport, education and personal social services.	47 district authorities responsible for housing, refuse collection, parks and sports grounds.

In Scotland the new authorities are to take over from the existing bodies in 1975.

The Commonwealth

The Commonwealth grew out of the British Empire. All the states, nations and territories which belong to it today were once governed by men sent out from England who received their orders from London.

The transformation from dependence to independent nationhood usually followed this broad pattern:

Once British power was firmly established, the British Governor would try to draw local notabilities into the business of running the country, consulting them on important matters, and even appointing them to be his official advisers; in due course he would set up a legislative Council or Parliament, but he would make certain of being able to get his way in the last resort by allowing only a minority of its members to be elected by the local population and by appointing the majority himself; later on he would gradually increase the number of locally elected members until in the end there would be no officially appointed members left; at that stage London would usually surrender its powers to run the affairs of the country concerned, the leader of the majority in the Legislative Council or Parliament would become Prime Minister, the Governor would cease to play an active part in politics and, like the Queen in Britain, would be able to act only as advised by the Prime Minister.

The first countries to reach the top of the ladder of self-government were those settled by people of British or European stock. They were known as 'Dominions', and in defining their relationship to one another and to Britain, the Imperial Conference of 1926 described them as 'autonomous communities within the British Empire, equal in status, in no way subordinate one to another in any aspect of their domestic or foreign affairs, though united by a common allegiance to the Crown, and freely associated as members of the British Commonwealth of Nations.'

They were—apart from Britain—five in number:

Australia   Canada
Newfoundland (after a referendum joined Canada as a
    Province in 1949 and ceased being an independent
    Dominion)
New Zealand
South Africa (left the Commonwealth in 1961).

After the Second World War the number of countries which attained independent nationhood increased rapidly and, since many of them had populations which were not predominantly of British or European descent, it became customary to refer to the Commonwealth and not the British Commonwealth.

In January 1974 the following were fully independent members of the Commonwealth, in addition to those listed above:

India	Kenya	The Bahamas
Sri Lanka	Tanzania[1]	Barbados
Ghana	Malawi[2]	Mauritius
Nigeria	Malta	Swaziland
Cyprus	Zambia[3]	Tonga
Sierra Leone	Gambia	Western Samoa
Jamaica	Singapore	Fiji
Trinidad	Guyana[4]	Bangladesh
Uganda	Botswana[5]	Nauru
Malaysia	Lesotho[6]	

Former Names: [1] Tanganyika and Zanzibar.   [2] Nyasaland.
[3] N. Rhodesia. [4] Brit. Guiana. [5] Bechuanaland. [6] Basutoland.

(Burma became independent in 1948 but decided to leave the Commonwealth. Pakistan left the Commonwealth in January 1971.)

There are altogether 33 independent countries within the Commonwealth (including Britain). They form an association of countries. They are not a state or even a federation. There is no single parliament or government, no central defence force or executive power. They are no longer 'united by a common allegiance to the Crown'. For example, India, Ghana, Nigeria, Cyprus, Uganda, Kenya, Tanzania, Malawi and Zambia are republics although all recognise the Queen as Head of the Commonwealth. And there is no common foreign policy. Britain, Canada, Australia and New Zealand belong to military alliances designed to stop the spread of Communism; India, Ceylon, Ghana and Tanzania are 'uncommitted'.

The essence of the Commonwealth relationship is consultation, and the most important forms of consultation are the Commonwealth Prime Ministers' Conferences which, whenever possible, are held in London at least once every two years and now have a permanent home in Marlborough House, formerly the late Queen Mary's residence.

Other Commonwealth bonds:

Constant consultation between the Commonwealth delegations at the United Nations in New York.

Commercial ties and Imperial preferences.

Language (Many Commonwealth leaders with multilingual populations find that English is the only language in which they can talk to all their people.)

Common political traditions and habits of thought.

THE ENGLISH LANGUAGE   .   .   .   L   1–30

Some of the Technical Terms of Language—
An Emergency Guide to Punctuation—Foreign
Phrases and Classical Quotations—A Short List
of American Words and Phrases—A Dictionary
of British Writers.

MUSIC AND THE ARTS   .   .   .   .   M   1–34

Melody, Harmony and Rhythm — Music
History — The Instruments — Some Musical
Terms — A Brief History of the World's Arts
—Painters, Sculptors and Architects.

SPORT   .   .   .   .   N   1–58

Archery — Association Football — Athletics
— Badminton — Basketball — Billiards and
Snooker — Boxing — Cricket — Cross-Country
Running — Cycling — Equestrian — Fencing —
Gliding — Golf — Hockey — Ice Hockey — Ice
Skating — Lacrosse — Lawn Tennis — Motor
Cycling — Motor Racing — Netball — Rackets —
Rowing — Rugby League Football — Rugby
Union Football — Shooting — Ski-ing — Squash
Rackets — Swimming — Table Tennis — Volley
Ball — Walking — Water Polo — Yachting —
Other Olympic Results, 1972—Personalities.

THE ECONOMIC CRISIS   .   .   .   .   P   1–16

SOMETHING TO JOIN   .   .   .   .   R   1–14

A List of Youth Organisations—Morse Code
—Semaphore—Compass—Knots.

THE ARMED SERVICES, THE POLICE AND
FIRE BRIGADES   .   .   .   .   .   S   1–13

The Army—The Royal Navy—The Royal
Air Force—The Police—Fire Brigades—Relative Ranks: Sea, Land and Air—Decorations
and Medals.

THE LAW . . . . T 1–8

What is Law?—Rights, Duties—The Courts
—People in the Courts—The Cost of Going
to Law—The Action—Appeals—Where the
Law Comes From—The Subjects of Law—
Scottish Law.

NATURAL HISTORY . . . . . V 1–84

What Living Things are Made of—How living
Things Work—Reproduction and Heredity—
The History of Life on Earth—The Kinds of
Living Things—Nature Study and the Web of
Life.

MISCELLANY . . . . . . W 1–26

Time: Calendars and Clocks—British Flags—
A Note on Heraldry — Britain's Decimal
Coinage — Notes on Coins — Distance of
the Horizon—Seven Wonders of the Ancient
World—Roman Numerals—Greek and Rus-
sian Alphabets—Deaf and Dumb Alphabet—
Longest and Highest—A Guide to Some of the
Most Important Museums in Great Britain.

The World

1: ITS HISTORY

A Diary of World Events	2–48
An Index of Important Battles	49–50
Kings and Queens of Scotland	50
Historic Acts of Parliament	51–54
Explorations and Discoveries	54–58
British Prime Ministers	58–60
Presidents of the U.S.A.	61
The Royal Line	62–63
A Glossary of Political Terms	64–69
Government in Britain	70–72
The Commonwealth	72–75
The United Nations	75–78

A Diary of World Events

THE story of man, who first appeared on the Earth a little less than a million years ago, can be traced back only about 6,000 years. For earlier times there are no written records (nor have archaeologists made discoveries) to help the historian to form an accurate or detailed picture of human activity.

This diary is planned not only to be referred to if you are hurriedly searching for a particular event (or revising a particular period) but also to be read as a story. And a hair-raising story it is, with its empires rising and falling, its barbarian Franks and Goths and Vandals becoming the French and Germans and Italians of today, and the uneasy groupings of nations against one another becoming the enormous anxious grouping of our own time. Read the diary through immediately after looking at the chart of geological periods in the NATURAL HISTORY section (p. V34), and consider what a tiny pinch of time these 6,000 years are when measured against the total life of our planet. And remember, as you read, that the diary doesn't cease to be written simply because we have had to break off at 1974 to put it in this book. This diary is now your diary; History is your history.

The first reference to any historical figure in this account is printed in black type. So that if you are interested in, say, Napoleon, and come across his name in ordinary type, you will know that you are somewhere in the middle of his story, and must look back to **Napoleon** in order to find its beginning. The names of battles are printed in small capitals, like this: WATERLOO. If you wish to refer to a particular battle there is an index of battles at the end giving the dates under which you should look for them.

Some of the most important events of all, the passing of great Acts of Parliament and achievements of exploration and discovery, are omitted because they are dealt with separately elsewhere in this section.

B.C.

4000–3000 First settlements in the river valleys of the Nile in Egypt, the Tigris and Euphrates in Mesopotamia, the Indus in India and the Yellow River in China.

By 2000 Chinese civilisation, oldest in the world, covers practically the whole of China.

In the Indus valley the Dravidians have established an orderly system of government; they are often invaded, but out of the give and take of ideas between conquerors and conquered, Hinduism begins to emerge. In Mesopotamia the Sumerians have invented a form of writing (cuneiform),

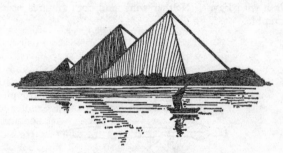

The Great Pyramids

divided the circle into 360°, a degree into 60 minutes and a minute into 60 seconds, and discovered how to extract copper and make bronze. Their knowledge lives on despite their absorption into the Babylonian Empire, whose best-known king, **Hammurabi**, extends the authority of Babylon as far as Syria and codifies his country's laws.

In the Nile valley the Egyptians have already built the Great Pyramids at Gizeh and the Sphinx (2600) and divided time into solar years.

The spread of knowledge from Egypt has helped to create the Minoan civilisation in Crete (named after the legendary king **Minos** (see DICTIONARY OF MYTHOLOGY), whose magnificent palace at Knossos was discovered in 1900).

In Britain the great stone circles at Stonehenge and Avebury are still used for religious worship.

1800–1700 First use in Egypt of papyrus, an early form of paper. Nile valley overrun by Hyksos ('princes of the desert').

The Babylonian empire is overrun by the Hittites; but there is conflict, lasting several centuries, between these and other invading tribes based on Babylon, Nineveh and other cities.

1580 Hyksos driven out of Egypt. Founding of the 'New Kingdom', under which Egypt is to be at her greatest.

1400 Moses leads the Israelites out of Egypt. Knossos destroyed by earthquake or enemies, and Cretan civilisation at an end.

1300–1200 Hittites, now controlling all Mesopotamia, discover how to smelt iron, equip their troops with iron weapons, and clash with Egypt. Neither wins, and both empires begin to crumble.

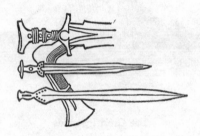

1180 Siege of Troy: one of the wars by which the ancestors of the ancient Greeks settled themselves round the Aegean, and the only one of which an account survives (in Homer's *Iliad*).

c. 1060–c. 970 David king of Israel.

c. 970–c. 940 Solomon king of Israel. He uses his enormous wealth, gained through trade, to build the Temple at Jerusalem.

800 The Phoenicians, whose cities of Tyre and Sidon are nearly 1,000 years old, found Carthage.

776 First Olympiad.

753 Rome founded.

750–550 Greek city states emerge on Greek mainland and around the coasts of Mediterranean and Black Sea.

691 Assyrians (already lords of Mesopotamia, Syria, Palestine, Arabia) conquer Egypt.

660 First Mikado in Japan.

612 Chaldeans conquer Assyrians and establish second Babylonian Empire.

597 Nebuchadnezzar, mightiest Chaldean emperor, captures Jerusalem and carries off the Jews into captivity.

594 Solon lays the foundations of Athenian democracy.

560 Buddha born.

551 Confucius born.

539–525 Cyrus, king of Persia, makes himself master of Asia Minor, captures Babylon, founds the Persian empire and allows the Jews to return to Jerusalem.

525 Cambyses, Cyrus's successor, conquers Egypt.

510 Rome becomes a republic.

490 Athens has helped Greek cities on the coast of Asia Minor to revolt—unsuccessfully—against their Persian overlords. **Darius I** of Persia lands a force in Greece to punish Athens; is beaten at MARATHON.

480 Xerxes makes a second attempt to crush Greece; exterminates a Spartan army under **Leonidas** at THERMOPYLAE and occupies Athens; but the Persian fleet is destroyed at SALAMIS.

479 Persians defeated at PLAETAEA.

461 Pericles becomes the most important person in Athenian politics. Under his leadership Greek civilisation, free of the Persian menace, has its 'golden age'; it is now that the Parthenon is built (447–438). But removal of the Persian danger leads to quarrelling among the Greek city states.

431–404 Peloponnesian War between Athens and Sparta, ending with capture of Athens.

The Parthenon

390 Gauls capture Rome except for the Capitol, but Romans regain the city by paying huge ransom.

359 Philip becomes king of Macedonia; sets out to make himself overlord of quarrelsome Greek cities.

338 Philip defeats combined armies of Athens and Thebes, becomes master of Greece.

336 Philip assassinated; succeeded by his son, **Alexander the Great**.

333 Alexander defeats **Darius III** of Persia and conquers Egypt, where he founds Alexandria.

327 Alexander extends his empire as far as the Indus.

323 Alexander dies; his empire is divided among his generals.

280 Pyrrhus, king of Epirus, aids Greek cities in S. Italy against Rome; defeats the Romans twice but himself suffers heavy losses (hence the term 'Pyrrhic victories', meaning victories won at great cost).

275 Defeating Pyrrhus, Rome becomes mistress of S. Italy, and thus comes into conflict with Carthage.

264 First Punic War between Rome and Carthage for control of Sicily.

260 Roman sea victory at MYLAE.

The Roman Empire at its furthest extent

256 Roman landing near Carthage repulsed.

246 Great Wall of China built.

241 Remainder of Carthaginian fleet defeated; Carthage sues for peace and loses control of Sicily.

238 Carthage sets out to create new empire in Spain.

225 Gauls invade Roman territory and are defeated. To prevent this happening again, Rome extends her frontiers northwards by conquering Cisalpine Gaul (modern Lombardy); is now mistress of all Italy.

219 Second Punic War. A 26-year old Carthaginian general, **Hannibal**, crosses the Alps into Italy, where he is unbeaten for 15 years.

217 Hannibal destroys a Roman army at LAKE TRASIMENE.

216 Hannibal destroys a second Roman army at CANNAE, but is unable to capture Rome itself.

210–206 Roman army wipes out Carthaginian forces in Spain and conquers the country.

204 Romans cross from Spain to Africa.

202 Hannibal returns to Africa to save Carthage, but is defeated at ZAMA.

201 Carthage surrenders her fleet and hands Spain over to Rome.

166 Tartar invasion of China.

149 Third Punic War. Uneasy at the steady recovery of Carthage, Rome resolves to destroy her rival.

146 Carthage destroyed.

102 **Marius** drives back invading German tribes.

91 Revolt of Italian cities belonging to Rome but with no say in government.

89 All Italians become Roman citizens.

88 Civil war in Rome between plebeians (people's party), led by Marius, and patricians (nobles), under **Sulla**. Sulla wins and Marius escapes to Africa.

87 While Sulla is fighting in Greece, Marius seizes power in Rome.

86 Marius dies.

82 Sulla returns, massacres his enemies, strengthens the power of the Senate, becomes dictator.

78 Sulla dies.

73 **Spartacus** leads revolt of 60,000 slaves.

71 **Crassus** crushes Spartacus revolt.

70 Crassus and **Pompey** reduce power of the Senate.

66–62 Pompey captures Jerusalem, conquers Syria and advances to the Euphrates.

60 Pompey, Crassus and **Caesar** divide the government of Rome's dominions between them, becoming the First Triumvirate (rule of three men). Caesar begins conquest of Gaul.

55 Caesar's first visit to Britain.

53 Crassus defeated and killed by Parthians.

51 Caesar completes conquest of Gaul.

49 Caesar crosses the Rubicon, boundary of his own command, to overthrow Pompey, now his only rival.

48 Caesar defeats Pompey at PHARSALUS. Pompey escapes to Egypt and is murdered.

44 Caesar is murdered.

43 **Octavian**, Caesar's nephew, **Antony** and **Lepidus** form Second Triumvirate.

42 Octavian and Antony defeat **Brutus** and **Cassius**, chief plotters against Caesar. The government of Rome's dominions is divided, Octavian taking the West, Antony the East (which he rules from Egypt with **Cleopatra**) and **Lepidus** Carthaginian Africa.

31 Octavian defeats Antony and Cleopatra at ACTIUM.

30 Deaths of Antony and Cleopatra.

27 Octavian, now known as Augustus, becomes first Roman emperor.

4 True date of birth of **Jesus**.

A.D.

14 Augustus dies.

30 Jesus crucified.

43 Emperor **Claudius** sends force to conquer Britain. The South is soon subdued, despite resistance from **Caractacus,** who is captured and sent to Rome. The Romans work their way northwards.

61 **Boadicea**, queen of the Iceni, revolts against Romans, burns their settlement at London; but her army is annihilated and she takes poison.

68 **Nero**, last emperor of the house of Augustus, commits suicide.

70 Emperor **Titus** captures and destroys Jerusalem, drives the Jews from the Holy Land.

79 Pompeii and Herculaneum destroyed in eruption of Vesuvius.

82 Agricola, governor of Britain, attempts conquest of Scotland.

93 Trajan adds Dacia (modern Rumania) and Mesopotamia to Roman empire, now at its largest.

117 Hadrian tries to keep barbarians out of Roman territories by building permanent fortifications, including 70-mile-long wall (Hadrian's Wall) from Tyne to Solway.

164–80 Plagues ravage Roman and Chinese empires.

180 Century of war and disorder begins for Rome, during which a succession of generals, many not even Roman by birth, are made emperors by troops in their pay. Perpetual invasions by Franks, Goths, Parthians, Vandals and Huns.

226 Artaxerxes founds new dynasty in Persia.

284 Diocletian, last Roman emperor to persecute Christians, re-organises the empire with two joint emperors and two subordinate emperors.

312 Constantine defeats his joint emperor, **Maxentius**, and becomes sole emperor in West.

313 Constantine legalises Christianity; later makes it State religion.

324 Constantine defeats emperor in the East, becomes sole ruler of Roman world.

328 To celebrate victory, Constantine founds 'new Rome' by enlarging ancient Greek city of Byzantium, calls it Constantinople.

330 Constantine moves capital to Constantinople.

337 Constantine dies, and empire is again ruled by succession of joint (and rival) emperors.

379 Theodosius the Great, emperor in the East, drives Goths from Greece and Italy.

382 Theodosius makes peace with Goths.

394 Theodosius becomes last sole emperor of Roman world.

395 Theodosius dies; division of empire into West and East becomes final.

407 As barbarians pour into Western empire, Roman legions are withdrawn from Britain in last attempt to defend Rome. Britain is left easy prey to Angles and Saxons.

410 Visigoths under **Alaric** plunder Rome. Waves of barbarians sweep into Spain, Portugal, Italy, Gaul and North Africa.

434 Attila becomes king of the Huns, Mongolians whose invasion of Europe is death-blow for Western empire.

449 Hengist and **Horsa**, Jutish chiefs, invade England, set up kingdom in Kent.

451 Invading Gaul, Attila is defeated by army of Goths and Romans at CHALONS.

452 Attila invades Italy; is persuaded by **Pope Leo I** to spare Rome.

453 Attila dies.

455 Vandals sack Rome. In next twenty years ten different emperors rule.

476 Last Roman emperor deposed; Western empire comes to an end.

482 Clovis, king of Salian Franks, makes himself first king of Frankland (France), with Paris as his capital.

496 Clovis baptised; Franks become Christians.

527 Justinian, whose codification of Roman law is basis for much later Western law, becomes emperor in Constantinople. Attempting re-conquest of Western Empire, he recovers North Africa, S.E. Spain and Italy.

536 Belisarius, Justinian's famous general, captures Rome.

565 Justinian dies.

568 Lombards invade Italy, settle in the north.

570 Birth of **Mohammed**.

590 Gregory the Great becomes Pope; declares Rome supreme centre of the Church.

597 St Augustine lands in England, baptises **Ethelbert**, king of Kent.

601 St Augustine becomes first archbishop of Canterbury.

c. 616 Mohammed proclaims himself the only true prophet of Allah.

618 Great T'ang dynasty founded in China.

628 Mohammed writes to all rulers of the earth, demanding that they acknowledge the One True God, Allah, and serve Him.

632 Mohammed dies; his friend **Abu Bakr**, first Caliph ('successor'), leads Arabs out of the desert to achieve Mohammed's aim of making the world submit to Islam.

637 Arabs defeat Persians at KARDESSIA. Soon after, Mesopotamia, Syria, Palestine and Egypt fall to them.

638 Jerusalem surrenders to Arabs.

Education (Many Commonwealth universities are linked to British universities in order to ensure high academic standards. Moreover, many Commonwealth countries continue to have their doctors, scientists, engineers, administrators and soldiers trained in Britain.)

Sport (Cricket and cricketing language are familiar in countries like Britain, Australia, New Zealand and the West Indies, but hardly outside the Commonwealth.)

Despite the rapid increase since the end of the Second World War in the number of fully independent countries within the Commonwealth, there still remain, in almost every part of the world, territories which continue to be dependent on Britain. Some are well advanced in self-government; others are little more than small island communities, fortresses, anchorages or former coaling stations which may have difficulty in surviving as fully independent states. The still dependent territories include:

In Africa:

Rhodesia (illegally declared independent in 1965 by its then Prime Minister, Mr. Smith, but no country in the world has recognised his claim to independence)

In the Atlantic:

Bermuda   Falkland Islands
St Helena

In the Caribbean:

Leeward Islands   Windward Islands

Five of the larger island units in these two groups—Antigua, Dominica, Grenada, St Lucia and the island group of St Kitts, Nevis and Anguilla—have in 1967 been granted the new status of 'Associated States', i.e. complete self-government except in foreign and defence policy. St. Vincent now also belongs to this group.

In the Mediterranean:

Gibraltar

In and around the Indian Ocean:

Aldabra Is.   Seychelles

In the Far East:

Brunei   Hong Kong

In the Pacific:
British Solomon Islands   Pitcairn Islands
Gilbert and Ellice Islands
New Hebrides (under joint Anglo-French administration)

Total population of the Commonwealth: about 950
million.

The United Nations

The United Nations came into existence on October 24, 1945,
and every year October 24 is celebrated as United Nations' Day
throughout the world.

The aims of the United Nations are set out in its Charter in
these words: 'to save succeeding generations from the scourge
of war . . . to reaffirm faith in fundamental human rights, in the

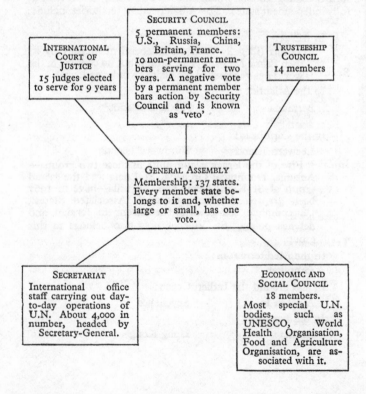

SECURITY COUNCIL
5 permanent members:
U.S., Russia, China,
Britain, France.
10 non-permanent mem-
bers serving for two
years. A negative vote
by a permanent member
bars action by Security
Council and is known
as 'veto'

INTERNATIONAL
COURT OF
JUSTICE
15 judges elected
to serve for 9 years

TRUSTEESHIP
COUNCIL
14 members

GENERAL ASSEMBLY
Membership: 137 states.
Every member state be-
longs to it and, whether
large or small, has one
vote.

SECRETARIAT
International office
staff carrying out day-
to-day operations of
U.N. About 4,000 in
number, headed by
Secretary-General.

ECONOMIC AND
SOCIAL COUNCIL
18 members.
Most special U.N.
bodies, such as
UNESCO, World
Health Organisation,
Food and Agriculture
Organisation, are as-
sociated with it.

dignity and worth of the human person, in the equal rights of men and women and of nations large and small, and to establish conditions under which justice and respect for the obligations arising from treaties and other sources of international law can be maintained, and to employ international machinery for the promotion of the economic and social advancement of all peoples'.

> Members of the U.N. in 1945: 51 countries
> Members of the U.N. in 1975: 137 countries.

The principal organ of the U.N. is the General Assembly. Around it are grouped the other five main organs of the U.N.:

General Assembly All other U.N. bodies report to it. It controls the U.N. budget and assesses each country's contribution. It elects new members on the recommendation of the Security Council. On 'important' questions, i.e., questions affecting the world's peace and security or the election of new members or the budget, a two-thirds majority of those present and voting is essential before any action can be taken. It meets every year in regular session beginning on the third Tuesday in September.

Security Council It is primarily responsible for keeping international peace and security. Any nation—whether a member of the U.N. or not—may bring a dispute or threat to peace to its attention and ask it to take action. Any of the five permanent members can block action by voting 'No'. This is known as the veto. Its ten non-permanent members are elected by the General Assembly.

International Court of Justice Its 15 judges are elected by the General Assembly on the recommendation of the Security Council. They consider legal disputes brought before them by nations which cannot agree between themselves. They also give advice on international law when asked to by the General Assembly, the Security Council or other U.N. bodies.

Trusteeship Council It looks after the interests of non-self-governing territories in different parts of the world which have been placed under the trusteeship of the U.N. Its aim is to help these territories towards full self-government as quickly as possible.

Secretariat It consists of international civil servants who, while they belong to it, must forget their national loyalties and work only for the best interests of the U.N. The head of the

Secretariat is the Secretary-General, who is appointed by the General Assembly on the recommendation of the Security Council, usually for a five-year term.

The U.N. has had four Secretaries-General:

1. Trygve Lie, of Norway (1945–1953).
2. Dag Hammarskjoeld, of Sweden (1953–1961. Killed in an air crash in Africa).
3. U Thant, of Burma (1961–1971).
4. Kurt Waldheim, of Austria (1972–).

Economic and Social Council (ECOSOC) Its aim is to establish lasting world peace by helping the poor, the sick, the hungry, the illiterate in all parts of the globe. It is responsible for assisting under-developed countries and promotes health and education schemes. In a broad sense it supervises the work of many special U.N. bodies like the U.N. Educational, Scientific and Cultural Organisation (UNESCO), the International Bank for Reconstruction and Development, the International Labour Organisation (I.L.O.), the Food and Agriculture Organisation (F.A.O.), the U.N. International Children's Emergency Fund (U.N.I.C.E.F.) and the International Atomic Energy Agency which seeks to help countries by encouraging and supporting the use of atomic energy for peaceful development purposes.

Location of U.N. Headquarters: New York.

Official languages in which the U.N. conducts its business: Chinese, English, French, Russian, Spanish.

FURTHER READING

The Making of Man, by I. W. Cornwall (Phoenix House)

Looking at History, by R. J. Unstead (A. & C. Black)

History: Civilisation from the Beginning (Macdonald Illustrated Library)

Larousse Encyclopaedia of Ancient and Medieval History and *Larousse Encyclopaedia of Modern History* (Paul Hamlyn)

The Story of Britain, by R. J. Unstead (A. & C. Black)

Boys and Girls of History, by Eileen and Rhoda Power (Dobson)

A History of Everyday Things in England (4 books), by Marjorie and C. H. B. Quennell (Batsford)

The Story of the United Nations, by Katharine Savage (Bodley Head)

The World

2: ITS GEOGRAPHY
(*including Its Weather*)

THE WORLD

The Earth: Some Facts and Figures	2
The Oceans and Seas: Their Areas and Depths	3–5
The Continents: Their Areas and Populations	5–7
The Largest Islands	7
Countries of the World by Continents	8–23
The Largest Cities	24
The Highest Mountains	24
Highest and Lowest Points in each Continent	26
Principal Volcanoes	26–28
Lakes of the World	28
Principal Rivers of the World	29
Great Waterfalls	29–30
Great Ship Canals of the World	31
Principal Languages	31
Distances by air between some of the World's chief cities	32–33

GREAT BRITAIN

The Counties:	
England	34–35
Wales	35
Scotland	36–38
Northern Ireland	38
Other British Isles	38
Largest Cities	38
Highest Mountains, Largest Lakes	39
Important Rivers	39–40
London Boroughs	40
London Postal Districts	41–42

A DICTIONARY OF GEOGRAPHICAL TERMS	43–51
THE WEATHER	52–56

GEOGRAPHY, which literally means 'writing about the earth', is the science of the physical world. It includes in its scope the earth's surface, land and sea, and the features and products of both of these. It deals with natural divisions, like continents or mountain ranges; and political divisions, like countries and towns. This brings it inside the borders of History. It deals with those factors, like the climate and surrounding atmosphere, which directly affect the earth and sea and their products. This introduces Meteorology and Physics. It deals with both natural and man-made products, which makes it an important part of Economics, and links it with Agriculture. It describes the influence of nature on man, and of man on nature. So that it overlaps Anthropology and Sociology.

THE EARTH: *some facts and figures*

The Earth is the fifth largest of the nine major planets (the others are Mercury, Venus, Mars, Jupiter, Saturn, Uranus, Neptune and Pluto) and the third in distance from the sun— about 93,000,000 miles. In shape, it is almost, but not quite, a sphere, being slightly flattened at the poles, as well as being rather pear-shaped, with the pear's stalk at the North Pole.

About seven tenths of the Earth's outer crust are covered with water, this water forming the four oceans and the seas. The other three tenths are land, and comprise the six continents and innumerable islands. The whole surface is blanketed by a layer of air known as the atmosphere. This air is formed of various gases, without which nothing on earth would be able to live. Changes and movements within the atmosphere, together with the rays from the sun, are responsible for our weather.

There are well over 3,000,000,000 people living on earth, of whom well over half live in the continent of Asia.

Polar diameter (i.e. from pole to pole through the earth's centre), 7,900 miles.

Equatorial diameter (between points on the equator exactly opposite one another), 7,926·5 miles.

Equatorial circumference, 24,901·8 miles.
Total surface area (estimated), 196,950,000 sq. miles.
Area of land, 57,312,000 sq. miles.
Area of sea, 139,638,000 sq. miles.
Total mass (weight), about 6,588,000,000,000,000,000,000 (i.e. 6,588 million million million) tons.

THE OCEANS AND SEAS

The four oceans together with the seas cover about seven-tenths of the earth's surface. All the oceans form one vast mass of water which is divided, for convenience, into the Pacific, the Atlantic, the Indian and the Arctic. *Seas* are smaller, more self-contained portions of the ocean, like the Mediterranean Sea, which is almost entirely surrounded by land. Some seas, like the Caspian, are completely surrounded, but the water is nevertheless salt, not fresh.

The greatest known ocean depth (35,948 ft., just off the Philippines), is about a mile more than the greatest land height (Mt. Everest, 29,028 ft.). The average depth of the ocean (12,451 ft.) is much greater than the average height of the land above sea-level (2,300 ft.).

The floor of the ocean, like the land, has many ridges and valleys. Where it adjoins the great land masses, on what is called the *Continental Shelf*, it is relatively shallow; but it soon plunges steeply down the *Continental Slope* into the *Deep-Sea*

Plain, which forms most of the ocean floor and varies in depth
from 12,000 to 18,000 ft.; here and there dropping into enormous
cracks and valleys known as the *Deep Trenches*.

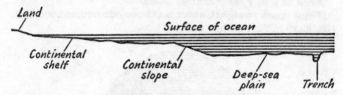

The origin of the Continental Shelf has not yet been explained.
It might be expected that the abrupt Continental Slope would
come at the water's edge, rather than anything up to a hundred
miles out from the land. One possible reason is that the water
level has risen, or the land level fallen, during the course of
millions of years. Or it may be that the continental boundary
did originally come at the slope, but that the sea has gradually
worn away the land and left the original boundary far behind.

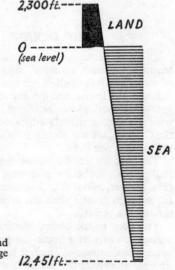

The Average Height of Land
Compared with the Average
Depth of Ocean

OCEANS AND MAIN SEAS: *Their Areas and Depths*

Ocean or sea	Area (sq. miles)	Average depth (ft.)	Greatest depth (ft.)
Oceans:			
Pacific	63,801,668	14,048	35,948
Atlantic	31,839,306	12,880	30,246
Indian	28,356,276	13,002	22,968
Arctic	5,440,197	3,953	17,850
Seas:			
Malay Sea	3,144,056	3,976	21,342
Caribbean Sea	1,063,340	8,172	23,748
Mediterranean Sea	966,757	4,878	16,798
Bering Sea	875,753	7,714	13,422
Gulf of Mexico	595,760	4,961	12,744
Sea of Okhotsk	589,807	2,749	11,154
East China Sea	482,317	617	10,500
Hudson Bay	475,762	420	1,500
Sea of Japan	389,074	4,429	12,276
Andaman Sea	307,954	2,854	12,392
North Sea	222,124	308	1,998
Black Sea	178,378	3,160	6,864
Red Sea	169,073	1,611	7,254
Baltic Sea	163,059	189	1,380

You won't find the Malay Sea on the map. It consists of the following seas: Sulu, Celebes, Molucca, Halmahera, Ceram, Banda, Arafura, Timor, Flores, Bali, Java, Savu and South China; the following gulfs: Thailand, Tomini and Boni; and the following straits: Malacca, Singapore and Macassar.

THE CONTINENTS

A continent is a large mass of land, not broken up by a large stretch of sea. The Earth's land surface is made up of six such

continents, as well as a large number of islands. The continents
and islands fit into four main divisions:

(1) an immense landmass, nearly all of it in the eastern
hemisphere, consisting of the continents of *Europe*, *Asia* and
Africa;

(2) a smaller landmass, the *Americas*, in the western hemisphere; this is sometimes divided into two continents, North
America and South America;

(3) two large island continents in the southern hemisphere,
Australia and *Antarctica*;

(4) a great number of islands.

Generally, islands are regarded as belonging to the nearest
continent. The far-flung islands of the Pacific, however, are
usually grouped with Australia, New Zealand and New Guinea
in the continent of *Oceania*.

Although the ice that forms over it in winter makes it fairly
solid, the Arctic is a sea, not a continent. The ice and snow
covering the Antarctic, however, have formed above land which
rises above sea level.

More than half of all the land in the world is uninhabitable—it
is rock, desert, tundra, dense jungle, swamps or is covered with
ice. Less than half of the remainder is suitable for cultivation.

Nearly one-half of the people in the world live on one-
thirtieth of the total area of land. There are immense areas (like
the Northern Territory of Australia and the North-West Territories of Canada) with only one inhabitant to every 25 or 50
square miles; and other areas (like East Pakistan and England)
where more than 750 persons, on the average, are crowded into
each square mile of land.

The total world population is about 3,711,000,000. At
the beginning of the century it was about a third of that
figure. This enormous increase in population makes many
people anxious about overcrowding and possible shortage of
food in the future. But many experts say that there is no real
need to worry, since science is not only converting what was
thought to be useless land (and even parts of the sea) into fertile
soil, but is also constantly getting more nourishment from
resources already available. There is also new anxiety lest the
world runs short of oil, before the full development of new
sources for energy.

The Continents: Area and Population

Continent	Area (sq. miles)	Population
Europe	1,903,000	466,000,000
Asia *	16,661,000	2,104,000,000
U.S.S.R.	8,649,000	245,000,000
Africa	11,683,000	354,000,000
America	16,241,000	522,000,000
Oceania	3,286,000	19,800,000

Total World Population: 3,711,000,000

* Excluding figures for U.S.S.R. which are given separately and including European and Asiatic Turkey.

The Largest Islands

Island	Ocean	Continent	Area (sq. miles)
Australia	Indian–Pacific	Oceania	2,948,366
Greenland	Atlantic–Arctic	N. America	839,782
New Guinea	Pacific	Oceania	316,861
Borneo	Pacific	Asia	285,000
Baffin Is.	Arctic	N. America	236,000
Malagasy	Indian	Africa	227,737
Sumatra	Indian	Asia	161,612
Honshu	Pacific	Asia	88,919
Great Britain	Atlantic	Europe	84,186
Victoria Is.	Arctic	N. America	80,450
Celebes	Indian	Asia	73,160
South Island, N.Z.	Pacific	Oceania	58,093
Java	Indian	Asia	48,534
North Island, N.Z.	Pacific	Oceania	44,281
Cuba	Atlantic	N. America	44,206
Newfoundland	Atlantic	N. America	42,734
Ellesmere Is.	Arctic	N. America	41,000
Luzon	Pacific	Asia	40,420
Iceland	Atlantic	Europe	39,758
Mindanao	Pacific	Asia	36,537
Hokkaido	Pacific	Asia	34,276
Novaya Zemlya	Arctic	Asia	32,000
Ireland	Atlantic	Europe	31,839
Hispaniola	Atlantic	N. America	29,536
Tasmania	Pacific	Oceania	26,215

THE COUNTRIES OF THE WORLD BY CONTINENTS

The following tables tell you what the areas and populations of the countries are; the names of their capitals; and the populations of the capitals.

Of course, the number of people in any country is changing every day: so we have given approximate figures, based on the latest counts (or *censuses*).

Note: The Commonwealth is a free association of independent states, with a total area (excluding the United Kingdom) of 9,902,356.6 sq. miles. Member countries are:

United Kingdom	Lesotho
Canada	Malawi
Australia	Malaysia
New Zealand	Malta
Bahamas	Mauritius
Bangladesh	Naura
Barbados	Nigeria
Botswana	Sierra Leone
Cyprus	Singapore
Fiji	Sri Lanka
Gambia	Swaziland
Ghana	Tanzania
Grenada	Trinidad and Tobago
India	Uganda
Jamaica	Zambia
Kenya	Tonga
	Western Samoa

EUROPE AND THE MEDITERRANEAN

Country	Area (sq. miles)	Population	Capital	Population of Capital
Albania	10,629	2,075,000	Tirana	50,000
Andorra	180	25,000	Andorre	8,500
Austria	32,393	7,391,000	Vienna	1,614,841
Belgium	11,755	9,691,000	Brussels	1,075,000
Bulgaria	42,796	8,524,000	Sofia	927,823
Cyprus	3,500	632,000	Nicosia	108,000
Czechoslovakia	49,381	14,435,613	Prague	1,082,500
Denmark	16,576	4,879,000	Copenhagen	1,378,000
Finland	117,975	4,598,336	Helsinki	526,896
France	212,736	50,770,000	Paris	2,590,000
Germany				
West	95,707	61,809,000	Bonn	278,778
East	41,571	17,043,000	E. Berlin	1,200,000
Gibraltar	2	26,833	Gibraltar	20,000
Greece	51,182	8,768,641	Athens	2,540,241
Hungary	35,912	10,415,000	Budapest	1,959,000
Iceland	39,758	210,352	Reykjavik	83,831
Irish Republic	26,633	2,971,000	Dublin	566,034
Italy	117,471	54,025,000	Rome	2,842,616
Liechtenstein	62	22,000	Vaduz	4,270
Luxembourg	999	348,000	Luxembourg	78,000
Malta, Gozo	122	322,000	Valetta	15,547
Monaco	$\frac{1}{2}$	23,490	Monaco	2,422
Netherlands	12,868	13,259,000	Amsterdam	807,472
Norway	125,183	3,918,000	Oslo	477,476
Poland	121,131	32,889,000	Warsaw	1,308,100

Country	Area (sq. miles)	Population	Capital	Population of Capital
Portugal	35,700	8,545,120	Lisbon	783,000
Rumania	91,671	20,469,658	Bucharest	1,488,328
San Marino	23	19,000	San Marino	2,500
Spain	185,205	34,032,801	Madrid	3,150,000
Sweden	173,426	8,115,426	Stockholm	1,306,762
Switzerland	15,944	6,269,800	Berne	162,405
Turkey (in Europe)	9,250	3,166,000	see Asia	1,440,779
United Kingdom of Great Britain and Northern Ireland	94,283	55,521,534	London	7,739,024
U.S.S.R. (in Eur.)	1,226,548	130,079,000	Moscow	7,172,000
R.S.F.S.R. (Eur.)	225,000	47,126,000	Moscow	1,693,000
Ukraine		9,002,000	Kiev	955,000
Byelorussia	81,090	3,128,000	Minsk	386,000
Lithuania	25,174	2,364,000	Vilnius	743,000
Latvia	24,903	1,356,000	Riga	371,000
Estonia	17,610	3,569,000	Tallinn	374,000
Moldavia	13,200		Kishinev	
Vatican City		1,000	Vatican City	1,000
Yugoslavia	98,386	21,500,000	Belgrade	1,204,000

ASIA

Country	Area (sq. miles)	Population	Capital	Population of Capital
Afghanistan	250,000	16,516,000	Kabul	500,000
Bahrain	213	216,000	Manama	89,608
Bangladesh	55,126	75,000,000	Dacca	1,900,000
Bhutan	18,000	1,010,000	Thimpu	—
Brunei	2,226	141,497	Bandan Seri Begawan	38,000
Burma	261,789	28,874,000	Rangoon	3,186,866
China				
Mainland	4,300,000	732,000,000	Peking	7,570,000
Taiwan (Formosa)	13,890	15,353,000	Taipei	1,921,736
Hong Kong	404	4,103,500	Victoria	767,000
India	1,259,765	547,367,926	Delhi	4,065,698
Indonesia	815,865	129,000,000	Djakarta	4,576,009
Iran (Persia)	628,060	28,448,000	Teheran	3,150,000
Iraq	171,599	9,498,000	Baghdad	2,690,000
Israel	7,993	3,230,000	Jerusalem	301,000
Japan	142,748	103,265,000	Tokyo	11,403,744
Jordan	34,750	2,460,000	Amman	583,000
Khmer Republic	70,000	7,100,000	Phnom Penh	2,000,000
Korea				
North	46,814	13,300,000	Pyongyang	286,000
South	38,452	31,460,000	Seoul	5,509,993
Kuwait	5,800	733,000	Kuwait	300,000
Laos	89,320	2,700,000	Vientiane	174,000

Country	Area (sq. miles)	Population	Capital	Population of Capital
Lebanon	4,300	2,645,000	Beirut	555,000
Malaysia	130,000	10,434,000	Kuala Lumpur	550,000
Sarawak	48,000	977,000	*Kuching*	63,491
Sabah	30,000	656,000	*Kota Kinabalu*	41,830
Maldive Islands	115	114,000	Malé	13,610
Mongolia (Outer)	604,095	1,240,000	Ulan Bator	195,300
Nepal	54,362	11,289,000	Katmandu	353,756
Oman	82,000	750,000	Muscat	7,650
Pakistan	364,737	56,830,000	Islamabad	80,000
Philippines	114,830	39,102,000	Manila	1,399,583
Qatar	8,000	170,000	Doha	100,000
Saudi Arabia	870,000	7,200,000	Riyadh	450,000
Singapore	224	2,110,400	Singapore	551,200
Sri Lanka	25,332	12,747,755	Colombo	557,252
Syria	72,234	6,294,000	Damascus	2,500,000
Thailand (Siam)	198,247	36,000,000	Bangkok	7,000
Timor (East)	7,329	590,000	Dili	7,000
Turkey (in Asia)	286,857	32,501,000	Ankara	1,449,779
United Arab Emirates	32,000	240,000		
U.S.S.R. (in Asia)				
R.S.F.S.R. (Asia)	5,357,954	130,697,000	*see Europe*	
Kazakhstan	1,072,797	13,235,000	Alma Ata	753,000
Turkmenistan	189,370	2,223,000	Ashkhabad	259,000
Uzbekistan	159,170	12,143,000	Tashktne	1,424,000
Kirghizia	75,900	3,003,000	Frunze	442,000
Tadzhikistan	55,700	2,987,000	Dushanbe	388,000

Country	Area (sq. miles)	Population	Capital	Population of Capital
Georgia	37,570	4,734,000	Tbilisi	907,000
Azerbaijan	33,460	5,219,000	Baku	1,292,000
Armenia	11,900	2,545,000	Erevan	791,000
Vietnam North	63,344	21,340,000	Hanoi	800,000
South	65,709	17,867,000	Saigon	2,500,000
Yemen	75,000	6,000,000	Sana'a	120,000
Yemen P.D.R.	180,000	1,598,000	Aden	250,000

Notes

1. This map is drawn to Mercator's Projection, a convenient method for showing all the countries of the world, but also very misleading in some ways. See under **Projections**, page B49.

2. For an explanation of the International Date Line see page B46.

AFRICA

Country	Area (sq. miles)	Population	Capital	Population of Capital
Afars and Issas	9,000	125,000	Djibouti	62,000
Algeria	851,077	13,547,000	Algiers	943,000
Angola	481,351	5,673,046	St Paul de Luanda	346,763
Botswana	275,000	620,000	Gaborone	18,000
Burundi	10,747	3,475,000	Bujumburu	70,000
Cameroun	143,500	5,836,000	Yaounde	180,000
Cape Verde Islands	1,557	272,071	Praia	6,000
Central African Republic	238,767	1,518,000	Bangui	301,793
Chad	461,202	4,000,000	Port Lamy	126,000
Congo	129,960	2,100,000	Brazzaville	156,000
Dahomey	47,144	2,948,000	Porto Novo	85,000
Egypt	386,000	34,000,000	Cairo	5,126,000
Equatorial Guinea	11,000	286,000	Malabo	9,000
Ethiopia and Eritrea	398,350	26,000,000	Addis Ababa	800,000
Gaboon	101,400	500,000	Libreville	31,000
Gambia	4,003	374,000	Banjul	27,809
Ghana	91,843	8,545,000	Accra	851,614
Guinea	94,885	3,890,000	Conakry	120,000
Ivory Coast	124,471	5,400,000	Abidjan	600,000
Kenya	224,960	10,890,000	Nairobi	509,000
Lesotho	11,716	1,000,000	Maseru	30,000
Liberia	43,000	1,500,000	Monrovia	110,000
Libya	679,358	1,869,000	Tripoli	331,947
Malagasy	228,500	8,000,000	Tananarive	400,000
Malawi	45,000	4,700,000	Zomba	19,666

Country	Area (sq. miles)	Population	Capital	Population of Capital
Mali	464,751	4,929,000	Bamako	150,000
Mauritania	419,121	1,140,000	Nouakchott	18,000
Mauritius, etc.	809	855,271	Port Louis	142,270
Morocco	173,746	15,379,259	Rabat	374,809
Mozambique	297,731	7,376,000	Lourenço Marques	441,363
Niger	492,778	4,030,000	Niamey	100,000
Nigeria	339,169	79,960,000	Lagos	1,000,000
Portuguese Guinea	13,948	487,448	Bissau	6,000
Réunion	970	436,000	St Denis	65,614
Rhodesia	150,333	5,780,000	Salisbury	490,000
Rwanda	10,169	3,500,000	Kigali	4,273
St Helena	47	4,722	Jamestown	1,475
Ascension Is.	34	1,231	Georgetown	
Tristan da Cunha	45	280	Edinburgh	
S. Tomé and Principé	372	73,811	Sao Thome	3,187
Sénégal	75,730	3,780,000	Dakar	581,000
Seychelles	156	52,650	Victoria	13,736
Sierra Leone	27,925	2,180,355	Freetown	128,000
Somalia	256,000	2,730,000	Mogadishu	220,000
South Africa	472,685	21,448,172	Pretoria, Cape Town	1,096,597
S.W. Africa	317,725	746,328	Windhoek	60,000
Spanish Presidios:				
Ceuta	5	67,187	—	
Melilla	72	64,942	—	
Sahara	125,000	63,000	Villa Cisneros	250

Country	Area (sq. miles)	Population	Capital	Population of Capital
Sudan	967,000	15,312,000	Khartoum	135,000
Swaziland	6,704	465,000	Mbabane	18,500
Tanzania	363,708	12,926,000	Dar es Salaam	306,090
Togo	21,893	2,089,000	Lomé	148,000
Tunisia	48,330	5,409,000	Tunis	1,127,000
Uganda	93,981	10,400,000	Kampala	331,000
Upper Volta	105,800	5,514,000	Ouagadougou	125,000
Zaire	905,000	21,637,000	Kinshasa	1,300,000
Zambia	291,000	4,054,000	Lusaka	238,000

NORTH AMERICA

Country	Area (sq. miles)	Population	Capital	Population of Capital
Bahamas	4,004	193,000	Nassau	112,000
Barbados	166	241,296	Bridgetown	18,789
Belize	8,900	122,000	Belmopan	3,500
Bermuda	21	53,000	Hamilton	3,000
Canada	3,851,809	21,568,310	Ottawa	536,000
Cayman Islands	100	10,652	George Town	5,000
Costa Rica	23,421	1,800,000	San José	216,167
Cuba	46,736	8,553,000	Havana	1,755,360

Country	Area (sq. miles)	Population	Capital[1]	Population of Capital
Dominica	290	74,000	Roseau	11,924
Dominican Republic	19,332	4,012,000	Santo Domingo	817,000
El Salvador	8,259	3,541,000	San Salvador	337,141
Grenada	688	105,000	St. George's	8,400
Guadeloupe	688	323,000	Point à Pitre	39,000
Guatemala	42,042	5,400,000	Guatemala	790,311
Haiti	10,714	4,768,000	Pt.-au-Prince	300,000
Honduras	43,227	2,535,000	Tegucigalpa	225,000
Jamaica	4,411	1,953,472	Kingston	572,653
Leeward Is.				
Antigua and Barbuda	171	65,000	St Johns	13,000
Monserrat	33	12,905	Plymouth	1,230
St Kitts-Nevis-Anguilla	168	51,000	Basseterre	15,897
Virgin Is.			Charleston	1,530
		10,500	Road Town	2,183
Martinique	421	332,000	Fort-de-France	99,051
Mexico	763,944	48,313,000	Mexico City	8,000,000
Netherlands Antilles	382	223,819	Willemsted	—
Nicaragua	57,143	2,300,000	Managua[1]	—
Panama	28,576	1,428,082	Panama City	418,000
Panama Canal Zone	371	51,000	Balboa	—
Puerto Rico	3,435	2,913,000	San Juan	485,100
St Pierre and Miquelon	93	5,000	St Pierre	—
Trinidad and Tobago	1,980	1,010,000	Port-of-Spain	93,954
Turks and Caicos	166	6,000	Grand Turk	2,000

[1] Almost totally destroyed, 1972; population, 1970, 318,000

Country	Area (sq. miles)	Population	Capital	Population of Capital
United States	3,548,974	203,211,926	Washington, D.C.	756,510
Virgin Is. (U.S.)	132	62,468	Charlotte Amelie	12,740
Windward Is.				
St Lucia	233	110,000	Castries	40,000
St Vincent	150	92,000	Kingstown	22,000

SOUTH AMERICA

Country	Area (sq. miles)	Population	Capital	Population of Capital
Argentina	1,079,965	23,360,000	Buenos Aires	8,352,900
Bolivia	424,162	4,658,000	La Paz	553,000
Brazil	3,288,063	93,000,000	Brasilia	544,862
Chile	286,397	10,000,000	Santiago	4,000,000
Colombia	439,997	22,000,000	Bogotá	2,512,000
Ecuador	116,270	7,000,000	Quito	700,000
Falkland Is.	4,618	1,957	Stanley	1,079
Guyana	83,000	713,233	Georgetown	168,000
Guiana, French	34,740	48,000	Cayenne	20,000
Paraguay	157,006	2,314,000	Asuncion	437,000
Peru	514,059	14,000,000	Lima	3,600,000

Country	Area (sq. miles)	Population	Capital	Population of Capital
Surinam	55,400	480,000	Paramaribo	2,183,935
Uruguay	72,172	2,500,000	Montevideo	110,000
Venezuela	352,143	10,721,522	Caracas	1,173,114

OCEANIA

Country	Area (sq. miles)	Population	Capital	Population of Capital
American Samoa	76	28,000	Pago Pago	1,251
Australia	2,974,581	13,091,300	Canberra	165,300
Cocos Is.	5	654	—	
Lord Howe Is.	7	260	—	
Norfolk Is.	13½	86,200	Kingston	
British Solomon Is.	11,500	160,998	Honiara	11,191
*Canton and Enderbury	7	—	—	—
Fiji	7,036	541,000	Suva	54,157
French Polynesia	1,520	109,000	Papeete	15,220
Gilbert and Ellice Is.	360	54,000	Tarawa	10,616
Guam	209	105,000	Agana	
Nauru	8	7,000	Nauru	
New Caledonia	9,546	98,000	Noumea	12,000
New Hebrides	5,700	89,031	Vila	5,500

*uninhabited since 1968

Country	Area (sq. miles)	Population	Capital	Population of Capital
New Zealand	109,736	2,909,916	Wellington	328,800
Western Samoa	1,133	131,000	Apia	25,000
Tonga Group	269	92,360	Nuku'alofa	20,000
Midway Islands	2	2,220	—	
Wake Island	3	1,647	—	

ANTARCTICA

By the Treaty of Antarctica. signed in December 1959, the following countries agreed to freeze all their claims to Antarctic territory for thirty years, without giving them up: Argentina, Australia, Belgium, Chile, France, Great Britain, Japan, New Zealand, Norway, the Republic of South Africa, the U.S.A. and the U.S.S.R.

The aim of the treaty was to allow the research and peaceful co-operation that had started during the International Geophysical Year to continue in this scientifically important area.

The areas given here (except for the Australian and New Zealand claims) are only rough estimates.

Claimant country	Name of claim or area	Limits	Approx. area (sq. miles)
Australia	Australian Antarctic Territory	45° E.–160° E. from 60° S. to Pole (except Adelie Land)	2,472,000
France	French Antarctica and Southern Lands (four groups of Is. in South Pacific Ocean; Adelie Land)	136° E.–142° E. from 60° S. to Pole	178,000

Claimant country	Name of claim or area	Limits	Approx. area (sq. miles)
Great Britain	Falkland Is. Dependencies (S. Shetlands, S. Orkneys, S. Sandwich, minor is. and Graham's Land)	20° W.–80° W. from 58° S. to Pole (and 20° W.–50° W. from 50° S. to 58° S.)	590,000
New Zealand	Ross Dependency	160° E.–150° W. from 60° S. to Pole	160,000
Norway	Queen Maud Land	20° W.–45° E., from shore of continent to Pole	950,000
Argentina		25° W.–73° W. from 60° S. to Pole	
Chile		53° W.–90° W. from 60° S. to Pole	
Unclaimed	Ellsworth Highland, Marie Byrd Land	80° W.–150° W., shore of continent to Pole	750,000

THE WORLD'S LARGEST CITIES

City and Country	Population	City and Country	Population
New York*	11,571,899	Seoul, Korea	5,509,993
Tokyo	11,403,744	Cairo, Egypt	5,126,000
Shanghai*, China	10,820,000	Philadelphia*, U.S.A.	4,817,914
Buenos Aires*,		Djakarta*, Indonesia	4,750,000
Argentina	8,352,900	Rio de Janeiro*,	
Mexico City, Mexico	8,000,000	Brazil	4,296,782
Peking, China	7,570,000	Tientsin, China	4,280,000
London*, England	7,418,020	Detroit*, U.S.A.	4,199,931
Moscow, U.S.S.R.	7,061,000	Delhi, India	4,065,698
Los Angeles*,		Leningrad*,	
U.S.A.	7,032,075	U.S.S.R.	4,002,000
Chicago*, U.S.A.	6,978,947	Santiago, Chile	4,000,000
São Paulo, Brazil	5,901,533	Lima, Peru	3,500,000
Bombay*, India	5,850,000	Berlin, Germany	3,284,000

* Seaport

THE WORLD'S HIGHEST MOUNTAINS

Peak	Location	Height (ft.)
Everest	Nepal–Tibet	29,028
Godwin Austen (K2)	Karakoram (India)	28,250
Kanchenjunga	Nepal–Sikkim	28,146
Makalu	Nepal–Tibet	27,824
Dhaulagari	Nepal	26,811
Nanga Parbat	N. W. Kashmir	26,629
Nanda Devi	Tibet, nr. India	25,645
Kamet	India–Tibet	25,447
Minya Konka	Sinkiang (China)	24,900
Communist Peak	U.S.S.R.	24,590

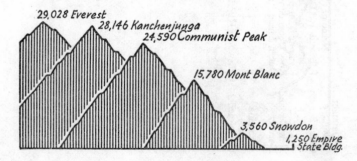

29,028 Everest
28,146 Kanchenjunga
24,590 Communist Peak
15,780 Mont Blanc
3,560 Snowdon
1,250 Empire State Bldg.

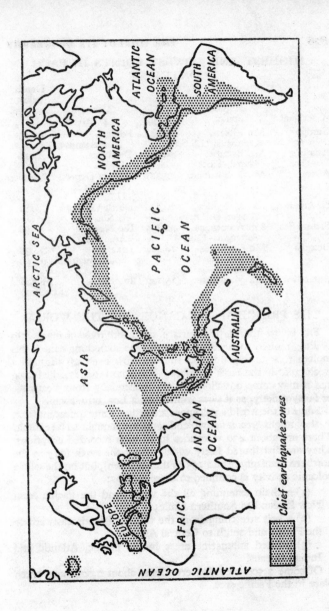

Chief earthquake zones

HIGHEST AND LOWEST POINTS IN EACH CONTINENT

Continent	Highest point	Height	Lowest point	Depth below sea-level (ft.)
Europe	Mt. Elbrus, Caucasus, U.S.S.R.	18,481	Polders, Netherlands (2)	12–15
Asia	Mt. Everest, Nepal–Tibet	29,028	Dead Sea, Jordan	1,286
Africa	Mt. Kilimanjaro (Kibo Peak), Tanzania	19,321	Qattara Depression, Egypt, U.A.R.	436
N. America	Mt. McKinley, Alaska, U.S.A.	20,320	Death Valley, U.S.A.	282
S. America	Mt. Aconcagua, Argentina–Chile	22,835	Rio Negro, Argentina	98
Oceania	Mt. Carstensztoppen, New Guinea	16,404	Lake Eyre, South Australia	38
Antarctica	Mt. Markham	15,100	Interior	8,200 (ice-filled)

THE PRINCIPAL VOLCANOES OF THE WORLD

Far below the earth's surface the solid rock changes into boiling, molten rock. From time to time something causes this molten rock to expand, and thus to blow itself up through a weak point in the earth's surface. The liquid rock is called lava, and it may come out violently, as occasionally from Vesuvius, or fairly quietly, as it does from Mauna Loa, on Hawaii.

Some of the world's volcanoes are active, some quiescent (that is, they might *become* active) and some are thought to be extinct. There are about 430 volcanoes in all with recorded eruptions. They are distributed fairly widely about the earth (275 in the northern hemisphere and 155 in the southern), but on the whole volcanic activity is confined to three regions:

(1) a chain extending all the way round the Pacific from New Zealand to Southern Chile;

(2) a belt stretching from the Canary Islands eastward to the Pacific and south to Central Africa;

(3) isolated submarine areas in the Pacific, Atlantic and Indian Oceans.

Of some 2,500 recorded eruptions, about 2,000 have taken place in the Pacific area.

THE PRINCIPAL VOLCANOES OF THE WORLD

I. Active

Volcano	Height (ft.)	Volcano	Height (ft.)
Cotopaxi (Ecuador)	19,613	Colima (Mexico)	12,631
Popocatapetl (Mexico)	17,887	Fuego (Guatemala)	12,582
Sangay (Ecuador)	17,749	Kerintji (Indonesia)	12,484
Tungurahua (Ecuador)	16,512	Santa Maria (Guatemala)	12,362
Cotacachi (Ecuador)	16,197	Rindjani (Indonesia)	12,225
Klyuchevskaya (U.S.S.R.)	15,912	Semeru (Indonesia)	12,060
Purace (Colombia)	15,604	Ichinskaya (U.S.S.R.)	11,834
Wrangell (Alaska, U.S.A.)	14,005	Atitlan (Guatemala)	11,565
Tajmulco (Guatemala)	13,812	Nyiregongo (Congo)	11,384
Mauna Loa (Hawaii, U.S.A.)	13,675	Irazu (Costa Rica)	11,260
Cameroons (Nigeria)	13,350	Slamat (Indonesia)	11,247
Tacana (Guatemala)	13,333	Spurr (Alaska, U.S.A.)	11,070
Erebus (Antarctica)	13,200	Raung (Indonesia)	10,932
Acatenango (Guatemala)	12,992	Etna (Sicily)	10,784

II. Quiescent

Volcano	Height (ft.)	Volcano	Height (ft.)
Kilimanjaro (Tanganyika)	19,321	Sundoro (Indonesia)	10,285
Misti (Peru)	19,031	Balbi (Solomon Is.)	10,171
Pichincha (Ecuador)	15,712	Apo (Philippine Is.)	9,690
Kronotskaya (U.S.S.R.)	12,238	Marapi (Indonesia)	9,551
Lassen (U.S.A.)	10,466	Tambora (Indonesia)	9,353
Welirang (Indonesia)	10,354	Paricutin (Mexico)	9,100

III. Believed Extinct

Volcano	Height (ft.)	Volcano	Height (ft.)
Aconcagua (Argentine–Chile)	22,835	Demavend (Iran)	17,604
Chimborazo (Ecuador)	20,610	Karisimbi (Congo)	15,020
Orizaba (Mexico)	18,701	Mikeno (Congo)	14,780
Elbrus (U.S.S.R.)	18,526	Fujiyama (Japan)	12,395

LAKES OF THE WORLD

Lake	Location	Area (sq. miles)	Length (miles)	Salt or fresh
Caspian Sea[2]	U.S.S.R.–Iran (Asia–Europe)	170,000	680	Salt
Superior	U.S.A.–Canada	31,820	383	Fresh
Victoria	Uganda–Kenya–Tanzania	26,200	200	Fresh
Aral Sea[1]	Kazakhstan Republic, U.S.S.R.	26,166	265	Salt
Huron	U.S.A.–Canada	23,010	247	Fresh
Michigan	U.S.A.	22,400	307	Fresh
Baikal	U.S.S.R.	13,197	385	Fresh
Tanzania	Congo–Zambia, Tanzania–Burundi	12,700	420	Fresh
Great Bear	Canada	12,000	195	Fresh
Great Slave	Canada	11,170	325	Fresh
Nyasa	Malawi–Tanzania–Mozambique	11,000	350	Fresh
Erie	U.S.A.–Canada	9,940	241	Fresh
Winnipeg	Canada	9,398	260	Fresh
Ontario	U.S.A.–Canada	7,540	193	Fresh
Chad[2]	Niger–Chad–Cameroun–Nigeria	7,200	—	Fresh

[1] Classified as lakes, despite their names, as they are completely landlocked.
[2] In flood, Lake Chad becomes the world's largest fresh-water lake, covering 50,000 square miles.

PRINCIPAL RIVERS OF THE WORLD

River	Continent	Approx. length (miles)	Flow (cu. ft./sec.) where known	Outflow into:
Nile	Africa	4,145	420,000	Mediterranean Sea
Amazon	S. America	3,900	7,200,000	Atlantic Ocean
Yangtze Kiang	Asia	3,100	770,000	Pacific Ocean
Lena	Asia	2,800	—	Arctic Ocean
Congo	Africa	2,718	2,000,000	Atlantic Ocean
MacKenzie	N. America	2,635	450,000	Arctic Ocean
Mekong	Asia	2,600	600,000	South China Sea
Amur	Asia	2,600	—	Gulf of Tartary
Ob–Irtish	Asia	2,600	—	Gulf of Ob/Pacific
Hwang Ho (Yellow)	Asia	2,600	116,000	Yellow Sea (Pacific)
Niger	Africa	2,550	—	Atlantic Ocean
Yenisei	Asia	2,550	—	Arctic Ocean
Missouri	N. America	2,475	(see Mississippi)	Mississippi River
Mississippi	N. America	2,470	513,000	Gulf of Mexico
La Plata Parana	S. America	2,300	2,800,000	Atlantic Ocean
Murray–Darling	Australia	2,300	13,000	Southern Ocean
Volga	Europe	2,290	350,000	Caspian Sea
Yukon	N. America	1,979	—	Bering Sea
St Lawrence	N. America	1,945	400,000	Atlantic Ocean
Rio Grande	N. America	1,800	5,180	Gulf of Mexico

THE WORLD'S GREAT WATERFALLS
In Order of Height (Single Leaps Only)

Waterfall	Country	River	Height (ft.)
Angel Falls	Venezuela	Tributary of Caroni River	3,212
Ribbon Falls	California, U.S.A.	Tributary of Yosemite River	1,612
King George VI	Guyana	Urshi River	1,600

Waterfall	Country	River	Height (ft.)
Upper Yosemite	California, U.S.A.	Yosemite Creek	1,430
Tugela (highest fall)	Natal, Republic of S. Africa	Tugela River	1,350
Gavarnie	Pyrenees, France	Gave de Pau	1,385
Wollomombi	New South Wales, Australia	Wollomombi River	1,100
Takakkaw	British Columbia, Canada	Tributary of Yoho River	1,000
Staubbach	Switzerland	Pletschen River	980
Mardola	Norway	Elkesdals Lake	974
Vettisfoss	Norway	Utla River	856
Chirombo	Zambia	Ieisa River	880
King Edward VIII	Guyana	Semang River	840
Gersoppa	India	Sharavati River	830
Sutherland	New Zealand	Arthur River	815

In Order of Volume

Waterfall	Country	River	Height (ft.)	Average annual flow (cu. ft./sec.)
Guaira or Sete Quedas	Brazil–Paraguay	Alto Parana River	130	470,000
Khon	Laos-Khmer	Mekong River	70	410,000
Niagara	U.S.A.–Canada	Niagara River	167	212,000
Paolo Afonse	Brazil	Sao Francisco River	192	100,000
Urubupunga	Brazil	Alto Parana River	40	97,000
Iguazu	Argentina–Brazil	Iguazu River	237	61,660
Patos-Maribondo	Brazil	Rio Grande	115	53,000
Victoria	Zambia and Rhodesia	Zambesi River	354	38,430
Grand	Labrador	Hamilton River	245	35,000
Kaieteur	Guyana	Potaro River	741	23,400

GREAT SHIP CANALS OF THE WORLD

Canal	Year opened	Length miles	Depth feet	Width feet
Amsterdam (Netherlands)	1876	16·5	23	88
Corinth (Greece)	1893	4	26.25	72
Elbe and Trave (Germany)	1900	41	10	72
Gota (Sweden)	1832	115	10	47
Kiel (Germany)	1895	61	45	150
Manchester (England)	1894	35·5	28–30	120
Panama (U.S.A.)	1914	50·5	45	300
Princess Juliana (Netherlands)	1935	20	16	52
Saulte Ste. Marie (U.S.A.)	1855	1·6	22	100
Saulte Ste. Marie (Canada)	1895	1·11	22–25	142
Suez (Egypt)	1869	100	34	197
Welland (Canada)	1887	26·75	25	200

PRINCIPAL LANGUAGES OF THE WORLD

There are probably over 2,000 languages spoken today. Nobody can say the exact number, since many are spoken only by small groups and tribes and have never been recorded on paper. About two thirds of the world's population speak twelve principal languages. The second twelve languages listed here account for about half the remaining population.

Language	Speakers (millions)	Language	Speakers (millions)
Mandarin (China)	493	Italian	58
English	291	Urdu (Pakistan and India)	54
Russian	167	Cantonese (China)	45
Hindi	162	Javanese (Indonesia)	42
Spanish	155	Ukrainian (mainly U.S.S.R.)	41
German	123		
Japanese	98	Telegu (India)	41
Bengali (India, Pakistan)	85	Wu (China)	39
Arabic	82	Tamil (India and Ceylon)	37
Portuguese	80	Min (China)	36
French	73	Korean	35
Malay	71		

DISTANCES BY AIR BETWEEN SOME OF THE WORLD'S CHIEF CITIES, IN MILES

	Amsterdam	Brussels	Buenos Aires	Cairo	Calcutta	Copenhagen
Amsterdam	—	98	7,124	2,041	4,731	393
Brussels	98	—	7,050	1,993	4,761	469
Buenos Aires	7,124	7,050	—	7,368	10,279	7,517
Cairo	2,041	1,993	7,368	—	3,533	1,986
Calcutta	4,731	4,761	10,279	3,533	—	4,390
Copenhagen	393	469	7,517	1,986	4,390	—
Dublin	467	487	6,853	2,473	5,160	770
Geneva	424	331	6,892	1,755	4,748	708
Johannesburg	5,614	5,528	5,028	3,908	5,263	5,736
Karachi	3,718	3,723	9,151	2,210	1,355	3,443
London	231	218	6,921	2,194	5,319	608
Madrid	908	818	6,268	2,081	4,962	1,280
Montreal	3,421	3,452	5,629	5,424	7,600	3,606
New York	3,635	3,657	5,305	5,603	7,918	3,845
Paris	253	162	6,892	1,997	4,877	630
Rome	812	737	6,947	1,321	4,482	955
Singapore	6,529	6,556	9,858	4,696	1,801	6,191
Stockholm	703	787	7,820	2,115	4,200	324
Sydney	10,349	10,399	7,311	8,949	5,678	9,967

	Dublin	Geneva	Johannesburg	Karachi	London	Madrid
Amsterdam	467	424	5,614	3,718	231	908
Brussels	487	331	5,528	3,723	218	818
Buenos Aires	6,853	6,892	5,028	9,151	6,921	6,268
Cairo	2,473	1,755	3,908	2,210	2,194	2,081
Calcutta	5,160	4,748	5,263	1,355	4,962	5,319
Copenhagen	770	708	5,736	3,443	608	1,280
Dublin	—	740	5,885	4,179	279	905
Geneva	740	—	5,201	3,632	468	627

	Dublin	Geneva	Johannesburg	Karachi	London	Madrid
Johannesburg	5,885	5,201	—			
Karachi	4,179	3,632	4,393	—		
London	279	468	5,650	3,938	—	
Madrid	905	627	5,045	4,140	774	—
Montreal	2,965	3,669	8,047	6,989	3,241	3,451
New York	3,171	3,853	7,976	7,260	3,443	3,581
Paris	486	254	5,439	3,808	215	655
Rome	1,184	444	4,812	3,297	908	844
Singapore	6,962	6,524	5,378	2,942	6,760	7,069
Stockholm	1,004	1,029	5,949	3,342	899	1,603
Sydney	10,695	10,425	6,845	6,841	10,575	10,980

	Montreal	New York	Paris	Rome	Singapore	Stockholm	Sydney
Amsterdam	3,421	3,635	253	812	6,529	703	10,349
Brussels	3,452	3,657	162	737	6,556	787	10,399
Buenos Aires	5,629	5,305	6,892	6,947	9,858	7,820	7,311
Cairo	5,424	5,603	1,997	1,321	4,696	2,115	8,949
Calcutta	7,600	7,918	4,877	4,482	1,801	4,200	5,678
Copenhagen	3,606	3,845	630	955	6,191	324	9,967
Dublin	2,965	3,171	486	1,184	6,962	1,004	10,695
Geneva	3,669	3,853	254	444	6,524	1,029	10,425
Johannesburg	8,047	7,976	5,439	4,812	5,378	5,949	6,845
Karachi	6,989	7,260	3,808	3,297	2,942	3,342	6,841
London	3,241	3,443	215	908	6,760	899	10,575
Madrid	3,451	3,581	655	844	7,069	1,603	10,980
Montreal	—	333	3,430	4,107	9,201	3,658	9,955
New York	333	—	3,621	4,282	9,534	3,919	9,949
Paris	3,430	3,621	—	697	6,667	949	10,534
Rome	4,107	4,282	697	—	6,224	1,234	10,136
Singapore	9,201	9,534	6,667	6,224	—	5,997	3,914
Stockholm	3,658	3,919	949	1,234	5,997	—	9,697
Sydney	9,955	9,949	10,534	10,136	3,914	9,697	—

Great Britain and Northern Ireland

THE COUNTIES: *Their Areas and Populations*

Note: The list that follows this note gives the new counties or shires, their areas and populations as they have been since April, 1974, when the provisions of the Local Government Act, 1972, came into force. This Act brought some old counties to an end, rearranged the area and boundaries of others, and introduced new counties and districts.

England is now divided into six metropolitan counties and districts: Greater Manchester, Merseyside, S. Yorkshire, Tyne and Wear, W. Midlands, W. Yorkshire. Besides these, there are 39 non-metropolitan counties: Avon, Bedfordshire, Berkshire, Buckinghamshire, Cambridgeshire, Cheshire, Cleveland, Cornwall, Cumbria, Derbyshire, Devon, Dorset, Durham, E. Sussex, Essex, Gloucestershire, Hampshire, Hereford and Worcester, Hertfordshire, Humberside, I. of Wight, Kent, Lancashire, Leicestershire, Lincolnshire, Norfolk, N. Yorkshire, Northamptonshire, Northumberland, Nottinghamshire, Oxfordshire, Salop, Somerset, Staffordshire, Suffolk, Surrey, Warwickshire, W. Sussex, Wiltshire.

In Wales, the local government areas are now: Clwyd, Dyfed, Gwent, Gwynedd, Mid Glamorgan, Powys, S. Glamorgan, W. Glamorgan.

England

National Capital: London

County or Shire	Administrative Headquarters	Area (acres)	Population
Avon	Bristol	231,000	909,000
Bedford	Bedford	305,026	463,000
Berkshire	Reading	307,176	657,600
Buckinghamshire	Aylesbury	464,000	497,000
Cambridgeshire	Cambridge	842,412	519,830
Cheshire	Chester	573,835	880,941
Cleveland	Middlesborough	43,948	572,400
Cornwall	Truro	876,295	383,390
Cumbria	Carlisle	1,682,323	474,750
Derbyshire	Matlock	650,092	893,600
Devonshire	Exeter	1,612,323	459,280
Dorset	Dorchester	664,116	561,663
Durham	Durham	601,977	610,650
Essex	Chelmsford	907,849	1,386,290
Gloucester	Gloucester	770,297	571,070
Greater Manchester	Manchester	317,347	2,770,000
Hampshire	Winchester	932,000	1,438,000
Hereford & Worcester	Worcester	970,000	595,000

County or Shire	Administrative Headquarters	Area (acres)	Population
Hertford	Hertford	403,816	940,630
Humberside	Kingston-upon-Hull	867,784	841,610
Kent	Maidstone	921,665	1,426,410
Lancashire	Preston	742,438	1,350,480
Leicestershire	Leicester	630,851	809,890
Lincoln	Lincoln	1,454,273	512,000
Greater London	S.E.1.	390,305	7,353,810
Merseyside	Liverpool	160,000	1,636,938
Norfolk	Norwich	2,362,900	625,700
Northampton	Northampton	585,009	478,000
Northumberland	Newcastle-upon-Tyne	1,244,000	279,500
Nottinghamshire	Nottingham	520,956	682,570
Oxfordshire	Oxford	645,314	521,480
Salop	Shrewsbury	862,458	345,860
Somerset	Taunton	854,488	395,000
Staffordshire	Stafford	657,200	751,640
Suffolk	Ipswich	940,800	564,000
Surrey	Kingston-upon-Thames	408,859	995,930
Sussex, East	Lewes	443,627	660,720
Sussex West	Chichester	498,321	636,500
Tyne & Wear	Newcastle	—	2,790,000
Warwick	Warwick	489,300	109,284
West Midlands	Birmingham	—	2,790,000
Wight, Isle of	Newport I.O.W.	94,141	109,284
Wiltshire	Trowbridge	860,099	495,280
Yorkshire North	Northallerton	2,055,000	655,000
Yorkshire South	Barnsley	385,760	1,320,919
Yorkshire West	Wakefield	503,863	2,077,896

Wales

National Capital: Cardiff

Clwyd	Mold	599,000	371,000
Dyfed	Carmarthen	1,425,000	315,000
Gwent	Newport, Gwent	340,356	440,479
Gwynedd	Caernarvon	955,000	224,354
Mid Glamorgan	Cardiff	251,732	533,310
Powyss	Llandrindod Wells	1,255,000	99,000
South Glamorgan	Cardiff	102,807	389,916
West Glamorgan	Swansea	201,476	371,867

Scotland

National Capital: Edinburgh

Aberdeen	Aberdeen	1,252,267	142,949
Angus	Forfar	546,861	99,126

County or Shire	Administrative Headquarters	Area (acres)	Population
Argyll	Inverary	1,990,521	58,941
Ayr	Ayr	724,234	367,491
Banff	Banff	403,054	43,589
Berwick	Duns	292,535	20,911
Bute	Rothesay	139,711	12,606
Caithness	Wick	438,833	27,754
Clackmannan	Alloa	34,937	45,852
Dumfries	Dumfries	688,112	88,012
Dunbarton	Dumbarton	154,362	242,067
East Lothian	Haddington	170,971	56,639
Fife	Cupar	322,878	334,345
Inverness	Inverness	2,695,094	90,816
Kincardine	Stonehaven	242,460	26,837
Kinross	Kinross	52,392	6,834
Kirkcudbright	Kirkcudbright	574,024	27,780
Lanark[1]	Glasgow	535,862	635,631
Midlothian[1]	Edinburgh	201,046	151,954
Moray	Elgin	304,931	52,640
Nairn	Nairn	104,251	8,679
Orkney	Kirkwall	240,848	17,228
Peebles	Peebles	222,240	13,524
Perth	Perth	1,595,804	126,357
Renfrew	Paisley	143,829	364,967
Ross and Cromarty	Dingwall	1,977,254	59,700
Roxburgh	Newton St. Boswells	425,564	42,211
Selkirk	Selkirk	171,209	20,715
Stirling	Stirling	288,349	210,936
Sutherland	Golspie	1,297,913	12,556
West Lothian	Linlithgow	76,859	110,814
Wigtown	Stranraer	311,984	27,453
Zetland	Lerwick	352,337	18,053

Northern Ireland
National Capital: Belfast

County	Assize Town	Area (acres)	Population (1971)
Antrim	Belfast	702,954	352,549
Armagh	Armagh	312,773	133,196
Down	Downpatrick	609,035	310,167

[1]Aberdeen, Edinburgh, Glasgow and Dundee are each classified as a County of a City. Their populations, not included in the above, were estimated in 1971 as: Aberdeen 178,441; Dundee 182,467; Glasgow 897,848; Edinburgh (1973 figs) 448,682

County	Assize Town	Area (acres)	Population (1971)
Fermanagh	Enniskillen	420,211	49,960
Londonderry	Londonderry	512,513	130,296
Tyrone	Omagh	779,545	138,975
County Boroughs:			
Belfast		15,357	353,700
Londonderry		2,200	51,200

Other British Isles

Island	Capital or chief town	Area (acres)	Population
Isle of Man	Douglas	145,325	49,743
Channel Islands:			
Jersey	St. Helier	28,717	72,532
Guernsey	St. Peter Port	15,654	52,708
Alderney	St. Anne's	1,962	1,686
Great Sark	—	1,035	} 590
Little Sark	—	239	

BRITAIN'S LARGEST CITIES

City and Aerodromes [1]	Population
London (B.A.A.)	7,379,014
Birmingham (M)	1,087,660
Glasgow (M)	897,848
Leeds (M)	748,070
Liverpool (M)	589,000
Sheffield —	565,500
Manchester (M)	533,561
Bradford (M. See Leeds)	462,900
Edinburgh (B.A.A.)	448,682
Bristol (M)	425,203
Belfast (S)	353,700
Coventry (M)	336,000
Newcastle-upon-Tyne —	299,800
Nottingham —	294,700
Leicester —	287,350
Kingston-upon-Hull —	285,970
Cardiff —	283,680
Stoke-on-Trent —	260,140

[1] S: owned and operated by State; B.A.A.: operated by British Airports Authority; M: owned and operated by Municipal Authority.

BRITAIN'S HIGHEST MOUNTAINS AND LARGEST LAKES

Peak	County	Height (ft.)	Lake	County	Area (sq. miles)
		England			
Scafell Pike	Cumbria	3,210	Winder-mere	Westmorland–Lancs.	10
		Wales and Monmouthshire			
Snowdon	Gwynydd	3,560	Bala	Merioneth	4
		Scotland			
Ben Nevis	Inverness	4,406	Loch Lo-mond	Dunbarton–Stirling	27
		Northern Ireland			
Slieve Donard	Down	2,796	Lough Neagh	Antrim–London-derry–Tyrone–Armagh	150

IMPORTANT RIVERS OF BRITAIN

River	Length (miles)	Rises in:	Flows to:
Severn	220	Plynlimmon, Dyfed	Bristol Channel
Thames	209	Cotswold Hills, nr. Cirencester	North Sea
Trent	170	N. Staffordshire	Joins Ouse to form R. Humber
Great Ouse	156	Near Brackley, Northants.	The Wash
Wye	130	Plynlimmon	Severn, nr. Chepstow
Tay	117	Grampian Mts., N. Argyllshire	Firth of Tay
Spey	110	Grampian Mts., Inverness	Moray Firth
Clyde	106	S. Lanark (union of Daer and Potrail Water)	Firth of Clyde
Tweed	97	Tweedsmuir Hills, S. Peebles	North Sea, at Scot.–Eng. border
Dee	87	Cairngorm Mts., W. Aberdeenshire	North Sea (at Aber-deen)
Ribble	75	Pennine Chain, W. Yorkshire	Irish Sea (nr. South-port)
Dee	70	Merioneth, N. Wales	'Sands of Dee', Irish Sea

River	Length (miles)	Rises in:	Flows to:
Mersey	70	Pennine Chain (union of Goyt and Tame at Stockport)	Irish Sea (at Liverpool)
Tees	70	Cross Fell, Cumbria	North Sea
Forth	66	S. Perth, N.E. side of Loch Lomond	Firth of Forth
Towy	66	Hills between Cardigan and Radnor	Carmarthen Bay
Eden	65	Pennine Chain (Cumbria–Yorks.)	Solway Firth (Irish Sea)
Wear	65	Pennine Chain (W. Durham)	North Sea
Derwent	60	N. of the Peak (Derby)	Trent
Ouse	60	Yorks. (union of Swale and Ure)	Joins Trent to form R. Humber
Tamar	60	Devonian Hills (Devon)	English Channel (at Plymouth)
Derwent	57	Yorkshire moors	Ouse (between Selby and Goole)
Exe	54	Exmoor (N. Devon)	English Channel (Exeter)
Teifi	53	Llyn Teifi, N.E. Dyfyd	Cardigan Bay (at Cardigan)
Tyne	45	Northumberland (union of N. and S. Tyne)	North Sea (at Tynemouth)

LONDON BOROUGHS

The London County Council and the County Council of Middlesex, together with existing Borough Councils, ceased to exist on 31 March 1965, and were replaced by the Greater London Council. The area is now divided into the following boroughs and the Cities of London and Westminster.

INNER LONDON:

Camden (Hampstead, Holborn, St. Pancras)
Greenwich (Greenwich and part of Woolwich)
Hackney (Hackney, Shoreditch, Stoke Newington)
Hammersmith (Fulham, Hammersmith)
Islington (Finsbury, Islington)
Lambeth (Lambeth and part of Wandsworth)
Lewisham (Deptford, Lewisham)
Royal Borough of Kensington and Chelsea
Southwark (Bermondsey, Camberwell, Southwark)
Tower Hamlets (Bethnal Green, Poplar, Stepney)
Wandsworth (Battersea and part of Wandsworth)

OUTER LONDON:

Barking (Parts of Barking, Dagenham)
Barnet
Bexley
Brent
Bromley
Croydon
Ealing
Enfield
Haringey
Harrow
Havering
Hillingdon
Hounslow
Merton
Newham
Redbridge
Richmond upon Thames
Royal Borough of Kingston upon Thames
Sutton
Waltham Forest

LONDON POSTAL DISTRICTS

Abbey Wood	S.E.2
Acton	W.3
Anerley	S.E.20
Balham	S.W.12
Barnes	S.W.13
Battersea	S.W.11
Bethnal Green	E.2
Blackheath	S.E.3
Bow	E.3
Brixton	S.W.2
Brockley	S.E.4
Camberwell	S.E.5
Catford	S.E.6
Charlton	S.E.7
Chelsea	S.W.3
Chingford	E.4
Chiswick	W.4
Clapham	S.W.4
Clapton	E.5
Cricklewood	N.W.2
Deptford	S.E.8
Dulwich	S.E.21
Ealing	W.5
Earls Court	S.W.5
East Dulwich	S.E.22
Eastern Central (Head) District	E.C.1-4
Eastern (Head) District	E.1
East Finchley	N.2
East Ham	E.6
Eltham	S.E.9
Finchley, Church End	N.3
Finsbury Park	N.4
Forest Gate	E.7
Forest Hill	S.E.23
Fulham	S.W.6
Golders Green	N.W.11
Greenwich	S.E.10
Hackney	E.8
Hammersmith	W.6
Hampstead	N.W.3
Hanwell	W.7
Hendon	N.W.4
Herne Hill	S.E.24
Highbury	N.5
Highgate	N.6
Holloway	N.7
Homerton	E.9
Hornsey	N.8
Kennington	S.E.11
Kensington	W.8
Kentish Town	N.W.5
Kilburn	N.W.6
Lee	S.E.12
Lewisham	S.E.13
Leyton	E.10
Leytonstone	E.11
Lower Edmonton	N.9
Maida Hill	W.9
Manor Park	E.12
Mill Hill	N.W.7
Mortlake	S.W.14
Muswell Hill	N.10
New Cross	S.E.14
New Southgate	N.11
Northern (Head) District	N.1
North Finchley	N.12
North Kensington	W.10
North-Western (Head) District	N.W.1
Norwood	S.E.19

Notting Hill	.	.	W.11	Tooting . . .	S.W.17
Paddington (Head)				Tottenham . .	N.17
District	.	.	W.2	Upper Edmonton .	N.18
Palmer's Green	.		N.13	Upper Holloway .	N.19
Peckham	.	.	S.E.15	Victoria Docks and	
Plaistow .	.	.	E.13	North Woolwich .	E.16
Poplar .	.	.	E.14	Walthamstow .	E.17
Putney .	.	.	S.W.15	Walworth . .	S.E.17
Rotherhithe	.	.	S.E.16	Wandsworth . .	S.W.18
St John's Wood	.		N.W.8	West Brompton .	S.W.10
Shepherd's Bush	.		W.12	West Ealing .	W.13
South-Eastern (Head)				Western Central	
District	.	.	S.E.1	(Head) District .	W.C.1–2
Southgate	.	.	N.14	Western (Head)	
South Kensington	.		S.W.7	District . .	W.1
South Lambeth	.	.	S.W.8	West Kensington .	W.14
South Norwood	.		S.E.25	West Norwood .	S.E.27
South Tottenham	.		N.15	West Wimbledon .	S.W.20
South-Western				Whetstone . .	N.20
(Head) District	.		S.W.1	Willesden . .	N.W.10
Stockwell	.	.	S.W.9	Wimbledon . .	S.W.10
Stoke Newington	.		N.16	Winchmore Hill .	N.21
Stratford	.	.	E.15	Woodford and South	
Streatham	.	.	S.W.16	Woodford . .	E.18
Sydenham	.	.	S.E.26	Wood Green . .	N.22
The Hyde	.	.	N.W.9	Woolwich . .	S.E.18

A Dictionary of Geographical Terms

Aborigines The earliest known inhabitants of a country.

Alluvium The fine sand or soil deposited in low places by running water.

Antipodes Two places precisely opposite one another on the earth, such as Barfleur in Normandy and Antipodes Island, south-east of New Zealand. At antipodes the hours and seasons are reversed, so that when it is midnight in summer in Barfleur it is noon in winter on Antipodes.

Archipelago A group of islands.

Atoll A coral reef, typical of the Pacific Ocean, shaped like a ring or horseshoe round a lagoon.

Aurora borealis The Northern lights; an electrical discharge seen by night over the higher latitudes of the northern hemisphere.

Axis The imaginary line running from pole to pole through the centre of the earth.

Bar A collection of gravel, sand or mud at the mouth of a river.

Basin The area of land drained by a river and its tributaries.

Bayou A marshy creek or offshoot to a river or lake which remains swampy because of floods and lack of drainage.

Blowhole A hole in the roof of a seaside cave through which air and sometimes water are forced by the rising tide.

Beaches, Raised Line of former sea shore left dry through a rise in the land.

Bore or **Eagre** A tidal wave arising in the estuaries of certain rivers.

Butte A flat-topped hill, like a MESA but smaller.

Canyon A narrow, deep gorge, with steep sides, cut by a river through soft rock in a dry region. The biggest and best known is the Grand Canyon of the Colorado River, U.S.A.

Cape A headland or piece of land jutting out into the sea.

Cataract A large waterfall, or series of waterfalls.

Col A mountain pass or neck.

Continental drift The movement by which, according to one theory, the continents arrived at their present positions after breaking off from a single original mass of land. The main

B43

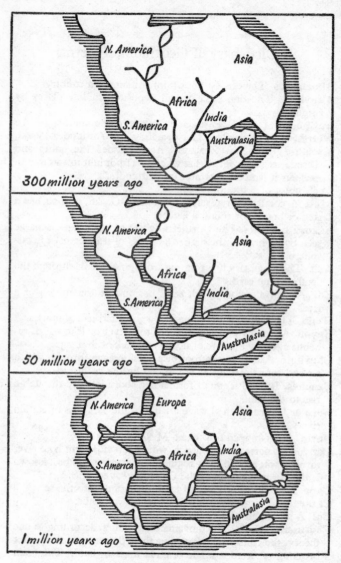

Continental Drift

argument in favour of the theory is that the shores of the continents fit together fairly well, like pieces of a jig-saw puzzle.

Contour A line joining places of the same height above sea-level; in a map they help to show the shapes of the land.

Coral Reef A barrier, lying at or just below the surface of the sea, built up of the skeletons of immense numbers of small creatures called coral polyps.

Couloir A steep, narrow gorge on the side of a mountain.

Crater The funnel-shaped hollow at the top of the cone of a volcano.

Crevasse A crack in a glacier or ice sheet.

Date Line The line that follows roughly the 180° meridian from Greenwich, and marks the point where according to international agreement the day begins. When a ship crosses this line eastwards it goes forward a day; westwards, it goes back a day.

Delta A fan-shaped tract of flat land at the mouth of a river, made up of silt and other material brought down from upstream and deposited there. The soil of deltas is usually very rich.

Doldrums The term for a region of calms and baffling winds near the equator.

Dunes Mounds formed by wind-blown sand.

Earthquake A movement of the earth, caused either by volcanic activity below the surface or by a large area of earth, weaker than that which surrounds it, slipping a little downwards. Earthquakes need not be severe. In some parts of the Pacific they are a daily, and not especially frightening, occurrence.

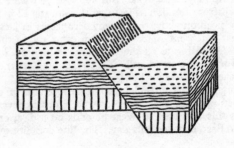

Erosion The wearing away of the land by sun, wind, rain, frost, running water, moving ice and the sea.

Fault A break in the earth's crust along which movement has taken place—usually, but not always, vertically—so that the layers (strata) of the two rock faces no longer match. It is often along a fault that earthquakes occur.

Fiord A long, narrow inlet of the sea, with steep sides, scooped out in ages past by glaciers. A fiord is usually very deep, becoming shallower towards its mouth.

Föhn Wind A warm, dry wind blowing down the sides of mountains facing away from the prevailing wind. It is best known in the valleys of the northern Alps. Other föhn winds are the Chinook (the eastern side of the Rocky Mountains, Canada and the U.S.A.); the Nor'Wester (New Zealand) and the Samoon (Iran).

Geysers Hot springs which shoot jets of hot water and steam into the air at regular or irregular intervals.

Glaciers Masses of ice that move very slowly down a valley towards the sea, propelled by gravity, carrying rock material with them.

Horse Latitudes Regions of calms and variable winds between latitudes 25° and 40° N. and S.; so-called because becalmed sailors whose food was running out used to throw their horses overboard.

Icebergs Masses of ice that have broken off from glaciers and are afloat in the sea. Only about one-ninth of an iceberg is above the surface.

International Date Line Generally, every country sets its time according to the rising and setting of the sun. So that anywhere in the world the sun is at its highest at about 12 o'clock midday, *local time*. But suppose you were to travel due west from London so fast that the sun stayed in the same relative position above you (many aeroplanes in fact do this) and that you went right on till you came round to London again. According to all the local times you passed through, time would have stood still. Yet in fact your journey would have taken twenty-four hours.

By international agreement, a line has been drawn down the meridian opposite that of Greenwich, and whenever anyone crosses this line East to West he adds on a day; or if from West to East, he takes off a day. The line does not quite keep

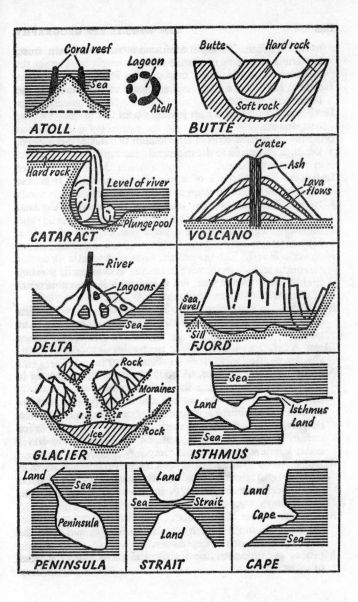

to the meridian. To avoid confusion it has been drawn round any lands or groups of islands where it might have upset the calendar too much. (See map on page B15.)

Isobars Lines on a map joining places of the same average barometric pressure.

Isotherms Lines on a map joining places of the same average temperature.

Isthmus A narrow strip of land joining two large land areas or joining a peninsula to the mainland. Examples: the isthmuses of Panama and Suez.

Latitude The distance of a place north or south from the equator, measured in degrees of the MERIDIAN.

Littoral The seashore, the land along the coast, or the land lying between the levels of high and low tide.

Longitude The distance of a place east or west of a given MERIDIAN.

Magnetic North The pole of the lines of magnetic force that run north and south through the earth. It changes its position slightly from year to year, but in general it is in an area north of Canada, roughly at longitude 97° W. and latitude 71° N.

Meridian An imaginary circle on the earth's surface passing through the two poles; on it all places have noon at the same time.

Mesa A flat, table-like mass with steep sides all round. Eventually, by wearing away, mesas becomes BUTTES.

Meteor or Shooting Star. A body of matter flying around in outer space which enters the earth's atmosphere. It usually travels so fast that the friction caused by passing through the atmosphere burns it up quickly. Some big ones, however, do survive the journey and reach the earth. These are called *meteorites*. One of the biggest fell in Arizona, blowing a crater a mile wide and 600 ft. deep.

Mirage An optical illusion, caused by the presence of layers of air of different density, in which the image of a sheet of water may appear over the desert, or images of ships and icebergs, upside-down, over polar waters.

Monsoons Winds of the Indian Ocean and nearby lands blowing from the north-east in October to March, and from the south-west in April to September.

Moraine A continuous line of rocks and gravel along the edges of a glacier.

Oasis An area in the desert made fertile by the presence of water.

Pampas Dreary expanses of treeless, grassy plain and salt marshes in Argentina.

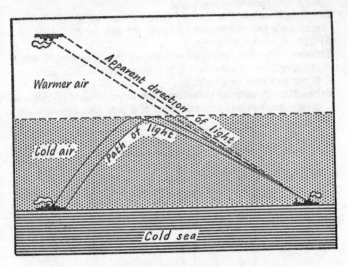

Peninsula A tract of land almost surrounded by water.

Pothole A hole worn in solid rock, usually at the foot of a waterfall, by the constant grinding of a stone, kept in motion by the current.

Prairie The almost flat, mostly treeless grasslands of North America. Similar areas are the steppes of the U.S.S.R., the pampas of Argentina and the veld of South Africa.

Projections Ways of representing the earth's surface on a map. Because the earth is round, any map distorts the area it represents (just as flattening out an orange peel distorts its original shape). Only a globe can be really accurate.

Different types of projection have been worked out, each suited to a particular purpose. The two main ones are Conical and Cylindrical. The former shows each hemisphere as a cone which has been unrolled. A Cylindrical Projection shows the earth as though it were an unrolled cylinder. Mercator's

projection, used on page B14, is cylindrical. Its main fault is
that it makes the Equator out to be the same length as all
other latitudes, even those near the Poles, which are really
only a few miles long. Thus countries near the Poles appear
far larger than they really are.

Roaring Forties The seaman's name for the steady north-west
anti-trade winds between latitudes 40° and 60° S.

Sierra A mountain range.

Sirocco The hot, dry and sometimes dusty southerly wind
blowing from the Sahara; it is experienced in North Africa,
Sicily and southern Italy.

Stalactite A column of mineral matter, particularly calcium
carbonate, hanging from the roof of a cave like a giant icicle.

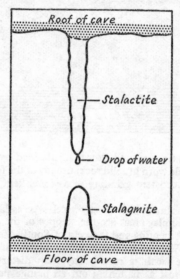

Stalagmite A column of calcium carbonate rising from the
floor of a cave, formed by water containing the mineral falling
from the roof or from a STALACTITE.

Strait A narrow band of sea connecting two large sea areas.
Example: the Straits of Gibraltar, connecting the Atlantic and
the Mediterranean.

Trade Winds Regular steady winds in the tropics, between latitudes 30° N. and 30° S., blowing to the equator.

Tropics The tropic of Cancer (line of latitude 23½ degrees North) and the Tropic of Capricorn (line of latitude 23½ degrees South) are, respectively, the northernmost and southernmost lines on which the sun's rays shine vertically.

Tsunami The correct name for what is often wrongly called a tidal wave, namely, a huge sea wave sometimes experienced along the coasts of the oceans (as in Japan and Chile in 1960) and caused by earthquakes on the ocean floor.

Typhoon A violent, destructive whirlwind blowing in the China Seas from August to October.

Whirlpool A circular eddy in the sea produced by the coming together of two currents, or in a river by the way the channel is formed.

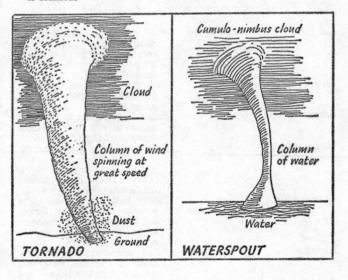

Weather

CLOUDS

There are three principal formations of cloud that can easily be recognised from the translations of their Latin names: **stratus**, a flat layer; **cumulus**, a heap, pile or pack; and **cirrus**, meaning a lock of curly hair. These often combine, as the list shows, in other formations. It may be helpful to remember that **alto** means high and **nimbo** or **nimbus** means rain.

TYPES OF CLOUD

Type	Usual range of height of base in feet	Description
Cumulus	1,000–1,500	Flat base, high rounded tops. Small, white, scattered puffs mean fair weather, but heavy, deep clouds often become cumulo-nimbus.
Stratus	Up to 500–2,000	Unbroken grey layer; looks like fog that has lifted from the ground.
Stratocumulus	1,000–4,500	Broad layer arranged in round masses or rolls, often so close together that their edges join.
Nimbostratus	Near surface to 20,000	Dark grey with a base that is the same throughout. Often gives continuous rain or snow; if these do not reach the ground the cloud appears to trail.
Cumulonimbus	Up to 2,000–5,000	Heavy, dark, very tall—as high as 3 miles. Tops often spread out in anvil-shape. Thunderstorm cloud; gives showers of rain, snow, hail, etc.
Altocumulus	6,500–20,000	Small, thin rounded patches, resembling cumulus, sometimes so close together their edges meet.
Altostratus	6,580–20,000	Sheet or veil, sometimes thin, but sometimes so thick it blocks out the moon or even the sun, when it normally indicates continuous rain.

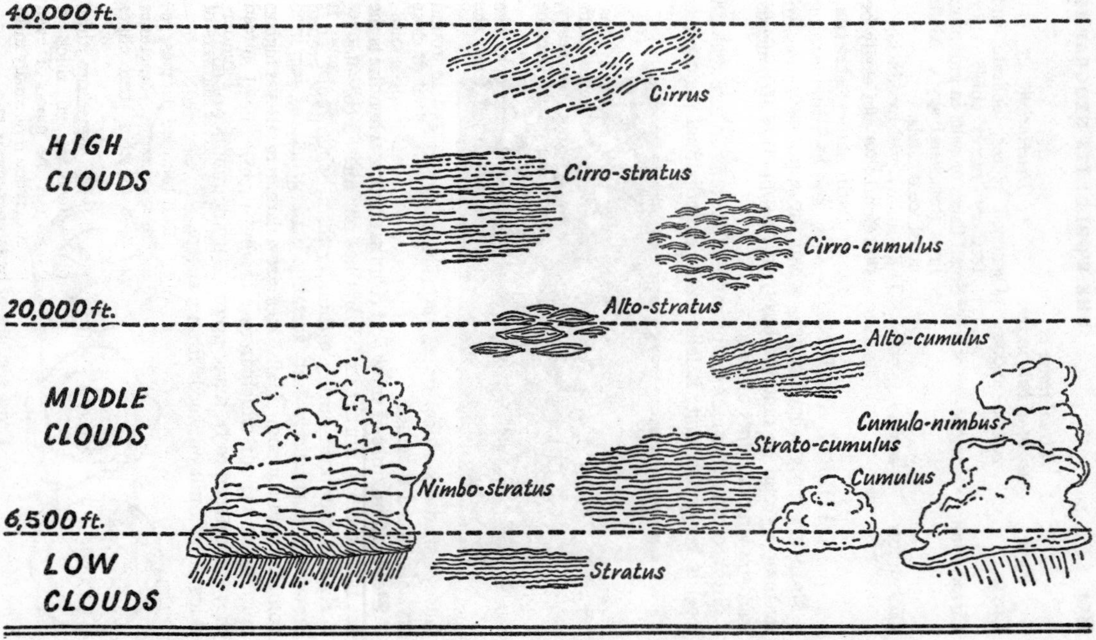

Cirrus

Cirro-cumulus

Cirro-stratus

Alto-cumulus

Alto-stratus

Cumulo-nimbus?

Cumulus

Strato-cumulus

Nimbo-stratus

Stratus

40,000 ft.

HIGH CLOUDS

20,000 ft.

MIDDLE CLOUDS

6,500 ft.

LOW CLOUDS

Type	Usual range of height of base in feet	Description
Cirrus	20,000–40,000	Detached pieces, delicate and feathery ('mares' tails').
Cirrocumulus	20,000–40,000	Small flakes or rolls in groups or lines ('mackerel sky'). Made up of ice crystals.
Cirrostratus	20,000–40,000	Thin, milky veil producing a ring of light round the moon.

OTHER INFLUENCES ON WEATHER

Rain is simply what happens when the water droplets that make up a cloud become too heavy to be supported by the up-ward-moving currents of air.

Snow occurs when the temperature of the atmosphere at cloud level is below freezing; it falls either as individual ice crystals

(always with six sides) or as snowflakes composed of several crystals joined together.

Sleet is a mixture of snow and rain that occurs when the snow has been melting during its fall but has not melted completely.

Hail is produced during a thunderstorm, when moist air is drawn up particularly fast, forming hard pellets of ice in a cumulonimbus cloud. Hailstones grow larger as they pick up more water vapour which freezes around them. Sliced in half they can be seen to be made up of a varying number of coats or skins of ice built outwards from a centre.

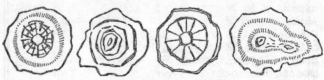

Cross sections of hailstones

Dew is what results when at night the ground releases the heat it has stored up during the day, and the air on or just above it becomes cooler. When the temperature falls below a certain point the water vapour on the ground or on nearby objects like blades of grass forms the drops of water we call dew.

Hoar Frost is frozen dew.

Fog is a thick mass of small water drops in the lower air, resulting from condensation. In cities the water drops are often mixed with particles of dust and smoke; when the mixture is really detestable it earns the name of *smog*.

Mist is simply a thinner version of fog.

Land fogs occur mainly in autumn and winter and **sea fogs** in spring and summer. This is because the sea takes in and gives off the sun's heat much more slowly than the land, and begins to lose the previous summer's heat (thus cooling the air above it and causing fog) only after the winter has passed.

Thunder is produced by the expansion of air due to the tremendous heat of lightning flashes.

Lightning is an electrical discharge from a thunder-cloud, which generates electricity much as a power station does.

SOME VIOLENT KINDS OF WEATHER

Typhoons and **hurricanes** are caused by tropical cyclones. These cyclones occur where the pressure of the atmosphere has sunk very much lower than that of the surrounding air. Around its calm centre—known as the 'eye' of the storm—winds of hurricane force (that is, of speeds greater than 75 m.p.h.) blow continuously. Cyclones cause immense damage in the tropics. They occur most often in the seas off China (typhoons), but nearly as often in the West Indies (hurricanes).

Whirlwinds are like cyclones, having an area of low pressure at their centres, but they are very much smaller, consisting of columns of air whirling very rapidly round an axis that is vertical or nearly so. In the desert they can cause **sandstorms**.

A **tornado** is an extremely violent whirlwind.

A **waterspout** is a tornado occurring at sea; a portion of cloud looking like an upside-down cone reaches down from the base of a thunder-cloud to where it meets a cone of spray raised from the sea to form a continuous column or spout between sea

and cloud. In the days of sailing-ships waterspouts were known
to tear ships to pieces.

WORLD WEATHER RECORDS

Record	Degree or amount	Where recorded	When recorded
Highest shade temperature	(57·8° C.) 136° F.	San Louis, Mexico	1933
Lowest temperatures	(−88·3° C.) −127° F.	Vostok, Antarctica	1960
	(−74·5° C.) −102·1° F.	Near S. Pole	1957
	(−67·7° C.) −89·9° F.	Oimekon, Siberia	1933
Highest average annual temperature	(31·1° C.) 88° F.	Lugh, Somalia	Over 13 years
Lowest average annual temperature	(−51·1° C.) −60° F.	Near S. Pole	—
Maximum rainfall (24 hours)	73·62 in.	Cilaos, Ile de Réunion	1952
Maximum rainfall (one month)	366·14 in.	Cherrapunji, India	1861
Maximum average annual rainfall	471·68 in.	Kauai, Hawaii	1912–49
Minimum average annual rainfall	0·02 in.	Arica, Chile	43-year average

BRITISH WEATHER RECORDS

Highest temperature	100·5° F. (38·1° C.)	Tonbridge, Kent	1868
Lowest temperature	−17° F. (−27° C.)	Braemar, Scotland	1895
Maximum rainfall (24 hours)	11 in.	Martinstown, near Dorchester	1955
Maximum annual rainfall	257 in.	Sprinkling Tarn, Cumberland	1954
Minimum annual rainfall	9·29 in.	Margate	1921
Maximum wind velocity	177 m.p.h.	Shetlands	1962

FURTHER READING

A Dictionary of Geography, by W. G. Moore (Penguin)
Standard Encyclopædia of the World's Oceans and Islands, ed.
  Anthony Huxley (Weidenfeld & Nicolson)
The Observer's Book of The Weather (Warne)

The World

3: ITS FAMOUS PEOPLE
(*Actual and Mythical*)

A Dictionary of Famous People   2–33
Names in the News   34–42
A Dictionary of Mythology   43–50

In *A Dictionary of Famous People* are to be found short biographies of the great men and women of both the distant and the recent past. In *Names in the News* short notes are given about celebrated persons now living. Those in *A Dictionary of Mythology* were, of course, never alive at all, in any ordinary sense—they are the gods and goddesses found in the myths and legends of ancient peoples.

A Dictionary of Famous People

WHEN the story of a man's life, his biography, is told very briefly it is called a potted biography. The biographies in this section have been potted and then potted again. They are meant to answer the following questions: 'Who was he?' 'When did he live?' 'Where did he come from?' 'What did he do?' For fuller details you should, of course, consult either a separate biography of your man (or woman) or one of the big encyclopaedias that are devoted entirely to telling the stories of famous lives. (For famous Britishers the best source of all is the *Dictionary of National Biography*.)

Left out of this section are most of those people whose achievements are mentioned elsewhere; for example,

> Kings and Queens of England and Scotland (HISTORY);
> British writers (THE ENGLISH LANGUAGE);
> Explorers and discoverers (HISTORY);
> Painters, sculptors and architects (THE ARTS).

In the case of other historical figures, dates of birth and death are given and you are advised to 'see HISTORY'—which usually means the DIARY OF WORLD EVENTS. In some instances people who appear elsewhere in the book are treated fully here (e.g. Captain Scott); this is because there is something important to add that has not been said in the other section where the mention occurs.

The letter *c.* before a date (e.g. *c.* 450 B.C.) is short for the Latin *circa*, 'about', and means that the date is not certainly known.

Aeschylus (*c.* 525–456 B.C.), Greek tragic dramatist.

Akbar, Jalal-ud-din Mohammed (1542–1605), greatest of the Mogul emperors.

Alaric 1st (376–410), King of the Visigoths, who sacked Rome.

Alban, St, lived in the last part of the 3rd century; served as soldier in Rome, was converted to Christianity and, returning to Britain to preach, was martyrised.

Alcibiades (*c.* 450–404 B.C.), Athenian statesman and general, pupil of Socrates.

Alcott, Louisa May (1832–88), American writer, author of *Little Women*.

Alexander II (1818–81), Czar of Russia who emancipated the serfs; assassinated by Nihilists.

Alexander the Great (356–323 B.C.), see HISTORY.

Alfred the Great (849–99), see HISTORY.

Ampére, André Marie (1775–1836), French mathematician, the first to propound the electro-dynamic theory.

Andersen, Hans Christian (1805–75), Danish storyteller and poet; author of famous fairy tales.

Andrew, St, one of Jesus' disciples, and patron saint of Scotland; commemorated on 30 November.

Anselm, St (1033–1109), Archbishop of Canterbury; quarrelled with William Rufus about the authority of the Pope, but regained his position under Henry I.

Antonius Marcus (Mark Antony) (*c.* 83–30 B.C.), see HISTORY.

Aquinas, Thomas, St (*c.* 1225–74), Italian religious teacher and philosopher.

Archimedes (*c.* 287–212 B.C.), Greek mathematician, physicist and inventor; made many discoveries in mechanics (notably the lever) and invented the Archimedean screw. Killed during siege of Syracuse by Romans.

Aristophanes (*c.* 450–*c.* 385 B.C.), greatest of the Greek comic dramatists.

Aristotle (384–322 B.C.), Greek philosopher and pupil of Plato; took the whole field of knowledge as his subject.

Arkwright, Sir Richard (1732–92), pioneer of British cotton industry.

Augustine, St (354–430), religious philosopher and teacher.

Arnold, Thomas (1795–1842), headmaster of Rugby; regarded as the creator of the modern Public School system. The original of the headmaster in *Tom Brown's Schooldays*.

Arthur (*c.* 600), Celtic warrior about whom a great deal of legend has collected.

Attila (*c.* 406–53), king of the Huns, see HISTORY.

Attlee, 1st Earl (1883–1967), Deputy Prime Minister, 1942–5; Prime Minister, 1945–51.

Augustine, St, missionary monk sent to Britain in 597; first Archbishop of Canterbury. Died in 604.

Augustus Caesar (63 B.C.–A.D. 14), first Emperor of Rome; see HISTORY.

Bach, Johann Sebastian (1685–1750), great German composer.

Bacon, Francis, Lord Verulam (1561–1626), English philosopher and statesman; Attorney-General under Elizabeth, Lord Chancellor under James I; author of *Novum Organum* and *Essays*.

Bacon, Roger (*c.* 1214–94), Franciscan friar, the first man in modern times to insist on the importance of experiment in science.

Baden-Powell, Lord (1857–1941), famous for his defence of Mafeking during Boer War; founded Boy Scouts (1908) and Girl Guides (1910).

Baird, John Logie (1888–1946), pioneer of television.

Bakewell, Robert (1725–95), pioneer of modern agriculture.

Ball, John (d. 1381), English priest who was a leader of the Peasants' Revolt.

Balzac, Honoré de (1799–1850), great French novelist; author of 80 novels with the general title of *La Comédie Humaine*.

Banks, Sir Joseph (1744–1820), English botanist and 'father of Australia'.

Barnado, Dr Thomas (1845–1905), devoted his life to the welfare of homeless children; founder of the homes named after him.

Baudelaire, Charles (1821–67), French poet, whose work has had an immense influence on modern poetry.

Becket, St Thomas à (1118–70), see HISTORY.

Bede, 'The Venerable' (*c.* 673–735), monk and historian, 'the father of English history'.

Beethoven, Ludwig van (1770–1827), German composer.

Bell, Alexander Graham (1847–1922), inventor of the telephone.

Benedict, St (*c.* 480–544), founded the Order of Benedictine monks.

Bentham, Jeremy (1748–1832), radical writer and thinker; helped develop the Utilitarian philosophy that the aim of politics should be 'the greatest happiness of the greatest number'.

Berlioz, Hector (1803–69), French composer.

Bernard, St (923–1008), Cistercian monk, patron saint of mountaineers.

Bernhardt, Sarah (1845–1923), famous French tragic actress.

Bismarck, Prince Otto (1815–98), see HISTORY.

Blake, Robert (1599–1657), Parliamentary general in the Civil War; admiral in the wars against Holland and Spain.

Blériot, Louis (1872–1936), French inventor and aviator; first to fly the English Channel, 1909.

Blondin, Charles (1824–97), French tight-rope walker famous for his crossing of the Niagara Falls.

Boadicea (d. A.D. 62), see HISTORY.

Boccaccio, Giovanni (1313–75), Italian novelist and poet; author of the *Decameron*.

Bolivar, Simon (1783–1830), 'the Liberator'; revolutionary who broke Spanish power in South America; first president of Venezuela and Dictator of Peru.

Boone, Daniel (1734–1820), American explorer and settler.

Booth, William (1829–1912), founder and first general of the Salvation Army.

Borgia, Cesar (1476–1507), son of Pope Alexander VI, made himself ruler of Romagna by murdering those who stood in his way. Banished by Pope Julius II and died in the invasion of Castile.

Botha, General Louis (1862–1919), Boer general who became first Premier of South Africa.

Boyle, Robert (1627–91), English scientist; the first man to distinguish between a mixture and a compound. Author of Boyle's Law (see DICTIONARY OF SCIENCE AND MATHEMATICS).

Bragg, Sir William (1862–1942), English scientist who received the 1915 Nobel Prize with his son, **Sir Lawrence Bragg** (b. 1890), for their work on X-rays and crystal structures.

Brahms, Johannes (1833–97), German composer.

Brecht, Bertold (1898–1959), German dramatist and poet, author of *The Threepenny Opera*.

Bright, John (1811–89), famous Radical statesman and orator, and one of those responsible for the introduction of Free Trade.

Brown, Sir Arthur Whitten (1886–1948), made the first trans-atlantic flight in 1919 with Sir John Alcock.

Brown, John (1800–1859), fanatical opponent of slavery in America. He was hanged for having incited slaves to rebel, and his death was a signal for the outbreak of the Civil War.

Bruce, Robert (1274–1329), see HISTORY.

Brummell, George (1778–1840), 'Beau Brummell', leader of fashion in English society when George IV was Prince Regent.

Brunel, Isambard Kingdom (1806–59), engineer and steam-ship-designer: constructed Clifton Suspension Bridge and much of the G.W. Railway.

Brunel, Sir Mark Isambard (1769–1849), father of Isambard, and constructor of the Thames tunnel.

Brutus, Marcus (85–42 B.C.), see HISTORY.

Buddha (Sidharta Gautama), the founder of Buddhism in the 6th century B.C.

Burghley, William Cecil, Lord (1520–1598), principal adviser to Queen Elizabeth for 40 years.

Burke, Edmund (1729–97), political philosopher, statesman and orator: most famous for his attacks on the French Revolution.

Byrd, William (1543–1623), English composer.

Cabot, John (c. 1455–c. 1498), see EXPLORATIONS AND DISCOVERIES.

Cabot, Sebastian (c. 1493–1557), see EXPLORATIONS AND DISCOVERIES.

Caesar, Caius Julius (c. 101–44 B.C.), see HISTORY.

Calvin, John (1509–64), French religious reformer who preached his severe doctrine (Calvinism) in Geneva, where he created a Protestant republic.

Campbell, Sir Malcolm (1885–1948), racing driver who held land and water speed records.

Canute the Great (995–1035), see HISTORY

Carnegie, Andrew (1835–1919), son of poor Scottish weaver who became American multi-millionaire; gave away most of his money to benefit the public, especially by the founding of libraries.

Cartier, Jaques (1491–1557), see EXPLORATIONS AND DISCOVERIES.

Casabianca, Louis de (c. 1754–98), captain of a French war-ship at the Battle of the Nile; he and his 10-year-old son refused to leave the burning ship and died together.

Cassius, Caius (d. 42 B.C.), see HISTORY.

Catherine the Great (1729–96), Empress of Russia; came to the throne by deposing and murdering her husband, the weak

Peter; carried Russia's frontiers by conquest to the Black Sea and the borders of Germany.

Cato, Marcus Porcius (234–149 B.C.), Roman statesman, soldier and writer: opposed the luxurious living of his times.

Cavell, Edith (1865–1915), British nurse shot by the Germans for helping wounded British soldiers to escape from Belgium.

Cavour, Count Camillo de (1810–61), one of the founders of modern Italy.

Caxton, William (*c.* 1422–91), founder of the first English printing press.

Cecilia, Saint, the patron saint of music: martyrised *c.* A.D. 176.

Cervantes, Saavedra, Miguel de (1547–1616), Spanish novelist, author of *Don Quixote.*

Charlemagne (742–814), see HISTORY.

Charles V (1510–58), Holy Roman Emperor who ruled Austria, the Netherlands and Spain.

Chatham, William Pitt, Earl of (1708–78), statesman and Parliamentarian, in control of English policy during Seven Years War.

Chekhov, Anton (1860–1904), great Russian dramatist and short-story writer; author of *The Cherry Orchard,* etc.

Chippendale, Thomas (*c.* 1717–79), famous furniture designer.

Chopin, Frédéric (1810–49), Polish composer and pianist.

Churchill, Sir Winston (1874–1965), British statesman and author: Prime Minister 1940–45 and 1951–55.

Cicero, Marcus Tullius (106–43 B.C.), most eloquent of the Roman orators.

Cierva, Juan de la (1895–1936), Spanish engineer who invented the autogiro.

Claudius I (10 B.C.–A.D. 54), Roman Emperor; erected many great buildings; visited Britain; murdered by his wife Agrippina.

Clemens, Samuel Langhorne ('Mark Twain') (1835–1910), American writer and humorist, author of *Tom Sawyer* and *Huckleberry Finn.*

Cleopatra (69–30 B.C.), see HISTORY.

Clive, Robert, Lord (1725–74), English general, victor of Plassey, who laid the foundations of the British empire in India.

Cobbett, William (1762–1835), politician, social reformer and writer, author of *Rural Rides*.

Cobden, Richard (1804–1865), statesman, economist and advocate of Free Trade.

Cody, Samuel (1861–1913), the first man to fly in Britain, 1908.

Cody, William (1846–1917), American showman known as 'Buffalo Bill'.

Coke, Sir Edward (1552–1634), great English jurist.

Coke, Thomas William (1752–1842), pioneer of scientific farming.

Columbus, Christopher (1451–1506), see EXPLORATIONS AND DISCOVERIES.

Confucius (*c.* 551–479 B.C.), the most celebrated of the Chinese philosophers.

Cook, Capt. James (1728–79), see EXPLORATIONS AND DISCOVERIES.

Copernicus, Nicholas (1473–1543), Polish founder of modern astronomy; author of the Copernican theory that the planets revolve round the sun.

Corneille, Pierre (1606–84), French tragic dramatist.

Cortes, Hernando (1485–1547), Spanish conqueror of Mexico.

Cranmer, Thomas (1489–1556), first Protestant Archbishop of Canterbury; see HISTORY.

Crispin, St (3rd century), patron of shoemakers: commemorated on 25 October.

Croesus (d. *c.* 546 B.C.), last king of Lydia (part of modern Turkey), celebrated for his fabulous wealth.

Crockett, Davy (1786–1836), American frontiersman; fought in Congress for a fair deal for the Red Indians; killed at the Battle of Alamo.

Cromwell, Oliver (1599–1658), see HISTORY.

Cruikshank, George (1792–1878), famous book illustrator and caricaturist.

Cunard, Sir Samuel (1787–1861), founder of the shipping company which became the Cunard Line.

Curie, Pierre (1859–1906) and **Marie** (1867–1934), pioneers of the science of radioactivity, and first to isolate radium.

Daguerre, Louis (1789–1851), French inventor of the earliest photographic process (the daguerrotype).

Daimler, Gottlieb (1834–90), German inventor with N. A.

Otto of the Otto gas engine, and also of the motor-car named after him (see CARS).

Dalton, John (1766–1844), English scientist who discovered atomic theory.

Damien, Father Joseph (1840–89), Belgian missionary who volunteered to look after lepers in Honolulu, and himself died of the disease.

Dante Alighieri (1265–1321), greatest of the Italian poets, author of the *Divine Comedy*.

Danton, Georges (1759–94), President of the Committee of Public Safety during the first French Revolution; supplanted by Robespierre and guillotined.

Darius I (548–485 B.C.), see HISTORY.

Darling, Grace (1815–42), English lighthouse-keeper's daughter famous for saving a shipwrecked crew by putting out with her father in a small boat.

Darnley, Earl of (1545–67), Mary Queen of Scots' second husband, murdered after Mary had entered into an intrigue with Bothwell.

Darwin, Charles (1809–82), English naturalist whose *Origin of the Species* first set out the theory of evolution by means of natural selection.

David (1038–970 B.C.), king who united Israelites in Canaan.

David, St (6th century), patron saint of Wales.

Davis, Jefferson (1808–89), President of the Confederate States during the American Civil War.

Davy, Sir Humphrey (1778–1829), scientist who invented miners' lamp.

Debussy, Claude (1862–1918), French composer.

De Gaulle, General Charles (1890–1970), led Free French in Second World War; President of France, 1958–69.

De Havilland, Sir Geoffrey (1882–1965), a pioneer of civil and military aviation.

Democritus (*c.* 460–357 B.C.), Greek philosopher to whom the conception of the atomic theory is attributed.

Demosthenes (385–322 B.C.), most famous of the Athenian orators; he roused the Athenians to resist Philip of Macedon.

Descartes, René (1596–1650), French philosopher and mathematician.

Diaghilev, Sergei (1872–1929), Russian ballet impresario and founder of the Ballets Russes.

Diocletian (245–313), Roman Emperor under whom the Christians were ruthlessly persecuted; see HISTORY.

Diogenes (412–322 B.C.), Greek philosopher who scorned wealth and social conventions and is said to have lived in a tub.

Disraeli, Benjamin (Earl of Beaconsfield) (1804–81), see HISTORY.

Dominic, St (1170–1221), founder of the Order of Dominicans, or Black Friars.

Dostoeivsky, Feodor (1821–81), one of the greatest Russian novelists, author of *Crime and Punishment*.

Drake, Sir Francis (c. 1540–96), see HISTORY.

Dumas, Alexandre (1802–70), prolific French novelist and dramatist, author of *The Count of Monte Cristo* and *The Three Musketeers*.

Dunstan, St (909–88), famous Abbot of Glastonbury and Archbishop of Canterbury, who lived through seven reigns.

Duval, Claude (1643–70), notorious French-born highwayman, hanged at Tyburn.

Dvorak, Antonin (1841–1904), Czech composer.

Edison, Thomas Alva (1847–1931), inventor of electric lighting and the gramophone.

Eiffel, Alexandre (1832–1923), French engineer who built the Eiffel Tower and the locks on the Panama Canal.

Einstein, Albert (1879–1955), German mathematical physicist and one of the greatest of all men of science; author of the theory of relativity.

Elgar, Sir Edward (1857–1934), English composer.

Emmet, Robert (1778–1803), Irish patriot; he led a rebellion in 1803, and was executed for high treason.

Empedocles (c. 500–c. 430 B.C.), Greek philosopher, founder of a school of medicine which regarded the heart as the seat of life.

Epicurus (342–270 B.C.), Greek philosopher who taught that pleasure was the chief good of man and was to be attained through the practice of virtue.

Erasmus, Desiderius (1466–1536), Dutch scholar and philosopher, one of the great figures of the Renaissance.

Essex, Robert Devereux, Earl of (1567–1601), Queen Elizabeth's favourite; he conspired against her and was executed.

Euclid (c. 330–c. 260 B.C.), Greek mathematician who laid the foundations of modern geometry.

Euripides (480–406 B.C.), great Athenian tragic dramatist.

Evelyn, John (1620–1706), famous for his diaries, and one of the founders of the Royal Society.

Fabius Maximus ('Cunctator') (d. 203 B.C.), the Roman dictator who saved Rome from Hannibal by deliberately avoiding battle. From this policy comes the term 'Fabian tactics'.

Fabre, Jean (1823–1915), French naturalist, life-long observer of the habits of insects.

Fahrenheit, Gabriel (1686–1736), German physicist, inventor of the method of grading a thermometer which bears his name.

Faraday, Michael (1791–1867), English physicist and chemist, founder of the science of electro-magnetism.

Fawkes, Guy (1570–1606), a Yorkshire Catholic, one of the conspirators in the Gunpowder Plot; he was captured in the cellar of Parliament House, tried and executed.

Ferdinand of Spain (1452–1516) and **Isabella** (1451–1504), see HISTORY.

Flaubert, Gustave (1821–80), one of the greatest French novelists.

Fleming, Sir Alexander (1881–1955), discoverer of penicillin.

Fokker, Anthony (1860–1939), famous Dutch airman and aeronautical engineer.

Ford, Henry (1863–1947), founder of the Ford Motor Co. and pioneer of the cheap motor-car.

Forester, Cecil Scott (1899–1966), author, creator of Hornblower.

Fox, Charles James (1749–1806), Whig statesman who favoured American independence and opposed the war with France.

Fox, George (1624–91), founder of the Society of Friends (the Quakers).

Francis of Assisi, St (1182–1226), founder of the Franciscan Order of monks; lover of flowers, animals and birds.

Franklin, Benjamin (1706–90), American statesman, philosopher and scientist; played an important part in framing the constitution of the U.S.A.; invented the lightning conductor.

Frederick I (c. 1123–90), Holy Roman Emperor and German national hero; drowned on his way to the Third Crusade.

Frederick II (the Great) (1712–86), King of Prussia; see HISTORY.

Freud, Sigmund (1856–1939), Austrian psychiatrist and founder of psycho-analysis.

Frost, Robert (1874–1963), distinguished American poet.

Fry, Elizabeth (1780–1845), Quaker prison reformer.

Galen, Claudius (131–201), Greek physician, who made important discoveries in anatomy.

Galileo (1564–1642), great Italian mathematician, physicist and astronomer.

Galton, Sir Francis (1822–1911), founder of eugenics and inventor of the device of finger-print identification.

Galvani, Luigi (1737–98), Italian physicist and doctor, who demonstrated the principle of animal electricity.

Gandhi, Mohandas Karamchand (1869–1948), great Indian patriot, social reformer and teacher, driving spirit of the movement for national independence.

Garibaldi, Giuseppe (1807–82), Italian patriot who fought for the unification of Italy.

Garrick, David (1717–79), the leading tragic actor of his day.

George, St, patron saint of England; believed to have been a champion of Christianity during the days of Diocletian, and to have been martyrised in A.D. 303.

Gershwin, George (1898–1937), American jazz pianist and composer; wrote *Rhapsody in Blue* and the Negro opera, *Porgy and Bess.*

Gibbons, Grinling (1648–1720), celebrated wood-carver and sculptor.

Gilbert, Sir William Schwenck (1836–1911), English humorist and playwright, best remembered for the famous Savoy operas, in which he collaborated with Sir Arthur Sullivan.

Gladstone, William Ewart (1809–98), see HISTORY.

Glendower, Owen (1359–1415), Welsh chieftain who opposed Henry IV.

Gluck, Christoph von (1714–87), composer, born in Bohemia.

Goethe, Johann Wolfgang von (1749–1832), the most celebrated German writer; novelist, poet, philosopher and scientist.

Gordon, Charles, General (1833–85), see HISTORY.

Gordon, Lord George (1751–93), instigator of the Anti-Popery riots of 1780.

Gorki, Maxim (1868–1936), Russian novelist.

Grace, Dr William (1845–1915), famous cricketer who dominated the game for over 40 years. Altogether he scored 54,896 runs, including 126 centuries, and took 2,876 wickets.

Grahame-White, Claude (1879–1959), the first Englishman to be granted a British certificate of proficiency in aviation, 1909.

Grant, Ulysses Simpson (1822–85), the most famous American general of the Civil War; twice President of the U.S.A.

Gregory, St (257–336), founder of the Armenian Church; his festival is 9 March.

Gregory the Great, St (*c.* 540–604), one of the most important of the Popes, 590–604.

Gregory XIII (1502–85), Pope who introduced the Gregorian calendar.

Grenville, Sir Richard (1541–91), Elizabethan sea-captain who, with his one ship, the *Revenge*, fought a fleet of Spanish warships in 1591 and died on the deck of the *San Pablo*.

Grieg, Edvard (*c.* 1843–1907), Norwegian composer.

Grey, Lady Jane (1537–54), see HISTORY.

Grimaldi, Joseph (1779–1837), great English clown.

Grimm, the brothers **Jakob** (1785–1863) and **Wilhelm** (1786–1859), German philologists and folk-lorists who collected the famous fairy-tales.

Gustavus Adolphus (1594–1632), King of Sweden; see HISTORY.

Gwynn, Nell (1650–87), the dancer and actress who became mistress to Charles II.

Hadrian (76–138), see HISTORY.

Hakluyt, Richard (*c.* 1552–1616), geographer; first of the English naval historians.

Halley, Edmund (1656–1742), Astronomer Royal; made first magnetic survey of the oceans, and discovered the comet named after him.

Hampden, John (1594–1643), one of the leaders in Parliament's quarrel with Charles I.

Handel, George Frederick (1685–1759), composer.

Hannibal (247–183 B.C.), see HISTORY.

Hardicanute (1019–42), son of Canute the Great, and the last Danish king of England; imposed the tax known as Danegeld.

Hardie, James Keir (1856–1915), first Socialist M.P. (1892).

Hargreaves, James (d. 1778), inventor and pioneer of modern wool industry.

Haroun-al-Rashid (763–809), the most famous Caliph of Baghdad; hero of the *Arabian Nights*.

Harris, Joel Chandler (1848–1908), American author of the Uncle Remus stories.

Harte, Francis Bret (1839–1902), American poet and author, famous for his stories of Californian mining life.

Harvey, William (1578–1657), English doctor who discovered circulation of the blood.

Hastings, Warren (1732–1818), first Governor-General of India; impeached on charges of cruelty and corruption and acquitted after a trial stretching over 7 years.

Havelock, Sir Henry (1795–1857), hero of the relief of Cawnpore and Lucknow in the Indian Mutiny.

Hawke, Edward, Lord (1705–81), victorious admiral in the battle of Quiberon, fought against the French in a storm, 1759.

Hawkins, Sir John (1532–95), Elizabethan naval officer, vice-admiral in the battle with the Spanish Armada.

Hawthorne, Nathaniel (1804–64), American novelist, author of *The Scarlet Letter*.

Haydn, Franz Joseph (1732–1809), Austrian composer.

Heine, Heinrich (1797–1856), German lyric poet.

Hemingway, Ernest (1898–1961), American novelist, author of *A Farewell to Arms* and *For Whom the Bell Tolls*.

Henry the Navigator (1394–1460), Portuguese prince who inspired many voyages of exploration down the Atlantic coast of Africa.

Hepplewhite, George (d. 1786), one of the four great 18th-century cabinet-makers (the others were Chippendale, Robert Adam and Sheraton).

Hereward the Wake, the last of the Saxon chiefs to hold out against the Normans.

Herod the Great (*c.* 73–4 B.C.), King of Judea under the Romans; to him is attributed the massacre of the innocents.

Herodotus (*c.* 485–425 B.C.), Greek historian, called 'the father of history'.

Herschel, Sir John (1792–1871), celebrated astronomer.

Herschel, Sir William (1738–1822), father of the last-named; discoverer of the planet Uranus and the satellites of Saturn.

Hill, Sir Rowland (1795–1879), originator of the penny post.

Hippocrates (*c.* 460–*c.* 370 B.C.), Greek physician: the 'father of medicine'. Rules of conduct for doctors are still based on his Hippocratic Oath.

Hitler, Adolf (1889–1945), see HISTORY.

Hobbes, Thomas (1588–1679), English philosopher, advocate of strong government, author of *Leviathan*.

Homer (*c.* 700 B.C.), most famous of all epic poets, and regarded as the author of the *Iliad* and the *Odyssey*; seven Greek towns vie for the honour of having been his birthplace.

Hood, Samuel, Lord (1724–1816), British admiral who captured Toulon and Corsica, 1793.

Hopkins, Sir Frederick Gowland (1861–1947), English biochemist noted for his work on proteins and vitamins.

Horace (65–8 B.C.), great Roman satirist and poet.

Houdini, Harry (1873–1926), American locksmith who went on the stage as an expert in escaping from handcuffs, locked rooms, etc.

Howard, John (1726–90), prison reformer.

Howe, Richard, Earl (1726–99), British admiral who won a famous victory ('the Glorious First of June') over the French in 1794 off Brest.

Hugo, Victor (1802–85), great French poet, dramatist and novelist, author of *Les Miserables* and *The Hunchback of Notre Dame*.

Hume, David (1711–76), Scottish historian and philosopher.

Hunter, the brothers **William** (1718–83) and **John** (1728–93), both famous Scottish physicians, who made many discoveries in anatomy. John is regarded as the founder of modern surgery.

Huss, John (1369–1415), Bohemian religious reformer, whose death by burning alive led to a half century of civil war.

Huxley, Thomas Henry (1825–95), English naturalist and ardent supporter of the theory of evolution of Charles Darwin (*q.v.*).

Ibsen, Henrik (1828–1906), Norwegian writer, one of the world's greatest dramatists.

Innocent III (1160–1216), powerful Pope who initiated the 4th Crusade.

Irving, Sir Henry (1838–1905), great English actor, and the first to be knighted.

Ivan the Terrible (1530–84), first Czar of Russia, who earned his name by his cruel treatment of his subjects.

Jackson, Andrew (1767–1845), American general, twice President of the U.S.A.

Jackson, Thomas (1824–63), most successful general on the Southern side in the American Civil War; known as 'Stonewall' Jackson for the dogged fight he put up at the First Battle of Bull Run.

James, Henry (1843–1916), great Anglo-American novelist.

Jefferson, Thomas (1743–1826), drew up the American Declaration of Independence; twice U.S. President.

Jeffreys, George, Lord (1648–89), judge notorious for his harsh judgements, especially during the so-called 'Bloody Assize', held to try the followers of the Duke of Monmouth who had rebelled against James II.

Jenghiz Khan (1162–1227), Mogul ruler who twice conquered China and drove the Turks back into Europe.

Jenner, Edward (1749–1823), English country doctor who discovered vaccination as a means of preventing smallpox.

Jerome, Jerome K. (1859–1927), humorous writer, author of *Three Men in a Boat*.

Jesus Christ (*c.* 4 B.C.–A.D. 30 or 33), the founder of Christianity; born at Bethlehem, the first-born of His mother Mary. According to Matthew, His birth was miraculous and Joseph was His foster-father. He learned His father's trade of carpentry at Nazareth, and began His mission when He was about thirty. A summary of His teaching is found in the Sermon on the Mount.

Joan of Arc, St (1412–31), see HISTORY.

John, St, the Baptist (executed A.D. 28), the forerunner of Jesus Christ.

Johnson, Amy (1904–41), first woman aviator to fly solo from England to Australia.

Jones, John Paul (1747–92), Scottish mariner who commanded the American fleet during the War of Independence.

Josephine, Empress (1763–1814), wife of Napoleon I until he divorced her and married Marie-Louise.

Julian the Apostate (331–63), Roman Emperor who professed Christianity until the last two years of his life, when he tried to re-establish paganism.

Jung, Carl (1875–1961), Swiss psychiatrist.

Justinian I (*c.* 483–565), see HISTORY.

Kant, Immanuel (1724–1804), German scientist and philosopher.

Kean, Edmund (1787–1833), one of the greatest English tragic actors.

Kelvin, William Thomson, Lord (1824–1907), scientist and inventor; made important discoveries in the field of thermodynamics (the branch of physics dealing with heat).

Kemble, Frances ('Fanny') (1809–93), noted actress, and member of a famous theatrical family, which included her father, **Charles Kemble** (1775–1854), her uncle **John Philip Kemble,** a famous tragic actor, and her aunt Mrs Siddons (*q.v.*).

Kennedy, John Fitzgerald (1917–63), President of the United States from 1961 until his assassination at Dallas, Texas, in November 1963.

Kepler, Johann (1571–1630), German astronomer who worked out the laws of planetary motion.

Khayyam, Omar (11th century), Persian poet and mathematician, whose *Rubaiyat* was translated by the English poet, Edward Fitzgerald.

Kidd, Captain William (*c.* 1645–1701), famous pirate whose crimes were committed under cover of the British flag. Hanged at Execution Dock in London.

Kitchener, Horatio, Lord (1850–1916), reconquered the Sudan (1897); Commander-in-Chief in the Boer War; Secretary of State for War, 1914–16. Drowned when the troopship *Hampshire* was sunk by a mine.

Knox, John (1505–72), see HISTORY.

Kruger, Paul (1825–1904), President of the Transvaal who was leader of the Boers in the bitter quarrel with the British that led to the Boer War.

Kruschev, Nikita Sergeyevich (1894–1971), Russian Prime Minister, 1958–64. See HISTORY.

Kublai Khan (1216–94), Mogul Emperor, grandson of Jenghiz Khan; he greatly extended the empire and lived in extraordinary splendour.

Lafayette, Marie-Joseph, Marquis de (1757–1834), French statesman and general, who took an active part in the American War of Independence.

La Fontaine, Jean de (1621–95), French poet and fablewriter.

Lamarck, Jean Baptiste, Chevalier de (1744–1829), French naturalist, author of a theory of the evolution of animals, known as Lamarckism.

Landseer, Sir Edwin (1802–73), most famous English animal painter of his day; designed the lions which are part of the Nelson Monument in Trafalgar Square.

Lanfranc (*c.* 1005–89), Archbishop of Canterbury in the time of William the Conqueror.

Langton, Stephen (1151–1228), Archbishop of Canterbury; one of the leaders of the group that compelled King John to sign the Magna Carta.

Lasker, Emmanuel (1868–1941), world chess champion, 1894–1921.

Latimer, Hugh (c. 1485–1555), Bishop of Worcester, one of the founders of English Protestantism; burned at the stake at Oxford.

Laud, William (1573–1645), Archbishop of Canterbury; favourite and chief minister of Charles I; tried for treason and executed under the Long Parliament.

Lavoisier, Antoine (1743–94), French chemist who gave oxygen its name and was the first to establish that combustion is a form of chemical action; guillotined during the French Revolution.

Laurence, John, Lord (1811–79), marched to the relief of Delhi in the Indian Mutiny.

Lawrence, Thomas Edward ('**Lawrence of Arabia**') (1888–1935), British soldier and archaeologist; led the Arabs against the Turks in the First World War; described his campaign in *Seven Pillars of Wisdom*.

Leacock, Stephen (1869–1944), Canadian economist and humorous writer.

Lee, Robert Edward (1807–70), Commander-in-Chief of the Southern forces in the American Civil War.

Leibnitz, Gottfried (1646–1716), discovered, independently of Newton, the differential calculus.

Leicester, Robert Dudley, Earl of (1531–88), favourite of Queen Elizabeth and leader of the English forces in the Low Countries, 1585–7.

Lenin, Vladimir Ilyich (1870–1924), see HISTORY.

Leonidas, King of Sparta when Greece was invaded by Xerxes, 480 B.C.; killed leading the defence of the Pass of Thermopylae.

Lesseps, Ferdinand, Vicomte de (1805–94), French engineer responsible for building the Suez Canal.

Lilburne, John (1614–57), English politician and pamphleteer, leader of the Levellers during the English Revolution.

Lincoln, Abraham (1809–65), President of the United States whose pronouncement against slavery led to the outbreak of the Civil War. Soon after the victory of the North, he was assassinated while at the theatre by a fanatical anti-abolitionist, John Wilkes Booth.

Linnaeus, Carl (1707–78), Swedish naturalist, founder of modern botany; he devised a system for naming and classifying plants and animals (see NATURAL HISTORY).

Lister, Joseph, Lord (1827–1912), English surgeon who first established the need for antiseptics in surgical operations.

Liszt, Franz (1811–86), Hungarian composer and pianist.

Livy (59 B.C.–A.D. 17), great Roman historian.

Lloyd George, David, Earl of Dwyfor (1865–1945), see HISTORY.

Locke, John (1632–1704), English philosopher and founder of empiricism, which is the doctrine that all knowledge is derived from experience.

London, John ('Jack') (1876–1916), American novelist, author of *White Fang, Call of the Wild*.

Longfellow, Henry Wadsworth (1807–82), American poet, author of *Hiawatha*.

Lonsdale, Earl of (1857–1944), distinguished sportsman who presented the Lonsdale belts for boxing.

Lope de Vega, Felix (1562–1615), Spanish dramatist and author of more than 2,000 plays.

Louis XIV (1638–1715), King of France for 72 years; called *le grand monarque* (the great king), he gave expression to the idea of absolute monarchy, in which the king claims complete power over his subjects. See HISTORY.

Louis XVI (1754–93), see HISTORY.

Loyola, St Ignatius (1491–1556), founder of the Order of Jesuits.

Luther, Martin (1483–1546), see HISTORY.

Macadam, John (1756–1836), inventor of the Macadam process of road-making.

Macaulay, Thomas Babington, Lord (1800–59), celebrated historian and poet, author of *History of England* and the *Lays of Ancient Rome*.

Macbeth, King of Scotland immortalised by Shakespeare; he reigned from 1040 to 1057.

Macdonald, Flora (1722–90), Scottish Jacobite who sheltered Prince Charles Edward after his defeat at Culloden Moor, 1746.

Machiavelli, Niccolo (1469–1527), Florentine statesman and historian; author of *The Prince*, which describes how a ruler may build up his power.

Macready, William Charles (1793–1873), the greatest tragic actor of his day.

Magellan, Ferdinand (*c.* 1480–1521), Portuguese navigator; see EXPLORATIONS AND DISCOVERIES.

Malory, Sir Thomas (*c.* 1430–70), compiled the *Morte D'Arthur*, which tells the story of King Arthur and his Knights of the Round Table.

Malthus, Thomas Robert (1766–1834), English economist, who regarded the growth of the population as a danger, and proposed that marriage should be discouraged.

Marat, Jean-Paul (1743–93), one of the leading figures in the Reign of Terror during the French Revolution; assassinated by Charlotte Corday.

Marconi, Guglielmo, Marchese (1874–1937), Italian engineer, inventor of the first practical method of wireless telegraphy.

Marco Polo (see **Polo, Marco**).

Marcus Aurelius (121–180), Roman Emperor who drove off the barbarians, and was famous for his wisdom and his taste for philosophy and literature.

Maria Theresa (1717–80), Empress of Austria, Queen of Bohemia and Hungary; see HISTORY.

Marie Antoinette (1755–93), daughter of Maria Theresa, and wife of Louis XVI of France; see HISTORY.

Mark Antony (see **Antonius, Marcus**).

Marlborough, John Churchill, Duke of (1650–1722), perhaps the greatest of all British soldiers; see HISTORY.

Marx, Karl (1818–83), German philosopher and economist, on whose teaching and writings Communism is based; author of *Das Kapital*.

Masaryk, Thomas (1850–1937), founder and first President of Czechoslovakia.

Maupassant, Guy de (1850–93), famous French novelist and short-story writer.

Maxim, Sir Hiram (1840–1916), inventor of the automatic quick-firing gun named after him.

Maxwell, James Clerk (1831–79), Scottish physicist who formulated the electro-magnetic theory of light; his work made wireless possible.

Mazzini, Giuseppe (1805–72), Italian patriot who worked for the independence and unification of his country.

Mendel, Gregor (1822–84), Austrian botanist and monk whose study of the common garden pea resulted in the law of heredity known as the Mendelian law.

Mendelssohn, Jakob Ludwig Felix (1809–47), German composer.

Mercator, Gerhardus (1512–94), Flemish geographer who simplified navigation by inventing a system of projection in which the longitudes are represented by equidistant parallel lines and the degrees of latitude by perpendicular lines parallel to the meridian.

Mesmer, Friedrich (1733–1815), German doctor who developed the system of animal magnetism known as 'mesmerism'.

Metternich, Prince (1773–1859), Austrian statesman who led the conservative resistance to the ideas of progress spread by the French Revolution.

Mill, John Stuart (1806–73), writer on politics, economics and philosophy, and one of the founders of modern liberalism.

Millikan, Robert Andrew (1868–1953), American physicist who discovered cosmic rays.

Miltiades (d. 489 B.C.), one of the leaders of the Athenians against the Persians at Marathon.

Mithridates (c. 132–63 B.C.), King of Pontius from 120 to 63 B.C., implacable enemy of the Romans; he spoke 22 languages and, surrounded by enemies, was said to have made himself immune from all poisons.

Mohammed (c. 570–632), the founder of the Moslem religion; see HISTORY.

Molière (Jean Baptiste Poquelin) (1622–73), the greatest of the French comic dramatists.

Monk, George, Duke of Albemarle (1608–69), general and admiral who fought in the Anglo-Dutch wars; having fought on Cromwell's side against the Royalists, he later helped to restore Charles II to the throne.

Montaigne, Michel de (1533–92), great French essayist.

Montcalm, General Louis, Marquis de (1712–59), French commander in Canada, defeated by Wolfe.

Monteverdi, Claudio (1568–1643), Italian composer.

Montezuma II (1466–1520), last Aztec ruler of Mexico, Emperor when Cortes invaded the country.

Montfort, Simon de, Earl of Leicester (1208–65), powerful baron who forced Henry III to grant the first English Parliament; see HISTORY.

Montgolfier, Joseph (1740–1810) and **Jaques** (1745–99), French brothers who made many ascents in balloons inflated by heated air.

Montrose, James Graham, Marquess of (1612–50), general who raised the Highlands in support of Charles I and II.

Moore, Sir John (1761–1809), British general killed during retreat to Corunna in the Peninsular War.

More, Sir Thomas (1478–1535), Lord Chancellor under Henry VIII who was executed for refusing to take the Oath of Supremacy; wrote *Utopia*.

Morgan, Sir Henry (c. 1635–88), Welsh buccaneer who preyed on the Spaniards in the Caribbean; captured Panama in 1671.

Mountevans, Admiral Lord (1881–1957), British sailor and explorer known as 'Evans of the Broke'; wrote *South with Scott*.

Mozart, Wolfgang Amadeus (1756–91), Austrian composer.

Mussolini, Benito (1883–1945), Fascist dictator of Italy, 1922–43; see HISTORY.

Nansen, Fridtjof (1862–1930), Norwegian explorer and organiser of relief for victims of the First World War.

Napoleon I (Bonaparte) (1769–1821), see HISTORY.

Nasser, Gamel Abdel (1918–70), President of the United Arab Republic, 1958–70.

Napoleon III (1808–73), see HISTORY.

Nelson, Horatio, Viscount (1758–1805), England's greatest naval commander; see HISTORY.

Nero, Claudius Caesar (37–68), Roman Emperor whose reign is notorious for his cruelty and wild living.

Newton, Sir Isaac (1642–1727), probably the greatest of all scientists; famous for his work on the nature of white light the calculus and gravitation; wrote the *Principia*.

Ney, Marshal (1769–1815), one of Napoleon's generals.

Nicholas II, Czar of Russia (1868–1918); shot with his family by the revolutionaries, 16 July 1918.

Nicholas, St (4th century), patron saint of Russia; associated (as Santa Claus) with Christmas.

Nietzsche, Friedrich (1844–1900), German philosopher, who believed that the mass of people must be led by the few Supermen.

Nightingale, Florence (1820–1910), creator of modern nursing and hospital reformer; the 'lady with the lamp' of the Crimean War.

Nijinsky, Vaslav (1890–1950), great Russian ballet dancer, Polish-born.

Nobel, Dr Alfred (1833–96), Swedish inventor of dynamite; in his will he left money for the annual prizes named after him (for work done for the benefit of mankind in physics, chemistry, physiology and medicine, literature and peace).

Northcliffe, Lord (1865–1922), pioneer of modern journalism.

Nostradamus (Michel de Notre Dame) (1503–66), French astrologer.

Nuffield, Lord, William Richard Morris (1877–1963), pioneer motor-car manufacturer and philanthropist.

Oates, Captain L. E. G. (1880–1912), British explorer who was in the sledge party that accompanied Captain Scott in his dash for the South Pole. On the return journey the party became storm-bound, and Oates, badly frostbitten, walked out to his death in a blizzard rather than be a burden to his comrades.

Oates, Titus (1649–1705), informer against Roman Catholics in Charles II's reign.

O'Casey, Sean (1883–1964), Irish dramatist, author of *Juno and the Paycock*.

Offa, King of Mercia, reigned from *c.* 757 to 796; built an embankment from the Dee to the Wye, called Offa's Dyke.

Ohm, Georg (1787–1854), discoverer of a law of electric current known as Ohm's Law; see SCIENCE.

Otto, Nikolaus (1832–91), German engineer, inventor of the four-stroke cycle named after him; see CARS.

Ovid (43 B.C.–A.D. 18), Roman poet.

Owen, Robert (1771–1858), social reformer and factory owner; inspired the earliest Factory Acts, trade unionism and co-operative trading.

Paganini, Niccolo (1782–1840), Italian violinist whose virtuosity has become a legend.

Paine, Thomas (1737–1809), English revolutionary writer; after the publication of his *Rights of Man* he was forced to flee to France.

Palestrina, Giovanni de (1525–94), Italian composer.

Palmerston, Viscount (1784–1865), Whig Foreign Secretary, 1830–46; supported liberal uprisings throughout Europe; twice Prime Minister.

Pancras, St (3rd century), patron saint of children; martyrised at the age of fourteen.

Pankhurst, Emmeline (1858–1928), leader of movement for votes for women with her daughters **Dame Christabel** and **Sylvia**.

Paracelsus, Philippus (1493–1541), Swiss mystic and alchemist.

Parnell, Charles Stewart (1846–91), leader of the Irish National Party.

Pascal, Blaise (1623–62), French philosopher and mathematician; constructed the first calculating machine.

Pasteur, Louis (1822–95), French chemist and founder of the sciences of bacteriology and immunology; first to show that infectious diseases are caused by germs; devised the process of pasteurisation by which milk can be prevented from going bad.

Patrick, St (c. 389–c. 461), patron saint of Ireland.

Pavlov, Ivan (1849–1936), Russian physiologist; made many discoveries concerning the digestive system and the brain and nervous system.

Pavlova, Anna (1885–1931), great Russian ballet dancer.

Peel, Sir Robert (1788–1850), British statesman, founder of the modern police service; see HISTORY.

Penn, William (1644–1718), Quaker who founded Pennsylvania.

Pepys, Samuel (1633–1703), naval administrator and famous diarist.

Pericles (c. 490–429 B.C.), greatest of the Athenian statesmen; see HISTORY.

Pétain, Marshal Henri Philippe (1856–1951), hero of the defence of Verdun by the French in 1916; in 1940 signed armistice with the Germans, and in 1945 was condemned to death for treason; the sentence was commuted to life imprisonment.

Peter (the Great) (1672–1725), Czar of Russia who did much to modernise his kingdom; founded St Petersburg (now Leningrad).

Peter the Hermit (d. 1115), French monk who raised the army for the disastrous First Crusade.

Petrarch, Francesco (1304–74), Italian poet and scholar, creator of the sonnet.

Petrie, Sir Flinders (1853–1942), British Egyptologist.

Philip II of Macedonia (382–336 B.C.), conqueror of Greece and father of Alexander the Great; see HISTORY.

Philip II of Spain (1527–98), see HISTORY.

Piccard, August (1884–1962), Swiss physicist; ascended into stratosphere in a balloon, 1931 and 1932, and later explored the ocean in his bathysphere.

Pindar (522–443 B.C.), Greek lyric poet.

Pitman, Sir Isaac (1813–97), founder of the Pitman system of shorthand.

Pitt, William (1759–1806), British Prime Minister (at twenty-four, the youngest) throughout the period of the French Revolution and much of the war with France; see HISTORY.

Pizarro, Francisco (c. 1471–1541), Spaniard who conquered Peru with great cruelty; killed by his own soldiers.

Planck, Professor Max (1858–1947), German physicist whose law of radiation laid the foundation of the quantum theory.

Plato (427–347 B.C.), great Athenian philosopher, pupil of Socrates, teacher of Aristotle.

Plimsoll, Samuel (1824–96), M.P. who secured the passing of an Act of Parliament which defined a line (the Plimsoll Mark) above which the water must not rise when a ship is loaded. (See SHIPS.)

Plutarch (c. 46–120), Greek historian, author of *The Lives of Great Men of Greece and Rome*.

Poe, Edgar Allan (1809–49), American poet and short-story writer; wrote *Tales of Mystery and Imagination*, one of which, *The Murders in the Rue Morgue*, is among the earliest detective stories.

Polo, Marco (1254–1324), Venetian explorer; see EXPLORATIONS AND DISCOVERIES.

Pompey the Great (106–48 B.C.), Roman general; see HISTORY.

Priestley, Joseph (1733–1804), discovered and identified many of the common gases: discovered oxygen.

Proust, Marcel (1871–1922), French novelist; author of 15 novels with the general title, *A la Recherche du Temps Perdu* (*In Search of Lost Time*).

Ptolemy, Claudius (c. 90–168), Greek astronomer and geographer, born in Alexandria; according to the Ptolemaic system, the earth was the centre of the universe and the heavenly bodies revolved around it. (See COPERNICUS.)

Purcell, Henry (*c.* 1659–95), English composer.

Pushkin, Alexander (1799–1837), great Russian poet, author of *Eugene Onegin*.

Pym, John (1584–1643), Puritan statesman who led the campaign in the House of Commons against Charles I.

Pythagoras (*c.* 582–*c.* 507 B.C.), Greek scientist and mathematician; to him is attributed the discovery of the multiplication table, the decimal system and the square on the hypotenuse.

Rabelais, François (*c.* 1494–1553), French monk and satirical writer, author of *Gargantua* and *Pantagruel*.

Rachmaninov, Serge (1873–1943), Russian composer.

Racine, Jean (1639–99), French tragic dramatist.

Raffles, Sir Thomas Stamford (1781–1826), founder of Singapore, 1819; also of the Zoological Society of London.

Raleigh, Sir Walter (1552–1618), English statesman, poet, sailor and explorer; favourite of Queen Elizabeth; founded the colony of Virginia; was imprisoned in the Tower for 12 years, and there wrote a *History of the World*. Set free in 1615 to lead an expedition to Guiana in search of gold, he was unsuccessful; and on his return was executed.

Rasputin, Grigori (1871–1916), Russian monk who became all-powerful at the court of the last Russian Czar, Nicholas II.

Réamur, René (1683–1757), French chemist; inventor of the thermometer that bears his name.

Rhodes, Cecil (1853–1902), see HISTORY.

Richelieu, Cardinal Duc de (1585–1642), one of the greatest of French statesmen; Prime Minister to Louis XIII.

Ridley, Nicholas (1500–55), Bishop of London, burned at the stake with Latimer.

Rienzi, Cola di (1313–54), Roman patriot who led a popular rebellion in 1347.

Rilke, Rainer Marie (1872–1926), German lyric poet.

Rimbaud, Jean (1854–91), important modern French poet; all his poems were written between his 16th and 19th years.

Rizzio, David (*c.* 1540–66), Italian musician, favourite of Mary Queen of Scots; stabbed to death in her presence by the jealous Darnley.

Roberts, Field-Marshal Earl (1832–1914), English general who distinguished himself in the Afghanistan campaign; led the campaign against the Boers.

Robespierre, Maximilien (1758–94), French lawyer who was president of the Committee of Public Safety during the Reign of Terror; sent many people to the guillotine, but was himself overthrown and guillotined.

Rob Roy (Robert McGregor) (1671–1734), Scottish highlander noted for his brigandage.

Rockefeller, John Davison (1839–1937), oil magnate who was said to have been the richest man in the world.

Rodney, Lord (1719–92), English admiral, victor in two great battles in the wars with France and Spain, 1780 and 1782.

Roland, Madame (1754–93), one of the leading figures of the French Revolution; she was guillotined, and died pronouncing the famous words, 'Oh liberty, what crimes are committed in thy name!'

Rommel, Field-Marshal (1891–1944), German general; see HISTORY.

Roosevelt, Franklin Delano (1882–1945), four times U.S. President; see HISTORY.

Ross, Sir Ronald (1857–1932), discoverer of the parasite that causes malaria.

Rouget de Lisle, Claude Joseph (1760–1836), French poet who wrote the words and music of the *Marseillaise*.

Rousseau, Jean-Jacques (1712–78), French writer who urged a return to nature and argued that man was naturally good; his ideas had a great influence on the events of his time.

Rupert, Prince (1619–82), Royalist admiral and general; fought for his uncle, Charles I, against Cromwell's troops, and at sea for Charles II against the Dutch.

Russell, Bertrand (Earl Russell) (1872–1970), English philosopher and mathematician.

Rutherford, Lord (1871–1937), New Zealand-born scientist, author of the nuclear theory of the atom and the first man to split the atom.

Saladin (1137–93), Sultan of Egypt and Syria and Moslem hero of the Third Crusade; see HISTORY.

Santos-Dumont, Alberto (1873–1932), famous Brazilian airman, one of the pioneers of modern aviation.

Sappho (*c.* 611–*c.* 592 B.C.), the most famous poetess of the ancient world; a native of the Greek island of Lesbos.

Savonarola, Girolamo (1452–98), Florentine friar who denounced the corruption of his day and was burned at the stake.

Schiller, Johann Friedrich von (1759–1805), one of the greatest German dramatists and poets.

Schliemann, Heinrich (1822–90), German archaeologist who discovered the ruins of ancient Troy.

Schubert, Franz (1797–1828), Austrian composer.

Schumann, Robert (1810–56), German composer.

Schweitzer, Albert (1875–1965), famous musician and organist who became a doctor of medicine in order to devote his life to the work of a medical missionary in Equatorial Africa.

Scipio, Publius (Scipio Africanus the Elder) (c. 232–183 B.C.), Roman general who distinguished himself in the Second Punic War.

Scott, Captain Robert Falcon (1868–1912), polar explorer who commanded the Antarctic expeditions of 1901–4 and 1910. With a small party he reached the South Pole on 18 January 1912, only to find that Amundsen had reached it before him. On the return journey the party were stormbound, and all perished only 11 miles from their next depot.

Scott-Paine, Hubert (1891–1954), pioneer in the construction of flying-boats and high-speed motor-boats.

Selfridge, Harry Gordon (1858–1947), American whose famous shop in Oxford Street (opened in 1909) was the model for the modern British department store.

Shaftesbury, Anthony Ashley Cooper, Earl of (1801–85), the greatest social reformer of the 19th century; inspired changes in the treatment of lunatics, took part in the campaign against slavery and was largely responsible for the Factory Acts that forbade women and children to work underground in the mines and limited working hours.

Sheraton, Thomas (1751–1806), great English cabinet maker.

Sherman, General William (1820–91), great American soldier and leader of the famous 300-mile march across Georgia during the Civil War.

Sibelius, Jean (1865–1957), Finnish composer.

Siddons, Sarah (1755–1831), the greatest English tragic actress of her day.

Sidney, Sir Philip (1554–86), poet and soldier, one of Queen Elizabeth's favourites; killed fighting against the Spaniards at Zutphen.

Simpson, Sir James (1811–70), Scottish surgeon; first to use chloroform as an anaesthetic.

Smeaton, John (1724–92), rebuilder of the Eddystone lighthouse after its destruction by fire.

Smith, Adam (1723–90), political economist and first important advocate of free trade; author of *Wealth of Nations*.

Smuts, Field-Marshal Jan (1870–1950), South African soldier, who fought against the British in the Boer War, but afterwards worked for friendship with Britain. Prime Minister of South Africa, 1912–24 and 1939–48.

Sobieski, John (1629–96), King of Poland who freed Vienna from the Turks, 1683; see HISTORY.

Socrates (470–399 B.C.), Greek philosopher, whose teachings are known from the writings of his pupils, Xenophon and Plato. He taught people to think carefully and logically. Charged with corrupting the morals of the young, he was condemned to die by drinking hemlock.

Solomon (10th c. B.C.), son of David, ruler of Israel and Judah.

Solon (638–558 B.C.), great Athenian law-giver.

Somerset, Duke of (1506–52), Protector of England in early days of Edward VI's reign; later deposed and executed.

Sophocles (495–406 B.C.), popular Athenian dramatist; author of *Antigone, Electra, Oedipus*.

Soult, Marshal Nicolas (1769–1851), one of the most successful of Napoleon's marshals, and Wellington's opponent in the Peninsular War.

Spinoza, Benedict (1632–77), Dutch philosopher.

Stalin, Joseph (1879–1953), Soviet dictator from 1923 until his death; see HISTORY.

Stanley, Sir Henry Morton (1841–1904), explorer of Central Africa; in 1867, as a newspaper correspondent, he sought and found the missing David Livingstone.

Stendhal (Marie Henry Beyle) (1783–1842), French novelist.

Stephenson, George (1781–1848), English engineer, inventor of the first successful railway locomotive (see TRAINS).

Stevenson, Robert (1772–1850), lighthouse builder who invented the 'flashing' system of throwing light at sea.

Stowe, Harriet Beecher (1811–96), American author of *Uncle Tom's Cabin*, which helped to create strong feeling against slavery.

Stradivari, Antonio (1644–1730), Italian who was the greatest of all violin-makers.

Strafford, Thomas, Earl of (1593–1641), supporter of the authority of Charles I; abandoned by the King, he was impeached and executed.

Strauss, Johann (1825–99), Austrian composer.

Strauss, Richard (1864–1949), German composer.

Stravinsky, Igor (1882–1971), Russian-born American composer.

Strindberg, August (1849–1912), Swedish dramatist and novelist.

Sullivan, Sir Arthur (1842–1900), English composer; collaborator with W. S. Gilbert (*q.v.*) in the Savoy operas.

Sun Yat Sen, Dr (1867–1925), one of the leaders of the Chinese Revolution of 1911; President of the Chinese Republic, 1921–25.

Suvarov, Alexander (1730–1800), great Russian General.

Swedenborg, Emanuel (1688–1772), Swedish philosopher.

Tacitus, Caius (55–*c.* 120), Roman historian.

Tagore, Sir Rabindranath (1861–1941), Indian poet and philosopher.

Talleyrand-Périgord, Charles-Maurice de (1754–1838), Napoleon's Foreign Minister, 1797–1807.

Tamerlane (Timur the Lame) (1335–1405), founder of the Mogual dynasty in India; brutal conqueror of Turkestan, Persia and Syria.

Tarquin Superbus, the last king of Rome; banished 510 B.C.

Tasso, Torquato (1544–95), great Italian poet.

Telford, Thomas (1757–1834), Scottish road-maker and builder of canals and bridges, including the Menai Suspension Bridge.

Tell, William (14th century), legendary hero of the Swiss struggle for freedom against the Austrians.

Teresa, St (1515–82), Spanish nun famous for her austere life and her visions.

Terry, Dame Ellen (1848–1928), great English actress, long associated with Sir Henry Irving (*q.v.*).

Thales of Miletus (*c.* 624–565 B.C.), Greek philosopher who believed that water was the principal element.

Themistocles (*c.* 514–449 B.C.), Athenian soldier and statesman who defeated the Persian fleet at Salamis, 480 B.C.

Thomson, Sir Joseph (1856–1940), physicist and mathematician, discoverer of the electron.

Thoreau, Henry David (1817–62), nature-worshipping American philosopher; author of *Walden*.

Thucydides (*c.* 460–399 B.C.), greatest of the Greek historians.

Titus (40–81), Roman emperor, son of Vespasian; did much for the welfare of the Roman people, completed the Colosseum; see HISTORY.

Tolstoy, Count Leo (1828–1910), great Russian novelist; author of *War and Peace*, generally regarded as the greatest novel ever written.

Torquemada, Tomas de (1420–98), Inquisitor-General during Spanish Inquisition.

Toussaint L'Ouverture (1743–1803), Negro ex-slave who freed Santo Domingo (the Dominican Republic) from the French.

Trajan (*c.* 52–117), Roman emperor; did much to consolidate the Empire—work that was continued by his successor, Hadrian; see HISTORY.

Trotsky, Leon (1879–1940), one of the leaders of the Russian Revolution; in 1925 driven into exile in Mexico, where he was later assassinated.

Tschaikovsky, Peter Ilyitch (1840–93), Russian composer.

Turgenev, Ivan (1818–83), Russian novelist.

Tussaud, Madame Marie (1760–1850), Swiss who escaped from Paris at the time of the French Revolution and set up her exhibition of wax figures in London.

Tut-ankh-amen (*c.* 1350 B.C.), Egyptian Pharaoh whose tomb was discovered in 1922, with the mummy and the gold sarcophagus intact.

Twain, Mark (see **Clemens, Samuel**).

Tyler, Wat (d. 1381), leader of the Peasants' Revolt; see HISTORY.

Tyndale, William (*c.* 1492–1536), translator of the Bible; put to death for heresy.

Valentine, St, martyrised *c.* 273. The habit of sending Valentines is of pre-Christian origin, and is not connected with the saint.

Vaughan Williams, Ralph (1872–1958), English composer

Verdi, Giuseppe (1813–1901), Italian composer.

Verlaine, Paul (1844–1896), French poet.

Verne, Jules (1828–1905), French writer of early science fiction, author of *Twenty Thousand Leagues under the Sea*, *Round the World in Eighty Days*.

Vernier, Pierre (1580–1637), inventor of the sliding scale.

Vespasian (A.D. 9–79), Roman emperor; at one time commander of the Roman Army in Britain.

Vespucci, Amerigo (1451–1512), Italian navigator; the first map-makers gave his name to America.

Villeneuve, Pierre (1763–1806), commanded the French fleet against Nelson at Trafalgar.

Villon, François (1431–c. 1489), French poet.

Virgil (Publius Vergilius Maro) (70–19 B.C.), great Roman epic poet, author of the *Aeneid*.

Vitus, St (4th century), Roman Catholic saint and martyr; the custom of dancing before his shrine on his commemoration day, 15 June, gave rise to the name, St Vitus Dance, given to a nervous ailment.

Voltaire, François-Marie Arouet de (1694–1778), great and influential French philosopher and writer, author of *Candide*.

Wagner, Richard (1813–83), German opera composer.

Wallace, Alfred Russel (1823–1913), English traveller and naturalist; one of the founders of zoological geography; author of *Travels on the Amazon*.

Wallace, Sir William (c. 1270–1305), Scottish patriot; see HISTORY.

Warbeck, Perkin (1474–99), Pretender to the English Crown; claimed to be one of the princes murdered in the Tower; provided with an army by the French and the Scots, he invaded England in 1497, but was defeated and hanged.

Warwick, Richard Neville, Earl of (c. 1428–71), 'the King-maker'; see HISTORY.

Washington, George (1732–99), first President of the American Republic, 1789; see HISTORY.

Watt, James (1736–1819), great British engineer, designer of first efficient steam-engine.

Wedgwood, Josiah (1730–95), most famous of the English potters.

Wellington, Arthur Wellesley, Duke of (1769–1852), 'the Iron Duke'; see HISTORY.

Wesley, Charles (1708–88), hymn-writer, brother of John.

Wesley, John (1703–91), founder of Methodism.

Whitman, Walt (1819–92), American poet, author of *Leaves of Grass*.

Whittington, Richard (*c.* 1358–*c.* 1423), London apprentice who became four times Lord Mayor of London.

Whymper, Edward (1840–1911), first mountaineer to reach the summit of the Matterhorn.

Wilberforce, William (1759–1833), leading spirit of the successful campaign against the Slave Trade.

Wilkes, John (1727–97), popular Whig politician; expelled from the House of Commons, he was three times elected M.P. for Middlesex, being again expelled each time. In the end his opponents gave way and he was able to take his seat.

William I of Prussia (1797–1888), first German Emperor; see HISTORY.

William II (1859–1941), Emperor of Germany; see HISTORY.

William the Silent (1533–80), Prince of Orange who attempted to free Holland from the grip of Spain; assassinated; see HISTORY.

Wingate, Major-General Orde (1903–44), leader of the Chindit forces that operated behind Japanese lines in Burma during the Second World War. Killed in air crash.

Wolfe, General James (1727–59), British commander at the siege of Quebec, in which he was killed.

Wolsey, Cardinal Thomas (1471–1530), Archbishop of York and Chancellor to Henry VIII; see HISTORY.

Wright, Sir Almroth (1861–1947), discovered the system of inoculation against typhoid.

Wycliff, John (*c.* 1324–84), religious reformer; translator of the Bible.

Xenophon (430–355 B.C.), Greek historian and general, pupil of Socrates.

Xerxes (*c.* 519–465 B.C.), King of Persia; see HISTORY.

Ximenes, Francisco (1436–1517), succeeded Torquemada (*q.v.*) as Inquisitor-General in the Spanish Inquisition.

Young, Brigham (1801–77), Mormon leader and head of the Latter Day Saints of Salt Lake City.

Zeppelin, Ferdinand, Graf von (1838–1917), German inventor of the airship bearing his name.

Zola, Emile (1840–1902), great French novelist.

Names in the News

AT any one moment, thousands of our fellow men and women are 'names in the news'—enjoying the secure fame of, say, a great living composer, or the fleeting celebrity of a popular actor or a sportsman at the height of his career. Out of these thousands we have picked two or three hundred that we believe might be of special interest to readers of JUNIOR PEARS.

Of most of them, we can safely say that they are actors, or musicians, or writers, or whatever it may be: but there is at least one field in which what a man or woman actually *does* may change overnight—making hundreds of encyclopaedias for the moment, and in this respect, out-of-date. This is the field of politics, where a general election can turn all the members of the Government into members of the Opposition, or a cabinet reshuffle can lose half a dozen Ministers their jobs. Foreign Presidents and Prime Ministers present the same difficulty. So we must say of all political figures mentioned here that the positions they are said to hold were those they held towards the beginning of 1975, when this book was prepared for the printer.

A number of British and Commonwealth politicians have the title 'Rt. Hon.' (short for Right Honourable). This title is given to members of the Privy Council, a body that gives advice to the Queen.

Adamson, Campbell (b. 1922), Director-General, Confederation of British Industry.

Aga Khan (IV) (b. 1936), Imam of the Ismaili Moslems.

Amin, Idi (b. 1926), President of Uganda.

Amis, Kingsley (b. 1922), poet and novelist.

Archer, Peter (b. 1926), Solicitor-General.

Ardizzone, Edward (b. 1900), artist and illustrator.

Arlott, John (b. 1914), writer and broadcaster on cricket.

Armstrong, Neil (b. 1930), US astronaut; first man to set foot on the moon.

Ashcroft, Dame Peggy (b. 1907), actress.

Ashton, Sir Frederick (b. 1906), principal choreographer, Royal Ballet.

Attenborough, David (b. 1926), maker of zoological films.

Attenborough, Richard (b. 1923), producer and actor.

Avon, 1st Earl (Sir Anthony Eden) (b. 1897), Prime Minister, 1955–57.

Banda, Dr. Hastings (b. 1905), President of Malawi since 1966; Prime Minister, 1963–66.

Bannister, Dr. Roger (b. 1929), first man to run mile inside 4 minutes.

Beeching, Baron (b. 1913), Chairman of the British Railways Board, 1963–65.

Benn, Rt. Hon. Anthony Wedgwood (b. 1925), Secretary of State for Industry.

Bergman, Ingrid (b. 1917), Swedish-born actress.

Betjeman, Sir John (b. 1906), Poet Laureate.

Bhutto, Zulfika Ali (b. 1928), President of Pakistan since 1972.

Bliss, Sir Arthur (b. 1891), composer and Master of the Queen's Musick.

Bolt, Robert (b. 1924), dramatist.

Bonham Carter, Hon. Mark (b. 1922), Chairman, Community Relations Commission.

Boult, Sir Adrian (b. 1889), orchestral conductor.

Bradman, Sir Donald (b. 1908), Australian cricketer who during his career (1927–48) scored 28,067 runs in 338 innings, with 117 centuries and an average of 95·14.

Brandt, Willy (b. 1913), Chancellor of W. Germany, 1969–74.

Brezhnev, Leonid Ilyich (b. 1906), First Secretary of the Communist Party of the Soviet Union Central Committee since 1964.

Britten, Benjamin (b. 1913), composer.

Brook, Peter (b. 1925), producer, co-director of the Royal Shakespeare Theatre.

Burton, Richard (b. 1925), actor.

Callaghan, Rt. Hon. James (b. 1912), Foreign Secretary since 1974.

Callas, Maria (b. 1923), operatic soprano.

Carmichael, Ian (b. 1920), actor.

Carr, Rt. Hon. Robert (b. 1916), Home Secretary, 1972–74.

Carrington, Lord (b. 1919), Chairman, Conservative Party; Secretary of State for Defence, 1970–74.

Castle, Rt. Hon. Mrs. Barbara (b. 1911), Secretary of State for Social Services.

Castro, Dr. Fidel (b. 1917), Prime Minister of Cuba since 1959.

Chaplin, Sir Charles Spencer (b. 1889), London-born film comedian.

Cheshire, Group Captain Geoffrey, V.C. (b. 1917), famous pilot of Second World War; founder of Cheshire Homes for the Sick.

Chiang Kai-Shek (b. 1887), President of Nationalist China. See HISTORY.

Chou en-lai (b. 1898), Chinese Prime Minister since 1958.

Christie, Agatha (b. 1890), crime novelist; author of *The Mousetrap*, which has run longer than any other play in the history of the London theatre.

Clark, Lord (b. 1903), former Director, National Gallery; art critic and historian.

Coggan, Most Rev. and Rt. Hon. Donald (b. 1909), Archbishop of Canterbury since 1975.

Connery, Sean (b. 1930), actor.

Cosgrave, Liam (b. 1920), Prime Minister of Ireland.

Cowdrey, Colin (b. 1932), former England cricket captain.

Crosland, Rt. Hon. Anthony (b. 1918), Secretary of State for the Environment.

Curran, Sir Charles (b. 1921), Director-General, B.B.C.

Dali, Salvador (b. 1904), Spanish surrealist painter.

Davis, Colin (b. 1927), Musical Director, Royal Opera House, Covent Garden.

Dell, Edmund (b. 1921), Paymaster-General.

De Valera, Eamon (b. 1882), President of Ireland, 1959–73.

Dietrich, Marlene (b. 1904), German-born actress.

Douglas-Home, Rt. Hon. Sir Alec (b. 1903), Secretary of State for Foreign and Commonwealth Affairs, 1970–74; Prime Minister, 1963–64.

Du Maurier, Dame Daphne (b. 1907), author.

Elwyn Jones, Lord (b. 1910), Lord Chancellor.

Evans, Dame Edith (b. 1888), actress.

Ezra, Sir Derek (b. 1919), Chairman of National Coal Board since 1971.

Faulkner, Brian (b. 1921), Chief Minister, Northern Ireland Executive, 1974: Prime Minister 1971-72.

Fonteyn, Dame Margot (b. 1919), prima ballerina, Royal Ballet.

Foot, Michael (b. 1913), Secretary of State for Employment.

Ford Ge: ald (b. 1913), President of U.S.A. since 1974.

Franco, General Don Francisco (b. 1892), Head of Spanish State since 1936.

Freeson, Reg (b. 1926), Minister of Housing and Construction.

Fuchs, Sir Vivian (b. 1908), Director of British Antarctic Survey, 1958–73: led Commonwealth Trans-Antarctic Expedition, 1955–58.

Gandhi, Mrs. Indira (b. 1917), Prime Minister of India since 1966: daughter of Pandit Nehru, India's first Prime Minister.

Garbo, Greta (b. 1905), Swedish-born film actress.

George-Brown, Lord (b. 1914): as George Brown, Foreign Secretary, 1966–68.

Gielgud, Sir John (b. 1904), actor.

Giscard d'Estaing, Valery (b. 1926), President of France since 1974.

Grade, Sir Lew (b. 1906), chairman, A.T.V.

Greene, Graham (b. 1904), novelist.

Grimond, Rt. Hon. Joseph (b. 1913), leader of the Liberal Party, 1956–67.

Gromyko, Andrei (b. 1909), Foreign Minister, U.S.S.R.

Guinness, Sir Alec (b. 1914), actor.

Hailsham, Lord (b. 1907), Lord High Chancellor of Great Britain, 1970–74.

Hall, Peter (b. 1930), producer, Director of the National Theatre.

Harlech, Lord (b. 1918), President, British Board of Film Censors.

Harrison, Rex (b. 1908), actor.

Hart, Rt. Hon. Judith, Minister of Overseas Development.

Hartnell, Norman (b. 1901), dress designer.

Healey, Rt. Hon. Denis (b. 1917), Chancellor of the Exchequer.

Heath, Rt. Hon. Edward (b. 1916), Leader of the Conservative Party, 1964–75 Prime Minister, 1970–74.

Heenan, Cardinal John (b. 1905), Roman Catholic Archbishop of Westminster.

Helpmann, Sir Robert (b. 1909), dancer, choreographer, actor.

Hepworth, Dame Barbara (b. 1903), sculptor.

Heyerdahl, Thor (b. 1914), author and ethnologist, leader of Kon-Tiki expedition, 1947.

Hillary, Sir Edmund (b. 1919), mountaineer: with Sherpa Tensing, first to reach summit of Everest, 1953.

Hitchcock, Alfred (b. 1899), film producer and director.

Howell, Denis (b. 1923), Minister for Sport.

Howerd, Frankie (b. 1921), comedian.

Hoyle, Professor Sir Fred (b. 1915), mathematician, astronomer and writer.

Hunt, Lord (b. 1910), soldier and mountaineer; leader of the successful 1953 Mt. Everest expedition.

Hussein Ibn Talal (b. 1935), King of Jordan.

Hutton, Sir Leonard (b. 1916), first professional cricketer to captain England.

Innes, Hammond (b. 1913), writer.

Jackson, Glenda (b. 1936), actress.

Jenkins, Hugh (b. 1908), Minister for the Arts.

Jenkins, Rt. Hon. Roy (b. 1920), Home Secretary: Deputy Leader, Labour Party, 1970–72.

Joseph, Rt. Hon. Sir Keith (b. 1918), Secretary of State for Social Services, 1970–74.

Kaunda, Kenneth (b. 1924), President of Zambia.

Kenyatta, Jomo, President of Kenya since 1964.

Khama, Sir Seretse (b. 1921), President of Botswana.

Kissinger, Dr. Henry (b. 1923), Secretary of State, U.S.A.

Kosygin, Alexei (b. 1904), Chairman of the Council of Ministers of the U.S.S.R. since 1964.

Lancaster, Osbert (b. 1908), artist, writer and cartoonist.

Larkin, Philip (b. 1922), poet.

Lever, Harold (b. 1914), Chancellor of Duchy of Lancaster.

Lloyd, Rt. Hon. Selwyn (b. 1904), Speaker of the House of Commons.

Loren, Sophia (b. 1934), Italian film actress.

Lovell, Professor Sir Bernard (b. 1913), Director of Jodrell Bank Experimental Station, Cheshire.

Macmillan, Rt. Hon. Harold (b. 1894), Prime Minister, 1957–63.

Makarios III (b. 1913), Archbishop of Cyprus: President of the Republic of Cyprus since 1960.

Mao Tse-tung (b. 1893), Chairman of the Chinese Communist Party since 1936.

Mark, Sir Robert (b. 1917), Commissioner, Metropolitan Police.

Marsh, Rt. Hon. Richard (b. 1928), Chairman, British Railways Board since 1971.

Mason, Roy (b. 1925), Secretary of State for Defence.

Matthews, Sir Stanley (b. 1915), former professional footballer: first played for England 1934.

Maudling, Rt. Hon. Reginald (b. 1917), Home Secretary 1970–72; Deputy leader, Conservative Party, 1965–72.

Meir, Mrs. Golda (b. 1898), Prime Minister of Israel until 1974.

Menuhin, Yehudi (b. 1916), American violinist.

Miles, Sir Bernard (b. 1907), actor, founder of the Mermaid Theatre.

Milligan, Spike (b. 1919), comedian, writer.

Mills, John (b. 1908), actor and producer.

Mintoff, Dom (b. 1916), Prime Minister of Malta.

Montgomery, Field-Marshal Viscount (b. 1887), Commander of the 8th Army in North Africa and Italy, 1942–44; C.-in-C. British Forces, France and Germany, 1944–46. See HISTORY.

Moore, Henry (b. 1898), sculptor.

Morecambe, Eric (b. 1926), comedian.

Morris, John (b. 1932), Secretary of State for Wales.

Moss, Stirling (b. 1929), former racing motorist.

Mountbatten of Burma, 1st Earl (b. 1900), Chief of Combined Operations, 1942–43; Supreme Allied Commander, S.E. Asia, 1943–46; Viceroy of India, 1947; Chief of Defence Staff, 1959–65.

Muggeridge, Malcolm (b. 1903), journalist and broadcaster.

Mulley, Fred (b. 1918), Minister of Transport.

Murray, Lionel (Len) (b. 1922), General Secretary, Trade Union Congress since 1973.

Murdoch, Iris (b. 1919), novelist.

Nixon, Richard Milhous (b. 1913), President of the United States, 1969–74. See HISTORY.

Nunn, Trevor (b. 1936), Director, Royal Shakespeare Company.

Nureyev, Rudolf (b. 1939), ballet dancer.

Nyerere, Julius (b. 1922), President of Tanzania since 1964.

Olivier, Lord (Laurence Olivier) (b. 1907), actor, Director of the National Theatre, 1962–73, now Associate Director.

Orme, Stanley (b. 1923), Minister of State, Northern Ireland Office.

Osborne, John (b. 1929), playwright and actor.

O'Toole, Peter (b. 1934), actor.

Paul VI, His Holiness Pope (b. 1897), elected Pope in 1963.

Pears, Peter (b. 1910), singer.

Peart, Fred (b. 1915), Minister of Agriculture.

Pinter, Harold (b. 1930), actor and playwright.

Podgorny, Nikolai (b. 1903), President of U.S.S.R.

Pompidou, Georges (b. 1911), President of France.

Powell, Rt. Hon. Enoch (b. 1912), Minister of Health, 1960–63.

Prentice, Reg (b. 1920), Secretary of State for Education and Science.

Previn, André (b. 1929), composer and conductor.

Priestley, John Boynton (b. 1894), author and playwright.

Rabin, Yitzhak (b. 1922), Prime Minister of Israel.

Redgrave, Sir Michael (b. 1908), actor.

Redgrave, Vanessa (b. 1937), actress: daughter of Sir Michael Redgrave.

Rees, Merlyn (b. 1925), Secretary of State for Northern Ireland.

Richardson, Sir Ralph (b. 1902), actor.

Robson, Dame Flora (b. 1902), actress.

Rose, Sir Alec (b. 1908), sailed solo round the world, 1967–68.

Ross, William (b. 1911), Secretary of State for Scotland.

Rowling, Wallace (b. 1927), Prime Minister of New Zealand.

Rubinstein, Artur (b. 1888), pianist.

Ryle, Sir Martin (b. 1918), Astronomer Royal.

Sadat, Anwar (b. 1918), President of Egypt.

Sartre, Jean-Paul (b. 1905), French writer, philosopher and dramatist.

Schmidt, Helmut (b. 1918), Chancellor of W. Germany.

Schwarzkopf, Elisabeth (b. 1915), opera and concert singer.

Scofield, Paul (b. 1922), actor.

Scott, Sir Peter (b. 1909), artist, writer and naturalist; son of the explorer, Captain Scott.

Searle, Ronald (b. 1920), artist and cartoonist.

Secombe, Harry (b. 1921), singer and comedian.

Segovia, Andres (b. 1894), Spanish guitarist.

Sellers, Peter (b. 1925), actor.

Sheppard, Rt. Rev. David (b. 1929), Bishop of Liverpool: former English cricket captain.

Shore, Peter (b. 1925), Secretary of State for Trade.

Short, Rt. Hon. Edward (b. 1912), Lord President of the Council; Deputy leader, Labour Party.

Shostakovich, Dmitri (b. 1906), Russian composer.

Silkin, John (b. 1923), Minister for Planning and Local Government.

Silkin, Sam (b. 1918), Attorney-General.

Simenon, Georges (b. 1903), Belgian novelist, creator of the French detective, Maigret.

Sinatra, Frank (b. 1917), American singer and actor.

Smith, Ian (b. 1919), Prime Minister of S. Rhodesia from 1964; made illegal declaration of independence, November 1965.

Snow, Lord (b. 1905), author and scientist.

Solzhenitsyn, Alexander (b. 1918), Russian novelist.

Spence, Sir Basil (b. 1907), architect of the new Coventry Cathedral.

Spender, Stephen (b. 1909), poet.

Stewart, Rt. Hon. Michael (b. 1906), Foreign Secretary 1965–66 and 1968–70.

Sutherland, Graham (b. 1903), artist.

Sutherland, Joan (b. 1926), prima donna, Covent Garden Opera House.

Swann, Sir Michael (b. 1920), Chairman, B.B.C.

Taylor, Alan John Percivale (b. 1906), historian.

Thatcher, Margaret (b. 1925), Leader of the opposition; Secretary of State for Education and Science, 1970–74.

Thomson of Fleet, Lord (b. 1894), newspaper magnate, proprietor of *The Times*.

Thorndike, Dame Sybil (b. 1882), actress.

Thorpe, Rt. Hon. Jeremy (b. 1929), Leader of the Liberal Party since 1967.

Tito (Josip Broz) (b. 1892), President of Jugoslavia since 1953.

Trudeau, Pierre, (b. 1919), Prime Minister of Canada since 1968.

Tutin, Dorothy (b. 1931), actress.

Ustinov, Peter (b. 1921), actor, dramatist, producer.

Varley, Eric (b. 1933), Secretary of State for Energy.

Vorster, Balthazar (b. 1915), Prime Minister of S. Africa.

Wain, John (b. 1925), Professor of Poetry at Oxford University.

Waldheim, Kurt (b. 1918), Secretary-General, United Nations since 1972.

Walton, Sir William (b. 1902), composer.

Wedgwood, Dame Cicely Veronica (b. 1910), historian.

Welles, Orson (b. 1915), American actor, writer and producer.

Whitelaw, Rt. Hon. William (b. 1918), Deputy leader, Conservative Party; Secretary of State for N. Ireland, 1972–3.

Whitlam, Gough (b. 1916), Prime Minister of Australia.

Whittle, Air Commodore Sir Frank (b. 1907), developed gas turbine for jet propulsion.

Widgery, Lord (b. 1911), Lord Chief Justice of England.

Williams, Mrs. Shirley (b. 1930), Secretary of State for Prices and Consumer Protection.

Wilson, Rt. Hon. Harold (b. 1916), Prime Minister since 1974; led Labour Government, 1964–70.

Wise, Ernie (b. 1926), comedian.

Young, Brian (b. 1922), Director-General of the Independent Broadcasting Authority (I.B.A.).

A Dictionary of Mythology

The majority of the gods, goddesses and other mythological characters who appear in this list are Greek or Roman. Some, however, are Egyptian or Norse; and it is important to remember that, though the Greek and Roman myths are the most familiar to us, the Babylonians, the Hebrews, the Chinese, Japanese, Indians and many other peoples built mythical stories, and invented mythical characters, on the basis of their religious beliefs.

The fact that the Romans borrowed many of their myths from the Greeks, giving their own names to the gods, leads often to confusion. The following table shows, side by side, the Greek and Roman names of the principal gods and goddesses.

Greek	*Roman*
Aphrodite (goddess of love)	**Venus**
Apollo (god of light and the arts)	**Phoebus Apollo**
Ares (god of war)	**Mars**
Artemis (huntress)	**Diana**
Athene (goddess of wisdom)	**Minerva**
Cronus (father of Zeus)	**Saturn**
Demeter (goddess of corn)	**Ceres**
Dionysus (god of wine and revelry)	**Bacchus**
Eros (god of love)	**Cupid**
Hera (mother of the gods and goddess of marriage)	**Juno**
Hermes (messenger of the gods)	**Mercury**
Hestia (goddess of the hearth)	**Vesta**
Pan (god of the flocks)	**Faunus**
Poseidon (god of the sea)	**Neptune**
Zeus (father of the gods)	**Jupiter**

The printing of a name in small capital letters (e.g. VENUS) means that the mythical person named is the subject of a separate entry.

Achilles, King of the Myrmidons, most famous of the Greek heroes of the Trojan War.

Adonis, Greek god: a young man of great beauty, wounded by a boar and changed by APHRODITE into an anemone.

Aeneas, Trojan prince, hero of Virgil's *Aeneid*; the mythical ancestor of the Romans.

Aeolus, wind-god, who unchained the tempests.

Aesculapius, god of medicine.

Agamemnon, King of Mycenae, leader of the Greeks against Troy.

Ajax, Greek warrior at the siege of Troy.

Amazons, mythical race of war-like women.

Amphitrite, sea-goddess and wife of POSEIDON.

Ammon, Egyptian god.

Andromeda, daughter of the king of Ethiopia who, by claiming to be as beautiful as the NEREIDS, roused the anger of POSE-IDON, and was condemned to be devoured by a sea monster. She was saved by PERSEUS, who married her.

Antigone, daughter of OEDIPUS. When the king of Thebes forbade the burial of her brother, Polynices, she defied his order, and was buried alive in a cave; there she hanged herself.

Aphrodite, Greek goddess of love; she was said to have sprung from the foam of the sea.

Apollo, Greek and Roman god of light, the arts and divination; also called Phoebus.

Aquilo, the north wind.

Ares, the Greek god of war.

Argonauts, the fifty Greek heroes who, with JASON, sought the Golden Fleece in their ship the *Argo*.

Ariadne, daughter of MINOS of Crete; gave THESEUS the thread which enabled him to find his way out of the Labyrinth.

Artemis, Greek goddess and huntress.

Atalanta, Greek princess who declared she would marry only the man who could beat her at running; she was outrun by Milanion, who dropped three golden apples one after another to tempt Atalanta and slow her down.

Athene or **Pallas,** Greek goddess of wisdom.

Atlas, King of Mauretania who, for warring against ZEUS, was condemned to support the sky on his shoulders.

Bacchus, Roman god of wine.

Baldur, most beautiful of the Norse gods.

Bellerophon, Greek hero who caught PEGASUS, the winged horse, and killed the CHIMAERA.

Boreas, the north wind.

Calypso, nymph who delayed ODYSSEUS for seven years on his way home from Troy.

Cassandra, Trojan princess; she had the gift of prophecy, but was fated never to be believed.

Castor and Pollux, sons of ZEUS and Leda; they were transported to the heavens and became the constellation known as the Twins.

Centaurs, creatures, half-horse and half-man, living on Mt Pelion in Thessaly.

Cerberus, three-headed dog who guarded the gates of HADES.

Ceres, Roman corn goddess.

Charon, boatman who ferried the dead across the STYX.

Chimaera, fire-breathing monster, a mixture of lion, dragon and goat; slain by BELLEROPHON.

Circe, enchantress who turned ODYSSEUS' companions into swine.

Cronus, Greek name for SATURN.

Cupid, Roman name for EROS, the god of love.

Cybele, the 'great mother', goddess of nature.

Cyclops, one-eyed giants who forged ZEUS'S thunderbolts.

Danae, daughter of the king of Argos, visited by ZEUS in a shower of gold; mother of PERSEUS.

Daphne, nymph who was changed into a laurel-bush to save her from APOLLO.

Demeter, Greek goddess of the corn.

Diana, Roman goddess and huntress.

Dido, mythical queen who founded Carthage.

Dionysus, Greek god of wine and revelry.

Dryads, Greek goddesses of the forest.

Echo, nymph who, having displeased HERA, was changed into a rock and condemned to repeat the last words of those who spoke to her.

Electra, sister of ORESTES.

Elysium, or **the Elysian fields,** the Greek and Roman paradise.

Endymion, beautiful youth who was loved by the moon.

Erebus, the dark subterranean region below which was HADES.

Eros, the god of love.

Euphrosyne, one of the three GRACES.

Eurydice, wife of ORPHEUS.

Eurus, the south-east wind.

Fates, the three goddesses, Clotho, Lachesis and Atropos, who were in charge of human destinies; they weaved the web of each man's life, which ended when Atropos cut the thread.

Fauns, Roman gods of the fields.

Flora, goddess of flowers and gardens.

Freya, Norse goddess of love.

Furies or **Eumenides,** goddesses whose mission was to punish human crimes.

Gorgons, three sisters, MEDUSA, Euryale and Stheno, who had the power to change into stone all who looked at them.

Graces, the three goddesses, EUPHROSYNE, Aglaia and Thalia, who were regarded as the bestowers of beauty and charm.

Hades, the Greek god of the infernal regions; also the infernal regions themselves.

Harpies, winged monsters with women's faces and long claws.

Hector, most valiant of the defenders of Troy: killed by ACHILLES.

Hecuba, wife of PRIAM, King of Troy; nineteen of her children were killed during the siege.

Helen, Greek princess of great beauty; her removal to Troy by PARIS was the cause of the Trojan War.

Helicon, Greek mountain consecrated to the MUSES.

Hera, wife of ZEUS and goddess of marriage.

Heracles, Greek demi-god.

Hercules, Roman name for HERACLES.

Hermes, Greek messenger of the gods.

Hesperides, daughters of ATLAS, guardians of the golden apples stolen by HERCULES.

Hestia, Greek goddess of the hearth, known to the Romans as Vesta.

Horus, falcon-headed Egyptian god.

Hygieia, Greek goddess of health.

Hymen, god of marriage.

Icarus, son of Daedalus; his father made for them both wings fastened with wax. Icarus flew too near the sun; the wax fastenings melted, and he fell into the sea and was drowned.

Irene, Greek goddess of peace.

Iris, the rainbow, a messenger of the gods.

Isis, Egyptian goddess of medicine, marriage and agriculture.

Ixion, thrown into Hell by ZEUS and condemned to be bound to a flaming wheel everlastingly revolving.

Janus, Roman god of beginnings (hence *Januarius*, the first month of the year); he was able to see both the future and the past and is always represented with two heads.

Jason, Greek hero and leader of the ARGONAUTS, who won the Golden Fleece.

Juno, wife of JUPITER and goddess of marriage.

Jupiter, Roman name for the father of the gods and king of heaven.

Lethe, one of the rivers of Hell; all who drank its waters became forgetful of the past.

Mars, Roman god of war.

Medea, witch who married JASON and, when he left her, took her revenge by devouring their children.

Medusa, one of the three GORGONS. She offended MINERVA, who turned her hair into serpents. PERSEUS cut off her head and carried it with him to turn his enemies into stone.

Menelaus, King of Sparta and husband of HELEN of Troy.

Mercury, messenger of the gods.

Midas, King of Phrygia to whom the favour was granted that everything he touched turned into gold. When this happened even to his food, he prayed for the power to be taken away.

Minerva, Roman goddess of wisdom and the arts.

Minos, King of Crete who demanded an annual tribute of young men and women from Athens; they were sent into the Labyrinth and devoured by the Minotaur.

Mnemosyne, goddess of memory and mother of the MUSES.

Muses, nine goddesses who presided over the arts: Clio (History), Euterpe (music), Thalia (comedy), Melpomene (tragedy), Terpsichore (dancing), Erata (elegaic poetry), Polymnia (lyric poetry), Urania (astronomy), Calliope (eloquence and epic poetry).

Naiads, nymphs presiding over rivers and springs.

Narcissus, beautiful youth who pined away for love of his own reflection and was turned into a flower.

Nemesis, Greek goddess of vengeance and retribution.

Neptune, Roman god of the sea.

Nereids, nymphs of the Mediterranean.

Notus, the south wind.

Oceanides, nymphs of the sea.

Oceanus, Greek god of the sea.

Odin, or **Wotan,** father of the Norse gods.

Odysseus, King of Ithaca, one of the heroes of the siege of Troy, whose many adventures on his return home are described in Homer's *Odyssey*. The Romans called him ULYSSES.

Oedipus, King of Thebes, who, discovering that he had unwittingly killed his father and married his mother, blinded himself.

Orestes, son of AGAMEMNON and Clytemnestra. When Agamemnon was killed by Clytemnestra, Orestes was saved by his sister ELECTRA, who then drove him to kill his mother in revenge.

Orion, giant hunter; killed by ARTEMIS, he became one of the constellations.

Orpheus, great musician of Greek myth; went into Hades in search of his dead wife, EURYDICE, and so charmed the infernal spirits with his music that they returned Eurydice to him on condition that he should not look behind him until he had left the lower world. He broke this condition and was torn to pieces.

Osiris, Egyptian god, protector of the dead.

Pales, Roman goddess of flocks and shepherds.

Pan, goat-footed Greek god who presided over the flocks.

Pandora, the first woman to be created. ATHENE made her wise; ZEUS gave her a box full of evil things. On earth she married Epimetheus, the first man; then opened the box and so released all the ills from which men suffer.

Paris, Trojan prince who took HELEN from her husband and so caused the Trojan War. Appointed to choose the most beautiful of the three goddesses, HERA, ATHENE and APHRODITE, he chose the last, thus bringing down on Troy the hatred of the other two.

Parnassus, Greek mountain sacred to the MUSES.

Pegasus, winged horse that sprang from the blood of MEDUSA.

Penelope, wife of ODYSSEUS. During his long absence she was pressed to choose a new husband, and promised to do so when she had finished weaving a tapestry; but every night she undid the work she had done that day.

Perseus, son of ZEUS and DANAE. He and his mother were cast adrift and came to the country of King Polydectes. The king, hoping to get rid of Perseus, sent him to bring back MEDUSA's head.

Phaethon, son of the Sun-God, whose father allowed him to drive the sun-chariot for one day only; he was unable to manage the horses, and ZEUS, angered, struck him dead.

Pleiades, the seven daughters of ATLAS who killed themselves in despair and were turned into stars.

Pluto, King of HADES and god of the dead.

Polyphemus, the most famous of the CYCLOPS; he imprisoned ODYSSEUS, who escaped by blinding him.

Pomona, goddess of fruits and gardens.

Poseidon, god of the sea.

Priam, the last King of Troy, killed in the sack of the city.

Procrustes, robber who fitted his victims to a bed, stretching them or lopping their limbs to do so. Slain by THESEUS.

Prometheus, the god of fire. Having formed the first man of clay, he stole fire from heaven to bring him to life. ZEUS had him chained to a mountain, where his liver was devoured every day by a vulture, but grew again every night. He was freed by HERACLES.

Proserpina, wife of PLUTO and mother of the FURIES.

Proteus, sea god who could change his shape at will.

Psyche ('the soul'), beautiful maiden loved by CUPID.

Pygmalion, King of Cyprus who fell in love with a statue of a woman he had made himself.

Remus, brother of ROMULUS.

Romulus, thrown with his brother REMUS into the Tiber at birth; washed ashore and adopted by a she-wolf. Romulus founded Rome (the traditional date is 753 B.C.).

Saturn, husband of CYBELE and father of JUPITER. A promise made to Titan forced him to eat his children when they were born. Cybele saved Jupiter by putting a stone in his place. Jupiter dethroned his father and Saturn took refuge in Latium, where he showed men how to cultivate the land.

Satyrs, the companions of BACCHUS.

Sirens, monsters, half-woman and half-bird, who lived on the rocks between the isle of Capri and the coast of Italy. By the sweetness of their singing they lured sailors to destruction.

Sisyphus, founder of Corinth, who for his greed and dishonesty was condemned after death to roll a stone for ever uphill; as soon as it got to the top it rolled down again.

Styx, the river flowing round HADES, over which CHARON ferried the dead.

Tantalus, King of Lydia condemned for ever to hunger and thirst.

Tartarus, the lowest region of HADES.

Telemachus, son of ODYSSEUS who set out in search of his father.

Theseus, Greek hero who, among his many adventures, killed the Minotaur (see MINOS).

Themis, goddess of justice.

Thor, the Norse god of war.

Titans, sons of the Heaven and the Earth. Rebelling against the gods, they attempted to climb to Heaven by piling mountain upon mountain; but they were destroyed by JUPITER's thunder-bolts.

Triton, one of the sea-gods.

Ulysses, Roman name for ODYSSEUS.

Venus, the Roman goddess of beauty and love.

Vulcan, Roman god of fire.

Zephyrus, the west wind.

Zeus, Greek name for the father of the gods.

A Dictionary of Science and Mathematics

Abacus A digital computing device of ancient origin consisting of counters strung on wires, one wire for each digital position.

Aberration Deviation from perfect image formation in an optical or equivalent system due to imperfect machining.

Absolute Temperature A temperature scale based on Charles's Law of the expansion of gases. Any gas cooled down at constant pressure *must* cease to be a gas above $-273°$ C. This is called *absolute zero*, and the scale based on this is the absolute scale. It is symbolised in formulae and equations by T. The Kelvin Scale is the same as the absolute scale.

TEMPERATURE CONVERSIONS

Fahrenheit	Centigrade	Absolute or Kelvin (K.)
−459·4	−273·0	0
−148·0	−100·0	173
−112·0	−80·0	193
−76·0	−60·0	213
−40·0	−40·0	233
−4·0	−20·0	253
0	−17·8	255·2
32·0	0	273
50·0	10	283
68·0	20	293
86·0	30	303
104·0	40	313
122·0	50	323
140·0	60	333
158·0	70	343
176·0	80	353
194·0	90	363
212·0	100	373
1,292·0	700	973
1,472·0	800	1,073
1,832	1,000	1,273
2,192	1,200	1,473
2,732	1,500	1,773
3,092	1,700	1,973
3,632	2,000	2,273

Acceleration The rate of change of velocity, expressed in metres per second per second, or feet per second per second, etc. Negative acceleration = retardation.

Accumulator A type of electric cell or battery that can be recharged. The commonest sort has special plates of lead peroxide for the positive and lead for the negative, with dilute sulphuric acid as the liquid.

Acid Acids are a very important group of chemical compounds. Examples of inorganic acids are hydrochloric acid (HCl), nitric acid (HNO_3), and sulphuric acid (H_2SO_4). Organic acids such as acetic acid ($CH_3 \cdot COOH$) usually contain the *carboxyl* group, COOH. All acids contain *replaceable* (or *acidic*) hydrogen in their molecules (though in organic acids, only the hydrogen in COOH is acidic), and the most characteristic reaction of acids is for this hydrogen to be replaced by a metal to form a *salt* (q.v.). Some metals react directly with acids to give a salt and hydrogen gas while another example of this kind of reaction is the neutralisation of an acid by a *base* (q.v.) to give a salt and water. E.g. Potassium hydroxide (a base) reacts with dilute nitric acid to give potassium nitrate (a salt) and water. Here the potassium replaces the acidic hydrogen which goes into making the water. The reason why acids so readily lose their acidic hydrogen is that in solutions of acids to a great extent the hydrogen is already separate from the rest of the molecule in the form of positive hydrogen ions.

Acids have a sour taste and when concentrated can be very corrosive and dangerous to handle. *Indicators* (q.v.) can be used to test whether a solution is acidic or not: e.g. in the presence of an acid, blue litmus turns red.

Acoustics The study of sound.

Adsorption The taking-up of a gas by a solid in such a way that a layer of gas only one molecule thick is held firmly in the surface of the solid. Adsorption is an essential part of some chemical phenomena, including catalysis.

Alkali A *base* (q.v.) that is soluble in water, e.g. the hydroxides of sodium and potassium (caustic soda and caustic potash). Alkalis can be identified in solution by means of *indicators* (q.v.).

Alpha Radiation (Alpha Rays, α-Rays) This is a stream of particles that are the nuclei of helium atoms. They are emitted from radioactive substances. Some emitters of alpha rays are: uranium, radium, plutonium. Alpha rays have such little penetrating power that a sheet of paper will stop them, but where they do penetrate they have intense effects.

Alternating Current See RADIO AND TELEVISION

Altimeter An instrument used to measure height above the Earth.

Ampere (A) The S.I. unit of electric current.

Analog Computer A computer in which numerical quantities are represented by physical quantities, e.g. the numbers between 1 and 2 may be represented by the corresponding voltages between 1 volt and 2 volts. Another example of an analog computer is the slide rule in which numbers are represented by lengths.

Angle Formed by two lines meeting at a point. The angle ABC—written $\angle ABC$ or $A\hat{B}C$— is θ. Angles are measured
(i) in *degrees* anti-clockwise with 360° to the full circle.
(ii) The other system, more used in algebra and geometry, is in *radians*, where one radian is the angle the radius of a circle, r, drawn along the circumference, makes at the centre. Since the circumference of a circle is $2\pi r$, there are 2π radians to a full circle or 360°.

Trigonometrical values: in the triangle ABC $B = \theta$, $C = 90°$ or $\dfrac{\pi}{2}$

Then sine or $\sin \theta = \dfrac{AC}{AB}$

Cosecant or $\operatorname{cosec} \theta = \dfrac{1}{\sin \theta} = \dfrac{AB}{AC}$

cosine or $\cos \theta = \dfrac{BC}{AB}$

Secant or $\sec \theta = \dfrac{1}{\cos \theta} = \dfrac{AB}{BC}$

Tangent or $\operatorname{Tan} \theta = \dfrac{AC}{BC}$

Cotangent or $\cot \theta = \dfrac{1}{\tan \theta} = \dfrac{BC}{AC}$

Since ABC is a right angled triangle, by Pythagoras' theorem $AB^2 = AC^2 + BC^2$. It follows that $\sin^2\theta + \cos^2\theta =$

$$\frac{AC^2 + BC^2}{AB^2} = 1$$

Similarly $\sec^2\theta - \tan^2\theta = 1$; $\operatorname{cosec}^2\theta - \cot^2\theta = 1$.

The numerical values of all these functions have been calculated for all angles and can be found in books of mathematical tables.

Angular Acceleration: rate of change of angular velocity (q.v.).

Angular Distance: the angle which two points or bodies subtend at the point of observation. Often used in astronomy. The a.d. between the two points A and B as measured from C is $\theta°$

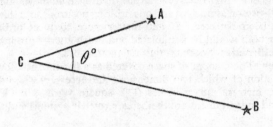

Angular Velocity: rate of motion through an angle about an axis. Measured in degrees, revolutions, radians per unit time. The angular velocity of a point in radians/unit time can be calculated by dividing its linear velocity *perpendicular* to the line joining it to the axis by the length of the line. The a.v. of A about C is $\dfrac{v}{r}$ radians/sec.

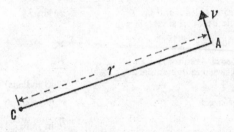

Angstrom (Å) Unit of length. 1 angstrom $= 10^{-10}$ m $= 10^{-8}$ cm $= 3.9 \times 10^{-9}$ inches. 1 inch $= 2.54 \times 10^{8}$ Å. Used in atomic physics e.g. to measure the wavelengths of X-rays (0.1 Å to 10 Å) or the distance between atoms in molecules and crystals (the distance between copper atoms in copper metal is 3.4 Å).

Anion A negatively charged atom or radical (group of atoms).

Anode Positive electrode. See ELECTROLYSIS.

Anti-matter Particles like electrons, protons and neutrons all have corresponding anti-particles: anti-electrons (called *positrons*), anti-protons and anti-neutrons. It is possible that somewhere in the universe there exists anti-matter composed entirely of anti-particles (e.g. an anti-hydrogen atom would have an anti-proton as nucleus and one orbiting positron), but this has never been detected. If anti-matter were to meet ordinary matter both would be annihilated and much energy produced.

Archimedes See PRINCIPLE OF ARCHIMEDES.

Area The amount of space covered as a flat expanse, for the calculation of which two dimensions are necessary. Units are square metres, square inches ($\square$), square yards, etc. Units for land measurement are the hectare (metric system) and acre.

AREAS OF COMMON SHAPES

Figure	Area
Rectangle, sides a and b	ab
Triangle, sides a, b, c, vertical height h. $\quad s = \frac{1}{2}(a + b + c)$	$\frac{1}{2}bh$ $\sqrt{s(s - a)(s - b)(s - c)}$
Trapezoid, parallel sides a and c	$\frac{1}{2}h(a + c)$
Parallelogram, sides x and y, θ = angle between sides	$xy \sin \theta$
Circle, radius r	πr^2
Sector of circle, radius r, θ = angle between radii boundaries	$\dfrac{r^2\theta}{2}$ (θ in radians)
Segment of circle	$\dfrac{r^2}{2}(\theta - \sin \theta)$ (θ in radians)
Ellipse, semi-axes a and b	πab
Surface of sphere, radius r	$4\pi r^2$
Surface of cylinder, height h, radius r	(1) $2\pi rh$ (curved surface only) (2) $2\pi r(h + r)$ (total surface)
Surface of cone, slant height l, radius r	(1) πrl (curved surface) (2) $\pi r(l + r)$ (total surface)

Arithmetical Progression Series of quantities in which each term differs from the preceding by a constant *common difference*. An A.P. in which the first term is a, the common difference d, the number of terms n and the sum of n terms S has:

$$S = a + (a + d) + (a + 2d) + (a + 3d) + \cdots \\ + (a + (n - 1)d)$$

$$= \frac{n}{2}\{2a + (n - 1)d\}$$

Armature The coil or coils—usually rotating—of an electric motor or dynamo.

Atmosphere Normal or Standard. Unit of pressure = pressure which will support a column of mercury 760 mm. or 29·92 in. high at 0° C, sea-level at Lat. 45°. 1 Normal atmosphere = 1·0132 Bars = 14·72 lb./sq. in. = 101,320 N/sq.m.

Atom The smallest particle of an element still retaining the chemical properties of that element.

It consists of a positively charged heavy nucleus surrounded by negatively charged electrons, which move in orbits very similar to the way in which planets move round the sun. The positive charge on the nucleus exactly balances the total negative charge of all the surrounding electrons when the atom is neutral.

The nucleus consists of two types of particle very strongly held together—protons and neutrons. A proton carries one unit of positive charge. A neutron has no charge. The mass of a neutron is very slightly more than the mass of a proton.

The chemical properties of the atom are determined by the electrons, which in number, of course, are equivalent to the proton charge in the nucleus. So if a proton is removed from (or added to) the nucleus of an atom it is no longer the same element. The addition or subtraction of neutrons, however, makes no difference to the chemical properties.

The number of protons (and the corresponding number of electrons) determines the element. An atom of carbon, for example, has six planetary electrons, an atom of copper twenty-nine, an atom of uranium ninety-two. The simplest atom is that of hydrogen, whose nucleus is one proton and which has one planetary electron.

Atomic Number A number that tells the number of protons in the nucleus of an atom and therefore the number of planetary electrons. A list of elements start with hydrogen of atomic number 1 and continues in series 1, 2, 3, 4, etc.

Atomic Pile Original name for a *nuclear reactor* (q.v.).

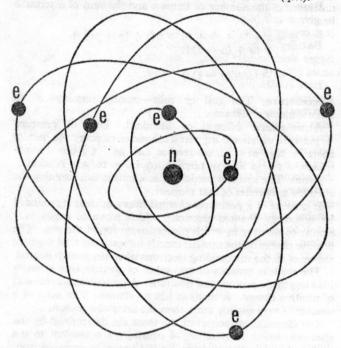

CARBON ATOM

Schematic diagram, 6 planetary electrons, 2 on inner orbits, 4 on outer orbits. These four are the valency electrons. The nucleus has 6 protons and 6 neutrons all very close together in the one body, which carries almost all the mass of the atom.

Atomic Weight A number showing how heavy the atom of an element is compared with the isotope carbon 12 taken as 12·0000. Owing to the facts that when atomic nuclei fuse to make another element energy is given out, and therefore mass lost, and many elements are mixtures of isotopes of different weights, the atomic weight is rarely a whole number.

Avogadro's Law Equal volumes of all gases under the same conditions of temperature and pressure contain equal numbers of molecules.

Base A chemical substance which reacts with an *acid* (q.v.) to give a *salt* (q.v.) and water only. Bases may be insoluble (e.g. copper II oxide) or soluble (see *alkali*).

Battery A number of electric cells joined together to give a bigger electromotive force. Thus three dry cells, each 1·5 V, in series give 4·5 V.

Beta Radiation (Beta Rays, β-Rays) A stream of very fast electrons emitted by some radioactive substances. These electrons come from the nucleus by breakdown of neutrons, not from the planetary electrons. Beta rays are more penetrating than alpha rays, the most energetic of them being capable of penetrating 1 mm. of lead. Because of their penetrating power they are used for the measurement of thickness in industry, e.g. the thickness of the tin layer on iron in tinplate.

Binary numbers A system of numbers in which the only digits used are 0 and 1. In the familiar decimal system the number 268 can be read as $2 \times 10^2 + 6 \times 10^1 + 8 \times 10^0 = 200 + 60 + 8 = 268$. In the binary system powers of 2 are used instead of powers of 10. Thus $1101 = 1 \times 2^3 + 1 \times 2^2 + 0 \times 2^1 + 1 \times 2^0 = 8 + 4 + 0 + 1 = 13$. The numbers up to 15 are:

1	0001	6	0110	11	1011
2	0010	7	0111	12	1100
3	0011	8	1000	13	1101
4	0100	9	1001	14	1110
5	0101	10	1010	15	1111

Binary numbers are used in digital computers since an electrical circuit can represent a 0 or a 1 depending on whether it is off or on.

Binomial Theorem One of the most important theorems in algebra, leading to many sorts of series. It states that the expression $1 + x$ raised to the power of n (i.e. $(1 + x)^n$) can be written in the form $(1 + x)^n = 1 + nx + \dfrac{n(n - 1)x^2}{1 \cdot 2} + \dfrac{n(n - 1)(n - 2)x^3}{1 \cdot 2 \cdot 3} +$ etc.

If **n** is a positive integer (i.e. a positive whole number) this expansion is valid for any **x**, and the series ends after **n** + 1 terms. If **x** is between − 1 and 1, the binomial expansion is valid for all **n** (positive or negative, integer or fraction). In this case the expansion is an infinite series which however adds up to a finite number.

Black hole The term used to describe immensely dense stars with gravitational fields so powerful that no radiation can

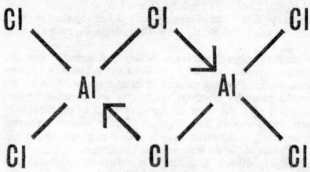

DATIVE BOND

The arrows indicate the giving of electrons by chlorine to aluminium. These arrowed lines show dative bonds, the ordinary lines covalent bonds.

escape from them, and hence invisible but believed to lie at the centre of the Milky Way and elsewhere in the Universe.

Bond The method of binding together of atoms to form molecules. Three types of bond account for most compounds. They are:

    (*a*) Electrovalent bond (ionic, polar);
    (*b*) Covalent bond (non-polar, homopolar);
    (*c*) Dative bond (co-ordinate, semipolar).

ELECTROVALENT BOND

The sodium, less one electron, is positive. The chlorine with an extra electron is negative.

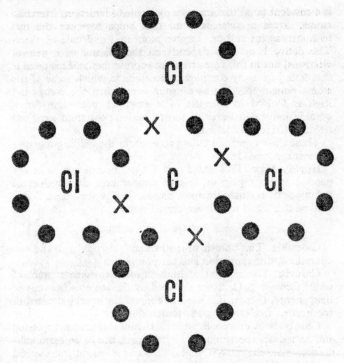

COVALENT BOND

The seven electrons of chlorine are shown as dots, the four electrons of carbon as x's.

The electrovalent bond exists in simple compounds where one atom needs an electron and the other gives it. Thus a sodium ion is positively charged when giving an electron and a chlorine ion is negatively charged when it accepts an electron. In solution these ions exist separately, but in the solid the positive binds to the negative in a crystal structure. The covalent bond works differently. It is created by the giving of an electron from each atom in such a way that each shares the pair of electrons thus formed. This accounts for the binding of atoms that are not ionised in solution and atoms that are the same. For example, it is a covalent bond that makes a molecule of hydrogen from two atoms. It is a covalent bond that holds together the two hydrogen atoms and one oxygen atom in a molecule of water. The dative bond also depends on the sharing of a pair of electrons, but in this case one atom supplies both. This bond is that found in many complex compounds in which some of the atoms remain together as a group even when the compound itself is ionised in solution. For example, potassium ferrocyanide ionises in water to form positive potassium ions and negative 'ferrocyanide' ions.

These three types of binding account for the holding-together of most compounds.

Boyle's Law This states that if a gas is compressed or expanded without gain or loss of temperature the product of volume and pressure remains constant. If P is pressure and V is volume the law is usually expressed thus:

$$PV = K \text{ (where } K \text{ is a constant)}$$

Calculus The branch of mathematics dealing with the two operations, differentiation and integration.

Calorie The amount of heat required to raise 1 gram of water through $1°$ C. Now replaced by the joule as the unit of heat energy, though still used to express the energy content of foodstuffs. 1 calorie $= 4.187$ joules.

Catalysis A process in which a chemical reaction is speeded up, sometimes tremendously, by the presence of an extra substance, called the catalyst, that is the same chemically at the end of the reaction as it is at the beginning. Many industrial processes depend on catalysis. A simple example is the quick combination of hydrogen and oxygen into water where platinum is present. It is believed that the catalysis in this case is due to adsorption on the surface of the platinum.

Cation A positively charged atom or radical (group of atoms).

Cell A source of electricity caused by chemical action. A primary cell is one that cannot be recharged once its electrolyte or electrodes are used up. A simple primary cell consists of zinc and copper in dilute sulphuric acid. The copper is the positive electrode and the zinc the negative. This is the simple voltaic cell. It is of no use for practical work. A dry cell of the normal type consists of zinc as the negative pole or electrode, in the form of the container, with a jelly of ammonium chloride as the electrolyte and a central carbon rod as the positive pole or electrode. This gives 1·5 V. Many other dry cells have been developed for use in rockets and satellites. A fuel cell is one in which primary fuels or derivatives of them are used. A solar cell is not really chemical. It consists of a special substance that generates electricity when light shines on it.

A secondary cell can be recharged. See ACCUMULATOR.

Centripetal force The force acting on a body constrained to move in a curved path. For a body of mass m travelling in a circle of radius r at velocity v the force is $m \cdot v^2/r$ and directed towards the centre of the circle.

Charles's Law The law that determines the effect of heat on a gas when the pressure is kept constant. It states that the volume of a gas (*any* gas) increases by a certain fixed amount ($\frac{1}{273}$ of its volume at $0°$ C.) for every degree Centigrade rise in temperature. Another way of stating this today is to say that the volume of a gas, if the pressure is constant, is directly proportional to its absolute temperature.

Coefficient In mathematics this means the number that indicates how many of a thing there are. For example, $2x$ means 2 of the thing called x, and 2 is the coefficient of x. In physics and technology the word coefficient is used to indicate a constant value of importance. For example, the coefficient of linear expansion for a material, the coefficient of friction between two chosen substances, etc.

Colloid A material that does not dissolve in a liquid is usually deposited on the bottom if the particles are big enough. If the particles are small enough, however, they remain in suspension though individually invisible, kept up by the random movements of the molecules of solvent. Particles as small as this are said to be colloidal, and the suspension they form is a colloidal solution. The range of size of colloidal particles is between 0·0000001 and 0·00005 cm. (between 1 and 500 nanometres).

Colour The sensation when the eye receives certain wavelengths of light. Ordinary 'white' light consists of electromagnetic radiation of many different wavelengths from about 4,000 Angstroms to about 7,000 Angstroms. If these are spread out as in a spectrum so that only a portion enters the eye at a time, then as the eye moved along the spectrum from the short-wavelength end to the long-wavelength end colour is seen, going from violet to red through a series usually given as seven, namely, violet, indigo, blue, green, yellow, orange, red. These are the colours of the rainbow. Actually this is a very rough-and-ready description. If tiny separate parts of the spectrum are exposed one at a time hundreds of different hues can be seen.

The colours of everyday objects are caused by selective absorption of parts of the spectrum of white light.

Complex Numbers Algebraic expressions such as $x + iy$ where x and y are real, and i is the square root of -1. The real part is x and iy is the imaginary part of the number. In equations involving complex numbers the real and imaginary parts are equated separately, otherwise operations are normal.

Compound A substance that consists of chemical elements bonded together. Examples: the elements sodium and chlorine when combined together chemically make sodium chloride (common salt), a compound.

Conductor An electrical conductor is a material that conducts electricity easily, such as the metals. The best conductor is silver and the next best copper.

Conversion Table

1 cm. = 0·3937 in.	1 yd. = 0·9144018 m.
1 m. = 39·37 in.	1 sq. in. = 6·451626 sq. cm.
1 sq. cm. = 0·1549997 sq. in.	1 sq. yd. = 0·8361307 sq. m.
1 sq. m. = 1·195985 sq. yd.	1 acre = 0·404687 hectare
1 hectare = 2·7104 acres	1 cu. yd. = 0·7645594 cu. m.
1 cu. m. = 1·3079428 cu. yd.	1 gal. = 4·5434 litres
1 litre = 0·22009 gal. or	1 quart = 1·1358 litres
0·88036 quarts	1 bushel = 36·37 litres
1 kg. = 2·204622341 lbs.,	1 lb., Avoirdupois =
Avoirdupois	0·4535924277 kg.
1 in. = 2·54005 cm.	

These figures are very exact. Quick, very rough answers can be obtained by the methods below:

To Turn

Metres into feet multiply by $3\frac{1}{4}$
Feet into metres multiply by 3 and divide by 10
Metres into yards add $\frac{1}{10}$
Yards into metres subtract $\frac{1}{10}$
Kilometres into miles multiply by 5 and divide by 8
Miles into kilometres add $\frac{3}{8}$ of the number of miles
Square metres into square yards add $\frac{1}{5}$

Square yards into square metres subtract $\frac{1}{6}$
Square kilometres into square miles multiply by 2 and divide by 5
Square miles into square kilometres multiply by $2\frac{3}{5}$
Cubic metres into cubic yards add $\frac{1}{3}$
Cubic yards into cubic metres subtract $\frac{1}{4}$
Kilogrammes into pounds (Avoirdupois) add $\frac{1}{10}$ and multiply by 2
Pounds into kilogrammes subtract $\frac{1}{10}$ and divide by 2
Litres into pints add $\frac{3}{4}$
Pints into litres multiply by 3 and divide by 5

Cosine In trigonometry the cosine of an angle (other than the right angle) in a right-angled triangle is the ratio of the side next to the angle to the hypotenuse. Cos $90° = 0$, cos $60° = 0·5$, cos $45° = 0·707$, cos $30° = 0·866$.

Cosmology The study of the evolution and structure of the universe, nowadays carried out with the aid of radio as well as optical telescopes.

Cryogenics The science of producing and maintaining very low temperatures and the study of properties of matter at those temperatures. Modern cryogenics dates from 1908 when helium, the gas with the lowest boiling point at atmospheric pressure ($-269°$ C), was first liquefied. Since then many remarkable effects have been discovered: e.g. *superconductivity* (q.v.).

Crystallography The science which deals with the regular structure of crystals. Often investigated by X-rays.

Current Electric current is the rate of flow of electric charge. In a metallic conductor this flow is due to electrons, which drift along between the metal atoms. As electrons are negatively charged, they are going in the opposite direction to the direction of current usually accepted. A current of 1 A is approximately 6 million billion electrons per second.

Decibel See RADIO AND TELEVISION.

RELATIVE DENSITIES OF COMMON SUBSTANCES

Metals		Liquids at 15° C.	
Steel	7·6–7·8	Acetone	0·79
Brass	8·4–8·7	Alcohol	0·79
Aluminium	2·70	Ether	0·74
Copper	8·89	Glycerine	1·26
Lead	11·34	Oil (lubricating)	0·9–0·92
Titanium	4·5	Turpentine	0·87
Mercury	13·6	Blood	1·04–1·067
		Water at 4° C.	1·00

Miscellaneous Solids			*Gases at N.T.P.*	
Celluloid	.	.	1·4	Air	.	.	.	0·00129
Glass	.	.	2·4–2·8	Argon	.	.	.	0·00178
Ice	.	.	0·92	Carbon dioxide	.	0·00198
Paraffin Wax	.	0·9	Helium	.	.	0·000179
Brick	.	.	2·1	Hydrogen	.	.	0·00009
Coal (soft)	.	.	1·3	Methane	.	.	0·000717
Diamond	.	.	3·5	Oxygen	.	.	0·00143
Rubber	.	.	0·97–0·99		
Balsa wood	.	0·12–0·2		
Ebony	.	.	1·19		
Lignum vitae	.	1·25		
Oak	.	.	0·74		
Boxwood	.	.	0·93		
Cork	.	.	0·24		

Density The mass per unit volume of a substance. It can be expressed in kilograms/cubic metre, tons/cubic yard, pounds/cubic foot, etc. The density of a substance varies with temperature. Often the *relative density* or *specific gravity* is used. This is the ratio of the density of a substance to that of water at 4° C. and is therefore simply a number. The density of water at 4° C. is 1000 kg./m³ or 1 gm./c.c. The two densest substances are osmium and iridium.

Deoxyribonucleic acid (DNA) The molecule found in the nucleus of nearly all living cells which carries the genetic code responsible for determining the organism's structure.

Digital computer Any device which performs calculations on numbers represented digitally.

Direct Current (D.C.) A current passing in the same direction all the time round a circuit. It can vary in size, but not in direction.

Dispersion The name given to the splitting-up of light into the spectrum by a prism or lens.

Dissociation The reversible splitting-up of a chemical compound into parts. *Thermal dissociation* may occur when a compound is heated: e.g. ammonium chloride dissociates into the gases ammonia and hydrogen chloride on heating. *Electrolytic dissociation* into charged ions may occur when a compound is dissolved in water: e.g. hydrogen chloride gas dissolves in water to give hydrochloric acid which is dissociated into positive hydrogen ions and negative chloride ions.

Dyne See FORCE and NEWTON.

Electrode The name given to the part by means of which electricity is led into or away from a gas or liquid. The negative electrode is the cathode and the positive one the anode.

Electron Elementary particle with small mass and unit negative electric charge. Electrons orbit the nucleus of an atom much as the planets orbit the sun.

Electromagnetic Waves Waves that consist of varying electrical and magnetic quantities travelling along at the speed of light. Light, radio waves, X-rays, gamma rays, are all electromagnetic radiation. (See RADIO AND TELEVISION.)

Electromotive Force (e.m.f.) The electrical pressure developed by a cell, battery or generator which enables them to produce an electric current in a circuit. Measured in volts.

Electrolysis The movement of ions to form an electric current in an electrolyte, usually as the result of an applied electric potential. Negative ions move towards the anode and positive ions towards the cathode. As a result, gases may be liberated or metal deposited. When metal is deposited on the cathode the process is called electroplating.

Elements The chemical units of which compounds are made. There are 92 naturally occurring chemical elements, though some have never been prepared, and a number have been made artificially (transuranic elements) to extend the list to 103 or more.

THE ELEMENTS

Atomic number	Name	Symbol	Atomic weight	Relative densities (gases at N.T.P.)
1	Hydrogen	H	1·008	0·0000899
2	Helium	He	4·003	0·0001785
3	Lithium	Li	6·939	0·534
4	Beryllium	Be	9·012	1·85
5	Boron	B	10·811	2·34
6	Carbon	C	12·011	Diamond 3·52 Graphite 2·25 Amorphous 0·5–1·0
7	Nitrogen	N	14·007	0·0012506
8	Oxygen	O	15·999	0·0014290
9	Fluorine	F	18·998	0·0016970
10	Neon	Ne	20·183	0·008999
11	Sodium	Na	22·990	0·97
12	Magnesium	Mg	24·312	1·75
13	Aluminium	Al	26·982	2·70
14	Silicon	Si	28·086	2·33

Atomic number	Name	Symbol	Atomic weight	Relative densities (gases at N.T.P.)
15	Phosphorus	P	30·974	Yellow 1·82 / Red 2·20
16	Sulphur	S	32·064	Monoclinic 1·96 / Rhombic 2·07
17	Chlorine	Cl	35·453	0·00321
18	Argon	A	39·948	0·0017837
19	Potassium	K	39·102	0·862
20	Calcium	Ca	40·08	1 55
21	Scandium	Sc	44·956	3·0
22	Titanium	Ti	47·90	4·54
23	Vanadium	V	50·94	6·11
24	Chromium	Cr	52·00	7·18
25	Manganese	Mn	54·94	7·21
26	Iron	Fe	55·85	7·87
27	Cobalt	Co	58·93	8·9
28	Nickel	Ni	58·71	8·9
29	Copper	Cu	63·54	8·95
30	Zinc	Zn	65·37	7·14
31	Gallium	Ga	69·72	5·90
32	Germanium	Ge	72·59	5·32
33	Arsenic	As	74·92	5·73
34	Selenium	Se	78·96	Red 4·45 / Grey 4·80
35	Bromine	Br	79·909	3·12
36	Krypton	Kr	83·80	0·003733
37	Rubidium	Rb	85·47	1·53
38	Strontium	Sr	87·62	2·55
39	Yttrium	Y	88·905	4·46
40	Zirconium	Zr	91·22	6·5
41	Niobium	Nb	92·906	8·57
42	Molybdenum	Mo	95 94	10·2
43	Technetium	Tc	99	—
44	Ruthenium	Ru	101·07	12·2
45	Rhodium	Rh	102·91	12·4
46	Palladium	Pd	106·4	12·0
47	Silver	Ag	107·87	10·5
48	Cadmium	Cd	112·40	8·65
49	Indium	In	114·82	7·31
50	Tin	Sn	118·69	7·31
51	Antimony	Sb	121·75	6·69
52	Tellurium	Te	127·60	6·25
53	Iodine	I	126·904	4·94
54	Xenon	Xe	131·30	0·005887
55	Caesium	Cs	132·905	1·90
56	Barium	Ba	137·34	3·5
57	Lanthanum	La	138·91	6·15
58	Cerium	Ce	140·12	6·77
59	Praseodymium	Pr	140·907	6·77
60	Neodymium	Nd	144·24	7·00

Atomic number	Name	Symbol	Atomic weight	Relative densities (gases at N.T.P.)
61	Prometheum	Pm	147	—
62	Samarium	Sm	150·35	7·54
63	Europium	Eu	151·96	5·25
64	Gadolinium	Gd	157·25	7· 0
65	Terbium	Tb	158·92	8·23
66	Dysprosium	Dy	162·50	8·54
67	Holnium	Ho	164·93	8·78
68	Erbium	Er	167·26	9·05
69	Thulium	Tm	168·93	9·31
70	Ytterbium	Yb	173·04	6·97
71	Lutecium	Lu	174·97	9·84
72	Hafmium	Hf	178·49	13·3
73	Tantalum	Ta	180·95	16·6
74	Wolfram	W	183·85	19·3
75	Rhenium	Re	186·2	21·0
76	Osmium	Os	190·2	22·5
77	Iridium	Ir	192·2	22·4
78	Platinum	Pt	195·09	21·4
79	Gold	Au	196·97	19·3
80	Mercury	Hg	200·59	13·55
81	Thallium	Tl	204·37	11·85
82	Lead	Pb	207·19	11·34
83	Bismuth	Bi	208·98	9·75
84	Polonium	Po	210	9·32
85	Astatine	At	211	—
86	Radon	Rn	222	0·009725
87	Francium	Fr	223	—
88	Radium	Ra	226·05	5·0
89	Actinium	Ac	227·05	—
90	Thorium	Th	232·12	11·7
91	Protactinium	Pa	231·05	15·37
92	Uranium	U	238·07	18·95
93 *	Neptunium	Np	237	20·25
94 *	Plutonium	Pu	239	19·84
95 *	Americium	Am	241	13·67
96 *	Curium	Cm	242	—
97 *	Berkelium	Bk	243–250	—
98 *	Californium	Cf	251	—
99 *	Einsteinium	Es	246, 247, 249, 251–256	—
100 *	Fermium	Fm	250, 252–256	—
101 *	Mendelevium	Md	256	—
102 *	Nobelium	No	254	—
103 *	Lawrencium	Lr	257	—
104 *	Kurchatovium(?)	Ku	—	—
105 *	Hahnium(?)	—	—	—

* These are called transuranic elements. They have all been artificially created, often in negligibly small amounts, by means of nuclear reactors or machines such as cyclotrons.

Elementary Particle Electrons, protons and neutrons are the familiar elementary particles that make up atoms and nuclei. However, many other particles smaller than atoms are now known to exist, though high energy *particle accelerators* (q.v.) are usually needed to create them. Many of these fundamental or elementary particles are very short-lived and decay into more stable particles or gamma rays in a minute fraction of a second. Examples of these elementary particles are the *neutrino* (a particle with no mass and no charge), the π-*mesons* (which help to explain how the protons and neutrons in a nucleus stay together) and heavier particles like the Σ (*sigma*) and the Ω⁻ (*omega minus*). The list of elementary particles keeps growing, and surprises keep appearing. In 1974 two new particles (called *psi* particles) were discovered which lived a thousand times longer than any theory expected that they should.

Energy The capacity of a body or substance for doing work. It can exist in a number of forms e.g. mechanical, potential, heat, chemical, electrical, radiant and nuclear energy. The law of conservation of energy states that energy is never lost or gained but only changes from one form to another.

In driving a car to the top of a hill, work is done against the force of gravity and the car gains *potential* energy. This is converted into *kinetic* energy of motion as the car freewheels down the hill. Friction at the moving parts causes wastage of energy as *heat* energy and the car would slow down without the engine which converts *chemical* energy stored in the petrol into kinetic energy.

Einstein showed that matter is a form of energy. In nuclear fission and fusion, matter is converted into energy according to the formula $E = m \cdot c^2$ (m = mass, c = speed of light). This is the origin of the energy released in nuclear bombs and in the sun. The sun's energy reaches the earth in the form of *radiant* energy (heat and light rays).

All forms of energy are now measured in joules. Calories were formally used to measure heat energy. The c.g.s. unit of energy is the *erg* = 10^{-7} joules.

Useful formulae:

Kinetic energy = $m \cdot v^2/2$ (m = mass of body, v = velocity of body).

Change in potential energy = $m \cdot g \cdot h$ (m = mass, g = gravitational acceleration, h = change in vertical height).

Electrical energy $= V \cdot I \cdot t$ ($V =$ voltage, $I =$ current, $t =$ time).

Change in heat content $= m \cdot s \cdot (T_2 - T_1)$ ($m =$ mass, $s =$ specific heat, $T_2 =$ final temperature, $T_1 =$ initial temperature).

Equivalent Weight The equivalent weight of an element is the number of units by weight of it that will combine with, or displace, 1 unit of hydrogen or 8 units of oxygen. It is therefore equal to the atomic weight divided by the valency. The equivalent weight of an acid is the weight of acid containing unit weight of replaceable hydrogen (see acid), and that of a base is the the weight of base required to neutralise the equivalent weight of an acid.

Erg See ENERGY.

Expansion Most substances expand on being heated, and each has its own capacity for such expansion. The coefficient of linear expansion is the figure that is used for finding how much a substance expands in one direction

$$l_2 = l_1 (1 + \alpha t)$$

Where l_1 is the length at the first temperature, t is the rise in temperature in degrees Centigrade, α is the coefficient of linear expansion and l_2 is the length at the second temperature.

A similar relationship exists for volume expansion. If $V_1 =$ volume at first temperature, $t =$ rise in temperature in degrees Centigrade, β is the coefficient of cubical expansion and $V_2 =$ the volume at the second temperature

$$V_2 = V_1 (1 + \beta t)$$

For solids $\beta = 3\alpha$ approximately.

Fission The splitting of a thing into two more or less equal parts. In nuclear fission, the nucleus of an atom splits into two parts accompanied by the release of nuclear energy and one or more neutrons. Fission may occur spontaneously or by the nucleus being hit by a neutron, but only occurs readily in certain *fissile* materials such as uranium 235 and plutonium 239. It is possible that the neutrons released during fission can hit other nuclei and bring about further fission. This process can be repeated and result in a runaway *chain reaction* with an enormous build up of energy. However, a chain reaction can only occur if the amount of fissile material is above a *critical size*, so that the number of neutrons continues to rise despite some escaping and some hitting nuclei without causing fission. Atomic bomb explosions are uncontrolled chain reactions of this kind. But nuclear fission can be controlled in *nuclear reactors* (q.v.) and used as a source of energy.

Fluorescence The property of some substances to absorb light of one wavelength and emit light of a longer wavelength: e.g. fluorescein, an organic compound whose solution in alkalis glows bright green due to fluorescence. In fluorescent lighting tubes, the electric current causes mercury vapour to emit ultra-violet light, which then excites fluorescent substances on the sides of the tube to emit visible light. Unlike *phosphorescence* (q.v.), fluorescence stops as soon as the original illumination stops.

Force That which makes a body change its state of rest or uniform motion in a straight line. Units are the newton (S.I. system), the dyne (c.g.s. system) and the poundal (f.p.s. system). Force (p), mass (m) and acceleration (f) are related by the equation $p = mf$ (Newton's second law of motion).

Formulae (not dealt with under separate entries, see AREA, VOLUME, BINOMIAL THEOREM, etc.).

Circumference of circle $= 2\pi r$ (or πd).

Mechanics

Falling bodies

Where g = gravity = 9·8 (in m. per sec. per sec.); u = initial velocity (in m. per sec.); v = final velocity (in m. per sec.); h = height (in m.); t = time (in sec.).

$$v = u + gt$$
$$h = \frac{u + v}{2}t$$
$$h = ut + \tfrac{1}{2}gt^2$$
$$g = \frac{v - u}{t}$$
$$2gh = v^2 - u^2$$

Time of swing of pendulum : $t = 2\pi\sqrt{\dfrac{l}{g}}$ where t = time of complete swing (once in each direction) (in sec.); l = length of pendulum (in m.); g = gravity.

Useful Factors

$(a + b)^2 = a^2 + 2ab + b^2$

$(a - b)^2 = a^2 - 2ab + b^2$

$a^2 - b^2 = (a + b)(a - b)$

$a^3 + b^3 = (a + b)(a^2 - ab + b^2)$

$a^3 - b^3 = (a - b)(a^2 + ab + b^2)$

$x^4 + x^2y^2 + y^4 = (x^2 + xy + y^2)(x^2 - xy + y^2)$

$a^3 + b^3 + c^3 - 3abc =$
$$(a + b + c)(a^2 + b^2 + c^2 - ab - bc - ca)$$

$a^2(b - c) + b^2(c - a) + c^2(a - b) =$
$$-(a - b)(b - c)(c - a)$$

$bc(b - c) + ca(c - a) + ab(a - b) =$
$$-(a - b)(b - c)(c - a)$$

$a(b^2 - c^2) + b(c^2 - a^2) + c(a^2 - b^2) =$
$$(a - b)(b - c)(c - a)$$

Quadratic Equation

$ax^2 + bx + c = 0.$ Solution:

$$\frac{-b \pm \sqrt{b^2 - 4ac}}{2a}$$

Geometrical Progression

pth term $= ar^{p-1}$

Sum to n terms $= a\dfrac{r^n - 1}{r - 1}$ or $a\dfrac{1 - r^n}{1 - r}$

Sum to infinity when $-1 < r < 1 = \dfrac{a}{1 - r}$

Arithmetical Progression

Last term $= a + (n - 1)d$

Sum to n terms $= \dfrac{n}{2}[2a + (n - 1)d]$

Simple Interest

$$I = \frac{P \times R \times T}{100}$$

Friction The force that resists the movement of one surface over another. It results from the fusing together of high points of contact between the surfaces. To overcome the fusion force must be used. The coefficient of friction is the ratio of the force required to make one surface slide to the weight of the body. In many machines friction is a nuisance because it uses up energy in the form of heat and damages the surfaces; hence the use of a lubricating fluid to keep the surfaces apart. Hence also ball-bearings and roller-bearings, which reduce friction enormously.

Friction is often useful, as in brakes, which depend on heavy friction to reduce motion.

Fusion In chemistry and physics, the melting of a solid substance. In nuclear physics it means *nuclear* fusion, which is the joining together of the nuclei of two atoms to make a different atom. When this happens with the light elements, such as hydrogen, deuterium (heavy hydrogen) and tritium, energy is released in the process. This is what happens in the sun, and it is what physicists hope to achieve in *thermonuclear fusion* in order to produce electrical power from heavy hydrogen obtained from sea-water.

Gamma Radiation (Gamma Rays, γ-Rays) Radiation of the same nature as X-rays and light, i.e. electromagnetic radiation, but of much shorter wavelengths. It is emitted by some radioactive substances, e.g. cobalt 60, and is the most penetrating of all radiation.

Gas Laws The combination of Boyle's Law and Charles's Law into one equation:

$$PV = RT$$

where P = pressure; V = volume; T = absolute temperature; R = gas constant = 8·314 joules per degree per mole.

Gram-Atom The weight in grams equivalent to the atomic weight. For example, the atomic weight of oxygen is 16, so a gram-atom of oxygen is 16 grams.

Gram-equivalent The weight in grams of a substance equal to the *equivalent weight* (q.v.).

Gram-molecule The weight in grams equivalent to the molecular weight of an element or compound. For example, the molecular weight of H_2SO_4 is 98, so a gram-molecule of H_2SO_4 is 98 gm.

Gravity Every object attracts every other object with a force directly proportional to the product of the masses of the objects and inversely as the square of the distance between them. If m_1 is the mass of one object, m_2 the mass of the other, d the distance between them, then the gravitational force $F = \dfrac{km_1m_2}{d^2}$, where k is a constant.

For objects on or near the earth, the mass of the earth is very much greater than an object, and so the gravitational force between them makes the object 'fall' towards the earth. The acceleration as it does this is called the acceleration due to gravity. At the Earth's surface this is 9·8 m. per sec. per sec. in the S.I. system and 32 ft. per sec. per sec. in the f.p.s. system.

Half-life The time for half the nuclei in a sample of radioactive material to decay. This ranges from a fraction of a second for some man-made radioisotopes to 4,510 million years for Uranium 238. (See ISOTOPE.)

Heat Energy possessed by a substance in the form of random motions of the atoms which make up the substance. In a redhot piece of iron the atoms are vibrating back and forth very fast, and so the iron contains more heat than when it is cold and the atoms are moving much less fast. However, heat must not be confused with *temperature* (q.v.). The adding of heat to a substance usually causes a rise in temperature but the amount of this rise depends on the mass and *specific heat* (q.v.) of the substance. Adding heat to a substance may cause a *change of state* (e.g. a solid melting to a liquid) without a change in temperature (see *latent heat*). Measured in *joules* (q.v.).

Heavy water Water in which the hydrogen is replaced by the *isotope* (q.v.) deuterium and hence written as D_2O rather than H_2O. The nucleus of ordinary hydrogen is simply one proton, while that of deuterium is one proton and one neutron.

Hologram A photograph taken with the light from a laser which, when even a small part of it is illumined by laser light, reconstitutes the entire picture. The discovery of Professor Denis Gabor of Imperial College, London, for which he was awarded the 1971 Nobel prize for Physics.

Indicator A substance added in small quantities to a chemical reaction which shows when the reaction is complete by a sudden change of colour. The most familiar indicators change colour depending on whether a solution is acidic or alkaline: e.g. litmus is red in acids but blue in alkalis, and phenolphthalein is colourless in acids but purple in alkalis.

Infra-red Light This is the 'light', though invisible, with wavelengths longer than those of visible light and in the range 7,500–100,000 Angstroms, or, 0·75–10 micrometres. Infra-red radiation has a heating effect and can be detected at great distances by modern crystal detectors. Every warm body emits infra-red radiation.

Insulator A material, such as glass, rubber, porcelain, plastics, that has no free electrons, and so will not allow electric current to pass when an e.m.f. is applied.

Interferometer A device in which the phenomenon of interference of light or radio waves is used as a tool in astronomy, metrology and spectroscopy.

Ion An electrically charged atom or group of atoms.

Ionisation The electrification of an element or compound by the loss or gain of an electron or electrons. It occurs chiefly in liquid solutions and gases subjected to electric discharge. A mass of ionised gas is called a *plasma*.

Isotope One of two or more forms of the same chemical element, differing from other isotopes only in atomic weight. The difference is due entirely to the addition or subtraction of neutrons from the nucleus. Examples: The hydrogen atom has one proton and one planetary electron. Add a neutron to the nucleus and it becomes twice as heavy. It is heavy hydrogen or deuterium. Add another neutron and it becomes tritium, three times as heavy as the normal hydrogen. All three isotopes are hydrogen so far as the chemistry is concerned. Many elements have several stable isotopes (tin has ten). It is customary to give the mass number of an isotope after the name in order to indicate which isotope is present, e.g. uranium 238, uranium 235, plutonium 239, etc.

Every element can be made to have radioactive isotopes, called *radioisotopes*. Many of these are used in science and industry because they emit radiation (alpha, beta or gamma). A few elements have naturally occurring radioisotopes.

FAMILIAR RADIOISOTOPES

Name	Type of radiation	Half-life
Carbon 14	beta	5,000 years
Phosphorus 32	beta	14·3 days

Name	Type of radiation	Half-life
Cobalt 60	beta, gamma	5·3 years
Strontium 90	beta	25 years
Iodine 131	beta, gamma	8 days
Caesium 137	beta, gamma	33 years
Radium 226	alpha, gamma	1,590 years
Uranium 235	alpha	880 million years
Uranium 238	alpha	4,510 million years
Plutonium 238	alpha	2,400 years

Joule The S.I. unit of energy or work. It is the work done when 1 newton acts through 1 metre. Replaces the calorie as the unit of heat energy. 1 joule = 0·239 calories.

Laser A device for producing an intense, narrow beam of light, in which all the waves are in step. The atoms of some gases, if electrically excited, can be persuaded by a 'trigger' pulse of light of a certain wavelength to emit more light of the same wavelength. If such a gas is put into a tube with accurately parallel mirrors at each end, and triggered, the light waves will run up and down, getting stronger as they pass over and re-trigger the atoms of the gas. If some of the light is allowed to escape at one end it emerges in such a narrow beam that a laser can shine a spot only a mile or so across on the moon, and so intense it can burn through steel. An even more interesting possibility is the use of the laser in communications. Since a beam of light has an enormously higher frequency than the shortest radio wave, and since the amount of information a beam can carry is proportional to its frequency, a light beam, if it can be *modulated* (See RADIO AND TELEVISION: modulation), should be able to carry as many as a thousand television channels. (See Aircraft, Rockets and Missiles: SATELLITES, Communications.)

Latent heat The latent heat of fusion (vaporisation) is the amount of heat required to turn unit mass of a solid (liquid) into liquid (gas) at the same temperature. The latent heat of fusion of ice is 335 joules per gram; the latent heat of vaporisation of water is 2257 joules per gram.

Lens A piece of transparent material, usually glass, shaped and polished to have curved surfaces. The commonest are a double-convex lens and a double-concave lens. Every combination of two of the following surfaces is possible: convex, concave, plane.

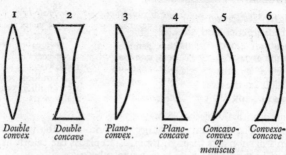

1, 3 and 5 are convergent; 2, 4 and 6 are divergent

A single lens like this is known as a thin lens, and simplified approximate formulae can be used. The principal focus is then the point where parallel rays parallel to the axis come to a point. The distance from the centre of the lens to the point image is called the focal length.

Lens are of two sorts whatever their surfaces. One sort makes rays of light *converge* when they pass through the lens; the other sort makes rays of light *diverge*.

The focal length of a convergent lens can be found very simply by getting an image of a distant object and the distance from lens to image is then the focal length.

The equation of a simple lens, where u = distance of object from centre of lens, v = distance of image from centre, f = focal length, and distances are considered positive when measured *against* the direction the light is travelling, is:

$$\frac{1}{v} - \frac{1}{u} = \frac{1}{f}$$

All measurements are positive when taken from lens to a *real* image or object.

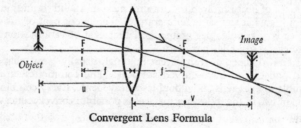

Convergent Lens Formula

Light Radiation that affects our eyes and we 'see'. It is electromagnetic, and the wavelengths of visible light extend from about 4,000 Angstroms (blue) to about 7,000 Angstroms (red). It is customary to speak of all electromagnetic radiation of near wave-lengths to these as 'light', even though it causes no sensation on the eye.

Magnifying Power The magnifying power of a single convex used with the eye as a magnifying glass equals 1 plus $\frac{25}{f}$, where f equals focal length in centimetres.

The magnifying power of an astronomical telescope or a Galileo-type telescope is the focal length of the objective divided by the focal length of the eyepiece.

Mass The mass of a body is proportional to the amount of matter in it. It is *not* the same as *weight* (q.v.), because $W = M . g$ where g = gravity.

Mathematical Signs

Is equal to	$=$	Is approximately equal to	$\doteqdot$
Is not equal to	$\neq$	Is identical to	$\equiv$
The difference between	$\sim$	The sum of	Σ
Greater than	$>$	Varies as	$\propto$
Not greater than	$\not>$	Angle	$\wedge$
Less than	$<$	Infinity	∞
Not less than	$\not<$		

Metals As commonly understood, metals are the substances that are good conductors of heat and electricity, are lustrous when polished and so on. In chemistry, however, a metal is characterised as having a tendency towards losing electrons and thus becoming positively charged. This definition means that only a very few of the elements are not metals.

Microscope A device for getting a magnified image of very small objects. A single magnifying glass is therefore a simple microscope.

A compound microscope consists of two lenses, one of short focal length, the objective, one of long focal length, the eyepiece. The object is placed in the plane of the principal focus.

The magnifying power is found by multiplying the power of the objective by that of the eyepiece. The power of the objective is the *optical tube length* divided by the focal length of the objective. The optical tube length is taken for modern microscopes as being 18 cm. So if, for example, the focal length of an objective is 0·5 cm., then the magnifying power is 36. An eyepiece with a magnification of 3 will then give a total magnification of 108.

The eyepiece and objective are complex lenses, not simple ones, in order to correct for the various errors that a simple lens inflicts on the image, errors that become more and more important as the magnification is increased.

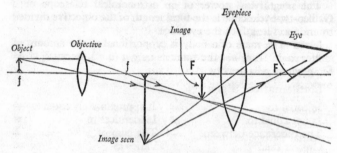

Geometrical Diagram of Microscope

Microscope, Electron A microscope which substitutes beams of electrons for beams of light to form a very greatly magnified image of an object. Electron microscopes are just becoming available which are able to photograph living organisms, and to provide three-dimensional photographs.

Mole The amount of substance that contains as many elementary units as there are in 0·012 kg. of carbon 12. The number of such units is *Avogadro's number* = 6·023 × 10²³.

Molecule The smallest unit of a chemical compound to retain its identity. If split up, the results are the atoms of elements of which it is compounded. A single element can exist in molecular form. For example, hydrogen can be atomic or molecular. In the latter case two atoms of hydrogen are combined into a molecule.

Momentum The product of a body's mass and velocity.

Neutron One of the fundamental particles of nature. Its mass is slightly greater than that of a proton, but the neutron carries no electrical charge. Because of this it is not acted on by the electrical forces in an atom, and so can penetrate more easily. A neutron is therefore a good nuclear projectile. It is the causing agent in nuclear *fission* (q.v.). Neutrons are produced in immense numbers in a *nuclear reactor* (q.v.).

Newton (N) The S.I. unit of force. It is the force that would give a mass of 1 kg. an acceleration of 1 metre per second per second. The force of gravity on a mass of 1 kg. is 9·8N. Replaces the dyne as the unit of force. $1 N = 10^5$ dynes.

Normal Solution A solution of which 1 litre (1,000 c.c.) contains one *gram-equivalent* (q.v.) of a substance. Indicated by N, e.g. N-hydrochloric acid means normal hydrochloric acid solution in water. Used for quantitative analysis. A more dilute solution is one-tenth normal, shown by $N/10$.

Normal Temperature and Pressure (N.T.P.) Normal temperature is taken as 0° C., normal pressure as 76 cm. of mercury. These together give a standard set of conditions for comparing the behaviour of gases.

Nuclear Reactor An apparatus in which a nuclear fuel undergoes *fission* (q.v.) under controlled conditions. The essential parts of a nuclear reactor are: (a) the fuel, which is usually in the form of rods and may be plutonium, natural uranium or enriched uranium (uranium in which the proportion of fissile U-235 to non-fissile U-238 has been made higher than in natural uranium), (b) the *moderator*, which is placed between the fuel rods with the purpose of slowing down the fast neutrons produced during fission so that they produce further fission more readily (moderators commonly used are graphite or *heavy water* (q.v.)), (c) *control rods* (often of cadmium) which absorb neutrons and slow down the rate of fission thus preventing a runaway chain reaction, (d) the *coolant*, which is a fluid (such as carbon dioxide gas or liquid sodium) that is pumped in pipes through the reactor core to remove the vast quantities of heat generated during fission (this heat may be used to generate electricity), (e) a very thick shield of concrete, steel and water to prevent dangerous radiation from escaping from the core. The *fast breeder reactor* is a reactor which 'breeds' more nuclear fuel at the same time as producing energy by fission. This is possible because a fast neutron produced by fission can be absorbed by a non-fissile U-238 nucleus giving a U-239 nucleus which then decays radioactively into fissile plutonium. The reactor at Dounreay, Scotland is of this type. Nuclear reactors will be a very important source of electricity in the future but an outstanding problem is what to do with the dangerous radioactive waste products.

Nucleus Means the centre part of anything. Used chiefly to mean the heavy centre part of an atom. Every atomic nucleus consists of protons and neutrons, with the exception of ordinary hydrogen, the nucleus of which is one proton. Examples: oxygen, 8 protons 8 neutrons; iron, 26 protons 30 neutrons; radium, 88 protons 138 neutrons.

Ohm (Ω) The S.I. unit of electrical resistance. If an e.m.f. is expressed in volts and the current in a circuit expressed in amperes, then volts divided by amperes gives the resistance in ohms.

Ohm's Law The law of electrical circuits that states that the current is directly proportional to the applied e.m.f. Ohm's Law is obeyed in most circuits of elementary electrics and electronics.

Particle Accelerator A machine which accelerates *elementary particles* (q.v.) near to the speed of light by means of electric and magnetic fields. The resulting beams of high energy particles are allowed to hit stationary atomic targets or to meet other beams of particles head on. By observing the products of such collisions, much is learnt about elementary particles and the atomic nucleus.

Periodic Table A table grouping the elements so that certain chemical and physical properties are repeated at regular intervals. It is arranged in horizontal *periods* and vertical *groups*. Elements in one group have similar physical and chemical properties, e.g. fluorine, chlorine, bromine, iodine, all in sub-group *b* of group VII and called the *halogens*.

Phosphorescence Light emitted by some substances without heating, some as the result of irradiation with ultra-violet light or other light, some as the result of chemical action, e.g. phosphorescent organisms in sea-water and creatures like fireflies and glow-worms. See FLUORESCENCE.

Plasma Physics The study of gas in a highly ionised state— the state in which most of the universe exists and from which atomic scientists are hopeful of extracting electric power by a process of controlled fusion equivalent to a controlled hydrogen bomb explosion.

Polymer A compound consisting of a chain of repeated molecular units. It is formed from the individual *monomer* units by the process of polymerisation. Natural polymers include rubber and proteins while synthetic polymers include many plastics (e.g. polythene) and artificial fibres (e.g. nylon).

Power The rate of doing work or using energy. The S.I. unit is the *watt*, equal to 1 joule per second. In electrical circuits the power in watts is found by multiplying the volts by the amperes. The horse-power was formally used in mechanics. 1 horse-power = 746 watts.

Pressure The force or weight per unit area acting on a surface. Measured in newtons per square metre (S.I. units), kilograms per sq. m. or pounds per sq. in. etc. Atmospheric pressure, that is the weight of air in a column of unit cross-sectional area up to the top of the earth's atmosphere, is roughly 15 lb. per sq. in. Pressure in gases is also expressed as the height of mercury (or other liquid) that the gas will support. A pressure of 0·76 m. (760 mm. or 29·921 in.) of mercury is equivalent to 33·9 ft. of water. This is equivalent to 14·696 lb. per sq. in. or 10,332·3 kg. per sq. m. To turn kilograms weight to newtons multiply by 9·8, the gravitional acceleration in metres per sec. per sec. A *bar* is equivalent to 100,000 newtons per sq. m. High pressures, especially in gases, are measured in kilobars. A *torr* is equivalent to 1 mm. of mercury and is used to measure low pressures in gases.

CONVERSION TABLE OF PRESSURES

Cm. of Hg	In. of Hg	Millibars	Kg./sq. m.	Lb./sq. in.
71·2	28	942	9,650	13·74
73·7	29	976	9,970	14·2
75·5	29·7	1,000	10,220	14·55
76·2	30	1,019	10,400	14·8
78·7	31	1,052	10,750	15·3

Principle of Archimedes When a body is suspended in a liquid its apparent loss in weight is equal to the weight of liquid displaced.

Projectile Body thrown or projected. If v is the initial velocity, a the angle of projection, g gravity, the projectile moves in a parabola. The following relationships are true:

$$\text{Total time of flight} = \frac{2v \sin a}{g}$$

PERIODIC

Period	Group 0	Group 1 A B	Group 2 A B	Group 3 A B	Group 4 A B
1		1 H 1·008			
2	2 He 4·003	3 Li 6·939	4 Be 9·012	5 B 10·811	6 C 12·011
3	10 Ne 20·183	11 Na 22·990	12 Mg 24·312	13 Al 26·982	14 Si 28·086
4	18 A 39·948	19 K 39·102 29 Cu 63·54	20 Ca 40·08 30 Zn 65·37	21 Sc 44·956 31 Ga 69·72	22 Ti 47·90 32 Ge 72·59
5	36 Kr 83·80	37 Rb 85·47 47 Ag 107·87	38 Sr 87·62 48 Cd 112·40	39 Y 88·905 49 In 114·82	40 Zr 91·22 50 Sn 118·69
6	54 Xe 131·30	55 Cs 132·905 79 Au 197	56 Ba 137·34 80 Hg 200·61	57 La 138·91 58–71 The rare earths ★ 81 Tl 204·37	72 Hf 178·49 82 Pb 207·19
7	86 Em 222	87 Fr 223	88 Ra 226·05	89 Ac 227	90 Th 232·12

★ The rare earths:

58 Ce 140·12	59 Pr 140·907	60 Nd 144·24	61 Pm 147	62 Sm 150·35	63 Eu 151·96	64 Gd 157·25

† The transuranium elements:

93 Np	94 Pu	95 Am	96 Cm	97 Bk	98 Cf	99 Einsteinium E

TABLE

Group 5 A	Group 5 B	Group 6 A	Group 6 B	Group 7 A	Group 7 B	Group 8		
7 N 14·007		8 O 15·999		9 F 18·998				
15 P 30·974		16 S 32·064		17 Cl 35·453				
23 V 50·94		24 Cr 52·00		25 Mn 54·94		26 Fe 55·85	27 Co 58·93	28 Ni 58·71
	33 As 74·92		34 Se 78·96		35 Br 79·909			
41 Nb 92·906		42 Mo 95·94		43 Tc 99		44 Ru 101·07	45 Rh 102·91	46 Pd 106·4
	51 Sb 121·75		52 Te 127·60		53 I 126·904			
73 Ta 180·95		74 W 183·85		75 Re 186·2		76 Os 190·2	77 Ir 192·2	78 Pt 195·09
	83 Bi 208·98		84 Po 210		85 At 211			
91 Pa 231		92 † U 238·07						

65 Tb 158·92	66 Dy 162·50	67 Ho 164·93	68 Er 167·26	69 Tm 168·93	70 Yb 173·04	71 Lu 174·97

100 Fermium Fm	101 Mendelevium Md	102 Nobelium Nb	103 Lawrencium Lr

Maximum height $= \dfrac{v^2 \sin^2 a}{2g}$

Horizontal range $= \dfrac{v^2 \sin 2a}{g}$

Proton The positive heavy particle of the nucleus of an atom; also the nucleus of a normal hydrogen atom.

Pulsar A type of radio star discovered in 1968 which gives out pulses of radio waves at very regular intervals. Believed to be composed of very densely packed neutrons.

Pythagoras Greek mathematician. The theorem of Pythagoras is the one that states that in a right-angled triangle the square on the hypotenuse is equal to the sum of the squares on the other two sides. See ANGLE.

Quasar (or quasi-stellar source) Much the brightest and most distant type of giant star so far discovered.

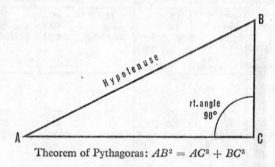

Theorem of Pythagoras: $AB^2 = AC^2 + BC^2$

Radical A group of atoms that stay together when a compound dissociates but yet not a stable group to qualify as a molecule, e.g. SO_4, NO_3, etc.

Radioactivity The spontaneous emission of radiation (alpha, beta or gamma) from a material, due to the break-up of the nuclei of the atoms. Materials that are abundantly radioactive are radium and uranium and some artificially made radioisotopes. Many materials, however, are known to have a tiny proportion of a radioactive isotope present, and these materials are everywhere—in food, plants, rocks, etc.

Reaction The correct name for what goes on when chemicals combine or split up.

Reagent Chemicals commonly used in chemical laboratories for experiments and analysis, such as dilute hydrochloric acid, ammonium hydroxide, dilute nitric acid, etc.

Reciprocal The reciprocal of a number y is one divided by y and is written $1/y$. E.g. the reciprocal of 4 is $1/4 = 0.25$.

Reflection The 'bouncing back' of light rays, heat rays, etc. The simple law of reflection is that the angle between the incoming ray and the perpendicular to the surface is equal to the angle between the reflected ray and the same perpendicular. This is expressed as: The angle of incidence = Angle of reflection. With flat or 'plane' mirrors the perpendicular is easy to draw in diagrams, but with curved reflecting surfaces the perpendiculars have to be arrived at by knowledge of the geometry of circles, parabolas, etc.

Such regular reflection is called mirror or specular reflection. At a roughened surface light is reflected in *all* directions and does not obey the above rules. This is called diffused or scattered reflection.

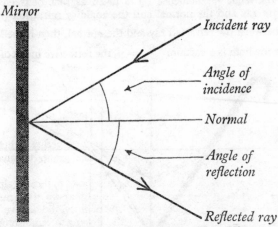

Specular or Mirror Reflection from a Plane Mirror

Refraction The sudden change of direction of light when passing from one transparent substance into another. A ray of light passing from air into water is bent towards the perpendicular, or normal.

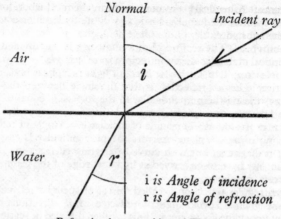

Refraction between Air and Water

If the angle of incidence (i) is taken as that between the incident ray and the normal and the angle of refraction (r) as that between the refracted ray and the normal, then if the less-dense medium is a vacuum $\frac{\sin i}{\sin r} = \mu$, the refractive index of the

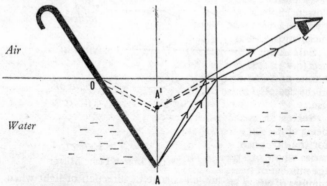

Apparent Bending of Walking-stick in Water Due to Refraction

The point A seems to be at A^1. Similarly with all points on OA so that the part immersed seems to be along OA^1.

substance. In ordinary experiments, as air is so little different from a vacuum for the passage of light, i is measured in air and r in the substance.

Resolving Power The power of an optical instrument or any optical system to deal with fine detail. The resolving power of a telescope is directly proportional to the diameter of the objective. Hence prismatic binoculars 8 × 40 are better than 8 × 25, the first figure being the magnifying power and the second the diameter of the objective in millimetres. The second binocular has the same magnifying power as the first but less resolving power, and so, though objects look just as big, the detail does not show up so well. The resolving power of the human eye is such that two point objects subtending an angle of about 1 minute at the eye can be seen separately, i.e. resolved.

Root This has two meanings in mathematics. (a) One of several equal factors of a number. Thus the square root $\sqrt{\ }$ or $^2\sqrt{\ }$ is one of two equal factors: e.g. $3 = \sqrt{9}$ (also written $9^{\frac{1}{2}}$) and $3 \times 3 = 9$. The cube root is one of three equal factors: e.g. $4 = ^3\sqrt{64}$ (also written $64^{\frac{1}{3}}$) and $4 \times 4 \times 4 = 64$. (b) The root of an equation in an unknown x is a particular value of x that satisfies the equation.

Root-mean-square The average value of a quantity that takes positive and negative values equally (e.g. an alternating current) is zero. If the values are squared, the mean found, and then the square root taken, the non-zero result is called the root-mean-square value.

Salt A salt is the compound formed when the hydrogen in an *acid* (q.v.) is replaced by a metal. Examples of a salt are potassium nitrate and calcium sulphate. Sodium chloride ($NaCl$) is a salt in the chemical sense but is also called common salt in everyday use.

Series In mathematics a series is a sum of many terms each being of the same form so that a general expression can be given for the nth term: e.g. $1 + 1/2 + 1/4 + 1/8 + 1/16 + \ldots$ is a series whose nth term is $1/2^n$. *Infinite series* are series in which the number of terms is without limit. Despite having an infinite number of terms, some infinite series sum up to a limiting value. Such series are called *convergent* (e.g. the series given above if continued to infinity adds up to the value 2). Series which are not convergent are called *divergent*.

Sine In trigonometry the sine of an angle (other than the right angle) in a right-angled triangle, is the ratio of the side opposite the angle to the hypotenuse. Sin 90° = 1, sin 60° = 0·866, sin 45° = 0·707, sin 30° = 0·5. See *Angle*.

S.I. Units The internationally recommended system of *units* (q.v.) in which the base units are:

Quantity	Name of unit	Symbol
length	metre	m
mass	kilogram	kg
time	second	s
electric current	ampere	A
temperature	kelvin	K
amount of substance	mole	mol
luminous intensity	candela	cd

Other quantities are derived by combining these units e.g. the S.I. unit of volume is the cubic metre (m), that of velocity the metre per second (m. s), that of energy the joule (m. kg. s) and that of electric charge the coulomb (A. s).

Specific Gravity See DENSITY.

Specific Heat The amount of heat in joules that must be added to unit mass of a substance to raise its temperature by 1° C. The table gives values for a gram of substance.

SPECIFIC HEATS OF COMMON SUBSTANCES

Aluminium	.	. 0·846	Alcohol	. .	. 2·428
Brass	. .	. 0·384	Chloroform	.	. 0·980
Copper	. .	. 0·389	Air	. . .	1·009[1]
Iron	. .	. 0·474	Carbon dioxide	.	0·846[1]
Rubber	. .	. 1·675	Oxygen	. .	. 0·911[1]
Wood	. .	. 1·675	Water	. .	. 4·187

[1] At constant pressure.

Spectroscope An apparatus in which light is dispersed by a triangular prism or diffracted by a diffraction grating to give bright vertical coloured lines on a dark background—the bright-line spectrum of the light. It consists normally of a rigid stand on which the prism is placed, a collimator, with a slit at one end to produce a beam of parallel light, and a telescope through which the spectrum is viewed. Telescope and collimator are rotatable on the graduated rigid prism table. By an arrangement of prisms in one special prism the spectrum comes through in the same straight line as the telescope and collimator. This is then a direct-vision spectroscope. There are many sorts of spectroscope, ranging from a small pocket-size direct-vision spectroscope to a piece of apparatus occupying a small room and used in industry for analysis. A spectrograph is a form of spectroscope in which the spectrum is photographed, and a mass spectrograph a form of spectrograph in which the quantities of light are measured.

Squares, Cubes, Square Roots, Cube Roots and Reciprocals See *Root*.

N	N^2	N^3	$\sqrt{N}$	$\sqrt[3]{N}$	$\frac{1}{N}$
1	1	1	1·0	1·0	1·0
2	4	8	1·414	1·26	0·5
3	9	27	1·732	1·442	0·3333
4	16	64	2·0	1·587	0·25
5	25	125	2·236	1·71	0·2
6	36	216	2·449	1·817	0·1667
7	49	343	2·646	1·913	0·1429
8	64	512	2·828	2·0	0·125
9	81	729	3·0	2·08	0·1111
10	100	1,000	3·162	2·154	0·1
11	121	1,331	3·317	2·224	0·0909
12	144	1,728	3·464	2·289	0·0833
13	169	2,197	3·606	2·351	0·0769
14	196	2,744	3·742	2·41	0·0714
15	225	3,375	3·873	2·466	0·0667
16	256	4,096	4·0	2·52	0·0625
17	289	4,913	4·123	2·571	0·0588
18	324	5,832	4·243	2·621	0·0556
19	361	6,859	4·359	2·668	0·0526
20	400	8,000	4·472	2·714	0·05
21	441	9,261	4·583	2·759	0·0476
22	484	10,648	4·69	2·802	0·0455
23	529	12,167	4·796	2·844	0·0435
24	576	13,824	4·899	2·885	0·0417
25	625	15,625	5·0	2·924	0·04
26	676	17,576	5·099	2·962	0·0385
27	729	19,683	5·196	3·0	0·037
28	784	21,952	5·292	3·037	0·0357
29	841	24,389	5·385	3·072	0·0345
30	900	27,000	5·477	3·107	0·0333
31	961	29,791	5·568	3·141	0·0323
32	1,024	32,768	5·657	3·175	0·0313
33	1,089	35,937	5·745	3·208	0·0303
34	1,156	39,304	5·831	3·24	0 0294
35	1,225	42,875	5·916	3·271	0·0286
36	1,296	46,656	6·0	3·302	0·0278

N	N^2	N^3	$\sqrt{N}$	$\sqrt[3]{N}$	$\dfrac{1}{N}$
37	1,369	50,653	6·083	3·332	0·027
38	1,444	54,872	6·164	3·362	0·0263
39	1,521	59,319	6·245	3·391	0·0256
40	1,600	64,000	6·325	3·42	0·025
41	1,681	68,921	6·403	3·448	0·024
42	1,764	74,088	6·481	3·476	0·0238
43	1,849	79,507	6·557	3·503	0·0233
44	1,936	85,184	6·633	3·53	0·0227
45	2,025	91,125	6·708	3·557	0·0222
46	2,116	97,336	6·782	3·583	0·0217
47	2,209	103,823	6·856	3·609	0·0213
48	2,304	110,592	6·928	3·634	0·0208
49	2,401	117,649	7·0	3·659	0·0204
50	2,500	125,000	7·071	3·684	0·02

Superconductivity This is the remarkable property of many metals and alloys to lose all electrical resistance below a certain critical temperature (usually within 20° of absolute zero). This means that an electric current can flow in a loop of the metal indefinitely without generating heat or decreasing in strength. Because of the low temperatures required (the metal is usually bathed in liquid helium) superconductivity is expensive to use on a large scale. But superconducting magnets which can produce very high magnetic fields without vast consumption of electrical energy are now quite widely used.

Surface Tension A force acting in the surface of a fluid, whether the surface separates one liquid from another or a liquid from a gas such as air. The force acts as if it were an elastic skin trying to reduce the area of surface. It is the surface tension that makes water climb up a narrow tube and makes a meniscus-shaped surface of water in any vessel. It is surface tension that makes water form into drops.

Surface tension is measured in newtons per metre. It varies with the temperature. The surface tension of pure water at 20° C. is 0·07275 newtons per metre.

Tangent In geometry a straight line touching (not cutting) a curve at only one point. In trigonometry the tangent of an angle (other than the right angle) in a right-angled triangle is the ratio of the side opposite the angle to the other side that is not the hypotenuse. Tan 0° = 0, tan 30° = 0·577, tan 45° = 1·0, tan 60° = 1·732, tan 90° = ∞.

Telescope An optical device for getting an image of a distant object much bigger than the object appears seen with the naked eye. (The image obtained is really much smaller than the actual object.) There are two simple types: the astronomical telescope and the Galilean telescope. The astronomical telescope has a very long focus convergent lens as objective and a very short

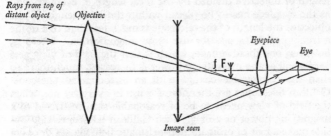

Rays from top of distant object   Objective   Eyepiece   Eye

f F

Image seen

Geometrical Diagram of Astronomical Telescope

F is focus of objective
f is focus of eyepiece

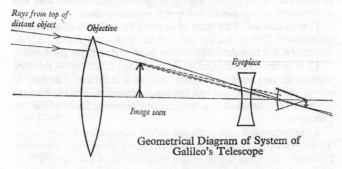

Rays from top of distant object   Objective

Eyepiece

Image seen

Geometrical Diagram of System of
Galileo's Telescope

focus convergent lens (or system of lenses) as eyepiece. The magnifying power is the focal length of objective divided by the focal length of eyepiece. The bigger the objective in diameter, the greater the resolving power. The image seen is inverted. Prisms can be inserted between the lenses to invert the image and at the same time make the light reflect along paths across and back and across and forward so that the length of the telescope can be short and the optical path long. The result is a prismatic monocular giving the image upright in relation to the object. Two of them make a pair of prismatic binoculars.

The Galilean telescope uses a long-focus convergent lens as objective and a short-focus divergent lens as eyepiece. The image is seen upright. The magnification is again the focal length of objective divided by the focal length of eyepiece, and as the eyepiece has to be placed within the focal length of the objective the length of the telescope is much less than that of the astronomical telescope for the same magnification. There is, however, one disadvantage, which is that the field of view gets very small as the magnifying power is increased, much more so than the comparable change with an astronomical telescope. Galilean telescopes are therefore for use in everyday life, when the field of view needs to be of reasonable size, restricted to a magnifying power of 2 or 3. Two Galilean telescopes side-by-side make a pair of ordinary non-prismatic field glasses or opera glasses.

All the above are refracting telescopes. Sir Isaac Newton designed a reflecting telescope to get over the difficulty of aberrations in the lenses needed for big magnification. All the very big observatory telescopes of today are reflecting ones.

Temperature The state of hotness or coldness of a body or substance. This is not the same as the heat energy of a body or substance, for this depends on the mass and the specific heat.

Thermocouple A kind of thermometer made by joining one wire at its two ends to another wire of a different material. If one junction is kept cool and the other heated, an electric current flows and can be used as a measure of the temperature of the hot junction.

Thermometer An instrument for measuring temperature. The commonest type of thermometer is a glass tube of extremely fine bore and thick walls with a bulb joined at the bottom containing mercury or some other liquid, which also reaches a certain distance up the tube. Warming makes the liquid expand up the tube; cooling makes it contract. A scale of numbers is arrived at by fixing two reference points, usually the melting point of ice and the boiling point of water.

Two temperature scales are in common use. One, called the Fahrenheit scale, has the melting point of ice at 32° and the boiling point of water at 212°. This is in general use in Britain and the U.S.A. The second scale is called Centigrade (Celsius in many European countries) and has the lower point at 0° and the upper at 100°. It is in use generally in many countries, and is international for scientific measurement.

To convert Fahrenheit to Centigrade, first subtract 32 and then multiply the result by $\frac{5}{9}$.

To convert Centigrade to Fahrenheit multiply by $\frac{9}{5}$ and then add 32.

Examples:

(1) 59° F., convert to ° C.
$$59 - 32 = 27; 27 \times \tfrac{5}{9} = 15° \text{ C.}$$

(2) 20° C., convert to ° F.
$$20 \times \tfrac{9}{5} = 36; 36 + 32 = 68° \text{ F.}$$

To convert ° C. to ° K. or absolute, add 273.

Liquid-in-glass thermometers are limited. Mercury freezes at −39° C.; ethyl alcohol boils at 78·3° C. So other devices must be used for very low and very high temperatures. For extreme temperatures a thermo-couple is frequently used, depending on the electricity generated when two dissimilar metals are joined and the junction heated or cooled. A platinum resistance-thermometer depends on the change of electrical resistance in platinum wire when it is heated. Modern materials called thermistors are also used. The resistance of such materials gets less as it is heated. So an electrical current increases.

Special thermometers of the liquid-in-glass sort are devised to read the minimum or the maximum temperature reached in a certain period of time. A clinical thermometer is a type of maximum thermometer in which the thread of mercury stays put at its highest because of a very narrow constriction at the base of the tube where it joins the mercury-supply bulb.

Trigonometry The branch of mathematics that deals with the properties of angles and the relationship between them, starting with the three ratios: sine, cosine, tangent. Further definitions: $\dfrac{1}{\text{sine}} = \text{cosecant}, \dfrac{1}{\text{cosine}} = \text{secant}, \dfrac{1}{\text{tangent}} = \text{cotangent}$, written cosec, sec and cot. See *Angle*.

Ultra-violet Light Light that is invisible to human beings and of shorter wavelength than visible light. Sometimes called 'dark light'. It is very active in affecting chemicals and causing fluorescence. It is present in the light from the sun, but much of it is filtered out by the earth's atmosphere. It is dangerous for the eyes. Range of wavelengths 1,800–4,200 Å. It is also present in mercury-vapour discharge light.

Units All physical quantities can be expressed in terms of five base units: mass (M), length (L), time (T), electric current and temperature. Thus volume = $L . L . L$, force = $(M . L)/(T . T)$. The magnitude of the base units is set by convention. In the c.g.s. system the base units are the centimetre (L), gram (M) and second (T). In the f.p.s. system they are the foot (L), pound (M) and second (T). The currently accepted system is the Système International d'Unités (see S.I. UNITS).

Vacuum Space which contains no matter. In practice unobtainable since, whatever the walls of the container were made of, the container would evaporate slowly and so destroy the vacuum. Usually very low pressures of air or other gases are called vacuums.

Valency The valency of an element is a number that tells in what proportions the element combines with other elements, and so can be used to work out molecular formulae of compounds. Elements of valency 1 (monovalent elements) include hydrogen, chlorine, silver and sodium; of valency 2 (divalent elements) include oxygen, magnesium and calcium; of valency 3 (trivalent elements) include aluminium and nitrogen; and of valency 4 (tetravalent elements) include carbon.

Oxygen being divalent means that one atom of it will combine with two atoms of monovalent hydrogen (giving water H_2O), or with one atom of divalent magnesium (giving MgO, magnesium oxide), or with 'half' an atom of tetravalent carbon (giving carbon dioxide, CO_2). Three atoms of oxygen combine with two of aluminium to give aluminium oxide Al_2O_3.

Valency is closely related to the theory of the chemical *bond* (q.v.) and is not always as simple as above. Many elements can combine with each other in a number of different ways: e.g. nitrogen and oxygen can give the oxides N_2O, NO, N_2O_3, NO_2, and N_2O_5 and two oxides of copper exist, CuO and Cu_2O.

Vapour Pressure A liquid loses atoms or molecules into its gaseous surround, usually air. When the pressure of these evaporated atoms or molecules is such that as many are returning to the material as are leaving it the vapour is saturated and its pressure is called the vapour pressure of the liquid. It increases with a rise in temperature and depends only on that temperature and the nature of the liquid. A volatile liquid has a high vapour pressure at ordinary temperatures. A liquid that has a low vapour pressure does not evaporate easily. On heating a liquid there comes a temperature at which the vapour pressure equals that of the atmosphere. It then boils.

VAPOUR PRESSURES OF SOME LIQUIDS AT 20° C. IN MM. OF MERCURY

Water	.	.	.	17·5	Benzene . . .	74·6
Mercury	.	.	.	0·0013	Chloroform . . .	161
Acetone	.	.	.	185	Ether	440
Alcohol	.	.	.	44·5	Carbon Tetrachloride .	91

Velocity In everyday use the same as speed, but in science and mathematics having the extra quality of being negative or positive to show *direction* in relation to any problem.

If u is the starting velocity, f the acceleration, then the velocity v after time t is given by $v = u + ft$. The distance travelled is given by $s = ut + \frac{1}{2}ft^2$. From these can be derived the equation $v^2 = u^2 + 2fs$.

Viscosity The internal friction of fluids, i.e. resistance to flow of one part over another. Examples: treacle, a very viscous fluid; ether, a liquid of low viscosity. Viscosity decreases with rise in temperature.

Volt The S.I. unit of electro motive force (e.m.f.), or potential difference or electrical pressure.

Volume The amount of space occupied by an object, expressed in cubic inches, cubic metres, cubic feet, etc.

VOLUMES OF COMMON SHAPES

Cube: l^3, where l = length of one side.

Rectangular prism: $l \times b \times d$, where l = length, b = breadth, d = depth.

Sphere: $\frac{4}{3}\pi r^3$, where r = radius.

Cylinder: $\pi r^2 l$, where r = radius of base, l = length of cylinder.

Cone: $\frac{1}{3}\pi r^2 h$, where r = radius of base, h = vertical height.

$\frac{1}{3}\pi r^2 \sqrt{l^2 - r^2}$, where l = length of sloping side.

Pyramid: $\frac{1}{3}$ area of base $\times h$, where h = vertical height.

Waves Many kinds of disturbance travel from one point to another as waves, for example, ripples on a water surface, pressure variations in air (sound) and electrical and magnetic disturbances (light). The important thing is that the disturbance varies periodically in both space and time. This can be understood by considering a water wave. If a water wave is photographed at one time it will look as in diagram (a) where the shape of the wave is repeated regularly and the distance, λ,

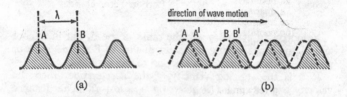

(a)   (b)

between successive crests is called the *wavelength*. If the wave is travelling from left to right with velocity v, at a slightly later time the picture will look as in (b) which has the earlier wave shape dotted in (the crest at A having moved to A^1). Moreover if we remain fixed at B, we have to wait a time T equal to λ/v before the crest originally at A reaches B. The time T between successive crests arriving at a given point is called the *period*. The reciprocal $1/T$ is the number of crests passing a point per second and is called the *frequency*, f. We have shown the important relationship

$$T = \lambda/v \text{ or } v = f.\lambda$$

which is true for all wave motions. It is important to note that it is the shape of the wave and the energy carried by it that moves from A to B and not the water itself. The water molecules are actually moving backwards and forwards in the direction at right angles to the direction the wave is travelling. For this reason, water waves are examples of *transverse* waves. *Longitudinal* waves, by comparison, are waves in which the particles are moving back and forth in the same direction as that in which the wave is moving e.g. sound waves.

All kinds of waves show the characteristic properties of *reflection* (q.v.), *refraction* (q.v.) and *diffraction*.

Weight The force of attraction exerted on a body by gravity. See *Mass*.

Weights and Measures, Tables of

Avoirdupois Weight

16 drams (*dr.*)	=	1 ounce (*oz.*)
16 ounces	=	1 pound (*lb.*)
14 pounds	=	1 stone (*st.*)
28 pounds	=	1 quarter (*qr.*)
4 quarters	=	1 hundredweight (*cwt.*)
20 hundredweights	=	1 ton (*tn.*)
100 pounds	=	1 central, or short hundredweight
2,000 pounds	=	1 short ton
7,000 grains	=	1 pound

Troy Weight

3·1683 grains (*gr.*)	=	1 carat
24 grains	=	1 pennyweight (*dwt.*)
20 pennyweights	=	1 ounce
12 ounces or 5,760 grains	=	1 pound

Apothecary's Weight, Dry

20 grains	=	1 scruple (℈)
3 scruples	=	1 drachm (ʒ)
8 drachms	=	1 ounce (℥)
12 ounces	=	1 pound (*lb.*)

Apothecary's Measure, Liquid

60 minims (*m.*) or drops	=	1 fluid drachm (fʒ)
8 fluid drachms	=	1 fluid ounce (f℥)
20 fluid ounces	=	1 pint
8 pints	=	1 gallon

Linear Measure

12 inches (*in.*)	=	1 foot (*ft.*)
3 feet	=	1 yard (*yd.*)
5½ yards	=	1 rod, pole or perch
40 poles	=	1 furlong (*fur.*)
8 furlongs	=	1 mile (*mi.*)
3 miles	=	1 league (*l.*)

Land Measure

7·92 inches	= 1 link (*li.*)
25 links	= 1 rod (*rd.*)
4 rods or 100 links	= 1 chain (*ch.*)
80 chains	= 1 mile

Square Measure

144 square inches (*sq. in.*)	= 1 square foot (*sq. ft.*)
9 square feet	= 1 square yard (*sq. yd.*)
30¼ square yards	= 1 square rod, pole or perch
40 square poles	= 1 rood (*r.*)
4 roods	= 1 acre (*ac.*)
640 acres	= 1 square mile (*sq. mi.*)

Land Square Measure

625 square links	= 1 square rod
16 square rods	= 1 square chain
10 square chains	= 1 acre

Cubic or solid Measures

1,728 cubic inches (*cu. in.*)	= 1 cubic foot (*cu. ft.*)
27 cubic feet	= 1 cubic yard (*cu. yd.*)

Liquid Measure

4 gills	= 1 pint (*pt.*)
2 pints	= 1 quart (*qt.*)
4 quarts	= 1 gallon (*gal.*)

Dry Measure

2 pints	= 1 quart
4 quarts	= 1 gallon
2 gallons	= 1 peck (*pk.*)
4 pecks	= 1 bushel (*bush.*)
8 bushels	= 1 quarter (*qr.*)
36 bushels	= 1 chaldron (*chal.*)
5 quarters	= 1 wey
2 weys	= 1 last

Circular Measure

60 seconds (″)	= 1 minute (′)
60 minutes	= 1 degree (°)
90 degrees	= 1 quadrant (*quad.*)
4 quadrants or 360 degrees	= 1 circle (o)

Miscellaneous Measures

1 gal. of pure water weighs 10 lb.
The gramme is the weight of 1 c.c. of pure water.
The litre is 1,000 c.c. of pure water, and weighs 1 kg.
A hand (in measuring a horse) is 4 in.
The British Thermal Unit (B.T.U.) is the amount of heat required to raise 1 lb. of water by 1° F.
A Therm is 100,000 B.T.U.
One horse-power is the power needed to raise 550 lb. 1 ft. in 1 sec.
The kilowatt is the power needed to raise 737·6 lb. 1 ft. in 1 sec. (746 watts = 1 h.p.).

Paper Measure

24 sheets = 1 quire
20 quires = 1 ream

(Stationers' reams are usually 480 sheets; printers' reams are 500 or 516 sheets.)

THE METRIC SYSTEM

Measures of Weight

10 milligrammes (mg.)	= 1 centigramme (cg.)
10 centigrammes	= 1 decigramme (dg.)
10 decigrammes	= 1 gramme (g.)
10 grammes	= 1 decagramme (Dg.)
10 decagrammes	= 1 hectogramme (hg.)
10 hectogrammes	= 1 kilogramme (kg.)

Linear Measure

10 millimetres (mm.)	= 1 centimetre (cm.)
10 centimetres	= 1 decimetre (dm.)
10 decimetres	= 1 metre (m.)
10 metres	= 1 decametre (Dm.)
10 decametres	= 1 hectometre (hm.)
10 hectametres	= 1 kilometre (km.)

Measures of Capacity

10 millilitres (ml.)	= 1 centilitre (cl.)
10 centilitres	= 1 decilitre (dl.)
10 decilitres	= 1 litre (l.)
10 litres	= 1 decolitre (Dl.)
10 decolitres	= 1 hectolitre (hl.)
10 hectolitres	= 1 kilolitre (kl.)

X-Rays Electromagnetic radiation of very short wavelength, ranging from a tenth of an Angstrom to 20 Angstroms. X-rays affect a photographic plate and cause fluorescence in some chemicals. They penetrate matter according to its density. They are used in medical practice for showing up growths, bone fractures, foreign bodies, etc., in the human body.

FURTHER READING

How Much and How Many: The Story of Weights and Measures, by Jeanne Bendick (Brockhampton Press)

Brains and Computers, by A. M. Andrew (Harrap)

The Second Book of Experiments, by Leonard de Vries (Murray)

Electricity, by Leslie Hunter (Burke)

Transistors Work Like This, by Egon Larsen (Phoenix)

The Young Scientist, ed. W. Abbott (Chatto & Windus)

The Magic of Electricity, by Sam Rosenfeld (Faber)

For the life stories of individual scientists: the *Immortals of Science* series (Chatto & Windus) and the *Lives to Remember* series (A. & C. Black)

The Atom, by Charles Hatcher (Macmillan)

Men who Changed the World: stories of invention and discovery, by Egon Larsen (Phoenix)

Science, ed. Dr J. Bronowski (Macdonald Illustrated Library)

The Double Helix, by James Watson (Weidenfeld and Nicolson)

The Biological Time Bomb, by Gordon Rattray Taylor (Thames and Hudson)

The New Materials, by David Fishlock (Murray)

The Naked Ape, by Desmond Morris (Cape)

Modern Cosmology, by Jagjit Singh (Pelican)

Men of Mathematics (Vols 1 and 2), by E. T. Bell (Pelican)

A Dictionary of Radio and Television

SOME of the terms used in discussing radio and television are general scientific terms (e.g. *ampere*, *ohm*) and if not found in this section should be looked for in the DICTIONARY OF SCIENCE AND MATHEMATICS.

Abbreviations

A—ampere
mA—milliampere (milliamp)
μA—microampere
V—volt
mV—millivolt
μV—microvolt
Ω—omega (capital) = ohm
MΩ—megohm
$\mu\Omega$—microhm
F—farad
μF—microfarad

W—watt
kW—kilowatt
mW—milliwatt
H—henry
mH—millihenry
μH—microhenry
A.C.—alternating current
D.C.—direct current
e.m.f.—electromotive force
R.M.S.—root-mean-square

Note: The above abbreviations are in accordance with the ruling of the British Standards Institution.

L.F.—low frequency
H.F.—high frequency
V.H.F.—very high frequency
R.F.—radio frequency
A.F.—audio frequency
R.C.C.—resistance–capacity coupling
S.G.—screen grid
D.C.C.—double cotton covered
S.C.C.—single cotton covered
D.S.C.—double silk covered
D.W.S.—double wound silk} synonymous terms
S.W.G.—standard wire gauge
S. pole—south pole

N. pole—north pole
L.T.—low tension
H.T.—high tension
G.B.—grid bias
Q.P.P.—quiescent push–pull

Aerial (Antenna) A conductor that can either send out or pick up radio waves and therefore can be the last stage of a transmitter or the first stage of a receiver. In its simplest form it is a metallic rod or wire but efficient, directional aerials can be of complicated design.

A transmitter operating on long or medium waves has an aerial that is a high wire leading through the transmitter to the ground. For waves as short as, or shorter than, those used for television the antenna is free of any earth connection and the length of rod forming the antenna is related to the wavelength. The commonest relationship is that the antenna is a half the wavelength. The usual design is of two rods in line, each rod just under a quarter wavelength long, the two ends at the middle being where the line joining the antenna to the transmitter or receiver is placed. This is the *half-wave dipole* or Hertzian antenna.

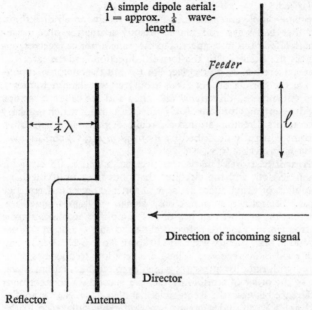

A simple dipole aerial:
l = approx. ¼ wavelength

Feeder

$\frac{1}{4}\lambda$

ℓ

Direction of incoming signal

Director

Reflector   Antenna

A dipole with one reflector and one director

The B.B.C. television video signal is transmitted in London on a wavelength of 6·67 m. or 21 ft. 10½ in. A half-wave antenna would therefore have a total length of 10 ft. 11¼ in. In practice, owing to end-effects, so that the effective length is slightly bigger than the physical length, the antenna would be about 10 ft. 5 in. long.

The audio signal for television is on a different wavelength from that of the video signal, so an aerial correctly designed for one will not be accurate for the other. In practice, a compromise is often made.

If the electrical component of the electromagnetic wave being transmitted or received is vertical, then the half-wave antenna is vertical. If the electrical component is horizontal the antenna is horizontal. Some of the B.B.C. regional television signals and all its V.H.F. frequency-modulation signals are horizontally polarised.

Single-dipole antennae transmit and receive in all directions. Another half-wave rod placed exactly a quarter of a wave-length *behind* but unconnected to the transmitter or receiver, en-hances the efficiency in the forward direction, and the extra rod is called a reflector. Rods placed in *front* of the operative dipole, and at the correct distance (*not* a quarter wavelength but less), also enhance the directional efficiency and are called directors.

Alternating Current (A.C.) Electric current which regularly reverses its direction around a circuit. A particular alternating current is usually described by its *frequency* (q.v.) and its *root-mean-square* value (q.v.).

Amplification This is the electronics and radio term for magnification, and the circuitry that does the amplifying is an amplifier, of which there are several sorts. The radio-frequency or R.F. amplifier amplifies only signals of high frequencies, whereas the audio-frequency or A.F. amplifier amplifies signals of frequencies ranging between about 50 and 15,000 cycles per second in high-fidelity work and to about 8,000 cycles per second in a good radio receiver. These are very low frequencies com-pared with radio frequencies, which even on the medium waves are of the order of a million cycles per second. This enormous difference between the frequencies handled by an A.F. amplifier and an R.F. amplifier means a considerable difference in the circuits and valves used.

In radio and electronics and television, amplification involves the use of thermionic valves and transistors. Any one such valve or transistor with its associated circuit of resistors, capacitors and perhaps inductance, is called a *stage*. Each stage except the last in a radio receiver is designed as a voltage amplifier, but the final stage has to deliver power to a loudspeaker or the coils of a cathode-ray tube in a television receiver. This final stage is therefore a power amplifier.

The general principle of amplification is that an input alter-nating voltage, still at radio frequency if it is R.F. amplification but at audio frequency if it is A.F. amplification, is applied between the grid and cathode of a thermionic valve. The output is then taken from the anode circuit. If a transistor is used the input is in most cases (i.e. using common emitter connections) applied between base and emitter and the output taken between collector and emitter. In each case what is taken out is bigger than what is put in. The ratio of output to imput is called the *stage gain*.

The stage gain depends on the *amplification factor*, μ (mu), of the valve, the A.C. resistance of the valve, Ra, the *load*, and the type of coupling between stages. See VALVE.

Amplitude Modulation The addition of an audio-frequency signal to a carrier in such a way that the carrier amplitude varies in response to the signal. See MODULATION.

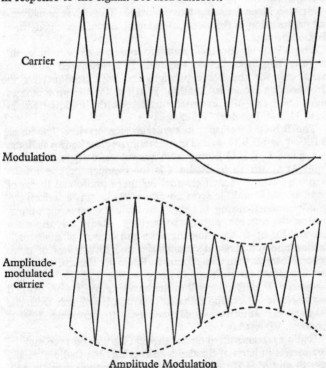

Carrier

Modulation

Amplitude-modulated carrier

Amplitude Modulation

Anode The positive electrode of an electrolytic cell or thermionic valve or discharge tube.

Audio Frequency (A.F.) This means a *frequency* (q.v.) within the range of sound wave frequencies audible to human ears. It can be taken as between 20 cycles per second and 20,000 cycles per second, though many people have a much smaller range than this. High-fidelity amplifiers are capable of reproducing from about 50 cycles per second to 15,000 cycles per second.

Automatic Gain Control A circuit device which automatically maintains the output of a stage almost constant, even though the input may be varying. It operates by the principle of *feedback* (q.v.), and is used in radio receivers to reduce the effect of *fading* (q.v.).

British Broadcasting Corporation The oldest broadcasting organisation in the world, developing out of a company first formed in 1922.

The B.B.C. broadcasts in sound to countries all over the world in forty languages beside English. It is organised into two parts, one for the home programmes, with headquarters in Broadcasting House in London, W.1, one for the programmes going overseas—the external services—with headquarters in Bush House, London, W.C.2.

The B.B.C. broadcasts in two television services, known as B.B.C.-1 and B.B.C.-2, and in four radio services known as Radio 1, 2, 3 and 4. B.B.C. Home radio was substantially re-organised from April 4th 1970. Radio 1 is the channel for pop music. Radio 2 is the principal channel for more traditional forms of popular music and for sport coverage. Radio 3 is a serious all-music channel during the day but includes items on drama, poetry, the arts etc. during the evening. Radio 4 is the main channel for up-to-the-moment news and current affairs broadcasting and for plays, documentaries and discussions of more general interest than those found in Radio 3. The radio services are broadcast on medium or long waves, and on very high frequency (V.H.F.). Details of the wavelengths used are printed in the *Radio Times*, and fuller information is available from the Engineering Information Department, Broadcasting House, London, W1A 1AA.

Radio 1 is transmitted on 247 metres; Radio 2 on 1500 metres, 202 metres in parts of Scotland, and on V.H.F.; Radio 3 on 464 metres and V.H.F.; Radio 4 on various medium wavelengths, and on V.H.F. Many of the V.H.F. programmes are transmitted in stereo. Radio 2 is to be found between 88–91 Mhz, Radio 3 between 90 and 93 and Radio 4 from 92–95 Mhz.

The External Services are mainly broadcast on short waves in the bands from 11–49 metres, but some of the services to Europe are broadcast on medium wavelengths and some of the short-wave programmes are relayed on medium wave from transmitters in Cyprus and various other parts of the world.

B.B.C.-1 television is transmitted on both the 405-line standard, and on the newer 625-line standard. B.B.C.-2 is transmitted only on 625 lines. The 405-line services are transmitted on V.H.F., the 625-line services on U.H.F., and in colour.

The B.B.C. has 20 local radio stations, all of which transmit on both V.H.F. and on medium-wave. They are as follows:

B.B.C. Radio Birmingham
(Pebble Mill Road, Birmingham B5 7S0)
B.B.C. Radio Blackburn
(King Street, Blackburn, Lancs. BB2 2EA)
B.B.C. Radio Brighton
(Marlborough Place, Brighton, Sussex BN1 1TU)
B.B.C. Radio Bristol
(3 Tyndalls Park Road, Bristol BS8 1PP)
B.B.C. Radio Carlisle
(Hilltop Heights, Carlisle, Cumberland)
B.B.C. Radio Derby
(56 St. Helens St., Derby DE1 3HY)
B.B.C. Radio Humberside
(9 Chapel St., Hull HU1 3NU)
B.B.C. Radio Leeds
(Merrion Centre, Leeds LS2 8NJ)
B.B.C. Radio Leicester
(Epic House, Charles St., Leicester LE1 3SH)
B.B.C. Radio London
(Harewood House, Hanover Sq., London W1R 0JD)
B.B.C. Radio Manchester
(33 Piccadilly, Manchester M60 7BB)
B.B.C. Radio Medway
(30 High St., Chatham, Kent ME4 4EZ)
B.B.C. Radio Merseyside
(Commerce House, 13/17 Sir Thomas St., Liverpool L16 BS)
B.B.C. Radio Newcastle
(Crestina House, Archbold Terrace, Newcastle-upon-Tyne NE2 1DZ)
B.B.C. Radio Nottingham,
(York House, Mansfield Road, Nottingham MG1 3JB)
B.B.C. Radio Oxford
(242/254 Banbury Road, Oxford OX2 7DW)

B.B.C. Radio Sheffield
(Ashdell Grove, 60 Westbourne Road, Sheffield S10 2QU)
B.B.C. Radio Solent
(South Western House, Canute Road, Southampton SO9 4PJ)
B.B.C. Radio Stoke-on-Trent
(Conway House, Cheapside, Hanley, Stoke-on-Trent, Staffs ST1 1JJ)
B.B.C. Radio Teesside
(91/93 Linthorpe Road, Middlesbrough, Teesside TS1 5DG)

Capacitance This is the property of a *capacitor* (q.v.) to store electric charge when a voltage is applied across the capacitor plates. The unit of capacitance is the *farad* (F), and a capacitor has a capacitance of one farad if it stores a charge of one coulomb when there is a voltage of one volt across it. The farad is too large for most practical purposes and it is normal to use the microfarad, μF (one millionth of a farad), and the picofarad, pF (one million millionth of a farad).

In understanding how a capacitor behaves in a circuit it is important to remember that electric current is the flow of electric charge. So whenever charge is moving into or out of a capacitor (i.e. the capacitor is *charging* or *discharging*) a current must flow. Also, the charge stored in a capacitor is always equal to the voltage across it times its capacitance.

Suppose a capacitor is connected in a circuit with a battery, a *resistor* (q.v.) and a switch. When the switch is open there is no voltage across the capacitor and therefore no charge stored in it. On closing the switch, current flows for a short time, charging up the capacitor until the voltage across it is equal to that of the battery. The insulating layer in the capacitor then prevents any further current flow. If the battery is now removed from the circuit, the capacitor discharges through the resistor and a current again flows for a short time (but in the opposite direction) until there is no voltage across the capacitor. If the battery is now reconnected, but with positive and negative reversed, the capacitor will again charge up (in the opposite direction to before) and current will again flow. Thus we can see that if we connect a capacitor to an A.C. generator whose voltage is regularly changing from positive to zero, zero to negative, and negative through zero to positive again, the capacitor will regularly charge up, discharge and recharge in the opposite direction. An alternating current will therefore flow even though there is an insulating layer in the capacitor. The A.C. is exactly of the same *frequency* (q.v.) as the voltage but the current maxima coincide with the voltage zeros: i.e. the voltage and current are 90° out of *phase* (q.v.). The magnitude of the current is given by V/X_C, where V is the voltage and X_C is called the *capacitive reactance*. For a capacitor of capacitance C farads and A.C. of frequency f, $X_C = 1/2\pi Cf$ ohms.

Capacitor A circuit component which has the property of *capacitance* (q.v.). The simplest form of capacitor is the parallel plate capacitor which consists of two plates of metal separated by an insulating material called a *dielectric*. The capacitance C is given by the formula

$$C = \frac{\varepsilon A}{d} \times \frac{10^{-9}}{36\pi} \text{ farads}$$

where A is the area of the overlapping plates, d is the distance between the plates and ε is a constant which depends on the dielectric used and is called the *dielectric constant*. For low values of capacitance the dielectric may be air (ε = 1). This is often the case for variable capacitors used in tuning radios. When the dial is turned, one set of plates interleaves with another set separated by air gaps and A in the above formula is increased or decreased. Higher value capacitors are made with ceramic, mica or paper dielectrics and may be rolled up for convenience.

Carrier Wave Electromagnetic waves of the frequencies of speech and music cannot be transmitted efficiently over long distances. So in telecommunications a wave of much higher frequency, the carrier wave, is used to 'carry' the desired signal by the technique of *modulation* (q.v.).

Cathode The negative electrode of an electrolytic cell or a thermionic valve or discharge tube.

Cathode-ray Tube This device is a glass envelope roughly conical in shape with a long neck in which a cathode emits electrons which travel towards a fluorescent screen on the large end of the envelope. A metal electrode in the neck is the anode to attract the electrons and speed them on their way to the screen. The cathode and focusing electrodes and anodes constitute the *electron gun*. When correctly designed a narrow intense beam of electrons travels to the screen and produces a tiny spot of light.

There are two main uses for a cathode-ray tube. One is with extra apparatus to make an oscilloscope, an apparatus that allows

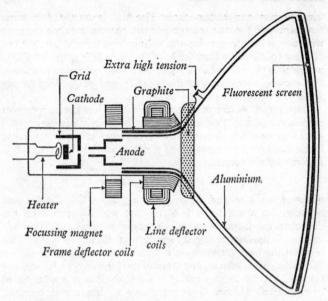

Grid

Cathode

Extra high tension

Graphite

Fluorescent screen

Anode

Aluminium

Heater

Focussing magnet

Frame deflector coils

Line deflector coils

A wide-angle television cathode-ray tube showing only
electrodes for a triode assembly

waves and oscillations to be seen as visible traces and measured.

The other use is in a television receiver. The electron beam is
forced to traverse the screen in lines, each successive line being
below the one before it, so that the whole of the working area of
the screen is *scanned*. In order to make the beam do this its movements are controlled by electromagnetic coils on the neck.

Circuit The name given to the arrangement of conductors,
capacitors, inductances, valves, etc., that make up the theoretical
picture of an electronics device. All these components are shown
in diagrams by conventional graphical symbols and the connecting wires by straight lines. The circuit diagram must be distinguished from the wiring diagram, which shows the natural
disposition, soldering points, etc., of the real components. The
circuit diagram merely tells the theory on which the behaviour
of the apparatus is based and can be calculated.

Coil Conducting wire wound on a former and used in A.C.

circuits as a source of *inductance* (q.v.). There may be many or few turns and the core may or may not be of a magnetic material, depending on the application. Coils are widely used in *tuning* (q.v.) circuits and as *chokes* when a high impedance to A.C. is required.

Colour Television The first British colour television broadcast was made on 2 July 1967, and the B.B.C.'s full colour service on B.B.C.2 opened on 2 December. Since then both B.B.C.1 and I.T.V. have begun transmitting a high proportion of colour programmes.

Condenser See CAPACITOR.

Crystal Detector An early form of rectifier consisting of a thin pointed wire (the 'cat's whisker') in contact with a *semiconductor* (q.v.) crystal. Used as a detector for radio waves prior to the invention of diode valves and *p–n junction* (q.v.) diodes.

Decibel A unit to indicate change of power, always taken from a convenient reference value and expressed as so many decibels up or down. A decibel is a tenth of a bel. The scale of decibels depends on the logarithms of the ratio of powers. The rise or fall in decibels = $10 \log \dfrac{P_2}{P_1}$, where P_2 is the second power and P_1 the first. If, for example, $P_2 = 2P_1$, then the second power is $10 \log 2$, (about) 3 decibels up.

DECIBEL TABLE
(Based on 1 milliwatt reference)

Milliwatts	Decibels	Milliwatts	Decibels
1	0	3·981	6
1·259	1	5·012	7
1·585	2	6·310	8
1·995	3	7·943	9
2·512	4	10·000	10
3·162	5		

Detection (Demodulation) The reverse process to *modulation* (q.v.): i.e. the separation of the original signal from the modulated *carrier wave* (q.v.). This is usually done in radio and television receivers (after changing from a frequency-modulated signal to an amplitude-modulated signal if necessary) by rectifying the high frequency signal to give a direct current varying at audio frequencies. See RECTIFICATION.

Diagrams There are certain standard graphical symbols used in electrical, electronic, radio and television circuit diagrams. Straight lines indicate conducting connections (lengths of copper wire when an amateur is wiring up a piece of apparatus).

Diode This means 'two electrodes' and refers to a component that will allow the passage of an electric current in one direction only and hence can be used for *rectification* (q.v.). The diode may be a thermionic valve with only a cathode and an anode or a semiconductor *p–n junction* (q.v.).

Doping The adding of small quantities of impurities to a *semiconductor* (q.v.). Adding of antimony or arsenic to germanium gives *n-type* germanium. This has a higher conductivity (see *resistivity*) than undoped germanium because the impurity atoms bring extra electrons which are readily available for carrying electricity. Adding aluminium or indium to germanium gives *p-type* germanium. This also has an increased conductivity but due to the presence of positively charged *holes* which, like electrons, can carry electricity. See P–N JUNCTION and TRANSISTOR.

Early Bird The world's first commercial communications satellite, launched by the United States in the spring of 1965.

Earth A term much used in radio and electronics. For ordinary circuits, including telephone and distribution lines, the earth, being a conductor of electricity, though a poor one, can be used as the return wire to complete the circuit. For circuits involving electromagnetic oscillations and waves the earth is the conductor to which the transmitter or receiver is connected, the antenna being the other. Thus when medium or long radio waves are used the antenna system is a long, high wire or system of wires and the earth connection is a system of wires buried in the ground. For an ordinary receiver the water pipe is a good enough earth. The word 'earth' is also used, however, to mean the common metallic connection to all the circuits, frequently the metal chassis on which everything is mounted. The advantage of an earth connection is that stray currents use the earth as a 'sink' and in receiving weak signals on medium and long waves the signal is increased. Modern receivers frequently need no earth connection at all. Transmission and reception of television signals and any others using dipole antennae make no use of an earth connection.

Electric Field An electric field is a region of space in which an electric charge experiences a force.

Electromagnetic Waves (EM waves). Waves (see DIC-
TIONARY OF SCIENCE) consisting of both electric and magnetic
quantities varying regularly in space and time and travelling
together at the speed of light.

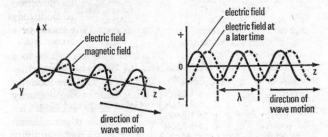

(a) Simplified diagram
    of an electromagnetic
    wave

(b) Diagram showing how
    the electric field varies

Diagram (a) gives an instantaneous picture of an EM wave. The
electric field (q.v.) is in the x-direction and oscillates between
$+$ve and $-$ve values as in diagram (b). The *magnetic field*
(q.v.) is in the y-direction and varies in a similar way. The
whole wave travels in the z-direction at the speed of light so that
at a later time the electric field will vary as shown dotted in (b).
The wavelength, λ, is the distance between one crest and the
next. The frequency, f, is the number of oscillations per second
at a given point. These are related to the speed of light, c, by
the equation

$$c = f.\lambda$$

The value of c for EM waves in free space, c_0, is 3×10^8 m
per sec. or 186,000 miles per sec. Note that EM waves do not
need a medium through which to travel, unlike sound waves.
EM waves do of course travel through other materials but at a
velocity c_0/μ where μ is the refractive index of the material.

EM waves have very different properties depending on the
wavelength. Different names are given to different ranges of
wavelength, and these make up the *Electromagnetic Spectrum*.
(see DICTIONARY OF SCIENCE for *Gamma rays, Ultra-violet light,*
etc).

WAVELENGTHS AND FREQUENCIES

λ	n	λ	n
2,000 m.	150 kc/s	50 m.	6 Mc/s
1,000 m.	300 kc/s	10 m.	30 Mc/s
500 m.	600 kc/s	3 m.	100 Mc/s
300 m.	1,000 kc/s	1 m.	300 Mc/s
	(1 Mc/s)	10 cm.	3,000 Mc/s
200 m.	1,500 kc/s	3 cm.	10,000 Mc/s
100 m.	3,000 kc/s	1 cm.	30,000 Mc/s
	(3 Mc/s)	5 mm.	60,000 Mc/s

THE ELECTROMAGNETIC SPECTRUM

Wavelength	Frequency	Name
0·01 Å	3×10^{14} Mc/s	
0·1 Å	3×10^{13} Mc/s	Gamma rays and X-rays
10 Å	3×10^{11} Mc/s	
100 Å	3×10^{10} Mc/s	Ultra-violet light
4,000 Å	$7 5 \times 10^{8}$ Mc/s	Visible light—violet / red
7,500 Å	4×10^{8} Mc/s	Infra-red light
1,000,000 Å	3×10^{6} Mc/s	
(0·01 cm.)		
0·1 cm.	300,000 Mc/s	Radio waves from millimetre
1,000,000 cm.	30 kc/s	waves to long waves

Fading The variation in strength of a received radio signal. Medium waves suffer from this at night when the ground ray and the sky ray are received together and the sky ray is varying. Short waves suffer from it because of variations in the conditions of the reflecting ionosphere. It can be reduced in a receiver by automatic gain control.

Farad The S.I. unit of capacitance.

Feed Back This is the feeding back from a later part of a circuit to an earlier part. The feedback may be negative, in which case it stabilises, reduces amplification and, if it varies according to the input, provides automatic gain control. If the feedback is positive it can produce instability and even oscillation but increases amplification.

Ferrite A material made like a ceramic, i.e. by baking at a high temperature. It is made of a number of oxides, including iron oxide, and can be designed so that it has any magnetic properties desired. Moreover, it can be moulded into any shape. The magnetic coils used on the cathode-ray tubes of television receivers are wound on ferrite cores. A long rod of ferrite inside a coil constitutes a ferrite 'aerial' for a small radio receiver.

Filter A circuit device for passing oscillations of only certain desired frequencies, e.g. low-pass filter, high-pass filter, band-pass filter (for passing only a band of frequencies and cutting off everything of higher and lower frequencies).

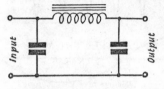

LOW-PASS FILTER: the higher the frequency the more easily it is short-circuited. The lower the frequency the more easily it is passed on.

HIGH-PASS FILTER: the higher the frequency the more easily it is passed on. The lower the frequency the more easily it is short-circuited

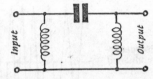

Frequency An alternating quantity (such as an alternating current or a radio wave) consists of repeated *cycles*, one cycle being the sequence of variation of the quantity from zero to maximum positive, from maximum positive through zero to maximum negative and then back to zero. The number of such cycles per second is called the frequency and is measured in *hertz* (one hertz is the same as one cycle per second).

Frequency Modulation (F.M.) A special way of making a *carrier wave* (q.v.) take an audio-frequency variation. Instead of the amplitude of the carrier being made to vary, the frequency is made to vary instead. It is done on V.H.F. transmissions by the B.B.C. to give a high-quality signal fairly free of interference by locally-made electrical noise. An F.M. receiver must have extra circuitry to transform the signal into an amplitude-modulated one for audio-frequency amplification in the usual way. The two stages needed are called the *limiter* and *discriminator*, usually combined into one stage called the *ratio detector*.

Galvanometer An instrument which measures small electric currents.

Ganging The mechanical coupling of variable capacitors in order to tune two or more circuits with one dial.

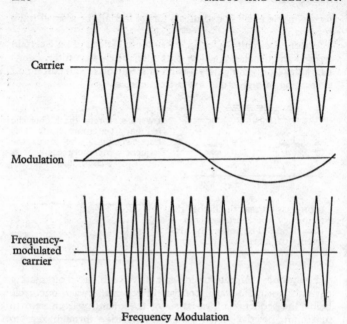

Carrier

Modulation

Frequency-
modulated
carrier

Frequency Modulation

Graphical Symbols There is a convention for representing in circuit diagrams the many sorts of components involved in electronics, radio and television. Most of these are now standardised, but some still have a few variations.

GRAPHICAL SYMBOLS

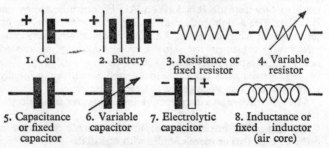

1. Cell

2. Battery

3. Resistance or fixed resistor

4. Variable resistor

5. Capacitance or fixed capacitor

6. Variable capacitor

7. Electrolytic capacitor

8. Inductance or fixed inductor (air core)

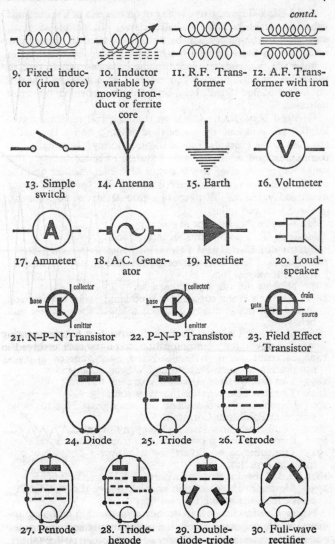

9. Fixed inductor (iron core)

10. Inductor variable by moving iron-duct or ferrite core

11. R.F. Transformer

12. A.F. Transformer with iron core

13. Simple switch

14. Antenna

15. Earth

16. Voltmeter

17. Ammeter

18. A.C. Generator

19. Rectifier

20. Loud-speaker

21. N-P-N Transistor

22. P-N-P Transistor

23. Field Effect Transistor

24. Diode

25. Triode

26. Tetrode

27. Pentode

28. Triode-hexode

29. Double-diode-triode

30. Full-wave rectifier

Grid Bias The negative volts put on the grid of a thermionic valve to establish how it shall behave. In simple circuits, especially in the past, small batteries were used to provide the bias. But in most circuits the bias is effected by the drop in voltage across a resistor placed in the cathode-to-earth part of the valve circuit. Bias is also needed by transistors, though no longer called 'grid' bias, and this is provided by small batteries.

Ground Ray Radio waves on the long and medium wavelengths are sent out by an earthed antenna and travel along attached to the ground. This is the ground ray. It provides the commonest and most widespread system of broadcasting. The range varies according to the power of the transmitter and the nature of the ground over which it travels. For the sort of power in use today, the reliable range of a ground ray can be up to two or three hundred miles.

Half-wave Aerial See AERIAL.

Henry (*H*) The S.I. unit of inductance.

History of Radio and Television, *Some Important Dates*

1864 James Clerk Maxwell originates the theory of electro-magnetic waves.

1884 Nipkow invents a scanning disc.

1888 Heinrich Hertz succeeds in producing waves by electrical means and makes many discoveries about their nature and behaviour.

1894 Sir Oliver Lodge at Oxford gives the first public demonstration of wireless communication over a few hundred yards.

1896 Marconi comes to England and establishes radio communication between Penarth and Weston-super-mare.

1897 The first wireless signalling company formed.

1898 The first paid wireless messages sent.

1901 Marconi in Newfoundland receives signals from his radio station at Poldhu in Cornwall.

1922 The British Broadcasting Company founded.

1926 Baird transmits moving pictures over a short distance.

1927 Transmission of pictures by wire over a distance of 250 miles in America.

1929 B.B.C. begins first experimental T.V. transmissions.

1936 Alexandra Palace station opened to give the world's first public high-definition T.V. service.

Hum Continuous, low frequency *noise* (q.v.) in audio equipment usually originating from the mains supply and caused, for example, by inadequate earthing or an unsmoothed power supply.

I.B.A. The Independent Broadcasting Authority (formerly the Independent Television Authority) was set up as the result of the Television Act 1954 to provide a service, additional to that of the B.B.C., for broadcasting entertainment, disseminating information, religious and educational programmes. The Authority receives no revenue through licence fees but derives its income through advertising. The first transmission started in September 1955.

Programmes are produced by 15 programme companies in 14 separate areas. National news bulletins for all areas are provided by Independent Television News, a non-profit-making company in which all the programme companies are shareholders. The programme companies under contract with the Authority for the six-year period from the end of July 1968 are:

Anglia Television (East of England); ATV Network (Midlands); Border Television (The Borders and Isle of Man); Channel Television (Channel Islands); Grampian Television (North-East Scotland); Granada Television (Lancashire); Harlech Television (Wales and West of England); London Weekend Television (London weekends from 7 p.m. Friday); Scottish Television (Central Scotland); Southern Independent Television (South of England); Thames Television (London weekdays to 7 p.m. Friday); Tyne Tees Television (North East England); Ulster Television (Northern Ireland); Westward Television (South-West England); and Yorkshire Television (Yorkshire).

Impedance (Z) The word used to represent for A.C. circuits the equivalent of *resistance* (q.v.) in a D.C. circuit. The impedance depends on the actual resistance and the *reactance* (q.v.) due to capacitance and inductance. Impedance has the same relationship to e.m.f. and current as resistance. So

$$I = \frac{E}{Z}$$

Inductance Whenever a coil has a varying magnetic field through it, an e.m.f. is set up in the coil causing a current to flow if the circuit is complete. This is known as *induction* and was discovered by Faraday. Whenever an electric current flows in a coil, a magnetic field is created through the coil. Therefore a varying current in a coil will produce a varying magnetic field through the coil and, by induction, will give rise to an induced current in the coil. However, the induced current is always in a direction which opposes the effect of the original current. This opposition to the passage of a varying current is called *inductive reactance* and depends on (a) the rate of change of current in the coil and (b) the *self inductance* (L) of the coil, which is a quantity that takes into account the diameter of the coil, the number of turns and the nature of the core. L is measured in *henries* and a coil has an inductance of one henry if a current varying at the rate of one ampere per second induces in the coil an e.m.f. of one volt. If A.C. of frequency f flows through a coil of inductance L, the inductive reactance (X_L) is $2\pi fL$ ohms, so that with an applied e.m.f. of V volts, the current will be $V/2\pi fL$ amps. By induction it is possible for a varying current in one coil to cause an induced current to flow in another coil. This is known as *mutual inductance* and is the basis of *transformers* (q.v.).

Inductance Capacitance Circuit (L-C Circuit) In an A.C. circuit the voltage across an inductor leads the current through it by 90° (see PHASE), while that across a capacitor lags the current by 90°. This behaviour leads to interesting effects in both the series L–C circuit, in which an inductor is connected in series with a capacitor, and the parallel L–C circuit, in which an inductor is connected in parallel with a capacitor. In the series circuit, because the current through each component is the same, the voltage across the capacitor is 180° out of phase with that across the inductor. This means that the two voltages will cancel out if they are of the same magnitude. In the parallel circuit, because the voltage across each component is the same, the current through the capacitor is 180° out of phase with that through the inductor and the currents will tend to cancel each other out. The condition for complete cancellation is the same in each case, namely that the inductive reactance (X_L) equals the capacitive reactance (X_L), where both quantities depend on the frequency f of the electricity.

Now, $X_L = 2\pi fL$ and $X_c = 1/2\pi fC$
so if $X_L = X_c$
then, $2\pi fL = 1/2\pi fC$
                          $f^2 = 1/4\pi^2 LC$
                          $f = 1/2\pi\sqrt{LC}$

This special frequency is called the *resonant frequency*. At the resonant frequency in the series circuit, the combination of

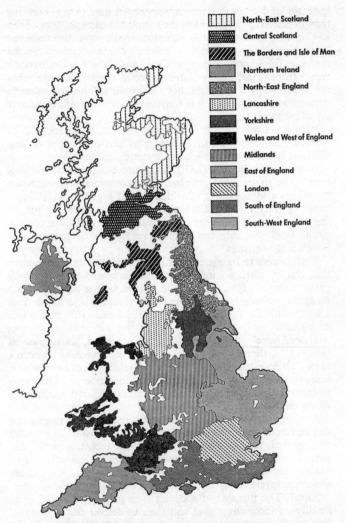

⦀⦀⦀	North-East Scotland
▨	Central Scotland
◤	The Borders and Isle of Man
▨	Northern Ireland
⦙⦙	North-East England
⦂	Lancashire
▨	Yorkshire
■	Wales and West of England
⦀	Midlands
▨	East of England
▨	London
▨	South of England
≡	South-West England

I.B.A. Television Transmission Areas

inductor and capacitor present no opposition to the current, though resistance in the wires does limit the current. The series *L–C* circuit is known as an acceptor circuit as, at the resonant frequency, the opposition to current is at a minimum. At the resonant frequency in the parallel circuit, the total current is zero. In practice, however, resistance in the wires means that the cancellation is not exact, but the circuit still has a maximum opposition to current at this frequency. It is therefore called a rejector circuit.

Because of this peculiar behaviour of series and parallel *L–C* circuits, they are used in *tuning* (q.v.) and other applications where it is necessary to pick out a particular frequency.

Integrated Circuit (I.C.) I.C.s are complete circuit elements (e.g. an amplifier), the individual components (transistors, capacitors and resistors) of which are all together on a single 'chip' of silicon. As individual containers for each component are not required and very little power is needed to make the circuit work, the chip can be made very small (up to 100 components per sq. mm.).

Intermediate Frequency (I.F.) This is the fixed frequency that results when an incoming signal is mixed with a locally generated oscillation. The I.F. in Britain for the *superhet* (q.v.) reception of long waves and medium waves is 470 kc/s. The I.F. for B.B.C. V.H.F. frequency modulation programmes is 10·7 Mc/s.

Ionosphere High above the earth's surface, starting at 70 miles or so, there are deep layers of gas electrified by the sun's rays. These electrified atoms and molecules affect radio waves and are known under the general term 'ionosphere'. The ionosphere varies daily and seasonally and according to the behaviour of the sun.

Medium waves are reflected from its lowest layers during the day and from higher layers at night (when the lowest layers have disappeared, this giving good intensity of reception some distance away). Short waves are reflected from the ionosphere and enable long-distance communication to take place. Very short waves penetrate the ionosphere and are lost.

Load The purpose of a circuit is to generate a signal or to modify an incoming signal and then to deliver the new signal into another apparatus known as the load. The load takes energy from the circuit that 'drives' it and the nature of the load (e.g.

its impedance) alters the behaviour of the circuit. The load for an audio amplifier is usually a loudspeaker, and that for a radio transmitter is an *aerial* (q.v.).

Loudspeaker A device for turning electrical variations into variations of air pressure that reach the ears. There is commercially only one widely-used type—the moving-coil loudspeaker. In this a magnet, usually a permanent magnet, has an annular gap. On this gap floats a tiny light coil of fine wire. This moves according to the current flowing through it.

For an ordinary commercial loudspeaker the ability of the loudspeaker is usually restricted to about a range of 100–5,000 cycles per second. By special construction a loudspeaker can be made to cover a wider range than this, and a combination of loudspeakers can be made to cover from 30 to 15,000 cycles per second.

The loudspeaker is, of course, the final stage of a sound-radio receiver or the audio part of a television receiver.

Magnetic Field A region of space in which a magnet experiences a turning force (couple). Magnetic fields are produced by permanent magnets and electric currents.

Magnetometer An instrument for measuring the intensity of a magnetic field.

Maser A device for the amplification of electromagnetic waves. Used in radioastronomy for amplifying the very small signals received from distant radio galaxies, and for picking up the signals received from communications satellites.

Measuring Instruments To measure current an ammeter (milliammeter, microammeter) is used. For voltage (e.m.f., potential difference) a voltmeter is used. For resistance it is an ohmmeter that is required.

Microelectronics Microelectronics is concerned with the miniaturisation of electronic circuits. This is achieved by use of *integrated circuits* (q.v.) and *printed circuits* (q.v.), which enable complicated circuits (as in computers) to be kept to a very small size.

Microphone An apparatus for changing pressure waves in air (sound) into electrical variations. There are several sorts, such as the crystal microphone, the ribbon microphone, the moving-coil microphone, etc.

Microwave An electromagnetic wave with a wavelength between fifty and one-fiftieth of a centimetre.

Modulation This is the term for changing a carrier wave in such a way that it has with it the audio-frequency variations corresponding to speech or music. *Amplitude modulation* (q.v.) occurs when a carrier increases and decreases in amplitude. *Frequency modulation* (q.v.) occurs when a carrier varies in *frequency* according to the amplitude of the current from the microphone.

For reception of radio-telephony the modulation must be separated from the carrier. This is usually called *detection* (q.v.), but is sometimes called demodulation.

Molniyas The name given to the first series of Russian communications satellites.

Noise In electronic equipment, noise is unwanted hissing, humming and crackling heard as a background to the wanted signal. Noise may be generated by the equipment itself (for instance due to the random thermal motions of electrons), and this is particularly troublesome in high frequency circuits carrying small signals. An important factor in such circuits is therefore the *signal-to-noise ratio* which needs to be large if the noise is not going to swamp the signal. Noise may also be picked up from outside sources, e.g. mains *hum* (q.v.) and 'atmospherics' in radio receivers.

Ohm's Law The most important law of simple electrical circuits. It states simply that one electric current is directly proportional to the applied e.m.f. That is

$$I = \frac{E}{R}$$

where I = current; E = e.m.f.; R = resistance.

From this relationship come all the laws of elementary electrical circuits.

Oscillation An oscillation is one complete cycle of a regularly varying quantity. See *frequency*.

Oscillator An electronic circuit designed to generate continuous *oscillations* (q.v.). This is usually achieved by connecting an *inductance–capacitance circuit* (q.v.) to a valve or transistor amplifier and arranging positive *feedback* (q.v.) to keep the oscillations going. The *frequency* (q.v.) of the oscillations depends on the values of capacitance and inductance in the $L–C$ circuit. Oscillators have numerous uses e.g. to generate the *carrier wave* (q.v.) needed to transmit radio signals.

Parallel A method of connecting circuit components. If components have ends ab, a_1b_1 a_2b_2, etc., then they are connected in parallel if all the *a*'s are joined together and all the *b*'s joined together. If electric cells of the same e.m.f. are joined in parallel, the total e.m.f. is that of any one of them but greater power is available from cells connected in this way. The diagram shows how to calculate the resultant resistance (or capacitance) when resistors (or capacitors) are connected in parallel. See *series*.

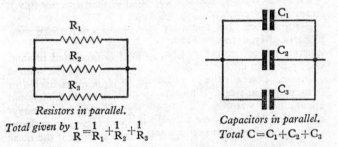

Resistors in parallel.
Total given by $\dfrac{1}{R} = \dfrac{1}{R_1} + \dfrac{1}{R_2} + \dfrac{1}{R_3}$

Capacitors in parallel.
Total $C = C_1 + C_2 + C_3$

Phase This is a term which describes the time relationship of two oscillatory currents or waves of the same *frequency* (q.v.). If both are zero together, increase to their maximum positive together and subsequently remain in step, the two oscillations are said to be *in phase*. If, when oscillation (a) is at its maximum positive, oscillation (b) is zero, then (b) is said to be 90° *out of phase* with (a). The diagram shows the case of (b) *lagging* (a) by 90° (or equivalently (a) *leading* (b) by 90°) because when (a) is at

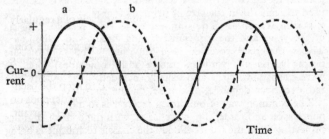

Two oscillations out of phase by 90° or one quarter of a cycle;
(b) 'lags' on (a)

its maximum positive, (b) is zero but increasing towards its maximum positive. If when (a) is at its maximum positive, (b) is at its maximum negative, then (a) and (b) are said to be *180° out of phase* and if combined would cancel each other out completely provided they were of the same magnitude. A phase difference of 360° means that the oscillations are again in phase as an oscillation merely repeats itself every 360°.

Piezoelectricity Electric current produced by mechanical stimulation of crystals.

p–n junction The boundary between a piece of *n*–type and a piece of *p*–type *semiconductor* (q.v.). (See *doping*). The *p–n* junction has the property of *rectification* (q.v.), and is therefore widely used in *diodes* (q.v.).

Power Power is the rate of doing work or using energy and is measured in *watts*. The rate of work done by an electrical apparatus in watts is equal to the voltage across it (in volts) multiplied by the current through it (in amps).

Prefixes Standard prefixes are:

$$p = \text{1 million-millionth} = \text{pica, e.g. 2 picafarads, 2 pF}$$
$$n = \text{1 thousand millionth} = \text{nano, e.g. 4 nanoseconds, 4 ns}$$
$$\mu = \text{1 millionth} = \text{micro, e.g. 3 microamperes, } 3\mu\text{A}$$
$$m = \text{1 thousandth} = \text{milli, e.g. 6 milliamperes, 6 mA}$$
$$k = \text{1 thousand} = \text{kilo, e.g. 10 kilovolts, 10 kV}$$
$$M = \text{1 million} = \text{mega, e.g. 10 megacycles, 10 Mc/s}$$

Printed Circuit This is an insulating board with a layer of copper on one side. The copper is dissolved away except along protected paths which then act as connections between components mounted on the board. Photographic methods are often used to scale down the size of printed circuits.

Radio Receiver The simplest valve radio receiver consists of the valve and the associated tuning circuit and telephones. The commercial receiver is a superhet. The controls are normally: on–off, volume, tuning and (sometimes) tone. A wave–change switch is also usually included. The quality of a radio receiver depends, of course, on the circuitry.

The common way of building a receiver is to mount the components on and under a metal chassis, with the control spindles projecting from the front. Today the chassis technique is being replaced by a board on which connections are printed, i.e. a *printed circuit* (q.v.).

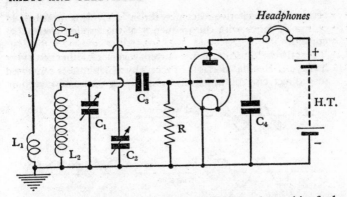

A one-valve receiver for medium-wave reception, using positive feed-back (reaction) *via* L_3 to increase the sensitivity. $C_1 = C_2 = 0.0005\mu F$ max; $C_3 = 0.0003\,\mu F$; $C_4 = 0.001\,\mu F$; $R = 2M\Omega$. Coils wound with No 28 D.C.C. wire on 2 in. diameter cylinder, $L_1 = 15$ turns, $L_2 = 75$ turns, $L_3 = 40$ turns. L_1 is spaced from L_2 with matchsticks and wound over it

Radio Waves in Use

Names commonly used

Frequency	Wave-lengths	Wavelength range	Frequency range
Low frequency	Long waves	Above 600 m.	Below 500 kc/s
Medium frequency	Medium waves	200–600 m.	500–1,500 kc/s
High frequency	Short waves	10–80 m.	3,750 kc/s to 30 Mc/s
V.H.F. Very-high frequency	Ultra-short waves	Band I 4·41–7·32 m.	41–68 Mc/s
		Band II 3–3·43 m.	87·5–100 Mc/s
		Band III 1·39–1·72 m.	174–216 Mc/s
U.H.F. Ultra-high frequency		Band IV 51–63 cm.	475–585 Mc/s
		Band V 31–49 cm.	610–960 Mc/s
	Micro-waves	7·5 mm.–15 cm. Divided into several bands—S Band, X Band, J Band, etc.	2,000–40,000 Mc/s

Reactance (X) This is the term for the effect of capacitance or inductance in cutting down current. It is given the symbol X, usually with suffixes L and C to denote whether it is inductive reactance or capacitative reactance, thus X_L, X_C. It is measured in ohms. It varies with the frequency of the applied alternating current.

Rectification Alternating current reverses its direction every half cycle. Rectification is the process by which A.C. is converted to a direct current which always flows in the same direction.

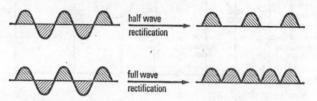

half wave
rectification

full wave
rectification

This is achieved by the use of rectifiers or *diodes* (q.v.) which allow current to pass through them in one direction only. In the *half wave* rectifier the $-ve$ half of the cycle is simply suppressed, while in the *full wave* rectifier, the $-ve$ half of the cycle is inverted so as to flow in the desired direction.

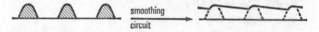

smoothing
circuit

Rectification is very important because the mains supply is A.C. while most electronic circuits need a D.C. supply. However to be suitable, the rectified supply has to be *smoothed* so that the voltage is nearly constant.

Resistance This is the tendency for all materials to oppose the flow of an electric current and to convert electrical energy into heat. It is measured in ohms and the resistance of a conductor depends, in simple cases, on the *resistivity* (q.v.) of the material and the dimensions of the conductor. A resistance of R ohms carrying a current of I amps converts electrical energy into heat at the rate of I^2R watts.

Resistivity This is the resistance (measured in microhms) of a cubic centimetre of material, and is a measure of how badly the material conducts electricity. The reciprocal of resistivity is *conductivity*, a measure of how well a material conducts electricity. Copper and other metals are good conductors, with a low resistivity which increases with temperature. Glass and plastics are insulators with a very high resistivity. Between these limits lie *semiconductors* (q.v.).

RESISTIVITIES

Resistivity

Aluminium	.	2·82	Amber .	.	5×10^{16}
Brass .	.	About 8	Celluloid	.	2×10^{10}
Copper	.	1·72	Plate glass	.	2×10^{13}
Iron .	.	9·8	Mica (clear)	.	4×10^{16}
Magnesium	.	4·46	Paraffin wax	.	3×10^{18}
Nichrome	.	About 100			
Nickel .	.	7·24			
Steel, hardened	.	About 45			
Tin .	.	11·4			

Resistor An electronic component used in a circuit to provide a known *resistance* (q.v.). Both fixed and variable resistors are very widely used.

Resonance When an *inductance–capacitance circuit* (q.v.) responds at a maximum to one frequency only, it is said to be in resonance with a signal of that frequency. *Tuning* (q.v.) consists of selecting the point of resonance.

Root-mean-square (R.M.S.) The average value of a quantity that takes positive and negative values equally (e.g. an alternating current) is zero. If the values are squared, the mean found and then the square root taken, the non-zero result is called the R.M.S. value. Because the heating effect of an electric current depends on the square of the current, the R.M.S. of an A.C. is equal to the constant D.C. needed to produce the same heating effect as the A.C. The peak value (or amplitude) of an A.C. is $\sqrt{2} = 1·414$ times the R.M.S. value.

Scanning The traversing of a scene or screen by a spot of light in an orderly fashion. It is scanning in successive lines in a very short time that allows a scene to be turned into electrical variations by a television camera and then into a pattern of light on a television-receiver screen.

Selectivity The ability of a radio receiver to tune to one radio station without interference from stations with nearby wavelengths.

Semiconductor A material whose *resistivity* (q.v.) is much higher than that of metals but much less than that of insulators. E.g. the elements germanium, silicon and selenium and the compounds copper oxide and indium antiminide. Semiconductors have three special electrical properties which make them very useful. (a) Unlike metals, the conductivity of semiconductors can be increased by the addition of small quantities of impurities. This is called *doping* (q.v.), and is the basis behind all modern semiconductor devices such as the *transistor* (q.v.). (b) Some semiconductors (notably selenium) increase their conductivity if light is shined on them. This is useful in photocells and in copying by the process of *xerography*. (c) Over some temperature ranges, semiconductors increase their conductivity very fast with increasing temperature, and can therefore be used where sensitivity to temperature is needed.

Series A method of connecting circuit components such that they are joined end to end. The current through each component is therefore the same, though the voltage across each will differ.

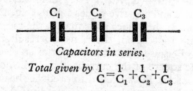

Resistors in series. Total $R = R_1 + R_2 + R_3$

Capacitors in series.

Total given by $\dfrac{1}{C} = \dfrac{1}{C_1} + \dfrac{1}{C_2} + \dfrac{1}{C_3}$

The diagram shows how to work out the total resistance (capacitance) when resistors (capacitors) are connected in series. See *parallel*.

Sky Ray Radio waves going out into space and not following the ground.

Sound Sound is the sensation felt when our ears pick up pressure waves (i.e. sound waves) transmitted through a gas or other fluid from a vibrating source (e.g. a violin string). Sound waves through a gas consist of alternate compressions and rarefactions of the gas travelling along at the speed of sound. This is 332 metres per second or 760 miles an hour in air. The *pitch* of sound heard depends directly on the *frequency* (q.v.) of vibration of the source. Thus the note middle C corresponds to a

frequency of vibration 256 cycles per second. The octave higher
is always double the frequency.

Music and speech are built up from a large number of simple
waves of different frequencies all mixed together. Even a single
note played on a violin, say, consists of a lowest frequency which
is called the *fundamental* (and corresponds to the pitch of the
note), as well as a number of higher frequencies present in lesser
strength. These are called *harmonics* and they determine the
tone or quality of the note heard. This is why audio equipment
sensitive to frequencies up to 15,000 cycles per second is needed
for the faithful reproduction of sound.

Superhet The superheterodyne receiver. This is the
common commercial type for sound and television. It enables
high *selectivity* (q.v.) suitable for today's overcrowded air to be
obtained without too much loss of quality.

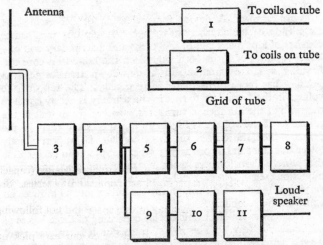

BLOCK DIAGRAM OF SUPERHET TELEVISION RECEIVER: 1. Frame Time
Base. 2. Line Time Base. 3. R.F. Amplifier. 4. Frequency Changer.
5. I.F. Amplifier. 6. Video Detector. 7. Video Amplifier. 8. Sync.
Separator. 9. I.F. Amplifier. 10. Audio Detector. 11. Audio Amplifier

The principle is to mix two oscillations together in a frequency-changer in such a way that no matter what the frequency
of the incoming signal is, the outgoing frequency from the

frequency-changer is always the same, the *intermediate frequency* (q.v.). At this fixed frequency it is comparatively easy to make satisfactory band-pass filters and transformers.

Symbols For the mathematical treatment of current, e.m.f., etc., symbols in the form of letters are used:

λ = lambda = wavelength
n or f = frequency
v = velocity
R = resistance
I = current
E = e.m.f.
R_a = A.C. resistance of valve

μ = mu = amplification factor of valve, sometimes written m.
g = mutual conductance of valve
L = inductance
C = capacitance

Telstar The first television satellite, orbited by the United States.

Transformer A device for increasing or decreasing the magnitude of an alternating voltage. A step-up transformer consists of a primary coil of few turns and a secondary coil of a larger number of turns both wound on the same iron core but forming separate circuits. In a step-down transformer the primary has more turns than the secondary. The ratio of the voltage in the secondary to that in the primary is nearly equal to the ratio of the number of turns in the secondary to that in the primary. If the voltage is higher in the secondary than in the primary then the current in the secondary is proportionately lower than that in the primary, so that the power in each coil is the same. Transformers work by means of electromagnetic induction (see *inductance*). The A.C. in the primary produces a varying magnetic field through the secondary and so induces an e.m.f. in the secondary.

Transistor An electronic device consisting of three layers of *semiconductor* (q.v.). The *n–p–n* transistor has two layers of *n*–type semiconductor sandwiching a layer of *p*–type, and the *p–n–p* transistor has two layers of *p*–type sandwiching one of *n*–type (see DOPING). In either case, the middle layer is called the *base* and the outer layers are called the *collector* and *emitter*. The transistor is principally used as an amplifier, since a small current flowing in the base–emitter circuit can be used to control a much larger current in the emitter–collector circuit.

The transistor was invented in 1948 and since then has rapidly been replacing the *valve* (q.v.) in electronic circuits. The advantage of using transistors is that they can be made very small and reliable since they do not require the vacuum tube, the heater or the high voltage power supply necessary for valves.

Triode A thermionic valve with three electrodes—cathode, grid, anode.

Tuning In a radio receiver the frequency of the radio station heard is determined by the resonant frequency of an *inductance-capacitance circuit* (q.v.). By varying the capacitance in the circuit, the resonant frequency is changed and so different stations can be selected. See RESONANCE.

Valve (Thermionic Valve) This is an evacuated glass bulb containing a cathode, an anode and from zero to four other electrodes called grids. The cathode is heated (usually by a separate heating filament) and emits electrons. These electrons will only be attracted to the anode if it has a positive voltage with respect to the cathode, otherwise they will be repelled and no current will flow. Thus the simple two-electrode valve (the diode) can be used for *rectification* (q.v.). The triode valve has a perforated grid between the anode and cathode. The voltage applied to the grid now controls the electron flow between the cathode and anode. But because the grid is much closer to the cathode than the anode, small changes in the grid voltage bring about the same change in the cathode–anode current as much larger changes in the anode voltage. Hence amplification of voltages can be achieved, the amplification factor μ being the ratio of the change in anode voltage to the change in grid voltage to bring about the same change in cathode–anode current. More grids can be added to give tetrodes, pentodes etc. for special purposes. See GRID BIAS.

Video The word indicating the vision side of a television signal.

Watt (*W*) The S.I. unit of electrical *power* (q.v.).

FURTHER READING

A Dictionary of Electronics (Penguin)

Transistors Applied, by H. E. Kaden (Philips)

Electronic computers, by S. H. Hollingwood and G. C. Totill (Pelican)

Physics of Semi Conductors, by J. D. Suchet (Van Nostand)

The Annual Register of World Events (Longmans) (For information about progress in world-wide communications, year by year).

Radio Communication Handbook (The Radio Society of Great Britain)

A Dictionary of Aircraft, Rockets and Missiles

(with a section on Astronomy)

Astronomy   38-44

Abbreviations

A.P.U.	Auxiliary Power Unit
A.S.I.	Airspeed Indicator
A.T.C.	Air Traffic Control
C.A.A.	Civil Aviation Authority
D.F.	Direction Finder
E.A.S.	Equivalent Air Speed
F.A.A.	Federal Aviation Agency (U.S.A.)
F.A.I.	Fédération Aeronautique Internationale
I.A.S.	Indicated Air Speed
I.C.A.O.	International Civil Aviation Organisation
I.L.S.	Instrument Landing System
R.A.E.	Royal Aircraft Establishment
R.Ae.C.	Royal Aero Club
R. Ae.S.	Royal Aeronautical Society
R/T	Radio-telephony
S.B.A.C.	Society of British Aerospace Companies
T.A.S.	True Air Speed
V.F.R.	Visual Flight Rules
V.O.R.	V.H.F. Omni-range Beacon
V.T.O.L.	Vertical Take-off and Landing (q.v.)

Aerofoil The geometry of a section through a wing, rotor blade or tailplane so shaped that it can contribute lift.

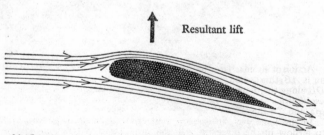

Resultant lift

Air flow over an aerofoil surface, caused by forward motion of the aerofoil, results in a reduction of pressure above the upper surface and a slight increase of pressure beneath. Thus there is a resultant lift at right-angles to the direction of the air flow.

F2

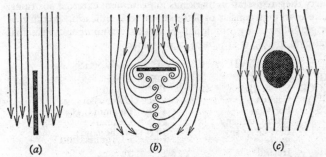

Air action on a flat plate and a stream-lined obstacle. In (*a*) the plate is edge-on and the air flows smoothly past. In (*b*) the plate is face-on and a large area of low pressure and turbulence is produced, slowing down the air. In (*c*) a crudely stream-lined object allows the air to flow round the surface.

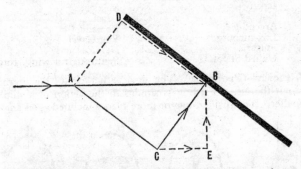

Action of air on a flat plate drawn forward. If the pressure due to the air is *AB*, this can be resolved into *CB*, at right-angles to the plate, and *DB* along the plate. *CB* can be resolved into *EB at right-angles to the air direction* and *CE* in the same direction as the air. *EB* represents the *lift*, and *CE* the *drag*.

In the same way, an aerofoil inclined at an angle of attack *DBA* to airflow in the direction *AB* will produce lift *EB* which will be additional to the lift already produced by its cambered upper surface.

Aircraft Markings All civil aircraft must be registered and carry their registration markings in prominent external positions. The markings consist of letters/numbers indicating country of origin followed by individual aircraft letters/numbers. Principal national markings are given in the table.

CIVIL AIRCRAFT MARKINGS

AP	Pakistan	OE	Austria
CCCP	Soviet Union	OH	Finland
CF	Canada	OK	Czechoslovakia
CS	Portugal	OO	Belgium
D	West Germany	OY	Denmark
DM	East Germany	PH	Netherlands
EC	Spain	PP	Brazil
EI	Ireland	SE	Sweden
ET	Ethiopia	SP	Poland
F	France	SU	Egypt
G	United Kingdom	SX	Greece
9G	Ghana	TC	Turkey
HA	Hungary	TF	Iceland
HB	Switzerland	VH	Australia
I	Italy	VT	India
JA	Japan	XA	Mexico
LN	Norway	4X	Israel
LV	Argentine	YR	Romania
LX	Luxembourg	YU	Yugoslavia
LZ	Bulgaria	ZK	New Zealand
N	United States	ZS	South Africa

Airscrew (Propeller) The device that draws an aircraft through the air. Its action is similar to the action of a ship's propeller. It consists of two or more blades inclined at an angle

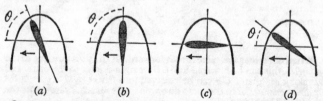

(a)   *(b)*   *(c)*   *(d)*

Section of propeller blade end-on, looking towards the hub. The angle between the line of the blade and the transverse axis of the hub is a measure of the pitch. The pitch is coarser in *(a)* than in *(d)*. In *(b)* it is coarsest and the propeller is said to be feathered. In *(c)* there is no pitch at all and the propeller achieves nothing. The arrow in each case indicates the direction in which the blade-section is supposed to be travelling for the hub to be going forward.

to the axis. In rotation the speed of the tip of a blade is greater than that of a part nearer the hub. This makes the resultant direction of air, due to the combination of forward aircraft speed and propeller rotation, change all the way along the blade. To remedy this to some extent the blade is twisted so that the tip is nearer position (c) in the diagram than the root, which may be in position (d).

As the forward speed of an aircraft changes so does the efficiency of the propeller. The higher the forward speed, the coarser should be the propeller pitch. Propellers are therefore made so that the pitch can be varied by the pilot to suit the conditions and are known as variable-pitch propellers.

Air-speed Indicator Speed through the air increases the pressure on the front. A small tube directed into the air, called a Pitot tube, can be used to direct the air-stream to a pressure-measuring device. At the same time a closed tube with holes in its sides can be used to measure the static atmospheric pressure. The difference between the two is an indication of air-speed.

Altimeter The normal height-measuring instrument is an aneroid barometer. As the atmospheric pressure decreases with height above the earth's surface, the decrease can be used as an indication of height. The drop is approximately 1 in. on the barometer for 1,000 ft. up to about 5,000 ft. Such an altimeter measures only height above sea-level, and the zero must be adjusted to suit prevailing conditions.

The radio altimeter relies on the reflection of radio signals to give the true height above the actual ground being flown over.

Artificial Horizon An instrument to assist a pilot flying blind to know when he is flying on an even keel. It depends on a gyroscope to maintain a picture of an aircraft in a horizontal position between two horizontal lines. As the aircraft changes its attitude so the picture changes.

Atmosphere The layer of gas round the earth. It consists chiefly of oxygen and nitrogen, but there are also small quantities of other gases, such as carbon dioxide, argon, helium, etc.

The pressure of the atmosphere is greatest at sea-level. It gets less and less the farther one goes away from the earth, but not in direct proportion to the height. The temperature also gets less with height up to about 36,000 ft., when it reaches $-57°$ C. and stays at this. This level is called the tropopause. Below it is the troposphere. Above it is the stratosphere.

The atmosphere is not a gas with constant characteristics. So a *standard atmosphere* has been agreed on internationally. Figures for height records, etc., must be reduced to the standard conditions. The pressure at sea-level of this standard atmosphere is 14·7 lb./square in. or 29·75 in. of mercury. The temperature is taken as 59° F. or 15° C.

THE STANDARD ATMOSPHERE

Altitude (ft.)	Pressure (lb./in.²)	Temperature (° C.)
100,000	0·152	
90,000	0·245	
80,000	0·397	Ambient temperature
70,000	0·642	remains constant
60,000	1·038	above 36,000 ft.
50,000	1·679	
40,000	2·717	
35,000	3·455	−54·342
30,000	4·361	−44·436
25,000	5·450	−34·530
20,000	6·750	−24·624
15,000	8·291	−14·718
10,000	10·104	−4·812
8,000	10·913	−0·850
5,000	12·226	5·094
4,000	12·691	7·075
3,000	13·170	9·056
2,000	13·664	11·038
1,000	14·172	13·019
Sea-level	14·696	15·000

(lb./in² = pounds to the square inch)

Autogiro The trade name for a type of rotating-wing aircraft invented by Juan de la Cierva. The wing or rotor is not driven by an engine.

Automatic Pilot A device whereby an aircraft will fly automatically on an even keel on a prescribed course without the attention of the pilot. Any roll or yaw or pitch or change in direction is indicated by the instruments, and signals are sent by servo mechanisms to make the necessary change to rudder or elevator.

More elaborate automatic pilots can also maintain a rate of climb or descent or a constant height.

Ballistic Missiles See MISSILES.

Boundary Layer The layer of air close to the surface of an aerofoil. It is very thin. The airflow at the leading edge is usually laminar, i.e. parallel to the surface, but farther back it is broken up and the resulting turbulence produces drag. Several attempts have been made to avoid this, one important one being an arrangement for sucking in air through surface holes in the aerofoil.

British Aircraft Manufacturers

Aviation Traders (Engineering) Ltd
British Aircraft Corporation Ltd with factories at Bristol; Preston; Stevenage; Weybridge; and Hurn, near Bournemouth
Britten-Norman (Bembridge) Ltd (Member of the Fairey Group)
Campbell Aircraft Ltd
Cierva Rotorcraft Ltd
Crosby Aviation Ltd
W. H. Ekin (Engineering) Co Ltd
Hawker Siddeley Aviation Ltd with principal factories at Bitteswell; Brough; Chester; Hamble; Hatfield; Kingston-upon-Thames; and Woodford
Nipper Kits and Components Ltd
Rollason Aircraft and Engines Ltd
Scottish Aviation Ltd
Short Brothers & Harland Ltd
Wallis Autogyros Ltd
Westland Aircraft Ltd

Consol A long-range navigational aid capable of use over 1,000 miles of sea or 700 miles of land by day, more at night.

It is worked by the erection of five permanent beacons sending out signals of dots and dashes on medium frequencies—in the range of 950–1,150 m. These five are in Bushmills (Northern Ireland), Plonéis (France), Stavanger (Norway), Lugo (Spain), Seville (Spain). All but the last work 24 hours a day. Tables and charts are issued to give the true bearings of any signal according to the number of dots (or dashes) heard before what is called the equi-signal. The charts at present are for the Arctic, Rockall, British Isles, Reykjavik, Azores, Lisbon–Berne.

The air navigator has merely to tune in to the correct wavelength, count the dots or dashes, look up his chart or table and so get a direction line. Two such direction lines, for two of the transmitting beacons, will give him a fix.

Decca Navigator A navigation aid for ships and aircraft relying on ground stations transmitting signals on low frequencies (the range goes from 70 to 130 kc/s). Any one Decca chain has four ground transmitters, all controlled by one of them, the master, so that signals shall be sent out in phase from each transmitter. The three 'slaves' are called purple, green and red.

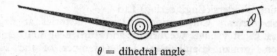

θ = dihedral angle

Curved lines on a chart indicate where two signals from the master and one 'slave' are in phase. There are three systems of lines—purple, green and red. The aircraft getting a red 'in-phase' signal knows that it is on one of the red lines. A 'green' or 'purple' in-phase signal shows that the aircraft is either on a green line or a purple line. Where two lines cross is the position. The radio receiver also assesses how much out of phase two signals are, and thus gives positions not limited to the lines. A pen automatically marks the position on a moving chart. So the track of the aircraft is visible all the time to its navigator.

There are 12 Decca chains in Europe, 4 in Canada, 1 in the United States, 1 in Japan, 2 in India and 2 in the Persian Gulf.

Dectra is a long-range adaptation of the system for long haul flight such as on the North Atlantic route. There are refinements and variations for this purpose such as the provision of additional range information.

Delta Wing A wing planform which forms the shape of a triangle. It has many of the aerodynamic advantages of a swept-back wing but is structurally more efficient.

Dihedral Angle The angle between the wing and the horizontal, looking head-on at the aircraft. Most aircraft have some dihedral angle which tends to stabilise roll.

Drag The force resisting the motion of an aircraft through the air. It can be broken down into two parts: induced drag caused inevitably with lift (q.v.) by the pressure differences over the wing: and parasitic drag caused by turbulence (q.v.)

due to roughness of the skin, interference of airflow round different parts of the aeroplane, projections such as aerials, radomes, cockpits.

Escape Velocity The velocity that a body must have to get away from the gravitational pull of earth. It is given by the equation

$$V = \sqrt{2gR}$$

where R = distance from centre of earth; g = acceleration due to gravity at distance R.

For ordinary purposes the escape velocity from the earth is taken as about 7 miles a second or 11·2 km. a second. At this velocity a projectile will follow a parabolic course and never return to earth.

Free Fall The state of non-resistance to a gravitational field. This happens with a body falling towards the earth before it enters the earth's atmosphere. It happens with a satellite in orbit. A passenger inside a vehicle in free fall has the sensation of being weightless, because the vehicle is not resisting the gravitational field. Anyone falling from a height towards the ground feels the air resistance and so is not exactly in free fall, though nearly so. In the 'weightless' condition a man jumping up will hit the ceiling. He will have no sense of balance. Men can experience this state for a few seconds only in an aircraft making a loop when the speed is enough for centrifugal force to balance the earth's gravitational force. Crews have been weightless for much longer periods in manned space vehicles.

Fuels For rockets see under PROPELLANT.

Petrol is used in piston engines, but gas turbines (jet engines, turboprops, turbofans) burn a kerosene or paraffin-based fuel.

g The acceleration due to gravity, which on the surface of the earth is taken as roughly 32 ft. per sec. per sec. or 981 cm. per sec. per sec. It is also taken as a unit of acceleration for discussions of the forces acting on rockets and airmen and astronauts. An airman, for example, flying at 500 m.p.h. along a curved path of 1 mile radius would experience a centrifugal force equivalent to an acceleration of 5 g.

Gas Turbine See JET PROPULSION.

Gravity The force of attraction between bodies according to the law of gravitation, which states that any two bodies in the universe attract each other with a force that is directly proportional to the product of the masses and inversely proportional to the square of the distance between them. That is

$$\text{Force} = \frac{km_1m_2}{d^2}$$

k is the gravitational constant $= 6 \cdot 67 \times 10^{-8}$ in c.g.s. units.

Calculation from this shows that the acceleration due to gravity (g) at the earth's surface is about 32 ft. per sec. per sec. This varies, however, with geographical position, and gets very much less with height above the earth's surface.

Guided Missiles See MISSILES.

Gyroscope Used in many navigational instruments in aircraft and ships. It consists essentially of a heavy wheel spun by an electric motor or a turbine and rotating at high speed. It has two properties: (i) if it is supported in frictionless gimbals so that it can rotate freely in all three dimensions, it will remain parallel to its original position, i.e. it has 'rigidity in space': (ii) if it is not supported in gimbals but is made to turn it will *precess* and exert a force proportional to the rate of turn—a measure of the force being a measure of the rate of turn. This is used, for example, to correct gunsights for the movement of the aircraft.

Both these properties can be combined: if a gyro is held in one direction in its gimbals so that it has to turn with the earth it will precess until it points North and the N–S axis of the earth's rotation is parallel to its own axis. It will then continue to point North, and can be used as a genuine compass.

Heat Barrier Currently a major problem in the advance of aircraft speeds. At sufficiently high speeds the kinetic energy of the air flowing past the aircraft is turned into appreciable heat energy, and the temperature of the aircraft skin at Mach 3 can reach the melting point of steel. Aircraft to travel at these speeds therefore must be made of heat-resisting materials, and the crew, passengers and electronic gear must be refrigerated.

Helicopter This is an aircraft that can rise vertically by the use of rotating wings. These wings, very long and narrow, are aerofoils, and constitute the rotor. When this is in action the lift provided by the passage of the blades through the air propels the aircraft vertically. The engine-power has to be enough to provide lift for the whole weight of the aircraft.

For forward movement the plane of the rotor is tilted down-

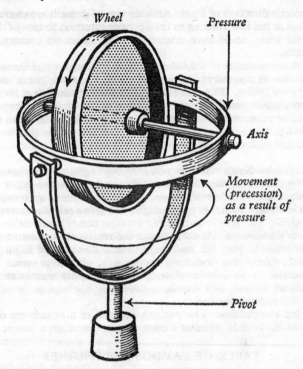

Wheel

Pressure

Axis

Movement (precession) as a result of pressure

Pivot

A gyro in gimbals. Pressure on the axis makes the whole support move round. If this pressure is supplied by a weight that points towards the centre of the earth the axis will always point in the same direction in relation to the earth.

ward in front. This is achieved by altering the pitch of the rotor blades so that as each passes through the rear part of the rotation its pitch is increased and as it passes through the front part of the rotation its pitch is decreased. The unequal thrusts tilt the machine downwards and forwards.

As the helicopter body is free to rotate it tends to go round in the opposite direction to that of the rotor. To overcome this in the classic helicopter type a tail rotor is fixed on one side. The pitch of this can be varied to give control for turning the heli-

copter's direction of flight. Another way of doing it is to have a
rotor at the rear rotating in the opposite direction to that of the
front rotor, or to have counter-rotating rotors on concentric
shafts.

A development of the helicopter is that using normal forward
engines as propellers for forward flight, the rotor being used
only for lifting. This was the method used in the Fairey Roto-
dyne, which could go from city-centre to city-centre carrying a
load of passengers (the biggest of ordinary helicopters takes no
more than a couple of dozen passengers) at a speed roughly comparable with that of twin-engined airliners current at that time.

Inertial Navigation A system of dead reckoning navigation
independent of outside sources. It depends on two types of
instrument—accelerometers and gyroscopes. Three gyroscopes
set in three directions at right angles will give a reference system
in space. The accelerometers tell the direction of acceleration in
three dimensions. As they change the results are calculated by
computer to give the true position and direction of flight in
space. Air-speed indicators, compasses, altimeters—none is
essential to an inertial system. Until recently restricted to
military aircraft and missile applications, the system is now
in full scale airline use.

Jet Propulsion The pushing forward of a vehicle by the
rapid backwards efflux of a mass of gas. In effect, a rocket is

TABLE OF FAMOUS JET ENGINES

Makers	Name	Maximum thrust (lb.)
Rolls-Royce	Spey (military) RB.168–25R	12,250 (dry)
	RB.211–524	48,000
Rolls-Royce Bristol	Viper 600	3,750
	Olympus 593	38,050 (dry)
	Pegasus 11	21,500
Pratt & Whitney	JT8D–15	15,500
	JT9D–20	49,400
U.S. General Electric	TF39	41,100
	CF6–50A	49,000
	F101	30,000
U.S.S.R.	Kuznetsov NK–8–4	22,270
	Kuznetsov NK–144	28,660
	Soloviev D–30KU	25,350

working by jet, but the expression is usually restricted to the gas turbine. The first jet engine was built by Sir Frank Whittle at the beginning of the last war, and flew in the Gloster E28/39 experimental jet aircraft in 1941.

The gas turbine works by sucking air in at the front, compressing it, mixing vaporised fuel—usually paraffin—with it, igniting the mixture, making the burning gases flow through a turbine to drive the compressor by a shaft, and letting them escape in a jet to drive the aircraft. In most large modern gas turbines the compressor and turbine are *axial*: that is, they consist of many small blades set on a drum moving in between stationary blades mounted on a closely-fitted casing. Small gas turbines have a centrifugal compressor. In a ramjet the forward motion of the engine is used to compress the incoming air sufficiently for combustion to take place. This can happen only at very high speeds—about three times the speed of sound.

Lift Vertical force due to the flow of air round an aerofoil. Three-quarters of it, roughly speaking, is composed of suction due to low pressure on the upper surface of the aerofoil: the other quarter is due to pressure underneath. The lift increases with the *angle òf attack* (q.v.) until the aerofoil stalls.

Mach Number A number which relates the speed of an aircraft to the speed of sound in the same conditions. Mach 1, the speed of sound is taken as 1,094 ft. per sec. in air at NTP, so under the same conditions Mach 2 would be 2,188 ft. per sec. and Mach 3, 3,282 ft. per sec., and so on. Mach 1 is 761 m.p.h. at ground level but due to fall in pressure is only 660 m.p.h. at 36,000 ft. (tropopause).

Missiles Missiles are, of course, anything thrown, but today they almost invariably mean the powerful weapons that depend mainly on rocket-engines for their propulsion. They are classified into strategic and tactical; short, medium, intermediate or intercontinental in range; ballistic or guided; use, whether surface-to-air, air-to-air, etc.

Missiles as weapons are inextricably mixed up with space research, for the same basic missiles, without the warhead and modified electronically, serve to launch satellites.

Ballistic missiles are those that travel most of the way on a trajectory like that of any projectile. Guidance is used at first to set such a missile on course. Then the rocket burns out and the rest of the missile travels a natural course to target. They are classified as ICBM—intercontinental ballistic missile, and IRBM —intermediate-range ballistic missile.

Guided missiles are controlled for all or most of the way to their target. Some are guided all the way by radio signals from the ground. Others are steered by automatic celestial navigation, inertial systems or Doppler radio (which depends on a change of frequency when a source is approaching or receding) or radar. Missiles for short ranges at moving targets have homing devices, whether radar or the reception of radiation (radio or infra-red) from the target.

The number and naming of missiles has reached such a pitch that no list of missiles is worth giving, so soon are so many out of date. Mention may be made, however, of the U.S. Atlas, an ICBM of great range, the booster for several satellite launchings, and used for the first man-in-orbit scheme of the U.S.A.—Project Mercury, on February 20, 1962, when Colonel John H. Glenn completed three orbits and returned unharmed.

Navigation The method of steering a vehicle in a desired direction. In aircraft and ships the magnetic compass is used, but the gyro-compass (see GYROSCOPE) is more usual. Other methods of navigation depend on special radio techniques, such as the Decca Navigator (*q.v.*), or the Consol (*q.v.*), or on inertial systems (*q.v.*).

The basic methods are still those that sailors use—*dead reckoning* and *celestial*. The first depends on a record of courses, speeds and the estimated effect of wind to give a track from the place of departure to the estimated present position. The second uses observations of stars, the sun and moon to give an exact position. Neither of these is much use to a modern aircraft: the errors of dead reckoning, which in a ship or slow aeroplane were not too serious, are vast at high speeds: and the calculations of celestial navigation take so long that the position is irrelevant by the time it is found. Both systems have been mechanised: the first into the *inertial system* (q.v.), the second into a device which observes stars and calculates the aircraft's position instantaneously.

Orbit The name given to the closed path of a satellite round the earth or any body round any other. The earth is in orbit round the sun, the moon (and some artificial satellites) in orbit round the earth. Usually an orbit is an ellipse.

Propellant The name given to the materials used in rocket engines. They can be divided into two classes—liquid and solid, though the possibility of ionic propulsion and nuclear propulsion do not come into this division.

Liquid propellants consist mostly of a fuel and an oxidant. The fuel can be paraffin, petrol, alcohol, hydrazine, aniline or other liquid that can be oxidised to form enormous volumes of gas. The oxidant can be liquid oxygen, red fuming nitric acid, hydrogen peroxide, fluorine or any other yet to be announced. The V2 used on London during the Second World War was fuelled by liquid oxygen and alcohol.

There are a few single liquid propellants, even though chemically they are mixtures.

There are also solid fuels. The simplest is, of course, gunpowder. There is also cordite. Other solid fuels include: (*a*) J.P.N., a mixture of nitrocellulose, nitroglycerine, diethyl phthalate, carbamite, potassium sulphate, carbon and wax; (*b*) galcit, a mixture of potassium perchlorate and a fuel such as asphalt; (*c*) N.D.R.C., a mixture of ammonium picrate, sodium nitrate and resin.

Research continues for better and better fuels. Some are naturally kept secret even when discovered.

The 'goodness' of a propellant is measured as *specific impulse*, given by the equation

$$\text{Specific impulse} = \frac{\text{Thrust in pounds}}{\text{Rate of loss of mass in pounds}}$$

It is related to the exhaust velocity of gas by the equation

$$\text{Specific impulse} = \frac{\text{Exhaust velocity}}{g}$$

Propeller See AIRSCREW.

Radar A system of communication based on the transmission and reception of a radio wave broken into short groups called pulses. It was developed during the Second World War, first in Britain then in the U.S.A. Its earliest purpose was merely the detection of enemy aircraft.

The display is on the screen of a cathode-ray tube. In its simplest form this consists of a 'blip' on a horizontal line of light to indicate the departure of the signal and a second blip to indicate its return. The time between these is measurable on the screen, and as radio waves travel at 186,000 miles a second the distance of the reflecting object can be arrived at very quickly.

From this first elementary radar a whole system of remarkable developments has come. Today radar signals may be used to operate radio beacons that are triggered off only when they receive the signal, to produce complete 'map' pictures of the ground below, and so on.

The wavelength in the first radar was several metres, but since then systems using centimetric waves have given much greater precision.

Automatic viewing of the land below by radar is used for the navigation of some missiles.

An aircraft-approach aid depending on radar is G.C.A., ground controlled approach, now referred to as P.A.R., precision approach radar. The ground operator uses radar to see how far the aircraft deviates in azimuth and elevation from the correct approach path to the runway. From this information he can instruct the pilot by radio to make what corrections are needed to keep the aircraft on the correct approach. Two types of radar are in use for air traffic control—primary and secondary radar respectively. The first of these employs a rotating beam on the ground to determine the position of aircraft in the area by detecting the energy reflected by the aircraft when illuminated by the radar beam. The second type, S.S.R., secondary surveillance radar, uses its radar beam to trigger a reply from a transponder carried in the aircraft. The replies can be coded to give such information as aircraft identity and height, for example, thus giving the controller more information for his task. Radar is also used in aircraft and on the ground to provide information on weather conditions such as heavy storms which are important to the pilot.

Records Records recognised officially have to be made according to certain fixed rules and all attempts are under the control of the Fédération Aeronautique Internationale (F.A.I.). Unofficially a number of aircraft have flown faster than the official record shows, but not under the permissible conditions.

The official World Records as at August 1, 1974, are:

Speed in straight line over 15 to 25 km. Col. Robert L. Stephens and Lt.-Col. Daniel Andre (U.S.A.F.) at Edwards

Air Force Base, California, in a Lockheed YF-12A May 1, 1965, 2,070 m.p.h.

Altitude. Alexander Fedotov, U.S.S.R., in an E-266 (MiG-25), 118,898 ft., on July 25, 1973.

Distance in a straight line. Major Clyde P. Evely, (U.S.A.F.), in a Boeing B-52H Stratofortress, on January 10–11, 1962, between Okinawa and Madrid, 12,532·3 miles.

Distance in a closed circuit. Captain William M. Stevenson, (U.S.A.F.), in a Boeing B-52H Stratofortress, Seymour Johnson Air Force Base–Bermuda–Sondrestrom (Greenland)–Anchorage (Alaska)–March Air Force Base–Key West–Seymour Johnson Air Force Base, June 6–7, 1962, 11,337 miles.

Altitude in sustained horizontal flight. Col. Robert L. Stephens and Lt.-Col. Daniel Andre (U.S.A.F.), in a Lockheed YF-12A over a 15 to 25 km. course at Edwards Air Force Base, California, on May 1, 1965, 80,257·9 ft.

Speed in closed circuit. M. Komarov, U.S.S.R., in an E-266 (MiG-25) over a 500-km. circuit at Podmoskovnoe, on October 5, 1967, 1,852·6 m.p.h.

Re-entry This means re-entry into the earth's atmosphere. All discussions of space travel depend on the solution of the problem of how a vehicle in orbit at speeds of thousands of miles an hour can get back to earth safely. This is the problem of losing speed near the ground and of getting through the earth's atmosphere without burning up.

The problem has been solved by the U.S.A. and Russia. Each has brought space vehicles out of orbit and retrieved them.

The solution of the first stage, the entry into the atmosphere at high speed, has been so far to have a fairly blunt-nosed vehicle with an outer skin that burns up. In the few minutes of travel such a burn-up of the outside can save the inside. The solution of the final stage so far has been the use of a parachute released at a certain height.

Problems of the re-entry of a vehicle large enough to hold a man have led to other possible solutions. One is to let the impact energy be largely dissipated in a shock-wave. Another is to shape the vehicle so that it goes like a glider into a very shallow dive. The speed is thus much reduced.

Reciprocating Engine Another name for piston engine, in

which the rotation of a shaft is arrived at from the in-and-out action of pistons in cylinders. All early aero engines were piston engines.

Rocket A rocket is a vehicle driven by a type of engine that does not depend on air. It is therefore able to function in outer space.

The action is that fuels called propellants are burned to create intense volumes of gas, and this gas is shot out of the only opening in the rocket—the rear. The resultant pressure of the gases is therefore forward. So the rocket travels. The simplest rocket used in fireworks has gunpowder or similar fuel lit by a fuse when on the ground.

As the rocket travels upwards it loses the fuel that is being consumed. So the total weight gets less and the rocket accelerates more and more until all the fuel is spent. The weight at starting must be great, because all the fuel is there. The ratio of

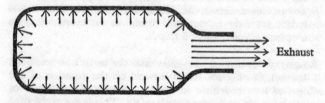

The propulsion system of a rocket. The fuel burns to form very quickly immense volumes of gas, which expand to press on the surroundings. The only outlet is at the rear. So the resultant pressure, shown by arrows, is forwards.

this initial mass to the final mass when the fuel is gone is called the *mass ratio*. The velocity at the end is given by the equation

$$V = c \log_e R$$

where R = mass ratio; c = jet velocity.

Turned into common logarithms, this becomes

$$V = 2 \cdot 3 \, c \log_{10} R$$

The bigger the final velocity must be, the more fuel there must be and the bigger (and heavier) must be the casing and rocket-engine apparatus. Consequently the practice has become necessary, for space research, of using rockets in several stages.

Then when the first stage, or booster, is burned out its heavy container can be automatically thrown away. The next rocket stage then starts to fire with all the advantages of height and speed reached with the help of the booster. So it can be smaller. Thus a composite rocket of several stages can be built up.

Rockets need an immense amount of engineering and electronics for the many controls needed if they are to achieve anything other than going up in smoke.

Largest known spacecraft launcher, the American Saturn V, weighs 3,000 tons at launch and is 365 ft. high. The Rocketdyne J-2 liquid hydrogen engines produce 1,000,000 lb. thrust. Saturn V placed the three-man Apollo 11 spacecraft on the moon.

Satellites Any body in orbit round a bigger body is a satellite. The moon is a satellite of the earth, and the earth can be described as a satellite of the sun.

Artificial satellites are man-made objects put into orbit, usually round the earth.

To get a satellite into orbit round the earth it must be launched parallel to the earth's surface, high above the earth's atmosphere, at sufficient speed. If the speed is too little the intended satellite will fall back to earth. If the speed is above the escape velocity (*q.v.*) it will fly off into space. Between a certain minimum velocity, depending on the height, and the escape velocity, there is a range of velocities that will take a satellite into orbit. This range at a height of 300 miles is from about 4·9 to 6·9 miles per sec., at 400 miles from 4·7 to 6·7 miles per sec. and at 1,000 miles from 4·45 to 6·3 miles per second. A vehicle launched at the lower speed would just orbit on a circular orbit, whereas one launched at exactly the higher speed would depart on a parabolic path.

If launched into orbit at a speed between these values (for the correct height) the vehicle would travel on an ellipse, being farthest away from the earth at one end and nearest at the opposite end.

The satellite must be launched more or less parallel to the earth. This is done by radioed instructions from the ground. Clearly, enormous rocket power is needed to get a satellite up to the launching height.

Since the successful orbital flight of the Russian Sputnik 1 in October 1957, many thousand known successful satellites have been launched; others have been launched secretly. Many of these have since come out of orbit; the time a satellite lasts depends on how deeply it dips into the earth's atmosphere. At 100 miles high a satellite might last a week before air resistance slowed it down and burnt it up; at 800 miles it could last indefinitely.

The amount of machinery in orbit is getting immense: as well as the existing satellites, there are the same number of last stage boosters, discarded fairings; one rocket blew up in orbit and produced no fewer than 200 fragments. The situation is also complicated by the chattering of the earlier satellites, which, although they have finished their missions, cannot be switched off, and their radio transmitters go on using valuable wavelengths.

Satellites serve several purposes; here is a short guide. (The unqualified type-names refer to U.S. machines.)

Physical Research—Designed to study electrical and magnetic fields at high altitudes, the emission of atomic particles and X-rays from the sun.

Navigation—Transit, Anna. The first named emits precisely timed radio signals as a navigational aid for Polaris submarines and other ships. The Anna series of satellites are used for surveying and mapping the positions of the continents on the globe.

Reconnaissance—Big Bird satellites carry cameras to watch military activity in hostile countries.

Communications—The first Telstar, launched in 1962, was a failure; but its successor allowed television viewers in Europe to see live events in America such as the Negro Freedom March on Washington, and President Kennedy's funeral. Satellites can pass on television, voice and telegraph channels at great distances; but at the moment it is uncertain how best to set up a world-wide satellite communications system. The difficulty is in choosing a height for the orbits. Low level repeaters like Telstar pass so quickly overhead that they are in range of stations on either side of the Atlantic for only about 20 minutes at a time. A considerable number would be necessary, and the ground stations would have to keep shifting their aim from one to the other. An alternative is a set of three satellites so high that they can see right round the globe to each other, and appear to stand still in the sky over the same three spots. This makes the tracking problem easier, but the relaying transmitters in the satellites must be more powerful to cope with the increased range. Another snag about the synchronous satellite (so called because it does one orbit in 24 hours, the time it takes the earth to rotate once) is that signals take an appreciable time to make the round trip, so it would be difficult to hold a telephone conversation.

A curious result of this satellite work is that the competing telephone and telegraph cables are being intensively developed, and look as though they will be able to compete effectively. One interesting possibility here is the use of laser light beams (see LASER, p. D27) in silvered tubes under the oceans—these will have such an enormous information capacity that one tube could carry all the telephone and telegraph links across the Atlantic, and have room for 1,000 television bands and more.

Mancarrying—American and Russian satellites have carried men—and a woman—into orbit and safely back. This is the most spectacular feat in space, but from the scientific point of view probably the least valuable.

SATELLITES PLACED IN ORBIT DURING 1974

Satellite	Launcher	Weight lb.	Purpose	Country	Date
Cosmos 628	Skean	?	Military	U.S.S.R.	17.1.74
Skynet 2A	Thor-Delta	?	Comm.	U.K.	19.1.74
Cosmos 629	Vostok core	9,000	Reconn.	U.S.S.R.	24.1.74
Cosmos 630	Vostok core	?	Reconn.	U.S.S.R.	30.1.74
Cosmos 631	Skean	?	Military	U.S.S.R.	6.2.74
Cosmos 632	Vostok core	?	Reconn.	U.S.S.R.	12.2.74
USAF 07A	Titan 3B-Agena D	6,600	Reconn.	U.S.A.	13.2.74
Tansei 2	Mu 3C	140	Sc.	Japan	16.2.74
San Marco 4	Scout	?	Sc.	Italy	18.2.74
Cosmos 633	Sandal	900	Sc.	U.S.S.R.	27.2.74
Meteor 16	Vostok core	?	Weather	U.S.S.R.	5.3.74
Cosmos 634	Sandal	900	Sc.	U.S.S.R.	5.3.74
Miranda/X4	Scout	205	Sc.	U.K.	9.3.74
Cosmos 635	Vostok core	?	Reconn.	U.S.S.R.	14.3.74
USAF 15A	Thor-Burner 2	430	Weather	U.S.A.	16.3.74
Cosmos 636	Vostok core	?	Reconn.	U.S.S.R.	20.3.74
Cosmos 637	Proton core	?	Comm.	U.S.S.R.	26.3.74
Cosmos 638	Vostok core	?	Soyuz test	U.S.S.R.	3.4.74
Cosmos 639	Vostok core	?	Reconn.	U.S.S.R.	4.4.74
USAF Big Bird ⎫		30,000	Reconn.	⎫	
Capsule 20B ⎬	Titan 3D	130	Pick-a-back	⎬ U.S.A	10.4.74
Capsule 20C ⎭		130	Pick-a-back	⎭	
Cosmos 640	Vostok core	?	Reconn.	U.S.S.R.	11.4.74
Westar 1	Long-Tank Thor Delta	?	Western Union Comm.	U.S.A.	13.4.74
Molniya 1AC	Vostok core	2,200	Comm.	U.S.S.R.	20.4.74
Cosmos 641 ⎫		90	Military	⎫	
Cosmos 642 ⎪		90	Military	⎪	
Cosmos 643 ⎪		90	Military	⎪	
Cosmos 644 ⎬	Skean	90	Military	⎬ U.S.S.R.	23.4.74
Cosmos 645 ⎪		90	Military	⎪	
Cosmos 646 ⎪		90	Military	⎪	
Cosmos 647 ⎪		90	Military	⎪	
Cosmos 648 ⎭		90	Military	⎭	

Satellite	Launcher	Weight lb.	Purpose	Country	Date
Meteor 17	Vostok core	?	Weather	U.S.S.R.	24.4.74
Molniya 2J	Vostok core	2,750	Comm.	U.S.S.R.	26.4.74
Cosmos 649	Vostok core	?	Reconn.	U.S.S.R.	29.4.74
Cosmos 650	Skean	?	Military	U.S.S.R.	29.4.74
Cosmos 651	Scarp	?	Military	U.S.S.R.	15.5.74
Cosmos 652	Vostok core	?	Reconn.	U.S.S.R.	15.5.74
Cosmos 653	Vostok core	?	Reconn.	U.S.S.R.	15.5.74
Cosmos 654	Scarp	?	Military	U.S.S.R.	17.5.74
SMS 1	Long-Tank Thor Delta	?	Weather	U.S.A.	17.5.74
Intercosmos 11	Skean	?	Sc.	U.S.S.R.	17.5.74
Cosmos 655	Skean	?	Military	U.S.S.R.	21.5.74
Cosmos 656	Vostok core	14,550	Soyuz test	U.S.S.R.	27.5.74
Cosmos 657	Vostok core	?	Reconn.	U.S.S.R.	30.5.74
ATS 6	Titan 3C	?	Sc.	U.S.A.	30.5.74
Explorer 52	5-stage Scout	60	Sc.	U.S.A.	3.6.74
Cosmos 658	Vostok core	?	Reconn.	U.S.S.R.	6.6.74
USAF 42A	Titan 3B-Agena D	6,600	Reconn.	U.S.A.	6.6.74
Cosmos 659	Vostok core	?	Reconn.	U.S.S.R.	13.6.74
Cosmos 660	Skean	?	Military	U.S.S.R.	18.6.74
Cosmos 661	Skean	?	Military	U.S.S.R.	21.6.74
Salyut 3	Proton core	41,000	Unmanned space station	U.S.S.R.	24.6.74
Cosmos 662	Sandal	900	Sc.	U.S.S.R.	26.6.74
Cosmos 663	Skean	?	Military	U.S.S.R.	27.6.74
Cosmos 664	Vostok core	?	Reconn.	U.S.S.R.	29.6.74
Cosmos 665	Vostok core	?	Comm.	U.S.S.R.	29.6.74
Meteor 18	Vostok core	?	Weather	U.S.S.R.	9.7.74
Cosmos 666	Vostok core	9,000	Reconn.	U.S.S.R.	12.7.74
Timation 3	Atlas Burner	?	Sc.	U.S.A.	14.7.74
Aeros 2	Scout	?	Sc.	Germany	16.7.74
Molniya 2K	Vostok core	2,750	Comm.	U.S.S.R.	23.7.74
Cosmos 667	Vostok core	9,000	Reconn.	U.S.S.R.	25.7.74
Cosmos 668	Sandal	900	Sc.	U.S.S.R.	25.7.74
Cosmos 669	Vostok core	9,000	Reconn.	U.S.S.R.	26.7.74
Molniya 1S	Proton core	?	Comm.	U.S.S.R.	29.7.74
Cosmos 670	Vostok core	?	Soyuz test	U.S.S.R.	6.8.74
Cosmos 671	Vostok core	9,000	Reconn.	U.S.S.R.	7.8.74
USAF 63A	Thor-Burner 2	430	Weather	U.S.A.	9.8.74
Cosmos 672	Vostok core	?	Soyuz test	U.S.S.R.	12.8.74
USAF 65A	Titan 3B-Agena D	?	Reconn.	U.S.A.	14.8.74
Cosmos 673	Vostok core	?	Military	U.S.S.R.	16.8.74
Cosmos 674	Vostok core	9,000	Reconn.	U.S.S.R.	29.8.74
Cosmos 675	Skean	?	Military	U.S.S.R.	29.8.74
ANS-1	Scout	?	Sc.	Holland	30.8.74
Cosmos 676	Skean	?	Military	U.S.S.R.	11.9.74
Cosmos 677		90	Military		
Cosmos 678		90	Military		
Cosmos 679		90	Military		
Cosmos 680	Skean	90	Military	U.S.S.R.	19.9.74
Cosmos 681		90	Military		
Cosmos 682		90	Military		
Cosmos 683		90	Military		
Cosmos 684		90	Military		
Cosmos 685	Vostok core	9,000	Reconn.	U.S.S.R.	20.9.74
Cosmos 686	Sandal	900	Sc.	U.S.S.R.	26.9.74
Westar 2	Long-Tank Thor Delta	?	Western Union Comm.	U.S.A.	10.10.74
Cosmos 687	Skean	900	Sc.	U.S.S.R.	11.10.74
Aeriel 5	Scout	?	Sc.	U.K.	15.10.74
Cosmos 688	Vostok core	9,000	Reconn.	U.S.S.R.	18.10.74
Cosmos 689	Skean	?	Military	U.S.S.R.	18.10.74
Cosmos 690	Vostok core	?	Sc.	U.S.S.R.	22.10.74
Molniya 1AD	Vostok core	2,200	Comm.	U.S.S.R.	24.10.74

Satellite	Launcher	Weight lb.	Purpose	Country	Date
Cosmos 691	Vostok core	9,000	Reconn.	U.S.S.R.	25.10.74
Meteor 19	Vostok core	?	Weather	U.S.S.R.	28.10.74
USAF Big Bird		30,000	Reconn.		
Capsule 85B	Titan 3D	130	Pick-a-back	U.S.A.	29.10.74
Capsule 85C		?	Pick-a-back		
Intercosmos 12	Skean	900	Sc.	U.S.S.R.	31.10.74
Cosmos 692	Vostok core	9,000	Reconn.	U.S.S.R.	1.11.74
Cosmos 693	Vostok core	?	Reconn.	U.S.S.R.	4.11.74
NOAA 4		750	Weather	U.S.A.	
Oscar 7	Two-stage	64	Comm.	Australia	15.11.74
Intasat 1	Thor Delta	44	Sc.	Spain	
Cosmos 694	Vostok core	9,000	Reconn.	U.S.S.R.	16.11.74
Cosmos 695	Sandal	900	Sc.	U.S.S.R.	20.11.74
Molniya 3A	Vostok core	3,300	Comm.	U.S.S.R.	21.11.74
Intelsat 4F	Atlas-Centaur	?	Comm.	U.S.A.	21.11.74
Skynet 2B	Uprated Thor Delta	?	Military	U.K.	23.11.74
Cosmos 696	Vostok core	9,000	Reconn.	U.S.S.R.	27.11.74
Cosmos 697	Vostok core	9,000	Reconn.	U.S.S.R.	13.12.74
Meteor 20	Vostok core	?	Weather	U.S.S.R.	17.12.74
Cosmos 698	Skean	?	Military	U.S.S.R.	18.12.74
Symphonie 1	Uprated Thor Delta	?	Comm.	Germany	19.12.74
Molniya 2L	Vostok core	2,750	Comm.	U.S.S.R.	21.12.74
Cosmos 699	Scarp	?	?	U.S.S.R.	24.12.74
Salyut 4	Proton core	41,000	Unmanned space station	U.S.S.R.	26.12.74
Cosmos 700	Skean	?	Military	U.S.S.R.	26.12.74
Cosmos 701	Vostok core	9,000	Reconn.	U.S.S.R.	27.12.74

Abbreviations: Sc.—scientific, and includes a great variety of experiments on cosmic particles, meteorites, light, magnetism, etc.
Comm.—Communications, also abbreviated comsat.

The list above includes all Earth satellites known to have been launched successfully during 1973. Details of satellite weight and purpose are often withheld for reasons of military security.

SPACE PROBES LAUNCHED TO DECEMBER 1974

Probe	Type	Country	Date
Pioneer 1	Lunar	U.S.A.	11.8.58
Pioneer 3	Space	U.S.A.	6.12.58
Lunik 1	Lunar	U.S.S.R.	2.1.59
Pioneer 4	Lunar	U.S.A.	3.3.59
Lunik 2	Lunar impact	U.S.S.R.	12.9.59
Lunik 3	Lunar orbit and photography of far side of moon	U.S.S.R.	4.10.59
Pioneer 5	Solar	U.S.A.	11.3.60
Venus Probe		U.S.S.R.	12.2.61
Ranger 1	Space	U.S.A.	23.8.61
Ranger 2	Space	U.S.A.	18.11.61
Ranger 3	Lunar	U.S.A.	26.1.62
Ranger 4	Lunar impact	U.S.A.	23.4.62
Mariner 2	Passed close to Venus 15.12.62 and radioed back much information	U.S.A.	27.8.62
Ranger 5	Moon photography and hardland, but missed	U.S.A.	18.10.62
Mars 1	Mars study, failed	U.S.S.R.	1.11.62
Luna 4	Moon study	U.S.S.R.	2.4.63

Probe	Type	Country	Date
Ranger 6	Moon photography and hard land; cameras failed	U.S.A.	2.2.64
Zond 1	Venus probe	U.S.S.R.	2.4.64
Ranger 7	As before: successful	U.S.A.	31.7.64
Ranger 8	As before: successful	U.S.A.	20.2.65
Ranger 9	As before: successful	U.S.A.	21.3.65
Luna 5	Moon photography: failed to make soft landing	U.S.S.R.	12.5.65
Luna 6	Missed moon	U.S.S.R.	8.6.65
Zond 3	Photography of far side of moon	U.S.S.R.	15.7.65
Luna 7	Failed to make soft landing on moon	U.S.S.R.	4.10.65
Mariner 4	Photography of Mars	U.S.A.	28.10.64
Zond 4	Photography of Mars: cameras failed	U.S.S.R.	14.7.65
Luna 9	First soft landing on moon, pictures of lunar surface	U.S.S.R.	31.1.66
Luna 10	Lunar orbiter launched from earth orbiting platform	U.S.S.R.	31.2.66
Surveyor model	Failed to achieve simulated lunar trajectory	U.S.A.	8.4.66
Surveyor 1	First U.S. soft landing on moon, TV pictures transmitted	U.S.A.	30.5.66
Lunar Orbiter 1	To survey Apollo landing sites, crashed on moon surface	U.S.A.	10.8.66
Pioneer 7	Solar	U.S.A.	17.8.66
Luna 11	Second Soviet lunar satellite, scientific research	U.S.S.R.	24.8.66
Surveyor 2	Second U.S. attempt soft landing, crashed when vernier rocket failed	U.S.A.	20.9.66
Luna 12	Third Soviet in lunar orbit, radiation and photographs	U.S.S.R.	22.10.66
Surveyor model 3	Dummy launched on simulated lunar trajectory	U.S.A.	26.10.66
Lunar Orbiter 2	Fifth lunar satellite taking photographs	U.S.A.	6.11.66
Luna 13	Soft landing, transmitted TV pictures, forced rod into surface to test strength	U.S.S.R.	21.12.66
Lunar Orbiter 3	Sixth lunar satellite taking photographs. Weight 860 lb.	U.S.A.	5.2.67
Surveyor 3	Second U.S. lunar landing Ocean of Storms. TV pictures and soil samples. Weight 617 lb.	U.S.A. (on moon)	17.4.67 20.4.67
Lunar Orbiter 4	Seventh lunar satellite taking TV pictures	U.S.A.	4.5.67
Explorer 34	Interplanetary probe with radiation counters. Weight 163 lb.	U.S.A.	24.5.67
Venus 4	Interplanetary probe on un-	U.S.S.R.	12.6.67

Probe	Type	Country	Date
	disclosed mission. 2,433 lb.		
Mariner 5	Probe passing Venus at 2,000 miles. Weight 540 lb.	U.S.A.	14.6.67
Surveyor 4	Lunar landing, failed by loss of contact	U.S.A.	14.7.67
Explorer 35	Eighth lunar satellite monitoring wind, magnetic field, particles. Weight 230 lb.	U.S.A.	19.7.67
Lunar Orbiter 5	Ninth lunar satellite to map 'far side'. Weight 860 lb.	U.S.A.	1.8.67
Surveyor 5	Forced landing in Sea of Tranquillity. TV pictures and soil samples. Weight 616 lb.	U.S.A. (on moon)	8.9.67 11.9.67
Surveyor 6	Fourth U.S. lunar landing Sinus Medii. TV pictures. Moved on lunar surface. Weight 617 lb.	U.S.A. (on moon)	7.11.67 10.11.67
Pioneer 8	Solar flares study. Interplanetary orbit. Weight 145 lb.	U.S.A.	13.12.67
Surveyor	Fifth U.S. lunar landing Crater Tycho. TV pictures. Soil analysis. Weight 617 lb.	U.S.A. (on moon)	7.1.68 10.1.68
Zond 4	Launch from orbital platform on lunar related test	U.S.S.R.	2.3.68
Luna 14	Fourth Soviet in lunar orbit radiation and photographs	U.S.S.R.	7.4.68
Zond 5	Out and return moon probe. Photographs and biological experiments	U.S.S.R. (behind moon)	14.9.68 18.9.68
Pioneer 9	Interplanetary probe. Solar particles, radiation, cosmic rays. With TTS 2	U.S.A.	8.11.68
Zond 6	Out and return moon probe. Skip re-entry	U.S.S.R. (moon) return	10.11.68 14.11.68 17.11.68
Venus 5	Interplanetary probe of 2,490 lb. Launched from orbital platform	U.S.S.R. (on Venus)	5.1.69 16.5.69
Venus 6	Interplanetary probe of 2,490 lb.	U.S.S.R. (on Venus)	10.1.69 17.5.69
Mariner 6	Probe passing Mars at 2,000 miles. Weight 850 lb.	U.S.A. (near Mars)	25.2.69 31.7.69
Luna 15	Orbiting lander spacecraft. In moon orbit 17.7.69. Crashed Mare Cisium	U.S.S.R. (on moon)	13.7.69 21.7.69
Zond 7	Out and return moon probe. Skip re-entry. Weight 6,000 lb.	U.S.S.R. (moon) return	7.8.69 11.8.69 14.8.69
Venus 7	Interplanetary probe with improved heat and pressure shield	U.S.S.R. (near Venus)	17.8.70 15.12.70
Luna 16	Unmanned lunar spacecraft. Landed in Sea of Fertility. Brought back soil sample	U.S.S.R. (on moon) (relaunch) (recovery)	12.9.70 20.9.70 21.9.70 24.9.70

Probe	Type	Country	Date
Zond 8	Unmanned test of manned. spacecraft. Free-return trajectory around moon. TV and photo equipment	U.S.S.R. (near moon) (recovery)	20.10.70 24.10.70 27.10.70
Luna 17	Unmanned lunar spacecraft Landed in Sea of Rains. Tests of 8-wheel Lunokhod-1 vehicle on surface	U.S.S.R. (on moon)	10.11.70 17.11.70
Mars 2	Scientific tests on interplanetary medium en route to Mars	U.S.S.R.	19.5.71
Mars 3	Weight 10,250 lb, enough to enter Mars orbit and soft land 1,800 lb.	U.S.S.R.	28.5.71
Mariner 9	Octagon, 2,150 lb, attempt to survey Mars photographically	U.S.A.	30.5.71
Luna 18	Went into lunar orbit, but lunar landing was a failure.	U.S.S.R.	2.9.71
Luna 19	Lunar orbiting craft	U.S.S.R.	28.9.71
Luna 20	Lunar landing craft—relaunched from moon 22.2.72 with soil sample	U.S.S.R.	14.2.72
Pioneer 10	Jupiter probe due at planet December 1973, then escape from solar system	U.S.A.	3.3.72
Venus 8	Venus probe, parachute landing July	U.S.S.R.	27.3.72
Luna 21	Unmanned lunar spacecraft. Completed 40 orbits of moon. Carried mobile Lunokhod-2 vehicle	U.S.S.R. (on moon)	8.1.73 15.1.73
Pioneer 11	Second Jupiter probe, due at planet January 1975, then escape from Solar System	U.S.A.	6.4.73
Explorer 49	Radio astronomy Explorer B is a cylinder with four paddles and four aerials, with retro rocket	U.S.A. (moon orbit)	10.6.73 15.6.73
Mars 4	Similar to Mars 2 and Mars 3, but no landing capsule. Was 2,200 km. behind Mars on 10.2.74. Orbital engine failed	U.S.S.R.	21.7.73
Mars 5	Went into Mars orbit to act as data relay for Mars 6 and Mars 7 landers	U.S.S.R. (Mars orbit)	25.7.73 12.2.74
Mars 6	Mars landing probe; capsule launched 6.3.74 but failed to transmit data	U.S.S.R.	5.8.73
Mars 7	Mars landing probe; capsule launched 9.3.74 but missed planet by 13,000 km.	U.S.S.R.	9.8.73
Mariner 10	Dual purpose probe, flew past Venus 5.2.74 and due to pass Mercury 29.3.74	U.S.A.	3.11.73
Luna 22	Lunar orbiting craft, extend-	U.S.S.R.	29.5.74

Probe	Type	Country	Date
	ing photographic mission of Luna 19 from 130 miles altitude		
Luna 23	Lunar landing craft, intended to collect soil sample but was damaged in landing Mare Crisium, 6.11.74	U.S.S.R.	28.10.74
Helios 1	Solar probe intended to reach perihelion about 15.3.75	Germany	10.12.74

MANNED SPACE VEHICLES LAUNCHED TO DECEMBER 1974

Name	Orbits or time	Country	Crew	Date
Vostok 1	1 orbit	U.S.S.R.	Gagarin	12.4.61
Freedom 7	No orbit	U.S.A.	Sheppard	5.5.61
Liberty Bell 7	No orbit	U.S.A.	Grissom	21.7.61
Vostok 2	17 orbits	U.S.S.R.	Titov	6.8.61
Friendship 7	3 orbits	U.S.A.	Glenn	20.2.62
Mercury Atlas 7	4 hr. 56 min.	U.S.A.	Carpenter	24.5.62
Vostok 3	3 days 22 hrs.	U.S.S.R.	Nikolayev	11.8.62
Vostok 4	2 days 22 hrs.	U.S.S.R.	Popovitch	12.8.62
Mercury Atlas 8	9 hrs. 13 min.	U.S.A.	Schirra	3.9.62
Sigma 7	22 orbits (manually controlled descent after instrument failure)	U.S.A.	Cooper	15.5.63
Vostok 5	81 orbits, 5 days	U.S.S.R.	Bykovsky	14.6.63
Vostok 6	48 orbits	U.S.S.R.	Valentina Tereshkova	15.6.63
Voskhod 1	16 orbits, 24 hrs. 17 mins.	U.S.S.R.	Komarov, Yegorov, Feoktikov	12.10.63
Voskhod 2	18 orbits	U.S.S.R.	Belyaev, Leonov[1]	18.3.65
Gemini 3[2]	3 orbits	U.S.A.	Grissom, Young	23.3.65
Gemini 4	62 orbits, 97 hrs. 50 mins.	U.S.A.	McDivitt, White[3]	3.6.65
Gemini 5	120 orbits, 190 hrs. 56 mins[4] (3,338,000 mls.)	U.S.A.	Cooper, Conrad	21.8.65
Gemini 6 &	26 hours	U.S.A.	Schirra, Stafford	15.12.65
Gemini 7[5]	206 orbits, 330 hrs. 25 mins. (5,716,000 mls.)	U.S.A.	Borman, Lovell	4.12.65

[1] Leonov was the first man to leave a spaceship and float freely in outer space.
[2] Gemini 3 was a manoeuvrable spacecraft and changed its flight path three times.
[3] White was the second man and the first American to step out into space.
[4] The approximate time that would be required to fly to the moon, briefly explore and return to earth.
[5] These spacecraft carried out a successful rendezvous in orbit, approaching to within 6 feet of each other and flying in formation for more than 2 circuits of the earth.

Name	Orbits or time	Country	Crew	Date
Gemini 8	4 orbits, 10 hrs. 18 mins.	U.S.A.	Armstrong, Scott	16.3.66
Gemini 9	48 orbits, 72 hrs. 21 mins.	U.S.A.	Stafford, Cernan	3.6.66
Gemini 10	44 orbits, 70 hrs. 48 mins.	U.S.A.	Young, Collins	18.7.66
Gemini 11 [6]	48 orbits, 71 hrs. 18 mins.	U.S.A.	Conrad, Gordon	12.9.66
Gemini 12 [7]	63 orbits, 94 hrs. 26 mins.	U.S.A.	Aldrin, Lovell	11.11.66
Soyuz 1	17 orbits, 24 hrs. 37 mins.	U.S.S.R.	Komarov [8]	23.4.67
Apollo 7	10 days 20 hrs. Live TV, rendezvous with booster	U.S.A.	Schirra, Eisele, Cunningham	11.10.68
Soyuz 3	3 days 23 hrs. Rendezvous with Soyuz 2, no docking	U.S.S.R.	Beregovoy	26.10.68
Apollo 8	6 days 3 hrs. First manned flight around moon	U.S.A.	Borman, Lovell, Anders	21.12.68
Soyuz 4	2 days 23 hrs. Docking target for Soyuz 5	U.S.S.R.	Shatalov	14.1.69
Soyuz 5	3 days 1 hr. Docked with Soyuz 4. Two cosmonauts transferred for re-entry.	U.S.S.R.	Volynov Khrunov Yeliseyev	15.1.69
Apollo 9	10 days 1 hr. LM manned flight for 6 hrs. for lunar manoeuvres	U.S.A.	McDivitt Scott Schweikart	3.3.69
Apollo 10	8 days. LM manned flight for 8 hrs in 60 n.m. lunar orbit	U.S.A.	Stafford Young Cernan	18.5.69
Apollo 11	8 days. LM 'Eagle' vehicle for man's first landing on the moon, 20 and 21.7.69	U.S.A.	Armstrong Aldrin Collins	16.7.69
Soyuz 6	5 days. Rendezvous trials of three Soyuz craft in Earth orbit	U.S.S.R.	Shonin Kubasov	11.10.69
Soyuz 7	5 days. Rendezvous trials as above	U.S.S.R.	Filipchenko Volkov Gorbatko	12.10.69
Soyuz 8	5 days. Rendezvous trials as above	U.S.S.R.	Shatalov Yeliseyev	13.10.69
Apollo 12	10 days. LM 'Intrepid' vehicle on	U.S.A.	Conrad Gordon	14.11.69

[6] First orbit docking achieved.   [7] Docking achieved on third orbit.
[8] Komarov was first in-flight space fatality when parachute shroud lines became entangled.

Name	Orbits or time	Country	Crew	Date
	moon 19 and 20.11.69		Bean	
Apollo 13	6 days. LEM 'Aquarius' vehicle used as lifeboat for crippled service module	U.S.A.	Lovell Haise Swigert	11.4.70
Soyuz 9	17 days long-duration flight. Craft weighed 14,220 lb.	U.S.S.R.	Sevastyanov Nikolayev	1.6.70
Apollo 14	10 days. Landing in Fra Mauro highlands. Use of wheeled cart. Exploration of Cone Crater	U.S.A.	Shepard Mitchell Roosa	31.1.71
Soyuz 10	2 days. Docked with Salyut but trouble with hatch prevented transfer	U.S.S.R.	Rukavishnikov Shatalov Yeliseyev	22.4.71
Soyuz 11	24 days. Rendezvous with Salyut. Mission ended with death of cosmonauts	U.S.S.R.	Dobrovolski Volkov Patseyev	6.6.71
Apollo 15	12 days. Landing in Apennines. Use of Lunar Roving Vehicle. Exploration of Hadley Rille	U.S.A.	Scott Worden Irwin	26.7.71
Apollo 16	11 days. Landing in Descartes highlands 17 mile exploration in LVR2	U.S.A.	Young Duke Mattingly	16.4.72
Apollo 17	12 days. Landing in Taurus-Littrow area LRV3—found volcanic evidence	U.S.A.	Cernan Evans Schmitt	7.12.72
Skylab 2	First manned flight to Skylab space station (launched 14.5.73). Deployed sail to reduce temperature and released solar panel. Manned duration 28 days to 22.6.73	U.S.A.	Conrad, Kerwin, Weitz	25.5.73
Skylab 3	Second manned flight to Skylab space station. Record manned duration 59 days to 25.9.73	U.S.A.	Bean, Lousma Garriott	28.7.73
Soyuz 12	First Soviet manned flight for two years, tested improved Soyuz. Manned	U.S.S.R.	Lazarev, Makarov	27.9.73

Name	Orbits or time	Country	Crew	Date
	duration 2 days to 29.9.73			
Skylab 4	Final flight to Skylab space station. Record manned duration 84 days to 8.2.74	U.S.A.	Carr, Pogue, Gibson	16.11.73
Soyuz 13	Verification of Soyuz modifications and for astronomy. Manned duration 8 days to 26.12.73	U.S.S.R.	Klimuk, Lebedev	18.12.73
Soyuz 14	Rendezvous and docking with Salyut 3 on 4.7.74. Manned duration 15 days to 19.7.74	U.S.S.R.	Popovich Artyukhin	3.7.74
Soyuz 15	Overshot Salyut 3 when booster overburned. Returned in 2 days.	U.S.S.R.	Sarafanov Demin	26.8.74
Soyuz 16	Successful rehearsal of ASTP mission. Manned duration 6 days to 8.12.74	U.S.S.R.	Filipchenko Rukavishnikov	2.12.74

Shock Wave When air moves over an obstacle faster than the speed of sound it no longer has time to be pushed gradually out of the way. Instead it changes its direction of motion in jumps: the lines along which these jumps occur are called shock waves, and separate regions of different pressure. The boom of a plane going through the sound barrier is simply its shock wave passing one's ears: the sudden change of pressure is heard as an explosion.

Sound Barrier A fanciful term dating from the immediate post-war period, denoting the sudden and often disastrous change of aerodynamic characteristics an aircraft experiences on reaching the speed of sound—or Mach 1. Nowadays these changes are allowed for in the design; passing Mach 1 is no longer a barrier, but a routine part of supersonic flight. See SHOCK WAVE.

Space Travel Exploration of other planets by man began in 1969 with the United States' Apollo 11 mission to the Moon. With its complete success the stage was set for other journeys to more remote planets and for more extensive exploration of the Moon itself.

All that was required of Neil Armstrong, Edwin Aldrin, and Michael Collins, the astronauts on this first mission, was to effect a manned lunar landing, collect soil samples, set up scientific equipment, and return to Earth. Lift-off from Cape Kennedy was at 0932 local (1432 BST) on July 16. The S-1C stage burned with a 600 ft. tongue of flame for 2 min. 41·6 sec., taking the vehicle 50 miles downrange at 219,984 ft. altitude. The S-II second stage burned for nearly 7 min. and separated at a range of 888 miles and 609,980 ft. By this time the speed was 22,757 ft./sec. The S-IVB stage fired for 2 min. 25 sec., and 11 min. 50 sec. after lift-off Apollo 11 was in Earth orbit.

After one and a half orbits the S-IVB was fired for 5 min. 48 sec. to put Apollo 11 into translunar orbit at a speed of 35,538 ft./sec. The command module Columbia and the service module were then separated from the S-IVB and the lunar module assembly known as Eagle for the transposition and docking manoeuvre. The S-IVB was separated and inserted into orbit around the sun.

On July 17 a 3 sec. mid course correction was made and by this time the astronauts were sending back very fine TV transmissions in colour. A further burn on July 19 put the spacecraft into a lunar orbit, about 60 nautical miles from the surface. The lunar module LM undocked on Sunday July 20 and during the 13th orbit Mission Control cleared the LM to fire its descent engine. Armstrong used manual control to traverse a shallow crater strewn with rocks and the LM touched down at 2118 BST four miles down range of the predicted spot and 37 sec. late.

Mission Control gave the go-ahead to de-pressurise the LM at 0258 BST on July 21 and Armstrong stepped on to the moon surface at 0356 BST. 'That's one small step for man, one vast leap for mankind,' he said. Aldrin followed 19 min. later. They set up the TV camera so their activities could be seen on Earth. They erected the American flag and received radio greetings from President Nixon. A laser reflector and passive seismometer were set up, and the soil samples were obtained. Both astronauts were back in Eagle by 0612 BST. Take-off was at 1854 BST after 21 hr. 36 min. on the moon. They redocked with Columbia at 2235 and abandoned Eagle in lunar orbit. Splashdown in the Pacific was at 1751 BST on July 24, 11½ miles from the carrier USS *Hornet*.

Supersonic Flight Flight at speeds greater than Mach 1. It involves aerodynamic problems that are different from those of subsonic flight. No less troublesome are the problems of having to get from subsonic to supersonic speeds. Some of the adaptations already achieved are the sweptback wing with narrow section and small wing area. See SHOCK WAVE.

Turbofan Development of the jet engine in which a larger amount of air than is needed for combustion is taken in and mixed with the hot exhaust stream. The advantage is that the exhaust stream becomes heavier and slower so that it wastes less energy in turbulence (q.v.). Has better fuel consumption.

Turbo-prop The driving of propellers by gas turbines. This system, vibrationless and powerful, has proved successful for civil airliners, notably the Viscounts and Britannias.

Turbulence Air moves in two states: laminar flow—that is, in orderly streams; or turbulent flow—that is, in a disorderly mass of small swirls. Under general conditions, whether the flow will be laminar or turbulent depends on the value of the *Reynold's number*—a dimensionless function of the size of the object, the viscosity and the velocity of flow. Turbulent flow absorbs much more energy than laminar flow, and therefore aircraft designers try to prevent it occurring. It begins in the *boundary layer*, a thin skin of relatively stationary air close to the surface of the aeroplane. A promising system for preventing turbulence is to suck this layer away through fine holes in the skin.

Types of Aircraft, Some Outstanding Modern

RUSSIA

An-22 Antheus New long-range heavy transport. Four NK-12MA turboprops. Wing span 211 ft. An airbus version to carry 300–350 passengers is under development.

Il-62 Long-range jet transport powered by four NK-8-4 turbofans. Similar layout to VC10. Carries 186 passengers. Capable of non-stop flight from Moscow to New York.

MiG-25 (E-266) Twin jet all-weather fighter, NATO code 'Foxbat'. Large afterburning turbojets each rated at 24,250-lb. thrust. Closed circuit record holder (q.v.).

Tu-134 Medium-range transport with rear mounted D-30 turbofans of 14,990-lb. thrust. Seats for up to 72 passengers.

Tu-144 Supersonic transport powered by four Kuznetsov

NK-144 turbofans. Similar layout to Concorde. Carries up to 140 passengers. Max cruising speed Mach 2·35.

Tu-154 Medium/long-range transport powered by three 20,950-lb. thrust NK-8-2 turbofans. Carries up to 167 passengers.

Tu-28p 'Fiddler' Supersonic twin jet all-weather interceptor. Carries two large 'Ash' delta wing air-to-air missiles under each wing.

U.S.A.

Boeing 747 Four-jet heavy transport known as the 'Jumbo Jet'. Powered by four Pratt & Whitney JT9D-3 turbofans. Basic accommodation for 385 passengers, but capable of carrying up to 490 ten abreast.

Boeing 727 Short- to medium-range jet transport with three rear-mounted JT8D turbofans. 163–189 seats.

General Dynamics F-111 Swing-wing variable geometry fighter. Two Pratt & Whitney TF30 turbofans. Mach 2·5.

Lockheed L-1011 TriStar High density transport powered by three Rolls-Royce RB.211 turbofans. Up to 400 passengers.

Lockheed C-5A Heavy logistics transport. Four U.S. General Electric TF39 turbofans each 41,000-lb. thrust. Span 222 ft. Carries 100 tons of payload. For U.S.A.F. Military Airlift Command.

McDonnell Douglas F-4M Phantom R.A.F. version of multi-role supersonic fighter capable of more than Mach 2. Royal Navy Phantom is F-4K. Span 38 ft. 5 in. Two U.S. General Electric J79-GE-8 turbojets, 17,000-lb. thrust each with afterburning.

McDonnell Douglas DC-8 Four-jet passenger airliner. Super Sixty series have up to 251 seats. Pratt & Whitney or Rolls-Royce Conway turbofans.

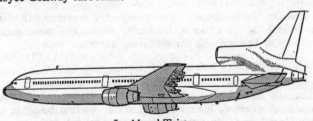

Lockheed Tristar

McDonnell Douglas DC-9 Twin turbofan short- to medium-range airliner. Seats for up to 139 tourist class passengers.

McDonnell Douglas DC-10 High density transport powered by three U.S. General Electric CF6-6 turbofans. Up to 345 passengers.

Rockwell International A-5 Vigilante Supersonic Mach 2 attack bomber. Span 53 ft. Two U.S. General Electric J79-GE-10 turbojets, 11,870-lb. thrust each (dry).

UNITED KINGDOM

British Aircraft Corporation

Concorde Supersonic transport designed and produced in co-operation with Aerospatiale in France. To fly faster than Mach 2. Four Rolls-Royce Bristol Olympus 593 engines. French prototype 001 flew March 2, 1969, and British 002 April 9, 1969.

Lightning Supersonic fighter powered by two Rolls-Royce Avon 210 turbojets each of 14,430-lb. thrust. Armed with two 30-mm. Aden guns and two Firestreak missiles.

VC10 Passenger four-jet airliner. Up to 151 seats. Super VC10 carries 163–174 passengers. Both powered by Rolls-Royce Conway turbofans. Maximum speed Mach 0·86.

One-Eleven Twin-jet short/medium range transport aircraft. New stretched 500 series aircraft seats up to 119 passengers. Rear-mounted Rolls-Royce Spey turbofans. 541 m.p.h.

Viscount Famous passenger airliner. Four Rolls-Royce Dart turboprop engines. Crew of two or three and up to 73 passengers. Range with maximum payload 1,725 miles. Maximum cruising speed 357 m.p.h.

Britten-Norman (Bembridge) Ltd.

Islander Twin-engined light transport carrying up to ten passengers, two 260 b.h.p. Lycoming O-540 engines. Speed 170 m.p.h. Trislander is three-engined version.

Hawker Siddeley Aviation Ltd.

Buccaneer Strike aircraft. Mk. 2B version powered by two 11,100-lb. thrust Rolls-Royce RB.168 Spey turbofans. Carries variety of weapons, including nuclear, in rotating bomb bay, plus Martel air-to-ground missiles on external pylons.

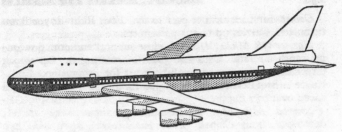

Boeing 747

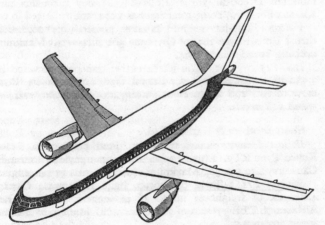

A300B European Airbus

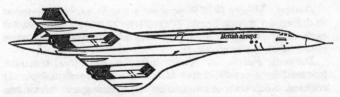

BAC/Aerospatiale Concorde

Comet First jet airliner ever to fly. Four Rolls-Royce Avon turbojets. Carries up to 101 passengers.

Harrier GR Mk. 1 V/STOL close support and armed reconnaissance aircraft. Uses two pairs of rotating nozzles which direct thrust downward for lift, or aft for propulsion. Rolls-Royce Bristol Pegasus 103 of 21,500-lb. thrust. Maximum level speed over 737 m.p.h.

Nimrod MR Mk. 1 Maritime reconnaissance aircraft developed from Comet. Four Rolls-Royce Spey Mk. 250 turbofans of 12,000-lb. thrust each.

Trident 3B Short/medium-haul three-jet airliner. Aft-mounted 11,960-lb. thrust Rolls-Royce Spey turbofans plus RB-162 booster. Tourist version has 152 seats.

Vulcan Four-jet medium bomber powered by 20,000-lb. thrust Rolls-Royce Bristol Olympus 301 turbojets. Maximum cruising speed Mach 0·94.

HS. 125 Srs 600 Twin-jet executive transport powered by 3,750-lb. thrust Rolls-Royce Bristol Viper 601 turbojets. Seats crew of two and up to eight passengers. Maximum cruising speed 518 m.p.h.

Short Brothers & Harland Ltd.

Belfast Heavy military transport. Four 5,730-e.h.p. Rolls-Royce Tyne RTy.12 turboprops. Maximum payload 80,000 lb. Can carry 150 troops. Maximum cruising speed 352 m.p.h.

Skyvan Srs 3 Twin turboprop light transport. Carries 4,600 lb. of freight or up to 18 passengers. Two Garrett AiResearch TPE 331-201 of 715 s.h.p. each. Maximum cruising speed 203 m.p.h.

FRANCE

Dassault Mirage IVA Supersonic strategic bomber designed to deliver an atomic bomb. Two SNECMA Atar 9K turbojet each rated at 14,770 lb. thrust with afterburning. Maximum speed Mach 2·2 at 36,000 ft.

Dassault Falcon 20 Twin turbofan executive transport powered by 4,315-lb. thrust U.S. General Electric CF700-2D engines. Seats crew of two and up to 14 passengers. Maximum cruising speed 536 m.p.h. at 25,000 ft.

Aerospatiale Caravelle Medium-range jet airliner. Two aft-mounted Rolls-Royce Avon turbojets. Super Caravelle has

Pratt & Whitney JT8D-1 turbofans and seats for up to 104 tourist class passengers. Maximum cruising speed 525 m.p.h.

HOLLAND

Fokker Fellowship Turbofan successor to turboprop Friendship. Short-haul transport with seats for up to 65 passengers. Two aft-mounted 9,850-lb. thrust Rolls-Royce Spey Mk. 555 engines. Maximum cruising speed 527 m.p.h.

Vertical Take-off and Landing (V.T.O.L.) A helicopter is a V.T.O.L. aircraft. The expression also includes newer devices concerned chiefly with getting fighters quickly off the ground without a long runway. There are several ways of getting vertical lift from jet engines. One is to have a deflecting plate that directs the jets down for take-off and is retracted to give horizontal jets when the machine is airborne. Another way, used in the Short SC-1, is to have separate engines for the vertical and horizontal thrusts. Designers in several countries are at work on their own ways of solving the problem of V.T.O.L.

Wind Tunnel An experimental device in which a wind is created by fans, and aerofoils and aircraft made accurately to scale are suspended in the wind. Instruments attached to the models measure lift, drag and other parameters at varying wind speeds.

Astronomy

Astronomical Measures The nearest star (Bungula in Centaurus) is 25,000,000,000,000 miles away. Measurements as huge as this become meaningless when given in miles, so stellar distances (distances between stars) were expressed until a short time ago in light-years. A light-year is the distance light travels in one year. The speed of light is 186,000 miles per second, so a light-year represents some 6,000,000,000,000 miles.

A newer astronomical measure of distance is the *parsec*, which is the distance at which the mean radius of the Earth's orbit would subtend an angle of 1 second. A parsec is rather more than 19,000,000,000,000 miles—or, roughly, 3¼ light-years.

Constellations On a cloudless night between 2,000 and 3,000 stars are visible to the unaided eye. With the help of one of the great astronomical telescopes (like the one on Mount Wilson in California) this number is increased to some 50,000,000.

The observable stars are divided into groups or constellations (a word that means 'star-groups').

THE CONSTELLATIONS

Those in capital letters are invisible from Great Britain

Scientific name	English name
Andromeda	The Chained Lady
ANTLIA	The Pump
APUS	The Bird of Paradise
Aquarius	The Water-Pourer
Aquila	The Eagle
ARA	The Altar
ARGO	Jason's Ship Argo
Aries	The Ram
Auriga	The Charioteer
Bootes	The Herdsman
Caelum	The Graving Tool
Camelopardalis	The Giraffe
Cancer	The Crab

Scientific name	*English name*
Canes Venatici	The Hunting Dogs
Canis Major	The Great Dog
Canis Minor	The Little Dog
Capricornus	The Horned Goat
Cassiopeia	The Lady in the Chair
CENTAURUS	The Centaur
Cepheus	Cassiopeia's Consort
Cetus	The Sea Monster
CHAMAELEON	The Chamaeleon
CIRCINUS	The Pair of Compasses
Columba	The Dove
Coma Berenices	Berenice's Hair
CORONA AUSTRALIS	The Southern Crown
Corona Borealis	The Northern Crown
Corvus	The Crow
Crater	The Cup
CRUX	The Southern Cross
Cygnus	The Swan
Delphinus	The Dolphin
DORADO	The Goldfish
Draco	The Dragon
Equuleus	The Little Horse
ERIDANUS	The River
Fornax	The Furnace
Gemini	The Twins
GRUS	The Crane
Hercules	The Legendary Strong Man
HOROLOGIUM	The Clock
Hydra	The Sea Serpent
HYDRUS	The Water Snake
INDUS	The Indian
Lacerta	The Lizard
Leo	The Lion
Leo Minor	The Little Lion
Lepus	The Hare
Libra	The Balance
LUPUS	The Wolf
Lynx	The Lynx
Lyra	The Lyre
MENSA	The Table Mountain
MICROSCOPIUM	The Microscope
Monoceros	The Unicorn
MUSCA	The Fly
NORMA	The Square
OCTANS	The Octant
Ophiuchus	The Serpent
Orion	The Giant Hunter
PAVO	The Peacock

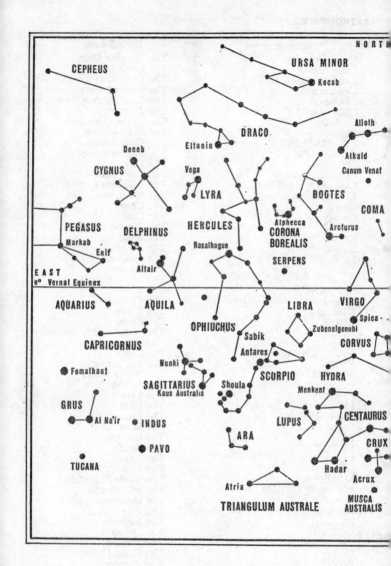

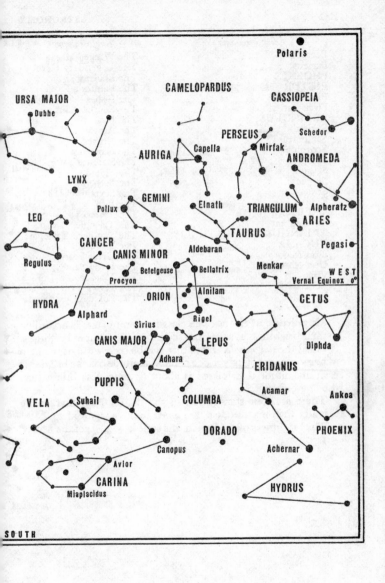

Scientific name	English name
Pegasus	The Winged Horse
Perseus	The Legendary Hero
PHOENIX	The Phoenix
PICTOR	The Painter's Easel
Pisces	The Fishes
Piscis Austrinus	The Southern Fish
RETICULUM	The Net
Sagitta	The Arrow
Sagittarius	The Archer
Scorpius	The Scorpion
Sculptor	The Sculptor's Workshop
Scutum	The Shield
Serpens	The Serpent
Sextans	The Sextant
Taurus	The Bull
TELESCOPIUM	The Telescope
Trinagulum	The Triangle
TRIANGULUM AUSTRALE	The Southern Triangle
TUCANA	The Toucan
Ursa Major	The Great Bear
Ursa Minor	The Little Bear
Virgo	The Maiden
VOLANS	The Flying Fish
Vulpecula	The Fox with the Goose

Magnitude of Stars The classification of stars is according to their brightness as seen from the earth. The unit of brightness is called the *magnitude*. Stars that can be seen without the help of telescopes are of magnitude 0–6. Magnitude 0 is the brightest; each magnitude that follows is about $2\frac{1}{2}$ times less bright than the one before it.

There are four stars (given in the list on F43) that, being brighter than magnitude 0, are given minus magnitudes.

The brightness of the Sun in this scale is −26·7; of the Moon, −11·2.

THE TWENTY BRIGHTEST STARS

Star	Constellation	Magnitude
Sirius	Great Dog	−1·43
CANOPUS	Jason's Ship Argo	−0·73
RIGIL KENTAURUS	Centaur	−0·27
Arcturus	Herdsman	−0·06
Vega	Lyre	0·04
Capella	Charioteer	0·09
Rigel	The Giant Hunter	0·15
Procyon	Little Dog	0·37
ACHERNAR	The River Eridanus	0·53
Betelgeuse	The Giant Hunter	0·90
AGENA	Centaur	0·66
Altair	Eagle	0·80
Aldebaran	Bull	0·85
ACRUX	Southern Cross	0·87
Antares	Scorpion	0·98
Spica	Maiden	1·00
Fomalhaut	Southern Fish	1·16
Pollux	Twins	1·16
Deneb	Swan	1·26
BETA CRUCIS	Southern Cross	1·31

The Solar System The centre of the Solar System is the Sun, our Earth being one of the planets revolving round it.

THE SUN

Diameter, miles	864,000
Mass, reckoning the Earth as 1	330,000
Density, reckoning the Earth as 1	0·25
Volume, reckoning the Earth as 1	1,300,000
Force of gravity on the surface, reckoning the Earth as 1	27·7
Period of rotation on its axis	25·38 days
Speed of rotation at its equator	4,407 m.p.h.
Surface area	12,000 times that of Earth
Volume	339,300,000,000,000,000 cu. miles
Mass	1,998,000,000,000,000,000,000,000,000,000 tons
Temperature	c. 10,000° F.
Height of biggest flames from the surface	286,000 miles

THE MOON

Diameter, miles	2,163
Surface area	14,660,000 sq. miles
Volume	5,300,000,000 cu. miles
Mass	78,000.000,000,000,000,000 tons
Speed in its orbit	2,288 m.p.h.
Estimated temperature, day	+214° F.
Estimated temperature, night	−250° F.
Force of gravity at surface, reckoning the Earth as 1	4/25
Time of revolution round the Earth	27 days 7 hr. 43 min. 11 sec.
Number of visible craters	30,000

THE PLANETS

	Average distance from the Sun (in miles)	Time taken to revolve round Sun	Diameter (in miles)
Mercury	36,000,000	88 days	3,100
Venus	67,200,000	224¾ days	7,700
Earth	93,000,000	365¼ days	7,927
Mars	141,500,000	687 days	4,200
Jupiter	483,300,000	11·86 years	88,700
Saturn	886,100,000	29·46 years	75,100
Uranus	1,783,000,000	84·01 years	29,300
Neptune	2,793,000,000	164·79 years	27,700
Pluto	3,666,000,000	248·43 years	3,600

Relative Gravitational Pull If the Earth's gravitational pull is reckoned as 100 the relative pull on the surface of the Sun and the other planets is:

Sun	.	.	.	.	2770	Jupiter	.	.	.	.	261
Mercury	.	.	.	38	Saturn	.	.	.	119
Venus	.	.	.	.	86	Uranus	.	.	.	.	88
Mars	.	.	.	.	38	Neptune	.	.	.	110

Motor Cars

Motorcycles, 3-wheelers, scooters and mopeds

MOTOR CARS

History and Development	2–8
How Cars Work	9–23
Engine	9–13
Transmission	14–17
Brakes	18–19
Body and Chassis	19–20
Steering	20
Electrical System	21–22
Suspension	22–23
Racing Cars	24–25
Land Speed Record	25
Identifying Cars	26–30
Group Manufacturers	31

MOTORCYCLES, 3-WHEELERS, SCOOTERS AND MOPEDS

History	33–35
How Motorcycles Work	35–38
The Frame	35
Engine	36–37
Ignition and Lighting	37
Brakes	37
Suspension	37–38
Controls	38
Motorcycle Sport	39
Scooters	40–41
Mopeds	41
Three-wheelers	42

1876 is perhaps the birth year of the motor car of today. It was then that the internal-combustion engine was developed to a workable form by Otto.

But the dream of the self-propelled carriage is a very old one. As far back as the sixteenth century, Johann Hautach made a vehicle propelled by coiled springs—a clockwork car. Steam carriages were also developed. The Frenchman Cugnot constructed a workable steam carriage in 1770—a three wheeler.

Cugnot Steam Carriage

Murdock, Dallery, Symington, Gurney and others all achieved a varying degree of success with steam-propelled carriages during the next fifty years (see models and drawings at the Science Museum). Gurney's steamer could climb Highgate Hill—a long, steep ascent—and in 1831 a Gurney coach ran regularly between Cheltenham and Gloucester at speeds up to 12 m.p.h. At the same time, Ogle and Summers built a car which achieved no less than 35 m.p.h. on the rough roads of that time—a speed greater than Stephenson's 'Rocket' locomotive of the same period, which had the advantage of running on rails.

But on the whole, these were triumphs that led nowhere. Opposition to any new kind of road vehicle was intense, and these early cars were constantly under attack from the highly organised horse-drawn coaching systems. Even more important, the first cars coincided with the almost fantastically rapid growth of Britain's railway systems: men with money chose to invest in railways, not horseless carriages.

Thus when Otto made a workable internal-combustion engine of the sort used in cars today, his achievement was of very little interest to Britain. Cars continued to be thought of as dangerous and unpleasant toys until the turn of the century. In France, however, Panhard and Levassor built a car round the new engine. There was activity in America, too, with petrol-driven cars such as the Duryea. In Germany, Benz constructed a petrol-engined three-wheeler (1885). Daimler made a two-cylinder V engine in 1889. Incidentally, the names Panhard and Daimler are still seen on motors today. Meanwhile in Britain what few cars there were had to proceed at walking pace behind a man carrying a red warning flag!

Prescott Steamer, 1903

Benz, 1885

In 1896 this ridiculous law was repealed (the London–Brighton run for Veteran cars celebrates the event each year) and motoring began to be taken more seriously in Britain.

At the turn of the century motorists had a choice of three sorts of self-propelled vehicle: steam, petrol-driven and electric. Electric cars were silent and very easy to manage, but useful only as town carriages. They could not go far without having their batteries recharged.

Steam cars were very numerous. Serpollet, White, Stanley and other manufacturers produced silent, fast and powerful vehicles with hill-climbing power that the petrol cars of the time could not approach. In addition, they involved none of the noisy and difficult gear-changing inseparable from the early petrol-engined cars. An American Stanley Steamer held the world speed record in 1906 at no less than $127\frac{1}{2}$ m.p.h.—an extraordinary speed, for petrol-driven road cars of the same date were not expected to reach more than 30 or 40 m.p.h.

But steam cars had their disadvantages. They were difficult to run. They used a lot of water. They could be very dirty. And it took up to 20 minutes to get steam up.

While the design of the steam car remained static and unchanging, the petrol car developed very rapidly indeed. Britain had an extremely advanced design in the Lanchester, a car that was many years before its time. A host of famous car makes, many of them still familiar, came into being—Peugeot, Singer, Sunbeam, Riley, Fiat and Rover among them.

Most important of all, petrol cars were developed that rivalled steam cars in speed and silence—and beat them in ease of operation and cost. The first Rolls-Royces (1905–10) in particular set an entirely new standard of refinement, luxury and (from the owner's point of view) simplicity. They were an example to all other makers of petrol cars and a clear indication that the days of the steam car were numbered. Another nail in the steam coffin was the self-starter—an American invention—which gave the petrol car an additional lead over the hard-to-start steamers.

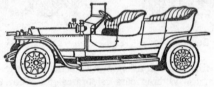

Rolls-Royce Silver Ghost

The Rolls-Royce was a craftsman-built car, individually made. In America Henry Ford started to build cars by mass-production: that is, in batches of thousands of cars, all made from interchangeable parts and assembled by largely unskilled labour. Ford's contribution to motoring development, although very different from that of the Rolls-Royce, was just as important. While Rolls-Royce set a new standard of perfection, Ford made cars available to people the world over. Motoring for the masses began with Ford.

By 1914 the car had settled into a pattern that has not changed very greatly. The engine was a multi-cylinder unit fed with controlled amounts of petrol and air by means of a jet carburettor (the earliest cars had a wick carburettor). The rear wheels drove the car and the front wheels steered it. Steering was effected by a wheel (earlier cars often had tillers) and braking by internal expanding hub brakes—though only on the rear wheels. Electricity was generally responsible for starting and lighting the most modern cars—and almost invariably responsible for engine ignition. The car's body and chassis were separate, although the first all-steel, 'unit construction' chassis bodies so common today had been produced. Early troubles of quick tyre wear and constant puncturing had been largely overcome.

During the First World War car design was neglected. Engine design advanced rapidly, however. In particular, many new and better metals were developed that allowed higher speeds within the engine and greater power development. It became apparent that the huge, thundering racing cars powered by massive engines were not necessarily the fastest; the comparatively tiny feather-weight racing cars of Ettore Bugatti—an immortal name—were beginning to steal the thunder. Smaller, lighter cars of fairly good performance and refinement began to appear. The Peugeot Bébé, designed by Bugatti, was a very early arrival. And in 1923 the first Austin 7 appeared. The Austin 7 and cars like it brought motoring for the masses to Europe just as the Model T Ford brought it to America. Motoring now became world-wide.

Model T Ford, 1927

Peugeot Bébé, 1913

Austin 7, 1926

By 1925 steam and electric cars had virtually disappeared from the scene. More and more saloon cars were being made. Economy cars of various sorts were successfully produced in huge numbers. Mass-production methods inevitably superseded hand fitting. Motoring was beginning to change people's habits and to expand their horizons.

Morris Cowley

During the next fifteen years the car finally overthrew the old order. For hundreds of years people had lived their lives within an area of a few square miles. A villager stayed in his village. But now the motor bus took him to other towns, other districts. Charabancs brought visitors to his village. More and more people could afford cars. Road networks covered whole countries and continents. The motor car that had started as a toy had become a near-necessity.

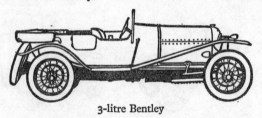

3-litre Bentley

Car development was comparatively undramatic during the period 1925–40. Family cars became much cheaper and shoddier. Sports cars increased their power and speed, but not violently. Racing became a nationally subsidised affair as well as a sport for rich amateurs. Luxury cars were smoother in outline but little else. Towards the end of the period, streamlining made an uneasy appearance as a styling feature, but had little effect on car performance. Citröen, the giant French manufacturer, developed a unit-built car with front-wheel drive that was to

Riley Falcon   Fiat 500, 1937

remain ahead of its time for twenty years. Other leaders in
design were Riley (small, comfortable, fast sports saloons from
1930 on); Lancia of Italy (small saloons of very advanced design,
including independent suspension for all four wheels—1937 on);
BMW of Germany (tubular backbone chassis frames, unusually
powerful engines); Fiat of Italy (the tiny 500-c.c. 'Topolino',
1937, the first miniature car to behave like a full-size model);
and MG (the sort of small and inexpensive sports car with which
Britain still leads the world).

Racing cars saw their peak development in the Mercedes-Benz
and Auto Union machines of Germany, which developed more
than 600 B.H.P.—a power that would take some beating today.

Mercedes-Benz Grand Prix racing car, 1937

American cars developed almost exclusively along the lines of
size, comfort and silence. Problems of more power from less
fuel—or of getting more passenger space in a compact vehicle—
were of little interest to American car-owners, who could get all
the petrol (and therefore power) they needed at very low prices.

Which brings the story to World War Two.

WORLD WAR TWO TO TODAY

After the Second World War, car production was at first resumed on pre-war lines. At first slowly, the designers and makers explored and incorporated new developments. The most important concerned suspension systems (q.v. this section), brakes (particularly discs, q.v.), tyres, luxuries such as radios and heaters, automatic transmissions, better fuels and tyres—and new layouts for cars. Another very important development was the rapid rise of the Japanese motor industry.

Today there is no such thing as a typical car. The family motorist can choose between rear-engine, rear-wheel-drive cars; front-engine, front-wheel-drive cars; front-engine, rear-wheel-drive cars. It is generally true to say that present-day cars offer more space, convenience and comforts, performance, mechanical reliability and fuel economy than old models, at the expense of greater complication, shorter life (the modern welded-up integral body/chassis rusts far too quickly) and more difficult servicing.

Particularly in this and other technically advanced countries, cars seem suddenly to have become too popular—too 'necessary' —too demanding. The worries facing the present-day motorist include the thousands upon thousands of other cars that threaten to bring him to a standstill; the rapidly increasing costs of running and maintenance (yet family life so often depends on the car); and the sudden realisation, all over the world, that the materials needed to construct and fuel a car are running dangerously short.

Volkswagen   Fiat 127

HOW CARS WORK

ENGINE

The Otto cycle (see History, above) is the name given to the four-stroke cycle of operation by which most car engines work. A very few cars use two-stroke engines.

With a four-stroke engine each cylinder is fired once during each two revolutions of the crankshaft. With a two-stroke engine, a cylinder fires at every revolution. Four-stroke engines use mechanically timed and driven valves to regulate the entrance and exit of gases into the cylinder. Two-stroke engines need no valves, and the flow of gases in and out of the cylinder is brought about by pressures within the engine itself. Today, the Wartburg is the only two-stroke car you are likely to see.

Four-strokes are generally smoother at low speed, more economical of fuel and capable of developing greater power from a given capacity.

Both engines work on a similar principle. One part of petrol is mixed with about 20 parts of air in a carburettor. This highly inflammable mixture is compressed by a piston rising within a cylinder. The piston has springy rings to ensure a gastight seal. When the mixture is exploded the piston is driven down. The piston is attached to a connecting-rod, in turn attached to a journal of the crankshaft. Thus the explosion drives the crankshaft round, and this movement is carried to the driving wheels (see Transmission). The action of the engine is therefore comparable to that of a man's arm cranking a car; the straight, up-and-down movement of his arm (his shoulder is the piston, his arm the connecting-rod) becomes a rotary or circular movement when applied to the crank.

Most European cars, both medium-sized and large, have four- or six-cylinder four-stroke engines with cylinders in line. Some 'baby' cars have fewer cylinders—the Fiat 500 has two. Big cars with six, eight or twelve cylinders may have V engines; if they did not the engines might be too long or their crankshafts too flexible. Some engines have opposing cylinders laid flat—a very space-saving arrangement.

All the engines described so far are Reciprocating engines— that is, they contain parts that go up and down, driving other parts that go round and round. Many attempts have been and

TWO STROKE CYCLE

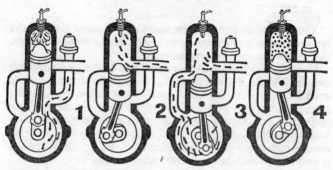

1. Ignition, induction.   2. Exhaust, crankcase charge compressed.
3. Exhaust, fresh charge enters cylinder.   4. Compression, partial
vacuum in crankcase.

are being made to construct engines with parts that all spin
(Rover long ago made a gas-turbine engine, for example). The
spinning, rotary engine should, in theory, be smoother and less
wasteful.

FOUR STROKE CYCLE

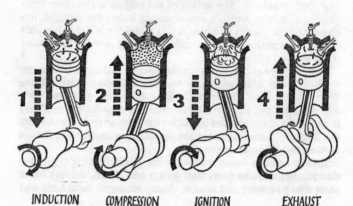

INDUCTION   COMPRESSION   IGNITION   EXHAUST

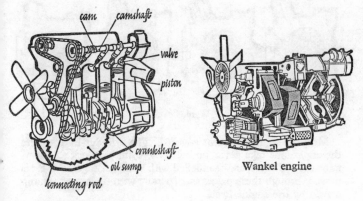

Four-cylinder, four-
stroke engine with
cylinders in line

Wankel engine

In fact, the Wankel engine is the only rotary design in international production. The drawing overleaf shows the Wankel
operating cycle. The lobes (shown shaded) describe patterns
within the casing of the engine that cause pressure/suction areas
for the mixture and exhaust. The advantages of the Wankel
engine include astonishing smoothness, but no manufacturer has
yet achieved fuel economy comparable with the piston engines'.

Lubrication Two stroke engines are lubricated by a small
amount of oil which is added direct to the petrol. As the mixture
must pass through the crankcase as well as to the cylinder, the
oil vapour provides enough lubrication for every part. The most
modern engines have a positive oil supply from a separate oil tank.

Four-stroke engines are elaborately lubricated from a reservoir
called the sump. Pure oil is drawn from the sump by an oil
pump which passes it under high pressure through channels
drilled through such components as the crankshaft, connecting-
rods and valve gear.

Cooling Car engines develop great heat, not only through the
explosions within the cylinder but also through friction of the
moving parts. This heat must be got rid of, either by cooling
with water or air.

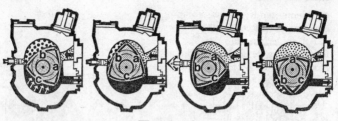

Wankel cycle

Most car engines are *water-cooled*. The cylinder-head, where the explosions take place, and also the cylinder block that contains the cylinders, are channelled with water passages. Water is passed through these passages, generally with the aid of a pump driven by the engine itself.

The constantly flowing water in the engine is cooled by the radiator, a grille of small water tubes supported by a lattice of fins. This is joined to the top and bottom of the engine by short lengths of rubber hose so that a loop circuit is formed. The radiator is exposed to the outside air, and may be further cooled by an engine-driven fan. Hot liquids always tend to rise above cool: so the hottest part of the radiator is the top, and the coolest the bottom. The flow of cooling water is thus from bottom to top of the engine and from top to bottom of the radiator.

Air Cooling The cylinders of an air-cooled car are covered with fins (as on a motor-cycle engine) which present a large area of coolable metal to the passing air. The fins are generally

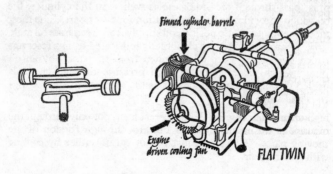

Finned cylinder barrels

Engine driven cooling fan

FLAT TWIN

supplemented by a powerful engine-driven fan to make sure of a good supply of cooling air even when the car is in heavy traffic.

Air-cooled engines need no cooling water, of course, and this is an advantage, as water may leak or freeze or cause corrosion. Air-cooling disadvantages include extra noise (water is a good sound damper) and the large amount of engine power needed to drive an adequate fan.

Surplus heat from either a water-cooled or air-cooled engine is generally used to warm the car interior.

Engine Power and Capacity *The size* of a car engine is described in terms of the amount of water that would be needed to fill all cylinders, with pistons down. In Europe we describe this amount in cubic centimetres (c.c.) or litres—thus 'Austin Maxi 1750', in which the engine is of approximately 1,750 c.c. capacity: or 'Riley 1½ litre', which was about 1,500 c.c. in capacity. 1,000 c.c. = 1 litre.

The old British description of cars as '10 h.p.', '16 h.p.', etc, is nowadays completely meaningless, and should be disregarded.

The power that an engine develops is described in Brake Horse Power or B.H.P. 'Austin A60' was so called because its engine developed approximately 60 B.H.P.

Capacity and power should not be confused. A racing-car engine of small capacity will develop considerable B.H.P.—probably four or five times as much as a family saloon of the same engine size. Both c.c. and B.H.P. must be known to get an idea of a particular engine.

Engine power depends on the rate at which it can digest fuel and get rid of the exhaust. Thus, the faster an engine can be made to turn—the more gulps of fuel it can consume—the more power it will deliver. Modern family-car engines often exceed 5,000 revolutions per minute. Modern racing-car engines may turn at 10,000 r.p.m. or even more.

To feed a family car with fuel, one carburettor may be enough. Sports and racing engines demand more fuel and therefore more carburettors to mix and deliver it. In the most modern high-performance engines, fuel injectors replace the carburettors. Yet more fuel may be given to the engine by a supercharger—a high-speed fan that forcibly feeds air to the carburettor (or mixture to the engine) under pressure.

TRANSMISSION

The power developed by a car's engine must be transmitted to its driving wheels through the clutch, gearbox, various drive shafts and a differential. All these parts are transmission parts.

The Clutch is used to join or separate the engine from the rest of the transmission. In starting a car from rest the clutch is 'let in' with a pedal so that the rapidly turning engine can *gradually* start the driving wheels turning without damage to other transmission parts. Use of clutch also simplifies gear changing.

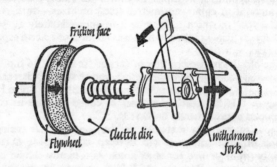

Friction face — *Flywheel* — *Clutch disc* — *withdrawal fork*

The clutch is made up of three disc-like plates, two joined to the engine and one to the transmission. When the clutch pedal is pushed the plates are separated. When the pedal is released the plates are pushed together by springs so that they join and become one. The plates are lined on their meeting faces with a friction material so that they can tolerate gradual engagement.

The Gearbox allows the driver to match the speed and power of the engine to the road conditions. Car engines work efficiently only when they are turning fast: thus a car with only top gear (highest) working would be unable to climb a hill, as the engine would steadily lose its speed and therefore its power. Exactly the same is true of a small child attempting to climb a steep hill on an adult's bicycle.

Most cars have four gears. A few have five. First is the lowest, used for starting the car from rest or for climbing steep hills.

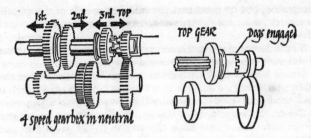

Top is used for easy cruising conditions and for maximum speed. Many cars today are fitted with—

Overdrive, in effect a separate gearbox that gives a very high gear. This allows high-speed cruising under easy conditions with the engine turning over slower than it would in normal 'top'.

The majority of cars still make use of a gearbox containing trains of gear-wheels that are engaged by a lever: the clutch helps the operation. But there have always been many other kinds of gearboxes, and recently more and more cars have—

Automatic Gears A car with a fully automatic gearbox has no clutch pedal, and the driver need only set a lever to select the *conditions* under which the car is to be operated. If he selects 'normal driving' he need do nothing further except brake or accelerate. The car itself will do whatever gear-changing is necessary. But although automatic gearboxes simplify driving, they themselves are inevitably complicated, as the basic gearbox must be controlled by electric, hydraulic and vacuum systems that relate engine conditions to the car's needs.

Other kinds of gearing include epicyclic '*preselectors*', in which the next gear wanted is 'dialled' for in advance; and the *variable-pulley* gearbox, in which belts are driven by two pulleys which change in relative size, and so give the most suitable of an infinite range of gears automatically, as in the DAF.

The Freewheel is a device that allows clutchless gear changing and also lets the car run free, as if de-clutched, when the throttle is closed. When the engine is accelerated the drive is taken up again.

Differential When a car turns a corner the inner of the two driven wheels travels a lesser distance than the outer, and therefore turns slower. On a very small and light car this might be acceptable; but on most cars the different speeds of the wheels would lead to excessive tyre wear, dangerous steering effects and wheel slip.

The differential is a mechanism that allows two wheels to turn at different speeds, yet both remain driven.

Drive Shafts and Universal Joints When the clutch has taken up the engine's power and the gearbox has adjusted it to road conditions there still remains the necessity to take the power to the driving wheels. How this is done depends on the lay-out of the car. Most cars have the engine at the front and the driving wheels at the back: in this case power is led to the differential, and thence to the driving wheels, through the *propeller shaft*. Generally, this shaft is a simple tube with a universal joint at either end. It may, however, be an enclosed unit in another tube which is joined to the rear axle.

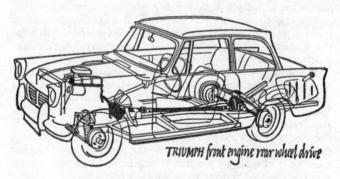

TRIUMPH *front engine rear wheel drive*

Two other shafts, called half-shafts, must then carry power from either side of the differential to each driving wheel. These may be enclosed in a rigid casing. If the car has independent rear suspension (described later) each shaft must have universal joints.

If the car is front-engined and front-wheel driven, or rear-engined and rear-wheel driven, then a propeller shaft is unnecessary. The drive can be taken from the differential straight to the rear wheels by two short shafts, each with universal joints.

Universal Joints allow a stiff shaft to transmit power through an angle, or through constantly changing angles.

They must be fitted to a propeller shaft because the rear

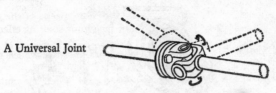

A Universal Joint

axle moves up and down on its springs while the gearbox remains stationary.

If the driving wheels are driven direct by shafts from the differential, then universal joints must be provided to allow for the wheels' up-and-down movements.

The three most commonly used universal joints are the flexible coupling, a rubber disc; the Hardy-Spicer type, which is comparable to gimbals; and the constant-velocity type, which uses metal balls running within tracks cut into two half-spheres, one cupping another.

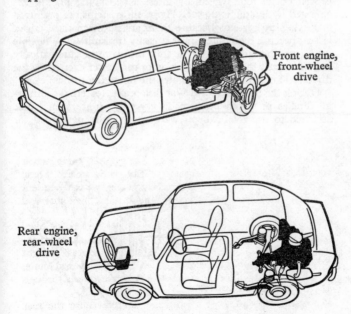

Front engine, front-wheel drive

Rear engine, rear-wheel drive

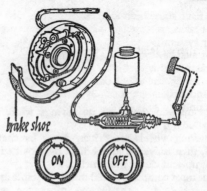

brake shoe

ON   OFF

BRAKES

Until recently, the great majority of the world's cars were braked on all four wheels by internal expanding hub brakes operated by hydraulic power. Hydraulic systems are preferred to mechanical systems because there are no mechanical power losses; because hydraulic power is easily transmitted by flexible tubes; and because each of the four brakes must automatically receive exactly the same proportion of the power exerted by the driver. The diagram above shows the operating principles.

During the Second World War disc brakes (external contracting brakes in which brake pads close like pincers on a disc attached to the road wheel) were successfully developed for

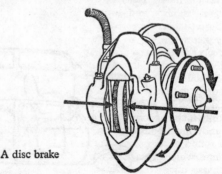

A disc brake

aircraft and have since been applied with great success to motor cars. Disc brakes are supplanting drum brakes.

Whatever system is used, an additional and separate braking system must also be supplied. This is called the 'parking brake' or 'hand-brake', and is used only to hold the car when at rest or to stop the car in the event of a failure of the main braking system. Hand-brakes are normally mechanically applied to the rear wheels only.

BODY AND CHASSIS

The chassis of a car is the framework that supports the body, engine and other components. This 'skeleton' is often visible in old sporting cars. However, the majority of present-day mass-

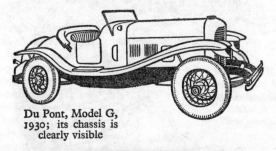

Du Pont, Model G,
1930; its chassis is
clearly visible

produced cars use the body itself as a chassis. The 'Unit Construction' modern car body is an all-metal welded box structure of great rigidity, and no separate chassis is needed. Sometimes additional local strength is given by a small chassis-like structure. Frequently the engine and perhaps the transmission and driving wheels are mounted on a small separate chassis that may be removed from the body very quickly and easily for servicing.

Although 'Unit Construction' is general, it is not the only method in use. Triumph mass-produced small cars with a separate chassis frame. Luxury-car makers must be able to supply a chassis on which various specialist coach-builders can fit individual bodywork. Sports and racing cars are often built up round a complicated arrangement of tubes called a Space Frame, which gives great rigidity with minimum weight; or with a chassis taking the form of a massive spine between engine and differential, with outriggers to hold bodywork and other components.

Sheet steel is the raw material of bodies for mass-produced cars. It can be formed in huge presses with great speed and economy. Sheet aluminium may also be used for parts that are not highly stressed (boot lids, for example).

Plastics bodies (fibreglass) are popular with small-production makers. The time and space needed to produce the bodies forbid large-scale production.

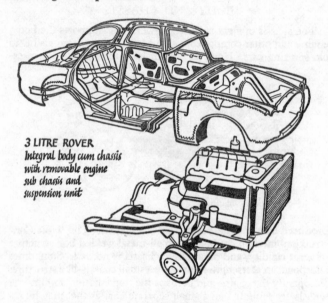

3 LITRE ROVER
*Integral body cum chassis
with removable engine
sub chassis and
suspension unit*

STEERING

Cars are steered by their front wheels: other lay-outs have been tried, but have never been successful.

A typical steering linkage consists of a steering wheel, whose motion is translated through the steering box to push the drop arm. This is connected by a drag link so that it steers one road wheel. The other road wheel is connected to the first by the track rod.

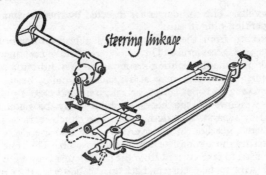

steering linkage

ELECTRICAL SYSTEM

The equipment of a car includes a complete electrical generating system, a storage battery to hold the electricity and a variety of systems and mechanisms that use it.

Electric power is supplied by dynamo or alternator, which is usually driven by belt from a pulley on the engine's crankshaft. The output of the dynamo or alternator charges the battery (usually 12-volt, but sometimes 6). A voltage regulator or cut-out keeps the output at a suitable level.

The battery stores electric power and passes it on demand. The greatest demand is that of the self-starter motor, which makes the battery supply enough power to turn over the engine quicker and for longer than a man could.

The petrol/air mixture within the cylinders is fired by sparking-plugs. These are supplied by the ignition coil with current stepped up in voltage from the battery's 6 or 12 volts to 6,000—

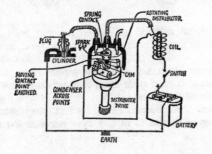

12,000 volts. The coil current is directed by the distributor to each sparking-plug in turn.

Electricity from the battery powers a host of other components and accessories. On a modern family car they will certainly include the lighting system, direction indicators, horn and panel lights; and may also include a radio, heater fan, additional fog and spot lamps, petrol pump and cigar lighter.

The windows or the hood—or both—may be raised and lowered by separate electric motors. The clutch, various panel instruments, gearbox and/or overdrive may also use electricity.

Electricity must complete a circuit to do a job. Thus one wire may be used to take current from the battery to a lamp bulb, and another wire to take current back to the battery. It is usual, however, to use the car itself as a conductor of current, thus halving the considerable amount of wiring.

SUSPENSION

Suspension is the word used to describe those parts of the car that join the road wheels to the chassis or body.

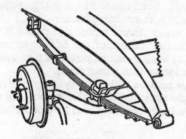

The traditional method of suspension was by leaf springs supporting an axle, and this method is still in common use for the rear axle.

Almost invariably today, the front wheels have independent front suspension (i.f.s.): with i.f.s., each wheel is free to behave independently of the other.

Independent rear suspension (i.r.s.) is also becoming increasingly common and is in any case necessary with a rear-engined car.

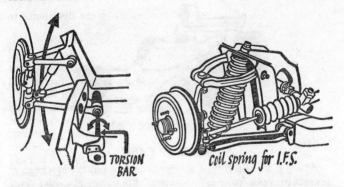

TORSION BAR

coil spring for I.F.S.

Springs may be in the form of leaves, coils, rubber units of various designs, or torsion bars (bars twisted along their length). Citroën introduced inert gas as a springing medium—rather as if the car were suspended on four footballs. Others followed.

Ride Controllers and Shock Absorbers If a car were suspended only on springs it would meet a bump, bounce over it and keep on bouncing. So-called shock absorbers or dampers let the spring do its work but prevent it from bouncing. They control the ride of the car and keep it steady.

With most cars, this control is the result of keeping each wheel steady. But ideally, it would be better to control the ride of the car as a whole: Citroën have gone a long way towards achieving this by linking each inert-gas suspension unit to the other by means of a hydraulic mechanism so that the behaviour of any one road wheel affects the behaviour of the others. The car is in fact self-levelling. Some British Leyland cars have front and rear wheels collectively sprung by liquid-filled tubes ('Hydrolastic').

Anti-roll Bars are used to link the behaviour of one road wheel to another. Thus on heavy cornering the heavily loaded outside wheels transfer some of their load to the inside wheels and the car remains more nearly level.

Tyres, while not part of the suspension, will affect its behaviour. Over- or under-inflation has drastic effects both on the way a car feels and how it behaves. Attempts have been and are being made to design tyres that will safely run 'flat' and tyres having renewable treads.

Formula 1 Tyrrell Ford

RACING CARS

Apart from the fun of it, motor racing has always been of enormous value to every motorist. Fuels, metals, oils, tyres, brakes—in fact, nearly every part of the ordinary car—all gain from the high-pressure testing and development that racing gives.

Grand Prix track racing is undertaken only by thorough-bred, out-and-out racing machines. The World Championship is decided by Grand Prix events. British cars and drivers have been consistently successful in the Grand Prix races of the last few years on circuits all over the world.

Track Racing also includes events for production cars, sports cars, Vintage and Veteran cars.

Road Racing includes the classic Le Mans—a sports-car race driven over a closed road circuit.

Rallies are typified by the classic Monte Carlo (not held in 1974) and by the Daily Mirror/RAC Rally of Great Britain—a five-day 2000+ miles event incorporating speed trials and forest stages. Starting point is York. The winners of the various classes are those who lose the fewest number of points. Motoring clubs throughout Britain hold Rallies.

Time Trials, Sprints, Hill Climbs, Rallycross, etc., are events that pit the driver 'against the clock'. The winners are those who cover a given distance, climb a certain hill or complete a number of circuits in the shortest time. Many such events are held throughout Britain.

Trials are winter events held over deserted country roads or in muddy fields and up hills. Often no one can complete the course, in which case the team that gets farthest wins. Special cars and skills are needed.

Club Racing takes place all over Britain and the world. In

'Goldenrod' (USA)—fastest wheel-driven car (409·69 mph.)

Britain such races are the proving grounds for new drivers. Cars range from true racing machines to Vintage Sports Cars.

Drag Racing. An American motor sport that has invaded Europe. Aim: to achieve the highest speed in a straight line over a short distance.

Formula Track Racing Cars True racing cars are defined by Formulae arrived at by internatonial agreement. The Formulae change frequently. At present these are in force:

Formula 1—3-litres unsupercharged or $1\frac{1}{2}$-litres supercharged engines in single-seater bodies.

Formula 2—Racing cars with single-seater bodies. Engine capacity up to 2000 c.c. Carburettor or injector, but not supercharger.

Formula 3—Max. 1600 c.c. Also 2 litre. Limited modifications. There are other such Formulae, mostly aimed at producing racing cars based on standard components, such as *Formulae Ford* (racing cars based on Ford engines) and *Formula 5000* (big cars, big engines); and classes for production motor vehicles, such as *Gran Turismo* (fast touring) and *Saloon* cars; also *Sports* cars. The popular *Group 1* is for standard production saloons.

LAND SPEED RECORD

Some important figures (wheel-driven cars):

			m.p.h.
5	Campbell	Sunbeam	150·9
6	Thomas	Higham Special	171·1

			m.p.h.
1927	Segrave	Sunbeam	203·8
1932	Campbell	Napier–Campbell Bluebird	254
1935	Campbell	Rolls-Royce–Campbell Bluebird	301·1
1938	Eyston	Eyston Thunderbolt	357·5
1947	Cobb	Railton	394·2
1965	Summers (USA)	Goldenrod	409·6

Not wheel-driven:

1970	Gary Gabelich	Blue Flame	622·4

Lotus Elite

IDENTIFYING CARS

Cars are identified and described in various ways. Engine capacity and power have already been discussed (see Engine). Descriptions such as saloon, convertible or station wagon are well known to you.

But every car also carries a variety of identity marks:

Registration Letters and Numbers (number plates) which are allotted to each new car by the County Council concerned. The same letters and numbers appear in the car's 'log book'— the official Registration Book. However many owners the car may have, its number plate never changes.

Chassis and Engine Numbers are among other details appearing in the log book. These are permanently stamped on cars of every nationality.

BMW 3.0 CSL

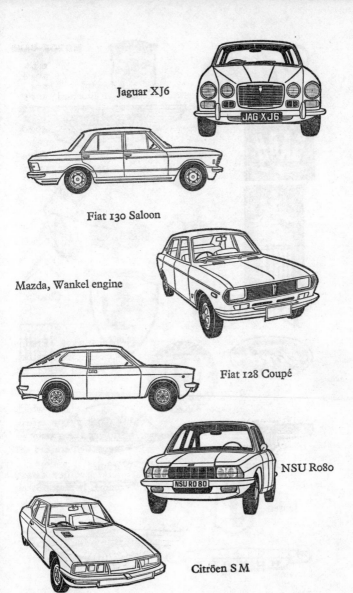

Jaguar XJ6

JAG XJ6

Fiat 130 Saloon

Mazda, Wankel engine

Fiat 128 Coupé

NSU Ro80

NSU RO 80

Citröen S M

Mercedes-Benz

Panhard

Peugeot

Skoda

Sunbeam

Volga

Gordon Keeble

International Registration Letters appear on a separate plaque fixed to the rear of a car when it is taken abroad. Among the most frequently seen are:

A	Austria	MC	Monaco
AUS	Australia, Norfolk Islands	MEX	Mexico
B	Belgium	N	Norway
BR	Brazil	NA	Netherlands (Antilles)
BRG	British Guiana	NL	Netherlands (Holland)
BS	Bahamas	NZ	New Zealand
BUR	Burma	P	Portugal
C	Cuba	PA	Panama
CDN	Canada	PAK	Pakistan
CH	Switzerland	PL	Poland
CL	Ceylon	PTM	Malaya
CY	Cyprus	RA	Argentina
D	Germany	RNR	Zambia
	(Federal Republic)	RSR	Rhodesia
DK	Denmark, Faroe Islands	S	Sweden
E	Spain, Canary Islands	SF	Finland
EAK	Kenya	SGP	Singapore
EAT	Tanganyika	SK	Sarawak
EIR	Republic of Ireland	SU	U.S.S.R.
ET	Egypt	SWA	South-West Africa
F	France	SYR	Syria
FL	Liechtenstein	T	Thailand
GB	Great Britain and	TN	Tunisia
	Northern Ireland	TR	Turkey
	(and GBA, Alderney;	TT	Trinidad and Tobago
	GBG, Guernsey; GBJ,	U	Uruguay
	Jersey; GBM, Isle of	USA	U.S.A.
	Man)	V	Vatican City
GR	Greece	WAG	Gambia
HK	Hong Kong	WAL	Sierra Leone
I	Italy, Sardinia, Sicily	WAN	Nigeria, British
IND	India		Cameroons
IR	Iran	WD, WG, WL, WV	
IRQ	Iraq		Windward Islands
IS	Iceland	YU	Yugoslavia
JA	Jamaica	YV	Venezuela
L	Luxembourg	ZA	Union of South Africa

Citroën GS

Ford Escort Rally Car

GROUP MANUFACTURERS

Many individual makers are members of a group of manufacturers. General Motors of the U.S.A., for instance, produces various makes of cars not only in America but throughout the world: Vauxhall in England and Opel in Germany are part of the General Motors Group.

In Britain many old names have been brought under group control:

British Leyland Motor Corporation   *Chrysler, United Kingdom*
      Austin   Hillman
      MG   Humber
      Morris   Chrysler
      Wolseley   Sunbeam
      Triumph
      Rover
      Jaguar
      Daimler

DAF 66 Estate

Audi 80/GT

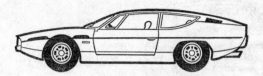

Lamborghini Mark III

FURTHER READING

Autocar Handbook, Motor Manual—and these magazines'
    annual Road Test compilations
The Observer's Book of Automobiles
Picture History of Motoring, L. T. C. Rolt
A History of the World's Sports Cars, R. Hough
About a Motor Car, Puffin Book (Penguin)
MAGAZINES—*Motor, Autocar, Motor Sport, Practical Motorist,
    Car, Motor Cycle*

PLACES TO VISIT

Science Museum, Kensington
National Motor Museum, Beaulieu, Hants

Porsche Turbo

Motorcycles, 3-wheelers, scooters and mopeds

1911 Zenith Gradua, J.A.P.   1922 Matchless twin
          engine

HISTORY

The history of the motorcycle begins, like that of the motor
car, with the internal combustion engine. Gottlieb Daimler,
pioneer of cars, can perhaps be credited with the first motorcycle
(1885) although an Englishman, Edward Butler, produced a
motor tricycle a year before.

Whatever its origins, the motorcycle took some time to
establish itself. The bicycling craze of the 1890's submerged
whatever interest there might have been in motorcycles. At the
turn of the century, however, social conditions changed radically
in every way. Times were ripe for motorisation of any sort—
bicycles included.

And indeed the first motorcycles were very similar to the
powered bicycles—the mopeds—of today. Like mopeds, they
were power-*assisted* vehicles. You pedalled when the motor
needed help. Later and more powerful machines remained as
simple as mopeds. They had no gears, or only two; there was no
kick-starter—you pedalled or ran alongside the machine to get it
going. Transmission was by belt (as it still is with certain
scooters and mopeds). Lighting was by acetylene—a romantic
but smelly and time-consuming method.

Suddenly, though, the motorcycle caught on. From 1910 on,
design developed fast. During the First World War, the motorcycle came into its own: motorcycle dispatch riders were popular
heroes and machines like theirs were greatly coveted when the
war ended.

In the 1920's, no fewer than 200 firms produced motorcycles.
The pattern of these machines did not change greatly for 20
years. Spring front-forks, electric lighting, greater power, the
kick-starter, three or four gears, a pillion—all these features were
adopted as standard.

The motorcycle thus emerged as an international form of transport, appealing particularly to those who enjoyed transport for its own sake (and there is still no more exhilarating way of getting about): and to those who wanted personal transport at rock-bottom prices.

1930 Scott Squirrel, water-cooled 2-stroke

1928 Coventry Victor twin

As we have said, the motorcycle began as a moped. Oddly enough this form of the motorcycle more or less disappeared from the scene—and the scooter, although it was invented soon after the First World War, was never commercially developed either. Three-wheelers, blending both motorcycle and car features, did make some progress. But the standard motorcycle was the most-used vehicle.

Harley Davidson

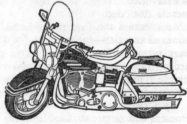

FROM WORLD WAR TWO TO TODAY

Wars leave nations poor. After the Second World War, everyone wanted personal transport and few could afford it. Two-wheelers became popular. The Moped, the minimal motorcycle, was developed to such a high standard of simplicity and reliability that it became, and remains, a permanent part of the world transport scene.

Italian companies invented the Motor Scooter, whose advantages included weather protection, a soft ride and simple controls. Perhaps it was the scooter craze that led manufacturers (particularly in Japan) to re-think the motorcycle and produce today's stylish, colourful, fully-sprung, lively yet docile machines, particularly in capacities from 125–350cc. Such machines killed off the scooter fashion.

The bigger machines have changed too. The old 'big bangers' still have their following, but world demand is for multi-cylinder designs of great sophistication and luxury. Self-starters, for instance, are common. Some major makers have announced motorcycles with Wankel engines (G12); these promise a new smoothness and freedom from vibration.

Almost certainly, the new crises in fuel, money, materials, parking space and public transport will lead to much greater use of all kinds of two-wheelers. Young people may stick to motorcycles instead of turning to cars. Commuters may well find it necessary to keep a small-capacity two-wheeler handy.

HOW MOTORCYCLES WORK

The Frame The wheels, engine and other parts of the machine are mounted in or on the frame—generally a double loop of steel tubing (the 'duplex' frame). Single steel tubes like a bicycle's are sometimes used; so are steel pressings. The engine is sometimes used as part of the frame. All those parts of the motorcycle that help it to roll or steer are called 'cycle' parts and are associated with the frame. The forks that hold the wheels are mounted on the frame—at the front, to the steering head, and at the rear by various methods (see **Suspension**).

The frame needs little or no attention other than polishing. But it is wise to go each week over all the nuts and bolts that hold components to it.

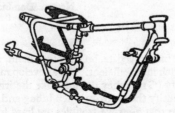

Duplex cradle frame

Engine Motorcycles and motor cars are very closely related mechanically. To avoid wasting space, we refer you back to the section on **Motor Cars** when talking about common features. Each reference is given like this—(G25)—which means, turn back to that page in the Cars section.

Like cars, motorcycles have either 2-stroke or 4-stroke (G9, 10) engines (a few have Wankel engines). There is endless argument about which is better. Two-stroke enthusiasts can claim lower first cost due to extreme mechanical simplicity (one could make a two-stroke engine with only three working parts!). They say too that 2-strokes 'slog' better at low revs up hills. And that as there is so little to go wrong, the 2-stroke is more reliable.

Villiers 200 c.c. 2-stroke, fan cooled,
with built-in ducting

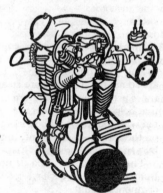

Norton 'Dominator' 99 4-stroke
twin

Four-stroke motorcyclists, on the other hand, argue that their engines are much more efficient. They develop more power from a given capacity (G13); they do not make the irregular popping noises that identify the 2-stroke when idling and use less petrol. They claim too that 2-stroke troubles are hard to track down in spite of the apparent simplicity of the working principle.

With very few exceptions, motorcycle engines are air-cooled (G11, 12) and have fins outside the cylinders. Engine capacity varies from less than 50 c.c. for moped engines to over 1000 c.c. on machines for the important American market. The vast majority of motorcycles have one or two cylinders but multi-cylinder machines are on the increase.

Motorcycle engines can be made to develop astonishing power for their size. 100 B.H.P. per litre is not uncommon (G13) which means that some of the 500 c.c. motorcycles you see on the road can develop as much power as a small car. A multi-cylinder 250 c.c. racing motorcycle may give as much as 180 B.H.P. per litre. Some racing engines reach 12,000 r.p.m. (G13).

Gearboxes Power from the engine is taken via a car-type clutch (G14) to a gearbox working in much the same way as a car's (G15) and for the same reasons (G14). Three or four gear ratios are usual, but five- and six-speed boxes are not uncommon. Some machines have a gear lever operated by hand, but the footchange—a centrally pivoted lever rocked down by the toe for downward changes, and by toe or heel for changes up—is usual. Automatic and infinitely variable gearboxes (G15) have been used on motorcycles and are not unusual on scooters and mopeds.

Final drive Almost always, the drive from engine to gear-box—the 'primary' drive—is by chain. So too is the final drive—although belts have been used in the past and may be again in the lightweights of the future in conjunction with automatic, scooter-type transmissions. A few makers have used shaft-drive on expensive and luxurious machines, but chain drive is the rule.

Ignition and Lighting Larger motorcycles and an increasing number of scooters use car-type electrical equipment (G21) complete with dynamo and battery.

A simpler and cheaper system for ignition and lighting is supplied by the Magneto—a machine which, like the dynamo, is rotated by the engine. Unlike the dynamo, a magneto delivers high-tension current—the current wanted at the sparking plug.

On smaller, simpler motorcycles, scooters and mopeds, the magneto is within the flywheel of the engine and the current it produces is used both for ignition and lighting.

Brakes Drum brakes (G18), mechanically operated by rods or cables, are the general rule, but discs are seen too.

Suspension The majority of motorcycles have telescopically-sprung front forks with dampers (G23) incorporated. The rear

wheel is mounted in a sprung pivoted fork or on a plunger
suspension system like a stubby version of the telescopic front
fork.

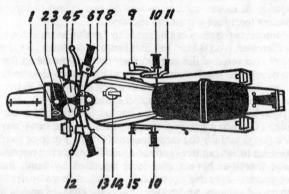

① Headlight control switch   ⑨ Rear brake pedal
② High beam indicator light   ⑩ Foot rests
③ Speedometer   ⑪ Kick starter pedal
④ Tachometer   ⑫ Clutch lever
⑤ Front brake lever   ⑬ Turn signal switch
⑥ Throttle grip   Horn button (below)
⑦ Emergency switch   ⑭ Fuel tank cap
⑧ Headlight control switch (above) ⑮ Gear change pedal
   Starter button (below)

Controls Here is a typical enough layout of the controls
found on a modern motorcycle. British machines often have
some reversed controls—the gear-change is on the left, and so on.
Some machines have rocking, heel-and-toe gear-change levers.
Most motorcycles have steering-column locks and quite a
number have lockable petrol-tank fillers. Old motorcycles had
controls not shown here; decompressors to help starting,
steering-head adjusters to alter the tension of the front suspension and so on. All machines, old or new, have a petrol tap (not
shown) which almost always has a position for 'reserve'.

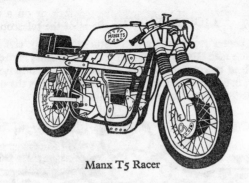

Manx T5 Racer

MOTORCYCLE SPORT

Grand Prix Racing International events—the World Championship Series—in France, Germany, Italy, Jugoslavia, Austria, Czechoslovakia, Holland, Belgium, Spain, Finland, Isle of Man TT, Sweden. 6 classes from 50 c.c. to 500 c.c. Also Sidecars.

Circuit racing (controlled by the ACU). National, regional and international. Formulae variable—designed to attract entries. F750, for basically roadster machines of 750 c.c., is internationally important.

Amateurs and club members are more likely to start with *Sprints* (clocked times); *Moto-cross* (125, 250 and 500 c.c.—also sidecar events) which is virtually the same thing as a *Scramble*— a race over rough territory; *Trials* (mixed territory, observed sections, competitors lose marks for each failure); or *Grass track racing* under ACU rules. All these events (and similar events for sidecar machines) are open to anyone who can get his entry accepted at Club, Local, National or International level. *Speedway* schools are held at Hackney and other venues. You hire a machine.

OSSA Trials machine

LIGHTWEIGHTS, SCOOTERS

The scooter represents a successful attempt to 'civilize' the motorcycle (see **History**, this section). Everything in the design should lead to comfort, silence, convenience, minimum maintenance, maximum enclosure. The ideal scooter is the one that demands least from its owner—often a girl.

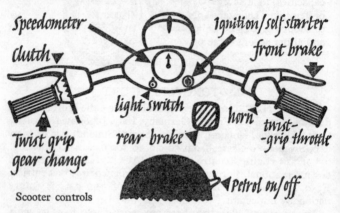

Scooter controls

Not so long ago, scooters were seen everywhere. Today, their place seems to have been taken by lightweight motorcycles or even, for short distances, by mopeds (q.v.) It is hard to account for the decline of the scooter but easy to understand the appeal of the lightweights. The best of them look, handle and brake better than scooters—and the choice is so enormous. For example, the commuter's Honda 50 (there are larger-engined

Honda ST70 FunBike

models) has a quiet 4-stroke engine, soft springing and some
weather protection; while the little Suzuki we show here
boasts a 5-speed gearbox and a 50 c.c. 2-stroke engine that is
claimed to develop 49 B.H.P. and give a top speed of 60-plus
mph!

The typical scooter had an engine capacity of something
between 125 and 200 c.c. Within or even well below these
capacities, today's lightweights offer you a choice of 'masculine'
or 'feminine' characteristics, suited to anything from Moto-Cross
to shopping trips . . . big or small wheels, fat or thin tyres . . .
and either scooter-type or motorcycle-type controls.

Suzuki 50 c. c.

MOPEDS

The moped ('motor + pedal') is basically a motorised bicycle
—and the simplest machines are adequately described in this
way. The more advanced mopeds, however, may have automatic, variable gears (or a 2, 3 or even 4-speed gearbox)—
excellent brakes—and springing front and rear.

Legally, a moped is a machine of 50 c.c. or less *with pedals*.
Without the pedals, motorcycle licensing restrictions about age
apply. The Yamaha Sixteener is legally a moped, but the rather
similar Suzuki 50 is not.

Puch Maxi S

THREE-WHEELERS

The aim of the 3-wheeler has always been to give the advantages of the light car with further advantages in terms of tax, fuel economy, first cost and 'garageability'. In this country, however, the importance of these advantages has lessened over the last few years. First cost is too near that of the cheapest four-wheeled cars (which have also increased their operating and economy efficiencies). Three-wheelers do not keep their value well—secondhand prices are low. There can be no doubt that the modern miniature car scores over the 3-wheeler in terms of quietness, comfort, carrying capacity, and, all too often, reliability. On the other hand, the 3-wheeler offers the motorcyclist one enormous advantage: he or she need not pass the car driving test to drive certain 3-wheelers. A motorcycle licence suffices.

There is no 'typical' 3-wheeler. It could be said that there are two main classes—those derived from motorcycles and those derived from motor cars—but even then, there is a great deal of overlap. The 'car' type of 3-wheeler is typified by the Reliant 'Robin' with its water-cooled 4-cylinder engine, or by the dashing little Bond 'Bug'. Both are virtually cars with a wheel missing. The Trojan, Messerschmidt, Peel and many others exemplify the other school—they could be called motorcycles or scooters with a wheel (and bodywork) added.

Bond 'Bug'

Railways

A Short History of Railways in Britain   2-7
Locomotives
    Steam: Some Classic Locos—The Last of the Line—
    How a Steam Locomotive Works—Locomotives and
    Modernisation—How a Diesel Locomotive Works—
    Electric Locomotives   7-20
Coaches—Brakes—Track—Signalling—Freight services
   —Railway Speeds—Channel Tunnel   20-32
Numbering   32
Preservation   32-33
Some British Railways Facts and Figures   33-34
World Railways: Facts and Figures   34

Locomotion No. 1

A SHORT HISTORY OF RAILWAYS IN BRITAIN

How Railways Began (1800–1850) Nobody knows when the first railway was built. The first mention of one, in which a special track of wooden rails was used, is found in the sixteenth century. Men had discovered that a cart or wagon ran more easily on a track than on the rough roads of the time. The earliest railways were purely local lines, no more than a few hundred yards long; with the coming of iron works and coal mines, they were used to help move wagonloads of material. The wagons were pulled by men or horses. One of the oldest mineral railways in the world, the Middleton Railway at Leeds, can trace its origin back to 1758; it survives today and is operated as a private line for freight by students of Leeds University.

The first railways to carry merchandise from one town to another were built early in the 1800s. The Surrey Iron Railway, from Wandsworth to Croydon, was approved by Parliament in 1801 and opened, for goods only, in 1804; while the first passenger-carrying railway in the world, the Oystermouth Railway from Swansea to Oystermouth (closed as recently as 1959), was opened in 1806. Both lines employed horses to pull the wagons or passenger trucks.

The Stockton & Darlington Railway was opened in 1825, followed in 1830 by the Liverpool & Manchester and Canterbury & Whitstable Railways.

At the time that these first railways were being built engineers were experimenting with steam locomotives—at first with little success. Richard Trevithick's road steam locomotive, one of the first effective models, was patented in 1802. It was followed two years later by his first rail steam locomotive, which ran on the Penydarren Iron Works tramway near Merthyr Tydfil. It was now that George Stephenson, one of the greatest railway engineers of them all, came upon the scene. At the time he was employed at Killingworth Colliery, Northumberland, and by 1815 he had built a type known as the 'Killingworth' locomotive, used on a number of colliery lines. A development of this type was built in 1825 for the Stockton & Darlington Railway by the newly founded firm of R. Stephenson & Co. This was the famous *Locomotion No. 1*, still in existence today.

The Stockton & Darlington was the first public railway in the world to use steam locomotives—though they were used only with goods trains. This line, regarded as the start of the present BR network, celebrated its 150th anniversary in 1975. In quest of suitable locomotives the Liverpool & Manchester Railway held trials in 1829 at Rainhill; the most successful entry was the *Rocket*, built by R. Stephenson & Co.

The Rocket

George Stephenson not only built locomotives but also surveyed, planned and engineered many railway routes.

The first trunk line was the London & Birmingham Railway, engineered by Robert Stephenson, George's son and partner, and completed in 1838. In the same year the Great Western Railway completed the first section of its line between London and Bristol. Railway schemes were now introduced by the hundred. All had to be submitted to Parliament for approval. Many were rejected; but many were approved.

The Battle of the Gauges From the beginning George Stephenson had had the foresight to realise that lines then only connecting neighbouring towns would one day be joined to form great trunk routes. He therefore standardised a gauge (the distance between the inner edges of the running rails) of 4 ft.

8½ in. for all the railways with which he was connected. This was a familiar gauge to Stephenson, since it was used on some colliery lines in the north-east. Other engineers, however, had their own ideas as to what the gauge should be. Isambard Kingdom Brunel, for example, engineer of the Great Western Railway, adopted a gauge of 7 ft. 0¼ in. for the line from London to Bristol, and many lines between London and the West of England and West Midlands were built to this 'Broad Gauge'. Very soon the immense disadvantages of using different gauges for neighbouring lines became obvious. At junction stations where standard and broad tracks met, passengers and goods had to be transferred from one train to another. In the end Parliament decreed that the standard gauge should be used for all main-line railways; and in 1868 the Great Western began to convert its tracks. During the period of change mixed-gauge tracks were used—these having three rails, one of which was common and the other two set to standard and broad gauge respectively; but broad-gauge tracks on the main line from London to Penzance remained until 1892, when the last stretch was converted in one week-end to standard gauge.

1850–1900 Gradually the pattern of railway routes became the one we know today. Small local companies soon realised the advantages of amalgamating with adjacent local lines and forming larger companies. Two of these amalgamations produced the Midland Railway in 1844 and the London & North Western Railway in 1846.

Meanwhile, more and more railways were built, many of them competing with other railways already in existence. Some companies were on friendly terms with their neighbours, but others were keen rivals and built railways simply in a spirit of competition. This explains why, today, some towns have more than one route to London or other big cities.

During the second half of the nineteenth century locomotives began to look less like the *Rocket*; boilers were made larger, chimneys shorter and cabs began to appear. By 1870 the locomotive had taken the shape familiar to our eyes today, and coaches had lost their resemblance to wagons.

1900–1970s By 1900 the main-line railway map was almost complete. The last main line to be built was the Great Central route to London from Nottingham and Leicester, opened in 1899. Apart from underground lines in London and one or two

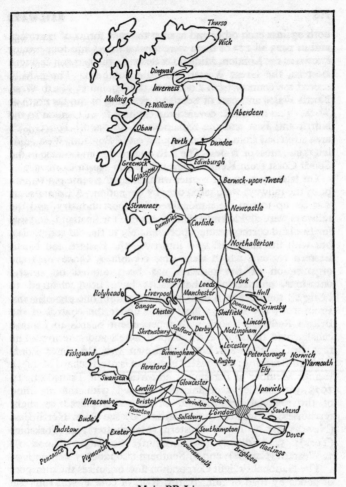

Main BR Lines

local lines built as late as the 1930s, building of new railways had then almost ceased. In fact, it was at this time that competition from road transport began to take traffic from the railway; first came the electric trams and, later, cars, lorries and buses. Railway companies could no longer afford to compete both against each other and against the new forms of transport, and in 1923 all 123 of them were amalgamated into four groups known as the London, Midland & Scottish, the London & North Eastern, the Great Western and the Southern. The L.M.S. served the country from London to the Midlands, North West, North Wales and part of Scotland, reaching to the far north at Wick. The L.N.E.R. covered the country from London to the North and East and the remainder of Scotland. The G.W.'s area stretched from London to the West of England, West Midlands and most of Wales. The S.R. operated from London to the South Coast from Kent to Devonshire and North Cornwall.

On January 1, 1948, together with canals and some road transport, the railways were taken over by the nation. A Commission was set up to run the nationalised transport industry, and the railways were divided into six regions, one for Scotland, and five for England corresponding approximately to the old companies, but with the L.N.E.R. split into two—the Eastern and North Eastern regions, which were later combined. Since 1948 the organisation of the railways has been altered on several occasions, and regional boundaries have been changed to bring all the lines in a particular area within one organisation. From 1963 the railways have come under the control of the British Railways Board, with independent boards to manage canals, road transport and transport hotels and catering. The first British Railways Board chairman was Dr. (later Lord) Richard Beeching; the present chairman is Mr. Richard Marsh, a former Member of Parliament and Minister of Transport. In 1975 yet another reorganisation started with the abolition of the regional organisation, which was replaced by eight territories: 1. Scottish (headquarters, Glasgow); 2. North East (Newcastle); 3. North Western (Manchester); 4. Yorkshire (York); 5. Midlands (Birmingham); 6. Anglia (London); 7. Western (Cardiff); and 8. Southern (London).

The National Freight Corporation now organises the transport of goods by road or rail. British Rail, of course, still runs the freight trains itself but you may see trains of container wagons bearing the name 'Freightliner' or the names of private firms.

For the last 20 years the railways of Britain have struggled to adapt themselves to the modern world. When he was Chairman of British Railways Dr. Beeching found that half the railway system carried about 95 per cent of the traffic while the other half carried the remaining 5 per cent and was losing money. The Beeching Plan, therefore, called for the closure of a large number of little-used lines, with passenger services taken over by buses. Many branch lines were closed and so, too, were some main lines. In some areas rail services provide a much better form of transport than buses, even though the trains are making a loss; during 1969 a system of payments was started in which the Government helps to off-set some of the losses by paying British Railways to continue the services. More recently the Government has made payments towards the building of new trains, for resignalling schemes and for track improvements. After some years of uncertainty on the future size of British Railways the Government decided at the end of 1973 that the system will remain at its present size.

During the ten years from 1960 to 1970 the British railway system changed considerably. As we shall see later, steam locomotives finally gave way to diesels and electrics in 1968, train speeds were higher than ever before and 100 m.p.h. became common, new types of signalling were brought into use on a large scale, and new operating methods introduced. In 1974 BR completed the electrification at 25,000 volts a.c. of the West Coast main line over the 401 miles between Euston and Glasgow.

LOCOMOTIVES

But for the steam locomotive, railways could not have been built on a large scale in mid-Victorian years. Steam locomotives reigned supreme on the railways of Britain for over a century until, at last, in the face of more modern forms of traction powered by diesel engines or electricity, the last steam loco-motive was withdrawn from BR's main lines in August 1968.

Steam: Some Classic Locomotives of the past.

Steam locomotives were classified according to the 'Whyte' table of wheel arrangements (see H9). In the days when there were 123 different companies the number of locomotive designs ran into hundreds. Yet the same wheel arrangements were adopted by many companies for locomotives on the same type of work. In late Victorian times 2–4–0 and 4–4–0 locomotives were used for passenger duties and 0–6–0 locomotives for goods trains and for shunting. In the first years of the present century locomotive designers began to think in terms of larger locomotives than had been used until then. Some railways built 4–4–2 (Atlantic)

Streamlined A4 Class ex-L.N.E.R.

locomotives for express duties and others had 4-6-os. The Great Western built a solitary 4-6-2 (Pacific) locomotive, but it was not very successful and was later rebuilt as a 4-6-0. After the grouping in 1923 designs were standardised and express passenger trains were built right up to the maximum size and weight

Coronation Class ex-L.M.S.

that the British loading gauge permitted. Some of the most famous express locomotives built during this period were the Great Western 'King' class 4-6-0, most powerful of all 4-6-0 designs; the L.N.E.R. streamlined 'A4' 4-6-2; the L.M.S. 'Coronation' class 4-6-2, which began as a streamlined engine; and the S.R. 'Merchant Navy' 4-6-2, a design which appeared in 1941 and was originally partly streamlined.

BR Types After nationalisation British Railways introduced twelve standard classes of steam locomotives. They were: three types of 4-6-2, for express passenger duties; two types of 4-6-0 for lighter express and intermediate passenger or freight working; three types of 2-6-0 for main-line and branch passenger or freight duties; a 2-6-4 tank for suburban passenger trains; two types of 2-6-2 tank for branch passenger and freight; and a 2-10-0 for heavy express or ordinary freight.

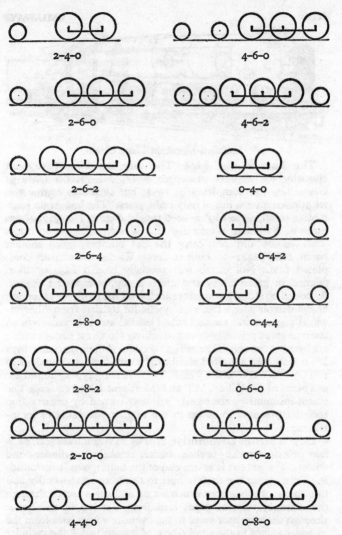

WHYTE CLASSIFICATION OF STEAM LOCOMOTIVE WHEEL ARRANGEMENTS

Modified Merchant Navy Class.

The Last of the Line The very last locomotive built specially for express passenger work, No. 71000 *Duke of Gloucester*, was completed in 1954; but even this engine was withdrawn after a life of only eight years. The last steam locomotive of all, a class '9' 2–10–0 freight engine, No. 92220, was built at Swindon Works for the Western Region in 1960. This engine did not carry the last number, since another batch, Nos. 92221–50, built at Crewe Works, was actually completed first. No. 92220 was specially named *Evening Star*, painted in green livery and given a copper-capped chimney. Although no steam locomotives are left on BR (with the exception of the narrow gauge line run by BR for tourists from Aberystwyth) you can still see and travel behind steam locomotives on the numerous privately-operated railways in Great Britain which are listed at the end of the railway section. Moreover, since 1972 BR has allowed a limited number of steam-hauled excursions to run on selected secondary main lines. Among types allowed are examples of the 'King', 'A4' and 'Merchant Navy' classes. The steam locomotives are mostly privately-owned by preservation societies but have to be up to the highest standards of maintenance.

How a Steam Locomotive Works A steam locomotive has five principal parts—firebox, boiler, smokebox, cylinders and wheels. The firebox is at one end of the boiler, which surrounds it. Tubes from the firebox pass to the front of the boiler and into the smokebox, from which smoke and gases escape through the chimney. Steam pipes lead from the top of the boiler through the regulator valve to the cylinder valves, and from the cylinder valves to the smoke-box. A piston inside the cylinder is connected to the driving wheels so that when it moves backwards and forwards the connecting-rods to the driving wheels

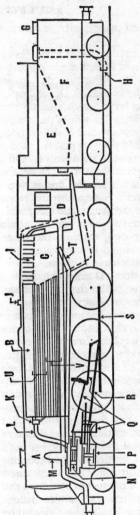

Simplified Diagram of British Railways 4-6-2 Express Steam Locomotive

A Smokebox
B Boiler
C Firebox
D Cab
E Coal space
F Water space
G Water tank filler
H Water pick up scoop for taking water at speed from
    troughs
I Firebox stays
J Safety valves
K Regulator valve operated by rodding from regulator
    lever in cab
L Steam pipe taking 'live' steam to cylinders

M Blast pipe for exhausting used steam from the
    cylinders out of the chimney
N Valve chest
O Piston
P Cylinder
Q Valve gear
R Connecting rod
S Coupling rod
T Brick arch
U Tubes carrying superheater elements. 'Wet' steam
    on its way from the regulator to cylinders passes
    through the superheater to dry it and make it
    more efficient
v Tubes to carry exhaust gases from firebox to smoke-
    box

make them turn. Engines have at least two cylinders, sometimes three or even four.

Coal is burnt in the firebox and heats the water in the boiler, turning it to steam. Because the steam cannot escape, pressure builds up. When the driver opens the regulator valve, steam passes through the pipe leading to the cylinders. Depending on the position of the driver's reversing lever, which operates part of the valve gear, the valves admit steam to one side of the pistons. The steam forces the piston to the opposite end of the cylinder, and the connecting-rods to the wheels push or pull the wheels round. When the steam has made its push the valves let it out of the cylinder into another pipe which leads it to the smoke-box. Here, with the smoke and gases from the fire, it is exhausted out of the chimney as a 'puff'. Meanwhile, the valves let in more steam to the other side of the piston, and this pushes the piston back again. So a continuous action is built up, steam pushing first on one side of the piston, then on the other, propelling it backwards and forwards and in turn causing the driving wheels to revolve and the locomotive to move.

Locomotives and Modernisation During the Second World War and the years immediately following, the railways were not able to replace old and worn-out equipment. Coal of a quality suitable for steam locomotives was becoming difficult to obtain and horribly expensive. It was difficult, too, to find men to train as firemen. So when, in 1955, the British Transport Commission announced an immense plan to modernise its locomotives, coaches, signalling and other equipment, part of the plan was that diesel and electric trains should replace steam locomotives, which would gradually disappear. Some trunk routes and suburban lines would be electrified; on others, diesel locomotives would haul express passenger and freight trains. Trains with diesel engines built on the coaches themselves (known as multiple-units) would be used for local and semi-fast journeys.

Diesel locomotives were originally classified by type according to horsepower but during 1968 British Rail introduced a new classification code in which each class is numbered between 1 and 55. Electric locomotive classes run from 70 to 86. Several manufacturers built diesel locomotives for British Rail (including British Rail themselves), and this means there are several designs for each power type. At the beginning of 1975 there were, in service, 19 basic main line diesel classes of all types, with a grand

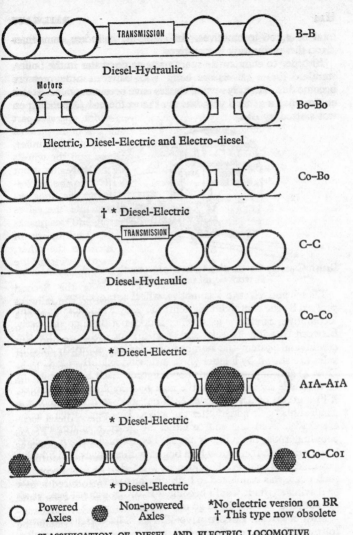

CLASSIFICATION OF DIESEL AND ELECTRIC LOCOMOTIVE
WHEEL ARRANGEMENTS

total of 2,506 locomotives. In addition, there are more than 1,100 diesel shunting locomotives.

In order to standardise spare parts some of the smaller non-standard diesel classes are being withdrawn as heavy repairs become due. Already several classes have been scrapped. At the end of 1971 a general withdrawal of most diesel-hydraulic types was started by BR.

Brush Class 47 Co-Co diesel-electric locomotive which can be found at work on all regions of British Rail.

Diesel and electric locomotive wheel arrangements are expressed by the continental system; the Whyte notation for steam locomotives cannot be used, since it does not distinguish clearly between driving wheels and non-driving wheels. In the continental system the number of axles are counted; driving axles are shown by a letter (A = 1 driving axle, B = 2, C = 3, D = 4) and unpowered axles by a figure. Each bogie or group of wheels is separated from the next by a hyphen. In addition, if in a group of driving axles each has its own driving motor a small suffix 'o' is added after the letter. If several driving axles are driven from one source either by gearing, shaft drive or coupling rods, no suffix is used. For example, if an electric locomotive has two four-wheel bogies with all axles individually powered it would be described as a Bo-Bo. If one motor on each bogie was connected to both driving axles by coupling rods or driving shafts it would become a B-B. In the last year or so the suffix 'o' has begun to go out of use.

How a Diesel Locomotive Works The diesel locomotive (or multiple-unit) power equipment is in two parts; the engine and the device for connecting the power output from the engine to the wheels, called the transmission.

The principle of the engine is the same for locomotives and multiple-units, but it is in the methods of transmission that variations occur. There are three of these: mechanical, hydraulic and electric.

The cylinders are the most important part of a diesel engine. There may be as few as four or as many as sixteen. Each has a piston sliding up and down inside it, connected to a crankshaft. Sometimes the pistons from two banks of cylinders drive a single crankshaft; in others, a cylinder may be open at both ends and have two pistons opposing each other, driving separate crankshafts connected by gearing. The diesel engine works by compression ignition. As the piston moves into the cylinder it compresses the air in the cylinder to a high pressure and to a very high temperature. Just before the piston stroke is completed a minute amount of fuel oil is injected into the cylinder by fuel pump, and the high temperature causes the fuel to ignite and explode, forcing the piston back. Several cylinders and pistons are arranged so that each fires in turn and, as one piston is rising to compress the air, the next will just be firing, the next driven half-way down, another at the end of its power stroke waiting to return to compress the air again. Generally four-stroke engines are used, in which the pistons make two strokes up and down for every one firing movement. The intermediate stroke cleans out the exhaust gas from the previous firing stroke and draws in fresh air for the next one.

The mechanical form of transmission employs a clutch and gearbox to transmit the drive from the output shaft of the engine to the wheels, just as in a motor-car. Its use in this country is limited to engines of less than about 400 h.p., and on British Rail is confined to some small shunting locomotives and to the multiple-unit rail-car sets, nearly all of which are equipped with this form of transmission.

The hydraulic system of transmission uses what is called a hydraulic torque converter. This consists of a cylindrical container filled with oil. Inside are two turbine wheels, one connected to the output shaft of the engine, the other to the shaft that drives the axles. They are mounted in such a way that when one turbine wheel (the impeller, driven by the engine) revolves, its blades force the oil into the blades of the second wheel and cause it to revolve and drive the locomotive wheels. Sometimes a locomotive may have more than one torque converter covering several speed ranges, or even an automatic gearbox in addition. Hydraulic transmission is used on a few British Rail shunting locomotives, some rail-car sets, but chiefly on some Western Region main-line diesel classes.

In the third system of transmission the diesel engine drives an electric generator which feeds current to electric motors

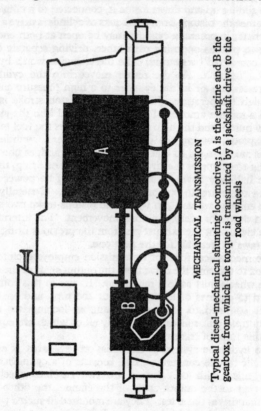

MECHANICAL TRANSMISSION

Typical diesel-mechanical shunting locomotive; A is the engine and B the gearbox, from which the torque is transmitted by a jackshaft drive to the road wheels

mounted on the locomotive axles. This is the most common system used on British Rail locomotives, and it is also in use on some Southern Region diesel multiple-unit trains.

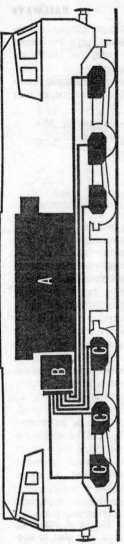

ELECTRIC TRANSMISSION

A typical diesel-electric locomotive; A is the diesel engine, which drives the generator, B, that provides current for C, the electric traction motors

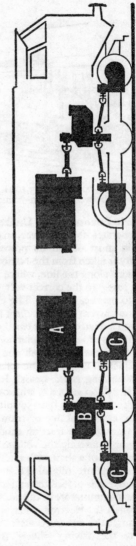

HYDRAULIC TRANSMISSION

A typical main-line diesel-hydraulic locomotive; A is the diesel engine, B the torque converter, from which the drive is transmitted by cardan shafts to C, the final axle drives

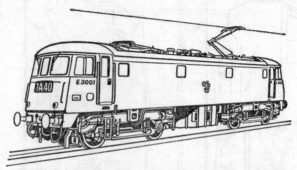

Bo-Bo 25,000 volt a.c. 3,200 h.p. electric locomotive for
services between Euston–Manchester/Liverpool/Glasgow

Electric Locomotives   Unlike a steam or diesel locomotive,
which generates its own power, an electric locomotive or multiple
unit train must obtain its power from some outside source.
Electricity is taken from the National Grid and passed to railway
sub-stations along the line, where it is transformed (and rectified
in many cases) to the correct voltage and fed either to conductor
rails or to overhead wires. The electric locomotives and trains
collect the current through *shoes* running on the conductor rail
or through a device called a *pantograph* which is mounted on the
roof and rubs along the underside of the conductor wire. The
current then passes through the control system and into the
electric traction motors. The return current is generally passed
into the running rails. British Rail have standardised electrification at 25,000 volts a.c. with overhead current collection except on the S.R. where the 750 volts d.c. third rail system is used.

An electric locomotive or train works by passing an electric
current through the traction motors. Speed can be varied by
reducing or increasing the voltage. In simple terms the traction
motor consists of a shaft with many coils of wire wound round it
called the armature, mounted inside an electromagnet. When an
electric current is passed through contacts on the armature shaft,
called the commutator, to the coils of wire in the armature, and
thus through the electromagnet, a magnetic attraction is set up
which causes the armature shaft to revolve. And as this shaft is
geared to the driving wheels, the whole process moves the
locomotive.

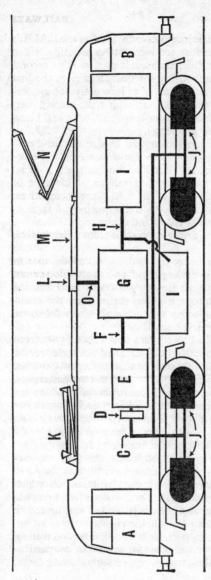

Simplified Diagram of British Rail Main Line Bo-Bo Electric Locomotive Operating on 25,000 Volts Alternating Current from Overhead Contact Wire

A Cab No. 1
B Cab No. 2
C Relatively low voltage direct current (about 1900 volts)
D Control equipment
E Main rectifier
F Relatively low voltage alternating current (about 2000 volts)
G Main transformer
H Low voltage alternating current (240 volts)
I Other equipment, such as compressor and ejector motors

for train brakes, and air-operated control apparatus, lighting on locomotive, train heating and control equipment
J Traction motors
K Second pantograph not in use (most locomotives have only one pantograph)
L Circuit breaker
M Supply from pantograph
N Pantograph collecting electricity from overhead wire
O High voltage alternating current (25,000 volts)

Seven types of a.c. electric locomotive are used on the L.M.R.'s electrified main lines; the first 100 locomotives are sub-divided into five classes built by different manufacturers. The second 100 are of all one class embodying the best features of the first 100 locomotives. The seventh class of 34 locomotives, considerably more powerful than the earlier 200, with 5,100 horse power, has been built for the electrification between Crewe and Glasgow, which includes steep gradients.

Another type of modern locomotive is the electro-diesel, used on the Southern Region. This works as an electric locomotive when running on an electrified line but has a diesel engine for running on non-electrified sidings. This type of locomotive, together with some of the S.R. diesel locomotives, can work certain Southern express trains push–pull fashion, that is with the locomotive at either end of the train. When the locomotive is pushing the driver controls it from a driving cab in the leading coach.

More electrification is being planned for suburban lines in cities. Some lines will run underground, and some will be rapid transit systems which will use lightweight trains more like the trams found in some European cities, rather than the traditional, somewhat heavy electric multiple-unit trains found on existing BR suburban electric lines.

Coaches Modern main-line coaches weigh about 32–34 tons each, are 64 ft. 6 in. long over the body ends and 9 ft. wide over the body (9 ft. 3 in. if you count the door handles). Corridor coaches seat 48 or 64 second-class passengers or 42 first-class passengers. The latest coaches are of 'integral' construction in which the coach body is self-supporting without a heavy underframe. For about the last eight years all new second class coaches have been of the open pattern, that is with pairs of seats on each side of a central passageway. BR's latest coaches are 75 ft. long.

In 1971 BR made history by introducing trains with fully air-conditioned coaches on ordinary services; until then they had been used for only a few special luxury expresses on which supplementary fares were charged. On air-conditioned coaches the windows do not open and the air is filtered and heated or cooled before being circulated inside the coach.

Brakes If you want to stop a train it's not much good turning off the power alone; a train can coast for several miles, particularly if it is running downhill, without appreciably slowing down.

A train's brakes usually consist of blocks which, when applied, press hard on the treads of the wheels. Latest freight wagons and a few electric multiple-units have disc brakes—special brake pads which press against discs on the axle. The means of applying and releasing them is by variations in air pressure. There are two systems in use: one employing a vacuum to hold the brakes off, and opening it to the atmosphere to apply them; and the other using compressed air to do the same thing.

The *vacuum brake* has been standardised on locomotive-hauled trains on BR until recent years. Throughout every passenger train and many freight trains runs an air-tight pipe flexibly connected between coaches and to the locomotive it-self. Connected to this 'train pipe' by a branch pipe on each coach is a cylinder containing a piston. The piston is connected by rodding to the brake blocks. A vacuum pump or ejector on the locomotive draws air out of the system which releases the brake; admission of air to the train pipe by the driver's brake valve applies the brakes. The difference in air pressure above and below the piston causes it to move up or down and in turn the brake blocks press against the wheels or move away when released.

If a passenger operates the alarm signal or a train becomes uncoupled accidentally and breaks the flexible train pipe be-tween the coaches, air enters the brake system automatically and applies the brakes.

The *compressed-air brake* is more complicated, but works on the principle that the release of compressed air will apply the brakes. All electric trains in Great Britain use the air brake and, in the latest multiple-units, this is applied and released elec-trically—a much quicker process—although there is still auto-matic application in case of emergency. Air brakes are used on 'Freightliner' goods trains and are gradually being adopted as the new standard type on locomotive-hauled passenger trains. The brake system on these trains uses two pipes running throughout the train, one to apply the brakes when the compressed air is let out through the driver's brake valve, the other full of high pres-sure compressed air to release them.

Track The rails used on early railways were of cast iron; but for very many years now the track has been made of steel. Until the 1950s *bull-head* was used almost exclusively on British railways and is still in use on many lines. This has a cross-section rather like a figure 8. It is laid in cast-iron *chairs* and held by wooden blocks or 'keys' wedged between the rail and the side of the chair. The chairs are bolted to wooden sleepers, and the sleepers themselves are held in position by granite ballast.

Since about 1946 the place of bull-head as a standard rail has been taken by what is called *flat-bottomed rail*. This, as its name suggests, has a flat base and is capable of standing upright without support. It is held in position by *baseplates*, and the rail and baseplates are spiked, clipped or bolted to the sleeper.

Rails are normally 60 ft. long and are supported by 24 sleepers to a length: there are 2,112 sleepers in one mile of track. Each length is joined to the next by *fishplates*—lengths of steel plate about 2 ft. long bolted through the rail ends with four bolts. When new track is laid, small gaps are left between rail ends to allow for expansion in hot weather. The holes through which the fishplate bolts pass are oval, to allow the rail to expand slightly.

Welded track is now used extensively in Britain. In this type of track the 60ft lengths of rail are welded together into one piece, often $\frac{1}{2}$ mile or even one mile in length without a break. In the previous paragraph we mentioned that gaps allow for the rails to expand in hot weather. If special measures are not taken, continuously-welded rail would be badly distorted when it expands in very hot weather. To overcome this difficulty welded rail is nearly always carried on concrete sleepers which are so heavy that the rail is held tightly in position. The sleepers are spaced slightly closer at about 26 for every 60 ft. Moreover, soon after it is laid the rail is heated artificially to average summer-time temperatures, starting at one end and working through to the far end. As the rail is heated it expands, and is fastened down tightly in its expanded form. In subsequent hot weather, therefore, it will not expand any more; in cold weather it tries to contract but since it is rigidly held it is unable to do so. In some ways it is like a piece of elastic which has been pulled tight and stretched a little. The engineers responsible for heating the rail try to fix it in position at a temperature about half-way between the extremes of cold in winter and heat in summer.

A new form of track in which sleepers and ballast are replaced by a solid bed of reinforced concrete paving to which the rails are attached is being tried out experimentally by British Railways for possible use on future high speed lines.

Signalling First, the signals themselves. *Semaphore signals*, with an arm about 5 ft long, are still used on many lines. *Stop* signals have a red arm with a white vertical stripe near the left end, and at night show a red light for danger and green for clear. *Distant* signals have a yellow arm with a vee notch cut from the left-hand end and a black vee stripe near the end. At night they show a yellow light at caution and green for clear. These signals give the driver an advanced indication of the next stop signals ahead. All semaphore signals have the arm horizontal for danger or caution. Some signals, nearly all on the Western Region, have the arm lowered at about 45 degrees to show clear, but most semaphore signal arms are inclined 45 degrees above horizontal for clear. Most main lines now have *colour-light signals* without arms, in which the indications are given by coloured lights—red, danger; yellow, caution; double-yellow, preliminary caution; and green, clear.

All passenger lines on British Rail are worked on the 'absolute block' system of signalling. In this, each line is divided into sections ('block sections'); where mechanical signalling is used, there is usually a signal box wherever sections meet.

The principle is that there shall never be more than one train in a block section on one line at a time. The signal boxes are equipped with 'block instruments' and bells for each line, so that signalmen in neighbouring boxes can keep each other fully informed about the passage of a train through the sections they control. The block instrument has a dial resembling a clock face but without any figures. The dial is marked with three panels; one says 'line blocked', another 'line clear' and the third 'train on line'. The indications are given by a needle pivoted in the centre. Normally the needle is vertical and pointing to the 'line blocked' panel. When deflected to the right ('twenty minutes to two' position) it points to the 'line clear' indication; to the left ('twenty minutes past ten') it points to 'train on line'. The needle is operated by an electro-magnet when the signalman turns a switch on the block instrument to the appropriate position. The indication is electrically repeated by the block instrument applying to the same section in the signal box at the other end of the section.

When a signalman wants to signal a train he must carry out

the routine laid down by regulations in which he 'offers' the train by coded bell signals to the next signalbox ahead and if the line is clear the signalman there 'accepts' the train by a repetition of the bell signal. Bell signals are exchanged when the train enters and leaves the section of line between the two boxes and indicators show whether the section is clear or occupied by a train.

At one time the safety of trains depended solely on the correct operation of the block system by the signalmen: but today, lines carrying fast, frequent services are equipped with additional safeguards to prevent a signalman from forgetting a train. Many of these devices are worked by the trains themselves from what are known as track circuits. A track circuit is an electrically-insulated section of line which has a weak electric current passed through the running rails and connected to an electro-magnetic relay at one end of the section. As a train passes over the line, its wheels short-circuit the current, which is cut off from the relay. The relay arm therefore falls away from the magnet and makes contact with other electrical circuits, which can be used to operate such equipment as locks on signal and point levers and can prevent a signalman from pulling a signal lever to clear a signal when a train is standing on a track circuit ahead of it.

The track circuit is in fact the basis of all modern signalling, because it allows the signalman to 'see' trains several miles away. In mechanical signalling, where the signalman works points and signals from levers which operate rods or wires, Government regulations limit the mechanical operation of points to no more than 350 yds from the signal box. Thus, at big junctions, several signal boxes are often needed to control the layout. But with electric operation of points and signals there is no limit, and signal cabins can be arranged to work points and signals several miles away. Track circuits are used to show the signalman the positions of trains by lights on a track diagram in the signal cabin. Track circuits are also used to initiate the operation of barriers at level crossings, the ones in which barriers automatically lower across half the road when a train is coming. This type of crossing, which also has flashing lights to stop cars and pedestrians when a train is approaching, is gradually replacing the old type with swing gates. By the way, NEVER try to pass over a crossing when the barriers are down.

Modern signal cabins have been introduced on many sections of British Rail as part of the modernisation plan. In some, the signals and points are controlled from banks of thumb-switches. But in the most recent cabins the controlling miniature push-buttons or thumb-switches are placed in their appropriate positions on a diagram which consists of a replica of the track layout. The buttons usually work on the route-setting principle; that is, the operation of two buttons will set up a complete route—the equipment checking first that no other train is on the line concerned, then changing the points needed for the route and finally clearing the signal.

Illustrated overleaf is part of a modern signalling panel. To set up a route the signalman turns the thumb-switch at the entrance to a signal section and presses a button at the end of it. When the route is set, white lights are illuminated on his diagram along the track concerned so that he can see the path the train will take. As the train passes along the route, the lights change from white to red to show the signalman the position of the train. After the train has passed the signalman restores the thumb-switch to its normal position until it is needed again and the white lights are extinguished. Where there is a junction, the button he presses determines the route that is set. For example, in the illustration, if he wants to send a train on the up relief line into the up goods lines he will turn switch 4 and press button D. That sets the route from signal 4 to signal 6. He then turns switch 6 and presses button F. The points will be set, signal 6 will clear and the white diagram lights will show the route set as far as signal 8. If instead the train was to continue straight up the relief line he would still turn switch 6 but press button E. Three routes are shown set up in the illustration—up relief to up goods; up main to up relief (switch 2 button E) and down main (switch 1 button A). Other switches and buttons for shunting movements have been omitted for clarity.

The signalmen in these modern cabins advise each other of approaching trains by the train describer. Usually the describer displays a code of figures and letters indicating the train's classification (see page H27), its destination and its number. The code is set up on the describer by the signalman who dials the code on a telephone-type dial or operates push buttons. The code description automatically moves from aperture to aperture along the track diagram in step with the train, so the signalman can see its description at a glance. When the train continues on its way towards the next signal cabin its description is automatically

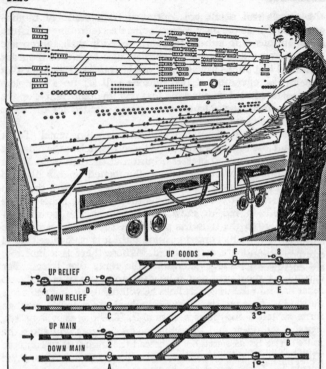

passed to the describer there so that the signalman knows what train is approaching him. He can watch its progress, too, from his track circuit diagram. Usually there are several automatic signal sections controlled solely by track circuits between the areas worked by the push-button panels. Colour-light signals are installed throughout the 401 miles between Euston and Glasgow, as part of electrification, mostly controlled from centralised power signalboxes supervising long sections of line. There are only 6 signal boxes between Euston and Nuneaton—a distance of 97 miles, and over the 220 miles from the Warrington area to Glasgow only five signal boxes. One of the latest signal boxes on BR, that at Motherwell, completed in 1974, controls no less than 123 route miles.

Most British Rail main lines, whether equipped with semaphore or colour light signals, are fitted with 'A.W.S.'—the automatic warning system. This device, situated at all semaphore distant signals and nearly all colour-light signals, gives the driver an audible advice of the indication shown by the signal. A bell rings in the cab if the signal is clear; if it is at caution a horn sounds and the brakes are applied automatically unless the driver acknowledges the warning. More advanced than AWS is a new sophisticated form of signalling in which the signals ahead (if indeed lineside signals are retained) or the condition of the line ahead and the safe running speed are displayed continuously in the driver's cab. This form of signalling is essential for high speed running over 100 m.p.h. It can be achieved by pairs of wires laid along the centre of the track which transmit signalling codes to a train passing above by induction—a form of magnetism. If the wires are crossed at, say, 100 metre intervals the transmitted code operates a counter on the train which shows the distance travelled. Similar in function are transponders—small packs of equipment located at intervals as required along the line which are energised by a coded signal from a passing train and reply with coded details about that location.

BRITISH RAIL DIESEL AND ELECTRIC TRAIN CLASSIFICATION HEADCODES

The BR four-character headcode uses a figure, a letter, and two figures. The first figure denotes the type of train as in the following table; the letter occupying the second position indicates the destination area of the train and varies from region to region; the figures in the third and fourth positions indicate the route or the train number.

1 Express Passenger or Newspaper train; Breakdown or Snowplough train going to clear line.
2 Ordinary Passenger train; Breakdown train not going to clear line.
3 Express Parcels train composed of vehicles permitted to travel at 90 m.p.h. or over.
4 Freightliner, Parcels train, company or express freight permitted to travel at 75 m.p.h. or over.
5 Empty coaching stock train.
6 Fully fitted freight, parcels or milk train.
7 Express Freight train not fully brake fitted.
0 Light Engine; Light Engines coupled; Engine with not more than two brake vans.
8 Freight train not fully brake fitted.
9 Unfitted freight train or train requiring to stop in section.

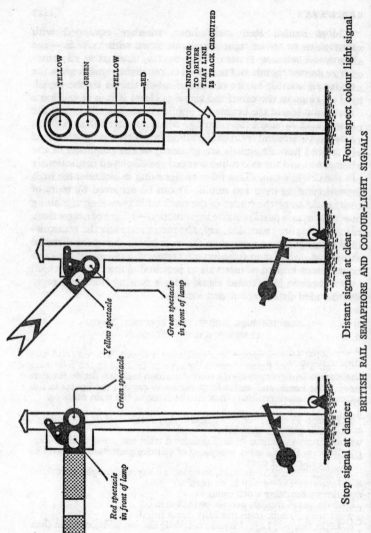

RAILWAYS

YELLOW

GREEN

YELLOW

RED

INDICATOR
TO DRIVER
THAT LINE
IS TRACK CIRCUITED

Four aspect colour light signal

Yellow spectacle

Green spectacle
in front of lamp

Distant signal at clear

Green spectacle

Red spectacle
in front of lamp

Stop signal at danger

BRITISH RAIL SEMAPHORE AND COLOUR-LIGHT SIGNALS

The next stage beyond that is the introduction of automatic speed control. Already automatic trains which drive themselves after the train operator has pressed the start button are at work on London's Victoria Line underground route. Modern signalling is an essential part of our future railway system which will have many trains timed at maximum speeds of 125 or 150 m.p.h.

Freight Services Goods wagons on British Rail have not changed very much in size since the early days of railways, 100 years or so ago. The normal open wagon or covered goods van is still a four-wheeler of about 16 ft. in length, although open wagons for carrying coal are now of all-steel construction instead of wood. One reason for the continuity in size has been the limitation of some goods stations and sidings throughout the country. Some short loading platforms are designed for only one wagon at a time, and sidings in some places can only be reached by short turntables or traversers. Wagon tipplers for lifting and turning wagons upside down can handle only very short wagons. Thus, while coaches have developed into long bogie vehicles, goods wagons have remained about the same size.

But these small wagons are not suited to today's high speeds and the new operating methods now being adopted by the railways. Until a few years ago the normal British goods train was slow moving, with each wagon or group of wagons starting from different stations and terminating at different stations. There were several thousand goods stations which handled all the different types of freight traffic. Very often a wagon would pass through two, three or even more marshalling yards on its journey. The basic division of a goods train was a single wagon. But under Dr. Beeching new methods of operation were investigated. Many small stations and goods yards were closed and freight trains were reorganised to run between main centres without remarshalling. Lorries collect and deliver freight from factories and shops to the main goods stations.

British Rail developed the Freightliner train for carrying goods. These consist of long flat bogie wagons, able to travel at up to 75 m.p.h., for carrying containers. They run as block trains, that is without intermediate remarshalling, between big cities all over the country, for example between London and Liverpool, Manchester, Edinburgh and Aberdeen, Birmingham and Glasgow, Plymouth and London and so on. The containers are loaded in the factory or warehouse, then taken by lorry to the goods station where the container is lifted on to one of the railway wagons. One wagon can often carry up to three containers. When loaded the train sets off on its journey. At the other end the containers are again taken by road to their destination. While they are being unloaded at the factory or warehouse, other containers are being put on to the train which quickly makes another journey.

Coal in special hopper wagons and oil in tank wagons is also taken in block loads, from a colliery or port to a power station or oil storage depot. Some of the latest wagons used in block trains are large bogie types weighing 100 tons fully loaded.

Railway Speeds *The Record-Holders*

Railway speeds in the last few years have increased, but until now British trains have not normally exceeded 100 m.p.h., with averages of 80–90 m.p.h. The first 100 m.p.h. run by rail ever was claimed for the Great Western's 4-4-0 *City of Truro*, which was said to have reached 102·3 m.p.h. on May 9, 1904, with a Plymouth to London mail. This has since been disputed, and L.N.E.R. 4472 *Flying Scotsman* made the first authentic 100 m.p.h. run in 1934.

The world's speed record for steam locomotives is held by Great Britain's No. 60022 *Mallard*, which, in July 1938, reached 126 m.p.h. with a test train between Stoke and Peterborough on the L.N.E.R. main line. The world's rail-speed record for any form of traction is 205 m.p.h., achieved in March, 1955, by the French electric locomotives Nos. BB–9004 and CC–7107 between Bordeaux and Dax. But already the Japanese have gone beyond the 100 m.p.h. speeds at one time thought to be the practicable limit for trains in daily service, with regular speeds of up to 130 m.p.h. on the Tokaido line between Tokyo and Osaka, built specially for high-speed running and opened in 1964. During 1972 the Japanese opened a second high-speed railway, the New San Yo line on which trains run regularly up to 155 m.p.h. and the French introduced a gas turbine train designed to run at 180 m.p.h.

The German, Italian and French railways also are experimenting with trains at 125 m.p.h. on existing main lines, and there is talk of even higher speeds. British Rail is now undertaking research into a new type of high-speed lightweight train powered by gas turbines or electric motors in an endeavour to increase train speeds to 125–150 m.p.h. using existing track. This

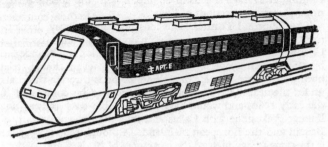

British Railways Experimental Advanced Passenger Train for
150 m.p.h. running

train, known as the Advanced Passenger Train, APT for short,
will have special suspension and the coach bodies will tilt as the
train goes round curves. The APT is not likely to be in service
until the late 1970s. Before the APT comes into service we shall
see another new type of train, the HST—High Speed Train.
It will be of more conventional type but with a diesel locomotive
at each end of every train, and will travel up to 125 m.p.h. It
was the first of the HST units on a trial run in June 1973 which
captured the world's speed record for diesel traction by reaching
141 m.p.h. between York and Northallerton.

French Railways now operate some of the fastest regular
trains in Europe, in terms of start-to-stop average speed, for
one of their trains is timed over the 41 miles from Arras to
Longueau in 29 mins, an average of 84·8 m.p.h. Two other
trains, the 'Mistral' and the 'Cisalpin', cover the 195 miles
between Paris and Dijon at averages of 82·5 and 81·4 m.p.h.
respectively, while 'The Aquitaine' covers the 360 miles from
Paris to Bordeaux at an average of 90 m.p.h. with a top speed of
125 m.p.h.

The German Federal Railway also has some fast runs. At the
top of the list is the electrically-hauled 'Rheingold' express,
which runs the 83 miles from Karlsruhe to Freiburg at an
average speed of 83·3 m.p.h., with top speeds of 100 m.p.h.

For comparison, the fastest British Rail's trains over long
distances are those of the London Midland electrified line from
Euston to Liverpool and Manchester and the East Coast main
line from King's Cross to Edinburgh, both of which have trains

running at average speeds of 80 m.p.h. with top speeds of 100 m.p.h. over long sections of line.

The Channel Tunnel The most exciting railway development of the late 1970's almost certainly would have been the Channel Tunnel which after years of preparation was abandoned by the British Government early in 1975 even though trial boring had started to test tunnelling methods through the chalk under the sea. The Tunnel was expected to be completed in the early 1980s and would have had a double-track railway line linking Folkestone with Calais and thus the railway systems of Britain and the European mainland. Although the track gauge is the same (1·432 metres) the clearances of bridges and stations are about 300 millimetres narrower and lower in Britain so that through trains from the Midlands and North of England to such places as Paris, Brussels or Cologne would have been formed of British-size trains.

But the Channel Tunnel bores (there would be two for the trains, one for each line) would allow even larger trains so that the car-ferry trains carrying road vehicles through the Tunnel would have been more than 12 ft wide and about 16 ft high.

Locomotive numbering on BR In 1973 BR started renumbering its entire fleet of locomotives (except for its three steam locomotives) into a new series in which the locomotive class number forms the first two figures of the complete number. Shunting locomotives are numbered in classes 01 to 13, main line diesel locomotives in classes 20 to 55 and electric locomotives from 71 to 87 though with gaps as some classes have been withdrawn. The first locomotive in each class will be numbered 001. Thus the lowest numbered locomotive is a shunter 01.001, the high-powered Deltic locomotives which haul the expresses on the East Coast main line will be 55.001 to 55.022, and the latest electric locomotives on the Euston-Glasgow line 87.001—87.035. The HST power cars are in class 252.

Preservation Although British Rail no longer runs regular steam locomotives on main lines, steam locomotives are by no means extinct in Britain. Over the last few years as steam engines have been withdrawn many have been sold to private owners for preservation. Some are not in working order and can be seen only as static exhibits at museums. Others, including several large express locomotives, are kept in working order ready to run on BR main line special trips.

Numerous smaller tank and tender engines can be seen running on standard gauge lines operated by preservation societies or private companies. These branches are all in private ownership and new railway companies have been formed to operate services mainly as tourist attractions. Most employ volunteer railway enthusiasts to help run and maintain the line under the guidance of a few professional engineers and other railway staff.

Lines run by private railway companies with steam locomotives.

Standard gauge

Name	Location
Bluebell Railway	Horsted Keynes–Sheffield Park (Sussex)
Dart Valley Railway	{ Totnes–Buckfastleigh (South Devon) Paignton–Kingswear (South Devon)
Keighley & Worth Valley	Keighley–Oxenhope (Yorkshire)
Middleton Railway	Leeds
Severn Valley	Bridgnorth–Hampton Loade–Bewdley (Shropshire)
Lakeside Railway	Windermere Lakeside–Haverthwaite
North Yorkshire Moors	Grosmont–Pickering
Kent & East Sussex Railway	Tenterden–Bodiam

Narrow gauge

Name	Location
Festiniog Railway	Portmadoc–Dduallt (Blaenau Festiniog) (Caernarvonshire)
Talyllyn Railway	Towyn–Abergynolwyn (Merioneth)
Welshpool & Llanfair	Llanfair Caereinion–Castle Caereinion (Montgomery)
Ravenglass & Eskdale	Ravenglass–Dalegarth (Cumberland)
Romney, Hythe & Dymchurch	Hythe–Dungeness (Kent)
Sittingbourne & Kemsley	Sittingbourne (Kent)
Fairbourne	Fairbourne (Merioneth)
Llanberis Lake	Llanberis (Caernarvonshire)
Snowdon Mountain	Llanberis (Caernarvonshire)
Vale of Rheidol (BR)	Aberystwyth–Devils Bridge (Cardiganshire)

NOTE: Some other lines are attempting to complete arrangements to resume services as this edition closed for press.

SOME BRITISH RAILWAYS FACTS AND FIGURES

Largest station area	Clapham Junction	27¾ acres
Largest number of platforms	Waterloo	21

Busiest railway junction	Clapham Junction	2,500 trains each 24 hours

Steepest Main-line Gradients:

	Lickey Incline	1 in 37·7 (nearly 2 miles)
	Exeter (between St David's and Central stations)	1 in 31·3 (7½ chains)
	Dainton Bank (near summit)	1 in 37 (12 chains)
Highest altitude	Druimuachdar	1,484 ft. above sea-level
Longest Bridge	Tay Bridge	2 miles 364 yd.
Longest Tunnel	Severn Tunnel	4 miles 628 yd.

Total number of locomotives in service (November 1974)	Diesel: 3,624
	HST diesel power cars 2
	Electric: 352
	Narrow gauge steam: 3

WORLD RAILWAYS

Facts and Figures

The total mileage of the world's railway routes is nearly 700,000, of which nearly one-third (227,244) is in the U.S.A.

The country with the longest individual railways is Canada. The Canadian National Railways have 23,500 miles of line; the Canadian Pacific Railway, 20,900.

British Rail route mileage open for traffic at the beginning of 1974 (the latest date for which figures are available) is 11,326. The total track mileage is 29,387. Of the route mileage 2,151 is electrified.

The journey between Moscow and Vladivostok, on the Trans-Siberian Railway (nearly 6,000 miles, taking 9 days) is the longest that can be taken without changing trains.

The longest stretch of perfectly straight line in the world runs for 328 miles across the Nullarbor Plain, Australia.

The highest railway station in Europe is 11,333 ft. above sea-level, on the Jungfrau Railway in Switzerland.

The highest railway stations in the world are in Chile (15,817 ft.) and Peru (15,806 ft.).

The world's longest tunnel (other than underground systems) is the Simplon No. 2 opened in 1921, 12 miles 559 yards long. It will be exceeded in 1975 by the new Seikan Tunnel linking the Japanese Islands of Honshu and Hokkaido which will be nearly 22 miles long.

Ships

Sailing Ships   2
Identifying Ships   2–4
Ship's Flags and Signals   4–6
Measures of Wind and Wave   6–7
Biggest Ships   7–8
Fastest Atlantic Crossings   8–9
Naval Vessels   10–13
The Hovercraft   13
Nautical Terms   14–18

SAILING SHIPS

What Is a Ship? An odd question? Well, strictly speaking the word applies only to vessels with three or more masts, all of them *square-rigged*. And a vessel is square-rigged when its main sails are square and are stretched by yards suspended by the middle at right angles to the mast. The other kind of rigging is *fore-and-aft*—that is, the sails are turned so that they run lengthwise of a ship. Look at the picture of sailing-ships: you'll see that one rigged fore-and-aft on the mizzen mast (the mast at the back) is a *barque*. Rig her fore-and-aft on the main mast, too, with only the foremast square-rigged, and she is a *barquentine*. A two-masted vessel with a square rig on both masts and a boom mainsail (you'll see what that is in the picture) is a *brig*; rig the main mast fore-and-aft, and she's a *brigantine*. A vessel rigged entirely fore-and-aft is a *schooner*; give her a square top sail and she's a *topsail schooner*.

Note: Despite what we've said about the strict meaning of the word 'ship', we shall use it in this section, as everyone in practice does, to mean any sea-going vessel.

IDENTIFYING SHIPS

Every shipping company has its own 'house' flag and distinguishes its ships by a particular colour scheme and marking of the funnels and the hull. Ships of the Union-Castle Line, for instance, have lavender-coloured hulls and black and red funnels; those of Canadian Pacific have white hulls with a green line and are green from the loaded water line to the unloaded water line (this area is called the boot topping). P. & O. liners also have white hulls, but can be distinguished by their yellow funnels and the line's own distinctive flag.

You can often tell the company a ship belongs to from its name. For instance, an 'Empress' or a 'Duchess' will be Canadian Pacific; a 'Castle' will be Union-Castle. A name ending in '-ia' almost certainly means the ship is a Cunarder—few vessels

Fore-and-aft Schooner

Topsail Schooner

Brig

Brigantine

Barque

Barquentine

Cutter

belonging to this great line have had any other ending for over a hundred years. White Star used to be associated with the '-ic' ending (*Oceanic*, and the ill-fated *Titanic*), but this is now associated with Shaw Savill. Other lines prefer to stick to certain initial letters; for example, the Royal Mail Steam Packet Co. has an A class and an O class. As to O's—you will find it easy to make a long list of Orient Line ships beginning with that letter.

SHIP'S FLAGS AND SIGNALS

The International Code On the sea, with its traffic of ships from all parts of the world, there must be no barriers of language. The International Code enables ships to communicate with one another no matter what tongue is spoken on board.

A set of signal flags consists of 26 alphabetical flags, 10 numeral pennants (a pennant is a flag that's triangular instead of rectangular), 3 substitutes and the answering, or code, pennant.

Now, every ship at sea has signal letters assigned to it. There are four of these in every case, the first letter or first two letters indicating the nationality of the ship. (For example, British ships' signal letters begin with G or M.)

If you want to signal to a particular ship you first hoist the flags that make that ship's signal letters. If you don't do this, it will be understood that you are addressing all ships within signalling distance.

Ships receiving a signal have to hoist their answering pennant *at the dip* (that is, about half-way up) when they see each flag hoisted, and *close up* (that is, as high as it will go) when they have understood it. The ship sending the message hoists its own answering pennant to show that the message is completed.

The substitutes are used to repeat a letter. If, for example, one wanted to use the letter A three times in a single group of flags, one would clearly need three complete sets of flags to do it, were it not possible to use the substitutes.

All the signal flags have special meanings when flown alone. For example:

A—Flown by man-of-war when on full-speed trial.
B—'I am taking on or discharging explosives.'
G—'Pilot wanted.'

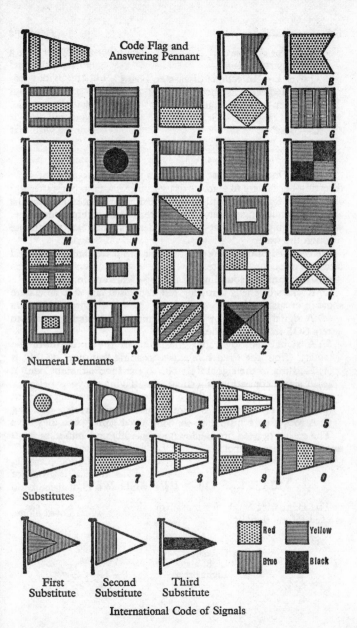

Code Flag and
Answering Pennant

A B

C D E F G

H I J K L

M N O P Q

R S T U V

W X Y Z

Numeral Pennants

1 2 3 4 5

6 7 8 9 0

Substitutes

First
Substitute

Second
Substitute

Third
Substitute

Red   Yellow

Blue   Black

International Code of Signals

H—'Pilot on board.'

P—Departure flag.

Q over L—'Infectious disease on board.'

W—'Medical assistance required.'

Y—'I am carrying mails.'

N and C together—SOS.

C—'Yes.'

N—'No.'

Sirens One short blast on a ship's siren means that she is directing her course to starboard, two short blasts to port, three short blasts for engines full-speed astern. In fog one long blast at intervals not longer than two minutes means a ship is under way, two long blasts that she is under way but not moving through the water.

Distress Signals (*a*) A gun or other explosive signal fired at intervals of about a minute.

(*b*) A continuous sounding of any fog-signal apparatus.

(*c*) Rockets or shells throwing red stars fired one at a time at short intervals.

(*d*) A signal by radio or any other method consisting of the letters SOS in Morse Code.

(*e*) A signal sent by radio consisting of the spoken word 'Mayday' (from the French *m'aidez*, meaning 'help me').

(*f*) Hoisting of the signal flags NC in the International Code.

(*g*) A signal consisting of a square flag having above or below it a ball or anything resembling a ball.

(*h*) Flames on the ship (as from a burning tar barrel).

(*i*) A rocket parachute flare showing a red light.

The ensign hoisted upside down is generally understood as an unofficial distress signal.

MEASURES OF WIND AND WAVE

The **Beaufort Scale** for measuring the force of winds at sea is used internationally.

Scale No.	Wind force	M.p.h.
0	Calm	1
1	Light air	1–3
2	Light breeze	4–7

Scale No.	Wind force	M.p.h.
3	Gentle breeze	8–12
4	Moderate breeze	13–18
5	Fresh breeze	19–24
6	Strong breeze	25–31
7	Near gale	32–38
8	Gale	39–46
9	Strong gale	47–54
10	Storm	55–63
11	Violent storm	64–72
12	Hurricane	73–82
13	Hurricane	83–92
14	Hurricane	93–103
15	Hurricane	104–114
16	Hurricane	115–125
17	Hurricane	126–136

Wave Scale

		Height of waves, crest to trough (ft)
0	Calm	
1	Calm	$\frac{1}{4}$
2	Smooth	$\frac{1}{2}$–1
3	Smooth	2–3
4	Slight	3–5
5	Moderate	6–8
6	Rough	9–13
7	Very rough	13–19
8	High	18–25
9	Very High	23–32
10	Very High	29–41
11	Phenomenal	37–52
12	Phenomenal	45 and over

Note: The highest sea in the Bay of Biscay is 27 ft. In mid-Atlantic the waves will sometimes top 40 ft.

THE WORLD'S BIGGEST SHIPS

	Flag	Tons	Length (feet)	Built
Oil Tankers:				
Globtik Tokyo	British	238,252	1,243·0	1973
Globtik London	British	238,207	1,243·0	1973
Nisseki Maru	Japanese	184,855	1,138·6	1971
Arteaga	Spanish	163,795	1,139·0	1972
Butron	Spanish	163,790	1,139·0	1973
Venoil	Liberian	152,327	1,115·5	1973
Venpet	Liberian	152,327	1,115·5	1973
Svealand	Swedish	152,068	1,108·0	1973

	Flag	Tons	Length (feet)	Built
Universe Iran	Liberian	149,623	1,132·8	1969
Universe Japan	Liberian	149,623	1,132·8	1969
Universe Korea	Liberian	149,623	1,132·8	1969
Universe Portugal	Liberian	149,623	1,132·8	1969
Universe Ireland	Liberian	149,609	1,132·8	1968
Universe Kuwait	Liberian	149,609	1,132·8	1968
Lauderdale	British	143,959	1,101·2	1972
Naess Ambassador	British	143,875	1,101·2	1972
Adele	Liberian	143,686	1,140·0	1971

Passenger Liners:

	Flag	Tons	Length (feet)	Built
France	French	66,348	1,035·0	1961
Queen Elizabeth II	British	65,863	963·0	1969
United States	U.S.A.	50,924	990·0	1952
Canberra	British	45,733	818·5	1961
Oriana	British	41,915	804·0	1960
Rotterdam	Netherlands	37,783	748·6	1959
Nieuw Amsterdam	Netherlands	36,982	758·5	1938

FASTEST ATLANTIC CROSSINGS BEFORE 1900

Date	Port	Ship	Time
1862	Queenstown	Scotia	9 days
1869	Queenstown	City of Brussels	8 days
1882	Queenstown	Alaska	7 days
1889	Queenstown	City of Paris	6 days
1894	Queenstown	Lucania	5½ days
1897	Southampton	Kaiser Wilhelm	6 days

THE BLUE RIBAND: RECORD ATLANTIC CROSS-INGS BY SCREW STEAMSHIPS SINCE 1900

Westward

Date	Ship	European port	d.	Time h.	m.*	Speed (knots)	Sea miles
1900–1	Deutschland (G)	Southampton	5	11	54	23·15	3,044
1907 } 1910 }	Lusitania (B)	Queenstown	{ 4	— 11	40	24·00 25·88	— —
1908 } 1911 }	Mauretania (B)	Queenstown	4	10	41	26·06	—

* Days, hours, minutes.

Date	Ship	European port	Time d.	h.	m.*	Speed (knots)	Sea miles
1929	*Mauretania* (B)	Cherbourg	4	21	44	26·9	3,162
1929	*Bremen* (G)	Cherbourg	4	17	42	27·83	—
1930	*Europa* (G)	Cherbourg	4	17	06	27·91	3,157
1933	*Rex* (It.)	Gibraltar	4	13	58	28·92	3,181
1935	*Normandie* (F)	Bishop's Rock	4	3	02	29·98	3,015
1936} 1938}	*Queen Mary* (B)	Bishop's Rock	{4 3	0 21	27 48	30·14 30·99	2,939 2,907
1952	*United States* (U.S.)	Bishop's Rock	3	12	12	34·51	2,906

* Days, hours, minutes.

Eastward

Date	Ship	European port	Time d.	h.	m.	Speed (knots)	Sea miles
1900–1	*Deutschland* (G)	Eddystone Light	5	7	38	23·51	3,082
1904	*Kaiser Wilhelm II* (G)	Eddystone Light	5	8	16	23·58	—
1907} 1910}	*Lusitania* (B)	Queenstown	{ 4	— 15	 50	23·61 25·57	— —
1908} 1911}	*Mauretania* (B)	Queenstown	4	13	41	25·89	—
1924	*Mauretania* (B)	Cherbourg	5	1	49	26·25	3,198
1929	*Mauretania* (B)	Plymouth	4	17	50	27·22	3,098
1929} 1933} 1933}	*Bremen* (G)	Cherbourg	{4 4 4	14 17 16	30 43 15	27·91 28·14 28·51	3,084 — 3,199
1935} 1937}	*Normandie* (F)	Bishop's Rock	{4 4	3 0	25 06	30·35 30·99	— 2,978
1936} 1938}	*Queen Mary* (B)	Bishop's Rock	{3 3	23 20	57 42	30·63 31·69	— 2,938
1952	*United States* (U.S.)	Bishop's Rock	3	10	40	35·59	3,144

Note: G = Germany; B = Britain; It. = Italy; F = France; U.S. = United States.

NAVAL VESSELS

In general Warships are usually painted grey, except in wartime when they are 'dazzle-painted' in patches of colour (grey, brown, blue) as a form of camouflage. Unlike a merchant ship, a warship has no raised deck at the stern. Propulsion is usually either by steam turbine or oil-fired water-tube boilers: some have diesel engines and a few have gas turbines. Nuclear power has been mainly confined to submarines, with such exceptions as the Soviet Union's ice-breaker *Lenin* and the U.S. passenger-freighter *Savannah*, both government-owned ships. The larger warships have an elaborate system of bulkheads (running the length and breadth of the ship) to enable them to continue floating after accidents or direct hits. The aircraft carrier and the cruiser are armoured (the latter having three or four inches of armour with about two inches of deck plating): smaller ships have no armour, relying on their speed and manoeuvrability. A warship's *standard displacement* is a measurement made when it is ready for sea with ammunition and stores, but omitting fuel and reserve feed water. *Load displacement* refers to the ship ready for sea with all stores, fuel and ammunition.

Aircraft Carrier. *Ark Royal*, 1955. 808 ft

Main Types: The Aircraft Carrier No attacking guns: usually 4.5-in. or 40 mm. guns and some A.A. guns for self-defence. Latest developments include steam catapults and rocket assistance for take-off: the Deck Landing Projector Sight, which is an aid to landing: non-skid decks. The largest carriers are American (the *Enterprise* has a load displacement of 83,350 tons). The only remaining British carrier (which will continue as a fixed-wing carrier until the late 1970's) is the *Ark Royal* (standard displacement, 43,000 tons: 808 ft long: speed, 31 knots: over 40 aircraft).

Cruiser. *Blake,* 1961. 565ft

The Cruiser A general-purpose warship, fast and heavily armed. The largest are American. The two ships of the *Tiger* class are the last big all-gunned ships: the place of guns will be taken in future by guided missiles. The Royal Navy has 2 cruisers in the Operational Fleet, *Tiger* and *Blake* which have both been converted for helicopter-carrying.

Destroyer. Battle class, 1947. 379 ft

The Destroyer A small warship, very fast and man-oeuvrable. Used on general duties and also as mine-layers, radar pickets and on anti-submarine patrols. Destroyers are organised in flotillas, the leader having a black band round the top of the forward funnel. The Royal Navy has nine guided missile destroyers, the largest destroyers in the Fleet (standard displacement, 5,200 tons: 520 ft long: speed, 32 knots: armed with 4 4.5-in. guns, 1 Seaslug guided weapon launcher, 2 Seacat short range guided weapons, and 6 21-in. torpedo tubes). Eight of these are in the Operational Fleet, one is in reserve. Six Type 42 destroyers are under construction.

Frigate.   Leopard class, 1957.   Diesel.   340 ft

The Frigate A term used of a great variety of ships of 1,000
to 2,300 tons. Used on anti-submarine patrols and as escorts to
merchant ships. Some of the latest are designed to act as anti-
aircraft ships in the protection of convoys. The Royal Navy has
60 frigates in the Operational Fleet or engaged on trials and
training. Seven more are under construction.

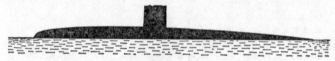

Submarine.   *Dreadnought,* nuclear propelled.   266 ft

The Submarine Underwater warship, long pressurised hull
and small superstructure consisting of the bridge and conning
tower. In conventional submarines diesel engines are used on
the surface, electric motors when submerged. The Royal Navy
has 32 submarines in the Operational Fleet, including four
Polaris submarines (*Resolution, Repulse, Revenge and Renown*)
and eight Fleet submarines (*Dreadnought, Churchill, Conqueror,
Courageous, Swiftsure, Valiant, Warspite* and *Sovereign*). The
Fleet submarines have a standard displacement of 3,500 tons, an
American pressurised water-type reactor driving steam turbines,
a length of 285 ft and a speed of about 30 knots. Four Fleet
submarines are under construction.

Other ships in the Operational Fleet include the Royal
Navy's two assault ships, which can carry an Army battalion and
a brigade group H.Q., landing craft, and R.A.F. as well as R.N.
helicopters. There are also 2 commando ships, 1 ice patrol ship
and 42 ships which constitute the Mine Counter-measure Force.

Submarine.   Porpoise class, 1958.   295 ft

Refitting or in reserve are 17 mooring, salvage and boom vessels, 2 seaward defence boats, 2 fleet maintenance ships, 1 submarine depot ship, 1 royal yacht/hospital ship. There are also 84 fleet support and auxiliary vessels, ranging from minesweeper support ships to fleet replenishment tankers.

THE HOVERCRAFT

The most striking first applications of the hovercraft principle have been on water rather than on land. The hovercraft travels on a cushion of air created between the underside of the vessel and the water or land. The world's first commercial hovercraft service was established in 1962 when British United Airways began carrying passengers over the 19 miles of water between Wallasey and Rhyl. The craft used, a Vickers VA-3, covers the distance with 24 passengers at a speed of about 60 knots. The world's biggest hovercraft, the **Mountbatten**, weighing 165 tons, owned by British Rail and carrying 254 passengers and 30 cars, began flying between Dover and Boulogne in August, 1968.

FURTHER READING

All About Ships and Shipping, ed. E. P. Harnack (Faber)
Boy's Book of World-Famous Liners (Hughes)
Ships and Aircraft of the Royal Navy. H.M.S.O. C.P. 38, available at R.N. Recruitment Centres

Sailing vessel under way

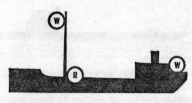
Steam vessel, less than 150 ft long, under way

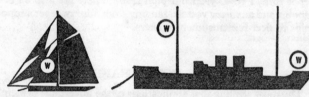
Sailing vessel or steam vessel under 150 ft long, at anchor

Vessel over 150 ft long, at anchor

Lights at sea:
G—Green
R—Red
W—White

Steam vessel, over 150 ft under way

Small pulling boat under way

A vessel not under command

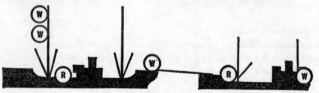
Vessel towing another

NAUTICAL TERMS

abaft, behind.

abeam, opposite the centre of the ship's side.

admiral, from the Arabic *Amir-al-Bahr,* Commander of the Seas.

aft, towards the stern.

alee, away from the wind; to put the helm over to the lee side of the boat.

avast, hold fast, stop; from the Italian *basta,* enough.

ballast, weight put in a ship or boat to help keep her stable; nowadays, usually sea-water.

batten down, to fix tarpaulins to the hatches with iron battens and wedges.

beam, the width of a ship at her widest part.

belay, to make a rope fast to a cleat or belaying pin.

bells are struck to give the time every half-hour, starting anew at each change of watch. 12.30 is one bell; 1, two bells; 1.30, three bells; and so on until 4, which is eight bells; then the pattern is repeated from 4.30, one bell, to 8, eight bells; 8.30 being one bell again, and 12 noon and midnight, eight bells.

bilge, the broadest part of a ship's bottom.

binnacle, the case in which the compass is housed.

boom, a spar for stretching the foot of a sail; any long spar or piece of timber.

bow, the front or forepart of a ship.

bowsprit, a spar projecting from the bow.

bulkhead, a partition dividing a cabin or hold.

bulwark, a ledge round the deck to prevent things falling or being washed overboard.

cable, a sea measure of 100 fathoms.

cleat, a piece of wood or metal fastened on parts of a ship, and having holes or recesses for fastening ropes.

coaming, the rim of a hatchway, raised to prevent water from entering.

companion, a wooden hood over a hatch.

companion-ladder, steps leading down to a cabin.

coxswain, a petty officer in charge of a boat and crew (a 'cock' was a small rowing boat).

davits, iron fittings that project over a ship's side for hoisting a
   boat.

Davy Jones' locker, the bottom of the sea. There are three
   possible explanations for this term:

> 1. Davy Jones was a noted pirate, given to putting his
> victims over the side.
>
> 2. In Negro language 'duffy' or 'davy' is a ghost, and
> 'Jones' means 'Jonah'.
>
> 3. The Hindu goddess of death is called Deva Lokka.

deadlights, a storm-shutter for a cabin window.

displacement, the quantity of water displaced by a boat afloat.

dog watch, a division of the usual four hour's watch, to make a
   change of watches; from 4 to 6 and 6 to 8 p.m.

draught, the depth to which a ship sinks in the water.

fathom, a nautical measure of 6 ft.

fender, a buffer made of bundles of rope, cork or other material,
   to prevent a ship from scraping against a pier when moored.

fid, a wooden tool used for separating the strands of a hemp or
   nylon fibre rope in splicing.

first watch, 8 p.m. till midnight.

flukes, the part of an anchor that hooks into the sea bed.

fore-and-aft, lengthwise of a ship.

forecastle (fo'c'sle), the forepart of the ship under the main-
   deck, the crew's quarters. The term is a survival from the old
   days when high wooden castles were built on each end of a
   fighting ship. The *aftercastle* is a term no longer used, but it
   is interesting to note that the cleaning gear for the after parts
   of ships in the Royal Navy is still stamped AX, the old sign for
   'aftercastle'.

galley, a ship's kitchen.

grapnel, a small anchor with several claws or arms.

halyards, ropes by which sails are hoisted.

hatch, the cover for a hatchway.

hatchway, the opening in a ship's deck into the hold, or from
   one deck to another.

hawse, the bows or forward end of a ship.

hawser, a small cable; a large rope.

Jacob's ladder, a ladder with rope sides and wooden treads.

knot, one nautical mile per hour; 6.80 ft.

lanyard, a short rope used for fastening or stretching.

larboard, the port side: the term was officially banned in 1844, and 'port' substituted, to avoid confusion with 'starboard'.

lee, the sheltered side of a ship.

leeway, the distance a ship is driven to leeward of her true course.

marline spike, an iron tool used for separating the strands of a rope in splicing.

middle watch, from midnight till 4 a.m.

nautical, or sea mile, one-sixtieth of a degree measured at the equator.

night watch, 4 p.m. to 8 p.m.

offing, to seawards; towards the horizon.

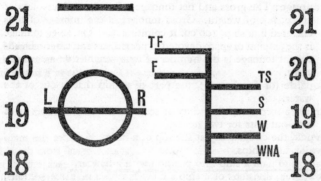

The line and the circle are the original Plimsoll Mark. The top line is the Deck Line. TF = Tropical Fresh Water. F = Fresh Water. TS = Tropical Summer. S = Summer. W = Winter. WNA = Winter North Atlantic. LR = Lloyd's Register. The figures show the amount of water the ship is drawing. They are 6 in. high and the bottom of the figure represents the foot.

Plimsoll line, a line 18 in. long running through a ring painted on both sides of a merchant ship. A ship may be safely loaded until this line is awash. It is named after Samuel Plimsoll, who was responsible for bringing it into use.

poop, the raised after-part of a ship.

port, the left side of a ship looking forward.

quarter, a ship's sides near the stern.

quarter-deck, the after end of the upper deck.

ratlines, the rope steps placed across the shrouds to enable sailors to go aloft.

scuppers, holes in a ship's sides for draining water from the decks.

shrouds, very strong wire ropes which support the masts on both sides.

splicing, joining two ropes by weaving together the untwisted strands.

starboard, the right side of a ship looking forward.

stay, a rope supporting the mast or a spar.

stern, the rear end of a ship.

superstructure, the parts of a ship built above the upper deck.

taffrail, the rail on the counter, or projecting stern, of a ship.

tonnage: The gross and net tonnage of a ship are measures of space, not of weight. Gross tonnage is the number of tons enclosed in a ship, 100 cu. ft counting as 1 ton. Net tonnage is the amount of space devoted to passengers and cargo. Dead-weight tonnage is the number of tons weight that a ship can carry.

topside (or **freeboard**), the part of a ship that is out of the water.

trick, a turn or spell of duty at sea. A trick at the wheel or as look-out lasts for two hours.

truck, the circular cap at the top of a mast.

waist, amidships.

warp, to haul a ship into position with a hawser.

watches, divisions of a ship's crew into two or three sections, one set having charge of the vessel while the others rest. Day and night are divided into watches of four hours each, except the period from 4 p.m. to 8 p.m., which is divided into two dog-watches of two hours each. Men not included in the watches are known as 'Daymen'.

weather side, the side of a ship on which the wind is blowing.

weigh, to heave up the anchor.

yawing, the swinging of a ship's head first in one direction and then in another, due to bad steering or to a high sea.

NAUTICAL MEASURES

6 ft	= 1 fathom
600 ft	= 1 cable
6,080 ft or 2,026·6 yd	= 1 nautical mile
3 nautical miles	= 1 league

The English Language

Some of the Technical Terms of Language	2–5
An Emergency Guide to Punctuation	6–8
A Dictionary of Foreign Phrases and Classical Quotations	9–18
A Short List of American Words and Phrases	19–25
A Dictionary of British Writers	26–30

SOME OF THE TECHNICAL TERMS OF LANGUAGE

THESE are a few of the terms you will meet, and need, when you are thinking or talking about language. It is largely for the sake of those of you who are studying foreign and classical languages that we have included terms like *inflexion*, *gender* and *case*. They are now of little concern to the ordinary user of English; and for this we have to thank William the Conqueror. He brought with him to England not only his capacity for castle-building and strong government but also the French language. This became the official language of England for nearly 300 years. The result was that English for that period escaped from the hands of writers and teachers, who tend to fix a language in all its formality, and passed into the care of the ordinary people, who, by the time it got back into official use, had gaily lopped off nearly all the difficult word-endings, inflexions and marks of gender and case.

affix, a syllable, not a word in itself, which can be added to an existing word in order to change its meaning. See PREFIX and SUFFIX.

alliteration, the use in a phrase or sentence of words that begin with, or contain, the same letter or sound: e.g.

> Lord Lundy from his ear*l*iest years
> Was *f*ar too *f*reely moved to tears.

anagram, a re-arrangement of the letters of a word or phrase which produces another word or phrase: e.g. 'Florence Nightingale' becomes, 'Flit on, cheering angel'.

antecedent, a word which determines the form of another word coming later in the sentence: e.g. in 'Few boys would say that they enjoy washing behind their ears', *boys* is the antecedent of the pronoun *they*, which therefore must be in the plural.

antithesis, words arranged to stress a contrast: e.g. 'To err is human, to forgive divine.'

antonym, a word whose meaning is directly opposite to that of another word: e.g. *light* and *dark*, *large* and *small*, *clean* and *dirty.*

apposition, a second description of a person or thing placed side by side with the first, the second having grammatically the same value as the first: e.g. 'Jones, *captain of Wales*, scored the final try.'

auxiliary verb, a verb that has no meaning itself but helps to make the meaning of another verb: e.g. *will* in 'I will go', *do* in 'I do see what you mean'.

case, the grammatical function of a noun or pronoun: i.e. whether it is subject, object, genitive, etc. Case has almost vanished from the English language, but it is worth remembering that the *subject* is said to be *nominative*; the *object, accusative*; the *indirect object, dative*; and the *apostrophe form of the word* (Jean's, Jim's), *genitive.*

clause, a group of words containing subject and predicate but not expressing a complete idea: e.g. 'A marshal *who can rid the town of rustlers*—that's what we want.'

complement, a noun or adjective forming the predicate of a verb that cannot govern a direct object: e.g. 'He is *silly*', 'He became *captain.*'

conjugation, the inflexion (*q.v.*) of verbs.

declension, the inflexion (*q.v.*) of nouns or adjectives.

diaresis, the pronouncing of two successive vowels as separate sounds, often marked by the sign (¨) over the second: e.g. Chloë, aërated.

epigram, a short poem, especially one with a witty twist in it; any sharp, memorable saying.

epithet, an adjective.

etymology, the study of the origin of words.

euphemism, disguising a nasty fact with a nice name: e.g. saying 'he is putting on weight' when you mean 'he's getting fat'.

gender, the distinction of nouns according to sex. (As far as their own language is concerned, lucky Englishmen hardly have to bother about this.)

gerund, a noun formed from a verb by adding *-ing*: e.g. '*Walking* is good for you', '*Parking* is forbidden.'

homonym, a word that looks the same as another word but has a different meaning: e.g. *bear*, meaning 'carry' and 'a shaggy animal'; *peer*, meaning 'a lord' and 'peep'.

hyperbole, use of exaggerated terms for emphasis, as in 'a thousand thanks', 'he's got tons of money'.

indirect object, the person or thing towards whom an action is directed: e.g. 'I gave *him* a penny.'

inflexion, the change made in the form of words to show what grammatical part they play in a sentence: e.g. *him* is formed by inflexion from *he.*

litotes, deliberate understatement for effect: e.g. saying *not a few* when you mean *a great many.*

malapropism, named after Mrs Malaprop in Sheridan's play, *The Rivals.* 'She's as headstrong as an *allegory* on the banks of the Nile,' said Mrs Malaprop, meaning *alligator.* That is a malapropism: an attempt to use a difficult word and getting it wrong.

meiosis, general understatement—the opposite of hyperbole: e.g. 'Golly, this is *some* game' (meaning it's a terrific game), 'I *didn't half* enjoy it' (meaning you enjoyed it immensely).

metaphor, a telescoped simile (*q.v.*)—instead of saying something is like something else, you say it *is* that other thing. E.g. not 'Sir Jasper is like a fox', but 'Sir Jasper is a fox'. Language is full of metaphors: the *spine* of a book, a *blind* alley, saw-*teeth,* etc.

metonymy, naming something not by its own name, but by something closely associated with it: e.g. 'The Crown' for 'the Government'.

mixed metaphor, using together metaphors that don't match, with ridiculous results: e.g. 'Well, he's a dark horse, and he can paddle his own canoe.'

onomatopœia, the forming of a word so that it resembles the sound of the thing of which it is the name: e.g. *click, cuckoo, babble.*

oratio obliqua, indirect or reported speech: e.g. a friend says 'I am grateful' and you report this as: 'He said he was grateful.'

oxymoron, using together in one expression words that are contradictory: e.g. *bitter-sweet,* or 'he was a *happy pessimist*'.

palindrome, a word or sentence that reads the same backwards or forwards: e.g. 'Madam, I'm Adam.'

periphrasis, presenting an idea in a roundabout, wordy way.

phrase, any group of words, usually without a predicate.

predicate, the part of a sentence that tells you about, or describes, the subject.

prefix, an affix attached to the beginning of words: e.g. *dis-*, *un-*, *in-* in the words 'disappeared', 'uninterested', 'invaluable'.

prosody, the technique of verse—its rhyme, metre, etc.

pun, a play on words, different in meaning but the same in sound, so as to produce an amusing effect: e.g. Tom Hood's

> A cannon-ball took off his legs,
> So he laid down his arms.

(*Note*: A pun can be used seriously; there are several examples in Shakespeare.)

rhetorical question, a question that isn't asked in order to obtain an answer, but as a striking way of suggesting that the answer is obvious: e.g. 'Did you ever see such a rotten bowler as Smith?'

simile, likening one thing to another: e.g. 'The ice was like iron', 'He ran like the wind.'

spoonerism, getting the initial letters of words mixed up: e.g. the statement of the famous Dr Spooner (after whom this error was named) that an undergraduate had 'hissed all his mystery lectures'.

split infinitive, putting a word between the parts of the infinitive: e.g. 'to quickly run', 'to suddenly fall down'. A safe rule is to avoid it if it sounds clumsy, but not if it is the sharpest and neatest way of saying what you want to say.

suffix, an affix attached to the end of a word: e.g. *-ness*, *-ship*, *-able* in the words 'thinness', 'scholarship', 'bearable'.

syllepsis, e.g. 'He was kicking the football with determination and his left foot', 'She lost her spectacles and her temper'.

synecdoche, naming a part when you mean the whole: e.g. 'a fleet of a hundred sail' (meaning ships).

synonyms, words that are much the same in meaning and use: e.g. beautiful, handsome, good-looking; breakable, fragile, frail.

syntax, the part of grammar that deals with the way words are arranged in sentences.

tautology, unnecessary repetition: e.g. 'I have been *all alone by myself* for hours.'

AN EMERGENCY GUIDE TO PUNCTUATION

If you want to feel in a really dangerous, exposed position, sit down to write a simple, brief guide to punctuation—knowing that H. G. Fowler, in his *Modern English Usage*, devoted 1,000 worried words to the comma alone, and that punctuation is always to some extent an individual matter. However, this section, as warily as possible, sets down such rules as it is safe to pass on. It is meant as a simple, rough-and-ready guide for emergencies.

Remember: punctuation is only a way of helping your reader to understand the sense of what you write. In speech you make your meaning clear by your pauses and by the way your voice rises and falls (e.g. the listener knows when you're asking a question from the way your voice rises at the end of the sentence). Punctuation is simply a collection of devices for getting these pauses and these rises and falls of voice on to paper. (E.g. your rising voice at the end of a question is suggested by the question-mark.)

A. To mark where a sentence ends we use one of three stops:

    (i) a **full stop** (.) where the sentence is a statement;
    (ii) a **question mark** (?) where the sentence asks a question;
    (iii) an **exclamation mark** (!) where the sentence is an exclamation.

B. The **comma** (,) is the stop that stands for the little pauses after single words or groups of words. Read the following sentence aloud (it comes from *Huckleberry Finn*) and note how the commas mark the pauses and the ups and downs of your voice:

We went to a clump of bushes, and Tom made everybody swear to keep the secret, and then showed them a hole in the hill, right in the thickest part of the bushes.

Warning. Alas, it's not always as easy as this. If you've got tangled up in one of the comma's trickier uses, try pp. 96–99 in Eric Partridge's *You Have a Point There*.

C. A more definite pause in the sentence is marked by a **semicolon** (;). For example, you might write:

> *There was no football this afternoon; the weather was far too wet.*

You could say there are two sentences here; but (as has happened in the sentence you're now reading) the sense of each is so closely connected with the sense of the other that they gain from not being separated completely.

D. The **colon** (:) is generally used before a list of things or a quotation. E.g.

> *He told us what he had brought with him: a penknife, a fishing-rod, his lunch and half a pound of worms.*

or

> *Shakespeare wrote: 'To be or not to be, that is the question.'*

But *be warned*: some writers like to use the colon (as we have done in this sentence) where others would use a semi-colon.

E. **Inverted commas** or **quotation marks** (" ") are used (i) to mark off the actual words of a speaker where it is *those actual words* that you are writing down, e.g.

> *"Oh Lord," groaned the reader, "punctuation does seem difficult."*

or (ii) to mark off a quotation that comes inside a sentence: e.g.

> *When he got to "See how they run" he made little running movements with his fingers.*

Note: punctuation marks that don't belong to the quotation come outside the quotation marks. E.g.

> *Did I hear you recite "There was an old man of Kilkenny"?* (not *"There was an old man of Kilkenny?"*).

Warning: There are two kinds of inverted commas, (" ") and (' '). It doesn't matter which you use; but note the following:

> *Tom said, "Did I hear you recite 'There was an old man of Kilkenny'?"*

Where—as here—there's a quotation inside a quotation, use

your chosen mark for the main quotation and the other mark for
the quotation inside it.

F. **Dashes** (—) or **brackets** ( ) are used to enclose things
that are really said *aside*—in other words, they don't belong to
the main structure of the sentence. If I say:

> *He's a good boy and—as I was saying to his mother yesterday
> —his work has been excellent,*

my main sentence is *He's a good boy and his work has been
excellent. As I was saying to his mother yesterday* is said aside,
and goes either between dashes or between brackets.

G. The **apostrophe** (') is not so difficult as some people
make it (we knew a desperate little boy who'd grasped only that
it often accompanies the letter 's', and so put it in front of every
letter 's' he wrote, even in the middle of a word). There are two
main uses of the apostrophe:

> (i) to show possession: *George's book, Mr Davis's Jaguar*;
> (ii) to mark a missing letter: e.g. *don't* (*do not*), *it's* (*it is*).

(Of course, in *shan't* the apostrophe marks several missing
letters. In the eighteenth century it was written *sha'n't*.)

H. An important use of the **hyphen** (-) is to join words where
failing to join them would falsify one's meaning. E.g. a *gold
nibbed pen* is a pen made of gold with a nib in it; a *gold-nibbed
pen* is a pen (of whatever material) that has a gold nib.

FURTHER READING

You Have a Point There, by Eric Partridge
Mind Your Language! by Ivor Brown (Bodley Head)
Words! Words! Words! by Andrew Scotland (Cassell)
Modern English Usage, by H. G. Fowler (Oxford)

A DICTIONARY OF FOREIGN PHRASES AND CLASSICAL QUOTATIONS

It may seem odd to have a collection of words and phrases from other tongues in the middle of a section on THE ENGLISH LANGUAGE. But, rich though our own language is, we still find that certain things have been expressed most strikingly by the old Greeks or Romans or by modern Frenchmen. In some cases it is not simply that other nations have found a better way of saying something, but that there is a sort of historical flavour about a phrase that disappears if it is translated into English. 'Life is short, art is long' is somehow not quite the same thing as 'Vita brevis, ars longa'. Here, anyway, is a list of such phrases as are still in general use.

Abbreviations: Fr., French; Gr., Greek; Ger., German; It., Italian; L., Latin; Sp., Spanish.

à bas (Fr.), down, down with
ab extra (L.), from without
ab initio (L.), from the beginning
à bon marché (Fr.), good bargain, cheap
ab ovo (L.), from the egg
absit omen (L.), may there be no ill omen
ab uno disce omnes (L.), from one example you may judge the rest
ab urbe condita (L.), from the founding of the city: i.e. Rome, 753 B.C.
à cheval (Fr.), on horseback
à compte (Fr.), on account; in part payment
ad astra (L.), to the stars
ad Calendas Graecas (L.), at the Greek Calends—i.e. never, since the Greek had no Calends
à demi (Fr.), by halves, half
a Deo et rege (L.), from God and the king
à deux (Fr.), of two, between two, two-handed
ad finem (L.), to the end, towards the end

ad hoc (L.), for this purpose

ad hominem (L.), to the man, personal

a die (L.), from that day

ad infinitum (L.), to infinity

ad libitum (L.), at pleasure

ad majorem Dei gloriam (L.), for the greater glory of God

ad nauseam (L.), to the point where one becomes disgusted

ad rem (L.), to the point

ad valorem (L.), according to value

advocatus diaboli (L.), devil's advocate

aetatis suae (L.), of his (or her) age

affaire de coeur (Fr.), an affair of the heart

affaire d'honneur (Fr.), an affair of honour

a fortiori (L.), with stronger reason

à haute voix (Fr.), aloud

à jamais (Fr.), for ever

à la bonne heure (Fr.), in good time; all right; as you please

à la mode (Fr.), in fashion

à la mort (Fr.), to the death

al fresco (It.), in the open air

allez vous en! (Fr.), away with you!

alma mater (L.), benign mother—applied by old students to their university

alter ego (L.), one's second self

à merveille (Fr.), wonderfully

à moitié (Fr.), half, by halves

amor vincit omnia (L.), love conquers all

ancien régime (Fr.), the old order of things

anno Domini (L.), in the year of our Lord

anno mundi (L.), in the year of the world

annus mirabilis (L.), year of wonders

ante bellum (L.), before the war

ante meridiem (L.), before noon

à outrance (Fr.), to the bitter end

à pied (Fr.), on foot

à propos de bottes (Fr.), apropos of boots—i.e. beside the point

à propos de rien (Fr.), apropos of nothing

aqua vitae (L.), water of life

à quoi bon? (Fr.), what's the good of it?

arrière pensée (Fr.), a mental reservation
ars est celare artem (L.), true art is to conceal art
ars longa, vita brevis (L.), art is long, life is short
à tout prix (Fr.), at any price
au contraire (Fr.), on the contrary
au courant (Fr.), fully acquainted with
audi alterem partem (L.), hear the other side
au fait (Fr.), well acquainted with; expert
au fond (Fr.), at bottom
au grand sérieux (Fr.), in all seriousness
au naturel (Fr.), in the natural state
au pied de la lettre (Fr.), close to the letter; quite literally
au revoir (Fr.), goodbye; till we meet again
autres temps, autres moeurs (Fr.), other times, other manners
aux armes! (Fr.), to arms!
ave atque vale (L.), hail and farewell
à volonté (Fr.), at pleasure
basta! (It.), enough!
beau monde (Fr.), the world of fashion
bête noire (Fr.), a bugbear; your favourite hate
bien entendu (Fr.), of course; to be sure
bis (L.), twice; encore
bon diable (Fr.), good-natured fellow
bon goût (Fr.), good taste
bona fides (L.), good faith
bon mot (Fr.), a witty saying
bonne bouche (Fr.), a tasty morsel
bon ton (Fr.), the height of fashion
bon vivant (Fr.), one who lives well
bon voyage! (Fr.), a good journey to you!
caput (Ger.), utterly beaten, done for
carpe diem (L.), enjoy the present day
casus belli (L.), that which causes or justifies war
cause célèbre (Fr.), a notable trial
caveat emptor (L.), let the buyer beware
cave canem (L.), beware of the dog
cela va sans dire (Fr.), that goes without saying
c'est-à-dire (Fr.), that is to say
ceteris paribus (L.), other things being equal
chacun son goût (Fr.), every one to his taste

cherchez la femme! (Fr.), look for the woman; there's a woman at the bottom of it!

çi-devant (Fr.), before this; former

comme il faut (Fr.), as it should be; correct

compos mentis (L.), of sound mind; sane

compte rendu (Fr.), an account rendered; a report

coram populo (L.), in the presence of the public

cordon sanitaire (Fr.), a line of guards posted to keep contagious disease within a certain area

corpus delicti (L.), the substance of the crime or offence

coup d'état (Fr.), a sudden decisive blow in politics

coûte que coûte (Fr.), cost what it may

crême de la crême (Fr.), cream of the cream; the very best

cui bono? (L.), to whose advantage is it? who is the gainer?

cum grano salis (L.), with a grain of salt

de bonne grace (Fr.), with good grace; willingly

de facto (L.), from the fact; actual or actually

de gustibus non est disputandum (L.), there is no arguing about tastes

de haut en bas (Fr.), from top to bottom

dei gratia (L.), by the grace of God

de jure (L.), in law; by right

de mal en pis (Fr.), from bad to worse

de minimis non curat lex (L.), the law does not concern itself with very small matters

de mortuis nil nisi bonum (L.), speak nothing but good of the dead

de novo (L.), anew

deo volente (L.), God willing

de pis en pis (Fr.), worse and worse

de profundis (L.), out of the depths

de rigueur (Fr.), compulsory; indispensable

desunt cetera (L.), the rest is missing

de trop (Fr.), too much, or too many; superfluous

deus ex machina (L.), a god out of the machine; one who puts things right at a critical moment

dies irae (L.), day of wrath; the day of judgement

Dieu et mon droit (Fr.), God and my right

dolce far niente (It.), sweet-doing-nothing; pleasant idleness

Domine dirige nos! (L.), Lord, direct us!

Dominus illuminatio mea (L.), the Lord is my enlightening

double entendre (Fr.), a double meaning; a play on words

dramatis personae (L.), characters of the play

ecce! (L.), behold!

eheu fugaces . . . labuntur anni (L.), alas! the fleeting years slip away!

ejusdem generis (L.), of the same kind

embarras de richesses (Fr.), an embarassment of riches

en avant! (Fr.), forward!

en déshabillé (Fr.), in undress

en famille (Fr.), with one's family

enfant terrible (Fr.), a terrible child; a little terror

en fête (Fr.), festive; keeping holiday

en masse (Fr.), in a body; all together

en passant (Fr.), in passing; by the way

en plein jour (Fr.), in broad day

en rapport (Fr.), in agreement; in sympathy with

en règle (Fr.), in order; according to rules

en route (Fr.), on the way

entente cordiale (Fr.), cordial understanding

en tout cas (Fr.), in any case, at all events

en train (Fr.), in progress

entre nous (Fr.), between ourselves

e pluribus unum (L.), one out of many

errare est humanum (L.), to err is human

esprit de corps (Fr.), the animating spirit of a collective body, such as a regiment, school, etc.

et tu, Brute! (L.), and you, too, Brutus! (said to be Julius Caesar's last words)

Eureka! (Gr.), I have found it!

ex cathedra (L.), from the chair of office

ex curia (L.), out of court

exempli gratia (L.), by way of example

ex gratia (L.), as an act of grace

ex libris (L.), from the books

ex officio (L.), by virtue of his office

experientia docet (L.), experience teaches

experto crede (L.), trust one who has tried

ex post facto (L.), after the deed is done; retrospective

façon de parler (Fr.), way of speaking

fait accompli (Fr.), a thing already done

far niente (It.), doing nothing

faute de mieux (Fr.), for want of better

faux pas (Fr.), a false step; a slip in behaviour

favete linguis (L.), favour me with your tongues, i.e. be silent

felo de se (L.), a suicide

festina lente (L.), hurry slowly

fiat justitia, ruat coelum (L.), let justice be done, though the heavens fall

fiat lux (L.), let there be light

fidei defensor (L.), defender of the faith

flagrante delicto (L.), in the very act

floreat (L.), let it flourish!

fons et origo (L.), the source and origin

force majeure (Fr.), superior power; a force one cannot resist

fortiter in re, suaviter in modo (L.), forcibly in deed, gently in manner

gaudeamus igitur (L.), so let us rejoice!

gloria in excelsis (L.), glory to God in the highest

hic et ubique (L.), here and everywhere

hic jacet (L.), here lies

hinc illae lacrimae (L.), hence (come) those tears

hoc genus omne (L.), and all that sort (of people)

hoi polloi (Gr.), the many; the rabble

homme d'affaires (Fr.), a man of business

homme du monde (Fr.), a man of the world

honi soit qui mal y pense (Fr.), evil to him who evil thinks

honoris causa (L.), for the sake of honour; honorary

hors de combat (Fr.), unfit to fight

hors concours (Fr.), outside the competition

ich dien (Ger.), I serve

idée fixe (Fr.), a fixed idea

idem (L.), the same

id est (L.), that is

in camera (L.), in a (judge's private) room; in secret

index expurgatorius (L.), a list of forbidden books

in excelsis (L.), in the highest

in extenso (L.), at full length

in extremis (L.), at the point of death

infra dignitatem (L.), below one's dignity

in medias res (L.), in the midst of things

in memoriam (L.), in memory; to the memory of
in re (L.), in the matter of
in situ (L.), in its original position
in statu pupillari (L.), in the state of being a ward
integer vitae (L.), blameless of life
inter alia (L.), among other things
in toto (L.), entirely
in vino veritas (L.), there is truth in wine; truth is told by him
    who has drunk wine
ipse dixit (L.), he himself said it
ipsissima verba (L.), the very words
ipso facto (L.), in the fact itself; by this very fact
je ne sais quoi (Fr.), I know not what
laborare est orare (L.), work is prayer
lapsus linguae (L.), a slip of the tongue
lares et penates (L.), household gods
laudator temporis acti (L.), one who praises past times
laus Deo (L.), praise to God
lèse-majesté (Fr.), high treason
lettre de cachet (Fr.), a sealed letter; a royal warrant for arrest
    or imprisonment
lex talionis (L.), the law of retaliation
locum tenens (L.), a deputy
magnum opus (L.), a great work
male fide (L.), with bad faith; treacherously
mal à propos (Fr.), ill-timed
mariage de convenance (Fr.), marriage for advantage rather
    than love
mauvaise honte (Fr.), false modesty
mauvais sujet (Fr.), a worthless fellow
mea culpa (L.), by my own fault
memento mori (L.), remember that you must die
mens sana in corpore sano (L.), a sound mind in a sound
    body
meo periculo (L.), at my own risk
meum et tuum (L.), mine and thine
modus operandi (L.), plan of working
modus vivendi (L.), a way of living
mot juste (Fr.), exactly the right word
multum in parvo (L.), much in little
mutatis mutandis (L.), with necessary changes

nemo me impune lacessit (L.), no one hurts me with impunity

ne plus ultra (L.), nothing further; perfection

nil admirari (L.), to admire nothing, to be superior and self-satisfied

nil desperandum (L.), never despair

noblesse oblige (Fr.), rank imposes obligations; much is expected from people in high positions

nolens volens (L.), whether he will or not

noli me tangere (L.), don't touch me

nolle prosequi (L.), to be unwilling to prosecute

nom de guerre (Fr.), an assumed name

nom de plume (Fr.), a pen name

non compos mentis (L.), not of sound mind

nosce teipsum (L.), know thyself

nota bene (L.), mark well

nouveaux riches (Fr.), persons who have only recently become rich; upstarts

nulli secundus (L.), second to none

obiit (L.), he, or she, died

obiter dictum (L.), a thing said by the way

ora pro nobis (L.), pray for us

O sancta simplicitas! (L.), O sacred simplicity!

O! si sic omnia! (L.), Oh, would that all (had been done or said) thus!

O tempora! O mores! (L.), O the times! O the manners!

pace (L.), by leave of

panem et circenses (L.), (give us) bread and circuses! (the cry of the Roman populace)

par excellence (Fr.), eminently, by way of ideal

par exemple (Fr.), for example

pari passu (L.), with equal pace; together

peccavi (L.), I have sinned

pièce de résistance (Fr.), the best item

pied-à-terre (Fr.), temporary lodging

pinxit (L.), (he) painted (this)

pis aller (Fr.), the last or worst shift

poste restante (Fr.), to remain in the Post Office till called for

post hoc, propter hoc (L.), after this, therefore because of this (a false reasoning)

post mortem (L.), after death

prima facie (L.), on the first view

primus inter pares (L.), first among equals

proxime accessit (L.), he came next

quis custodiet ipsos custodes? (L.), who will watch the watchers?

qui s'excuse s'accuse (Fr.), he who excuses himself, accuses himself

quod erat demonstrandum (L.), which was to be proved

quod erat faciendum (L.), which was to be done

quot homines, tot sententiae (L.), so many men, so many opinions

rara avis (L.), a rare bird

reculer pour mieux sauter (Fr.), to draw back to take a better leap

reductio ad absurdum (L.), the reducing of a position to a logical absurdity

répondez, s'il vous plait (Fr.), reply, please

requiescat in pace (L.), may he (or she) rest in peace

revenons à nos moutons (Fr.), let us return to our sheep; let us return to our subject

ruat coelum (L.), let the heavens fall

rus in urbe (L.), the country in the town

sans peur et sans reproche (Fr.), without fear and without reproach

sans souci (Fr.), without care

satis verborum (L.), enough of words

sauve qui peut (Fr.), save himself who can

semper idem (L.), always the same

sic transit gloria mundi (L.), so passes away earthly glory

sic vis pacem, para bellum (L.), if you want peace, prepare war

sine die (L.), without a day being appointed

sine qua non (L.), without which, not; an indispensable condition

sotto voce (It.), in an undertone

status quo (L.), the state in which: things as they now are

stet (L.), let it stand; do not delete

sub judice (L.), under consideration

sub poena (L.), under a penalty

sub rosa (L.), under the rose; privately

sub specie (L.), under the appearance of

succès d'estime (Fr.), a success of esteem or approval (if not profit)

suggestio falsi (L.), a suggestion of something false

sui generis (L.), of its own kind; peculiar

summum bonum (L.), the chief good

sursum corda (L.), lift up your hearts

tabula rasa (L.), a blank tablet

tant mieux (Fr.), so much the better

tant pis (Fr.), so much the worse

tempora mutantur, nos et mutamur in illis (L.), the times are changing and we with them

tempus fugit (L.), time flies

terra incognita (L.), an unknown land

tertium quid (L.), a third something

tête-à-tête (F.), a private interview, a confidential conversation

tour de force (Fr.), a feat of strength or skill

tout à fait (Fr.), entirely

tout à l'heure (Fr.), instantly

tout de suite (Fr.), immediately

tu quoque (L.), you too

ubique (L.), everywhere

ultima Thule (L.), the utmost limit

ultra vires (L.), beyond one's powers

veni, vidi, vici (L.), I came, I saw, I conquered

verbum sat sapienti (L.), a word is enough for a wise man

via media (L.), a middle course

vice versa (L.), the terms being reversed

videlicet (L.), that is to say; namely

vi et armis (L.), by force and arms

virginibus puerisque (L.), for girls and boys

vis-à-vis (Fr.), opposite

viva voce (L.), by the living voice; orally

vogue la galère! (Fr.), come what may!

voilà tout (Fr.), that's all

vox et praeterea nihil (L.), a voice and nothing more

vox populi, vox Dei (L.), the voice of the people is the voice of God

A SHORT LIST OF AMERICAN WORDS AND PHRASES

The Americans, of course, speak English. But their English is no longer quite the English that is spoken in the British Isles: and sometimes the differences between the two can cause great puzzlement—especially when (as in *biscuit*) the word is the same but the meanings no longer match. This is a list of common words and phrases that are most likely to give rise to difficulties. Some of them, of course, find their way across the Atlantic every year; and it might be interesting to guess which ones, as they become familiar, will have to come out of this list in later editions.

aluminum, aluminium
attorney, lawyer
baggage-check, luggage-ticket
barkeep, barman
baseball park, a baseball playing-field
battery, the pitcher and catcher together in a baseball team
bill, banknote
billboard, hoarding
billion, 1,000,000,000 (as compared with the English billion, which is 1,000,000,000,000. This is said to be the only example of something bigger in English than in American)
cracker, biscuit
biscuit, a soft cake rather like a scone, never sweet, and served hot with butter
bit, 12½ cents
bone up, to swot up
boner, a howler
bootlegger, an illicit seller of liquor
bouncer, chucker-out
box, the rectangular space in which the pitcher stands at baseball
boxcar, a freight-car on the railway, enclosed and covered
brakeman, guard on a freight train
bug, any insect

bully, first-rate
bumper, railway buffers
bureau, dressing-table
buzz saw, circular saw
caboose, brake van on a goods train
cage, the special enclosure in which batting practice for baseball is carried on
cake, cake; but in the plural (**cakes**) it always means a kind of pancake
candy, sweets
candy-store, confectioners
car, a railway carriage or coach; sometimes the cage of a lift
cars (the), a train
carousel, roundabout
casket, coffin
check, cheque
check-room, cloakroom
checkers, draughts
chuckwagon, a wagon carrying food supplies for cowboys, pioneers, etc
clerk, sometimes a shop assistant
comfort station, public convenience
composition book, exercise book
conductor, guard on a passenger train
construction gang, gang of navvies on the railway
davenport, couch
depot, railway station (this use is now dying out)
derby (pronounced as spelt), a bowler hat
diamond, baseball field
dinner-pail, the container for a workman's or a schoolchild's midday meal
dirt wagon, dust cart
district attorney, public prosecutor
dooryard, backyard or back garden
doughboy, an infantry soldier
dove, dived
downtown, the business district in an American city (see **uptown**)
dresser, chest of drawers or dressing table
drug store, chemist's shop (soft drinks are sold there, too)
dry goods, articles of drapery, haberdashery, etc

duster, light overcoat or wrap
El, the elevated railway
engineer, engine driver
faucet, tap
fender, bumper of a car
first floor, ground floor
fixings, the garnishings of a meal
fraternity, an organisation of male students, usually designated by two or more Greek letters (e.g. the Phi Beta Kappa). See **sorority**
garbage can, dustbin
gas (short for **gasoline**), petrol
get next to, get wise to
given name, Christian name
gondola, railway wagon without sides or with very low sides
grab bag, lucky dip
grade, a division in American schools, similar to the English 'year'; also a mark in examinations
greenbacks, paper money
gridiron, a football field
guard, prison warder
haberdashery, articles for men's wear
hard sledding, a difficult task
hayseed, a yokel
highball, whisky and soda with broken ice in a tall glass
high-toned, stylish, superior
hogpen, a pig sty
home plate, base at first corner of the diamond in baseball; also the base at which the batter stands to bat
home run, or **homer,** a hit that allows the batter in baseball to make a circuit of all the bases without an error being made in handling the ball
homely, plain, ugly
homestead, a piece of land allotted under an Act of 1862 which gave possession of the land to any head of family who had lived on it for five years and had paid a small fee
homesteader, owner of a homestead
hood, the bonnet of a car
hundredweight, 100 lbs.
inaugural, the address made by a new President of the US on the day he takes office (**inauguration day**)

in short order, in no time, immediately

intermission, a school break

intersection, a street crossing

jag, a load (especially a load of liquor, more than the drinker can carry)

jail delivery, a mass escape from prison

janitor, a caretaker

jay, a simpleton

jug-handled, one-sided, unfair

jumping-rope, a skipping rope

keyman, a telegraphist

knock, to find fault with

line, a queue, a boundary

log-rolling, an agreement among politicians each to vote for some item of legislation desired by the others

longshoreman, a docker

lot, a plot of ground

luggage, empty baggage

lunch, a light snack taken at any time in the day

major, to specialise in a subject: an American student is said to major in the subject or subjects to which he gives most of his attention

make out, get along, manage

mean, seedy ('I feel mean tonight'): troublesome, inconvenient, unpleasant ('It was a mean, dirty job')

monkeyshines, capers

mortician, an undertaker

muslin, calico

name for, name after ('John was named for his uncle, Senator John Smith')

newsy, newsboy

night robes, night clothes

night stick, a policeman's truncheon

nine, a baseball team (compare the English 'cricket **eleven**')

nip and tuck, neck and neck, a close thing

notion department, the haberdashery section of an American department store

of, used in American in the sense of **before** a particular hour, e.g. 'At ten minutes of seven I got up'

Old Colony, Massachusetts

Old Dominion, Virginia

Old Glory, the American flag

overly, excessively

owl train, a train running in the small hours of the night

paddle, to spank, to smack

panhandle, a narrow strip of land within the boundaries of a state but projecting from the main body of that state. (Look at West Virginia in the atlas: this is called **the Panhandle State**)

pass up, to refuse, decline

patrolman, a policeman

patrol wagon, a prison van, Black Maria

pavement, roadway

pay dirt, the earth in which a miner finds gold

peek-a-boo, hide and seek

penny, a one-cent piece

pie, tart. (The English **pie** is sometimes called in America a deep pie.)

pilot, a cowcatcher on a train

pint, 16 fl. oz. (as compared with the English pint of 20 fl. oz.)

pitcher, the player in baseball who throws the ball to the batter; he tries to 'strike' the batter out, or to 'fan' him, i.e. to cause him to fail in three attempts to hit the ball

platform, one of the projecting ends of a railway car on which passengers step when entering a train. (American railway stations usually have no platforms in the English sense of the word.)

plug-hat, a silk hat

pocket-book, a purse

point, a nib

porch, a verandah on a house

porch climber, a cat burglar

precinct, a division of a city for police or electoral purposes

prison warden, a prison governor

push-pin, a drawing pin

pussyfoot, to attempt to achieve one's aims by concealing what one is up to

quarter, a 25-cent piece

quitter, a shirker

railroad, to get something done in a rush

realtor, an estate agent

river, this word in American is always behind the name of the river, never in front (e.g. Hudson River, Mississippi River)

robin, a red-breasted thrush

rock, a stone of any size

root for, to encourage a team by cheering it on

round-trip ticket, return ticket

roundabout, a short jacket worn by a boy

roundsman, a policeman

rubber, to crane one's neck in order to see or hear

rubberneck, someone standing and staring

rubbers, overshoes

sand, courage, grit

schedule, timetable (the **ch** is pronounced as a **k**)

scratch-pad, scribbling block

section, district of a town or city

sedan, a saloon car

sherbet, a kind of water ice

shingle, the signboard of a professional man

shower party, a party at which the hostess is showered with presents from her friends

sidewalk, a pavement

side-wheeler, a paddle-boat

slingshot, a catapult

sociable, a social gathering

socialize, to get together socially

sorority, an organisation of female students (see **fraternity**)

sourdough, a person who has spent one or more winters in Alaska

spark guard, a fire guard

spat, a slight quarrel

speakeasy, an illegal drinking-place

spool, a cotton reel

spur line, a branch railway line

stand, a witness box

stand pat, to sit tight

station agent, a stationmaster

station house, a police station

stem-winder, a keyless watch

stock-holder, shareholder

stoop, the platform at the top of a flight of steps leading to the front door of a house

stop over, to break a journey
street car, a tram
string, a shoelace
subway, an underground railway
sulky, a light two-wheeled one-horse carriage for one person
suspenders, braces
switch-tower, a signal-box
switchyard, a shunting yard
tag day, a flag day
tape needle, a bodkin
Thanksgiving dinner, a dinner eaten on Thanksgiving Day,
    the last Thursday in November. (Thanksgiving originated
    among the early American settlers, as an expression of their
    gratitude for their preservation.)
through; 'Monday through Friday', means from Monday to
    Friday inclusive
thumb tack, drawing pin
tightwad, a miser
ton, 20 cwt. but 2,000 lb.
toss and catch, pitch and toss
towerman, a railway signalman
truck, a lorry or van
tube, a wireless valve
uptown, the residential district in an American city (see **down-
    town**)
vest, waistcoat
vestibule train, a corridor train
vine, any creeping plant
wad, a sheaf of bank notes
waist, a blouse
washroom, a lavatory
wash rag, a face flannel
way station, an unimportant railway station
well-fixed, well-to-do
windshield, a wind screen
World Series, the most important series of competitions among
    American baseball teams

A DICTIONARY OF BRITISH WRITERS

This is a list of only the most famous of our writers, giving their dates, saying for which kind of writing they are most famous (as poet, novelist, dramatist or whatever it may be) and giving the name of their best-known work. The list was compiled by someone who would greatly have enjoyed saying more. ('Don't miss the *Canterbury Tales*. They're warm, funny, grave, full of unforgettable people and phrases, and, though it's worth getting used to the not-too-difficult Middle English of the original, there's a good modern translation published as a Penguin by Nevil Coghill.' That sort of thing.) But this is a list purely for reference—by, the compiler hopes, readers who are busy acquiring for themselves the desire to say more about a writer than that his dates were this or that, and his best-known work was that or this.

Addison, Joseph (1672–1719), essayist and dramatist.

Arnold, Matthew (1822–88), poet and critic. *The Scholar Gipsy*.

Auden, W. H. (1907–1973), poet.

Austen, Jane (1775–1817), novelist. *Pride and Prejudice*.

Bacon, Francis (1561–1621), essayist.

Barrie, Sir J. M. (1860–1937), novelist and playwright. *Peter Pan*.

Beaumont, Francis (1584–1616), dramatist, collaborated with John Fletcher (1579–1625). *Knight of the Burning Pestle*.

Beerbohm, Sir Max (1872–1956), essayist and critic.

Belloc, Hilaire (1870–1953), poet, essayist, historian and novelist. *Cautionary Tales*.

Bennett, Arnold (1867–1931), novelist. *Old Wives' Tale*.

Blake, William (1757–1828), poet. *Songs of Innocence* and *Songs of Experience*.

Borrow, George (1803–81), chronicler of gipsy life. *Lavengro*.

Boswell, James (1740–95), biographer, diarist. *Life of Dr Johnson*

Bridges, Robert (1844–1930), poet. *Testament of Beauty*.

Brontë, Charlotte (1816–55), novelist. *Jane Eyre*.

Brontë, Emily (1818–48), novelist. *Wuthering Heights*.

Browne, Sir Thomas (1605–82), essayist. *Religio Medici*.

Browning, Robert (1812–89), poet. *The Ring and the Book.*

Browning, Elizabeth Barrett (1806–61), poet. *Sonnets from the Portuguese.*

Buchan, John (1875–1940), novelist and historian. *Thirty Nine Steps.*

Bunyan, John (1628–88), author of *Pilgrim's Progress.*

Burns, Robert (1759–96), poet.

Butler, Samuel (1612–80), poet. *Hudibras.*

Butler, Samuel (1835–1902), novelist. *The Way of All Flesh.*

Byron, Lord (1788–1824), poet. *Don Juan.*

Campion, Thomas (1567?–1619), poet.

Carlyle, Thomas (1795–1881), historian and essayist. *The French Revolution.*

Carroll, Lewis (Charles Lutwidge Dodgson) (1832–98), author of *Alice in Wonderland.*

Chaucer, Geoffrey (1340?–1400), poet. *Canterbury Tales.*

Chesterton, G. K. (1874–1936), poet, essayist and novelist. The *Father Brown* stories.

Clare, John (1793–1864), poet.

Cobbett, William (1762–1835), essayist and social critic. *Rural Rides.*

Coleridge, Samuel Taylor (1772–1834), poet and critic. *Rime of the Ancient Mariner.*

Collins, Wilkie (1824–89), novelist. *The Moonstone.*

Collins, William (1721–59), poet.

Congreve, William (1670–1729), dramatist. *Way of the World.*

Conrad, Joseph (1857–1924), novelist. *Lord Jim.*

Cowley, Abraham (1618–67), poet.

Cowper, William (1731–1800), poet. *The Task.*

Crabbe, George (1754–1832), poet. *The Borough.*

Davies, W. H. (1870–1940), poet. *Autobiography of a Super-Tramp.*

Defoe, Daniel (1661?–1731), novelist. *Robinson Crusoe.*

Dekker, Thomas (1570?–1641?), dramatist.

De la Mare, Walter (1873–1956), poet and novelist.

De Quincey, Thomas (1785–1859), essayist and critic. *Confessions of an Opium-Eater.*

Dickens, Charles (1812–70), novelist. *David Copperfield.*

Donne, John (1573–1631), poet.

Doyle, Sir A. Conan (1859–1930), novelist. *Hound of the Baskervilles.*

Drayton, Michael (1563–1631), poet. *The Ballad of Agincourt.*

Dryden, John (1631–1700), poet and dramatist. *Absalom and Achitophel.*

Eliot, George (Mary Ann Evans) (1819–80), novelist. *Mill on the Floss.*

Eliot, T. S. (1888–1965), poet. *The Waste Land.*

Evelyn, John (1620–1706), diarist.

Fielding, Henry (1707–54), dramatist and novelist. *Tom Jones.*

Fitzgerald, Edward (1809–83), poet. *Rubaiyat of Omar Khayyam.*

Forster, E. M. (1879–1970), novelist. *Passage to India.*

Galsworthy, John (1869–1933), novelist. *The Forsyte Saga.*

Gaskell, Elizabeth Cleghorn (1810–65), novelist. *Cranford.*

Gay, John (1685–1732), poet. *The Beggar's Opera.*

Gibbon, Edward (1737–94), historian. *Decline and Fall of the Roman Empire.*

Gilbert, Sir W. S. (1837–1911), playwright and humorous poet. *The Bab Ballads.*

Gissing, George (1857–1903), novelist. *The Private Papers of Henry Ryecroft.*

Goldsmith, Oliver (1728–74), poet, essayist and playwright. *Vicar of Wakefield.*

Graves, Robert (b. 1895), poet and novelist.

Gray, Thomas (1716–71), poet. *Elegy in a Country Churchyard.*

Hardy, Thomas (1840–1928), poet and novelist. *Tess of the D'Urbervilles.*

Hazlitt, William (1778–1830), critic and essayist.

Herbert, George (1593–1633), poet.

Herrick, Robert (1591–1674), poet.

Hobbes, Thomas (1588–1679), philosopher. *Leviathan.*

Hood, Thomas (1799–1845), poet. *Song of a Shirt.*

Hopkins, Gerard Manley (1844–89), poet.

Housman, A. E. (1859–1936), poet. *A Shropshire Lad.*

Hudson, W. H. (1841–1922), novelist and naturalist. *Green Mansions.*

Hunt, Leigh (1784–1859), poet and essayist.

Jacobs, W. W. (1863–1943), novelist and short-story writer.

James, Henry (1843–1916), novelist. *Daisy Miller.*

Jefferies, Richard (1848–87), essayist and novelist. *Bevis.*

Johnson, Dr Samuel (1709–84), poet, critic and dictionary-maker. *Vanity of Human Wishes.*

Jonson, Ben (1573?–1637), poet and dramatist. *The Alchemist.*

Keats, John (1795–1821), poet. *Endymion.*

Kingsley, Charles (1819–75), novelist. *The Water Babies.*

Kipling, Rudyard (1865–1936), poet and novelist. *Jungle Tales.*

Lamb, Charles ('Elia') (1775–1834), essayist.

Landor, Walter Savage (1775–1864), poet.

Langland, William (1330?–1400?), poet. *Piers Plowman.*

Lawrence, D. H. (1885–1930), poet and novelist. *Sons and Lovers.*

Lear, Edward (1812–88), poet. *The Owl and the Pussycat.*

Lovelace, Richard (1618–58), poet.

Lytton, Lord (1831–91), novelist. *Last Days of Pompeii.*

Macaulay, T. B. (1800–59), historian. *History of England.*

Malory, Sir Thomas (*c.* 1470), author of *Morte d'Arthur.*

Marlowe, Christopher (1564–93), poet and dramatist. *Dr Faustus.*

Marryat, Frederick (1792–1848), novelist. *Children of the New Forest.*

Marvell, Andrew (1621–78), poet.

Masefield, John (1876–1967), poet and novelist. *Dauber.*

Massinger, Philip (1583–1640), dramatist. *New Way to Pay Old Debts.*

Meredith, George (1828–1909), novelist. *The Egoist.*

Milton, John (1608–74), poet. *Paradise Lost.*

Moore, George (1857–1933), novelist. *Esther Waters.*

Moore, Thomas (1779–1852), poet.

More, Sir Thomas (1478–1535), author of *Utopia.*

Morris, William (1834–96), poet. *The Earthly Paradise.*

O'Casey, Sean (1883–1964), dramatist. *Juno and the Paycock.*

Orwell, George (1903–50), essayist and novelist. *Animal Farm.*

Peacock, Thomas Love (1785–1866), poet and novelist.

Pepys, Samuel (1633–1703), diarist.

Pope, Alexander (1688–1744), poet. *Rape of the Lock.*

Raleigh, Sir Walter (1552–1618), poet.

Reade, Charles (1814–84), novelist. *Cloister on the Hearth.*

Richardson, Samuel (1689–1761), novelist. *Clarissa Harlowe.*

Rossetti, Christina (1830–94), poet. *Goblin Market.*

Rossetti, Dante Gabriel (1828–82), poet.

Ruskin, John (1819–1900), writer on art. *Stones of Venice.*

Scott, Sir Walter (1771–1832), poet and novelist. *The Waverley* novels.

Shakespeare, William (1564–1616), poet and dramatist. *Hamlet.*

Shaw, George Bernard (1856–1950), dramatist and critic. *St Joan.*

Shelley, Percy Bysshe (1792–1822), poet. *The Revolt of Islam.*

Sheridan, Richard Brinsley (1751–1816), dramatist. *The Rivals.*

Sidney, Sir Philip (1554–86), poet.

Skelton, John (1460?–1529), poet.

Smollett, Tobias (1721–71), novelist. *Roderick Random.*

Southey, Robert (1774–1843), poet and historian. *Life of Nelson.*

Spenser, Edmund (1552?–1599), poet. *Faerie Queene.*

Steele, Sir Richard (1672–1729), essayist.

Sterne, Laurence (1713–68), novelist. *A Sentimental Journey.*

Stevenson, Robert Louis (1850–94), poet and novelist. *Treasure Island.*

Suckling, Sir John (1609–42), poet.

Swift, Jonathan (1667–1745), author of *Gulliver's Travels.*

Swinburne, Algernon Charles (1837–1909), poet.

Synge, J. M. (1871–1909), dramatist. *Playboy of the Western World.*

Tennyson, Alfred, Lord (1809–92), poet. *Idylls of the King.*

Thackeray, William Makepiece (1811–63), novelist. *Vanity Fair.*

Thomas, Dylan (1914–53), poet. *Under Milk Wood.*

Thompson, Francis (1859–1907), poet. *The Hound of Heaven.*

Thomson, James (1700–48), poet. *The Seasons.*

Trollope, Anthony (1815–82), novelist. *The Warden.*

Vaughan, Henry (1622–95), poet.

Webster, John (1580?–1625?), dramatist. *Duchess of Malfi.*

Wells, H. G. (1866–1946), novelist. *Kipps.*

White, Gilbert (1720–93), naturalist. *Natural History of Selborne.*

Wilde, Oscar (1856–1900), poet, critic and dramatist. *Importance of Being Earnest.*

Wordsworth, William (1770–1850), poet. *Lyrical Ballads.*

Wycherley, William (1640?–1716), dramatist. *The Country Wife.*

Yeats, William Butler (1865–1939), poet.

Music and the Arts

Melody, Harmony and Rhythm	2–3
Music History	3–9
The Instruments	9–15
Some Musical Terms	16–17
The Plastic Arts—Pictures, Statues and Buildings:	
A Brief History	17–34

Music

VERY probably, music is historically the first of all the arts. After all, one often hears of babies who sing before they say their first word and who beat out rhythms before they sing. So it is easy to imagine a caveman grunting out some sort of music in an age when even speech—let alone writing—was unknown, and before the first cave paintings adorned the walls of his home.

There is another way in which music can claim to be the first of the arts. One writer put it this way: 'all other arts aspire to the condition of music'. By this, the writer meant that music is the freest of the arts. A writer must say what he means in precise words; a painter must make us a picture of something we recognise; a sculptor must present us with a form that has meaning. Or so it was until very recently. The musician, though, has never had to follow these rules because music has no meaning. He plays a fast tune on a trumpet and we all find it 'lively' or 'stirring'. He plays a slow tune on a violin and we all find it 'melancholy' or 'sad'. We even talk of 'pastoral' music—music that suggests green fields and blue skies. Yet music (as the musician would agree) has no meaning other than the meaning we agree to give it. The astonishing thing is that we all agree about its meaning!

Music, then, is free of the rules that bind the other arts. But there are several rules that apply to music. For instance: the basic recipe for all music includes Melody, Harmony and Rhythm.

Rhythm is the cornerstone of music. To prove this, try humming a very well-known tune (*Pop Goes The Weasel* will do) in a way that has all the notes of the melody in the right order, but with the rhythm deliberately distorted. Most people will find it impossible to recognise the tune. It will have lost its identity with its rhythm. Just the same thing happens when you break up the rhythm of a sentence. For example, you can take these words:

'*To let a firework off, blue paper must be lit*'

and by altering the rhythm, change their sense into:

'*To let: a firework. Off-blue paper. Must be lit.*'

Melody is the tune. Some melodies—*Greensleeves*, for instance—are so powerful that even drastic rhythm changes cannot conceal them.

Harmony is the structure of notes and chords that fill out the melody and add to its meaning. You could call harmonies the adjectives and adverbs of music. So if the melody is the noun 'cat', it is the harmonies that make the cat happy or sad, black or tortoiseshell.

Most tunes can be given a variety of harmonies. Yet musically gifted people generally agree on what is the right set of harmonies for a given tune—and they will certainly agree in disliking any wrong harmony or false chord they hear.

All the music we hear contains some—usually all—of the elements of rhythm, melody and harmony. One way of classifying musical instruments is to arrange them under the headings of Rhythm, Melody, Harmony. For instance, a drum is a Rhythm instrument; a flute is a Melody instrument; a guitar is a Harmony instrument because it plays chords. Put these three instruments together and you would have a band that could play many kinds of music.

If you are thinking of taking up a musical instrument, you will be wise to find out which sort suits your natural talents best —Melody, Harmony or Rhythm.

MUSIC HISTORY

Wherever history is recorded it is usual to find some record of music. A mural in the tomb of Rameses (about 1150 B.C.) shows players with large, elaborate harps. Another mural in Thebes shows a girl lute player. There is an Assyrian relief in the British Museum picturing a mixed orchestra of players.

All these random examples take us well back before the birth of Christ.

Going further afield and still further back to 2500 B.C., we know of a Chinese scholar called Ling Lun who codified the five tones of oriental music then in use and named each tone. Some tones, according to Ling Lun, were upper class and even royal; others were mere peasants! Oddly enough, this idea of naming tones by social qualities, degrees of nobility and so on, is found quite frequently in various periods and countries.

Moving nearer to our own age, there are endless references in fact and fiction establishing the unchanging importance of music throughout history. Everyone knows about David playing his harp to Saul—about the Pied Piper of Hamelin—about Red Indian war chants. Not everyone knows that the rich Romans had water organs; when people came to dinner, the water organ (*hydraulus*) played. Some people hated the noise and wrote peevish comments about it. Rather the same thing happens today with record players!

The tragedy is that although we know that there has always been music, we cannot hear the music itself. We know exactly how the Egyptians, say, looked and dressed. We can read their writings, study their religions, see their own models and paintings and tools in the museums. But we cannot know how their music *sounded*. In fact we can make no sense at all even of some of the earliest written music. We can roughly trace a melodic thread, but we do not know the rhythms or tones; or harmonies, if any. Ancient music is a mystery without a key.

Because of the lack of clearly written music, we can go back only comparatively few centuries to recapture the sound of old music. True, some melodies heard today are truly ancient, even ageless—the chants of Jewish temples, certain Indian pieces and the Catholic Church's Gregorian chants—but our sort of music is possibly an invention of the middle ages.

Written Music Our music is in the main based on the Diatonic scale which can be sung as Doh, Re, Mi, Fa, Sol, La, Ti, Doh. The notes are each a tone apart excepting Mi-Fa and Ti-Doh, which are a semitone (half tone) apart. Doh is the Tonic or 'home' note defining the music's key. Countless simple tunes (e.g., *Three Blind Mice*) employ only the 'natural' tones of the major Diatonic scale (there are minor scales too). Semitones enlarge the scale to 12 notes. Music not restricted to a key may be expressed by the Chromatic scale of 12 semi-tones.

Several ways of naming notes and writing music have been tried, of course. The simplest were based on sketching a tune like this:

Sing this sketch and with luck you will hear *God Save the Queen*.

To reduce the luck element, notes were named from A to G. Four or more 'stave' lines were added to align the written notes (today we use five, as shown below). This system was developed to its present-day form—an unsatisfactory form, incidentally, for our music uses 12 notes and five into twelve won't go.

A glance above will show you the result of this bad division. The middle C is the only note the two clefs have in common. If you look for any other note—A, for instance—it will occupy one position in the treble clef and a different position in the bass clef.

This system also forces us to use a variety of complicated correction signs. As you can see, our alphabet of notes runs

only from A to G—which makes seven notes; but as already
pointed out, ours is a 12-note music. To insert the other five
notes in written music, we have to make use of signs for sharps—
♯, flats—♭ and naturals—♮. But even then it does not work
out. Our scale includes notes that could be called either sharp
or flat! Here is an octave of notes from a piano:

* Is this note both B and C flat? † Is the black note F sharp
or G flat? And for that matter, is there any real difference
between D sharp and E flat? There is not on the piano,
naturally. But is there on a violin?

Fortunately we can ask the questions without answering them
here. It is enough to say that we live with our musical notation
because the cure—introducing a new system—would be worse
than the disease! Musicians are used to it, just as typists are
used to their typewriter keyboard's layout.

Music's Development From now on we almost ignore all
forms of music but our own European and American kinds—
that is, the 12-note forms played in various arrangements of
melody, harmony and rhythm.

As far as we know (we cannot be sure) this music first took a
wide hold of Europe from, say, the tenth century A.D. on.
Hucbald, a monk who lived until A.D. 930, describes a raw-
sounding two-voice harmony running in fifths (such as C and
G, D and A, etc). The effect of playing only in fifths is very
crude indeed.

John Cotton (A.D. 1130) wrote of music 'by at least two singers
in such a manner that, while one sounds the main melody, the
other colours it with other tones'. This suggests that polyphonic (many-voiced) music was only just beginning. Otherwise,
why did Cotton bother to explain it?

Polyphonic music developed fairly rapidly. By the fifteenth

and sixteenth centuries, minstrels' chants freed music of strict, almost mathematical forms and modes. New rhythms became acceptable. Harmonies were used for emotional as well as formal effects. Opera was reborn in Italy in about 1600. Instruments developed fast. Music schools were established. *Some important composers of the period: Monteverdi (opera) Byrd, Palestrina.*

In the seventeenth century, music almost began again with Bach, who developed past forms to an excellence that is still unsurpassed and also reached forward into the future both with his music and instruments (he virtually re-designed the organ, for example). Bach's impact on music is comparable with that of photography on graphic art—but Bach was also the age's supreme artist as well! *Important composers: Purcell, Handel, Bach.*

In the late eighteenth century, the modern symphony orchestra and its music came into being. Music began to move from so-called 'Classical' forms (that is, formal, variations-on-a-set-theme forms) into more free and spacious 'Romantic' forms. In our century, painting has received a very similar liberation: the painter of today need no longer draw to an academic formula—he can make his own rules and effects. *Typical 'classical' composers: Mozart, Gluck, Haydn.*

The rest of the story is probably best told by the names of nineteenth-century composers such as Beethoven, Mendelssohn, Berlioz, Schubert, Tchaikovsky, Brahms and others. All these are 'Romantic' composers in that they exploited and developed all that had gone before along their own individual lines; and also constantly strove to enlarge the range of effects and feelings that music and musical instruments convey. The restrictions put upon them, if any, were all self-imposed. They did not follow the Rules of the Game that existed in earlier centuries. They tried rather to change the game.

In our century, music has yet again started afresh. The very nature of 12-note music is in question. Why not a limitless scale? Or a number of different scales? Why follow any recognised form? Why accept the instruments of the orchestra as the only instruments—could not music be made electronically, without human instrumentalists?

Like painting, music need no longer be representational; it need no longer attempt to establish definite mind-pictures, as it generally did 60 years ago. Anything and everything that the listener agrees to accept as music—including arrangements of electronic noises—is now within the composer's scope.

Jazz When Pepys, the diarist, invited friends to his house for a musical evening 300 years ago, music was still at its formal stage. The Rules of the Game were known and followed. Thus the evening's music could be improvised on a formal theme understood by all the players present.

As music became more complicated, improvisation became less likely and less satisfactory. The written notes offered a more assured performance of more exciting and advanced music. Improvisation therefore slowly died.

It was revived by jazz players early in this century. The jazz player takes as his basis a set of harmonies that he and the others are familiar with—the chord structure of *Tea for Two*, for instance—and improvises melodies and counter melodies that fit those chords. Almost invariably, the improvisation is solidly supported by a firm and unchanging rhythm that locks the players together as they perform. This basis of firm harmonies and solid rhythm leaves the jazzman an enormous amount of freedom: and he makes the most of it. He plays round the melody. He adopts new instruments or alters old ones to fit his needs. He welcomes new sounds and ideas—indeed he will go out of his way to surprise his listeners.

The effect of jazz on other musical forms is already felt and felt strongly. Many modern 'classical' composers introduce jazz phrases and passages but seldom with success (the attempts of jazz musicians to use 'classical' forms and methods are equally poor). However, the sheer vitality, inventiveness and virtuosity of the best jazz musicians is heavily infectious. It is very probable that the jazz and 'classical' compositions of the future will move along tracks that meet here and there; and already, both schools are making similar experiments for similar purposes.

Popular Music Dance, 'pop', 'rock' and most other forms of popular music owe a lot to jazz. 'Folk' music, for instance, is often given jazz elements. However, pop is finding its own, unique 'voices' as the range of (particularly electronic) instruments and sound sources increases. Again, pop musicians are discarding the old recipes for making a tune and reaching out for new freedoms. A pop song of the 1930's had 32 bars, the modern pop song has any number.

No one can predict the future of popular music—but then, the whole idea of pop is that it should please now, this moment.

THE INSTRUMENTS

Instruments can be split into families and groups in various ways, most of them a little vague. For instance, the Flute is a Woodwind instrument—but most modern flutes are made of metal. However, here are some customary groupings:

STRINGS

Bowed The violin family, particularly the violin—viola—cello—string bass. But also the viols, which have frets.

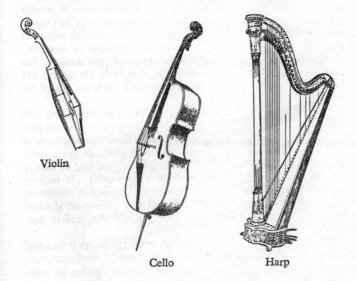

Violin

Cello

Harp

Hand or Plucked The harp. The guitar family—guitar in its 'classical' form with gut or nylon strings plucked with the fingers; or with steel strings plucked with a plectrum. Also banjo, ukelele, lute and many other fretted instruments.

Spanish ('Classic') Guitar   Venetian Lute

Keyboard Piano, harpsichord, klavier, spinet and many others.

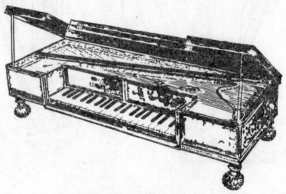

Spinettina: Augsburg, 17th century

WIND

Flute family—flute, piccolo and others, all blown transversely —that is, across a hole.

Recorder family. The various recorders, small and large; and many other instruments that you blown *down*, including the flageolet—a superior penny whistle—and various pipes.

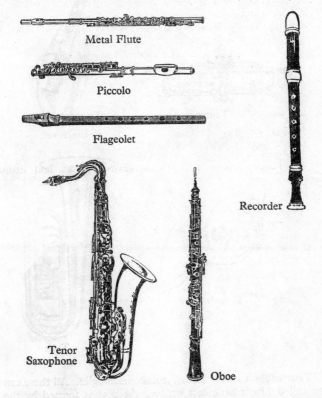

Metal Flute

Piccolo

Flageolet

Recorder

Tenor
Saxophone

Oboe

Bagpipes are wind instruments. They consist of a number of pipes blown by the player and also by an air reservoir, the bag. So there is some slight similarity with the—

Organ, which is an arrangement of various kinds of pipes and other sound producers fed air from a chamber that is kept filled by an air pump.

Reed instruments may have double reeds—oboes and bassoons—or, more commonly, single reeds, as in clarinets, saxophones.

BRASS WIND INSTRUMENTS

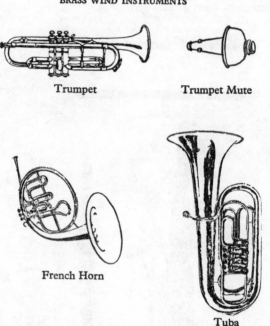

Trumpet

Trumpet Mute

French Horn

Tuba

Trumpets, cornets, horns, trombones, bugles. All these can be called **Lip** instruments because the note is formed by the player's lips—not by a reed, or whistle.

All lip instruments are, at heart, a posthorn to which something has been added. A bugle is a simple horn wound into coils.

A trumpet is a bugle with valves added to increase the number of notes obtainable. The French horn is a posthorn wound in circles and with valves to increase its range. The trombone literally shortens or lengthens itself (thus changing its pitch) when the player operates the slide. Naturally, there are many other differences and the posthorn idea is an oversimplification; but the fact remains that a trumpet with stuck valves or a trombone with a stuck slide reverts to the instrument that founded its family—and that basic instrument is a tapering tube with a mouthpiece, from which about five notes can be produced.

PERCUSSION INSTRUMENTS

Jazz Drum Kit

Include all forms of drums, cymbals, bells and other rhythm instruments—including the tunable kettle drums of the symphony orchestra, the jazz drummer's outfit, and the huge selection used by a Latin-American band.

Once again, the classification is a little vague. One could call a piano a percussion instrument—after all, its strings are hit by hammers.

Tympani

From the instruments described so far, one could form anything from a symphony orchestra to a folk group. Throughout
history and in every country, instruments have always been
basically what they are today. Walt Disney once made a short
film about the development of music called TOOT, WHISTLE,
PLUNK & BOOM (suggest that they show it at your school) which
made this point very well. There is really no *basic* difference
between a panpipes and a recorder, or a lyre and ukelele. The
differences lie only in additions, subtractions and modifications
made over many centuries.

Vibes

During the last hundred years, though, a completely new class of instruments has appeared. So let us have a new heading:

Electric, Electronic instruments (sometimes called Electrophones) produce their sounds either by amplifying sounds produced by ordinary instruments—the electric guitar is the best example—or by actually creating original sounds electrically, as in the electric organ. The organ in your local church is almost certainly partly electric; its action and air pump may be worked by electricity. But if it is a new instrument, then it is very probably 'electronic'. Its notes and tones have nothing to do with wind and pipes and everything to do with electronic tone generators, electric amplifiers and so on.

The future of such instruments is limitless. Most of the pop and beat music heard today would be almost inaudible if there were a power failure—most of the sound is made, and all of it amplified, by electric devices. The modern church organ, obviously, would be struck dumb if its power supply were cut. And many musicians are experimenting with *musique concrète*—music actually manufactured from recorded sounds, themselves probably of electronic origin.

Electric Guitar   Small Electric Organ

SOME MUSICAL TERMS

Many people are not clear about what is meant by the word 'Pitch', what the Conductor actually does and so on. Here are explanations of a few of these puzzles.

Ballad A song, often sentimental, that tells a story.

Bar Written music is divided into Bars by upright lines. Each bar contains so many beats. Count the beats and you will know the rhythm of the music. See MEASURE.

Beat Rhythmic pulse. A waltz has three beats to each bar.

Chamber Music Music for small instrumental groups— music that is best heard in a room, not a hall.

Conductor His function is not simply to make the orchestra play together, but rather to dictate *how* the music should be played. Two separate conductors will produce very different renderings of the same music from an orchestra.

Counterpoint, Contrapuntal Counterpoint is the combining of two or more melodies, played simultaneously. *Contrapuntal* is the adjective.

Fugue A contrapuntal composition for several parts—that is, instruments or voices.

Key Most music is written in the key of the composer's choice. The KEY SIGNATURE indicates to the player which key has been chosen. If the player sees F sharp written at the beginning of the music, he knows that his 'home key' is G— because the major scale of G is distinguished by possessing an F sharp. As the piece may not stick to its 'home key' of G, the composer will have to insert other sharps, flats and naturals as they occur. These are called Accidentals.

Measure A division of music in terms of beats. If there are three beats to the bar, then the writer will draw vertical lines at three-beat intervals and so divide his composition into Measures.

Notation To write a note filling a whole measure, you write a semi-breve, $\circ$. A minim, ρ, is worth half the time value of the semi-breve and the crotchet, ρ, worth half that. And so on to quaver, semi-quaver and demi-semi-quaver, etc.

Pitch The highness or lowness of a musical sound. Middle C is internationally agreed to have a frequency of 440. A note at the top of the piano, well above middle C, has a higher pitch. People with 'absolute pitch' are able to hear a note and name it correctly.

The Plastic Arts—Pictures, Statues and Buildings: A Brief History

As a representation of the development of men, art appeared in tangible forms (as pictures, carvings, buildings) only with the gradual evolution of man's self-awareness, remote ages ago. But though man seems to have existed for between one and two million years, art as we think of it dates only from fairly 'recent' times beginning around 50,000–30,000 B.C. We measure the quality of past civilisations from the surviving remains of the various forms of art through which man has expressed himself.

The advance of human society has not always been steady—there have been gaps and backslidings. But it does seem that, in different parts of the world at different times, there has been a gradual move towards a higher order in the acts and thoughts of men. Our own lives are built upon the effort that went into this growth, as we ourselves are building for those who are to come. And to understand a little of what this is about, we have to understand art. To help us to do so, there are critics. But critics, like anyone else, can be wrong, and sometimes very wrong. Take everything you see or hear or read about art (even what is written here) *cum grano salis* (see FOREIGN PHRASES AND CLASSICAL QUOTATIONS); and when in doubt, use your own good sense. It won't necessarily follow that you'll be right. In fact, to think you are certainly right may be most presumptuous, since to understand art, or anything else, requires hard work and hard thinking. But you will at least be making your *own* judgement, right or wrong. That is far better than accepting without question someone else's opinion.

We know very little about the beginnings of art; yet we can be fairly sure that it was not always thought to be something separate from life. Indeed, it was an embodiment of life. And we know that, though men were separated often by great distances, and each culture followed its own particular pattern, yet all these cultures shared a common background. The further back you go, looking at works of art on the way, the more you find these connections.

Around 7,000 B.C.—the time of the so-called Neolithic (New Stone Age) Revolution when men first started to farm instead of merely wandering and hunting—the great period of human endeavour had its beginnings. It was then that the first urban communities were founded—Jericho, Israel and Chatal Huyuk in Turkey. The main areas of ancient development were China, Egypt, Mesopotamia, the valley of the Indus and what is now the Gobi Desert.

China Civilisation proper here began in the Huangho Valley. In China the greatest emphasis in art was always on painting and

Chinese Bronze,
6–11th Century, B.C.

calligraphy (writing). While sculpture and architecture were important, and sometimes magnificent, they were not given the high regard they were given in the West. Recorded history dates from the Shan-Yin dynasty (1523–1028 B.C.), by which time superb bronzes were being produced. The Chou dynasty (1027–250 B.C.) saw the perfection of writing and the invention of porcelain, for which China has always been renowned. Shi-Hwang-Ti (246–206 B.C.) ruled an empire stretching from the Pacific to the Middle East (where contact was strengthened with western cultures), and built the Great Wall stretching east-west across his northern frontier for 1,400 miles. Possibly the most famous of all ancient Chinese artists was the painter **Ku'ai-chi** (*c.* A.D. 370), who was a master of delicate impressions of natural scenes.

Egypt Here, throughout her long history, the main emphasis was on massive works of architecture, sculpture and engineering. The ancient Egyptians had a genius for life-like portrait sculpture from earliest times (*c.* 3000 B.C.). The Ancient Kingdom (4400–2466 B.C.) established art in a formal sense, and the years 2800–1400 B.C. saw Egyptian culture at its richest. Artists created what they *knew* existed, not what they saw. (For instance, they painted the profile of a face and a full-face eye together in the same portrait.) Art, designed to impress, illustrated rather than decorated. Cheops built his famous 480-ft.-high pyramid at Gizeh around 2885 B.C. and repaired the already existing Sphinx. At Karnak in 2466 B.C. Amenemhat began building the Great Temple of Ammon, to which additions were made right down to the time of Alexander's conquest in 332 B.C. Between east and west, and under the Greek Ptolemies (323–30 B.C.), his capital Alexandria, with its arts and sciences, profoundly affected the whole world. Traditional Egyptian architecture (like Greek) was trabeated (beam and post), without arches and many-columned, with lotus flower capitals; although the arch was known. Walls were covered with painted or chiselled stylised people, hieroglyphics and realistic wild life. Perspective was not used although brilliant colours were. But their art ossified and was bound by convention. Only for a few decades of attempted religious reform under Akhnaton and Tut-ankh-Amen (c. 1350 B.C.) were the shackles broken by startlingly beautiful and original works, emphasising human rather than divine attributes.

Mesopotamia On the fertile plain between the Tigris and the Euphrates, tradition places the Garden of Eden. Of the two great cities, Babylon dates from 4000 B.C. and was destroyed by its rival, Nineveh, in 1275 B.C. Sargon (722–705 B.C.) brought law and culture to the land and built an immense palace at Khorsabad with 700 rooms raised above the plain on a 50-ft.-high platform. The Assyrians, lacking stone, invented the arch and the dome, covering their mud-brick walls with vividly coloured glazed bricks (Babylon) and finely carved bas-reliefs (Nineveh) that were, so to speak, the news-reels of the day, since they portrayed important events. The famous Hanging Gardens of Babylon were built by Nebuchadnessar II during a short but splendid revival of Babylonian culture between 597 and 538 B.C. Under the Persians (538–333 B.C.) art was rich but eclectic (that is, it borrowed ideas and forms from numerous sources). In the Palace of Persepolis decoration began to be confined to areas round windows and doors. Refined monarchs encouraged delicate carving, splendid ceramics and exquisite metalwork—art works which very much influenced Greece.

Greece Greek art flourished under the Minoans of Crete at Knossos and on the mainland at Mycenae until the Dorian in-

vasions, 1200 to 1100 B.C. These are the times immortalised by
the legends of Homer. Minoan art, influenced by Egypt, was of
high quality; the architecture was extravagant and luxurious.
About the earliest example of a purely classical building was the
Temple of Apollo in Corinth (535 B.C.), built in stone in a crude

Ionic

Corinthian

Doric

Doric style. (See illustration for the Doric and other main
orders of Greek architecture.) With the defeat of the Persian
invaders the greatness of Athens began (Pericles 461–431 B.C.)
and its expression in one of the golden ages of art.

The technique of foreshortening (attributed to the painter
Euthymides, whose work survives in the exquisite pots of the
'blackfigured' style) and the understanding of perspective (first
seen in the work of **Agatharchus**) were major discoveries.

The Parthenon (restored)

Apollodorus pioneered light-and-shade painting (called
chiaroscuro) and was followed by masters of realism (**Zeuxis,
Parrhasius, Apelles Hieron**), all mid-5th century fresco and
vase painters.

The Parthenon (447–432 B.C.), designed by **Ictinus** and
Callicrates, set a pattern for architecture that lasted till
the 19th century. Its sculptor, **Pheidias**, and his contemporary **Myron** capture in their work the sense of movement.

Praxiteles (350 B.C.) carved statues that attempted to create ideal rather than actual men. Portraiture began later in Alexander's time (336–323 B.C.) with sculptors like **Lyssipus** and **Scopas**, influenced, as in earlier times, by Egypt. As Athens waned and Alexandria and Rome waxed, sculptors working in Rhodes (**Agesander**) and Pergamum (Asia Minor), around

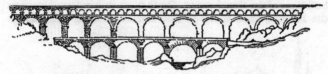

The Pont Du Gard Aqueduct

The Colosseum (restored)

The Arch of Janus

230–130 B.C., as their kings held back the invading Gauls, carved masterpieces of dynamic realism—The Laocoon, the Dying Gaul, the Venus of Milo.

Rome Much of the art of Rome was influenced by its colonial territories—notably Greece. But, particularly in architectural engineering, the Romans were brilliant developers of ideas. They drew, too, upon the artistic heritage left by their countrymen, the Etruscans, who had a genius for realistic portraiture and the representation of movement. Under Julius Caesar (60 B.C.) life-like sculpture flourished; the greatest Roman art was produced under Augustus (27 B.C.–A.D. 14). Painting was much used for decoration, so were walls and floors of mosaic work, inspired by the east. Architectural achievements were immense. In the 180-ft.-high Pont du Gard aqueduct at Nimes, in the South of France, arched stone anticipated the marvels of Gothic architecture; in Rome the concrete vaults of the Baths of Caracalla (A.D. 216) and of Diocletian (A.D. 306) established the Romans as structural wizards. The Pantheon (A.D. 120), whose dome is 142 ft high and still standing, anticipates the buildings of the Renaissance. On to these stupendous structures the Romans fixed sheets of fine marble, mosaics and, though

St Sophia

The Taj Mahal

they had no logical place, the non-structural classical orders. In the Colosseum (A.D. 70) the Doric, Ionic, Corinthian and Composite styles were set one above the other in a formula of design not broken until modern times. Romans made thousands of statues in gold, bronze and marble—most were Greek copies. A bronze of Nero (A.D. 54–68) was 111 ft. high. **Ludius** (10 B.C.) mastered perspective in huge frescoes.

Byzantine and Early Christians As Rome declined, Contantinople became the centre of world culture. The main link between imperial Rome and Christian Europe were the basilicas which, being places of law and commerce and not

pagan temples, were suitable for conversion to churches.
Trajan's Basilica in Rome (A.D. 98), (by **Apollodorus**), an ob-
long, formed the basis of church design; and the Basilica of
Constantine in Rome (A.D. 310), with its concrete vaults meeting
over a choir, was the prototype of Gothic vaulting.

Byzantine art became formal and stylised (that is, its manner
became fixed) because it was intended to convey the meaning of
the Gospels to the people with immense simplicity. Mosaics of

An Arabesque

A Porcelain Pot,
Ming Dynasty

this time are spectacular story books—notably those at S.
Apollinore Nuovo, Ravenna (A.D. 520), where clarity, not
observation of nature, was the ideal. Architects were daring and
inventive. At St Sophia in Constantinople (A.D. 537), built for
Justinian by **Anthemius** and **Isodorus**, the 180-ft.-high dome
was encrusted with gold mosaics and biblical scenes. St Mark's,
Venice (1042), was the climax of this glittering era, which ended
in the crusades.

Islam The debt the West owes to Islam is that, while their
own culture was forming, the Saracens, with their empire stretching from India to Spain and in touch with the East, preserved
with splendour and taste the ancient ideals of art. They evolved
the pointed arch, which triggered off Gothic vaulting; they
developed lavish, abstract surface decoration (arabesque). While
structure altered according to local influences, formal decoration

was unchanged. To the artists of Islam the interior was very much more important than the exterior. At Grenada, in Spain, caliph Abd-el-Walid (1309–54) created the splendidly luxurious Alhambra. In Constantinople Suleiman I, with his architect **Sinian**, established the pattern of all mosques with his domed Suleimaniyeh (1550), which was a smaller copy of S. Sophia. In India Sha Jehán built the shimmering white marble mauso-

Ribbed Vault

leum, the Taj Mahal (1630), one of the wonders of the world.

The East The culture of India combined with the traditions of China to produce immensely rich forms of art. In China the Tang dynasty (A.D. 618–907) was a period of sumptuous artistic expression. **Wu Tao-tze** sensuously painted the magic of movement; and **Li Chéng** (940–67) and his contemporary **Tung Yuan** painted only the essentials of superb landscapes. The Sung dynasty (960–1227) embraced an empire stretching as far as the Mediterranean and influenced, and was influenced by, the growing achievements of western artists. This was a time of great landscape painting. Fine austere pottery was produced, and painters like **Kuo Hsi** (1020–90), **Ma Yuän** and **Mu-Chi** (1215–70) used black ink and washes to capture the most fleeting impressions of the natural scene. Contact with Persia influenced the production of the blue and white pottery of the Ming dynasty (1368–1644). But under the Manchus (1644–1912) art, becoming fixed and formal and imitative, was slowly stifled. Classical Chinese art did, however, much influence western art after the Renaissance through the opening up of modern trade routes.

Pre-Gothic To call the times between Roman and Gothic the Dark Ages, as we do, is wildly misleading. This was a long period of gradual change, and it produced some of the most significant art in man's history. Artists were concerned with what they *felt*, not with what they knew. The court of Charlemagne at

Aix-le-Chapelle encouraged splendid works. Painting was confined to the illustration of manuscripts (e.g. the Book of Kells in
Ireland, 698). In sculpture and architecture two styles emerged:
that of the north of Europe, and that of the south.

While the Gothic Bayeux Tapestry was woven in Normandy
(1080), the cathedral at Pisa in Italy (begun 1063) was being
built in accord with ideas drawn from the architecture of

Windows (from *l* to *r*) Early English Lancet; Decorated;
Perpendicular

imperial Rome. The eleventh century saw the beginning of
daring and ceaseless architectural experiment. The introduction
of the Saracen pointed arch at S. Madeleine Vézelay in France
(1130) marked the beginning of Gothic vaulting; while in
Germany thin windows were being grouped together in first
attempts at tracery. Durham Cathedral, in England (1096), saw
the use of the first rib vault. Here stone ribs were placed across
semi-circular ends and diagonals of barrel vaults to support thin
roofing panels. It was the beginning of the Gothic revolution.
In Southern Italy and Sicily (the Crusade ports) eleventh-
century Norman artists began convering the walls and vaults of
their churches with 'new-realism' frescoes.

Gothic At its purest this is confined to northern Europe and
to the years 1150–1500—one of the greatest periods of art.
England, between 1000 and 1500, had a more complete sequence
of Gothic than any other country in Europe; its architecture gives
a complete picture of the slow evolution, and the flowering, of
Gothic. Sculpture flourished, and painting was subordinated
to it in the north of Europe.

The Norman period (1066–1189) is marked by bold, massive
architecture with semi-circular vaults and arches, round piers

and flat buttresses: e.g. the cathedrals at Norwich (1096), Durham (1096) and Peterborough (1117) and the Keep of the Tower of London. Early English (1189–1307), with tall lancet windows and steeply pitched roofs on groups of slender shafts, was less massive. Vaults became pointed, naves wider: e.g. the cathedrals at Lincoln (1185), Salisbury (1220) and parts of Westminster Abbey (1245). In the Decorated period (1307–1377) there is an emergence of ornate geometric and flowing

Norman Vault

tracery framing stained glass. Vaulting becomes complex, as can be seen in York (1261–1324), the biggest English cathedral. In the Perpendicular period (1377–1485) windows grow to an immense size. Fan vaults are numerous and are seen at their loveliest in Henry VII's chapel, Westminster, which really belongs to Tudor times, being finished in 1512.

French cathedrals were shorter and higher than their English counterparts, which were long and low. In Paris, Notre Dame (1163–1295) is High Gothic, and Rheims Cathedral (1212–1300) has one of the noblest façades in all Europe. French stained glass is spectacular. It is best seen at Chartres (1194–1260).

Renaissance This extraordinary period of history is marked by a return to realism strengthened by humanism—which can be defined as the belief that man, through thought, can control his own fate—and a convergence of the aims of art and science. In Tuscany, **Cimabue** (1240–1302) painted the change from Gothic to Renaissance. In the porch of Strasbourg Cathedral in Germany (1230) sculpture has already begun to turn its back on solemn symmetry and to tell a story; a feeling of life returns to the figures. In Tuscany, the painter and architect **Giotto di Bondone** (1266–1337), the sculptor **Nicolo Pisano** (1225–78), created figures as they *knew* they looked, and exploited the illusion of depth, so altering the whole outlook of art. Bridging these times of momentous change was the marvellous Florentine painter, **Fra Angelico** (1387–1455). In Siena, **Simone Martini** (1284–1344) revived realistic portrait painting; in Florence **Lorenzo Ghiberti** (1378–1455) did the same in bronze. **Melozzo da Forli** (1438–1494) painted extreme foreshortening, as did **Andrea Mantegna** (1431–1506).

The architect **Filippo Brunelleschi** (1377–1446) built the bold, immense dome over the Duomo (Cathedral) in Florence,

The Petit Trianon, Versailles

and established a new architectural form inspired by classical Rome. He also formulated the laws of perspective which were taken up by **Masaccio** (1401–28), a very great painter of austere and heroic art and one of the founders of the art of our own time. **Donatello** (1386–1466) produced powerful sculpture inspired by nature. In Rome **Leon Alberti** (1402–72) deliberately imitated the classical architects, and **Donato Bramante** (1444–1514) championed the grand classical manner epitomised by St Peter's in Rome. But architecture became obsessed rather with style than with structure—it became majestic theatre.

The Italian Renaissance fostered three of the world's greatest men. They were remarkable not only for their immense talent but also for the great range of their work. **Raphael (Raffaello Sanzio)** (1483–1520), one of the architects of St Peter's, was a painter, technically perfect, who symbolised the graceful Italian spirit. **Leonardo da Vinci** (1452–1519) rarely completed anything but experimented in subjects as diverse as from anatomy to engineering. He painted the Mona Lisa (1500) and the Last Supper (1497), and originated the concept that an artist should be a contemplative and creative thinker, similar to a saint or philosopher. **Michelangelo Buonarotti** (1475–1564) is astounding as painter, sculptor, poet, and architect-engineer. For four years, working alone, he painted the spectacular ceiling of the Sistine Chapel (1508–12) as well as the Last Judgement

(1536–41); and he designed and supervised the building of the majestic dome of St Peter's. His marble David (1504) personified the image of man the superhuman.

The new culture spread in France with the realistic sculpture of **Claus Sluter** (1380) and was taken up by painters like **Jean Fouquet** (1420–81), who combined it with traditional Gothic art to produce pictures that were excitingly dramatic. **Nicolas Poussin** (1594–1655) founded the Grand Manner in French baroque art ('baroque' means extravagantly and fantastically decorated) and was followed by **Claude Gellée** (1600–82), a prodigious painter of landscapes. Under the immense power of the State, architecture and civic design which influenced the whole of the western world evolved from the palaces at Fontaine-bleu (1528) and Versailles (1661–1756)—the latter built by **Le Vau** and **Jules Mansard.**

In the Netherlands the invention of oil painting by **Jan van Eyck** (1390–1441) replaced the ancient tempera technique (which used egg yolk as a binder), and his close attention to realistic and minute detail had a profound effect on the course of art. In Flanders **Rogier van der Weyden** (1399–1464) prevented the Gothic tradition of lucid design from being overwhelmed by this new form of painting, as did **Viet Stoss** (d. 1533) in woodcarving. **Pieter Brueghel** (1525–69) was followed by **Peter Paul Rubens** (1577–1640), who used brilliant colours and was a master of pomp and spectacle. **Frans Hals** (1580–1666) captured the magic of fleeting impressions in his portraits; and **Rembrandt van Rijn** (1606–69) observed and captured with unmatched skill and insight the reality of the people he painted. With **Jan Vermeer van Delft** (1632–75), art became more restrained, with emphasis on the detail rather than the mass.

In Spain art had to struggle against the restraints imposed by the Counter-Reformation, stronger here than anywhere else. But **El Greco (Domenicos Theotocopoulos)** (1541–1614) boldly disregarded natural forms in his strange, dramatic, visionary paintings. **Diego Velasquez** (1599–1660) painted the reality of natural things, and **Francesco Goya** (1746–1828) used his brush as a satirical weapon against a corrupt church and state.

In Germany the invention of printing in the fifteenth century decisively affected art. This was the age of the great engravers, with their infinite care for realism and detail. **Martin Schongauer** (1453–91) was followed by the innovator and reformer **Albrecht Dürer** (1471–1528) and the court painter to Henry VIII, **Hans Holbein** (1497–1543), who was a cunning observer of human character.

In England the Renaissance came slowly; but under Charles I the architect **Inigo Jones** (1573–1652) worked in the new style at Greenwich (1617) and in the Banqueting Hall, Whitehall (1619). **Sir Christopher Wren** (1632–1723) combined structural ingenuity with classical detail in St Paul's Cathedral (1675–1710),

St Paul's Cathedral

but thereafter architecture became a victim of merely fashionable, imitative ideas, culminating in the Gothic Revival, in which the logic of architecture was lost—for instance, devices invented during the great age of Gothic to support the structure were used as *decoration*, as in **Sir Charles Barry's** Palace of Westminster (1840). Other arts were detached, too, from the new machine age.

In miniature painting English artists excelled. **Nicholas Hillyarde** (1547–1619) and **Samuel Cooper** (1609–72) are the most famous miniaturists. **Sir Anthony van Dyck** (1599–1641) painted finely elegant, melancholy portraits of Stuart monarchs, but the first definitely English painter of genius was **William Hogarth** (1697–1764), a master of the casual moment and a fierce enemy of hypocrisy. A period of great landscapes and portraits flourished under **Sir Joshua Reynolds** (1723–92), **Thomas Gainsborough** (1727–88) and **John Constable** (1776–1837). The poet **William Blake** (1757–1837) was a painter of extraordinary visionary quality and one of the first truly modern painters; he was followed by the masterly experimenter with coloured light, **William Turner** (1775–1851)—the first westerner to depict Nature's changing moods.

Modern Architecture. In the nineteenth century European architecture, and British architecture in particular, saw a series of revivals of earlier styles, with the Gothic and the Classic styles both enjoying new popularity. **John Nash** (1752–1835) introduced the decorous and refined style known as Regency, still to be seen to advantage in the area of London's Regent's Park which he laid out.

It was **Thomas Telford** (1757–1834) in Britain, working in steel, and **Eugene Freyssinet** (1879–1962) in France, working in concrete, who pioneered the use of huge structural spans with economy of material which we now associate with modern architecture. The early twentieth century saw the birth of 'functional' architecture and the development of a clear, clean style with a structural frame of reinforced concrete in which floors, roofs and vertical supports form a homogeneous whole. Superfluous ornament was abandoned and the use of large glass windows increased. The three greatest architects of this century have been the Frenchman **Le Corbusier** (1887–1965), a master of form; the American **Ludwig Mies Van der Rohe** (b. 1886), a master of structure; and another American, **Frank Lloyd Wright** (1869–1959), a master of space. Other significant twentieth century architects include the Italian **Pier Luigi Nervi** (b. 1891), the American **Richard Neutra** (b. 1892) and the Briton **Basil Spence** (b. 1907).

Modern Art can be said to begin with the movement and painting which originated in France in the 1860s known as Impressionism. The Impressionists, influenced by Constable and Turner, tried in their work to capture a fleeting aspect of some scene, guided not by memory or knowledge but by their immediate 'impression' of it. The leading Impressionists include **Claude Monet** (1840–1926), **Pierre Renoir** (1841–1919) and Edgar Degas (1834–1917). Two nineteenth-century artists who grappled with the problem of achieving in paint an art form in time with their epochs were the Frenchman **Paul Cézanne** (1839–1906) and the American **James Whistler** (1834–1903).

Abstract art has dominated the twentieth century, at first with semi-abstract works which are based on nature but bear

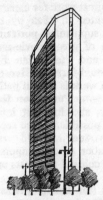

The Pirelli Building, Milan

little resemblance to natural forms, and later with pure abstract works which bear no relation to nature but which consist of shapes and colours of the artists' own invention. In this century pioneers have included the Spaniard **Pablo Picasso** (1881–1973), the Swiss **Paul Klee** (1879–1940), the Frenchman **Henri Matisse** (1869–1954) and the Russian **Vassily Kandinsky** (1886–1944), co-founder with the architect **Walter Gropius** (1883–1969) of the Bauhaus in Germany in the late 1920s.

In sculpture the Frenchman **Auguste Rodin** (1840–1917), the Rumanian **Constantin Brancusi** (1876–1957), the English-man **Henry Moore** (b. 1898) and the Englishwoman **Barbara Hepworth** (b. 1903) have worked in a revolutionary way in stone, wood and metal. With the action painting of the American **Jackson Pollock** (1912–1956) art entered an entirely new era. Here, at last, was Machine Age art.

In abstract art, the artist can use any materials or forms and may even throw or pour paint on to huge canvases laid on the floor, following what might be called the Law of Inspired

Chance. The purpose of other modern artists has been to speed social revolution: **Zadkine**, for example, sculpted the horrors of war in massive bronzes and **Kurt Schwitters** in the 1920s turned bits of trash (old magazines, bus tickets, labels) into pictures which he called anti-art, or Dada. What lay behind work like Schwitters' was a protest against romanticism and the belief that machines must work for men, not men for machines.

Photography, invented in 1822 by the Frenchman **J. N. Niépce,** has largely supplanted portraiture; and realism has become the concern of great movie-makers like the Swede **Ingmar Bergman** and the Italian **Federico Fellini** and photographers like **Henri Cartier-Bresson** and **Robert Capa** —men whose camera work is rich in pathos and a deep feeling for humanity. In pre-war Paris **Man Ray** experimented with abstract photography, showing that infinite arrangements of colour and form are possible. More recently, **Jean Tinguely** made crazy structures out of junk (old cars, tins, papers, pianos), protesting, as a number of contemporary artists have done, against the 'capitalist culture' that rests on a pattern of 'work—sell—buy—work'.

While some artists (for example, **Mark Rothko, Pevsner, Gabo** and **Victor Pasmore**) paint and construct delicate abstract images, beautiful in their own right, others continue to portray the natural objects and scenes that have caused them emotion. The key to most recent art is the preoccupation of artists with movement and space—direct results of mankind's technological achievements and his greater knowledge of the interior of things—not only their exterior. Contemporary art, influenced by television and the techniques and problems of the scientific age, is concerned with 'now' and, in searching for immediacy, artists have turned to kinetic art—with the impact of actual movement; op art—with the impact of visual illusions; and pop art—reflecting the impact of the pop culture of the 1960s and 1970s. Three of the leading contemporary British artists are **Francis Bacon, David Hockney** and **Bridget Riley.**

Famous artists not mentioned in the brief history are listed below. See also GUIDE TO SOME OF THE MOST IMPORTANT MUSEUMS IN BRITAIN.

Painters

Bellini, Giovanni (1431–1516), *Venetian*
Braque, Georges (1882–1963), *French*
Botticelli, Sandro (1444–1510), *Florentine*
Bosch, Hieronymus (1460–1516), *Dutch*
Canaletto (Giovanni) Antonio (1697–1768), *Venetian*
Caravaggio, Michelangelo da (1573–1610), *Italian*
Chagall, Marc (b. 1887), *French*
Chardin, Jean (1699–1779), *French*
Corot, Jean (1796–1875), *French*
Correggio, Antonio (1494–1534) *Italian*
Courbet, Gustav (1819–77), *French*
Dali, Salvador (b. 1904), *Spanish*
David, Jacques-Louis (1748–1825), *French*
Daumier (1808–79), *French*
Delacroix, Eugène (1798–1863), *French*
Duccio di Buoninsegna (1255–1318), *Italian*
Fragonard, Jean Honoré (1732–1806), *French*
Gauguin, Paul (1848–1903), *French*
Giogione (1478–1510), *Venetian*
Grünewald (1475–1528), *German*
Guardi, Francesco (1712–93), *Venetian*
Hokusai (1760–1849), *Japanese*
Ingres, Jean (1780–1876), *French*
John, Augustus (1878–1916), *English*
La Tour, Georges de (1593–1652), *French*
Lorenzetti, Pietro (active 1320–45), *Italian*
Manet, Edouard (1832–83), *French*
Mantegna, Andrea (1431–1506), *Italian*
Millet, François (1814–75), *French*
Modigliani, Amedo (1884–1920), *Italian*
Mondrian, Piet (1872–1944) *Dutch*
Nash, Paul (1889–1946), *English*
Parmigianino, Francesco (1503–40), *Italian*
Piero della Francesca (1416–92), *Italian*
Pollaiuolo, Antonio (1429–98), *Florentine*
Rossetti, Dante Gabriel (1828–82), *English*
Rousseau, Henri (1844–1910), *French*
Rowlandson, Thomas (1756–1827), *English*
Seurat, Georges (1859–91), *French*
Sickert, Walter (1860–1942), *English*
Sutherland, Graham (b. 1903), *English*
Thornhill, Sir James (1675–1734), *English*
Tiepolo, Battiste (1696–1770), *Venetian*
Tintoretto (1518–94), *Venetian*
Titian (1487–1576), *Venetian*
Toulouse-Lautrec (1864–1901), *French*
Uccello, Paolo (1396–1475), *Florentine*

Van Gogh, Vincent (1853–90), *Dutch*
Veronese, Paolo (1529–88), *Italian*
Watteau, Antoine (1684–1721), *French*
Watts, G. F. (1817–1904), *English*

Sculptors

Arp, Hans (1887–1966), *French*
Cellini, Benvenuto (1500–71), *Italian*
Epstein, Jacob (1880–1959), *English*
Gibbons, Grinling (1648–1720), *English*
Giacometti (1901–1966), *Swiss*
Houdon, Jean-Antoine (1741–1828), *French*
Lipchitz, Jacques (b. 1891), *French*
Quercia, Jacopo della (1374–1438), *Italian*
Robbia, Luca della (1400–82), *Italian*
Verrocchio, Andrea del (1435–88), *Italian*

Architects

Adam, Robert (1728–92), and his three brothers, *Scottish*. Built many country houses, including Syon House, Middlesex.

Bernini, Gianlorenzo (1598–1680), *Italian*. Sculptor and architect, St Peter's piazza, Rome.

Borromini, Francesco (1599–1667), *Italian*. Great Baroque designer.

Dudok, Willem (b. 1884), *Dutch*. Hilversum town hall.

Gaudi, Antoni (1852–1926), *Spanish*. Church of Sagrada Familia, Barcelona.

Jenny, William (1832–1907), *U.S.A.* Originator of steel-framed skyscrapers.

Mackintosh, Charles (1868–1928), *Scottish*. Pioneer modernist, Glasgow School of Art.

Morris, William (1834–96), *English*. Painter, decorator and handcraft revivalist.

Niemeyer, Oscar (b. 1907), *Brazilian*. Worked on United Nations building in New York and Brasilia.

Palladio, Andrea (1518–80), *Italian*.

Paxton, Sir Joseph (1801–65), *English*. Crystal Palace.

Perret, Auguste (1874–1954), *French*. Pioneered reinforced concrete.

Soane, Sir John (1753–1837), *English*. Bank of England.

Sullivan, Louis (1856–1924). *American*. Brilliant expounder of functional design.

Vanbrugh, Sir John (1664–1726), *English*. Blenheim Palace.

Vasari, Giorgio (1511–74), *Italian*. Important mainly as a writer.

Vitruvius, Marcus (100 B.C.), *Italian*. Famous writer of *De Re Architectura*.

Wyatt, James (1746–1813), *English*. Royal Military Academy, Woolwich.

Sport

AT the beginning of this section, sports are arranged alphabetically; under each heading are given details of governing bodies, championships and records. These are followed by a list of those results of the 1972 Olympics not recorded under particular sports. Finally, under 'Personalities', brief notes are given on some of the sportsmen who have made the greatest impression on the British scene in 1974–75.

Archery

Governing body: Grand National Archery Society, 20 Broomfield Road, Chelmsford, Essex, CM1 1SW.

Olympic Games 1972

Men	J. Williams (U.S.A.)	2,528 pts.
Women	D. Wilber (U.S.A.)	2,424 pts.

26th World Target Archery Championships 1971

Men (individual)	John Williams (U.S.A.)
Men (team)	U.S.A.
Women (individual)	Miss E. Gapchenko (U.S.S.R.)
Women (team)	Poland

British Target Championships 1974

Men	R. D. Matthews (Worcestershire)
Women	Miss P. M. Edwards (Kent)

Association Football

The Football Association was founded in 1863; the F.A. Cup competition was first held in 1871; official international matches have been played since 1872.

Governing bodies: Football Association (England), 16 Lancaster Gate, London, W2 3LW; Football Association (Scotland), 6 Park Gardens, Glasgow, G3 7YE; Football Association (Irish), 20 Windsor Avenue, Belfast, BT9 6EG; Football Association (Eire), 80 Merrion Square South, Dublin, 2; Football Association (Wales), 3 Fairy Road, Wrexham, LL13 7PS.

LEAGUE CHAMPIONS

1889	Preston North End	1898	Sheffield United
1890	Preston North End	1899	Aston Villa
1891	Everton	1900	Aston Villa
1892	Sunderland	1901	Liverpool
1893	Sunderland	1902	Sunderland
1894	Aston Villa	1903	Sheffield Wednesday
1895	Sunderland	1904	Sheffield Wednesday
1896	Aston Villa	1905	Newcastle United
1897	Aston Villa	1906	Liverpool

1907	Newcastle United	1949	Portsmouth
1908	Manchester United	1950	Portsmouth
1909	Newcastle United	1951	Tottenham Hotspur
1910	Aston Villa	1952	Manchester United
1911	Manchester United	1953	Arsenal
1912	Blackburn Rovers	1954	Wolverhampton
1913	Sunderland		Wanderers
1914	Blackburn Rovers	1955	Chelsea
1915	Everton	1956	Manchester United
1920	West Bromwich Albion	1957	Manchester United
1921	Burnley	1958	Wolverhampton
1922	Liverpool		Wanderers
1923	Liverpool	1959	Wolverhampton
1924	Huddersfield Town		Wanderers
1925	Huddersfield Town	1960	Burnley
1926	Huddersfield Town	1961	Tottenham Hotspur
1927	Newcastle United	1962	Ipswich Town
1928	Everton	1963	Everton
1929	Sheffield Wednesday	1964	Liverpool
1930	Sheffield Wednesday	1965	Manchester United
1931	Arsenal	1966	Liverpool
1932	Everton	1967	Manchester United
1933	Arsenal	1968	Manchester City
1934	Arsenal	1969	Leeds United
1935	Arsenal	1970	Everton
1936	Sunderland	1971	Arsenal
1937	Manchester City	1972	Derby County
1938	Arsenal	1973	Liverpool
1939	Everton	1974	Leeds United
1947	Liverpool	1975	Derby County
1948	Arsenal		

F.A. CUP WINNERS

1872	Wanderers	1888	West Bromwich Albion
1873	Wanderers	1889	Preston North End
1874	Oxford University	1890	Blackburn Rovers
1875	Royal Engineers	1891	Blackburn Rovers
1876	Wanderers	1892	West Bromwich Albion
1877	Wanderers	1893	Wolverhampton
1878	Wanderers		Wanderers
1879	Old Etonians	1894	Notts County
1880	Clapham Rovers	1895	Aston Villa
1881	Old Carthusians	1896	Sheffield Wednesday
1882	Old Etonians	1897	Aston Villa
1883	Blackburn Olympic	1898	Nottingham Forest
1884	Blackburn Rovers	1899	Sheffield United
1885	Blackburn Rovers	1900	Bury
1886	Blackburn Rovers	1901	Tottenham Hotspur
1887	Aston Villa	1902	Sheffield United

1903	Bury	1946	Derby County
1904	Manchester City	1947	Charlton Athletic
1905	Aston Villa	1948	Manchester United
1906	Everton	1949	Wolverhampton
1907	Sheffield Wednesday		Wanderers
1908	Wolverhampton	1950	Arsenal
	Wanderers	1951	Newcastle United
1909	Manchester United	1952	Newcastle United
1910	Newcastle United	1953	Blackpool
1911	Bradford City	1954	West Bromwich Albion
1912	Barnsley	1955	Newcastle United
1913	Aston Villa	1956	Manchester City
1914	Burnley	1957	Aston Villa
1915	Sheffield United	1958	Bolton Wanderers
1920	Aston Villa	1959	Nottingham Forest
1921	Tottenham Hotspur	1960	Wolverhampton
1922	Huddersfield Town		Wanderers
1923	Bolton Wanderers	1961	Tottenham Hotspur
1924	Newcastle United	1962	Tottenham Hotspur
1925	Sheffield United	1963	Manchester United
1926	Bolton Wanderers	1964	West Ham
1927	Cardiff City	1965	Liverpool
1928	Blackburn Rovers	1966	Everton
1929	Bolton Wanderers	1967	Tottenham Hotspur
1930	Arsenal	1968	West Bromwich Albion
1931	West Bromwich Albion	1969	Manchester City
1932	Newcastle United	1970	Chelsea
1933	Everton	1971	Arsenal
1934	Manchester City	1972	Leeds United
1935	Sheffield Wednesday	1973	Sunderland
1936	Arsenal	1974	Liverpool
1937	Sunderland	1975	West Ham
1938	Preston North End		
1939	Portsmouth		

FOOTBALL LEAGUE CUP WINNERS

1961	Aston Villa	1970	Manchester City
1962	Norwich City	1971	Tottenham Hotspur
1963	Birmingham City	1972	Stoke City
1964	Leicester City	1973	Tottenham Hotspur
1965	Chelsea	1974	Wolverhampton
1966	West Bromwich Albion		Wanderers
1967	Queen's Park Rangers	1975	Aston Villa
1968	Leeds United		
1969	Swindon Town		

SCOTTISH CUP WINNERS

1949	Rangers	1952	Motherwell
1950	Rangers	1953	Rangers
1951	Celtic	1954	Celtic

1955	Clyde	1966	Rangers
1956	Heart of Midlothian	1967	Celtic
1957	Falkirk	1968	Dunfermline
1958	Clyde	1969	Celtic
1959	St Mirren	1970	Aberdeen
1960	Rangers	1971	Celtic
1961	Dunfermline	1972	Celtic
1962	Rangers	1973	Rangers
1963	Rangers	1974	Celtic
1964	Rangers	1975	Celtic
1965	Celtic		

EUROPEAN CUP WINNERS

1957	Real Madrid	1967	Celtic
1958	Real Madrid	1968	Manchester United
1959	Real Madrid	1969	A.C. Milan
1960	Real Madrid	1970	Feyenoord
1961	Benfica	1971	Ajax
1962	Benfica	1972	Ajax
1963	A.C. Milan	1973	Ajax
1964	Inter Milan	1974	Bayern Munich
1965	Inter Milan		
1966	Real Madrid		

WORLD CUP WINNERS

1930	Uruguay	1958	Brazil
1934	Italy	1962	Brazil
1938	Italy	1966	England
1950	Uruguay	1970	Brazil
1954	Germany	1974	West Germany

OLYMPIC GAMES WINNERS

1908	United Kingdom	1948	Sweden
1912	United Kingdom	1952	Hungary
1920	Belgium	1956	U.S.S.R.
1924	Uruguay	1960	Yugoslavia
1928	Uruguay	1964	Hungary
1932	No competition	1968	Hungary
1936	Italy	1972	Poland

RECORDS

Championship wins: Arsenal and Liverpool eight times; Everton and Manchester United seven times; Aston Villa and Sunderland six times

Highest score in F.A. Cup: Preston North End 26, Hyde 0 (1887)

Highest score in Cup Final: Bury 6, Derby County 0 (1903)
Highest score by one man in League game: 10 goals, J. Payne
for Luton Town *v.* Bristol Rovers (1936)
Highest score by one man in Division I: 7 goals, E. Drake for
Arsenal *v.* Aston Villa (1935)
Highest score by one man in an international: 6 goals, G. J
Bambrick for Ireland *v.* Wales (1930)
Most goals during career: 550, by James McGrory (Glasgow
Celtic), 1922–38. **English record:** 434, by A. Rowley (West
Bromwich Albion, Fulham, Leicester City and Shrewsbury Town)
Most caps won by amateur: 62, by R. Haider (Kingstonian and
Hendon), 1966–73
Most caps won by a professional: Bobby Moore (West Ham
United), 108 for England
Most Welsh caps: I. Allchurch (Newcastle United, Cardiff City and
Swansea Town), 1950–66, 68
Most Scottish caps: G. Young (Glasgow Rangers), 1946–57, 53
Most Irish caps: T. Neill (Arsenal and Hull City), 1960–73, 59.

Athletics

Governing bodies: Amateur Athletic Association, 70 Brompton Road, London, SW3 1EE; Women's Amateur Athletic Association, 70 Brompton Road, London, S.W.3.

WORLD AND UNITED KINGDOM RECORDS
*(The records given here are those that have been
officially ratified as at 31st December, 1974)*

| | **Men** | |
	World	*United Kingdom*
100 metres	9·9 sec.	10·1 sec.
	J. Hines (U.S.A.)	D. Jenkins
	C. Green (U.S.A.)	B. Green
	R. Smith (U.S.A.)	
	E. Hart (U.S.A.)	
	R. Robinson (U.S.A.)	
200 metres	19·5 sec.	No record
(straight track)	T. Smith (U.S.A.)	
curved track)	19·8 sec.	20·3 sec.
	T. Smith (U.S.A.)	D. Jenkins
	D. Quarrie (Jamiaca)	

	World	*United Kingdom*
400 metres	43·8 sec.	45·2 sec.
	L. Evans (U.S.A.)	D. Jenkins
800 metres	1 min. 43·7 sec.	1 min. 45·1 sec.
	M. Fiasconaro (Italy)	A. Carter
1,000 metres	2 min. 16·0 sec.	2 min. 18·2 sec.
	D. Malan (S. Africa)	J. Boulter
1,500 metres	3 min. 33·1 sec.	3 min. 37·4 sec.
	J. Ryun (U.S.A.)	F. Clement
1 mile	3 min. 51·1 sec.	3 min. 55·3 sec.
	J. Ryun (U.S.A.)	P. Stewart
2,000 metres	4 min. 56·2 sec.	5 min. 8·2 sec.
	M. Jazy (France)	C. Robinson
3,000 metres	7 min. 37·6 sec.	7 min. 35·2 sec.
	E. Puttemans (Belgium)	B. Foster
2 miles	8 min. 13·8 sec.	8 min. 13·8 sec.
	B. Foster (G.B.)	B. Foster
3 miles	12 min. 47·8 sec.	12 min. 58·2 sec.
	E. Puttemans (Belgium)	D. Bedford
5,000 metres	13 min. 13·0 sec.	13 min. 14·6 sec.
	E. Puttemans (Belgium)	B. Foster
10,000 metres	27 min. 30·8 sec.	27 min. 30·8 sec.
	D. Bedford (G.B.)	D. Bedford
20,000 metres	57 min. 44·4 sec.	58 min. 39·0 sec.
	G. Roelants (Belgium)	R. Hill
30,000 metres	1 hr. 31 min. 30·4 sec.	1 hr. 31 min. 30·4 sec.
	J. Alder (G.B.)	J. Alder
1 hour	12 miles 1,610 yd.	12 miles 1,268 yd.
	G. Roelants (Belgium)	R. Hill
110 metres hurdles	13·1 sec.	13·5 sec.
	R. Milburn (U.S.A.)	B. Price
200 metres hurdles	22·5 sec.	23·0 sec.
	M. Lauer (W. Germany)	A. Pascoe
	G. Davis (U.S.A.)	
400 metres hurdles	47·8 sec.	48·1 sec.
	J. Akii-Bua (Uganda)	D. Hemery
3,000 metres steeplechase	8 min. 14·0 sec.	8 min. 22·6 sec.
	B. Jipcho (Kenya)	J. Davies
High jump	7 ft. 6½ in.	6 ft. 11¼ in.
	D. Stones (U.S.A.)	C. Boreham

	World	*United Kingdom*
Long jump	29 ft. 2½ in. R. Beamon (U.S.A.)	27 ft. L. Davies
Triple jump	57 ft. 2¾ in. V. Saneyev (U.S.S.R.)	54 ft. F. Alsop
Pole vault	18 ft. 5¾ in. R. Seagren (U.S.A.)	17 ft. 2¾ in. M. Bull
Shot-put	71 ft. 7 in. A. Feurbach (U.S.)	70 ft. 1½ in. G. Capes
Discus-throw	224 ft. 5 in. J. Silvester (U.S.A.) R. Bruch (Sweden)	213 ft. 1 in. W. Tancred
Hammer-throw	250 ft. 8 in. W. Schmidt (W. Germany)	233 ft. 9 in. B. Williams
Javelin-throw	308 ft. 8 in. K. Wolfermann (W. Germany)	278 ft. 7 in. C. Clover
Decathlon (10 events)	8,454 pts. N. Avilov (U.S.S.R.)	7,903 pts. P. Gabbett

Women

60 metres	7·2 sec. B. Cuthbert (Australia) I. Turova-Bochkaryeva (U.S.S.R.)	No record
100 metres	10·8 sec. R. Stecher (E. Germany)	11·1 sec. A. Lynch
200 metres	22·1 sec. R. Stecher (E. Germany)	23·0 sec. H. Golden
400 metres	51·0 sec. M. Neufville (Jamaica/G.B.) M. Zehrt (E. Germany)	51·8 secs D. Murray
800 metres	1 min. 57·5 sec. S. Zlateva (Bulgaria)	2 min. 1·2 sec. J. Allison
1,500 metres	4 min. 1·4 sec. L. Bragina (U.S.S.R.)	4 min. 4·8 sec. S. Carey
1 mile	4 min. 29·5 sec. P. Cacchi (Italy)	4 min. 37·0 sec. A. Smith
100 metres hurdles	12·3 sec. A. Ehrhardt (E. Germany)	13·0 sec. J. Vernon

	World	*United Kingdom*
High jump	6 ft. 4¾ in.	6 ft. 1½ in.
	J. Blagoyeva (Bulgaria)	B. Inkpen
Long jump	22 ft. 5½ in.	22 ft. 2¼ in.
	H. Rosendahl (W. Germany)	M. Rand
Shot-put	69 ft. 6¾ in.	53 ft. 6¼ in.
	N. Chizhova (U.S.S.R.)	M. Peters
Discus-throw	229 ft. 4 in.	190 ft. 4 in.
	F. Myelnik (W. Germany)	R. Payne
Javelin-throw	220 ft. 6 in.	182 ft. 5 in.
	R. Fuchs (E. Germany)	S. Platt
Pentathlon	4,932 pts.	4,801 pts.
(5 events)	B. Pollak (E. Germany)	M. Peters

THE MILE RECORD

Year	Name	Time
1884	George (G.B.)	4 min. 12·75 sec.
1915	Taber (U.S.A.)	4 min. 12·6 sec.
1923	Nurmi (Finland)	4 min. 10·4 sec.
1931	Ladoumègue (France)	4 min. 9·2 sec.
1933	Lovelock (New Zealand)	4 min. 7·6 sec.
1934	Cunningham (U.S.A.)	4 min. 6·8 sec.
1937	Wooderson (G.B.)	4 min. 6·4 sec.
1942	Hägg (Sweden)	4 min. 6·2 sec.
1942	Andersson (Sweden)	4 min. 6·2 sec.
1942	Hägg (Sweden)	4 min. 4·6 sec.
1943	Andersson (Sweden)	4 min. 2·6 sec.
1944	Andersson (Sweden)	4 min. 1·6 sec.
1945	Hägg (Sweden)	4 min. 1·3 sec.
1954	Bannister (G.B.)	3 min. 59·4 sec.
1954	Landy (Australia)	3 min. 57·9 sec.
1957	Ibbotson (G.B.)	3 min. 57·2 sec.
1958	Elliott (Australia)	3 min. 54·5 sec.
1962	Snell (New Zealand)	3 min. 54·4 sec.
1964	Snell (New Zealand)	3 min. 54·1 sec.
1965	Jazy (France)	3 min. 53·6 sec.
1966	Ryun (U.S.A.)	3 min. 51·3 sec.
1967	Ryun (U.S.A.)	3 min. 51·1 sec.

THE XXth OLYMPIC GAMES WINNERS
(Munich, 1972)
Men

100 metres	V. Borzov (U.S.S.R.)	10·1 sec.
200 metres	V. Borzov (U.S.S.R.)	20·0 sec.
400 metres	V. Matthews (U.S.A.)	44·7 sec.

800 metres	D. Wottle (U.S.A.)	1 min. 45·9 sec.
1,500 metres	P. Vasala (Finland)	3 min. 36·3 sec.
5,000 metres	L. Viren (Finland)	13 min. 26·4 sec.
10,000 metres	L. Viren (Finland)	27 min. 38·4 sec.
Steeplechase, 3,000 metres	K. Keino (Kenya)	8 min. 23·6 sec. (Olympic record)
Marathon	F. Shorter (U.S.A.)	2 hr. 12 min. 19·8 sec.
110 metres hurdle	R. Milburn (U.S.A.)	13·2 sec.
400 metres hurdle	J. Akii-Bua (Uganda)	47·8 sec. (world record)
High jump	Y. Tarmak (U.S.A.)	7 ft. 3¾ in.
Pole vault	W. Nordwig (E. Germany)	18 ft. 0½ in. (Olympic record)
Long jump	R. Williams (U.S.A.)	27 ft. 0½ in.
Triple jump	V. Saneyev (Bulgaria)	56 ft. 11¼ in.
Shot-put	W. Komar (Poland)	69 ft. 6 in.
Discus-throw	L. Danek (Czech.)	211 ft. 3 in.
Hammer-throw	A. Bondarchuk (U.S.S.R.)	247 ft. 8 in. (Olympic record)
Javelin-throw	K. Wolfermann (W. Germany)	296 ft. 10 in. (Olympic record)
Decathlon	N. Avilov (U.S.S.R.)	8,454 pts. (world record)
4 × 100 metres relay	U.S.A. (L. Black, R. Taylor, G. Tinker, E. Hart)	38·2 sec. (equals world record)
4 × 400 metres	Kenya (C. Asati, H. Nyamau, R. Ouko, J. Sang)	2 min. 59·8 sec.
20 km. walk	P. Frenkel (E. Germany)	1 hr. 26 min. 42·4 sec. (Olympic record)
50 km. walk	B. Kannenberg (W. Germany)	3 hr. 56 min. 11·6 sec. (Olympic record)

Women

100 metres	R. Stecher (E. Germany)	11·1 sec.
200 metres	R. Stecher (E. Germany)	22·4 sec. (equals world record)
400 metres	M. Zehrt (E. Germany)	51·1 sec. (Olympic record)
800 metres	H. Falck (W. Germany)	1 min. 58·6 sec. (Olympic record)
1,500 metres	L. Bragina (U.S.S.R.)	4 min. 01·4 sec. (world record)
100 metres hurdles	A. Ehrhardt (E. Germany)	12·6 sec. (Olympic record)

high jump	U. Meyfarth (W. Germany)	6 ft. 3½ in.
long jump	H. Rosendahl (W. Germany)	22 ft. 3 in.
shot-put	N. Chizhova (U.S.S.R.)	69 ft. 0 in. (world record)
discus-throw	F. Melnik (U.S.S.R.)	218 ft. 7 in. (Olympic record)
javelin-throw	R. Fuchs (E. Germany)	209 ft. 7 in. (Olympic record)
Pentathlon	M. Peters (G.B.)	4,801 pts.
4 × 100 metres relay	W. Germany (C. Krause, I. Mickler, A. Richter, H. Rosendahl)	42·8 sec. (equals world record)
4 × 400 metres relay	E. Germany (D. Kaesling, R. Kuehne, H. Seidler, M. Zehrt)	3 min. 23 sec. (world record)

Badminton

Governing body: Badminton Association of England, 81a High Street, Bromley, Kent, BRI IJY.

THOMAS CUP
(Men's International Championship)

		Venue
1961	Indonesia beat Thailand	Djakarta
1964	Indonesia beat Denmark	Tokyo
1967	Malaysia beat Indonesia	Djakarta
1970	Indonesia beat Malaysia	Kuala Lumpar
1973	Indonesia beat Denmark	Djakarta

ALL-ENGLAND CHAMPIONSHIPS
(Men's singles)

1960	Erland Kops	1969	R. Hartono
1961	Erland Kops	1970	R. Hartono
1962	Erland Kops	1971	R. Hartono
1963	Erland Kops	1972	R. Hartono
1964	K. A. Nielsen	1973	R. Hartono
1965	Erland Kops	1974	R. Hartono
1966	T. Huang	1975	S. Pri
1967	Erland Kops		
1968	R. Hartono		

UBER CUP
(Women's International Championship)

		Venue
1960	U.S.A. beat Denmark	Philadelphia
1963	U.S.A. beat England	Wilmington

1966	Japan beat U.S.A.	Wellington
1969	Japan beat Indonesia	Tokyo
1972	Japan beat Indonesia	Tokyo

ALL-ENGLAND CHAMPIONSHIPS
(Women's singles)

1960	J. Devlin	1969	H. Yuki
1961	Mrs. G. C. K. Hashman	1970	E. Takenaka
1962	Mrs. G. C. K. Hashman	1971	Mrs. E. Twedberg
1963	Mrs. G. C. K. Hashman	1972	Mrs. N. Nakayama
1964	Mrs. G. C. K. Hashman	1973	M. Beck
1965	U. Smith	1974	H. Yuki
1966	Mrs. G. C. K. Hashman	1975	H. Yuki
1967	Mrs. G. C. K. Hashman		
1968	Mrs. E. Twedberg		

INTER-COUNTY CHAMPIONSHIP

1960	Kent	1969	Surrey
1961	Surrey	1970	Surrey
1962	Surrey	1971	Surrey
1963	Surrey	1972	Surrey
1964	Essex	1973	Surrey
1965	Surrey	1974	Surrey
1966	Surrey	1975	Surrey
1967	Surrey		
1968	Surrey		

Basket Ball

Governing body: Amateur Basket Ball Association, P.O. Box I.W.3, Leeds 16.

OLYMPIC GAMES

1936	U.S.A.	1960	U.S.A.
1948	U.S.A.	1964	U.S.A.
1952	U.S.A.	1968	U.S.A.
1956	U.S.A.	1972	U.S.S.R.

NATIONAL CLUB CHAMPIONSHIP

1960	Central Y.M.C.A.	1969	Boreham Wood Bullets
1961	London University	1970	Liverpool & Bootle Police
1962	Central Y.M.C.A.	1971	Manchester University
1963	Central Y.M.C.A.	1972	Avenue (Chingford)
1964	Central Y.M.C.A.	1973	London Latvian SK
1965	Aldershot Warriors	1974	Sutton
1966	Oxford University	1975	Embassy All-Stars
1967	Central Y.M.C.A.		
1968	Oxford University		

Billiards and Snooker

Governing body: The Billiards and Snooker Association Control Council, Alexandra Chambers, 32 John William Street, Huddersfield, Yorkshire.

AMATEUR CHAMPIONSHIPS

English amateur, men 1975	N. Dagley
English amateur, women 1974	Mrs Vera Selby
English amateur snooker, 1975	S. Hood
English amateur snooker, women 1974	Mrs Vera Selby

Boxing

Governing bodies: British Boxing Board of Control, Ramillies Buildings, Hill's Place, London, W.1; Amateur Boxing Association, Clutha House, 10 Storey's Gate, London, S.W.1.

OLYMPIC GAMES WINNERS 1972

Heavyweight	T. Stevenson (Cuba)
Light Heavyweight	M. Parlov (Yugoslavia)
Middleweight	V. Lemechev (U.S.S.R.)
Light Middleweight	D. Kottysch (W. Germany)
Welterweight	E. Correa (Cuba)
Light Welterweight	R. Seales (U.S.A.)
Lightweight	J. Szczepanski (Poland)
Featherweight	B. Kousnetsov (U.S.S.R.)
Bantamweight	O. Martinez (Cuba)
Flyweight	G. Kostadinov (Bulgaria)
Light Flyweight	G. Gedo (Hungary)

WORLD PROFESSIONAL CHAMPIONS

Weight	as at 31/12/72	as at 31/12/73	as at 31/12/74
Heavy	J. Frazier (U.S.A.)	G. Foreman (U.S.A.)	M. Ali (U.S.A.)
Light Heavy	B. Foster (U.S.A.)	B. Foster (U.S.A.)	J. Conteh (Great Britain)
Middle	C. Monzon (Argentina)	C. Monzon (Argentine)	R. Valdez (Columbia)
Light Middle	K. Watima (Japan)	K. Watima (Japan)	O. Albarado (U.S.A.)
Welter	J. Napoles (Mexico)	J. Napoles (Mexico)	J. Napoles (Mexico)
Light Welter	A. Cervantes (Colombia)	B. Arcari (Italy)	P. Fernandez (Spain)

Weight	as at 31/12/72	as at 31/12/73	as at 31/12/74
Light	R. Duran (Panama)	R. Gonzales (Mexico)	G. Ishimatzu (Japan)
Junior Light	B. Villaflor (Philippines)	R. Arrendondo (Mexico)	K. Shibata (Japan)
Feather	J. Legra (Spain)	E. Jofre (Spain)	R. Chacon (U.S.A.)
Bantam	E. Pinder (Panama)	R. Herrera (Mexico)	R. Martinez (Mexico)
Fly	V. Borkorsor (Thailand)	C. Chionoi (Thailand)	S. Oguma (Japan)

WORLD HEAVYWEIGHT CHAMPIONS

1892	James J. Corbett (U.S.A.)	1949	Ezzard Charles (U.S.A.)
1897	Bob Fitzsimmons (Britain)	1951	Jersey Joe Walcott (U.S.A.)
1899	James J. Jefferies (U.S.A.)		
1905	Marvin Hart (U.S.A.)	1952	Rocky Marciano (U.S.A.)
1906	Tommy Burns (Canada)	1956	Floyd Patterson (U.S.A.)
1908	Jack Johnson (U.S.A.)	1959	Ingemar Johansson (Sweden)
1915	Jess Willard (U.S.A.)		
1919	Jack Dempsey (U.S.A.)	1960	Floyd Patterson (U.S.A.)
1926	Gene Tunney (U.S.A.)	1962	Sonny Liston (U.S.A.)
1930	Max Schmeling (Germany)	1964	Cassius Clay (U.S.A.)
1932	Jack Sharkey (U.S.A.)	1970	Joe Frazier (U.S.A.)
1933	Primo Carnera (Italy)	1973	George Foreman (U.S.A.)
1934	Max Baer (U.S.A.)	1974	Muhammad Ali (U.S.A.)
1935	James Braddock (U.S.A.)		
1937	Joe Louis (U.S.A.)		

BRITISH PROFESSIONAL CHAMPIONS

as at 31/12/74

Weight		Weight	
Heavy	B. Johnson	Light Welter	J. Singleton
Light Heavy	J. Conteh	Light	—
Middle	—	Feather	E. Armstrong
Light Middle	M. Hope	Bantam	D. Needham
Welter	J. Stracey	Fly	J. McCluskey

BRITISH AMATEUR CHAMPIONS 1975

Weight		Weight	
Heavy	G. McEwan	Light	P. Cowdell
Light Heavy	M. Heath	Feather	R. Beaumont
Middle	D. Odwell	Bantam	S. Ogilvie
Light Middle	C. Harrison	Fly	C. Magri
Welter	W. Bennett	Light Fly	A. Lawless
Light Welter	J. Zarachi		

RECORDS

Longest reigning world champion: Joe Louis
  (22nd June 1937—1st March 1949)
Longest reigning British heavyweight champion:
  Henry Cooper (12th January 1959—13th June 1970)

Cricket

Governing bodies: The Cricket Council, Lord's Ground, London, N.W.8; Women's Cricket Association, 34A Millway, Mill Hill, London, NW7.

TEST MATCHES

England v. Australia 1876–77 to 1975

The leading records of the series of matches are as follows:

Highest innings totals

903–7 dec.   By England at the Oval, 1938
729–6 dec.   By Australia at Lord's, 1930

Lowest innings totals

36   By Australia at Birmingham, 1902
45   By England at Sydney, 1886–87

Highest individual innings

364   L. Hutton for England at the Oval, 1938
334   D. G. Bradman for Australia at Leeds, 1930
311   R. B. Simpson for Australia at Manchester, 1964
307   R. M. Cowper for Australia at Melbourne, 1965–66
304   D. G. Bradman for Australia at Leeds, 1934
287   R. E. Foster for England at Sydney, 1903–4
270   D. G. Bradman for Australia at Melbourne, 1936–37

Most runs for a batsman in one rubber

England in England, 562 (av. 62·44) by D. C. S. Compton, 1948
England in Australia, 905 (av. 113·12) by W. R. Hammond, 1928–29
Australia in England, 974 (av. 139·14) by D. G. Bradman, 1930
Australia in Australia, 810 (av. 90·0) by D. G. Bradman, 1936–37

Batsmen scoring two centuries in a match

136 and 130   W. Bardsley for Australia at the Oval, 1909
176 and 127   H. Sutcliffe for England at Melbourne, 1924–25
119 n.o. and 177   W. R. Hammond for England at Adelaide, 1928–29

147 and 103 n.o.   D. C. S. Compton for England at Adelaide,
                                                            1946–47
122 and 124 n.o.   A. R. Morris for Australia at Adelaide, 1946–47

Bowlers taking nine or ten wickets in an innings

10 for 53   J. C. Laker for England at Manchester (2nd inns.), 1956
 9 for 37   J. C. Laker for England at Manchester (1st inns.), 1956
 9 for 121 A. A. Mailey for Australia at Melbourne, 1920–21

Bowlers taking fourteen or more wickets in a match

19 for 90   J. C. Laker for England at Manchester, 1956
16 for 137 R. A. L. Massie for Australia at Lord's, 1972
15 for 104 H. Verity for England at Lord's, 1934
15 for 124 W. Rhodes for England at Melbourne, 1903–4
14 for 90   F. R. Spofforth for Australia at the Oval, 1882
14 for 99   A. V. Bedser for England at Nottingham, 1953

Hat-tricks

For England   W. Bates at Melbourne, 1882–83
               J. Briggs at Sydney, 1891–92
               J. T. Hearne at Leeds, 1899

For Australia F. R. Spofforth at Melbourne, 1878–79
               H. Trumble at Melbourne, 1901–2
               H. Trumble at Melbourne, 1903–4

Most wickets taken by a bowler in one rubber

England in England, 46 (av. 9·60) by J. C. Laker, 1956
England in Australia, 38 (av. 23·18) by M. W. Tate, 1924–25
Australia in England, 31 (av. 17·67) by D. K. Lillee, 1972
Australia in Australia, 36 (av. 26·27) by A. A. Mailey, 1920–21

Record wicket partnerships by England batsmen

1st   323   J. B. Hobbs and W. Rhodes at Melbourne, 1911–12
2nd   382   L. Hutton and M. Leyland at the Oval, 1938
3rd   262   W. R. Hammond and D. R. Jardine at Adelaide, 1928–29
4th   222   W. R. Hammond and E. Paynter at Lord's, 1938
5th   206   E. Paynter and D. C. S. Compton at Nottingham, 1938
6th   215   L. Hutton and J. Hardstaff, jr., at the Oval, 1938
7th   143   F. E. Woolley and J. Vine at Sydney, 1911–12
8th   124   E. Hendren and H. Larwood at Brisbane, 1928–29
9th   151   W. H. Scotton and W. W. Read at the Oval, 1884
10th 130   R. E. Foster and W. Rhodes at Sydney, 1903–4

Record wicket partnerships by Australian batsmen

1st   244   R. B. Simpson and W. M. Lawry at Adelaide, 1965–66
2nd   451   W. H. Ponsford and D. G. Bradman at the Oval, 1934
3rd   276   D. G. Bradman and A. L. Hassett at Brisbane, 1946–47

4th	388	W. H. Ponsford and D. G. Bradman at Leeds, 1934
5th	405	S. G. Barnes and D. G. Bradman at Sydney, 1946–47
6th	346	J. H. Fingleton and D. G. Bradman at Melbourne, 1936–37
7th	165	C. Hill and H. Trumble at Melbourne, 1897–98
8th	243	C. Hill and R. J. Hartigan at Adelaide, 1907–8
9th	154	S. E. Gregory and J. McC. Blackham at Sydney, 1894–95
10th	127	J. M. Taylor and A. A. Mailey at Sydney, 1924–25

TEST CRICKET, 1877–1975

Summarised results (as at March 31, 1975)

	W.	D.	L.		W.	D.	L.
ENGLAND *v.*				**WEST INDIES** *v.*			
Australia	71	63	86	India	15	15	3
South Africa	46	38	18	Pakistan	4	3	3
West Indies	21	26	19	**NEW ZEALAND** *v.*			
New Zealand	23	24	0	England	0	24	23
India	22	20	6	Australia	1	2	4
Pakistan	9	17	1	South Africa	2	6	9
Rest of the World	1	0	4	West Indies	2	7	5
AUSTRALIA *v.*				India	2	7	7
England	86	63	71	Pakistan	1	9	5
South Africa	29	13	11	**INDIA** *v.*			
West Indies	19	10	6	England	6	20	22
New Zealand	4	2	1	Australia	3	6	16
India	16	6	3	West Indies	3	15	15
Pakistan	5	3	1	New Zealand	7	7	2
SOUTH AFRICA *v.*				Pakistan	2	12	1
England	18	38	46	**PAKISTAN** *v.*			
Australia	11	13	29	England	1	17	9
New Zealand	9	6	2	Australia	1	3	5
WEST INDIES *v.*				West Indies	3	3	4
England	19	26	21	New Zealand	5	9	1
Australia	6	10	19	India	1	12	2
New Zealand	5	7	2				

Greatest number of appearances in Test Cricket (as at March 31, 1975)

ENGLAND				ENGLAND (*contd.*)		
M. C. Cowdrey			118	L. Hutton		79
T. G. Evans			91	D. C. S. Compton		78
W. R. Hammond			85	A. P. E. Knott		74
K. F. Barrington			82	J. H. Edrich		73
T. W. Graveney			79	J. B. Statham		70

ENGLAND (*contd.*)

F. S. Trueman	. .	67
R. Illingworth	. .	66
P. B. H. May	. .	66
G. Boycott	. .	65
F. E. Woolley	. .	64
E. R. Dexter	. .	62
T. E. Bailey	. .	61
J. B. Hobbs	. .	61
W. Rhodes	. .	58
D. L. Underwood	. .	57
H. Sutcliffe	. .	54
F. J. Titmus	. .	53
A. V. Bedser	. .	51
E. Hendren	. .	51
K. W. R. Fletcher	. .	50
M. J. K. Smith	. .	50
G. A. R. Lock	. .	49
B. L. d'Oliveira	. .	48
L. E. G. Ames	. .	47
J. A. Snow	. .	47
J. C. Laker	. .	46
J. M. Parks	. .	46
M. Leyland	. .	41
H. Verity	. .	40
R. E. S. Wyatt	. .	40

AUSTRALIA

R. N. Harvey	. .	79
W. M. Lawry	. .	67
R. Benaud	. .	63
I. M. Chappell	. .	62
R. R. Lindwall	. .	61
G. D. McKenzie	. .	60
I. R. Redpath	. .	60
S. E. Gregory	. .	58
K. R. Miller	. .	55
W. A. Odfield	. .	54
K. D. Walters	. .	53
D. G. Bradman	. .	52
R. B. Simpson	. .	52
A. T. W. Grout	. .	51
W. W. Armstrong	. .	50
C. Hill	. .	49
V. Trumper	. .	48
C. C. McDonald	. .	47
A. R. Morris	. .	46
I. W. Johnson	. .	45
A. K. Davidson	. .	44
A. L. Hassett	. .	43

AUSTRALIA (*contd.*)

K. R. Stackpole	. .	43
P. J. Burge	. .	42
M. A. Noble	. .	42
N. C. O'Neill	. .	42
W. Bardsley	. .	41
W. A. Johnston	. .	40

SOUTH AFRICA

J. H. B. Waite	. .	50
A. D. Nourse, sen.	. .	45
B. Mitchell	. .	42
H. W. Taylor	. .	42
T. L. Goddard	. .	41
R. A. McLean	. .	40
H. J. Tayfield	. .	37
D. J. McGlew	. .	34
A. D. Nourse, jun.	. .	34

NEW ZEALAND

J. R. Reid	. .	58
B. E. Congdon	. .	50
B. Sutcliffe	. .	42
G. T. Dowling	. .	39
R. C. Motz	. .	32
V. Pollard	. .	32

PAKISTAN

Hanif Mohammad	. .	55
Imtiaz Ahmed	. .	41
Saeed Ahmed	. .	41
Intikhab Alam	. .	43
Mushtaq Mohammad	. .	38
Asif Iqbal	. .	34
Fazal Mahmood	. .	34
Nasim-ul-Ghani	. .	29
Mahmood Hussain	. .	27

WEST INDIES

G. Sobers	. .	89
R. B. Kanhia	. .	74
L. R. Gibbs	. .	61
F. M. Worrell	. .	51
W. W. Hall	. .	48
E. D. Weekes	. .	48
B. F. Butcher	. .	44
C. C. Hunte	. .	44
C. L. Walcott	. .	44

INDIA

P. R. Umrigar	.	.	59	V. Mankad	.	.	.	44
C. G. Borde	.	.	55	P. Roy	.	.	.	43
V. L. Manjrekar	.	.	55	R. G. Nadkarni	.	.	41
F. M. Engineer	.	.	46	M. L. Jaisimha	.	.	39
Mansur Ali Khan	.	.	46	B. S. Bedi	.	.	.	39

COUNTY CHAMPIONS

Since 1920		1951	Warwickshire
1920	Middlesex	1952	Surrey
1921	Middlesex	1953	Surrey
1922	Yorkshire	1954	Surrey
1923	Yorkshire	1955	Surrey
1924	Yorkshire	1956	Surrey
1925	Yorkshire	1957	Surrey
1926	Lancashire	1958	Surrey
1927	Lancashire	1959	Yorkshire
1928	Lancashire	1960	Yorkshire
1929	Nottinghamshire	1961	Hampshire
1930	Lancashire	1962	Yorkshire
1931	Yorkshire	1963	Yorkshire
1932	Yorkshire	1964	Worcestershire
1933	Yorkshire	1965	Worcestershire
1934	Lancashire	1966	Yorkshire
1935	Yorkshire	1967	Yorkshire
1936	Derbyshire	1968	Yorkshire
1937	Yorkshire	1969	Glamorgan
1938	Yorkshire	1970	Kent
1939	Yorkshire	1971	Surrey
1946	Yorkshire	1972	Warwickshire
1947	Middlesex	1973	Hampshire
1948	Glamorgan	1974	Worcestershire
1949	Middlesex & Yorks, tie		
1950	Lancs & Surrey, tie		

Since 1864 the title has been won outright by Yorkshire 31 times, Surrey 18, Nottinghamshire 12, Lancashire 8, Middlesex 5, Gloucestershire 3, Warwickshire 3, Worcestershire 3, Glamorgan 2, Hampshire 2, Derbyshire 1. Seven times it has been shared by Nottinghamshire 5, Lancashire 4, Surrey 2, Yorkshire 2, Gloucestershire 1, Middlesex 1.

RECORDS
Highest scores in first-class cricket: 499, Hanif Mohammed, for Karachi, 1958–59; 452 (not out), D. G. Bradman, for N.S.W., 1929–30; 443 (not out), B. B. Nimbalkar, for Maharashtra, 1948–49.

Highest score in England 424, A. C. MacLaren, for Lancashire, 1895

Highest scores in Test cricket: 365 (not out), by G. Sobers for W. Indies, 1958. 364, by L. Hutton for England, 1938

Most runs in first-class cricket: 61,237, between 1905 and 1934, by J. B. Hobbs

Highest team innings: Australia, Victoria 1,107 v. N.S.W., 1926–27; England, England 903 (for 7 dec.) v. Australia, 1938

Most runs in a day: Australians v. Essex, 1948, 721

Highest batting partnership: 577, by V. S. Hazare and Gul Mohammed, in India (1946–47)

Most runs in a season: 3,816, by Denis Compton (1947)

Most wickets in a season: 304, by A. P. Freeman (1928)

Highest number of wickets in a match: 19, by J. C. Laker, for England v. Australia (1956)

Most wickets during career: 4,187, by W. Rhodes, between 1898 and 1930

The only tie in Test Match history: West Indies 453 and 284, Australia 505 and 232, Brisbane, December 1960. Australia started the last possible over needing 6 runs with 3 wickets left.

Biggest win: Pakistan Western Railways beat Dera Ismail Khan by an innings and 851 runs, 1964–65

Most centuries in one season: D. C. S. Compton, 18 (1947)

Fastest scoring: P. G. H. Fender for Surrey v. Northamptonshire in 1920, 100 runs in 35 min.

Highest batting average in England: D. G. Bradman, 115·66 (1938). By an Englishman: G. Boycott, 100·12 (1971). In first-class games (1927–49) Bradman's figures were 338 inns., 117 centuries, 43 not outs, 28,067 runs, 95·14 average

Cross-Country Running

Governing bodies: English Cross-Country Union, 14 Windmill Hill, Ruislip, Middlesex; Women's Cross-Country & Race Walking Association, 10 Anderton Close, Bury, Lancashire.

ENGLISH CHAMPIONSHIP

Men

	Individual	Team
1970	T. Wright (Hallamshire H.)	Stoke City A.C.
1971	D. Bedford (Shaftesbury H.)	Shettleston Harriers
1972	M. Thomas (Thames Valley)	Tipton Harriers
1973	D. Bedford (Shaftesbury H.)	Gateshead A.C.
1974	D. Black (Small Heath)	Derby & County
1975	T. Simmons (Luton Utd.)	Gateshead Harriers

Women

	Individual	Team
1970	Mrs R. Ridley (Essex L.A.C.)	Cambridge Harriers
1971	Mrs. R. Ridley (Essex L.A.C.)	Coventry Godiva
1972	Mrs. R. Ridley (Essex L.A.C.)	Cambridge Harriers
1973	Mrs J. Smith (Barnet and District A.C.)	Cambridge Harriers
1974	Mrs. R. Ridley (Essex L.A.C.)	Barnet & District A.C.
1975	Mrs D. Nagle (Guinness A.C.)	Cambridge Harriers

INTERNATIONAL CHAMPIONSHIP

Men

	Individual	Team	Venue
1970	M. Tagg (England)	England	Vichy
1971	D. Bedford (England)	England	San Sebastian
1972	G. Roelants (Belgium)	England	Cambridge
1973	P. Paivarinta (Finland)	Belgium	Waregem
1974	E. de Berk (Belgium)	Belgium	Monza
1975	I. Stewart (England)	New Zealand	Rabat

Women

		Team	Venue
1970	Mrs D. Brown (U.S.A.)	England	Frederick
1971	Mrs D. Brown (U.S.A.)	England	San Sebastian
1972	J. Smith (England)	England	Cambridge
1973	P. Cacci (Italy)	England	Waregem
1974	P. Pigni (Italy)	England	Monza
1975	J. Brown (U.S.A.)	U.S.A.	Rabat

Cycling

Governing body: British Cycling Federation, 70 Brompton Rd, London, SW3 1EN.

1972 OLYMPIC GAMES WINNERS

1,000 m. T.T.	N. Fredborg (Denmark)
Sprint	D. Morelon (France)
Tandem sprint	U.S.S.R. (V. Semenets, I. Tselovalnikov)
4,000 m. individual pursuit	K. Knudsen (Norway)
4,000 m. team pursuit	West Germany
Road race	H. Kulper (Holland)
Road team T.T. 100 km.	U.S.S.R.

1974 WORLD CHAMPIONS

Men

Professional road race	E. Merckx (Belgium)
Amateur road race	J. Kowalski (Poland)

Professional sprint	P. Pedersen (Denmark)
Amateur sprint	A. Tkac (Czechoslovakia)
Professional 5,000 m. pursuit	R. Schuiten (Holland)
Amateur 4,000 m. pursuit	H. Lutz (W. Germany)
Professional 100 km. motor-paced	C. Stam (Holland)
Amateur hour paced	J. Breuer (W. Germany)
Amateur tandem sprint	V. Vackar & M. Vymazal (Czechoslovakia)
Amateur kilometre T.T.	E. Rapp (U.S.S.R.)
Amateur 100 km. team T.T.	Sweden
Amateur 4,000 m. team pursuit	W. Germany

Women (all amateur)

Road race	G. Gambillon (France)
Sprint	T. Piltsikova (U.S.S.R.)
Pursuit	T. Garkushina (U.S.S.R.)

RECORDS

Men's professional motor-paced 1 hour record: 44 mls. 261 yds., H. Damasse at Montlhery, 1956

Men's professional unpaced standing start 1 hour record: 49 km. 431·957 m., E. Merckx in Mexico, 1972

Men's amateur unpaced flying start 1 kilometre: 1 min. 1·1 sec., L. Borghetti in Mexico, 1967

Equestrian

Governing bodies: British Horse Society and British Show Jumping Association, National Equestrian Centre, Stoneleigh, Kenilworth, Warwickshire, CV8 2LR.

SHOW JUMPING

Olympic Games, 1972: Individual—G. Mancinelli (Italy)
    Team—W. Germany (H. Winkler, H. Steenken, F. Ligges, G. Wiltfang)
World Championships, 1974: Men—Hartwig Steenken (W. Germany)
    Ladies—Janou Tissot (France)
European Championships, 1973: Men—Paddy McMahon (G.B.)
    Ladies—Ann Moore (G.B.)
President's Cup, 1974: Great Britain
B.S.J.A. National Championship, 1974: Pip Nicholls on *Timmy*
Ladies' National Championship, 1974: Jean Davenport on *All Trumps*

HORSE TRIALS

Olympic Games, 1972: Individual—R. Meade (G.B.)
    Team—Great Britain (R. Meade, Lt. M. Phillips, Mary Gordon-Watson, Bridget Parker)

World Championships, 1974: Individual—Bruce Davidson (U.S.A.)
European Championships, 1974: Individual—A. Evdokimov
(U.S.S.R.) Team—U.S.A.
Badminton Horse Trials, 1975: Abandoned

DRESSAGE

Olympic Games, 1972: Individual—L. Linsenhoff (W. Germany)
Team—U.S.S.R. (Miss E. Patushkova, I. Kizimov, I. Kalita)
Senior Dressage Championship, 1974: Mrs. L. Johnstone on *El Farruco*
Dressage Horse of the Year, 1974: *El Farruco*

Fencing

Governing body: Amateur Fencing Association, The de Beaumont Centre, 83 Perham Road, London, W14 9SY.

1972 OLYMPIC CHAMPIONS, MEN

Foil	W. Wyoda (Poland)
Team Foil	Poland
Epee	C. Fenyvesi (Hungary)
Team Epee	Hungary
Sabre	V. Sidak (U.S.S.R.)
Team Sabre	Italy

WOMEN

Foil	A. Ragno-Lonzi (Italy)
Team Foil	U.S.S.R.

1974 ENGLISH CHAMPIONS

Men's foil	B. Paul (Salle Paul)
Men's foil team	Thames Fencing Club
Ladies' foil	Miss W. Ager (Salle Pearson)
Ladies' foil team	Ashton Fencing Club
Men's epee	E. O. Bourne (Salle Boston)
Men's epee team	Polytechnic
Men's sabre	R. Cohen (Salle Boston)
Men's sabre team	Polytechnic

Gliding

Governing body: British Gliding Association, Artillery Mansions, 75 Victoria Street, London, S.W.1.

World Records—Solo

Distance	1,460·8 km.	H. W. Grosse (W. Germany)	1972
Height	12,894 m.	P. Bikle (U.S.A.)	1961
Speed	(100 km. triangle) 155·06 km/h.	W. Neubert (W. Germany)	1970

Golf

Governing bodies: Royal and Ancient Golf Club, St Andrews, Fife, KY16 9JD; Ladies' Golf Union, 2 Fairways, Sandwich Bay, Kent.

OPEN CHAMPIONS
Since 1946

1946	Sam Snead (U.S.A.)	1958	P. Thomson (Australia)
1947	Fred Daly (Balmoral)	1959	G. Player (South Africa)
1948	Henry Cotton (Royal Mid-Surrey)	1960	Kel Nagle (Australia)
		1961	A. Palmer (U.S.A.)
1949	Bobby Locke (South Africa)	1962	A. Palmer (U.S.A.)
		1963	Bob Charles (N.Z.)
1950	Bobby Locke (South Africa)	1964	A. Lema (U.S.A.)
		1965	P. Thomson (Australia)
1951	Max Faulkner (un-attached)	1966	J. Nicklaus (U.S.A.)
		1967	R. de Vicenzo (Argentine)
1952	Bobby Locke (South Africa)	1968	G. Player (South Africa)
		1969	A. Jacklin (Potters Bar)
1953	Ben Hogan (U.S.A.)	1970	J. Nicklaus (U.S.A.)
1954	P. Thomson (Australia)	1971	L. Trevino (U.S.A.)
1955	P. Thomson (Australia)	1972	L. Trevino (U.S.A.)
1956	P. Thomson (Australia)	1973	T. Weiskopf (U.S.A.)
1957	Bobby Locke (South Africa)	1974	G. Player (South Africa)

RYDER CUP

1951	U.S.A.	1959	U.S.A.	1967	U.S.A.
1953	U.S.A.	1961	U.S.A.	1969	Tie
1955	U.S.A.	1963	U.S.A.	1971	U.S.A.
1957	Great Britain	1965	U.S.A.	1973	U.S.A.

WALKER CUP

1951	U.S.A.	1959	U.S.A.	1967	U.S.A.
1953	U.S.A.	1961	U.S.A.	1969	U.S.A.
1955	U.S.A.	1963	U.S.A.	1971	Great Britain
1957	U.S.A.	1965	Tie.	1973	U.S.A.

CURTIS CUP

1952	Great Britain	1960	U.S.A.	1968	U.S.A.
1954	U.S.A.	1962	U.S.A.	1970	U.S.A.
1956	Great Britain	1964	U.S.A.	1972	U.S.A.
1958	Great Britain	1966	U.S.A.	1974	U.S.A.

WORLD CUP

1960	U.S.A.	1965	South Africa	1970	Australia
1961	U.S.A.	1966	U.S.A.	1971	U.S.A.
1962	U.S.A.	1967	U.S.A	1972	Taiwan
1963	U.S.A.	1968	Canada	1973	U.S.A.
1964	U.S.A.	1969	U.S.A.	1974	U.S.A.

LADIES' BRITISH OPEN AMATEUR CHAMPIONSHIP

1970	Miss D. Oxley (G.B.)
1971	Miss M. Walker (G.B.)
1972	Miss M. Walker (G.B.)
1973	Miss A. Irvin (G.B.)
1974	Miss C. Semple (U.S.A.)

LADIES' CLOSE AMATEUR CHAMPIONSHIPS 1974

England:	Miss A. Irvin
Ireland:	Miss M. McKenna
Scotland:	Dr. A. Wilson
Wales:	Mrs. A. Briggs

Hockey

Governing bodies: British Hockey Board, The White House, Avenue Road, Duffield, Derby; Hockey Association of England, 70 Brompton Road, London SW3 1HB; All-England Women's Hockey Association, 160 Great Portland Street, London, W1N 5TB.

OLYMPIC WINNERS

1920	England	1952	India
1924	No competition	1956	India
1928	India	1960	Pakistan
1932	India	1964	India
1936	India	1968	Pakistan
1948	India	1972	W. Germany

COUNTY CHAMPIONSHIP

MEN		WOMEN	
1971	Staffordshire	1971	Herts. drew with Lancs.
1972	Wiltshire	1972	Essex

MEN		WOMEN	
1973	Surrey	1973	Lancashire
1974	Hertfordshire	1974	Lancashire
1975	Kent	1975	Leics. drew with Surrey

Ice Hockey

Governing body: International Ice Hockey Federation, 20 Bedford Street, London, WC2E 9HP.

OLYMPIC AND WORLD CHAMPIONSHIPS

		Venue
*1960	U.S.A.	Squaw Valley
1961	Canada	Geneva
1962	Sweden	Colorado Springs
1963	U.S.S.R.	Stockholm
*1964	U.S.S.R.	Innsbruck
1965	U.S.S.R.	Tampere
1966	U.S.S.R.	Ljubljana
1967	U.S.S.R.	Vienna
*1968	U.S.S.R.	Grenoble
1969	U.S.S.R.	Stockholm
1970	U.S.S.R.	Stockholm
1971	U.S.S.R.	Geneva
*1972	U.S.S.R.	Sapporo
1973	U.S.S.R.	Moscow
1974	U.S.S.R.	Helsinki
1975	U.S.S.R.	Dusseldorf

* Denotes Olympic Games

Ice Skating

Governing body: National Skating Association of Great Britain, Charterhouse, London, E.C.1.

WORLD RECORDS (*as at 31/12/74*)

Men

500 metres	L. Efskind (Norway)	38·0 sec.	1972
	L. Linkovesi (Finland)		
	E. Keller (W. Germany)		
	H. Borjes (Sweden)		
1,000 metres	A. Safranov (Norway)	1 min. 17·2 sec.	1974
1,500 metres	A. Schenk (Holland)	1 min. 58·7 sec.	1971
3,000 metres	A. Schenk (Holland)	4 min. 8·3 sec.	1972
5,000 metres	A. Schenk (Holland)	7 min. 9·8 sec.	1972
10,000 metres	A. Schenk (Holland)	14 min. 55·9 sec.	1971

Ladies

500 metres	S. Young (U.S.A.)	41·8 sec	1973
1,000 metres	T. Averina (U.S.S.R.)	1 min. 26·4 sec.	1974
1,500 metres	T. Averina (U.S.S.R.)	2 min. 14·0 sec.	1974
3,000 metres	S. Kaiser (Holland)	4 min. 46·5 sec.	1971

1972 OLYMPIC WINNERS (SAPPORO)

Figure Skating

Men	O. Nepela (Czechoslovakia)
Women	B. T. Schuba (Austria)
Pairs	I. Rodnina and A. Ulanov (U.S.S.R.)

Speed Events

Men's 500 metres	E. Keller (W. Germany)
Men's 1,500 metres	A. Schenk (Holland)
Men's 5,000 metres	A. Schenk (Holland)
Men's 10,000 metres	A. Schenk (Holland)
Ladies' 500 metres	A. Henning (U.S.A.)
Ladies' 1,000 metres	M. Pflug (West Germany)
Ladies' 1,500 metres	D. Holum (U.S.A.)
Ladies' 3,000 metres	S. Baas-Kaiser (Holland)

RECORDS

Only man to win five world titles and four Olympic gold medals (1923–31): Clas Thunberg (Finland)
Only woman to win four Olympic gold medals at one Olympiad (1964): Lidija Skoblikova (U.S.S.R.)

Lacrosse

Governing bodies: English Lacrosse Union, 170A London Road, Stockport, Cheshire, SK7 4DJ; All-England Ladies' Lacrosse Association, 70 Brompton Road, London S.W.3.

IROQUOIS CUP

1950	Old Hulmeians	1957	Old Mancunians
1951	Old Waconians	1958	Heaton Mersey
1952	Old Waconians	1959	Heaton Mersey
1953	Old Waconians	1960	Heaton Mersey
1954	Heaton Mersey	1961	Boardman and Eccles
1955	Old Waconians	1962	Old Hulmeians
1956	Cambridge University	1963	Mellor

1964	Old Hulmeians	1971	S. Manchester &
1965	Mellor		Wythenshawe
1966	S. Manchester &	1972	S. Manchester &
	Wythenshawe		Wythenshawe
1967	Mellor	1973	S. Manchester &
1968	Old Hulmeians		Wythenshawe
1969	Mellor	1974	Urmston
1970	Lee		

Lawn Tennis

Governing body: Lawn Tennis Association, Barons Court, London, W14 9EG.

WIMBLEDON CHAMPIONS

Since 1920

Men's Singles

1920	W. T. Tilden	1951	R. Savitt
1921	W. T. Tilden	1952	F. A. Sedgman
1922	G. L. Patterson	1953	E. V. Seixas
1923	W. M. Johnston	1954	J. Drobny
1924	J. Borotra	1955	M. A. Trabert
1925	R. Lacoste	1956	L. A. Hoad
1926	J. Borotra	1957	L. A. Hoad
1927	H. Cochet	1958	A. J. Cooper
1928	R. Lacoste	1959	A. Olmedo
1929	H. Cochet	1960	N. Fraser
1930	W. T. Tilden	1961	R. Laver
1931	S. B. Wood	1962	R. Laver
1932	H. E. Vines	1963	E. McKinley
1933	J. H. Crawford	1964	R. Emerson
1934	F. J. Perry	1965	R. Emerson
1935	F. J. Perry	1966	M. Santana
1936	F. J. Perry	1967	J. Newcombe
1937	J. D. Budge	1968	R. Laver
1938	J. D. Budge	1969	R. Laver
1939	R. L. Riggs	1970	J. Newcombe
1946	Y. Petra	1971	J. Newcombe
1947	J. A. Kramer	1972	S. Smith
1948	R. Falkenburg	1973	J. Kodes
1949	F. R. Schroeder	1974	J. Connors
1950	J. E. Patty		

Women's Singles

1920	Mlle S. Lenglen	1923	Mlle S. Lenglen
1921	Mlle S. Lenglen	1924	Miss K. McKane
1922	Mlle S. Lenglen	1925	Mlle S. Lenglen

1926	Mrs. L. Godfree	1954	Miss M. Connolly
1927	Miss H. Wills	1955	Miss A. Brough
1928	Miss H. Wills	1956	Miss S. Fry
1929	Miss H. Wills	1957	Miss A. Gibson
1930	Mrs. F. Moody	1958	Miss A. Gibson
1931	Frl C. Aussem	1959	Miss M. Bueno
1932	Mrs. F. Moody	1960	Miss M. Bueno
1933	Mrs. F. Moody	1961	Miss A. Mortimer
1934	Miss D. Round	1962	Miss K. Susman
1935	Mrs F. Moody	1963	Miss M. Smith
1936	Miss H. Jacobs	1964	Miss M. Bueno
1937	Miss D. Round	1965	Miss M. Smith
1938	Mrs. F. Moody	1966	Mrs. L. W. King
1939	Miss A. Marble	1967	Mrs. L. W. King
1946	Miss P. Betz	1968	Mrs. L. W. King
1947	Miss M. Osborne	1969	Mrs. P. F. Jones
1948	Miss A. Brough	1970	Mrs. B. M. Court
1949	Miss A. Brough	1971	Miss E. Goolagong
1950	Miss A. Brough	1972	Mrs. L. W. King
1951	Miss D. Hart	1973	Mrs. L. W. King
1952	Miss M. Connolly	1974	Miss C. Evert
1953	Miss M. Connolly		

DAVIS CUP

1950	Australia	1963	U.S.A.
1951	Australia	1964	Australia
1952	Australia	1965	Australia
1953	Australia	1966	Australia
1954	U.S.A.	1967	Australia
1955	Australia	1968	U.S.A.
1956	Australia	1969	U.S.A.
1957	Australia	1970	U.S.A.
1958	U.S.A.	1971	U.S.A.
1959	Australia	1972	U.S.A.
1960	Australia	1973	Australia
1961	Australia	1974	South Africa
1962	Australia		

WIGHTMAN CUP

1950	U.S.A.	1960	Great Britain
1951	U.S.A.	1961	U.S.A.
1952	U.S.A.	1962	U.S.A.
1953	U.S.A.	1963	U.S.A.
1954	U.S.A.	1964	U.S.A.
1955	U.S.A.	1965	U.S.A.
1956	U.S.A.	1966	U.S.A.
1957	U.S.A.	1967	U.S.A.
1958	Great Britain	1968	Great Britain
1959	U.S.A.	1969	U.S.A.

1970	U.S.A.	1973	U.S.A.
1971	U.S.A.	1974	Great Britain
1972	U.S.A.		

RECORDS

Longest match: M. Cox and R. Wilson (G.B.) beat C. Pasarell and R. Holmberg (U.S.A.) at Salisbury, Maryland, in the American Indoor Championships, 1968, after 6 hr. 23 min. playing time: 26–24, 17–19, 30–28

Largest number of games in Davis Cup singles: 86 in 1970; A. Ashe (U.S.A.) beat C. Kuhnke (W. Germany) 6–8, 10–12, 9–7, 13–11, 6–4

Largest number of games in a Wimbledon singles: 112, when R. Gonzales (U.S.A.) beat C. Pasarell (U.S.A.), 22–24, 1–6, 16–14, 6–3, 11–9 in 1969

Longest Wimbledon match: $5\frac{1}{4}$ hours, when Gonzales beat Pasarell

Greatest number of Wimbledon wins: William C. Renshaw (G.B.), 7 singles titles (1881–2–3–4–5–6–9) and 7 doubles (1880–1–4–5–6–8–9). Mrs. Helen Wills-Moody (U.S.A.) won the women's singles eight times

Greatest number of wins: Miss Elizabeth Ryan (U.S.A.), 19 titles (1914–34)

Motor Cycling

Governing body: Auto-Cycle Union, 31 Belgrave Square, London, SW1X 8QQ.

WORLD CHAMPIONS

	1972	*1973*	*1974*
		Road Racing	
50 c.c.	A. Nieto (Derbi)	J. de Vries (Kreidler)	H. van Kessel (Van Veen/ Kreidler)
125 c.c.	A. Nieto (Derbi)	H. Andersson (Yamaha)	K. Andersson (Yahama)
250 c.c.	J. Saarinen (Yamaha)	D. Braun (Yahama)	W. Villa (Harley David-son)
350 c.c.	G. Agostini (MV-Agusta)	G. Agostini (MV-Agusta)	G. Agostini (Yamaha)
500 c.c.	G. Agostini (MV-Agusta)	P. Read (MV-Agusta)	P. Read (MV-Agusta)

| Sidecar | K. Enders (BMW) | K. Enders (BMW) | K. Enders (Busch) |

Moto Cross

| 250 c.c. | J. Robert (Suzuki) | H. Andersson (Yamaha) | G. Moiseev (KTM) |
| 500 c.c. | R. de Coster (Suzuki) | R. de Coster (Suzuki) | H. Mikkola (Husqvarna) |

Speedway

| | I. Mauger (Jawa) | J. Szczakiel (Jawa) | A. Michanek (Jawa) |

BRITISH CHAMPIONS

	1972	*1973*	*1974*

Road Racing

125 c.c.	S. Machin (Yamaha)	A. Hockley (Yahama)	The Solo championship
250 cc..	S. Machin (Yamaha)	A. Rutter (Yamaha)	was won by: S. Woods
350 c.c.	M. Grant (Padgett Yamaha)	———	(Suzuki)
500 c.c.	J. Harvey (Kirby Metisse & TWS Suzuki)	———	
750 c.c.	D. Potter (Kuhn Norton)	D. Croxford (JP Norton)	
Three-wheeler	N. Hanks (BSA)	G. Boret (Renwick Konig)	M. Hobson (Yamaha)

Moto Cross

250 c.c.	A. Robertson (Husqvarna)	M. Davis (Bultaco)	J. V. Allan (Bultaco)
500 c.c.	B. Wade (Husqvarna)	J. Banks (Cheney BSA)	J. V. Allan (Bultaco)
Three-Wheeler	J. Turner (Triumph Wasp)	N. Thompson (Norton Wasp)	N. Thompson (Norton Wasp)

Speedway

| | I. Mauger (Jawa) | R. Wilson (Jawa) | E. Boocock (Jawa) |

RECORD

Winner of most World Championships: Giacomo Agostini (14, in 1966–74)

Motor Racing

Governing body: R.A.C. (Motor Sport Division), 31 Belgrave Square, London, SW1 8QH.

World Driving Championship 1974	E. Fittipaldi, (Brazil), *McLaren*
British Grand Prix 1974	J. Scheckter (S. Africa), *Tyrrell Ford*
Le Mans 24-hrs. 1974	H. Pescarolo (France), *Matra*
R.A.C. Rally 1974	T. Makinen (Finland) and H. Liddon (G.B.), *Ford Escort*
Monte Carlo Rally 1974	Not held

RECORDS

Winner of most World Championships: Juan Manuel Fangio (five, in 1951, 1954, 1955, 1956, 1957)
Winner of most Grand Prix: Jackie Stewart (26)
Winner of most Grand Prix in one year: Jim Clarke (seven, in 1963

Netball

Governing body: All-England Netball Association, 70 Brompton Road, London, S.W.3.

WORLD CHAMPIONS

1963	Australia beat New Zealand
1967	New Zealand beat Australia
1971	Australia beat New Zealand

INTER-COUNTY CHAMPIONSHIP

1951	Surrey	1960	Surrey	1969	Kent &
1952	Surrey	1961	Surrey		Surrey,
1953	Surrey	1962	Surrey		draw
1954	Surrey	1963	Surrey	1970	Kent
1955	Surrey	1964	Surrey	1971	Kent
1956	Surrey	1965	Middlesex	1972	Kent
1957	Surrey	1966	Surrey	1973	Kent
1958	Surrey	1967	Kent	1974	Kent
1959	Surrey	1968	Middlesex	1975	Essex

Rackets

Governing body: Tennis and Rackets Association, Cleeve House, Blewbury, Didcot, Oxon., OX11 9PB.

BRITISH ISLES OPEN CHAMPIONSHIP

1929	J. Simpson	1960	J. Dear
1932	Lord Aberdare	1962	G. Atkins
1933	I. Akers-Douglas	1968	J. Leonard
1934	A. Cooper	1970	C. J. Swallow
1936	D. Milford	1971	M. G. M. Smith
1946	J. Dear	1972	H. R. Angus
1954	G. Atkins		
1959	J. Thompson		

WORLD CHAMPIONSHIP

1903	J. Jamsetjhi (India)	1947	J. Dear (Queen's)
1911	C. Williams (Harrow)	1954	G. Atkins (Queen's)
1914	J. Soutar (U.S.A.)	1972	W. Surtees (U.S.A.)
1928	C. Williams (U.S.A.)	1973	H. R. Angus (Queen's)
1937	D. Milford (Marlborough)	1974	W. Surtees (U.S.A.)

Rowing

Governing body: Amateur Rowing Association, 6 Lower Mall, London, W6 9DJ.

THE GRAND CHALLENGE CUP

Between 1839 and 1929 the Cup was won 21 times by Leander, 12 times by London B.C., 7 times by Oxford University B.C., 4 times by Magdalen College, Oxford, 3 times by Thames R.C. and once each by Sydney R.C. and Harvard Athletic Association B.C. The winners since 1930 have been:

1930	London R.C.	1939	Harvard University, U.S.A.
1931	London R.C.		
1932	Leander Club	1946	Leander Club
1933	London R.C.	1947	Jesus College, Cambridge
1934	Leander Club		
1935	Pembroke College, Cambridge	1948	Thames R.C.
		1949	Leander Club
1936	F.C. Zurich R.C., Switzerland	1950	Harvard University, U.S.A.
1937	R. Wiking, Germany	1951	Lady Margaret B.C., Cambridge
1938	London R.C.		

1952	Leander Club	1963	London University
1953	Leander Club	1964	U.S.S.R.
1954	Club Krylia Sovetov, U.S.S.R.	1965	Ratzeburger, W. Germany
1955	University of Pennsylvania, U.S.A.	1966	T.S.C. Berlin, E. Germany
1956	Centre Sportif des Forces de l'Armée, France	1967	S. C. Wissenschaft DH f K, Leipzig
1957	Cornell University, U.S.A.	1968	London University B.C.
1958	Trud Club, Leningrad, U.S.S.R.	1969	S. C. Einheit, Dresden
1959	Harvard University, U.S.A.	1970	A. S. K. Vorwärts, Rostock
		1971	Tideway Scullers School
1960	Molesey B.C.	1972	W.M.F. Moscow, U.S.S.R.
1961	U.S.S.R. Navy		
1962	U.S.S.R. Navy	1973	Trud Kolomna, U.S.S.R.
		1974	Trud Kolomna, U.S.S.R.

DIAMOND SCULLS

First rowed 1844. Winners since 1950:

1950	A. D. Rowe (Leander)	1962	S. A. Mackenzie (Australia)
1951	T. A. Fox (Pembroke)		
1952	M. T. Wood (Australia)	1963	G. Kottman (Switzerland)
1953	T. A. Fox (London)	1964	S. Cromwell (U.S.A.)
1954	P. Vlasic (Jugoslavia)	1965	D. M. Spero (U.S.A.)
1955	T. Kocerka (Poland)	1966	A. Hill (Germany)
1956	T. Kocerka (Poland)	1967	M. Studach (Switzerland)
1957	S. A. Mackenzie (Australia)	1968	H. A. Wardell-Yerburgh (Eton Vikings)
1958	S. A. Mackenzie (Australia)	1969	H.-J. Böhmer (D.D.R.)
1959	S. A. Mackenzie (Australia)	1970	J. Meissner (W. Germany)
		1971	A. Demiddi (Argentina)
1960	S. A. Mackenzie (Australia)	1972	A. Timoschinin (U.S.S.R.)
1961	S. A. Mackenzie (Australia)	1973	S. Drea (Eire)
		1974	S. Drea (Eire)

UNIVERSITY BOAT RACE

Rowed on the river Thames between Putney and Mortlake: 4 miles, 374 yards.

1829	Oxford	1854	Oxford
1836	Cambridge	1856	Cambridge
1839	Cambridge	1857	Oxford
1840	Cambridge	1858	Cambridge
1841	Cambridge	1859	Oxford
1842	Oxford	1860	Cambridge
1845	Cambridge	1861	Oxford
1846	Cambridge	1862	Oxford
1849	Cambridge	1863	Oxford
1849	Oxford	1864	Oxford
1852	Oxford	1865	Oxford

1866	Oxford	1921	Cambridge
1867	Oxford	1922	Cambridge
1868	Oxford	1923	Oxford
1869	Oxford	1924	Cambridge
1870	Cambridge	1925	Cambridge
1871	Cambridge	1926	Cambridge
1872	Cambridge	1927	Cambridge
1873	Cambridge	1928	Cambridge
1874	Cambridge	1929	Cambridge
1875	Oxford	1930	Cambridge
1876	Cambridge	1931	Cambridge
1877	Dead heat	1932	Cambridge
1878	Oxford	1933	Cambridge
1879	Cambridge	1934	Cambridge
1880	Oxford	1935	Cambridge
1881	Oxford	1936	Cambridge
1882	Oxford	1937	Oxford
1883	Oxford	1938	Oxford
1884	Cambridge	1939	Cambridge
1885	Oxford	1946	Oxford
1886	Cambridge	1947	Cambridge
1887	Cambridge	1948	Cambridge
1888	Cambridge	1949	Cambridge
1889	Cambridge	1950	Cambridge
1890	Oxford	1951	Cambridge
1891	Oxford	1952	Oxford
1892	Oxford	1953	Cambridge
1893	Oxford	1954	Oxford
1894	Oxford	1955	Cambridge
1895	Oxford	1956	Cambridge
1896	Oxford	1957	Cambridge
1897	Oxford	1958	Cambridge
1898	Oxford	1959	Oxford
1899	Cambridge	1960	Oxford
1900	Cambridge	1961	Cambridge
1901	Oxford	1962	Cambridge
1902	Cambridge	1963	Oxford
1903	Cambridge	1964	Cambridge
1904	Cambridge	1965	Oxford
1905	Oxford	1966	Oxford
1906	Cambridge	1967	Oxford
1907	Cambridge	1968	Cambridge
1908	Cambridge	1969	Cambridge
1909	Oxford	1970	Cambridge
1910	Oxford	1971	Cambridge
1911	Oxford	1972	Cambridge
1912	Oxford	1973	Cambridge
1913	Oxford	1974	Oxford
1914	Cambridge	1975	Cambridge
1920	Cambridge		

Cambridge have won 68 times, Oxford 52 times.

OLYMPIC GAMES, 1972

Coxed fours	W. Germany (P. Berger, H.-L. Faerber, G. Auer, A. Bieri, U. Banter (cox))	6 min. 31·85 sec.
Coxless pairs	E. Germany (S. Brietzke, W. Mager)	6 min. 53·16 sec.
Single sculls	Y. Malishev (U.S.S.R.)	7 min. 10·12 sec.
Coxed pairs	E. Germany (W. Gunkel, J. Luche, K.-D. Neubert (cox))	7 min. 17·25 sec.
Coxless fours	E. Germany (F. Forberger, F. Ruehle, D. Grahn, D. Schubert)	6 min. 24·27 sec.
Double sculls	U.S.S.R. (A. Timoshinin, G. Korshikov)	7 min. 01·77 sec.
Eights	New Zealand	6 min. 08·94 sec.

RECORDS

Jack Beresford, Junior, won the Wingfield Sculls 7 times, 1920–26 and won medals in 5 successive Olympics
World professional titles record: W. Beach (Australia), 1884–87

Rugby League Football

Governing body: The Rugby Football League, 180 Chapeltown Road, Leeds, LS7 4HT.

WORLD CUP

1954	Great Britain	1970	Australia
1957	Australia	1972	Great Britain
1960	Great Britain		
1968	Australia		

CHALLENGE CUP COMPETITION

since 1950

1950	Warrington	1964	Widnes
1951	Wigan	1965	Wigan
1952	Workington Town	1966	St. Helens
1953	Huddersfield	1967	Featherstone Rovers
1954	Warrington	1968	Leeds
1955	Barrow	1969	Castleford
1956	St. Helens	1970	Castleford
1957	Leeds	1971	Leigh
1958	Wigan	1972	St. Helens
1959	Wigan	1973	Featherstone Rovers
1960	Wakefield Trinity	1974	Warrington
1961	St. Helens	1975	Widnes
1962	Wakefield Trinity		
1963	Wakefield Trinity		

Rugby Union Football

Governing bodv: Rugby Football Union, Twickenham, Middlesex, TW2 7RQ.

INTERNATIONAL CHAMPIONSHIP
since 1920

1920	England, Scotland and Wales, tie	1951	Ireland
1921	England	1952	Wales
1922	Wales	1953	England
1923	England	1954	England, France and Wales, tie
1924	England	1955	Wales and France, tie
1925	Scotland	1956	Wales
1926	Ireland and Scotland, tie	1957	England
1927	Ireland and Scotland, tie	1958	England
1928	England	1959	France
1929	Scotland	1960	England and France, tie
1930	England	1961	France
1931	Wales	1962	France
1932	England, Wales and Ireland, tie	1963	England
		1964	Scotland and Wales, tie
1933	Scotland	1965	Wales
1934	England	1966	Wales
1935	Ireland	1967	France
1936	Wales	1968	France
1937	England	1969	Wales
1938	Scotland	1970	France and Wales, tie
1939	England, Wales and Ireland, tie	1971	Wales
		1972	series not completed
1947	Wales and England, tie	1973	5-way tie
1948	Ireland	1974	Ireland
1949	Ireland	1975	Wales
1950	Wales		

COUNTY CHAMPIONSHIP
since 1960

1960	Warwickshire	1969	Lancashire
1961	Cheshire	1970	Staffordshire
1962	Warwickshire	1971	Surrey
1963	Warwickshire	1972	Gloucestershire
1964	Warwickshire	1973	Lancashire
1965	Warwickshire	1974	Gloucestershire
1966	Middlesex	1975	Gloucestershire
1967	Surrey and Durham		
1968	Middlesex		

VARSITY MATCH

since 1960

1960	Cambridge	1968	Cambridge
1961	Cambridge	1969	Cambridge
1962	Cambridge	1970	Oxford
1963	Cambridge	1971	Oxford
1964	Oxford	1972	Cambridge
1965	Drawn	1973	Cambridge
1966	Oxford	1974	Cambridge
1967	Cambridge		

MIDDLESEX SEVEN-A-SIDE TOURNAMENT

since 1951

1951	Richmond II	1964	Loughborough Colleges I
1952	Wasps	1965	London Scottish I
1953	Richmond I	1966	Loughborough Colleges I
1954	Rosslyn Park I	1967	Harlequins I
1955	Richmond I	1968	London Welsh I
1956	London Welsh I	1969	St. Luke's, Exeter I
1957	St. Luke's College, Exeter	1970	Loughborough Colleges I
1958	Blackheath	1971	London Welsh I
1959	Loughborough College	1972	London Welsh I
1960	London Scottish	1973	London Welsh I
1961	London Scottish I	1974	Richmond I
1962	London Scottish I	1975	Richmond I
1963	London Scottish I		

RECORDS

Most Caps: W. J. McBride (Ireland), 63; Ken Jones (Wales), 44;
D. M. D. Rollo (Scotland), 40 and H. F. McLeod (Scotland),
40; J. Pullen (England), 39

Highest international score: Wales beat France 49–14, 1910

Greatest winning margin: S. Africa beat France 55–6, 1906

Place kick record: 100 yd., at Richmond Athletic Ground, 1906, by
D. F. T. Morkel in an unsuccessful kick for S. Africa *v.* Middlesex.
67 yd., successful by Don Clarke in a club match at Roturua

Longest dropped goal: 90 yd. at Twickenham in 1932, by G. Brand
for South Africa *v.* England

Shooting

Governing bodies: National Rifle Association, Bisley Camp,
Brookwood, Woking, Surrey, GU24 0PB; National Smallbore
Rifle Association, Codrington House, Southwark Street, Lon-
don, S.E.1.

QUEEN'S PRIZE

1952	Major A. B. Kinnier Wilson (R.A.M.C.)
1953	Major N. W. McCaw (Rifle Brigade)
1954	Major G. E. Twine (Royal Artillery)
1955	L. R. Fenwick (City R.C.)
1956	Major G. E. Twine (Royal Artillery)
1957	J. R. C. Love (Kyle R.C.)
1958	Major R. A. Fulton (Royal Artillery)
1959	Lt. L. W. Mallabar (City R.C.)
1960	Sgt. G. Westling (Canada)
1961	W/O. N. L. Beckett (Canada)
1962	Philip Hall (South Norwood)
1963	Keith Pilcher (Surrey)
1964	A. Harris (Oxford University)
1965	Capt. J. Allen (Royal Marines)
1966	Major R. W. Hampton (Canada)
1967	J. Powell (Sussex R.A.)
1968	Capt. A. A. Parks (Canada)
1969	Major F. G. Little (Dean R.C.)
1970	G. F. Arnold (Dorking & District R.C.)
1971	R. M. Stevens (Ricochets R.C.)
1972	R. P. Rosling (City R.C.)
1973	Keith Pilcher (Surrey)
1974	Capt. F. C. Harriss

OLYMPIC GAMES, 1972

Free pistol	R. Shanaker (Sweden)	567 pts.
Small bore rifle (prone)	Ho Jun Li (N. Korea)	599 pts.
Small bore rifle (three positions)	J. Writer (U.S.A.)	1,166 pts.
Rapid-fire pistol	J. Zapedzki (Poland)	595 pts.
Clay Pigeon: Trench	A. Scalzone (Italy)	199 pts.
Skeet	K. Wirnhier (W. Germany)	199 pts.
Free rifle	L. Wigger (U.S.A.)	1,555 pts.
Moving target	L. Zhelezniak (U.S.S.R.)	569 pts.

Ski-ing

Governing body: National Ski Federation of Great Britain, 118 Eaton Square, London, SW1W 9AF.

1972 OLYMPIC GAMES (GRENOBLE)

Combined Alpine Ski Champions: *Men*—not held
Women—A.-M. Pröll (Austria)

BRITISH NATIONAL ALPINE CHAMPIONSHIPS

	Men	**Women**
1970	J. Vesey	G. Hathorn
1971	S. Varley	V. Sturge
1972	I. Penz	O. Chalvin
1973	S. Fitzsimmons	H. Carmichael
1974	K. Bartelski	T. Wallis
1975	S. Fitzsimmons	V. Iliffe

Squash Rackets

Governing bodies: Squash Rackets Association, 70 Brompton Road, London SW3 10X; Women's Squash Rackets Association, 345 Upper Richmond Road, Sheen, London SW14 8QN.

OPEN CHAMPIONSHIP

1950	Hashim Khan (Pakistan)	1963	Abu Taleb (Egypt)
1951	Hashim Khan (Pakistan)	1964	Abu Taleb (Egypt)
1952	Hashim Khan (Pakistan)	1965	Abu Taleb (Egypt)
1953	Hashim Khan (Pakistan)	1966	J. Barrington (amateur)
1954	Hashim Khan (Pakistan)	1967	J. Barrington (amateur)
1955	Hashim Khan (Pakistan)	1968	G. Hunt (Australia)
1956	Roshan Khan (Pakistan)	1969	J. Barrington (Ireland)
1957	Hashim Khan (Pakistan)	1970	J. Barrington (Ireland)
1958	Azam Khan (Pakistan)	1971	J. Barrington (Ireland)
1959	Azam Khan (Pakistan)	1972	J. Barrington (Ireland)
1960	Azam Khan (Pakistan)	1973	G. Hunt (Australia)
1961	Azam Khan (Pakistan)	1974	Qamar Zaman (Pakistan)
1962	Mohibullah Khan (Pakistan)		

AMATEUR CHAMPIONSHIP

1970	G. Allaudin (Pakistan)
1971	G. Allaudin (Pakistan)
1972	C. Nancarrow (Australia)
1973	M. Khan (Pakistan)
1974	J. Leslie (Great Britain)

WOMEN'S CHAMPIONSHIP

1949–58	Miss J. Morgan
1959	Mrs H. G. Macintosh
1960	Mrs G. E. Marshall
1961–64	Miss H. Blundell (Australia)
1965–74	Mrs B. McKay (Australia)

Swimming

Governing bodies: Amateur Swimming Association, Harold Fern House, Derby Square, Loughborough, Leicestershire, LE11 0AL; Channel Swimming Association, 'White Stacks', Walnut Tree Lane, Loose, Maidstone, Kent.

Men
WORLD AND UNITED KINGDOM RECORDS

(as at 31st December 1974)

	World	British
Freestyle		
100 metres	51·22 sec. M. Spitz (U.S.A.)	53·4 sec. R. B. McGregor
200 metres	1 min. 51·66 sec. T. Shaw (U.S.A.)	1 min. 56·17 sec. B. Brinkley
400 metres	3 min. 54·69 sec. T. Shaw (U.S.A.)	4 min. 4·39 sec. B. Brinkley
800 metres	8 min. 15·88 sec. S. Holland (Australia)	8 min. 33·01 sec. J. H. Carter
1,500 metres	15 min. 31·75 sec. T. Shaw (U.S.A.)	15 min. 54·78 sec. J. H. Carter
Breaststroke		
100 metres	1 min. 3·88 sec. J. Hencken (U.S.A.)	1 min. 5·74 sec. D. Wilkie
200 metres	2 min. 18·21 sec. J. Hencken (U.S.A.)	2 min. 19·28 sec. D. Wilkie
Butterfly		
100 metres	54·27 sec. M. Spitz (U.S.A.)	57·95 sec. B. Brinkley
200 metres	2 min. 0·7 sec. M. Spitz (U.S.A.)	2 min. 3·94 sec. B. Brinkley
Backstroke		
100 metres	56·3 sec. R. Matthes (E. Germany)	59·82 sec. C. Cunningham
200 metres	2 min. 1·87 sec. R. Matthes (E. Germany)	2 min. 8·25 sec. C. Cunningham

	World	British
Individual medley		
200 metres	2 min. 6·32 sec. D. Wilkie (Great Britain)	2 min. 6·32 sec. D. Wilkie
400 metres	4 min. 28·89 sec. A. Hargitay (Hungary)	4 min. 36·29 sec. B. Brinkley
Freestyle relay		
4 × 100 metres	3 min. 25·17 sec. U.S.A. National Team (A. Coan, M. Bottom, J. Montgomery, T. Hickcox)	3 min. 38·33 sec. English National Team
4 × 200 metres	7 min. 33·22 sec. U.S.A. National Team (Krumpholz, Bachhaus, Klatt, Montgomery)	7 min. 52·9 sec. English National Team
Medley relay		
4 × 100 metres	3 min. 48·16 sec. U.S.A. National Team (M. Stamm, T. Bruce, M. Spitz, J. Heidenreich)	3 min. 54·13 sec. British National Team

EUROPEAN RECORDS (*as at 31st December, 1974*)

Freestyle		
100 metres	51·77 sec. V. Bure	U.S.S.R.
200 metres	1 min. 53·10 sec. P. Nocke	W. Germany
400 metres	4 min. 1·27 sec. B. Gingsjoe	Sweden
800 metres	8 min. 32·82 sec. B. Gingsjoe	Sweden
1,500 metres	15 min. 54·57 sec. F. Peutze	E. Germany
Breaststroke		
100 metres	1 min. 4·61 sec. M. Kriukin	U.S.S.R.
200 metres	2 min. 19·28 sec. D. Wilkie	Great Britain
Butterfly		
100 metres	55·7 sec. R. Matthes	E. Germany
200 metres	2 min. 3·3 sec. H. Fassnacht	W. Germany

Backstroke

100 metres	56·3 sec. R. Matthes	E. Germany
200 metres	2 min. 1·87 sec. R. Matthes	E. Germany

Individual medley

200 metres	2 min. 6·32 sec. D. Wilkie	Great Britain
400 metres	4 min. 28·89 sec. A. Hargitay	Hungary

Freestyle relay

4 × 100 metres	3 min. 29·72 sec. National Team (Bure, Mazanov, Aboimov, Grivennikov)	U.S.S.R.
4 × 200 metres	7 min. 39·7 sec. National Team (Steinbach, Lampe, Meeuw, Nocke)	W. Germany

Medley relay

4 × 100 metres	3 min. 51·57 sec. National Team (Steinbach, Kusch, Meeuw, Nocke)	W. Germany

Women
WORLD AND UNITED KINGDOM RECORDS

(as at 31st December, 1974)

	World	British
Freestyle		
100 metres	56·96 sec. K. Ender (E. Germany)	1 min. 0·5 sec. A. E. Jackson
200 metres	2 min. 2·94 sec. S. Babashoff (U.S.A.)	2 min. 9·42 sec. S. Edmondson
400 metres	4 min. 15·77 sec. S. Babashoff (U.S.A.)	4 min. 29·17 sec. D. Walker
800 metres	8 min. 47·5 sec. J. Harshbarger (U.S.A.)	9 min. 17·41 sec. D. Simpson
1,500 metres	16 min. 33·94 sec. J. Turrall (Australia)	18 min. 43·2 sec. S. Edmondson
Breaststroke		
100 metres	1 min. 12·28 sec. R. Vogel (E. Germany)	1 min. 15·82 sec. A. Dickie
200 metres	2 min. 34·99 sec. C. Linke (E. Germany)	2 min. 43·11 sec. P. Beavan

	World	British
Butterfly		
100 metres	1 min. 1·88 sec. R. Kother (E. Germany)	1 min. 5·48 sec. J. L. Atkinson
200 metres	2 min. 13·76 sec. R. Kother (E. Germany)	2 min. 22·79 sec. D. Simpson
Backstroke		
100 metres	1 min. 2·98 sec. U. Richter (E. Germany)	1 min. 8·55 sec. M. Kelly
200 metres	2 min. 17·35 sec. U. Richter (E. Germany)	2 min. 26·2 sec. W. Burrell
Individual Medley		
200 metres	2 min. 18·97 sec. U. Tauber (E. Germany)	2 min. 26·86 sec. S. Richardson
400 metres	4 min. 52·42 sec. U. Tauber (E. Germany)	5 min. 6·71 sec. S. Richardson
Freestyle relay		
4 × 100 metres	3 min. 51·99 sec. United States National Team (K. Heddy, K. Peyton, A. Marshall, S. Babashoff)	4 min. 5·59 sec. English National Team
Medley relay		
4 × 100 metres	4 min. 13·78 sec. E. German National Team (U. Richter, R. Vogel, R. Kother, K. Ender)	4 min. 31·41 sec. British National Team

EUROPEAN RECORDS (*as at 31st December, 1974*)

Freestyle		
100 metres	56·96 sec. K. Ender	E. Germany
200 metres	2 min. 3·22 sec. K. Ender	E. Germany
400 metres	4 min. 17·83 sec. A. Franke	E. Germany
800 metres	8 min. 52·45 sec. C. Doerr	E. Germany
1,500 metres	17 min. 4·2 sec. N. Calligaris	Italy
Breaststroke		
100 metres	1 min. 12·55 sec. C. Justen	W. Germany
200 metres	2 min. 34·99 sec. C. Linke	E. Germany

Butterfly

100 metres	1 min. 1·99 sec.	
	R. Kother	E. Germany
200 metres	2 min. 13·76 sec.	
	R. Kother	E. Germany

Backstroke

100 metres	1 min. 3·08 sec.	
	U. Richter	E. Germany
200 metres	2 min. 17·35 sec.	
	U. Richter	E. Germany

Individual medley

200 metres	2 min. 18·97 sec.	
	U. Tauber	E. Germany
400 metres	4 min. 52·42 sec.	
	U. Tauber	E. Germany

Freestyle relay

4 × 100 metres	3 min. 52·45 sec.	
	National Team	E. Germany
	(K. Ender, A. Eife,	
	A. Huebner, S. Eichner)	

Medley relay

4 × 100 metres	4 min. 13·78 sec.	
	National Team	E. Germany
	(U. Richter, R. Vogel,	
	R. Koether, K. Ender)	

OLYMPIC WINNERS, 1972
Men

100 metres freestyle	M. Spitz (U.S.A.)	51·2 sec. *W.R.*
200 metres freestyle	M. Spitz (U.S.A.)	1 min. 52·8 sec. *W.R.*
400 metres freestyle	R. DeMont (U.S.A.)	4 min. 00·3 sec. *O.R.*
1,500 metres freestyle	M. Burton (U.S.A.)	15 min. 52·6 sec. *W.R.*
100 metres breaststroke	N. Taguchi (Japan)	1 min. 04·9 sec. *W.R.*
200 metres breaststroke	J. Hencken (U.S.A.)	2 min. 21·9 sec. *W.R.*
100 metres backstroke	R. Matthes (E. Germany)	56·6 sec. *O.R.*
200 metres backstroke	R. Matthes (E. Germany)	2 min. 02·8 sec. *O.R.*
100 metres butterfly	M. Spitz (U.S.A.)	54·3 sec. *W.R.*
200 metres butterfly	M. Spitz (U.S.A.)	2 min. 00·7 sec. *W.R.*

200 metres individual medley	G. Larsson (Sweden)	2 min. 07·2 sec. *W.R.*
400 metres individual medley	G. Larsson (Sweden)	4 min. 31·9 sec. *O.R.*
4 × 100 metres free-style relay	U.S.A. National Team (D. Edgar, J. Murphy, J. Heidenreich, M. Spitz)	3 min. 26·4 sec. *W.R.*
4 × 200 metres free-style relay	U.S.A. National Team (J. Kinsella, F. Tyler, S. Genter, M. Spitz)	7 min. 35·8 sec. *W.R.*
4 × 100 metres medley relay	U.S.A. National Team (M. Stamm, T. Bruce, M. Spitz, J. Heidenreich)	3 min. 48·2 sec. *W.R.*
Springboard diving	V. Vasin (U.S.S.R.)	594·09 pts.
Highboard diving	K. Dibiasi (Italy)	504·12 pts.

Women

100 metres freestyle	S. Neilson (U.S.A.)	58·6 sec. *O.R.*
200 metres freestyle	S. Gould (Australia)	2 min. 03·6 sec. *W.R.*
400 metres freestyle	S. Gould (Australia)	4 min. 19·0 sec. *W.R.*
800 metres freestyle	K. Rothammer (U.S.A.)	8 min. 53·7 sec. *W.R.*
100 metres breaststroke	C. Carr (U.S.A.)	1 min. 13·6 sec. *W.R.*
200 metres breaststroke	B. Whitfield (Australia)	2 min. 41·7 sec. *O.R.*
100 metres backstroke	M. Belote (U.S.A.)	1 min. 5·8 sec. *O.R.*
200 metres backstroke	M. Belote (U.S.A.)	2 min. 19·19 sec. *W.R.*
100 metres butterfly	M. Aoiki (Japan)	1 min. 3·3 sec. *W.R.*
200 metres butterfly	R. Kother (E. Germany)	2 min. 18·3 sec. *O.R.*
200 metres individual medley	S. Gould (Australia)	2 min. 23·1 sec. *W.R.*
400 metres individual medley	G. Neall (Australia)	5 min. 03·0 sec. *W.R.*
4 × 100 metres free-style relay	U.S.A. National Team (S. Neilson, J. Kemp, J. Barkman, S. Babashoff)	3 min. 55·2 sec. *W.R.*

4 × 100 metres medley relay	U.S.A. National Team (M. Belote, C. Carr, C. Dearduff, S. Neilson)	4 min. 20·8 sec. *W.R.*
Springboard diving	M. King (U.S.A.)	450·03 pts.
Highboard diving	U. Knape (Sweden)	390 pts.

Table Tennis

Governing body: English Table Tennis Association, 21 Claremont, Hastings, Sussex.

WORLD CHAMPIONSHIP

Men's Singles

1950	R. Bergmann (England)	1963	Chuang Tse-Tung (China)
1951	J. Leach (England)		
1952	H. Satoh (Japan)	1965	Chuang Tse-Tung (China)
1953	F. Sido (Hungary)		
1954	I. Ogimura (Japan)	1967	N. Hasegawa (Japan)
1955	T. Tanaka (Japan)	1969	S. Ito (Japan)
1956	I. Ogimura (Japan)	1971	S. Bengtsson (Sweden)
1957	T. Tanaka (Japan)	1973	H. En-tinh (China)
1959	Jung Kuo-Tuan (China)	1975	I. Jonyer (Hungary)
1961	Chuang Tse-Tung (China)		

Women's Singles

1950	A. Rozeanu (Rumania)	1961	Chiu Chung-Hui (China)
1951	A. Rozeanu (Rumania)	1963	K. Matsuzaki (Japan)
1952	A. Rozeanu (Rumania)	1965	N. Fukazu (Japan)
1953	A. Rozeanu (Rumania)	1967	S. Morisawa (Japan)
1954	A. Rozeanu (Rumania)	1969	T. Kowada (Japan)
1955	A. Rozeanu (Rumania)	1971	Lin Hui-Ching (China)
1956	T. Okawa (Japan)	1973	H. Yu-lan (China)
1957	F. Eguchi (Japan)	1975	Yung Sun Kim (N. Korea)
1959	K. Matsuzaki (Japan)		

SWAYTHLING CUP

1950	Czechoslovakia	1954	Japan
1951	Czechoslovakia	1955	Japan
1952	Hungary	1956	Japan
1953	England	1957	Japan

1959	Japan	1969	Japan
1961	China	1971	China
1963	China	1973	Sweden
1965	China	1975	China
1967	Japan		

CORBILLON CUP

1934	Germany	1955	Rumania
1935	Czechoslovakia	1956	Rumania
1936	Czechoslovakia	1957	Japan
1937	U.S.A.	1959	Japan
1938	Czechoslovakia	1961	Japan
1939	Germany	1963	Japan
1947	England	1965	China
1948	England	1967	Japan
1949	U.S.A.	1969	U.S.S.R.
1950	Rumania	1971	Japan
1951	Rumania	1973	S. Korea
1952	Japan	1975	China
1953	Rumania		
1954	Japan		

ENGLISH OPEN CHAMPIONSHIPS
Men's Singles

1970	S. Kollarovits (Czechoslovakia)
1971	T. Klamper (Hungary)
1972	S. Bengtsson (Sweden)
1973	S. Bengtsson (Sweden)
1974	K. Johansson (Sweden)
1975	A. Strokatov (U.S.S.R.)

Women's Singles

1970	Mrs. M. Alexandru (Rumania)
1971	Mrs. M. Alexandru (Rumania)
1972	Mrs. M. Alexandru (Rumania)
1973	Mrs. B. Radberg (Sweden)
1974	Mrs. M. Alexandru (Rumania)
1975	Miss E. Antonian (U.S.S.R.)

Volley Ball

Governing body: English Volleyball Association, 17 Merton Close, Oldbury, Warley, Worcs.

OLYMPIC WINNERS

Men		Women	
1964	U.S.S.R.	1964	Japan
1968	U.S.S.R.	1968	U.S.S.R.
1972	Japan	1972	U.S.S.R.

Walking

Governing body: Race Walking Association, 5 Carden Road, London S.E.15.

WORLD RECORDS

20,000 metres	1 hr. 24 m. 45 s.	B. Kannenberg (W. Germany)	1974
2 hours	16 miles 1,535 yd.	B. Kannenberg (W. Germany)	1974
30,000 metres	2 hr. 12 m. 58 s.	B. Kannenberg (W. Germany)	1974
20 miles	2 hr. 30 m. 38 6 s.	G. Weidner (W. Germany)	1974
30 miles	3 hr. 51 m. 48·6 s.	G. Weidner (W. Germany)	1973
50,000 metres	4 hr. 00 m. 27 2 s.	G. Weidner (W. Germany)	1973

OTHER BEST PERFORMANCES

3,000 metres	11 mins. 51·4 sec.	B. Junk (U.S.S.R.)	1952
2 miles	12 mins. 45·0 sec.	V. Hardmo (Sweden)	1945
5,000 metres	20 mins. 26·8 sec.	V. Hardmo (Sweden)	1945
5 miles	34 mins. 21·2 s.	K. Matthews (G.B.)	1960
10,000 metres	42 mins. 10·4 s.	G. Panitschkin (U.S.S.R.)	1958
7 miles	48 mins. 15·2 s.	V. Hardmo (Sweden)	1945
1 hour	8 miles 1,294 yd.	G. Panitschkin (U.S.S.R.)	1958
15,000 metres	1 hr. 4 mins. 22 s.	G. Panitschkin (U.S.S.R.)	1959
10 miles	1 hr. 9 m. 40·6 s.	K. Matthews (G.B.)	1964

Water Polo

Governing body: Amateur Swimming Association, Acorn House, 314 Gray's Inn Road, London, W.C.1.

OLYMPIC WINNERS

1900	Great Britain	1908	Great Britain
1904	U.S.A.	1912	Great Britain

1920	Great Britain		1952	Hungary
1924	France		1956	Hungary
1928	Germany		1960	Italy
1932	Hungary		1964	Hungary
1936	Hungary		1968	Yugoslavia
1948	Italy		1972	U.S.S.R.

Yachting

Governing body: Royal Yachting Association, 5 Buckingham Gate, London, SW1E 6JT.

Olympic Games, 1972

Finn	S. Maury (France)
Flying Dutchman	R. Pattisson, C. Davies (G.B.)
Tempest	V. Mankin, V. Dryrdyra (U.S.S.R.)
Star	D. Forbes, J. Anderson (Australia)
Soling	H. Melges, W. Bentsen, W. Allen (U.S.A.)
Dragon	J. Cuneo, T. Anderson, J. Shaw (Australia)

THE AMERICA'S CUP

Shamrock I lost to *Columbia* in 1899
Shamrock II lost to *Columbia* in 1901
Shamrock III lost to *Reliance* in 1903
Shamrock IV lost to *Resolute* in 1920
Shamrock V lost to *Enterprise* in 1930
Endeavour lost to *Rainbow* in 1934
Endeavour II lost to *Ranger* in 1937
Sceptre lost to *Columbia* in 1958
Gretel lost to *Weatherley* in 1962
Sovereign lost to *Constellation* in 1964
Dame Pattie lost to *Intrepid* in 1967
Gretel II lost to *Intrepid* in 1970
Southern Cross lost to *Courageous* in 1974

THE ADMIRAL'S CUP

1969	U.S.A.
1971	Great Britain
1973	Germany

The 1974 Round-the-World Yacht Race was won by *Sayula II*, of Mexico.

Olympic Games, 1972
(Munich)
(A list of winners not already noted under particular
games or sports)

Gymnastics

Governing body: British Amateur Gymnastic Association
23A High Street, Slough, Buckinghamshire.

Men

Combined exercises, individual	S. Kato (Japan)
Combined exercises, team	Japan
Floor exercises	N. Andrianov (U.S.S.R.)
Pommelled horse	V. Klimenko (U.S.S.R.)
Rings	A. Nakayama (Japan)
Long horse	K. Koeste (E. Germany)
Parallel bars	S. Kato (Japan)
Horizontal bars	M. Tsukahara (Japan)

Women

Combined exercises, individual	L. Turischeva (U.S.S.R)
Combined exercises, team	U.S.S.R.
Vault	K. Janz (E. Germany)
Uneven parallel bars	K. Janz (E. Germany)
Beam	O. Korbut (U.S.S.R.)
Floor exercises	O. Korbut (U.S.S.R.)

Modern Pentathlon

Individual	A. Balczo (Hungary)
Team	U.S.S.R.

Weightlifting

Governing body: British Amateur Weight Lifters' Association, 3 Iffley Turn, Oxford.

		Total
Flyweight	Z. Smalcerz (Poland)	743¾ lb.
Bantamweight	I. Foedli (Hungary)	831¾ lb. (world record)
Featherweight	N. Nourikian (Bulgaria)	887 lb. (Olympic record)
Lightweight	M. Kirzbinov (U.S.S.R.)	1,013¾ lb. (world record)
Middleweight	Y. Bikov (Bulgaria)	1,068¾ lb. (world record)
Light-heavyweight	L. Jenson (Norway)	1,118½ lb. (Olympic record)

Middle-heavyweight	A. Nikolov (Bulgaria)	1,157 lb. (Olympic record)
Heavyweight	Y. Talts (U.S.S.R.)	1,278¼ lb.
Super-heavyweight	V. Alexeyev (U.S.S.R.)	1,410¾ lb. (Olympic record)

Wrestling

Governing body: British Amateur Wrestling Association, 60 Calabria Road, London, N.5.

Freestyle

Light-Flyweight	R. Dmitriev (U.S.S.R.)
Flyweight	K. Kato (Japan)
Bantamweight	H. Yanagida (Japan)
Featherweight	Z. Abdulbekov (U.S.S.R.)
Lightweight	D. Gable (U.S.A.)
Welterweight	W. Wells (U.S.A.)
Middleweight	L. Tedioshvili (U.S.S.R.)
Light-Heavyweight	B. Peterson (U.S.A.)
Heavyweight	I. Yarygin (U.S.S.R.)
Extra-Heavyweight	A. Medved (U.S.S.R.)

Graeco-Roman

Light-Flyweight	G. Berceanu (Rumania)
Flyweight	P. Kirov (Bulgaria)
Bantamweight	R. Kazakoz (U.S.S.R.)
Featherweight	G. Markov (Bulgaria)
Lightweight	S. Khisamutdinov (U.S.S.R.)
Welterweight	V. Macha (Czechoslovakia)
Middleweight	G. Hegedus (Hungary)
Light-Heavyweight	V. Rezantsev (U.S.S.R.)
Heavyweight	N. Martinescue (Rumania)
Extra-Heavyweight	A. Roshin (U.S.S.R.)

Canoeing

Governing body: The British Canoe Union, 70 Brompton Road, London, SW3 1DT.

Slalom
Men

Kayak singles	S. Horn (E. Germany)
Canadian singles	R. Eiben (E. Germany)
Canadian pairs	W. Hofmann, R.-D. Amend (E. Germany)

Women

Kayak singles	A. Bahmann (E. Germany)

Regatta
Men

Kayak singles	A. Shaparenko (U.S.S.R.)
Kayak pairs	N. Gorbachev, V. Kratassyuk (U.S.S.R.)
Kayak fours	U.S.S.R.
Canadian singles	I. Patzaichin (Rumania)
Canadian pairs	V. Chessyunas, Y. Lobanov (U.S.S.R.)

Women

Kayak singles	Y. Ryabchinskaya (U.S.S.R.)
Kayak pairs	L. Pinayeva, E. Kuryshko (U.S.S.R.)

Handball
(Olympic Games)

1936   Germany
No further competitions until
1972   Yugoslavia

Judo

Governing body: The British Judo Association, 70 Brompton Road, London, SW3 1DR.

Heavyweight	S. Chochoshvili (U.S.S.R.)
Middle-heavyweight	S. Chochoshvili (U.S.S.R.)
Middleweight	S. Sekine (Japan)
Welterweight	T. Nomura (Japan)
Lightweight	T. Kawaguchi (Japan)
Open class	W. Ruska (Holland)

Personalities

Muhammad Ali: Muhammad Ali (formerly Cassius Marcellus Clay), born 17.1.1942 in Louisville, Kentucky, U.S.A., now lives in Chicago. He is 6 ft. 2½ in. tall, with black hair and brown eyes. Twice married, he has two children and is an ordained Muslim minister. As an amateur boxer he won several American titles, including a Golden Gloves competition, before gaining a gold medal in the 1960 Olympic Games as a light-heavyweight. In October 1960 he turned professional, and was still unbeaten when he won the world heavyweight championship from Sonny Liston on 25 February 1964. He successfully defended his title nine times before forfeiting it because of his reluctance to join the U.S. armed forces during the Vietnam war. In 1970 he made a 'comeback' and on 30 October 1974 he regained the world title by knocking out George Foreman at Kinshasa, Zaire; on 24 March 1975 he successfully defended it against Chuck Wepner. He is only the second man ever to regain the world heavyweight title.

John Conteh: Born 27.5.1951 in Liverpool, John Anthony Conteh is 6 ft. tall, with black hair and brown eyes, is unmarried, and now lives in London. He first started to box when he was 12. His most notable successes as an amateur include: A.B.A. middleweight champion, 1970; Commonwealth gold medallist, in 1970; representing England in the U.S.A. in 1970 (when he won three matches out of three) and also at the European Games in 1971, by which time he was boxing as a light-heavyweight; and winning the A.B.A. light-heavyweight championship in 1971. In 1971 he turned professional and to date has fought 27 matches, of which he has lost only one (on points). In March 1973 he became European light-heavyweight champion and on 1 October 1974 he won the world light-heavyweight championship by defeating Jorge Ahumada of Argentina. He successfully defended his title on 11 March 1975, against a challenge from Lonnie Bennett, of the U.S.A.

Johan Cruyff: H. Johan Cruyff was born in Amsterdam, Holland, on 25 April 1947. He is married, with three children—two girls and a boy—and at present lives in Barcelona, Spain. He started his career as a professional footballer playing for the Amsterdam team Ajax in 1964, and was badly missed when he left in 1973 to play for CF de Barcelona. Largely due to his talents, Barcelona became Spanish champions in 1974; they also reached the semi-final of the European Cup this year. Cruyff first played for the Dutch team in 1966 and has now been capped 28 times, having been the captain of the team for the past few years. He was the outstanding member of the Dutch World Cup team in 1974, when Holland was narrowly beaten by West Germany in the final. He has twice been elected European Footballer of the Year, in 1971 and 1973.

Brendan Foster: Born 12.1.1948 in Hebburn, Co. Durham, Brendan Foster is 5 ft. 10½ in. tall, with brown hair and grey eyes, and is married with no children. He lives in Gateshead, where he is Sports and Recreation Manager of Gateshead M.B.C. He started running at 14 and first represented England in the 1970 Commonwealth Games, where he won a bronze medal for the 1,500 metres. In the 1971 European Games he won another bronze medal over the same distance, and later that year set a British record for 2 miles. In the 1972 Olympic Games he finished fifth in the 1,500 metres. In 1973 he moved up to 5,000 metres, won his first A.A.A. title, won the Europa Cup Final over 5,000 metres, and set a world record for 2 miles (8 min. 13·8 sec.). During 1974 he set a world record for 3,000 metres (7 min. 35·2 sec.); won the 5,000 metres in the European Championships, set a British record for 1,500 metres and won a silver medal in the 5,000 metres at the New Zealand Commonwealth Games.

Reg Harris: Reginald Hargreaves Harris, O.B.E., was born on 1 March 1920 in Bury, Lancashire. He is 5 ft. 9 in. tall, with auburn hair and brown eyes. Married but without children, he now lives in Heaton, Staffordshire, and is a Sales Director. His cycling career started in 1934 and he won his first international track event in 1937. Since then he has won eleven British Amateur Track Championships and one World Amateur Sprint Championship, two Olympic silver medals (in 1948), and four World Professional Sprint Championships, as well as every professional Sprint Grand Prix. He has five British Professional Records and two World Records, as well as numerous track records throughout the world. In 1949 and 1950 he was elected Britain's Sportsman of the Year, and he was awarded his O.B.E. in June 1958. In 1974, forty years after his first race, he was the winner of the British Professional Sprint Championship.

Kevin Keegan: Joseph Kevin Keegan was born on 14 February 1951 at Armthorpe, near Doncaster. He is 5 ft. 8 in. tall, with dark brown hair and green eyes; he is married, and now lives near Mold, in North Wales. He started his career in football at the age of 16 as an apprentice professional at Scunthorpe United, and signed on as a full-time player a year later. He played almost 170 League games with the Lincolnshire club before transferring to Liverpool F.C. on 4 May 1971, for a fee of £35,000. Since joining Liverpool he has won a League Championship medal, a U.E.F.A. Cup medal and a Football Association Cup Winner's medal. He has also played 10 times for England.

Willie John McBride: William James McBride was born on 4 June 1940 at Toomebridge in N. Ireland. He is 6 ft. 3 in. tall, with fair hair and blue-grey eyes, and is married, with two children. He lives in Ballyclare, Co. Antrim, where he works as a bank manager. He did not play rugby until he was 17. In his last year at school he represented Ulster Schools in the Schools Introprovincial Championship, and on leaving school he joined the town club—Ballymena R.F.C.—to which he has belonged ever since. In 1960 he was selected for the Ulster senior team and in 1962 won his first cap for Ireland. Since then he has played in every international match except one (in 1964), and now has 63 caps to his credit. He has also been selected to play in five British Lions teams—in 1962, 1966, 1968, 1971 and 1974. He has played in 17 Test Matches for the Lions and captained the unbeaten 1974 team which won 23 out of its 24 matches in South Africa.

Alan Pascoe: Born 11.10.1947 in Portsmouth, Alan Peter Pascoe is 6 ft. 1 in. tall, with fair hair and brown eyes, and is married to the former British Sprint Champion Della James. They live in London, where he lectures in Physical Education. He began athletics seriously at 16. Whilst still at school he represented Great Britain in the 110 metres hurdles, and shortly afterwards was selected for the 1968 Mexico Olympics, where he equalled the British record but did not get through his heat! In 1969 he won a bronze medal at the European Games, and he gained a silver medal in the 1971 European Championships. At the Munich Olympics in 1972 he won a silver medal in the 4 × 400 metres relay. He now runs in the 400 metres hurdles, in which he came first at the Commonwealth games in New Zealand in 1974, as well as at the 1974 European Championships in Rome. He also won a silver medal in the 4 × 400 metres relay in New Zealand and a gold in the same event at Rome.

Gary Player: Gary Player was born on 1 November 1936 in Johannesburg, South Africa. He is 5 ft. 8 in. tall and weighs 10 st. 10 lbs. He is married, with six children, and still lives in Johannesburg. He became a professional golfer in 1953, his first major win being the South African Open in 1956. Since then, he has won an impressive string of major championships, including being both an individual and a team winner in the

World Cup in 1965. Perhaps his greatest achievement is to have won golf's four major championships: the U.S. Open (1965), the British Open (1959, 1968, 1974), the American P.G.A. (1962 and 1972) and the American Masters (1961 and 1974). Only three other golfers have ever done this. In 1974 he was particularly successful, winning both the Masters and the British Open, and for the fifth time in the last six years won over $100,000. He has now earned over $1,000,000 from playing golf.

Phil Read: Philip W. Read, born 1.1.1939 in Luton, is 5 ft. 10½ in. tall, has brown hair and brown eyes, and is married with four children, all boys. Apart from racing, he is the managing director of a motorcycling equipment business; he lives in Oxshott, Surrey. He rode his first race on 13 May 1956 at Mallory Park on a 350 c.c. BSA Gold Star, and his first win came in 1960 at the Manx Grand Prix, when he averaged 97·09 m.p.h. on a 500 c.c. Manx Norton. His first win in the important Isle of Man T.T. races was in 1961, riding a 350 c.c. Norton, and a 250 c.c. Yamaha brought him his first World Championship in 1964. To date he has 50 Grand Prix wins to his credit and seven World Championships—four on 250 c.c. machines, one on a 125 c.c. and two on 500 c.c., including the 1974 World Championship in this class.

Ian Stewart: Ian Stewart was born on 15 January 1949 in Birmingham, where he still lives. He is 5 ft. 10 in. tall, with brown hair and brown eyes, and is not married. He is a gun tester by profession. His early running successes include being European Indoor Champion over 3,000 metres in 1969 (in Belgrave); European Outdoor Champion over 5,000 metres in 1969 (in Athens); and Commonwealth Champion over 5,000 metres in 1970 (in Edinburgh). In 1971 he was injured, but recovered in time to participate in the Munich Olympic Games in 1972, where he won a bronze medal. He has been very successful in 1975, winning in quick succession the European 3,000 metres Indoor Championship (in Katowice) and the International Cross-Country Championship (in Rabat).

Colin Todd: Colin Todd was born on 12 December 1948 at Chester-le-Street in Co. Durham. He is 5 ft. 9 in. tall, with fair hair and blue eyes, and is married with two children, both boys; he lives in Derby. He signed for Sunderland F.C. when he was

15 years old, as an apprentice professional footballer, and signed
as a full-time player when he was 17. When still only 17 he
played his first team game for Sunderland, and went on to play
in nearly 200 League and Cup matches for them before being
transferred to Derby County for an estimated fee of £170,000,
at the age of 21. He has now been with Derby for five years, during which time he has won first division Championship medals—
in 1972 and 1975—and has five times played for England. In
1975 he was chosen as Footballer of the Year.

Derek Underwood: Derek Leslie Underwood, born 6.8.1945
in Bromley, Kent, is 6 ft. tall, has fair hair and is married, with
no children. He lives at Birling, near Maidstone, in Kent. He
first joined Kent County Cricket Club in 1962, making his début
for the first XI in 1963, when he became the youngest bowler to
take 100 wickets in his first season of first-class cricket. In 1964
he took 9 for 28 playing against Sussex, his best analysis; and
was awarded a County cap. He first played for England in 1966,
against the West Indies. In the same year he was elected best
young cricketer of the year, and in both that and the following
year he headed the national bowling averages. He has since
toured abroad every year. In 1968 he made the highest ever
score by an England No. 11 against Australia (45 not out), and in
1973 he and P. I. Pocock made a record tenth-wicket stand
against Pakistan of 55. In 1971 he took his 1,000th wicket in
first-class cricket, and his 100th Test wicket.

David Wilkie: David Andrew Wilkie was born on 8 March
1954 at Colombo, Sri Lanka (Ceylon), of British parents. He
is 6 ft. 1 in. tall, with brown hair and brown eyes, and is single.
At present he is studying marine biology in Miami, U.S.A. He
showed an aptitude for swimming at a very early age and joined
the Warrender Swimming Club in Edinburgh where he went
to school at the age of 11. His first representative honour came
when he was selected for the Great Britain swimming team in
the 1970 Commonwealth Games, in which he won a bronze
medal. This success was followed by winning a silver medal in
the 1972 Olympic Games, two golds and a silver in the 1974
Commonwealth Games in New Zealand and two golds in the
1974 World Championships in Vienna. He has held the World
Record for the 200 metres breaststroke and is currently the
holder of the World Record for the 200 metres individual medley.

The Economic Crisis

Britain in Crisis

When historians come to look back on the 1970s, almost certainly 1974 will appear in most of their accounts as the year of the economic crisis. They will take note of facts, such as rapidly rising prices, rocketing wage demands, the virtual collapse of the Stock Exchange, sudden shortages of essentials like petrol and sugar. These same facts have already persuaded many experts and ordinary citizens that Britain is on the edge of disaster. As yet, however, no one can be sure whether what the history books will record will be a real crisis of the magnitude, for example, of the Great Depression between World War I and World War II, or merely a crisis of opinion, a period when everyone *thought* there was a crisis but no one really suffered.

Certainly warnings that Britain faces disaster have been voiced regularly by politicians, economists and other commentators on the state of the nation. During most of the time life has proceeded as usual. In fact, over the last fifty years Britain has become richer than ever before. And everyone has benefited from better housing, education, medical care, holidays, diet and job opportunities. Against this background of prosperity, it may seem strange that Britain is in the midst of an economic crisis. Perhaps if no one believed in the crisis it would simply disappear!

Shares Crash

There was no room for such optimism during 1974 on the London Stock Exchange. Buyers and sellers of shares digested first a fuel crisis, when Arab countries decided to ration their oil, then another large increase in the price of oil; the miners went on strike; industry was forced to work a three-day week; companies formerly regarded as sound and well-managed began to go bankrupt. It was all too much. As a result, shares fell to their lowest level for over twenty years. The Stock Exchange, which quotes prices for all the shares of major companies and businesses in Britain, acts as a barometer of how businessmen feel about the economy. That is why, although shares do not play much of a role in most people's lives, what happens on the Stock Exchange is important. Such was the climate of despair in 1974 that no one wanted to buy shares in any of Britain's industries. The only activity in the market came from people who wanted to sell their shares—even at the prevailing low prices—for fear that the value of shares would drop even further.

At the end of 1974 it was possible to buy a share in British Leyland, Britain's biggest motor manufacturer, for less than the price of a packet of crisps. These shares—and others too—stood at a quarter of their value of only a year before. Such very low prices did not even represent the value of companies' buildings, machines and unsold finished goods. It was as if investors generally had decided that most firms were worth no more than their breaking up value (the money proceeds from a sale of all a

TYPICAL PRICE CHANGES
£1 in 1914 = 100p   :   £1 in 1974 = 10p

	MEAT	BREAD loaf	MILK per pint	EGGS per doz	BEER per pint	PETROL 1gal. 4-star	GAS per therm	ELEC. per unit
1914	4p	3p	1p	6p	1p	8p	$2\frac{1}{2}$p	$2\frac{1}{2}$p
1934	6p	3p	1p	10p	3p	7p	4p	1p
1954	8p	$3\frac{1}{2}$p	3p	17p	7p	$22\frac{1}{2}$p	7p	1p
1974	49p	13–$15\frac{1}{2}$p	5p	38p	15p	54p	11p	1·25p

SOURCE DAILY EXPRESS

This chart shows how the buying power of the pound has altered over the last sixty years. But as well as changes in the value of money, changes in production methods and wages have ensured that Britain's standard of living has risen more rapidly than the value of the pound has fallen. At the same time, national wealth has been spread more evenly throughout the population to reduce extremes of wealth and poverty. Everyone also works far shorter hours than in 1914.

company's assets, as happens on bankruptcy). Meanwhile, as if happily unaware of the value put upon their enterprise by the stock market, most firms carried on working and making profits. Not surprisingly, many government ministers and industrialists criticised the City (i.e. the City of London, the area around the Bank of England where the Stock Exchange and the big finance houses are situated). Share prices were said to be 'irrelevant', 'misleading', 'damaging to Britain'.

Perhaps there was truth in the criticism, because in the middle of January 1975 share prices suddenly went up. The next few weeks saw the biggest series of daily market rises within living memory. Investors recovered their nerve and buyers were queuing to purchase shares now regarded as being undervalued. However, at the time of writing (February 1975) share prices are still low compared with even a year ago, and very low compared with the peak levels of 1972. It is perhaps significant that nothing of real importance had happened in the world between the beginning and the end of January. The explanation is that there was a change of mood. Investors no longer felt that the whole of British industry was on the verge of bankruptcy or that the Labour Government was about to introduce widespread nationalisation (government take-over of companies). It was therefore safe to buy shares once more.

In economic matters, people's *expectations* are often as significant as actions or events. Throughout 1974 it had become increasingly clear that Britain's economy was suffering from a dangerously high level of inflation (i.e. the pound, measured by what it could buy, was becoming worth less and less). People became more worried about inflation than anything else. Then in January 1975 a rumour spread that the government was going to 'do something' about inflation. This rumour prompted a rise in shares. The publication of a government economic paper confirmed what everyone had been thinking, and this helped to keep shares high.

However, it is generally agreed that Britain's economy suffers from other ills besides inflation. Some economists even argue that inflation is merely a symptom of what is really wrong with the country and that it cannot properly be cured, for example, without improving the efficiency of industry and making radical changes in the management of the economy. In this respect, economists are rather like doctors examining a sick patient with a puzzling illness. They diagnose different causes of the illness and advise different cures. We will examine later some of these causes and cures.

What is Inflation?

Everyone knows that the cost of living is going up. For the housewife, the cost of everyday shopping in 1974 went up by over 19 per cent, the biggest increase ever. As the price of food rose,

RETAIL PRICES (Jan 1962:100)
THE UPWARD TREND

	1973	1974
Jan	171·3	191·8
Feb	172·4	193·2
Mar	173·4	194·9
Apr	176·7	201·6
May	178·0	204·4
Jun	178·9	206·5
Jul	179·7	207·4
Aug	180·2	208·6
Sept	181·8	210·0
Oct	185·4	215·0
Nov	186·8	218·8
Dec	188·2	221·6

so did the price of other goods. The price of petrol, for example, reached an all-time high of 72 pence per gallon (at 1 February, 1975), with further rises forecast. There were enormous rises in rates for houses, offices and factories. Many nationalised industries, such as the Post Office, British Rail and the Gas Corporation, announced price increases to be introduced during 1975. This is one aspect of inflation: goods and services cost more and everyone therefore gets less for their money. Between the first half of 1973 and the first half of 1974, six pence was knocked off the buying power of the pound.

In order to preserve living standards—buy the same goods, enjoy the same holidays and so on—everyone wants to increase his income. For most, this means higher wages. In fact, during 1974 basic wages (i.e. excluding overtime) went up by over 28 per cent. This rise was well above the rise in prices during the same period. So, many wage earners protected themselves from the effect of rising prices. However, there was no corresponding increase in production to pay for these higher wages. Sooner or later, the price of manufactured goods will have to go up because higher wages to workers make the goods more expensive to produce. That is another aspect of inflation.

At the time, the government was limiting industry's price rises. This meant that someone other than the *purchaser* of manufactured goods was paying for the increased wages of the workers who made the goods. In effect, companies paid for these wage increases by making lower profits. As a result, investors received a lower yield on their shares. This caused the value of shares in companies as quoted on the stock exchange to fall.

A seller of shares then normally makes a capital loss—he receives less for the shares than was paid for them. This is yet another aspect of inflation. Anyone on a fixed income also suffers during inflation. The income of old age pensioners, for example, is fixed by the government. So when prices go up, the value of the money they receive goes down. Of course, the value of everyone else's money has also gone down. But groups of people who can obtain higher payments for their work—whether professional fees or wages—can protect themselves. These are generally people who perform essential tasks that society cannot do without. Inflation thus benefits the strong at the expense of the weak. It also discourages saving and encourages spending, because anyone who saves money faces the certainty that it will buy less in the future.

How this process ends up is with run-away inflation or hyper-inflation, when the value of money depreciates so rapidly that it becomes almost worthless. This is what happened in Germany in 1922 and 1923. From 1914, when the value of the German mark stood at 4 marks to $1. (American), the German mark fell to 500 marks to the $ in 1922, and at the height of the inflation in

1923 several billion marks were required to buy a single dollar. By this time German shoppers needed suitcases full of bank notes to pay for goods. Half a pound of butter, for example, cost several million marks. In order to survive, many people lived by barter. Valuable possessions were exchanged for food and clothing. Savings and pensions were valueless. Understandably, Germany then went through a period of chaos. The shock to German society of inflation helped to discredit the then democratically-elected government and made possible the rise of extremist political groups and, finally, the dictatorship of Hitler and the Nazi Party. Even today, most of the countries with high inflation, such as Chile and Brazil, are governed by dictatorships. In Britain it is still hoped that inflation will be curbed. But the present rate of inflation has already given rise to fears about the future of our system of government and the ability of our institutions to cope with the problem. Many people already recognise that high inflation is a threat to democracy. According to one forecast, Britain's rate of inflation in 1975 could be as high as 25 per cent.

What Economists Think

The classic symptoms of inflation have been described as 'too much money chasing too few goods'. This might seem absurd, since during a period of high inflation no one thinks he has enough money and unless there is a shortage of things in the shops it is hard to recognise that there are too few goods. But when economists are explaining inflation they are examining the behaviour of the economy as a whole and assessing the relationship between what everyone produces (the Gross National Product) and what everyone earns: including wages, dividends from shares, interest from, for example, deposits in a building society and savings in the Post Office. This is called the National Income. Economists also consider exports and imports and the so-called balance of payments. If we export roughly the same amount of goods as we import we have a balance of trade. If what we pay for imports is equal to what we receive for our exports then we have a balance of payments. When we are thinking about this, it is important to consider the value of the pound against the currencies of our trading partners. If the value of the pound falls our imports cost more; equally our exports sell for less.

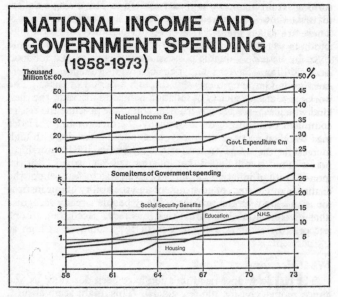

It is possible to have a balance of trade and a balance of payments deficit, both at the same time. This would happen, for example, if at the beginning of the year exports and imports roughly balanced out and then in the middle of the year the pound was devalued by 10 per cent but the volume of exports and imports remained the same. We would then be paying 10 per cent more for our imports and receiving 10 per cent less for our exports. Such a deficit would be *inflationary* unless we were either able to increase exports or reduce imports, or do a bit of both, so as to reach a balance once more. It is inflationary because we are getting goods (in this case imported goods) but not paying the full price for them. We are living on credit. A similar situation arises when, if we exclude exports and imports, expenditure on home-produced goods exceeds earnings at home. Normally, however, because Britain is a trading nation, if there is too much spending, we are spending more than we earn on both imported and home-produced goods. When the national accounts are drawn up other factors also have to be considered, such as our

earnings from insurance and banking and the profits sent back
to Britain from the foreign subsidiaries of British companies.
These are called invisible earnings. They are very substantial
and help to balance out what we overspend on imported goods.

So far we have not considered the role of money in the economy. We have seen how, in periods of inflation, prices and
earnings tend to go up; and that this is true even though nobody
works any harder and there is no real shortage of goods of the
kind which might force a rise in prices. At the same time nobody
complains of a shortage of pound notes. But if prices and earnings went up and the amount of money in circulation did not
increase at the same rate, there *would* be a shortage of pound
notes. The government solves this problem by printing more
money and by permitting the banks to lend more money. This
enables everyone to spend money they have not earned. Money
for economists therefore consists of notes and coins and credit.
The government can alter the supply of credit, just as it can control printing of notes, by restricting the amount banks are per-

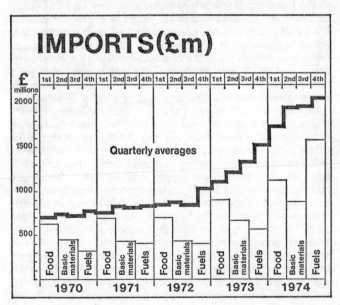

mitted to lend and by altering interest rates. If interest rates go up, fewer people want to borrow money because it costs them more to borrow. When the government tells banks to reduce their lending, and when interest rates go up, we have what is called a credit squeeze. If the squeeze works, inflation is eliminated because people can only spend what they earn.

In a model economy of the kind sometimes used by economists to illustrate their theories, there is no need for the government to tell the banks how much to lend, or interfere with interest rates. This is because anyone with an income is presumed to have a choice between spending and saving. When this imaginary person has bought the necessities of life, he then has a choice between saving the balance or spending it on luxuries. If he saves his surplus income by putting it on deposit with a bank, for example, he is paid interest. The bank then lends the money out (at a slightly higher rate), together with the savings of other savers, to an industrialist, for example, who wants to borrow money to buy new machines for his factory. In this theoretical world, the competing needs of savers and borrowers would balance out; and the balancing factor would be the rate of interest. If a lot of people did not want to spend all their income, there would be plenty of money to lend, and interest rates (the return savers get for saving and the cost borrowers pay for borrowing) would be low. When the demand for this money outstripped supply, then interest rates would go up in order to attract more savers to save, and so a balance would eventually be achieved.

In the real world such a balance is impossible because this simple money market between savers and borrowers is distorted by a variety of outside forces. These are the forces that cause inflation. In our theoretical economy above, there could never be too much money (including lending or credit) chasing too few goods, because demand and supply would always be forced into balance. No one can borrow more proportionately than someone else saves. No one can spend more than he earns unless he borrows what someone else has saved. In the same way, if there are fewer goods on the market than people wish to buy, their price will go up until fewer people want to buy them. And at the same time, higher prices would tempt industrialists to produce more because they can make a bigger profit. Eventually the right amount of goods at the appropriate price would be produced to ensure a balance between supply and demand.

Imagine what would happen if the conflicting forces of supply and demand just described were allowed to operate in the real world. Suppose there was a shortage of goods. Then in our model economy their price would shoot up. The prospect of higher profits would tempt manufacturers to produce more. They would hire more workers. Eventually too many goods would be produced. The production would be cut back and workers would be sacked. One minute the economy would be producing too little, and the next minute too much. This actually happened during the 19th century—and with appalling consequences for the working population, because every time there was a slump (production slowed down or ceased) millions were made workless. Nowadays such large-scale unemployment is unacceptable. In order to prevent unemployment, governments have learned to control the violence of trading cycles. Their main weapon is a technique known as 'demand management', the uses of which were first set out at length by the economist John Maynard Keynes.

As we have seen in our model economy, if for any reason demand for goods falls, industrialists produce less and this leads to unemployment of workers because fewer are required. In order to prevent unemployment, the government distorts the natural interplay of market forces, which would tend towards a balance of supply and demand, by boosting the level of demand. People are permitted to buy goods with money they have not earned, and the government itself spends money which it has not yet collected by way of taxes. When the government spends more money than it receives there is a *budget deficit*. Excessive government spending to keep up demand and prevent unemployment is called *deficit financing*. In this situation there is always 'too much money' and therefore by comparison 'too few goods': in other words—inflation.

Inflation, Growth and Productivity

Just as an ordinary person with, for example, an overdraft at the bank sooner or later has to repay what he has borrowed, so businessmen and governments must repay loans and make up for overspending by increasing income. A businessman typically increases income by making and selling more goods. And when all the businesses in the country are increasing sales and earnings, the government, which takes a proportion of those earnings in taxes, also increases its own income. In such circumstances, it is possible to repay debts and make up for overspending in one year by increasing production (and thereby income) in the next year. In most economies this is a continuous process. Production and earnings never quite catch up with overspending and debts. Inflation measures the size of the gap. The rate of inflation, therefore, is the percentage by which production (and therefore income) fails to keep pace with spending. When inflation is low (2–5 per cent, the typical annual rate until recently), so long as production and earnings are rising as well, it can be argued that no harm is done.

During a period of economic growth, when industry produces and sells more each year, these increased earnings enable workers to get higher wages and enable the government to collect more in taxes. Suppose a period of such growth lasted for five years, and inflation was at the rate of 5 per cent annually, then £1 at the start of the period would be reduced in terms of what it could buy to 82 pence at the end of the period. So long as production and earnings grow at a faster rate, everyone is *relatively* better off; and if they grow at the same rate, no one is worse off. Typically, a worker being paid £1 an hour at the beginning of the period might receive £1·50 an hour at the end of the period. Even though his pound is worth less in real terms (measured by what it can buy—i.e. 82 pence worth of goods), his real income has increased. Taking the value of the pound at the beginning of the period, the £1·50 he now earns is worth £1·23.

It is obvious, therefore, why all governments want their economies to grow. But we have already seen how most governments are committed to maintaining full employment and how they artificially boost demand (thereby directly causing inflation) to achieve this objective. Taking our five-year period above, how is it possible to increase production when the number of workers is fixed and all of them are employed at the start of the period? How can industrialists produce more goods without more workers? The answer is by increasing productivity. Each worker produces more (by working overtime, for example); the industrialist buys better machines which can make more goods and need fewer workers to operate them; managers become more efficient and so make better use of available resources. In most economies, economic growth is obtained by increasing productivity—each worker produces more, each machine produces more, and so on. Of course, there are times when the number of available workers *does* increase—due to changes in the birth rate, for example, and immigration. The impact of such changes, however, is small compared with the effect of rising productivity.

Until recently, many people have been blinded by the benefits of economic growth, and so have failed to observe its defects. Growing economies, for example, consume an increasing total of the world's natural resources (oil, coal, metals, wood, etc.) to make their products. The rich industrial countries buy more and more goods as the standard of living of their populations goes up. Soon everybody has a car, or two cars. Then the roads are clogged with traffic and, because everyone is buying more, there is more waste of every kind, from litter on the roadside to factory effluent which pollutes rivers and seas.

Slower Growth

Many governments are already aware of the need to restrict growth, if only to conserve the world's raw materials and halt pollution. This is difficult to achieve when governments themselves have become accustomed to spending more every year and the population expects—indeed demands—a rising standard of living. At the same time, many of the poorer countries which both supply the industrial states of the West with raw materials and serve as a market for their goods have grown tired of seeing their own resources exploited for the benefit of the citizens of other countries. They have banded together to obtain higher prices and restrict the rate at which their resources are consumed. In just over a year, for example, the Arab oil states recently effectively quadrupled the price of oil. In addition, the price of other raw materials has increased. It is this change of attitude within producer countries, rather than fear of the effects of pollution, which seems likely to slow down the growth of the economies of the industrial West.

Growth Stops

What happens when growth stops? We have already seen that when spending exceeds income there is inflation, which reduces the value of money. Real income (which measures what money can actually buy) can only be maintained by increased production.

Otherwise it makes no difference how much people are paid, how many pound notes the government prints. Without growth inflation is unsupportable. We saw earlier what happened to Germany in 1922–23.

In Britain the economy has already stopped growing. In addition, over the last fifteen years Britain's rate of growth has been much lower than that of the other major industrial countries. Between 1959 and 1972, these annual growth rates were as follows: Britain 3·1 per cent, Japan 11·0 per cent, France 5·8 per cent, Italy 5·5 per cent, Germany 4·9 per cent, United States 4·1 per cent, Canada 5·0 per cent. *In 1974 the British economy did not grow at all, and a virtually nil growth rate is forecast for 1975.* At present the government's budget deficit (the difference between income and expenditure) is £6,000 million, largely financed by loans from abroad. Total spending for 1975 has been estimated at around £76,000 million (assuming all income is spent) against domestic production estimated to be worth £70,000 million. So unless everyone spends less or industry produces more we will have to import extra goods to bridge this gap. This leads to a balance of payments deficit, puts pressure on the pound and makes necessary more foreign loans or devaluation of the pound, or both.

The orthodox answer to this grim situation is that Britain must spend less. But we have already seen what happens when spending is cut—demand for goods drops so less goods are produced and this leads to unemployment.

Politics

How much unemployment is acceptable is a political rather than an economic issue. This is probably the reason why most governments are committed to full employment, for fear that otherwise they would lose votes in elections and so fail to retain office. In Britain this fear has governed the policies of both Conservative and Labour governments. At the same time, the power of workers through organised trade unions has grown stronger. Like everyone else, the trade unions have become accustomed to a steadily-rising income. Many industrialists—because they have invested in expensive and complex machinery (called plant)—find it cheaper to yield to union wage demands rather than watch this plant sit idle. Normally, plant is bought with borrowed money: so whether it is being worked or not, the loan and the cost of raising the loan still has to be repaid. This is not to suggest that trade unions are responsible for Britain's present troubles; they are after all behaving no different from anyone else. Some economists argue that such strong pressure from trade unions is good for industry because ideally it forces businessmen to become more efficient and to make greater profits so that they can pay higher wages. That way everyone becomes richer.

But efficiency has a price. Generally, in an open market, an efficient firm can afford to charge lower prices for its goods and pay its workers higher wages compared with an inefficient firm. In time, therefore, the efficient are able to drive the inefficient out of business. And this causes unemployment. This principle, which affects competing firms within a country, also applies to countries which are competing with each other in the sale of goods abroad. One way of measuring the efficiency of one country's industries compared with the industries of another country is by comparing their economic growth and productivity. On this basis we have already seen that Britain has fallen behind the other major manufacturing countries. This is why, for example, the Japanese, one of the most efficient nations in the world, are able to sell so many of their cars in Britain. Their cars represent better value to purchasers here than British cars. The success of the Japanese and other foreign manufacturers of small cars means that British car makers have a smaller market for their goods. This helps explain the present poor state of the motor industry in Britain.

What is the Solution?

Despite the threat of unemployment many economists argue that Britain must reduce spending. Even if spending is not reduced, they point out that unemployment will inevitably follow the present inflationary policies because British firms will become increasingly uncompetitive on world markets. Their recipe for economic salvation also includes more investment by industry in new (and more productive machinery) and strict control of wage rates. Others argue that our problems are social and political rather than economic. Workers, for example, will not reduce their wage demands or work harder unless Britain's wealth is distributed more 'fairly'. Such thinkers tend also to view the making of profits by industry with dislike because some of these profits are given to shareholders in companies who thereby receive 'unearned' income. Many favour a state take-over of the major firms in British industry to ensure a 'fairer' distribution of profits. Another—and more recent view—is that our whole attitude to life must be altered. Instead of worrying about producing more, earning more and maintaining a high standard of living, everyone should settle for less. By halting growth, it is argued, everyone could lead a more relaxed life. We would produce less and also consume less. Everyone would have more leisure.

It is impossible to say which, if any, of these views will prevail. It may be that some typically British compromise will be worked out to take account of each.

In the meantime, the British economy is stagnant, wages and prices continue to rise and the government's budget deficit gets bigger and bigger. This is the economic crisis of 1974–75. It remains to be seen if it will mark a turning point in our politics and social affairs as well as in the economy.

Something to Join

A Section on Youth Organisations,
with notes on the Morse Code, Semaphore, Compass
and Knots.

ORGANISATIONS TO JOIN

(including some courses to apply for)

THIS is a list of some of the organisations that are either entirely for young people or have sections open to the young. A few of them (such as the Outward Bound Trust) provide courses only for those who have been specially recommended by the school or other authorities. Take particular note of the age limits for membership, which are given in most cases.

Air Training Corps A national organisation sponsored by the Ministry of Defence (R.A.F.) with the aim of promoting and encouraging in young men a practical interest in aviation and the R.A.F., providing training useful both in Service and civilian life, and developing, through the promotion of sports and pastimes in healthy rivalry, the qualities of leadership and good citizenship.

Amateur Athletic Association Controls athletics in England and Wales, with affiliated clubs throughout the country. Details of clubs, membership open to boys of 11 and over, and of training facilities, instructional booklets and coaching schemes from 70 Brompton Road, London SW3 1EE. This is also the address of the Women's Amateur Athletic Association.

Army Cadet Force The British Army's own voluntary youth organisation. Open to boys between the ages of 13 and 18. 58 Buckingham Gate, SW1E 6AN.

Boys' Brigade Object: 'The advancement of Christ's Kingdom among boys.' Juniors, 8–12 years; Company, 11–17; Seniors, 16–19.

Brathay Exploration Group Organises expeditions (surveying, field study in ornithology, botany, glaciology, archaeology and geography) in mountainous or remote country in the Lake District, the Shetland Isles and abroad to such places as Greenland, Kenya and Yugoslavia. Places divided equally between young people drawn from industry and others from schools of all kinds, nominated by their firms or schools. Camping, survey kit and expensive items of personal equipment are provided for expeditions. Fees: three-week expedition to Norway or Iceland £110; Shetland expedition £45; Lake District expedition £20. Age limits: 16–20.

The Brathay Field Study Centre organises one-week courses

for boys and girls studying for G.C.E. 'A' level in Geography of Biology. Good library and laboratory facilities and opportunities for carrying out individual study projects in the Lake District.

Further details from The Principal, Brathay Hall, Ambleside, Cumbria.

British Red Cross Society Gives training courses in first aid, nursing, hygiene, child care, accident prevention, etc. Puts this training into practice by helping old people, handicapped children and the deaf and blind, and in emergencies. Junior members also help at summer holidays for physically handicapped children. They are encouraged to make contacts with junior members abroad, and make Disaster Relief Kits. Age limits: Junior Red Cross, 5 to school leaving age. Adult Red Cross membership: 15 upwards. Headquarters: 9 Grosvenor Crescent, London, SW1X 7EJ.

British Sub-Aqua Club Devoted to underwater exploration, science and sport. Has over 500 branches in Great Britain. Minimum age: 15, but special Snorkeller Award Scheme for juniors. Applications to Director, British Sub Aqua Club, 70 Brompton Road, London, SW3 1HA.

British Trust for Ornithology A national society for all birdwatchers: invites members to take part in varied field investigations into bird biology and distribution, with emphasis on the interactions between man and birds: the common birds census, nest record scheme, Birds of Estuaries Enquiry, bird ringing (by special permit only after considerable training and practice), moult enquiry and other special enquiries including regular censuses of species such as the heron. Services to members include the quarterly journal 'Bird Study', the newsletter 'BTO News', national conferences—both general and specialist—regional conferences, local meetings in co-operation with local bird clubs, specialist courses in modern techniques, use of the lending library and the extensive reference library at Tring, and grants and awards for research. Annual subscription £3·50 p.a. (£1·40 p.a. for members under 21 or up to 25 if in receipt of full-time education.) Applications to the Membership Secretary, B.T.O., Beech Grove, Tring, Hertfordshire, Tel: Tring 3461.

Camping Club Youth Junior section of the Camping Club of Great Britain. Open to young people aged 12 to 17 inclusive. Entrance fee, 5p; annual subscription, 25p plus 3p VAT.

Camping at home and abroad. Instruction given. 11 Lower Grosvenor Place, London, SW1W OEY.

Concordia Youth Service Volunteers Runs international working camps to help with fruit picking and market gardening in Britain; also with the wine harvest, forestry and construction work on the Continent. Age limits for camps abroad: 18–30. Volunteers pay their own travel expenses. The age limit in British camps is 16–30, and the booking fee is £7·50. Applications to the Recruitment Secretary, Concordia, 11a Albemarle Street, London, W1x 4BE.

Council for British Archaeology Issues a *Calendar of Excavations* monthly from March until September with a final issue in January which enables anyone wishing to take part in excavations to get in touch with directors requiring voluntary helpers. For the over-16s only. Annual subscription to the *Calendar*: £1·25. C.B.A., 7 Marylebone Road, London, NW1 5HY.

Cyclists' Touring Club A national organisation, founded 1878 to protect and promote the interests of cyclists. Personal benefits include legal aid, third-party insurance, illustrated travel magazine and handbook, local cycle runs, clubrooms, social events, organised holiday tours. Junior membership (under 18): £1·25 a year including VAT. 69 Meadrow, Godalming, Surrey.

Field Studies Council Has ten Field Centres distributed over England and Wales. Courses, usually lasting a week, are organised from March to late October and include field work in archaeology, botany, geography, geology, zoology and art. Junior members (under 16) may attend only in groups with their teachers, but young people of 16 or over may also join suitable courses individually or in groups. Minimum annual subscription: 50p. Applications to Information Office, Preston Montford, Montford Bridge, Shrewsbury SY4 1HW.

Girls' Brigade A uniformed organisation for girls. Object: 'to help girls to become followers of the Lord Jesus Christ and through self-control, reverence and a sense of responsibility to find true enrichment of life.' National and International Headquarters: Brigade House, 8 Parsons Green, London, SW6 4TH.

Girl Guides Association Parallel organisation with the Scouts; U.K. membership of over three quarters of a million, world membership of over $6\frac{1}{2}$ million. Commonwealth

Headquarters: 17-19 Buckingham Palace Road, London, SW1W 0PT.

Junior Astronomical Society Aims to encourage people of all ages interested in astronomy and space. A quarterly journal, *Hermes*, includes articles on all aspects of astronomy and spaceflight. Regular meetings are held in London. There are special sections to help observers. Secretary: V. L. Tibbott, 58 Vaughan Gardens, Ilford, Essex, IG1 3PD.

Mountaineering Association Now amalgamated with the Youth Hostels Association (see page R7) which organises the mountaineering courses previously run by the Mountaineering Association.

National Council of YMCAs A world-wide organisation operating in eighty countries. Organises holiday and conference centres, national and regional camps, residential colleges, youth and community centres, and apprentice hostels. Age limits are fixed by local branches. Headquarters: 640 Forest Road, London, E17 3DZ.

National Federation of Young Farmers' Clubs Open to all young people between the ages of 10 and 26 who are interested in farming and the countryside. Headquarters: Y.F.C. Centre, National Agricultural Centre, Kenilworth, Warwickshire, CV8 2LG. Coventry 56131.

Outward Bound Trust Holds training courses at Aberdovey, Eskdale, Burghead, Ullswater and Ashburton to equip boys to face hazards and emergencies on the mountains and at sea. Also modified courses for girls. Applicants must be sponsored by employers, education authorities, youth organisations, etc., who may sometimes help financially. Courses last 26 days. Fees: juniors, £31·50; seniors, £35. The Trust now has facilities for training 4,000 boys and 500 girls a year. Age limits: boys, 14½-19½; girls, 16-20.

Quaker Work Camps, Friends Service Council Organises work camps in Britain and Ireland from July to mid-September lasting from 2 to 6 weeks each, and one or two short camps at Easter (1 to 2 weeks). Wide variety of work from manual, decorating, construction and conservation projects to running summer play schemes, residential holidays for mentally handicapped children, and work and study camps. Mixed international teams of 8-20 people. Minimum age 16, although this is raised to 18 or 19 in some cases. Handicapped participants are welcome. Volunteers pay their own travel expenses and pocket money, and those from Britain and Ireland are asked to contribute £2 a week towards their maintenance (except on 6 and 8 week camps). (Bursary help is available.) Volunteers who have taken part in Quaker Work Camps or related Quaker activities can be sent to work camps abroad. Applications from Britain and Ireland to Personnel Department, Friends Service Council, Friends House, Euston Road, London, NW1 2BJ. Volunteers from other countries should apply through a work camp organisation in their own country.

Ramblers' Association Works with the support of some 450 rambling clubs and 100 local groups throughout the country; publishes *Rucksack* three times a year and *Bed, Breakfast and Bus Guide* annually, supplying these free of charge to members. Loans 1/50,000 Ordnance Survey maps for small charge to members. Ordinary subscriptions: £2. Juniors (under 18 and full-time students): 80p. Applications to 1/4 Crawford Mews, York Street, London, W1H 1PT.

Partner organisation, **Ramblers' Holidays Ltd.,** organises walking and mountaineering holidays on the Continent: details from Wings House, Bridge Road East, Welwyn Garden City, Herts.

St John Ambulance Association and Brigade The Association Branch organises training courses in first aid and nursing, while the Brigade Branch is a uniformed organisation that encourages the study not only of first aid and nursing but also a variety of other subjects: among them, fire-fighting, sea- and boat-training, canoeing, camping, cooking, swimming and lifesaving. Summer training camps are held in most counties. Age limits: boys (ambulance-cadets) and girls (nursing cadets), 8–18. Headquarters: Registrar, G. W. Woodhill, M.B.E., 1 Grosvenor Crescent, London, SW1X 7EF.

Scout Association This firmly established youth movement offers a progressive and interesting system of character training for boys and young men. The movement embraces the following sections: Cub Scouts (8–10 inclusive), Scouts (11–15) and Venture Scouts (16–20). In addition to camping and other normal Scouting activities, a wide range of specialist subjects is made available . . . sailing, gliding, pot holing, climbing, underwater swimming, etc. Scouting exists in over 100 countries with a world membership of over 13 million. Headquarters: Baden-Powell House, Queen's Gate, London, SW7 5JS.

Sea Cadet Corps A voluntary youth organisation for boys between 12 and 18. Through its discipline and sea training the Corps sets out to help those who are considering a seafaring career. Although it is not a pre-service organisation and no cadet is obliged to become a sailor, the Corps is recognised by the Navy as providing excellent training for boys who subsequently join the Royal Navy or one of its Reserves. Headquarters: Broadway House, Broadway, Wimbledon, London, SW19 1RL.

White Hall Centre for Open Country Pursuits Courses run by the Derbyshire Education Committee in outdoor education, hillcraft, rock climbing, caving, camping, canoeing and mountain leadership. Open throughout the year. Minimum age: 14. Details from the Principal, White Hall Centre, Long Hill, Buxton, Derbyshire SK17 6SX.

Young Explorers' Trust (The Association of British Youth Exploration Societies) Seeks to promote and support expeditions for young people. Membership is open to groups and societies, however small, who are setting out to organise expeditions involving a significant element of exploration and discovery. The Trust offers an information service for expedition organisers, and meetings, study groups and training facilities are arranged. Overseas expeditions may apply for the Trust's approval, and grants are made annually to expeditions that reach the appropriate standard of organisation, safety and field tasks. Details from the Executive Officer, Young Explorers' Trust, 238 Wellington Road South, Stockport, SK2 6NW. 061–477–0898.

Young Ornithologists' Club Run by the Royal Society for the Protection of Birds for boys and girls up to 18. Runs courses, holds meetings, organises projects and encourages field work: publishes its bi-monthly magazine *Bird Life*. Subscriptions: individual £1·25; family, £1·50; also group membership for schools and clubs. Applications to The Lodge, Sandy, Beds.

Youth Hostels Associations These organisations have the object of helping young people on walking or cycling tours. In Britain and Ireland alone they maintain some 400 hostels where members are provided with beds and meals at very low rates. A number of Adventure Holidays are now arranged as introductions to new activities such as pony trekking, sailing, skin-diving, etc. Subscription: 5–16, 50p a year; 16–21, £1; 21 and over, £1·50. Plus VAT in each case. Headquarters:

England and Wales, Trevelyan House, St. Albans, Herts. *Scotland*, 7 Glebe Crescent, Stirling. *Northern Ireland*, 93 Dublin Road, Belfast, BT2 7HF.

Altogether in the 48 countries where the Youth Hostel movement flourishes there are over 4,000 hostels.

A British membership card (with photograph) is accepted in all countries affiliated to the International Youth Hostel Federation. The Y.H.A.'s sales department at 29 John Adam Street, Adelphi, London, WC2N 6JE, sells rucksacks, sleeping bags, tents, camping equipment, climbing kit, maps and guides.

Y.W.C.A. of Great Britain. Affiliated to the World Y.W.C.A., active in over 80 countries. Services in U.K. include accommodation for single young people and older women; clubs and community centres; opportunities to serve others; detached youth work and courses for school leavers and fifth and sixth formers. Headquarters: 2 Weymouth Street, London, W1N 4AX.

THE MORSE CODE

The Morse code consists of groups of dots and dashes ('shorts' and 'longs'), each group representing a letter or number. You can communicate in Morse by flashing a light, by sound (the imprisoned hero in a book, you remember, always taps it out with his shoe on the wall of his cell) or by using a flag. The dots should be made as short as possible, and the dashes should be three times as long as the dots.

The Morse Alphabet The letters that occur most often in English are given the shortest symbols. The words placed against the letters are used so that mistakes shall not arise because letters have similar sounds. (For instance, 'm' spoken sounds very like 'n', 'b' very like 'd' and so on.)

A for	Alfa	· —	K	Kilo	— · —
B	Bravo	— · · ·	L	Lima	· — · ·
C	Charlie	— · — ·	M	Mike	— —
D	Delta	— · ·	N	November	— ·
E	Echo	·	O	Oscar	— — —
F	Foxtrot	· · — ·	P	Papa	· — — ·
G	Golf	— — ·	Q	Quebec	— — · —
H	Hotel	· · · ·	R	Romeo	· — ·
I	India	· ·	S for	Sierra	· · ·
J for	Juliett	· — — —	T	Tango	—

U for Uniform	$\cdot\cdot-$		X	X-ray	$-\cdot\cdot-$
V Victor	$\cdot\cdot\cdot-$		Y	Yankee	$-\cdot--$
W for Whiskey	$\cdot--$		Z	Zulu	$--\cdot\cdot$

Numerals

1	$\cdot----$		6	$-\cdot\cdot\cdot\cdot$
2	$\cdot\cdot---$		7	$--\cdot\cdot\cdot$
3	$\cdot\cdot\cdot--$		8	$---\cdot\cdot$
4	$\cdot\cdot\cdot\cdot-$		9	$----\cdot$
5	$\cdot\cdot\cdot\cdot\cdot$		10	$-----$

Full stop (AAA) $\cdot-\cdot-\cdot-$
Apostrophe $\cdot----\cdot$
Oblique stroke $-\cdot\cdot-\cdot$
Brackets (KK) $-\cdot--\cdot-$
Short break $\cdot\cdot\cdot\cdot$
Beginning (CT) $-\cdot-\cdot-$
Hyphen $-\cdot\cdot\cdot\cdot-$
Inverted commas (RR) $\cdot-\cdot\cdot-\cdot$
Underline (UK) $\cdot\cdot--\cdot-$
Question (IMI) $\cdot\cdot--\cdot\cdot$
Long break (BT) $-\cdot\cdot\cdot-$
Ending (AR) $\cdot-\cdot-\cdot$
Finish of transmission for indefinite period (VA) $\cdot\cdot\cdot-\cdot-$

SEMAPHORE

It is immensely important in semaphore signalling that the angles should be clear and the arm and the wrist in a straight line. To ensure this, always press the first finger along the stick of the flag. Choose a position where you can be easily seen and a background that is as far away as possible—the sky being obviously the best.

Rules for Semaphoring At the end of each word you should drop the arms straight down in front of you—this is known as the 'ready' position—and pause. Should you make a mistake, give the 'annul' sign and begin the word again. ('Annul' means 'rub out', 'cancel'.) Before a number give the 'numeral' sign, and if you are going back to letters give the 'alphabet' sign before you do so.

When you are reading a message, acknowledge each word by making the letter 'A' (the 'general answer' sign). If you are

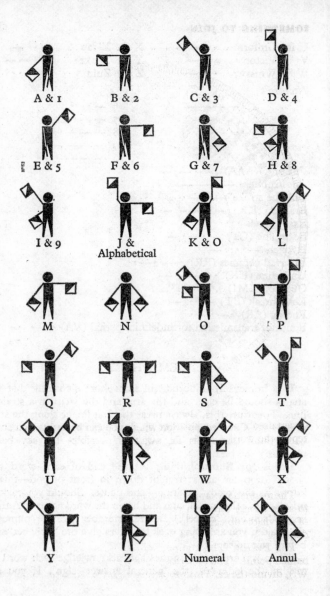

A & 1   B & 2   C & 3   D & 4

E & 5   F & 6   G & 7   H & 8

I & 9   J & Alphabetical   K & O   L

M   N   O   P

Q   R   S   T

U   V   W   X

Y   Z   Numeral   Annul

uncertain about a word, make no sign, and the sender will then repeat the word.

THE COMPASS

The magnetic compass is an instrument that enables navigators to steer in any direction required, and also shows the direction of any visible object. It is divided into points, quarter points and degrees.

The Points The compass circle is divided into thirty-two named points. The four main (or cardinal points, N., E., S. and W.), divide the card into four quadrants or quarters. Half-way between the cardinal points are the quadrantal points, N.E., S.E., S.W. and N.W. Half-way again between the cardinal and quadrantal points are the intermediate (three-letter) points, which are named from the cardinal and quadrantal points between which they lie, the cardinal points being named first; N.N.E., E.N.E., E.S.E., S.S.E., S.S.W., W.S.W., W.N.W., N.N.W. Between all these points are sixteen others (called 'by' points) which take their names from the nearest cardinal and quadrantal points.

For example, in the first quadrant (between N. and E.) the points are:

The cardinal	N.
The by-point next to it	N. by E.
The three-letter point half-way between N. and E.	N.N.E.
The by-point next to the half cardinal	N.E. by N.
The half cardinal	N.E.
The by-point	N.E. by E.
The three-letter point between E. and N.E.	E.N.E.
The by-point	E. by N.
The cardinal point	E.

Degrees The compass circle is also divided into degrees; it is in degrees (by what is called the **Quadrantal Notation**) that a course is usually given and steered. The card is divided into 360°, but is marked 0° at North and South and 90° at East and West. So N.E. would be given as N. 45° E. Gyro compass cards are marked right round from north through 90° (East), 180° (South), 270° (West) and 360° (North). This is called **Circular Notation**. Gyro compasses are carried in addition to magnetic compasses by most warships and many large merchant and passenger ships. The gyro, controlled by the earth's rotation, consists of a wheel turned at great speed by an electric motor. The points, with their equivalents in circular and quadrantal notation, are shown below.

Point	Circular	Quadrantal	Point	Circular	Quadrantal
N.	0	N.	N.E. by E.	56¼	N. 56¼ E.
N. by E.	11¼	N. 11¼ E.	E.N.E.	67½	N. 67½ E.
N.N.E.	22½	N. 22½ E.	E. by N.	78¾	N. 78¾ E.
N.E. by N.	33¾	N. 33¾ E.	E.	90	E.
N.E.	45	N. 45 E.	E. by S.	101¼	S. 78¾ E.

Point	Circular	Quadrantal	Point	Circular	Quadrantal
E.S.E.	112½	S. 67½ E.	S.W. by W.	236¼	S. 56¼ W.
S.E. by E.	123¾	S. 56¼ E.	W.S.W.	247½	S. 67½ W.
S.E.	135	S. 45 E.	W. by S.	258¾	S. 78¾ W.
S.E. by S.	146¼	S. 33¾ E.	W.	270	W.
S.S.E.	157½	S. 22½ E.	W. by N.	281¼	N. 78¾ W.
S. by E.	168¾	S. 11¼ E.	W.N.W.	292½	N. 67½ W.
S.	180	S.	N.W. by W.	303¾	N. 56¼ W.
S. by W.	191¼	S. 11¼ W.	N.W.	315	N. 45 W.
S.S.W.	202½	S. 22½ W.	N.W. by N.	326¼	N. 33¾ W.
S.W. by S.	213¾	S. 33¾ W.	N.N.W.	337½	N. 22½ W.
S.W.	225	S. 45 W.	N. by W.	348¾	N. 11¼ W.

KNOTS

The **Reef Knot** is both the firmest of knots and the quickest to untie. It is used for tying two ropes together.

The **Sheet Bend** is the best knot for tying together ropes of differing thickness. If the end is passed round again the knot becomes a **Double Sheet Bend**, which will neither stick nor jerk undone.

The **Clove Hitch** (an easy knot to make, as the picture shows) is used to make one rope fast to a larger one. When fastened to a pole or another rope it will neither slip up nor down.

The **Bowline** (used at sea for making a loop on a rope's end) makes a fixed loop that will never slip after the first grip. It can be safely used for making a halter for leading an animal.

The **Sheepshank** is used for temporarily shortening a rope.

The **Figure of Eight** is used at sea to prevent a rope un-reeving through a block.

The **Half-hitch** is used to tie ropes to poles.

The **Round Turn and Two Half-hitches** is used for securing a rope to a ring or a post.

The **Timber Hitch** is used for dragging timber along the ground.

The **Wall Knot** is a way of whipping, or finishing off, a rope that is unravelling. Take strand A and loop it back across the front of the rope; then take strand B and loop it over the end of strand A; finally looping strand C over the end of strand B and tucking its end into the loop formed by strand A. Finish by working the knot tight.

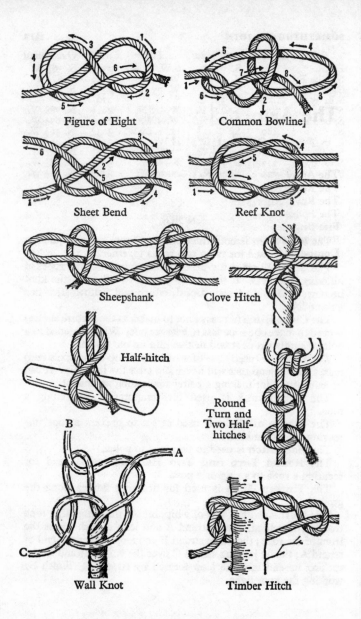

Figure of Eight

Common Bowline

Sheet Bend

Reef Knot

Sheepshank

Clove Hitch

Half-hitch

Round Turn and Two Half-hitches

Wall Knot

Timber Hitch

The Armed Services, The Police and Fire Brigades

The Army	2–5
The Royal Navy	5–7
The Royal Air Force	8–9
The Police	10–11
Fire Brigades	11
Relative Ranks—Sea, Land and Air	11
Decorations and Medals	12–13

The Armed Services

The present integrated Ministry of Defence was created on April 1, 1964, combining the four separate ministries previously responsible for armed service matters—The War Office, Admiralty and Air Ministry, and the former small administrative Ministry of Defence. The head of the Ministry is the Secretary of State for Defence, who is also chairman of the Defence Council—the permanent committee of military and civilian chiefs who determine defence policy.

THE ARMY

The man responsible for the detailed running of the Army is the Under-Secretary of State for the Army, a Member of Parliament, who in turn is responsible to the Secretary of State for Defence. The Under-Secretary controls the Army through the Army Board of the Defence Council and obtains expert military advice from the Chief of the General Staff (C.G.S.), who is the senior military member of the Board.

PRINCIPAL BRANCHES OF THE ARMY

The **Royal Armoured Corps** (R.A.C.), formed in 1939 by amalgamating the Cavalry and the Royal Tank Corps.

The **Royal Artillery** (R.A.) (the 'Gunners') who man both guns and missiles in Field and Air Defence roles.

The **Royal Engineers** (R.E.) (called the 'Sappers' from the days when they dug 'saps'—that is, trenches or mines that enabled the troops to advance towards the enemy). In general, their job is to help the Army to move. They make paths through minefields, provide means of crossing obstacles and carry out any necessary demolition and lay minefields in a withdrawal. They compile and print maps for the Army and the R.A.F. and operate the Army Postal Service.

The **Royal Corps of Signals** (R. Sigs.) is responsible for the Army's communications.

The **Infantry** is the fighting core of the Army and includes the Foot Guards, the Parachute Regiment and the Special Air Service Regiment.

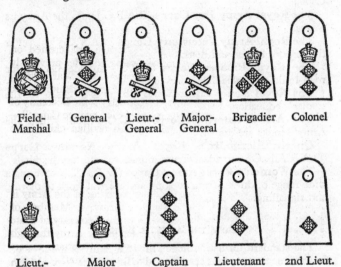

Field-Marshal   General   Lieut.-General   Major-General   Brigadier   Colonel

Lieut.-Colonel   Major   Captain   Lieutenant   2nd Lieut.

The **Royal Corps of Transport** (R.C.T.) replaced the Royal Army Service Corps in 1965.

The **Royal Army Medical Corps** (R.A.M.C.) came into being in 1857, after the Crimean War, as the Army Hospital Corps. Took its present name in 1898.

The **Royal Army Ordnance Corps** (R.A.O.C.) is responsible for providing the Army with food, equipment and stores—vehicles, clothing, ammunition, explosives, etc. Also provides clerical staff and mobile bath and laundry units on active service.

The **Royal Electrical and Mechanical Engineers** (R.E.M.E.) was formed in 1942 to meet the needs of mechanical warfare. Looks after and maintains tanks, vehicles, guns, radar, radios, instruments, etc.

The **Intelligence Corps** is a small branch consisting of men trained to collect intelligence (that is, largely information about an enemy or possible enemy).

The **Corps of Royal Military Police** (R.M.P.), the 'Red Caps'.

The **Royal Army Pay Corps** (R.A.P.C.) pays the Army its wages.

The **Royal Army Veterinary Corps** (R.A.V.C.) looks after the Army's horses and dogs.

The **Royal Pioneer Corps** (R.P.C.) provides labour for road-building, unloading stores, etc.

The **Royal Army Educational Corps** is in charge of the soldier's education.

The **Army Catering Corps** (A.C.C.), from which the Army's cooks are drawn.

Queen Alexandra's Royal Army Nursing Corps (Q.A.R.A.N.C.) provides women nurses for military hospitals.

The **Women's Royal Army Corps** (W.R.A.C.), covering a wide range of duties, from cooking and clerical work to driving and signalling.

HOW THE ARMY IS DIVIDED

The standard formation in the modern Army is the division. In wartime the divisions are grouped to form corps (two divisions

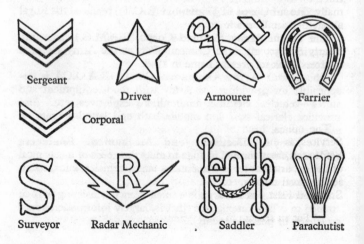

Sergeant

Driver   Armourer   Farrier

Corporal

Surveyor   Radar Mechanic   Saddler   Parachutist

Signaller   Sniper

Second Glider Pilot

or more), armies (two corps or more) and army groups (two armies or more).

A fighting division consists of two or three brigades, each of three or four armoured regiments or infantry battalions (normally one armoured regiment and three infantry battalions), altogether totalling about 17,000 men.

The fighting infantry unit of the Army is the battalion. Nearly 800 strong, it is divided into a Headquarters, Headquarters' Company and four Rifle Companies.

THE ROYAL NAVY [1]

The official head of the Navy (senior of the three Armed Services) is the Under-Secretary of State for the Royal Navy. Before the creation of the unified Ministry of Defence, the title of the department head was First Lord of the Admiralty. The senior naval member of the Navy Board is the Chief of Naval Staff and First Sea Lord.

[1] For an account of naval vessels, see the section on *Ships*.

HOW THE NAVY IS ORGANISED

Outside the Ministry of Defence, the Navy is under the command of two Commanders in Chief: Commander in Chief Fleet, who is responsible for all the Navy's ships, and Commander in Chief Naval Home Command, who is responsible for all the Navy's shore establishments, units ashore and the training of officers and ratings.

Ships and some submarines are based at four Base Ports, Portsmouth, Plymouth and Chatham in England and Rosyth in Scotland. The fleet is divided into two flotillas commanded by admirals; submarines are commanded by Flag Officer, Submarines; all are responsible to the Commander in Chief Fleet.

Under Commander in Chief Naval Home Command, establishments in the country are divided into regions which are commanded by admirals located at the four Base Ports and known as Flag Officers Portsmouth, Plymouth, Medway (Chatham), and Scotland and Northern Ireland (Rosyth).

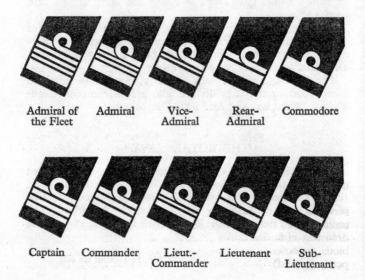

| Admiral of the Fleet | Admiral | Vice-Admiral | Rear-Admiral | Commodore |

| Captain | Commander | Lieut.-Commander | Lieutenant | Sub-Lieutenant |

Tactical
Communication
Rating

Gunlayer

Torpedo and
Anti-Submarine
Rating

Engineering
Mechanic

Air Mechanic

Petty Officer   Leading Rating

The administration and training of the Fleet Air Arm come
under the command of the Flag Officer, Naval Air Command.

The Corps of Royal Marines was founded in 1664 to
serve on sea and land. Today they provide four commando
units. Apart from serving in warships, the Marines are also
drawn upon for the crews of landing craft and for other amphi-
bious operations (that is, those carried out partly on sea and
partly on land).

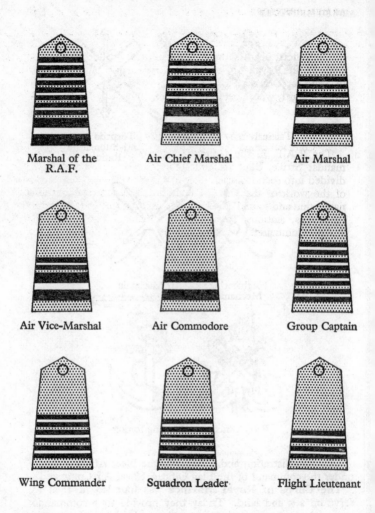

Marshal of the
R.A.F.

Air Chief Marshal

Air Marshal

Air Vice-Marshal

Air Commodore

Group Captain

Wing Commander

Squadron Leader

Flight Lieutenant

These are shoulder badges worn with battledress: with No. 1 dress (formal),
they are worn on the cuff as in the Royal Navy.

THE ROYAL AIR FORCE

The official head of the Air Force is the Under-Secretary of State for the Royal Air Force, who is responsible to the Secretary of State for Defence. He controls the Service through the Air Force Board, whose senior service member is the Chief of the Air Staff.

HOW THE AIR FORCE IS ORGANISED

The R.A.F. in the United Kingdom is organised in Commands: Strike, Support and Training. The Commands are divided into sections, each of which deals with a specific aspect of the work of the R.A.F.: operations, intelligence, training, navigation and so on. The Service's fighting units are organised in groups, stations, squadrons and flights. There are other R.A.F. Commands overseas, in West Germany and Cyprus.

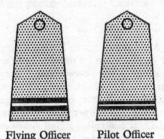

Flying Officer   Pilot Officer

Pilot's Wings

The Police

In May 1966, the Home Secretary announced plans to reduce the number of police forces in England and Wales from 117 to 49 (from 105 to 45 in England, and from 12 to 4 in Wales). In England and Wales the police are administered by the Home Office, in Scotland by the Scottish Home Office and Health Department, and in Northern Ireland by the Ministry of Home Affairs.

The main ranks in the police are constable, sergeant, inspector, superintendent and (in London) commander and deputy commander. The head of the Metropolitan Police Force is called the Commissioner; the head of a provincial force is called a Chief Constable.

Policewomen were first recruited during the First World War.

BRANCHES OF THE POLICE

The C.I.D. Most police forces have a Criminal Investigation Department. No officer can be recruited to this section until he has served for at least a few years as an ordinary uniformed constable. Ranks in the C.I.D. are the same as those in the uniformed police: e.g. detective-constable, detective-sergeant and so on.

In London, where one in every ten policemen belongs to this branch, the C.I.D. is controlled by an Assistant Commissioner, with the aid of a Commander and two Deputy Commanders. More than half of the staff of the C.I.D. are attached to police stations. The headquarters staff consists of Central Office (which deals with national and international crimes), the Criminal Record Office and Fingerprint Bureau, the Special Branch (which in war-time works with the forces in counter-espionage, and is also responsible for protecting important public persons), the Flying Squad and the Fraud Squad (whose job is to detect financial swindles).

The River Police A few forces (e.g. London, Liverpool, Glasgow) have sections of River Police, whose business is to prevent and detect stealing from craft on the river and from waterside premises, to deal with boats found adrift, to help vessels in difficulty, to come to the aid of drowning persons and to retrieve dead bodies, to prevent and detect smuggling and to prevent the pollution of the river.

The Thames Division in London has five river stations—at Wapping, Blackwall, Erith, Waterloo Pier and Barnes.

The Mounted Police These are used mainly for heading processions and controlling crowds.

Special Constables These are part-time unpaid men and women who are employed mainly to help in controlling crowds on special occasions. They have the same powers as full-time constables.

Fire Brigades

During the Second World War the 1,059 fire brigades in England and Wales were amalgamated into a single National Fire Service, and after the war an Act of Parliament created 125 brigades, each administered by the local authority. At the same time the 200 Scottish brigades were regrouped into eleven brigades.

In big cities the brigades are manned by full-time firemen; elsewhere some or all of the crews are part-timers.

The uniform of the British fireman is of dark-blue serge or cloth, with waterproof leggings and rubber or leather boots. The brass helmet of earlier times has given place to helmets made of leather or leather and rubber, which give much better protection against electric shock.

RELATIVE RANKS—SEA, LAND AND AIR

Army	Royal Navy	Royal Air Force
Field Marshal	Admiral of the Fleet	Marshal of the R.A.F.
General	Admiral	Air Chief Marshal
Lieutenant-General	Vice-Admiral	Air Marshal
Major-General	Rear-Admiral	Air Vice-Marshal
Brigadier	Commodore (1st and 2nd class)	Air Commodore
Colonel	Captain	Group Captain
Lieutenant-Colonel	Commander	Wing Commander
Major	Lieutenant-Commander	Squadron Leader
Captain	Lieutenant	Flight Lieutenant
Lieutenant	Sub-Lieutenant	Flying Officer
Second Lieutenant	Acting Sub-Lieutenant	Pilot Officer

Decorations and Medals

Victoria Cross (V.C.) (1856). *Ribbon*, crimson. (Until 1918 it was blue for the Royal Navy.) For conspicuous bravery. By order of Queen Victoria, who instituted the decoration, Victoria Crosses were struck from the metal of guns captured at Sevastopol during the Crimean War (see HISTORY: Diary of Events).

George Cross (G.C.) (1940). *Ribbon*, dark blue threaded through a bar adorned with laurel leaves. For gallantry. The G.C. is worn before all other decorations except the V.C., and is intended in the first place for civilians. It is awarded to servicemen, however, for actions for which military honours are not usually granted. It is given only for acts of the very greatest heroism.

The Distinguished Service Order (D.S.O.) (1886). *Ribbon*, red with blue edges. Given in recognition of special services in action to commissioned officers in the three services and (since 1942) the Mercantile Marine. A Bar may be awarded for any additional act of service.

Distinguished Service Cross (D.S.C.) (1914), for Warrant Officers and officers in the Royal Navy below the rank of Captain.

Military Cross (M.C.) (1914), for captains, lieutenants and Class I Warrant Officers in the Army.

Distinguished Flying Cross (D.F.C.) (1918), for officers and warrant officers in the R.A.F. and Fleet Air Arm; awarded for acts of gallantry when flying in active operations against the enemy.

Air Force Cross (A.F.C.) (1918), for acts of courage when flying, though not in active operations against the enemy.

Albert Medal (A.M.) (1866), for gallantry in saving life at sea or on land.

Medal for Distinguished Conduct in the Field (D.C.M.), for warrant officers, non-commissioned officers and men of the Army and R.A.F.

Conspicuous Gallantry Medal (C.G.M.), for warrant

officers and men of the Royal Navy, Mercantile Marine and R.A.F.

George Medal (G.M.) (1940), for acts of gallantry.

Distinguished Service Medal (D.S.M.), for chief Petty Officers, men and boys of all branches of the Royal Navy, Mercantile Marine and Royal Marines.

Military Medal (M.M.), for warrant and non-commissioned officers and men and women of the Army.

Distinguished Flying Medal (D.F.M.) (1918) and the **Air Force Medal** (A.F.M.), the equivalent of the D.F.C. and A.F.C. for warrant and non-commissioned officers and men.

King's Police and Fire Services Medal, awarded for distinguished service.

The Law

What is Law?   2–3
Rights, Duties   3
The Courts   3–4
How the Courts are Organised   4
Lower Courts   4–5
People in the Courts:
    The Judge   5
    Barristers   5
    Solicitors   5
    Parties   5
    Juries   6
The Cost of Going to Law   6
The Action   6–7
Appeals   7
Where the Law Comes From   7–8
The Subjects of Law   8
Scottish Law   8

What is Law? It is extremely difficult to say exactly what Law is. It is not a logical summing up of experience, like a law in science: it is an accumulation of orders and decisions and compromises, rooted deep in history. You could say that a law is an attempt to change human behaviour by means which ultimately involve the *force* of the State. By law, even a parking offender, if he keeps evading justice, may be brought to heel by *military action*. In fact, all our laws rely on force; but in our complicated society force is very much in the background.

Why do we obey laws? There is always the fear that we might be punished for a criminal offence, or sued for a civil one; but fear of being punished or sued is not even the main reason why we obey the hundreds of laws which affect us at practically every moment of every day. We obey them because we have been brought up to do so; because it is obvious that they are necessary; because this is a democracy and the laws as a whole are roughly how we want them.

It is natural to say 'obey' when we talk about Law, but it is a misleading word. Criminal laws indeed do have to be obeyed, but they are only a fraction of the total. There are many other laws that cannot be obeyed because they are not orders. For example, there is an Act of 1837 called the Wills Act which says that a will must be signed by the testator (the person making the will) in the presence of two witnesses who must be present at the same time. There is nothing in this to 'obey': if the will is not signed in this way, it is not a will: but no one can be punished. There are hundreds of laws of this sort which lay down procedures—that is, they say how things must be done: there are others which give permissions, or make definitions.

As you can see, it is perhaps impossible to say exactly what a law is: luckily this does not prevent us from obeying, using and understanding laws.

Rights, Duties When we look into it we find that much of the Law of England (though not necessarily of other countries) consists of statements about *rights*, *powers*, *duties* and *liabilities*. I have a *duty* not to steal from you—if I do, you automatically have a *power* to have me sent to prison. Again, you have a *right* not to be stolen from, and I am under a *liability* to you if I do.

This reasoning extends from criminal law to the other branches. When a lawyer says that someone *owns* something he means that that person has several rights, powers, duties and liabilities towards the thing. All of these can be dealt with separately: thus the owner of land can sell his *right* to use the land to another person, while keeping for himself the eventual ownership. This is called giving a lease, and under it he may well transfer to the other person the legal *duty* of making the land safe for visitors.

Our law makes very few clear, sweeping statements about life. Instead it consists of thousands of particular rules that often contradict one another. Oddly enough, this is an advantage, for it gives the Judges freedom to pick and choose among all the rules so that justice is done in a way that would be impossible had they to apply a fixed set of laws.

The Courts Part of the business of Government is to provide Courts of Law to keep the peace and to settle disputes. In the old days access to the Courts—that is, getting one's case heard in them—was difficult and expensive; nowadays—at least, in theory—they are free, and will hear the complaint of anyone who is within the United Kingdom.

They work in a formal way; their officers wear traditional clothes, and their methods and language are difficult for anyone who is not a student of the law. Anyone may go and listen to cases being decided—and everyone should, at least once, visit his local County or Magistrates Court, or the Law Courts in the Strand in London.

The Courts do not act of their own accord; cases have to be started either by making a charge in criminal matters or issuing a writ in civil matters. Once set in motion the Courts have considerable powers to compel the parties to a case and witnesses to attend and to give truthful evidence; to punish contempt (which is the legal name given to acts flouting the court's authority; for instance, refusal to give evidence, or to show respect for the judge) and to pronounce decisions and enforce obedience to those decisions.

Partly because the Courts are very traditional bodies, and partly to deal with the great involvement nowadays of Government in private affairs, the Courts are being replaced for some purposes by Administrative Tribunals. These are less formal, more flexible, and equally powerful bodies which differ from Courts in deciding not only *fact* and *law*, but also *policy*. For instance, the question of whether a landlord has allowed his houses to become slums involves more than the *law* defining a slum, and the *fact* of the condition of these houses; it also involves Government *policy* which decides at what point houses are so dilapidated that they have become slums and have to be replaced. Because of their independence of Government—see **Judges** below—the Courts are ill-suited for making this sort of decision. Tribunals decide an enormous variety of questions: from housing, to the siting of atomic power stations, to the release of the mentally ill from hospital.

How the Courts are Organised The supreme Judicial Authority and the ultimate Court of Appeal for Great Britain and Northern Ireland is the *House of Lords* (that is, all the peers who make up the House). In fact, only a dozen specially appointed *Lords of Appeal in Ordinary* hear cases which come before the House. Below them comes the *Court of Appeal*, staffed by the *Master of the Rolls* and eleven *Lords Justices of Appeal*. The *Court of Criminal Appeal* is staffed by the *Lord Chief Justice of England* and the Judges of the *Queen's Bench Division*. These three Courts hear appeals only: cases start in the *High Court of Justice*, which is divided into three Divisions: Queen's Bench, Chancery, Probate Divorce and Admiralty. There are 48 *puisne* Judges in the High Court (a *puisne* Judge is a junior Judge), and they can hear any kind of case. Until 1972, *Assizes* were held by Judges of the Queen's Bench touring the country three times a year. These Courts and the *Quarter Sessions* (part of the system of Lower Courts dealt with below, and consisting of magistrates sitting with a jury and having authority to hear more serious cases) have been replaced by a single Crown Court, served by a new bench of full-time Judges (Circuit Judges) and a limited number of part-time Judges known as Recorders.

Lower Courts The *County Courts* are widely distributed and hear small civil matters—limited in value to £750. They are staffed by 80 County Court Judges who sit periodically in all large towns. Procedure is simpler, quicker and cheaper than in the High Court, and they dispatch vastly more business. *Courts of the Justices of the Peace* hear mainly criminal matters, and are staffed by unpaid, part-time people who have no training in law. They dispatch innumerable petty cases, for example many traffic offences, and they also conduct preliminary examinations of more serious charges; if in such an examination they find there is a case to answer, they refer the matter to the Crown Court. Last of all there are *Coroner's Courts* in which a Coroner, who is a specially appointed barrister, solicitor or doctor, sits with a jury, and holds inquests on 'treasure trove', unexplained death and death in prison.

People in the Courts: The Judge The principal figure in a Court of Law—apart from Magistrates or Coroner's Courts— is the Judge, who has been appointed from among the leading barristers. He holds his office during 'good behaviour', and no English judge has been dismissed in modern times. Judges retire at 75, and are paid a handsome salary to attract the more successful barristers to the Bench and also to protect the Judges against the temptations of bribery.

Barristers Also officers of the Court, though they are employed by their clients, are the barristers—people who have passed examinations in Law, and been 'called to the Bar' by one of the Inns of Court. They are then privileged to appear in any Court on behalf of litigants (that is, persons going to law), who can of course argue their cases for themselves if they wish. Barristers have a double duty: to further their client's case, and to help the Court to enforce the rules of litigation and to come to a just decision. For instance, if a barrister discovered proof that the client he was defending on a criminal charge was guilty, he would be bound to tell the Court. But the barrister's main function is to present his client's case in court as well as he can: what that case is depends on—

Solicitors People who are faced with a court case go first to a Solicitor—a legal practitioner of much the same standing as the Barrister—who helps his clients prepare their cases, and engages barristers for them. In County and Magistrates' Courts, Solicitors can appear directly for their clients, but this is not so in the higher courts. Three quarters of most solicitors' jobs consist in keeping a client out of the courts by advising him, drafting his contracts, wills and leases and many other documents with such skill that disputes do not arise.

Parties There are two sides (parties) in a law case: in civil suits they are the *plaintiff*—who makes the complaint—and the *defendant*. In criminal cases they are the *prosecutor* and *defendant*. In an appeal, the party appealing is called the *appellant* and the other the *respondent*. Any person or corporate body— such as a Limited Company or a City Corporation—can sue or be sued. Children under age have equal rights at law, but they are represented in court by an adult 'next friend'.

Juries In serious criminal trials, and very occasionally nowadays at the request of one of the parties in civil suits, juries sit. A jury consists of twelve householders picked at random, who listen to the evidence and decide the facts of the case in answer to the Judge's questions. Their value lies in preserving common sense among the involved arguments of lawyers.

The Cost of Going to Law The disadvantage of our present system is the great expense of law suits. Although in theory the party at fault has to pay all the expenses of the case, *costs*— as this award is called—very seldom comes to more than a fraction of what has been spent. In civil suits the party with more money has a definite advantage: he can afford, if he loses at first, to appeal to higher and higher courts. Although there is a scheme which gives financial assistance to people involved in Law suits—they apply for *Legal Aid*—it is in general wise to avoid litigation.

The Action (This is the name given to the trying of a case). Every decision given in an English court is the result of a competition between the two sides. Each party brings its evidence and puts its arguments in turn, while the Judge sees fair play. The Judge is allowed in the end to decide the case only on what has been said before him in court—if one side has made a mistake and failed to make out a point which would have given them the decision it is not the Judge's responsibility to do it for them. The course of a trial moves rather like a game of tennis: one side makes a point—it is then up to the other to refute it, or to produce an explanation.

At the end of the evidence and argument the Judge asks the jury—if there is one—for their verdict on the facts; if there isn't a jury he gives his own decision. He then states the law he is going to apply, and makes his award. This takes several forms: in civil suits it is often *damages*—a money compensation for the wrong the defendant did the plaintiff. Less often defendants are ordered by *injunction* to do or to forbear from doing some action, or to deliver or return something of the plaintiff's, or to carry out an agreement. In criminal cases the Judges may—if the defendant is found guilty—discharge him, impose a fine, put him on probation (where he will be free but supervised by a probation officer), sentence him to a term of imprisonment, or, since the 1972 Criminal Justice Act, oblige him to undertake a number of hours of strenuous work for the community. Although criminals can be ordered medical and psychiatric treatment during, or instead of, imprisonment, it is often said that the courts lack sufficient means for dealing with criminals, and that prisons (which are very overcrowded, with a population of over 40,000 in England and Wales) are not the most suitable places for treatment.

Appeals In civil and criminal cases both sides may, with certain safeguards, appeal against the decision. The case is then heard before a Court of Appeal which hears no evidence but reviews the conduct of the trial and the accuracy of the Judge's finding of facts and law. Curiously enough there are many more appeals on points of law than on the facts: this is because finding the right law to apply can be a very difficult and uncertain business. The Appeal Court is free to alter or remove the award or sentence as it thinks fit.

Where the Law Comes From Our law comes from three separate sources: (i) Statutes; (ii) Decided Cases; (iii) Custom.

(i) *Statutes* are the Laws that Parliament makes. Bills—or proposals for new laws—are put before the House, and after they have been passed in three votes, usually after considerable alteration, they receive the *Queen's Assent* and become law. Government Departments make many orders under the authority of Statutes of *Acts of Parliament* which also have the force of law. It is not too difficult to know roughly what a statute means, but the courts are continually having to decide cases that Parliament hadn't thought about, and that might or might not come under a particular Act. Thus: Is a car-park a 'road'? Is a costermonger's barrow a 'place'? These questions look pointless to a non-lawyer, but to the parties involved they may mean imprisonment or great expense.

(ii) Our courts have developed a rule of following earlier decided cases, so that similar facts are treated in similar ways. The difficulty is for the Judge to decide which among the thousands of old cases he will apply. In fact there is considerable freedom of choice, and Judges can choose their cases to do 'substantial justice' (that is, to give the decision to the party who is really in the right despite legal technicalities which might appear to favour the other side).

Although Parliament has, in theory, a monopoly of law-making, the Judges do in this way make new law. For instance, up to 1932 it was thought that a manufacturer had no legal responsibility to the purchaser of his goods if they were faulty. But then a woman who found a rotten snail in her ginger beer and had become very ill as a result was able to persuade the House of Lords that the manufacturer was responsible for her illness. Although the House said it was following earlier cases, it altered the law in a very necessary way, and as thoroughly as if Parliament had done it.

(iii) Custom is now seldom appealed to. It relates mainly to land, and the alleged custom must be 'ancient, certain, reasonable and continuous'. Or in other words have existed since 1189, the beginning of legal memory.

The Subjects of Law Although the laws form a complete whole, and any Court can apply any part of the law, it is convenient to divide them roughly into groups: *Criminal*—which explains itself, and is much less important than it appears; *Contract*—agreements for selling, hiring, firing; *Tort*—compensation for injuries to person, reputation and property; *Real Property*—the ownership of land; *Personal Property*—the ownership of things; *Trusts*—obligations to hold or do something for another; *Constitutional*—concerned with Government, and the relation between the citizen and the State; *International*—concerned with relationships with foreign states and citizens. There are many smaller divisions.

Scottish Law. Compared with English Law, which applies in England and Wales, Scottish Law differs in a number of particulars and in its application. The supreme civil court of Scotland is still the House of Lords, but below it comes the *Court of Session*, whose Judges have the honorary title of Lord. The Appeal Court is called the *Inner House* and is presided over by the *Lord President* or by the *Lord Justice-Clerk*. Below the Court of Session are the *Sheriff Courts*, one of which is to be found in every county. The supreme criminal court is the *High Court of Justiciary*. There are also the *Burgh Courts* (for criminal cases) where the *Bailies* preside, and the *Justices' Courts* (for criminal and civil cases). In Scotland there are a number of differences in court procedure: for example, the Jury consists of fifteen people and may arrive at its verdict by a majority, and a verdict of 'Not Proven' is allowed. There is no Coroner: the *Procurator-Fiscal* inquires into all suspicious deaths.

Natural History

INTRODUCTION   2-3
    What is a Living Thing?—The Science of life

WHAT LIVING THINGS ARE MADE OF   3-11
    Cells—The Stuff of Life—Growth—Different Kinds
    of Cells—Different Kinds of Bodies

HOW LIVING THINGS WORK   11-24
    Energy—Different Ways of Getting Food—Diges-
    tion—How Food is Absorbed—Circulation in Plants
    —What the Blood Does—Breathing—Releasing
    Energy—Getting Rid of Waste—Controlling the
    Body

REPRODUCTION AND HEREDITY   24-29
    Kinds of Reproduction—Method of Fertilisation—
    After Fertilisation—Heredity—Linked Characters
    and New Characters

THE HISTORY OF LIFE ON EARTH   30-42
    Fossils—Dating the Rocks—The Beginning of the
    World—Life's Origins—Life Proliferates—The Great
    Ages of Life—Table of Earth History—Evolution

THE KINDS OF LIVING THINGS   43-76
    Classification—Viruses—Bacteria—Flagellata—Plant
    Kingdom—Fungus Kingdom—Animal Kingdom

NATURE STUDY AND THE WEB OF LIFE   76-84
    Nature Study—Animal Behaviour—The Breeding
    Season—Animal Language—The Web of Life—
    Britain's Natural Habitats—Equipment

INTRODUCTION

What Is a Living Thing?

Almost everywhere we can see living things. A fly buzzes about the lamp, mould grows on an old crust of bread, out of the window we can see trees and dogs and cats and people. Even that green scum on the old wall is a mass of tiny living plants. All these things are 'alive'—but what does 'living' really mean? Perhaps the best answer is that when a thing is alive it *does* certain things. All living things *eat* in some way. That is, they take substances into their bodies from outside, and transform them into their own body material. Then they *excrete*, getting rid of waste matter, and they *breathe*, absorbing oxygen, and they *grow*. Even a potato, which does not look lively, will suddenly sprout out shoots if it is kept warm and moist. And this shows yet another feature of living things—that they *respond* to things around them.

Finally, there is one very important thing which all living things do. They *reproduce* themselves. Human beings have babies, cats have kittens, trees have seedlings, mushrooms have baby mushrooms.

Living things also have *habits*. Even the humblest tiny living creature, microbe or mite, has a life story. Just for its own sake this life story is often fascinating, and it may be as fabulous as anything in the Arabian Nights. What could be more extraordinary than that the same little individual creature one day may be an egg, the next day a caterpillar, a few days later a chrysalis and then a butterfly? No human being has ever lived through such a series of changes (though the ancient Greeks thought that some of their gods and goddesses had turned into animals and plants and called this sort of happening a 'metamorphosis'—a changing of shape).

But, quite apart from its interest, the life story of a creature may be very important to us as well. The pretty little orange-and-black Colorado beetle is quite harmless—but in its first stage, or larva, it is the world's worst pest of potato plants. It has cost a great deal more money than the First World War.

V2

So it is useful to know which are our friends and which are our enemies in the world of living things.

The Science of Life

How does a slice of bread and butter get turned into bones and muscle and skin? Why do two red-haired parents always have red-haired children, while a brown-haired couple may have children with hair of any colour? Why, even, does a cat have *kittens*—what mechanism stops it from having a baby lobster? These are the sort of questions that men have asked from the beginning of history. But it is only in the last two or three hundred years that we have begun to get convincing answers. This is because men have only recently begun studying living things intensely, as a separate science—Biology, the Science of Life. And nowadays our knowledge has grown so great that 'Biology' is really no longer the name for a single science, but for a large number of separate sciences, all of which, however, deal with some aspect of living matter. There is Anatomy, for example, which is the study of the structure of living things—their bones and organs. There is Physiology, the study of how living things work—how we breathe, or digest our food, or grow. There is Systematics, which is the science of classifying living things; Psychology, which deals with thinking and behaviour; Ecology and Sociology, which study relationships between living things and their environment and with each other. All these sciences are aspects of Biology, and there are many others as well. Furthermore, in each field there are scientists who specialise in one particular problem. Yet the unity of the whole science of life is shown by the fact that often a discovery in one field applies in all the others as well. For instance, most of what we know about how human beings inherit blue eyes or red hair originally came from scientists working on fruit flies and the evening primrose.

WHAT LIVING THINGS ARE MADE OF

Cells

If we cut an exceedingly thin slice of the stem or leaf of a water plant, such as a water-lily or a pondweed, and put it under a microscope, a whole new world opens up before us. We see a number of little compartments, like the cells of a honeycomb.

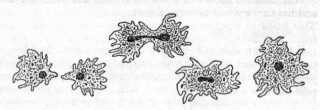

Amoeba, showing division

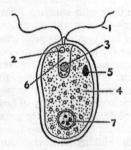

CHLAMYDOMONAS
1. Flagella
2. Contractile vacuole
3. Nucleus
4. Chloroplast
5. Eye spot
6. Central colourless cytoplasm
7. Pyrenoid

These compartments are, in fact, *called* cells, and each forms a tiny unit. The smallest, simplest living creatures consist of only one cell, and this is able to live and function all on its own as a separate individual. Larger living things are also made up of cells, countless billions and billions of them in the case of a man or a tree. But even the largest animal or plant starts life as a single cell—a fertilised egg cell.

Cells vary very much in size   Some, like bacteria cells, may be only about $\frac{1}{2000}$ mm. long, and require the most powerful microscope to examine them. The largest, produced by the sea-weed *Halicystis*, may be over $\frac{1}{2}$ in. in diameter, and fits nicely in the palm of the hand. Those of water plants in general are large and easy to examine, which is why we have chosen a pondweed leaf-cell. So that an animal cell can be compared with this typical plant cell, we illustrate an *amoeba*, which is a tiny animal that consists of only one cell.

Plant cells are usually more or less regular and fixed in shape, and have a rigid *cell wall* surrounding them made of cellulose. This helps to support the plant. Animal cells, on the other hand, vary much in shape, and they usually have only a thin membrane around them, though it may be very tough. In both cases, if the cell is alive, this surrounding wall or membrane is *permeable*. This means that water and dissolved substances can pass through it into the cell, or from the cell outwards.

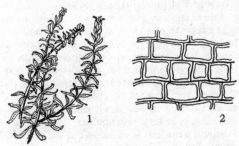

PONDWEED, ELODEA CANADENSIS
1. Plant; 2. Leaf cells

Inside the cell wall or membrane is a greyish, grainy, jelly-like substance, which is slowly moving, if we watch it closely. This substance is called *protoplasm*. In a fully grown plant cell it streams round and round the wall, while the space in the middle is usually filled with clear liquid. This space is called a *vacuole*. In an animal cell it usually fills the whole of the cell-space, while, instead of one big vacuole, there are several small round ones scattered about in the protoplasm.

The Stuff of Life

Protoplasm is the living substance of all plants and animals. In the right conditions it is able to perform all the functions of life—eating, breathing, excreting, moving, growing, responding, reproducing. Indeed, the living protoplasm inside our bodies and the bodies of other animals and plants is doing all these things all the time. One might well wonder what this marvellous stuff is made of. A large proportion (up to 97 parts in 100) is water; and in this water are dissolved and mixed up many different substances. There are salts and gases, and a number of complicated organic chemicals, which fall into four chief types— carbohydrates, fats, proteins and nucleic acids. The first three we are familiar with from the food we eat. Bread is largely a carbohydrate, butter, oil and the fat of meat are largely fat, while white of egg is pure protein, and lean meat also contains a large quantity. Such foods, derived from the protoplasm of animals and plants, are digested by our own bodies and turned into our own sort of protoplasm.

None of these substances is alive, yet, correctly mixed together in the right circumstances, they act upon one another to produce life. The key to this activity called life lies in the fourth of these substances we have mentioned—the nucleic acids. They seem to hold the protoplasm together and direct the way it works. Little particles of nucleic acids are scattered about in the protoplasm directing various activities. Mostly, however, the nucleic acids are all together in one lump called the cell *nucleus*. All living cells contain at least one nucleus. If we cut a cell in half, the half without a nucleus soon dies—but the other half recovers and goes on living. This gives some idea of how vital the nucleus is to the life of a cell. It shows that from the nucleus the whole cell can be re-created.

Growth

If we look through our microscope at a mass of living cells, eventually we are sure to see one that is dividing in two. First, we see that all the little dark particles in the nucleus come together into threads called *chromosomes*. Then these chromosomes assemble in the middle of the nucleus. Now each one splits into two, so that there are two sets instead of one. Then the two sets separate, going to opposite ends of the nucleus. Finally, the protoplasm all around also splits, and we have two new cells, each of which has a nucleus identical with that in the other, because it is formed from the exact division into two of the original nucleus.

It is in this way that all cells reproduce themselves. In one-celled creatures this division produces two new individuals, then when these divide there are four, then eight and so on. In many-celled creatures the two new cells do not separate, so this process makes the organism grow larger. In this way, an

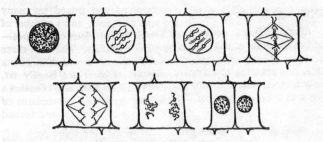

Mitosis (cell division)

enormous elephant or oak tree grows from a minute single fertilised egg cell. By the time a human baby is born, so many cells may be dividing in its rapidly growing body that a quarter of a million new cells come into existence every second.

Even when an animal is fully grown, cell-division does not stop. This is because individual cells get worn out and are replaced by young ones. In this way the body is constantly renewing and repairing itself. We can actually watch this repair work going on when we see how a cut heals by new cells growing over it. In human beings a big cut will not heal completely, but will leave a scar, while if we lose a finger or toe, or an arm, there is no chance that our bodies will replace it. In lower animals such as worms, however, a big piece may easily grow back into a whole new worm. This is because the cells in the worm's body retain their ability to grow and reproduce to a much larger extent than in higher animals. We can see this also in the case of various plants, where a tiny cutting or a piece of leaf may grow into a whole new tree. In higher animals, however, the cells in different parts of the body become highly *specialised*. By this we mean that they become highly developed for performing one function, such as excreting, or moving, but are unable to perform the others more than is barely necessary for keeping alive. But specialisation of cells also means that animals and plants can grow bigger bodies, because it allows the cells to be organised into different *organs* and *tissues*, each with a different kind of work to do.

Different Kinds of Cells

All the different activities of living are performed by a single cell in a minute animal like *Amoeba* or a tiny plant like *Chlamydomonas* (which also consists of a single cell). Remembering this, it is amazing to compare a human being and a tree, and see how in them the cells are specialised to do particular kinds of work in different parts of the body.

	Human	*Tree*
1. Support	Skeleton	Wood; roots and stem and branches
2. Movement	Muscles	Leaf; pulvini (occasionally)
3. Lubrication	Cartilage (e.g. knee cap)	—
4. Eating	Mouth	Leaf (produces food) Roots (absorption)
5. Protection	Skin	Cork
6. Digestion	Gut	Leaf and other tissue
7. Transport	Blood system	Xylem and phloem
8. Breathing	Lungs	Leaves
9. Storage	Fat tissue	Root
10. Excretion	Kidneys, rectum, skin	Wood and other by-products; leaves
11. Reproduction	Gonads	Flowers
12. Secretion	Glands	Glands
13. Control and response	Nervous system and hormones	Hormones

These tissues have cells which look very different from each other—as well they might, because they have such very different kinds of work to do. Here are a few among the innumerable kinds of specialised cells, together with the work they do:

	Human	*Tree*
Support	Bone cell	Xylem vessel
Movement	Muscle cell	Pulvinus cell
Feeding	Stomach cell	Leaf cell with plastids
Transport	Capillary wall cell Blood cell	Phloem sieve tube
Breathing	Lung cell	Stoma cells
Excretion	Kidney cell	Heavily lignified xylem cell
Reproduction	Sperm and ovum	Egg cell and pollen tube cell
Secretion	Gland cell	Gland cell
Storage	Fat cell	Potato tuber cell
Response and control	Nerve cell	Root tip cell
Protection	Skin cell	Cork cell

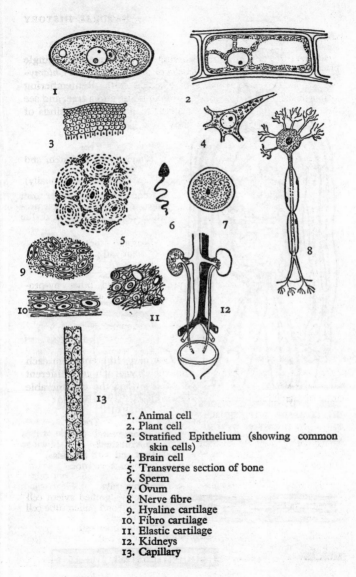

1. Animal cell
2. Plant cell
3. Stratified Epithelium (showing common
   skin cells)
4. Brain cell
5. Transverse section of bone
6. Sperm
7. Ovum
8. Nerve fibre
9. Hyaline cartilage
10. Fibro cartilage
11. Elastic cartilage
12. Kidneys
13. **Capillary**

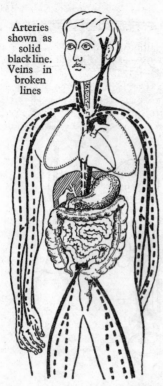

Arteries shown as solid black line. Veins in broken lines

Carbon dioxide and water form sugar in the leaves. Sugar provides energy for growth of the tree

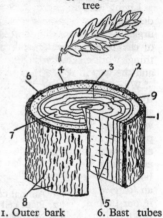

TREE AND CROSS SECTIONS TO COMPARE WITH HUMAN SHOWING DIGESTIVE SYSTEM, CIRCULATORY SYSTEM AND LUNGS

1. Outer bark
2. Inner skin and new wood
3. Annual rings
4. Cambium layer
5. Medullary rays
6. Bast tubes (shown as dots)
7. Sap wood
8. Lenticels
9. Heartwood

Involuntary

MUSCLE

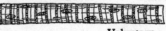

Voluntary

Different Kinds of Bodies

Not only do animals and plants have many different kinds of cells, but also the proportions of these vary from one to another, according to the sort of lives they lead. We have only to think of all the varied kinds of animals and plants there are, and where and how they live to see how true this is: the mole underground, the fish in the sea, the birds in the air; the oak tree, the cactus, the water-lily—to quote just a few examples. We will learn more about this later, in the section on the Web of Life.

HOW LIVING THINGS WORK

Energy

Living uses up energy. Even when we sit still we use a great deal of energy, for our heart and lungs and brain and digestive organs are still working, and all over our bodies untold millions of chemical changes are taking place. To discover how living things work means finding out where they get their energy from, and the way in which they use it.

When coal burns a chemical change takes place. Oxygen from the air combines with the substances in the coal and ash, smoke, water vapour and carbon dioxide gas are produced, while heat is given off. Heat is a form of energy, as we can prove by using this heat to boil water, and driving a steam engine with the steam produced. In this way we turn the heat-energy into work. Almost the same sort of thing happens in our bodies. Chemical changes take place in which oxygen from the air (carried by the blood) combines with various food substances in our tissues. Waste products equivalent to ash and smoke are produced, as well as water and carbon dioxide, and energy is liberated, some of it in the form of heat—which is why our bodies are warm.

Not all animals are warm-blooded, with a constant body temperature like that of mammals or birds. Indeed, most animals' bodies produce comparatively little heat while working; but warmth provides the optimum conditions for the body's workings, so such 'cold-blooded' creatures are much more dependent on climate and weather than are birds and mammals. It is the same with plants, whose life-processes need to be even less active than those of animals, because they do not need energy for moving around.

Different Ways of Getting Food

Except for certain lowly bacteria, all life on earth depends on plants. This is because plants are ultimately the sole source of food for all animals. Animals need complicated chemical substances—carbohydrates, proteins, fats—as their food, but they cannot manufacture them for themselves. They get them by eating other animals or plants—and only plants manufacture them in the first instance.

How plants make food is a mystery. But somehow *chlorophyll* (the green substance in their leaves) and other pigments they possess have the power of absorbing sunlight, and of using its energy in combining water and carbon dioxide gas to form glucose, a simple kind of sugar. This is the basic chemical reaction upon which all life depends:

$$6CO_2 \qquad + \qquad 6H_2O \rightarrow$$

(six 'molecules' or particles   (six molecules of water)
of carbon dioxide)

$$\rightarrow \quad C_6H_{12}O_6 \qquad + \qquad 6O_2$$

(1 molecule of glucose)   (six molecules of oxygen)

Later this glucose may be processed by the plant into starches, or other substances, such as fats or oils. Or it may be made into proteins by combination with various salts containing nitrogen. These substances may be built into the organism's own structure and protoplasm, or held as food reserves. The energy of sunlight is still in them, and when they are 'broken down' into smaller and simple molecules by recombining them with oxygen this energy is released, in the plant itself, or in an animal that has eaten it.

Digestion

The food that is burnt to provide energy in our bodies is not the food we have just eaten. Far from it. What we burn are food reserves stored in our tissues—in our muscles for example—and these reserves have got there only after a long series of processes. The first of these processes which food goes through when we eat it is digestion.

Digestion means dissolving. Before our intestines can absorb food it has to be dissolved. If we put a beefsteak or an apple into water it will not dissolve . . . not even if we chop it into tiny pieces. But if we pour the different digestive juices from our bodies on to it nearly all of it will be liquefied—the residue being those parts which our body cannot use.

The stages in which digestion takes place in our own bodies are as follows:

1. In the mouth food is chewed and broken up into smaller bits, and mixed with saliva. In the saliva are 'enzymes'— substances which produce a chemical change without themselves being altered. These saliva enzymes attack the starch in the food, and begin converting it into sugar. Starch really consists of big 'molecules' (or particles), made up of smaller molecules of sugar joined together chemically. What the enzyme does is add water to the starch molecules, which loosens the bonds which hold it together. One molecule of insoluble starch plus one molecule of water, in the presence of these saliva enzymes, 'break down' into six smaller soluble molecules of glucose (a kind of sugar). In this form it can easily be absorbed by the body.

2. From the mouth the food goes down the gullet into the stomach. Here it is mixed with 'gastric juice', which contains hydrochloric acid as well as another lot of enzymes. Just as starch molecules are built up of sugar molecules, so the molecules of proteins are built up of smaller molecules of amino acids. It is in the stomach that the breakdown of these protein molecules (which are the largest molecules known) begins.

3. From the stomach the food enters the small intestine, the upper part of which is called the duodenum. Here it comes in contact with the bile, a substance made by the liver, and stored before use in the gall bladder. The bile acts like soap upon the fats in the food, 'emulsifying' them, just as soap emulsifies grease and so enables us to clean our hands when they get greasy. The bile also helps to neutralise the stomach hydrochloric acid still left in the food.

4. In the middle and lower part of the small intestine digestion is completed by fluid from the pancreas, which continues the work of breaking down starches, fats and proteins, and of neutralising acid.

5. In the lower part of the small intestine, and in the large intestine or colon farther on, the dissolved food, and the water it is dissolved in, are absorbed through the walls of the intestine and pass into the blood stream. (The walls of this part of the intestine are lined inside with 'villi'; these are finger-like projections that increase the area through which absorption can take place.) The remaining solid waste, or 'faeces', is passed out of the body through the rectum and anus. The whole process takes up to 30 hours, though digestion itself only takes about $4\frac{1}{2}$ hours of this.

Not all animals digest food in this elaborate way. A one-celled animal like an Amoeba swallows tiny particles whole, and its entire process of digestion is carried out inside minute droplets of water in the protoplasm, called 'food vacuoles'. The Hydra breaks down its prey into particles, and then the cells lining its gut swallow these and digest them Amoeba-fashion, in food vacuoles. The starfish pushes its whole stomach out of its body, secretes its digestive juices on to its prey, liquefies it and then absorbs the resultant fluid. On the other hand, earth worms (and birds) have food storage 'crops' and 'gizzards'—special muscular compartments in which food is ground up with stones they have swallowed, before it is digested. Horses and cows have a whole extra stomach, called a 'rumen'. In this live bacteria which do part of their digestion for them, breaking down the hard cellulose of which grass is largely composed. After the bacteria have acted on the grass, the cow or horse then 'brings up' the food in the form of a 'cud', chews it and swallows it again into its true stomach, after which it is digested as in other animals. Termites, which eat wood, also have bacteria in their gut to help in breaking down the wood.

How Food Is Absorbed

When an animal has digested its food, how does the food get from its intestine into its blood? The answer is that it diffuses. If you put a lump of sugar into a cup of tea eventually the whole cup will be sweetened. This is because dissolved molecules in a liquid (or a gas) have a tendency to spread themselves evenly. If we now added a spoonful of salt, we would get a weird mixture, because the salt would also diffuse itself through the cup. Each substance, in other words, behaves independently of

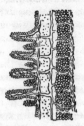

Lining of small intestine to illustrate osmosis in animals

the other. Now exactly the same thing happens with food in our
bodies. The starches, proteins and fats which we eat are
changed into sugars, amino acids and lipids, and these are dissolved in water in our intestine. There are many of them in the
intestine, but not many in the blood, so they tend to *diffuse*
through the membrane of the intestine wall and into the blood,
so to speak—a process which is known as *osmosis*. Now this
intestine wall membrane is only *semi-permeable*. This means
that the minute pores in it allow only certain molecules, because
they are small enough, to pass through. It is the same with the
membranes of many other tissues of the body. Not only so, but
some of these membranes can alter their permeability. By this
means, they can control the amount of a substance they let in.
But what happens, one might ask, when a tissue has the same
amount of, shall we say, fat in it as the blood has outside? How
does it keep on adding to its stores? The answer is that the blood
is carrying the fat in the form of small molecules of soluble lipids,
whereas the fat-filled tissue has it in the form of big molecules of
insoluble fat. So it is that by changing fats into lipids, starches
into sugars, proteins into amino acids and back again, and by
altering the permeability of its various membranes, our body can
control the flow and distribution of the food it gets. It can
build up a reserve of fat in one place, break one down somewhere else, repair a wound, supply a tired muscle with sugar and
so on.

In exactly the same way, plants, using simpler substances of
their own manufacture, move them from place to place, digesting

them and reassembling them as required. Only in insect-eating or carnivorous plants does something like animal digestion take place, but, even so, this is merely a supplement to normal plant-food manufacture.

Circulation in Plants

Plants even more than animals use their circulating food substances as a source of structural strength. The presence of dissolved sugars in cells causes water to enter and to inflate the cells until they are rigid—hence the collapse (or 'wilting') of leaves and herbaceous plants deprived of water.

Although trees are supported by the mechanical strength of their wood, the leaves in which they manufacture their foods are kept stiff by water pressure. In the case of very tall trees they may be over 200 ft. above the ground. Water reaches these leaves from the roots through tubular *Xylem* or wood vessels, composed of dead cells. In these vessels the water is continuous, right up to the liquid in the leaves. Water is always being lost from the leaves by evaporation—sometimes as much as half a tree's weight in a day. This loss increases the strength of the sugar solution in the leaf cells, and draws water into them from below. This creates a corresponding suction right down to the roots, causing them to absorb more water from the soil.

Meanwhile the sugar that is manufactured in the leaf cells all day long diffuses out of them into another conducting tissue, the *phloem*, forming the inner part of the bark, with living cells. In storage cells in various parts of the plant (in the stem and roots usually) this sugar is converted into starch. There is thus a steadily diminishing concentration of sugar in the phloem cells away from the leaves, causing the sugar to flow out of them. But this is not the whole picture, for plants move their food reserves about from place to place as they need them, and there is a continuous circulation going on.

What the Blood Does

Except for the smallest and simplest animals, such as the one-celled Amoeba, the sponges, sea-anemones, hydras and other similar creatures, getting food to the tissues by diffusion alone is too slow a process, for most animals are active and energetic, and need constant new supplies of food in different parts of their bodies. In response to this need animals higher than flatworms

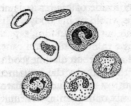

BLOOD CELLS

Top: Red corpuscles

Centre: (*l*) Lymphocyte;
(*r*) Monocyte

Bottom: Granulocytes

have developed a special 'tissue', called *blood*, which carries food round the body. The simplest animals with blood, such as roundworms, rely upon body-movements to circulate it. But higher up the scale of existence all animals have *hearts*, which are special pumps that force the blood round the body along definite channels.

Blood consists of a liquid, or 'plasma', in which are floating or moving countless cells of several different kinds. There are minute 'platelets', which help to 'clot' the blood, and so prevent us losing too much when we have a cut. There are large cells called white corpuscles, which eat bacteria that get into the blood and might cause illness. There are small white cells, which do repairs to the tissues. And lastly there are the red cells, shaped like tiny plates, by far the commonest of all. While food substances are mostly carried dissolved in the liquid part of the blood (or in the 'lymph', which is this same blood liquid separated from the blood cells and circulating separately to other parts of the tissues), the red blood cells have the job of carrying oxygen from the lungs to all parts of the body, and taking away carbon dioxide gas. They can do this very efficiently because they contain a pigment called haemoglobin, which combines with oxygen, and gives it up when it reaches the tissues. When it is carrying oxygen haemoglobin is bright red, which is why our arteries are red where they show beneath the skin. On the other hand, when it has given up its oxygen to the tissues haemoglobin is blue, which is why veins look blue, because they carry de-oxygenated blood back from the tissues to the heart and lungs.

Breathing

In a man the surface area of the inside of his lungs is about fifty times greater than that of the whole of his body. This is because the blood needs to be spread out in a thin film, separated from the air in the lungs by only the thinnest of membranes, if oxygen is to be efficiently absorbed and carbon dioxide given off. And just as blood is forced round the body by the heart, so the air in the lungs is forced in and out by muscular movement of the chest, so that fresh air, with plenty of oxygen, is available for our blood to extract the oxygen from. We can judge how efficiently our blood absorbs oxygen by filling our lungs and holding our breaths. In about three minutes practically all the oxygen has been taken up from the air in our lungs, our body needs more desperately, we feel dizzy and hastily gulp in fresh supplies.

Not all creatures have lungs, however. Insects have 'spiracles', little tubes with openings along the sides of their bodies, which divide into finer and finer branches, and carry air direct to the tissues of the body. By the movements of its body the insect pumps air in and out of its spiracles. But spiracles are not as efficient as blood for getting air to the tissues, and that is the chief reason why insects cannot grow much beyond a few inches long. The spiracle system simply cannot supply a larger body with enough oxygen.

Water-living creatures do not, of course, have lungs. They have gills, which may be inside their bodies, like the gills of fish, or freely waving and exposed, like the gills of tadpoles or marine worms. Gills, like lungs, are simply special areas of very thin skin where oxygen can diffuse into the blood—in this case oxygen dissolved in water, and not oxygen from the air. Many creatures actually absorb a fair amount of oxygen direct through the skins of their bodies. This happens, of course, in very simple animals which have no lungs or gills, but it also happens in animals like frogs. During the winter frogs 'hibernate': that is, they go to sleep; and they do this at the bottom of ponds, below the ice. While asleep their bodies do not need much oxygen, and they get all they need by diffusion through their skins. But during the summer, of course, when frogs live on land, they are air-breathing creatures with lungs like you or me.

Releasing Energy

You may well ask how all this food and oxygen that is circulating in the blood is actually used? The answer is, in three chief
ways: in building up òr repairing tissues, in building up stores
and reserves and in producing energy.

Our bodies are being repaired and rebuilt, broken down and
added to all the time. Molecule by molecule, the proteins of our
muscles, the lime of our bones and many far more complicated
ingredients of our tissues are being added to or taken away from.
If we take exercise, our muscles get bigger, if we give it up, our
reserves of fat suddenly increase. And all chemical changes
necessary to accomplish these things use energy.

Energy itself is stored up in the cells of the body, as electricity
is stored in a battery, in the form of chemicals which act upon
each other when the signal to do so is received. These chemicals
are a particular kind of phosphate. They break down into their
components, releasing energy, and then are reassembled again
by the breakdown of reserves of animal starch, or 'glycogen',
and oxygen-carrying chemicals, which in turn released lactic
acid into the blood. This lactic acid acts as a signal to the lungs
that more oxygen is needed, so that they work harder to supply
it, as when we pant as a result of hard effort. But in fact so long
as there is glycogen in a muscle it can go on running. After it
is used up, like a storage battery that has run down, it needs rest
and recharging.

Getting Rid of Waste

Apart from the solid indigestible waste matter that never
leaves the intestine until it is defaecated, all the building, repair
and energy-releasing that goes on in the body produces waste
products. The most important of these waste products is
ammonia (produced by the breakdown and repair of proteins)
because it is poisonous to living cells. In some simple water-
dwelling creatures ammonia merely diffuses out into the
surrounding water. In other animals it is turned to use: the
shells of crabs, for example, are made of *chitin*, the hair and nails
of human beings of *keratin*. Both these substances are compounds of ammonia, and represent clever ways of using it. But
most of the ammonia has to be got right out of the body.
In mammals it is usually combined in the blood with carbon

dioxide to form urea, and this is filtered out of the blood by the kidneys, and passed out of the body, by way of the bladder, as urine.

Carbon dioxide, apart from that combined with ammonia, is another waste product, and it is got rid of by diffusion through the lungs. Other waste matter, such as worn-out haemoglobin, is filtered out from the blood by the liver and spleen, and passed out into the intestine with the bile.

Plants also have their waste products. But except for gases, they do not excrete these, but turn them to use as building materials, for strengthening cell walls or other purposes.

Controlling the Body

Quite apart from their movements and habits, all the various activities going on in the bodies of animals have to be controlled and regulated. It would be an impossible position if we had consciously to tell our heart to beat, our individual tissues to take up or yield sugars, to adjust the strength or weakness of dilution of our blood and all the other thousand million activities which constitute living.

Some of this work is done by our nervous system, which has two chief parts, a section which works more or less automatically and a section which is under our conscious control. The conscious section directs our eyes to the book we are reading, the automatic does the focusing and the transmitting of the image to the brain. Even single-celled animals have what are known as nerve 'fibrils' in their protoplasm, while higher up the scale of life one finds definite nerve-cells. These are special cells, one end of which is prolonged into a nerve fibre, while the other has a bunch of 'nerve endings' which communicate with adjacent nerve cells. Simple animals such as a sea anemone have a network of nerve cells. Higher animals have a definite nerve cord, in which the nerve cells are concentrated. Higher up still in the animal scale, the front end of this nerve cord, in creatures like insects, is swollen into the beginnings of a brain. Of all invertebrates, the Octopus and Squid have the biggest brains.

Invertebrates, beside having no backbone, have their nerve cord lying along the lower side of their bodies. Vertebrates, on the other hand, have it along the dorsal, or back surface, and in a typical vertebrate it lies enclosed and protected by the spine,

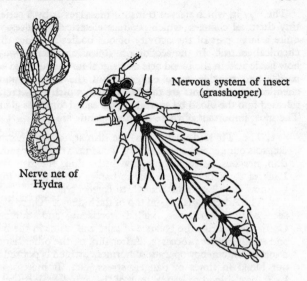

Nervous system of insect
(grasshopper)

Nerve net of
Hydra

while the brain is similarly enclosed and protected by the skull. This protection is very important, because nerve cells are the cells in the body to which repairs are most difficult, and we are born with our full set, and never grow any new ones. What we commonly call 'nerves' are not nerve cells at all, but bundles of fibres, which may be several feet long, coming from the nerve cells, all of which are lodged in the brain or spinal cord. If we sever a nerve in our arm, not a single nerve cell is lost, only a length of nerve fibre—but that in itself is an important loss.

Most of the signals from sense organs or from different parts of our body never even reach the brain, but are dealt with automatically by the spinal cord. But even if they do reach the brain, only a small part of them reach our consciousness. To what extent animals have what *we* call consciousness it is hard to tell. Certainly those parts of the brain which deal with memory, reasoning and learning are much better developed in human beings than in any animals. Scientists are beginning to think that the cleverest of all animals are probably whales and dolphins, followed perhaps by elephants.

The way in which nerves transmit messages is by a series of tiny chemical changes, which produce electrical impulses. But quite a large part of the activity of our bodies is under direct chemical control. In the section on 'Releasing Energy' we saw how lactic acid in the blood acts as a signal for the lungs to work harder and provide more oxygen. But the most important chemical control agents are the 'hormones', which are secretions released into the blood by special organs called 'ductless glands'. The most important of these ductless glands are:

1. The Thyroid gland, in the throat, whose hormone controls our general tempo of life. Too much thyroid produces thin, nervous, active people; too little, dull, sluggish types. Lack of thyroid hormone makes babies develop into idiots, but nowadays we know enough to correct this.

2. The Adrenal glands, on top of the kidneys. These glands secrete two hormones, called cortisone and adrenalin. Cortisone controls the balance of salts and water in the body, and various other processes. Adrenalin, on the other hand, is a sort of 'emergency operation' hormone, which is poured into our blood in times of danger, stress, etc. It increases the heart-beat, blood pressure, tone of the muscles, alertness and so forth, and enables us to cope better with an emergency.

3. The Pancreas, in the stomach region, regulates the amount of sugar in the blood, and prepares it for use either as fuel or for storage.

4. The Parathyroid, situated next to the thyroid, controls the way in which the body uses calcium in building and re-pairing bones, and the balance of phosphates in the tissues.

5. The Sex glands, situated in the region of the thighs, control reproduction and the bodily and character differences between males and females.

6. The Pituitary gland, situated under the brain, produces hormones which control the other glands.

Between the glands and the automatic nervous system all the incredible number of processes which we mean by 'living' are taken care of. This leaves the higher part of the brain free; and it is this higher part of the brain, especially the 'conscious' part, which man has used in building civilisations, writing books, studying the world that lies around him and speculating upon the meaning of his own life.

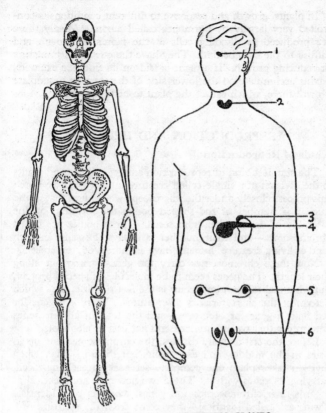

Human skeleton

DUCTLESS GLANDS

1. Pituitary
2. Thyroid and Parathyroid
3. Adrenals (above kidneys)
4. Islets of Langerhans in pancreas and glands in intestinal wall
5. Ovaries (in female)
6. Testes (in male)

In plants, growth and response to different conditions is controlled very largely by hormones called auxins. Mostly these are produced in dividing cells at the points of growth and diffuse to the cells behind. They have the effect of stimulating or reducing growth. If a plant is laid on its side, for example, auxins accumulate on the lower side of the stem and stimulate growth there, which causes the plant to bend upwards.

REPRODUCTION AND HEREDITY

Kinds of Reproduction

The simplest kind of reproduction among animals and plants is the division of a single-celled creature into two. If we watch this process closely under the microscope we see first that in the nucleus a number of rod-shaped bodies are forming, by the assembly of darker, denser material. These bodies are called chromosomes—and their number is always the same in each kind of living creature: humans have 46, horses 66, tomatoes 24.

Now these chromosomes carry the genes strung out along their length. The genes seem to be molecules of special protein, but what makes them important is the fact that it is they which determine the characteristics of creatures. There is a gene for red hair, a gene for blue eyes—and the total of all our genes determines that we are humans and not cats or elephants.

Before the cell actually divides, the chromosomes line up in pairs in the middle, and each splits lengthwise. Then when division takes place one complete set goes to each new cell, carrying its genes with it. These two new cells are identical as regards their chromosomes and genes, which is why Identical Twins are called identical—they come from the splitting of a single fertilised egg cell.

Similarly, when we plant a cutting from a tree its cells have the same kind of genes as the rest of the tree, and it grows into a tree which is identical, except in so far as wind, weather and site have influenced its growth.

In this kind of reproduction sex plays no part. It is called *asexual* or *vegetative* reproduction. *Sexual* reproduction is when a sex cell from each parent unites to form a single fertilised egg-cell, which then grows into a new creature. This new creature would obviously have twice the parental number of chromosomes

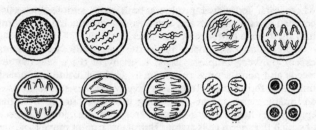

Meiosis (reduction division)

if it were not for the occurrence of a *reduction division* in the formation of the sex cells. When the chromosomes line up for division in the germ cells they split as usual, but then divide *twice*, giving four new cells instead of two, each with only half the normal number of chromosomes—such a cell being called 'haploid'. In the case of humans the sex cells have 23 chromosomes each—and only when they unite in fertilisation is the full, or 'diploid' number of chromosomes, 46, restored.

Methods of Fertilisation

In all animals and plants (except for the conifers and flowering plants) the male sex cell is free-swimming, propelling itself towards the female cell by lashing the water or seminal fluid with one or more whiplike *flagella* or *cilia*. In the lowest water-dwelling creatures the female cell may also be free-swimming, and the two cells may unite in mid-water. Even in highly advanced animals, such as fish like the herring, the female or egg cells, though no longer motile, are ejected into the water, where they are fertilised by the male sperms. But this is very wasteful—a female herring sheds many millions of eggs, only a small number actually get fertilised, and very few of these reach maturity. There is much greater certainty of survival in creatures which produce fewer eggs yet give them greater protection by keeping them inside the body until after fertilisation. This is accomplished by copulation—the two sexes come together, and the male introduces his sperm cells, together with a liquid in which they can swim, into the female by means of a tubular penis. In hermaphrodite animals like earthworms, where each individual produces both male and female cells, copulation is a double act, each worm introducing its sperm into the female entrance of the other.

Fertilisation takes place inside the parent also in all plants except the very simplest. Even in many of the algae, the sea weeds and pond-scums, the egg cells are held inside the parent until after fertilisation. In mosses, liverworts, ferns, club-mosses and many gymnosperms, including the huge Ginkgo tree, the egg-cell lies inside a flask-shaped 'archegonium', down the neck of which the sperm cells swim. But plants cannot move together for cross-fertilisation like animals, and free-swimming sperms have the disadvantage of needing water to swim in. In the highest plants of all, the conifers and flowering plants, this problem has been solved by the development of the 'pollen-tube': when the pollen grain alights on the stigma of the female flower a long tube grows out of it and down to the egg cell, carrying the male cell inside it.

This still does not solve the problem of getting the pollen grain to the female flower. Many are the devices that plants have adopted to achieve this end. In some, the pollen is blown by the wind, in others it is transferred by bees, butterflies, moths and other insects, or by birds or bats. And for each of these and yet other methods special devices have been evolved for ensuring its success. In the yucca plant, for example, pollen transfer is affected by a single moth, the yucca moth, whose eggs and caterpillars develop only in the yucca flowers. Neither moth nor plant could survive without the other.

After Fertilisation

When an egg is fertilised, the genes and chromosomes of the two parents are united, and an impetus is given which starts it dividing and developing into a new organism. Typically the divisions produce first of all a ball of cells—a 'blastula'—then one side folds in against the opposite wall, like a squashed tennis ball—the 'gastrula' stage—giving the little embryo an inner layer of cells as well as an outer. This inner layer or endoderm becomes the gut and internal organs as development continues, while the outer layer, or ectoderm, gives rise to the skin and nervous system. In between, a third layer appears, the meso-derm—and from this are produced the muscles, the blood, the connective tissue of the body and other parts. All this develop-

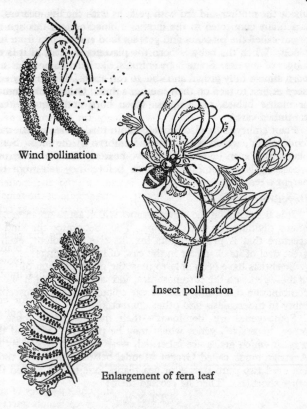

Wind pollination

Insect pollination

Enlargement of fern leaf

ment seems to be organised by cells in the top edge of the infolded gastrula, where later the head appears.

During this development the growing cells of nearly all animals are nourished by means of special food called yolk. They may also be protected by a hard or leathery shell, or by being kept inside the mother for part of their development; or indeed all of it, in the case of live-bearing animals such as guppy fish, some sharks, and grass snakes.

In placental mammals the highest stage of protection of all is reached, for in them the fertilised egg is not merely carried inside the mother and fed with yolk, as with the live-bearers, it is actually connected to the mother's blood system through an organ called the placenta and gets its food and oxygen from her blood. When the baby is born the placenta is shed, as it is no longer of any use. Some baby animals, like baby guinea pigs, are born almost fully grown and able to run about, though they still need at first to feed on their mother's milk. Others, like human or mouse babies, are helpless when born and require long, continued care.

Plant embryos are also provided with food, called in this case 'endosperm', which surrounds the embryo in the seed. Some plants may even be considered live-bearers, like the mangrove whose seeds sprout into seedlings before they fall from the parent tree.

Heredity

It is the genes on the chromosomes which act as organisers of how a dividing egg cell develops. They determine the kind of creature that is produced, its sex, its size, its colour, even a great deal of its character in the case of human beings.

Scientists have been able to map the exact position of many of these genes on the chromosomes, and say exactly which one or combination determines hair or eye colour, freckles or susceptibility to tuberculosis and other characters.

Some genes are 'dominant'—their qualities mask those of other, 'recessive', genes which may be present. This, and the way in which genes are inherited, were first discovered by an Austrian monk called Gregor Mendel between 1856 and 1865. He bred two pure strains of pea-plants, one tall (TT) and the other short (tt). Then he crossed them:

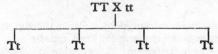

TT X tt

Tt   Tt   Tt   Tt

All the offspring were tall—because, of course, each had one dominant gene for tallness (T) and a recessive gene for shortness (t). Then he self-pollinated the offspring:

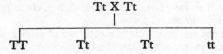

Tt X Tt

TT   Tt   Tt   tt

Three out of four of the third generation were tall, and one, having only recessive genes for shortness (tt), was short. By continued inbreeding he discovered that only one of the three tall plants bred true, that with two genes for tallness (TT), while the others continued to produce tall and short plants in the ratio of 3 to 1.

Mendel's pioneering researches were not appreciated until sixteen years after his death, when, in 1900, they were re-discovered. But since then they have provided the basis for the whole science of *Genetics*.

Linked Characters and New Characters

When characters are carried by genes on the same chromo-somes they are inherited together, and they are said to be 'linked'. A good example of linked characters are those carried by the sex-chromosomes, which are called the X and Y chromo-somes. Most females have two X chromosomes, most males an X and a Y (therefore it is the male which determines the sex of the offspring). The bodily qualities we associate with sex, such as the lion's mane, the cock's comb, are carried on the sex chromosomes, and are very constant, because these two chromo-somes are so unlike each other that there is little possibility of their inter-changing parts. But in the other chromosome pairs this does happen. It produces new combinations of qualities. If they are different enough from the normal they are called 'variations', and they may be very important, because sometimes they give an animal or plant a better chance of surviving than its fellows. When this animal or plant breeds, its offspring may inherit the variation, and also be more successful. By the accumulation of such successful variations new kinds of animals and plants come into existence.

Sometimes a totally unexpected variation occurs—because a completely new gene has suddenly appeared. When this happens it is called a 'mutation'. We know that X-rays can cause a mutation, but nobody is quite sure what causes them in nature. They are also a way in which new kinds of living things come into existence.

THE HISTORY OF LIFE ON EARTH

Fossils

If an animal dies and sinks to the bottom of a pond or stream or the sea it may rapidly get covered with mud or sand or other remains of animals or plants. In this way it or its shape may be preserved. It may decay, in which case only its skeleton is left, or it may be flattened under the pressure of the sediments accumulating above. Or it may be dissolved away, and its place taken by fine particles filtering into the mould. In this way, over a period of years, a fossil is formed. Some fossils are quite new. We can find fossil plants and animals only a few years old by digging below the surface of a peat bog. But once a fossil has been formed and is embedded deep in the rock, with luck it may survive for thousands and millions of years until erosion or digging bring it to the surface or geological changes destroy or alter it.

For centuries fossils have puzzled men. One can find fossil fish on the tops of mountains, fossil sea-shells embedded in the rocks of cliffs far inland. How did they get there? These fish and shells must have died at the time that the rocks were being formed, and clearly where these rocks are must have been under water at that time. From the evidence of fossils men began to see that the face of the earth has been constantly changing throughout time. What is more, many of these fossils were remains of creatures no longer existing on earth. Wise men decided that these must have been *Antediluvian monsters*, creatures destroyed by the great Flood of Biblical times. Some may indeed have been destroyed by that flood, but soon it became apparent that very different kinds of fossils were found in different kinds of rocks, so that there must have been not one, but hundreds of Floods.

As *Palaeontology*, the science of fossils, grew in the last century, and with it *geology*, the study of rocks, scientists learned that they could identify sedimentary rocks (i.e. rocks laid down by deposition under water) by the kinds of fossils in them. And they learned that these rocks occupied a definite sequence of positions (one above the other) and therefore of time of laying down. It was found that by studying each layer of rocks, from the first to the last, a history of life on earth could be obtained, showing the different kinds of living things which existed at different periods in the earth's history. From this it was but a short step to trying to date these rocks.

Dating the Rocks

Most fossils are found in sedimentary rocks, that is rocks laid down by the deposition of particles of sand or mud or other substance on the floor of the sea, the bottom of a lake or in a bog. Sometimes well-preserved fossils are found in volcanic and other rocks, but that is rare. In the case of Pompeii we have an entire fossil city, with many of its people, its dogs and cats and houses, all preserved by a smothering blanket of volcanic dust, ash and lava. We know from historical records that these fossils date from the great eruption of Mount Vesuvius in the year A.D. 79.

Where there are no such records dating is more difficult. By comparing the growth rings of trees, which vary in thickness according to the weather of each year, we can make a time scale going back about 3,000 years, and date the year in which the timber of Viking ships or Stone Age houses was felled. In lakes we can count the seasonal deposition layers left by melting snow and ice each spring back to about 15,000 years ago. For periods before that our estimates of age until recently had to be based on calculations of the rate at which particles in a given thickness of rock were deposited or worn away. Nowadays a more accurate method has been found. Because we know how fast radioactive carbon (called carbon 14) decomposes, we can date fossils up to about 30,000 years old by measuring the amount they contain against the amount they would have contained when alive, which is constant. Similarly, we can date rocks by measuring the amount they contain of uranium, which decomposes into lead, and of lead. The oldest rocks so dated are nearly 3,000 million years old.

The Beginning of the World

Scientists believe that the earth was born about 4,500 million years ago. For hundreds of millions of years after that there was no life. Terrible winds swept the bare harsh rocks of the earth's surface, appalling deluges of rain fell, because there was no vegetation cover to soften the sun's rays striking the surface. In the sedimentary rocks laid down during this vast lifeless era (which covered nearly half of the globe's history) we can see the splatter of raindrops, the ripple marks of ancient waves. But there is never any indication that might show the existence of life. Because of this, the rocks of this great region of time are known as 'Azoic' rocks—belonging to the period before there was life.

Life's Origin

About 2,700 million years ago the Archaeozoic Era began, and from then on rocks show traces, very uncertain and slight, of the existence of life, such as graphite deposits which only bacteria could produce. Conditions on the earth then were so different from what we know that it is hard to imagine ourselves back in those times. To give an example, we all know how quickly a dead branch, or a dead animal, disintegrates on the floor of a woodland. In a short while there is nothing left of it, though the mould beneath the spot has certainly been made richer. This disintegration and disappearance is caused by hundreds of tiny creatures, insects, mites, worms, bacteria, fungi.

Any rich organic matter is quickly broken down by these organisms into food for themselves and into salts and water. In those ancient times none of these organisms existed—so any rich organic matter that may have been formed by chemical interaction under the heat of the sun or the action of cosmic rays would remain undecomposed. Scientists believe that, because of this, chemical combinations were possible then in nature which never occur now only because the different stages towards them would soon be decomposed. Slowly, over the ages, a rich organic 'soup' was able then to develop on the earth, and when a certain size and complexity of chemical compound was reached, 'life' was one of its properties. The earliest of these living chemicals must have been very much like the viruses we know today—and which today are found only as parasites living in other living creatures. But these same viruses can be obtained in pure chemical form as crystals. They form the link between the living and the non-living.

From the 'virus' stage the next jump was to an organism like a great clump of viruses—the kind of organism that we know as bacteria. But these bacteria, like bacteria today, as they multiplied, would soon destroy the organic soup that has brought life into being. And so very early bacteria must have evolved which could manufacture their own food from simple ingredients like different salts and gases and water. By splitting different salts, or from the chemical reactions they set going, they obtained energy to do this. Bacteria of this type still exist today, and huge deposits of iron-ore indicate that such bacteria lived on earth long before there were other higher types of life.

Life Proliferates

The first few steps of life's progress took vast ages of time. Then a series of important stages were passed, and the process accelerated. Certain bacteria must have developed pigments with which they could absorb and use the energy of sunshine, using it to build up food from simple chemicals as plants do today. Similar bacteria, called purple bacteria, can be found alive today, while in the next group up from the bacteria, the flagellates, we find chlorophyll, the green pigment of most plants.

Flagellates are much bigger than bacteria, and they have one or more little whip-like processes with which they lash their way through the water. Among the flagellates we find kinds which make their own food, like plants. Other kinds decompose organic matter, like fungi, while yet others swallow their prey whole, like animals. They are a group in which life performed a whole series of experiments. All these kinds may be closely related to each other; so it is impossible to call them either plants or animals. They form a stage of life before plants and animals were clearly separated from each other. But we believe that both plants and animals are descended from flagellates. Indeed, we can find evidence of this in our own bodies, for human sperms, or male sex cells, still swim by means of long whip-like flagella, exactly as some flagellates do.

Through the vast Archaeozoic and Proterozoic Eras, some 2,200 million years long, a great development of living forms was taking place, though the traces of it which have come down to us are scanty. In the earliest of these rocks we find only traces of bacteria. Later appear various seaweeds, jelly-fish-like animals, simple worms. By the end of the age most of the main groups of backboneless animals, or Invertebrates, have appeared.

The Great Ages of Life

Suddenly, some 520 million years ago, in the rocks of the Cambrian period, appear the first signs of truly abundant life— Trilobites, Belemnites, Brachiopods, among creatures no longer found on earth, Sea-lilies among those we still have with us. In the succeeding eras, until the present day, life has continued to proliferate. From the sea, life moved on to land—first plants, like the simple, branching Psilophyton, and a few scorpions. Meanwhile in the water the first vertebrates had appeared—fish and fish-like animals with backbones, with highly developed nervous systems, with the potentiality of vast development in their make-up. Then they too began to colonise the land. Heavy sprawling creatures they must have been, with paddle-like fins that could scarcely be called limbs, and lungs improvised from stabilising swim-bladders. From the time of the appearance of land vertebrates, the history of life on earth is their story. In succeeding ages, among the great coal forests of the Carboniferous age, the dry deserts of the Permian, the grasslands of the Oligocene, amphibians, vast reptiles and mammals in turn flourished. Ferns, horsetails, club-mosses took turns in dominating the world's vegetation, and were finally all but replaced by the flowering plants and the conifers. Each new form of life was more successful than the preceding, because it was better adapted for survival. And all this time great climatic changes were taking place on earth, mountains were being built and then eroded away, seas filled and raised up, continents and islands appearing and disappearing.

The following table provides a summary of the chief events of earth history since the beginning of the world:

TABLE OF EARTH HISTORY
ERA AND AGE

Azoic Era

4,500–2,700 million years ago.
From the beginning of the world: rocks show no indications of the existence of life.

Archaeozoic Era

2,700–1,500 million years ago.
First signs of life (indications of bacteria and algae).

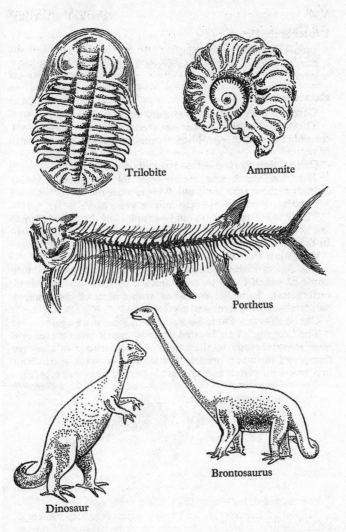

Trilobite

Ammonite

Portheus

Dinosaur

Brontosaurus

Proterozoic Era

1500–520 million years ago.

Rare remains of bacteria, sea weeds, sponges, jelly-fish, simple worms.

Palaeozoic Era

Cambrian Period—520–420 million years ago.

The first abundant fossils: seaweeds, jellyfish, sponges, sea cucumbers, starfish, sea-lilies, worms, molluscs, brachiopods, trilobites.

Ordovician Period—420–350 million years ago.

The first vertebrates appear—heavily armoured fish-like animals without true jaws, called Ostracoderms.

Silurian Period—350–320 million years ago.

The first life appears on land—simple, fork-branched plants, and scorpions. The first true fish, called Placoderms, appear. In the sea giant water scorpions (Eurypterids) grow 9 ft. long.

Devonian Period—320–275 million years ago.

The Age of Fishes: sharks, bony fish, and paddle-finned fish (some of which begin to crawl out on to land—the first land vertebrates). Land life flourishes, with forests of giant horse-tails, club-mosses, ferns and seed ferns.

Carboniferous Period—275–220 million years ago.

The Coal Age. Vast forested swamps, even in what are today's polar regions, produced thick beds of fossil wood (coal). Insects flourished, including dragon flies with 2¼-ft. wing-span. The first true land vertebrates appeared—amphibians and reptiles.

Pterodactyl

Permian Period—220–195 million years ago.

Trilobites, Eurypterids and many primitive, 'experimental' kinds of animals, such as the early amphibians, die out during drastic climatic changes, mountain-building cycles, etc. Reptiles flourish.

Mesozoic Era—The Age of Reptiles

Triassic Period—195–170 million years ago.

Reptiles dominate the earth. Some forms (such as the first crocodiles) take to living in the water. The first warm-blooded animals (mammals) appear.

Jurassic Period—170–140 million years ago.

Reptiles small and large swarm over the land (Diplodocus 100 ft. long, Brontosaurus, Tyrannosaurus and others), in the sea (Plesiosaurs 40 ft. long, Ichthyosaurs, Mosasaurs), and even in the air (Pterodactyls). The first flowering plants and the first birds appear, and many kinds of insects, including flies and termites.

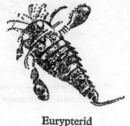

Eurypterid

Psilophyton

Cretaceous Period—140–70 million years ago.

Chalk, composed of lime deposited by or from the skeletons of minute plants and animals and accumulating at about 1 in. in 2,500 years, is laid down in 1,000-ft. thick beds in the warm shallow seas of this era. On land, flowering plants flourish, dominating the vegetation. Mysteriously, for no known reason, towards the end of the epoch many kinds of animals, including all the great reptiles, die out, leaving mammals and birds dominating the land, and fish again in the sea.

Cenozoic Era—The Age of Mammals

Tertiary Period—which breaks down into:
Eocene Epoch—70–50 million years ago.
Oligocene Epoch—50–35 million years ago.
Miocene Epoch—35–15 million years ago.
Pliocene Epoch—15–1 million years ago.

Giant horsetail with car-
boniferous ferns at base
of tree

Carboniferous ferns (horse-
tails and clubmosses)

Such mountain ranges as the Himalayas, the Alps, the Rockies, and the Andes arose during this era and the climate changed repeatedly, getting drier during the Oligocene, when grassland replaced large areas of forest. By the end of this era the world of living things that we know today had come into being, and many of the fish, insects, reptiles, molluscs and plants are identical. This was the era when the mammals and birds evolved fastest, many kinds appearing, dying out and being replaced by more successful types. (A good example is the evolution of the horse.)

Quaternary Period—the Age of Man

Pleistocene Epoch—1 million years ago to 25,000 years ago.

The great Ice Age. Four times during this period great ice-sheets up to 10,000 ft. thick advanced from the polar regions, covering much of Europe, Asia and North America, then re-treated again, giving warm 'interglacial' periods. During this period men first appeared, of several different species, but all of very primitive Stone Age or pre-Stone Age culture.

Holocene Epoch—25,000 years ago to the present day.

Only one species of man survives. He evolves rapidly in material culture, through ability to accumulate experience, from the Stone Age to the age of the Atom, controlling and altering the face of much of the earth, during the warm climate of this period (which may, in fact, be only an 'interglacial' period, to be followed by another ice-age).

Evolution

The different periods of geological history, and the different creatures to be found in their rocks, show plainly enough that life has changed through the ages. We can even find complete series showing how the horse, for example, evolved from an animal the size of a small dog.

The evidence of the rocks is not the only evidence we have for evolution. At an early stage in its development a human embryo can scarcely be distinguished from that of a fish or a tortoise. What is more, it even has gill slits, like those of certain fish. The process whereby animals repeat the earlier stages of their evolution during their development is called *recapitulation*. Then

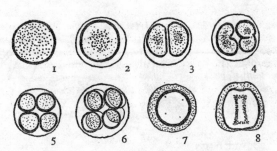

DEVELOPMENT OF SEA URCHIN AS TYPICAL OF ANIMAL
DEVELOPMENT

1. Unfertilized egg
2. Fertilized egg
3. Two-celled stage
4. Two cells, each divide
5. Four-celled stage
6. Eight-celled stage
7. Blastula—hollow ball
8. Gastrula—two layers

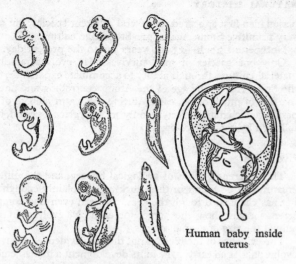

Human baby inside
uterus

COMPARISON OF EMBRYOS OF
HUMAN, TORTOISE AND FISH
Top: early stages. Centre: middle
stage. Bottom: late stage

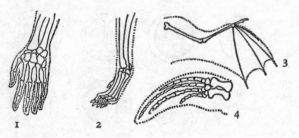

HOMOLOGIES

1. Man's hand
2. Dog's foot
3. Bat's wing
4. Whale's flipper

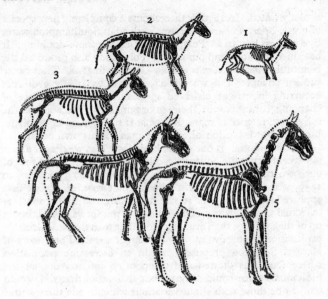

EVOLUTION OF THE HORSE

1. Eohippus (Eocene)
2. Mesohippus (Oligocene)
3. Merychippus (Miocene)
4. Pliohippus (Pliocene)
5. Equus (Pleistocene)

there is the evidence provided by examining anatomy. The appendix is a useless vestige of an organ in human beings, and we are scarcely aware of it until we get appendicitis. There seems little reason why we should have it unless it was once useful, as it is in many other creatures. Again we can find what are known as 'homologies' between apparently different structures—a bat's wing, a man's hand, a cat's foot, a whale's flipper, all contain bones which are manifestly the same, and show how the same structure has evolved for different uses. The geographical distribution of animals and plants can often not be explained unless we understand how they have evolved. And finally there is evolution going on all around us, which we can actually watch. In 1870 or thereabouts a completely new species of grass, *Spartina townsendii*, was evolved in Southampton water by a process known as 'Polyploidy' or chromosome-doubling. It has since spread round our coasts. Polyploidy also produced the beautiful *Primula kewensis* at Kew Gardens in 1898. These were sudden changes; but we can also find slow, steady evolution occurring in various observed species, under the influence of changing conditions in their environment, or because of the active interference of man. For what is stock breeding or plant-breeding but evolution directed by man for his own ends?

Today evolution is one of the basic facts that we accept about our world—that life on it is steadily changing, just as the face of our own countryside is changing. But only 100 years ago, in 1859, when Charles Darwin's book *The Origin of Species* first appeared, it was an idea so radical as to cause the fiercest intellectual war in history. Darwin's book put forward a summing up of the evidence then available, together with the first plausible explanation of how evolution was brought about. This theory of Natural Selection proposed that in an increasing population where food was limited and competition intense, not all the individuals born could survive, but that those that did would tend to be those with slight variations which made them better adapted than their fellows. With the amplifications that our modern knowledge of the science of Heredity has brought about, this theory stands today.

THE KINDS OF LIVING THINGS

Classification

From the earliest times men have given names to the animals and plants around them. These names helped men to distinguish one kind of thing from another, and also its properties and uses.

As civilisation advanced, as the world was explored, the mass of known plants and animals grew and grew, far beyond the bounds of simple comprehension. It was a Swede, Carl Linné, or Linnaeus (1707–78), who eventually devised the system of classification from which our modern methods are derived. He gave each separate organism two Latin names, the first or generic name to show what *kind* of creature it was, the second or *specific* name to show its exact *species*. Thus the tiger and the domestic cat are both kinds of cat. They are both therefore in the genus *Felis*. The tiger is *Felis tigris*, while the domestic cat is *F. domesticus*. The lion is also a kind of cat, but it is distinct enough to be separated a little more widely, and it is put into the genus *Panthera*, while the ocelot is similarly put in a separate genus, *Leopardus*. However, animals of the genus *Panthera* and the genus *Jaguar* are obviously closely similar to those of the genus *Felis*, so they are all grouped together in the cat *family*, the *Felidae*. Families in turn are grouped into *orders*, orders into *Classes*, classes into *Phyla* and phyla into *Kingdoms*. In this scheme our various cats are placed as follows:

Kingdom	Animalia		
Sub-kingdom	Metazoa		
Phylum (or division)	Chordata		
Sub-Phylum	Vertebrata		
Class	Mammalia		
Order	Carnivora		
Family	Felidae		
Genus	*Felis*	*Panthera*	*Leopardus*
Species	*F. tigris*	*P. Leo*	*L. pardalis*
	F. domesticus		(ocelot)
	(common cat)		

At first classification was merely a means of describing, identifying and labelling. But gradually it has come to be an attempt to show also the relationships between living things in the great scheme of evolution. But so many links in the chains of descent are missing that our attempts at such a truly 'natural' classification will probably never be final—they will change as each new discovery alters the picture.

A scheme showing the relationships between the different groups of living things would be as follows:

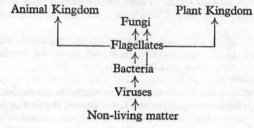

Viruses

The smallest, simplest of all living things, found only as parasites inside living tissue. Each virus particle is a single huge molecule of a highly complicated chemical substance belonging to the class of nucleo-proteins, and some viruses have been

VIRUS DISEASE

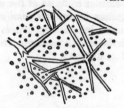

Rod shape crystals of
tobacco mosaic virus
(× 43,200)

As virus affects young
tobacco seedling leaves
become mottled and
deformed

prepared in pure chemical form as crystals. Yet, introduced into the appropriate living tissue, these crystals thrive and reproduce. Viruses stand half-way between the world of living and non-living matter, and scientists believe that the earliest forms of life must have been similar to viruses. Because viruses feed on the tissue of living creatures and sometimes produce poisonous waste products, they often cause serious diseases, such as small-pox, infantile paralysis, measles, chicken pox and various plant diseases, such as tobacco mosaic.

Bacteria

The smallest of all living things apart from viruses, the smallest being about $\frac{1}{2500}$ mm. long. Bacteria are notorious because some of them are parasites and cause diseases such as tuberculosis, pneumonia or typhoid, but there are many kinds very useful to man—indeed, it is doubtful if human life could exist without

BACTERIA

Nitrosomonas, showing flag-ella   Anthrax bacillus rods   Cholera spirals   Filaments

them. Some of the most important are the soil bacteria, which cause decay of plant and animal material, releasing food sub-stances for the use of plants, and the nitrogen-fixing bacteria, which enrich the soil with nitrogen compounds. Bacteria are mostly classified by their shape—rods, spirals, spheres, filaments, etc. A more natural classification might be by the way in which they obtain their food, some being even capable of photo-synthesis similar to that of plants.

Flagellata

A huge group of one-celled organisms without cell-walls, which propel themselves by lashing the water with one or more whip-like *flagella*. Much larger than the largest bacteria, in this group are forms which feed as animals, swallowing and digesting their prey; as plants, manufacturing sugars as they swim in the sunshine; and as fungi, causing decomposition and absorbing the juices produced. Many plants, animals and fungi have a 'flagellate' stage in their life history. It is best to regard the

Euglena

flagellates as a stage in evolution before the distinction between these three groups was clear, and from which they have in fact evolved. Common kinds: *Euglena*.

Plant Kingdom

Living things that make their food from simple inorganic substances, using the energy of sunlight. The cells are surrounded by a cellulose cell wall as well as a membrane. The body parts are not fixed in number in the higher forms.

Division 1—Algae Seaweeds and pond scums. Plants with one or many cells. In some seaweeds they may be organised into a body as much as 200 ft. long, which, however, has no division into true roots, stems or leaves, as in higher plants. Reproduction is by fragmentation, spores, or male and female cells.

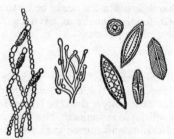

ALGAE

From *l* to *r*: Cyanophyta (blue green), **Chrysophyta** or diatoms
Phaeophyta

Class 1 Cyanophyta or blue-green algae. Microscopic one-celled or filamentous plants with a blue pigment as well as green chlorophyll dissolved in the sap. Found in ponds and on damp paths.

Class 2 Chrysophyta or diatoms. Chiefly single-celled, with a pill box-like case of silica, and yellowy-green pigments. Form yellowy scum on exposed mud-flats, etc. Chiefly they are plankton, floating near the surface of the sea, where they form one of the most important foods for larger creatures.

Class 3 Chlorophyta or green algae. Chiefly fresh-water pond-scums, etc. Bright green in colour, with chlorophyll as their only pigment, and starch as their food reserve. Their sex cells have two or four flagella. They are the group from which higher plants seem to have evolved.

From *l* to *r*: Chlorophyta (green algae), Geratium (yellow brown algae), Rhodophyta (red algae)

Class 4 Phaeophyta or brown algae. The common brown sea-weeds of the seashore, kelps, wracks, etc. They have a brown pigment as well as chlorophyll, and often a complicated life history, in which generations with a single set of chromosomes alternate with generations in which the cells have a double set.

Class 5 Pyrrophyta or yellow-brown algae. Mostly one-celled plants with a cell wall composed of jointed plates, and two flagella of unequal length. The chief group, the Dinoflagellates, are important floating or plankton plants.

Class 6 Rhodophyta or red algae. Red seaweeds, chiefly marine, with a red and a blue pigment as well as chlorophyll. Some live in deep water down to 200 ft. They have no free-swimming stages in their life-cycles.

Division 2—Bryophyta Mosses and liverworts. Land and fresh-water plants with many-celled bodies consisting of a flat, branching 'thallus' with 'rhizoids' instead of true roots. These plants have a life cycle in which there is an 'alternation of generations': the main plant, called the gametophyte, has a single set of chromosomes, and produces the sex cells, consisting of an egg cell in a flask-shaped organ called an archegonium, and sperm cells. The fertilised egg cell develops into the sporophyte generation, in which the cells contain a double set of chromosomes, and which lives parasitically on the gametophyte. In mosses one can see the sporophyte as a little

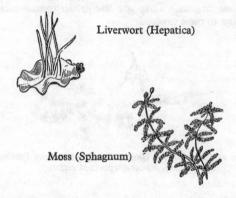

Liverwort (Hepatica)

Moss (Sphagnum)

long-stemmed capsule rising from the tips of the moss plants. The sporophyte produces spores by means of a cell division, which reduces the number of chromosomes to a single set, and these spores in turn develop into gametophytes.

Class 1 Hepaticae—liverworts, hornworts. Plants consist of a flat, branching thallus prostrate on damp ground or floating, or of a simple stem with midribless leaves. The spore capsules have organs called elaters, which twist and bend when wet and eject the spores.

Class 2 Musci—mosses. Small plants growing in damp places or in fresh water. They have stems bearing spirals of small midribbed leaves, and are anchored by water-absorbing 'rhizoids' at the base. Their spores germinate first into a *protonema*, from which develop the gametophytes.

PTERIDOPHYTA

From *l* to *r*: Psilotum, Lycopsida, Sphenopsida Equisetum, Filices

Division 3—Pteridophyta Fern-like plants. Land plants in which the chief generation, the sporophyte, with a double set of chromosomes, has true roots (except in Class 1), stems with a conducting system and leaves, and produces spores from which the small gametophyte generation grows. This in turn produces sex cells which fuse and grow into new sporophytes.

Class 1 Psilopsida. Plants with a creeping stem, small, scale-like leaves and no true roots. The two living kinds, *Psilotum* and *Tmesipteris*, are small branching plants growing in rich soil or hanging from trees, and found only in warm climates. They are especially interesting because they are closely related to the earliest known land plants, such as *Psilophyton*.

Class 2 Lycopsida. Plants with roots, stems clothed with small leaves in spirals, and cone-like reproductive organs at the branch tips. Some kinds were giant trees in the Coal Age. To-day they are all small herbs. *Isoetes*, the quill-wort, *Lycopodium*, the club-moss, and *Selaginella* are all found wild in Britain.

Class 3 Sphenopsida. Plants with roots, ribbed, jointed stems bearing whorls of leaves and cone-like reproductive organs on stalks at the top of the shoot. Some kinds, like the *Calamites*, were enormous trees in Coal Age times. *Equisetum*, the horse-tail, is found wild in Britain.

Class 4 Filicales—the ferns. Plants with roots and stems bearing large leaves, on the undersides of which the repro-ductive sporangia are formed. Some, like *Cyathea*, the tree fern, grow as big as small trees. Others are extremely small. *Osmunda*, *Hymenophyllum*, *Polypodium*, *Dryopteris* and many other kinds are all found in Britain.

GYMNOSPERM
Cedar

Division 4—Gymnospermae Plants producing naked ovules and seeds that have a single seed coat, usually in cones. Mostly trees, with well-developed wood and vascular system, many of them produce abundant resin. The gametophyte generation is reduced to a few cells in the pollen and perhaps some in the seed.

Class 1 Cycadeles. Plants with large, fern-like leaves usually, and usually separate male and female plants. The male sex cells are free-swimming; the cycads have spirals of huge palm-like leaves, and big central cones. They are widespread in the tropics, and sago is made from the pith of one kind. Of the other plants in this group, the Ginkgo is a large tree from western China, where it is almost extinct in the wild state, and the seed ferns are completely extinct.

Class 2 Coniferales. Conifer trees, with spreading branches, needle-shaped leaves, non-swimming male cells, and male and female cones on the same tree. This class includes all the firs, pines, larches, yews, junipers, etc., of cool forests.

Class 3 Gnetales. Three very dissimilar genera with opposite leaves and vessels in their wood, unlike all the other Gymno-sperms. Their ovules are borne in flower-like structures, not in cones. *Gnetum* is a tropical climbing plant, *Ephedra* is a small shrubby scaly-leaved plant found in warm countries, and *Welwitschia* is a peculiar-looking plant with long, strap-like leaves found only in a tiny area in the desert of South-West Africa.

Division 5—Angiospermae—Flowering plants. Plants with flowers, in which the ovule is enclosed in an ovary, and the seed has two seed-coats. There are conducting vessels, and the gametophyte generation has almost entirely vanished. The most abundant of all plants on land.

Poppy
(dicotyledon)

Iris
(mono-
cotyledon)

ANGIOSPERMS

FLOWER PARTS

1. Receptacle
2. Petal
3. Sepal
4. Stamen
5. Pistil
6. Stigma
7. Style
8. Ovary

Class 1 Monocotyledons. Plants characterised by the presence of only one cotyledon (seed-leaf) in their embryos. The leaves are parallel-veined and almost always have entire margins. The flower parts (sepals, petals, stamens and carpels) are always in three or a multiple of three. The sepals are often petal-like. The vascular system is in bundles scattered irregularly through the stem, so there is no secondary thickening as there is in the Dicotyledons. There are about 50,000 species of Monocotyledons, most of them herbs, divided into 11 orders. These orders include the bamboos, the bananas, the palms and the grasses, all families of great economic importance. They also include the

Liliaceae (the Lily family)
Amaryllidaceae (the Daffodil family)
Iridaceae (the Iris family)
Orchidaceae (the Orchid family)

which are of great importance to the gardener.

Class 2 Dicotyledons. Annual, biennal, ephemeral or perennial plants characterised by the presence of two cotyledons (seed-leaves) in their embryos. The leaves are net-veined, usually narrow at the base, and may be stalked or sessile. The flowers are sometimes composed of whorls with an indefinite number of segments, but most are either *pentamerous* (five, or a multiple of five, members to each whorl) or *tetramerous* (four, or a multiple of four, members to each whorl). The vascular system forms a ring round the stem. Perennials often take the form of shrubs or trees, and many are large trees. There are over 200,000 species of Dicotyledons. These fall into two groups—those with their petals separate (*polypetalous*) and those with their petals joined (*gamopetalous*)—and are divided into 44 orders.

It would be confusing and meaningless simply to list all 44 orders here. A study of plant classification cannot be made from a book alone. For the beginner the only way is to go into the countryside and examine the plants growing in their habitats. This cannot usefully be done without a guide and the best guide is a good Flora. The best Floras list all the most familiar, and many of the unfamiliar, plants classified in their orders, families, genera and species. Most elementary Floras ignore orders and begin with families, and these are more useful to the beginner. However, the following are some of the more important orders:

Ranales. Buttercup, magnolia, marsh marigold, laurel, tulip tree, etc.

Rosales. Rose, strawberry, blackberry, apple, cherry, pea, saxifrage, plane tree, etc.

Papaverales. Poppy, the cabbage family, mustard, mignonette, bleeding heart, etc.

Geraniales. Geranium, flax, nasturtium, the citrus family, rubber, etc.

Umbellales. English ivy, the carrot family, celery, cow-parsley, dogwood, etc.

Rubiales. Honeysuckle, teasel, madder, bedstraw, coffee, etc.

Campanulales. Bellflowers, the daisy family, lobelia, etc.

Caryophyllales. Pink, thrift, sea lavender, buckwheat, spinach, etc.

Ericales. Heath, heather, rhododendron, azalea, blueberry, etc.

Gentianales. Gentian, buddleia, olive, privet, ash, etc.

Polemoniales. Potato, forget-me-not, tobacco, phlox, petunia, etc.

Lamiales. Salvia, verbena, mint, teak, etc.

Scrophulariales. Snapdragon, gloxinia, mimulus, bladder-wort, acanthus, etc.

Fagales. Oak, beech, sweet chestnut.

Fungus Kingdom

Living things which obtain their food saprophytically, by decomposing organic matter and absorbing the resulting juices, or as parasites. Their bodies are usually built up of thread-like strands called hyphae, with many nuclei in the protoplasm between cross walls. They store their food as glycogen, like animals, not starch, as in plants. They reproduce by spores, or sexually.

Fungus Agaricus

Enlarged section of mushroom gill, showing basidia and two basidiospores

Division 1—Mycetezoa Slime moulds. Fungi in which the body is a naked mass of creeping protoplasm, except during the formation of spores, which have cellulose walls. Movement and feeding are by flowing protrusions of the protoplasm.

Class 1 Myxomycetes. Free-living forms, the protoplasm of which contains many nuclei, and which develop clearly defined fruiting bodies. *Physarum, Didymium, Stemonitis* are all common on the floors of damp woods.

Class 2 Phytomyxinae. Parasitic forms, living inside the tissues of plants. In reproduction the protoplasm simply divides up into a mass of spores, without any definite fruiting body.

Plasmodiophora causes the disease of cabbages known as 'club-root'.

Class 3 Acrasiales. Free-living forms, the protoplasm of which is actually an aggregate of many small individual organisms, each with its own nucleus. Reproduction is by a co-operative effort resulting in clearly defined fruit bodies. *Dictyostelium* is a common soil organism.

Division 2—Eumycota Fungi in which the body is a mass of thread-like strands called 'hyphae', with cell walls made of cellulose or chitin, and numerous nuclei between cross walls, where these are present.

Class 1 Phycomycetes—moulds. Simple fungi, some terrestrial, some parasitic, some living in fresh water. The hyphae usually have no cross walls. *Rhizopus* is the common black mould of stale bread, with spherical sporangia. *Saprolegnia* is the mould that covers dead insects in water.

Class 2 Ascomycetes. Mostly terrestrial fungi in which there is a characteristic club-shaped reproductive body called an 'ascus', typically with eight spores. Yeasts, truffles, morels, ergot, *Penicillium* (from which the important drug penicillin is derived) are all Ascomycetes.

Class 3 Basidiomycetes—Mushrooms, Puffballs, Rusts, Smuts, etc. Terrestrial and parasitic fungi in which the characteristic reproductive organ is called a 'basidium', and carries usually four spores, each on a stalk. *Agaricus campestris* is the common edible mushroom.

Class 4 Fungi Imperfecti. A provisional grouping of many fungi the typical reproductive bodies of which have never been seen—and which in some cases may even have lost the ability to produce typical reproductive bodies. 'Athletes' foot' is caused by one of these fungi.

Division 3—Lichenes These lichens are combinations between fungi and plants (algae). The fungus is usually an Ascomycete, though it is sometimes a Basidiomycete. It forms the main body of the lichen, anchors it to the ground, rock, tree-trunk or wherever it is growing, and absorbs and provides water to the algal cells, which manufacture food in the typical manner of plants, using the energy of sunlight, and pass some of this food back to the fungus. Every species of lichen contains exactly the same combination of fungus and algae. All the algae involved are known to be capable of living independently, but none of the fungi is. This alone indicates that the relationship is more favourable to the fungus than to the plant. When the fungus reproduces, its spores send out hyphae. These die if they do not chance upon cells of the right algae. When they do, a new lichen begins to develop.

Animal Kingdom

Living things that eat ready-made food. Their cells are enclosed in a membrane, and have no cell wall. The higher forms have a definite number of body parts. Typically they move about from place to place, or move their 'limbs' by muscle power, to obtain their food.

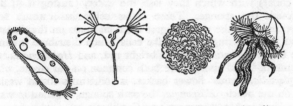

From *l* to *r*: Paramecium, Suctoria, Empongia, Aurelia

Subkingdom Protozoa—Single-celled animals

Phylum—Protozoa Microscopic one-celled animals. Their bodies have specialised parts, called 'organelles', equivalent to the organs of larger animals. They are found wherever there is moisture.

Class 1 Sarcodina—the amoebas. Free-living and parasitic animals which move and catch their food by pushing out their protoplasm into 'pseudopodia'. Some have shells, others skeletons. Includes the sun-animalcules, the radiolarians and the foraminifera.

Class 2 Sporozoa. Parasitic animals with complicated life histories. *Plasmodium* is the cause of malaria.

Class 3 Ciliata. The most complex of all one-celled animals, with highly organised systems of organelles for locomotion (waving hair-like cilia covering the body), excretion, contraction, control, feeding, etc. They usually have two nuclei. paramecium is common in infusions of hay.

Class 4 Suctoria. Protozoans which live fixed to one spot, capturing their prey by means of tentacles. They have free-swimming larvae which move by means of cilia. Some are parasites.

Subkingdom—Metazoa—Many-celled animals with at least two layers of unlike cells which may lose their boundaries in the adult state.

Phylum—Porifera Sponges. Sessile aquatic animals with two layers of cells, a skeleton and a system of pores, chambers and canals running through their bodies. These are lined with 'collar cells'—cells with a flagellum (surrounded by a sort of collar) with which they lash the water, causing it to flow through the sponge. These collar cells also capture food particles from the water, digest them and pass on the digested food to wandering amoeba-like cells which distribute it round the body. *Grantia*, which is bright red, and *Halichondria*, the crumb-of-bread sponge, are both common on our coasts, while *Euplectella*, Venus' flower basket, is sometimes found washed up on the beach. *Euspongia*, the bath sponge, is found in warm seas like the Mediterranean and Caribbean.

Phylum—Cnidaria Animals with two layers of cells, an internal, digestive layer reached through the central mouth, and an outer layer. Their tissues include a network of nerves, and special stinging cells. Most coelenterates are marine. They exist in two forms—a fixed or 'polyp' form and a free-swimming or 'medusa' (jelly-fish-like) form. To this phylum belong the jellyfish, such as the common jellyfish *Aurelia aurita* of our coastal waters, the sea anemones, sea ferns and corals, and the common fresh-water *Hydra*. Some kinds have a life-cycle in which both polyp and medusa stages alternate.

Phylum—Ctenophora The comb jellies. Marine animals which differ from the Coelenterates in having no stinging cells, and often in being 'two-sided' or bilaterally symmetrical. Some, like *Pleurobrachia*, the common sea gooseberry, have sticky tentacles; others, like *Beröe*, have not. All have eight plates of waving cilia with which they propel themselves and keep afloat.

Ctenophora

Trematoda fluke

Phylum—Platyhelminthes Flatworms. These are flat, bilaterally symmetrical animals with three layers of cells. They have no body cavity, no skeleton, no anus, no circulatory system. They live in the sea, fresh water, damp places and as parasites. They include *Planaria* worms, *Convoluta roscoffensis*, which lives on the food provided by algae embedded in its skin, and in return protects them (it is found along our southern coast) and many forms which cause dangerous diseases. The flukes are parasitic flatworms with complicated life histories. The Chinese liver fluke passes its larval stages first inside a water snail and then inside a fish, and when the fish is eaten the adult stage develops inside the human liver. *Bilharzia* is another important disease caused by a fluke. Tape-worms, which grow up to many yards in length, are also flatworms. They have segmented bodies and are parasites in the intestines of animals, including human beings. They also often have complicated life histories, with several 'hosts'.

Phylum—Nemertina Ribbon worms. These are mostly free-living worms found under stones on the seashore. They have an anus and a circulatory system, and capture their prey by throwing out a long muscular proboscis. *Lineus*, the bootlace worm, is common in Britain.

Phylum—Aschelminthes Small worm-like animals with a primitive form of 'coelom', or body cavity, and a tough outer skin or 'cuticle'. This phylum includes the Nematodes or round-worms, of which there are about half a million kinds, some of them (like the hookworm, *Trichina*, and *Filaria* worms) causing dreadful diseases. It also includes the hairworms and the rotifers, or wheel-animalcules, among many other forms.

Phylum—Acanthocephala Spiny-headed worms with a hooked proboscis and no digestive system, which live entirely as parasites. *Echinorhynchus proteus* lives first as a larva inside a small fresh-water crustacean, then as an adult hanging hooked to the intestines of ducks.

Phylum—Phoronida Tiny, hermaphrodite marine animals living in tubes as adults, and free-swimming as larvae. They and the succeeding phyla possess true body-cavities or 'coeloms'.

Phylum—Polyzoa Moss animals. They are tiny solitary or colonial marine animals, living in the compartments of tubes which they secrete, and capturing their prey by sweeping the water with tentacles: *Plumatella* is the commonest British form, often seen growing on the fronds of seaweeds.

Phylum—Brachiopoda Lamp shells. Marine animals with bivalve shell and sometimes a stalk, feeding by means of a ring of cilia at the mouth. *Terebratula* is a deep-water form found off our coasts. There are very few living examples, but over 30,000 extinct kinds.

Phylum—Annelida Segmented worms. These have their bodies divided into segments, a longitudinal alimentary canal and nerve cord (with an enlarged portion at the front end), and have a closed blood circulation. In this phylum are the:

1. *Polychaeta* Sand worms and lug worms. Marine worms with a distinct head and bristly appendages on each segment, with which they swim or crawl, and some of which live in tubes. Many of these have extraordinary mating habits, like the Palolo worm of the Pacific, whose front end breaks off, swims to the surface of the sea and mates once a year on the last quarter of the October–November moon. *Nereis*, the bristle worm, *Arenicola*, the lug worm, and *Sabella*, the tube-dwelling fan-worm, are British forms of Polychaetes.

2. *Oligochaeta* Comprises the earthworms and potworms like *Lumbricus terrestris*, our common earthworm, and the pond-living Tubifex worm, most of which live by swallowing earth or mud and digesting the organic contents.

3. *Hirudinea* The leeches, parasitic worms that suck blood, attaching themselves to their prey by suckers.

4. *Archiannelida* Small marine worms like simplified polychaetes. *Protodrilus* lives under stones on sandy shores.
   Sipunculoidea, or peanut worms.
   Echiuroidea—sac-shaped marine worms with a long proboscis. Of these *Bonellia* has larvae which develop into

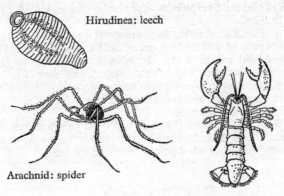

Hirudinea: leech

Arachnid: spider

Crustacea: lobster

tiny parasitic males if they find an adult female. But if they do not, they become females!

Phylum—Arthropoda This consists of animals with segmented bodies, each segment of which typically has a pair of jointed legs. Typically all arthropods have an external skeleton of hard chitin, which they have to burst out of, or 'moult', from time to time in order to grow bigger. They have well-developed sense organs, particularly eyes, and nervous systems, and their body cavity forms an open blood-circulation system.

The Arthropods form the largest Phylum in the animal kingdom in number and variety of forms. They are divided into six classes:

1. *Onychophora* Worm-like animals found in the tropics in damp spots, and considered by many scientists to be intermediate between Arthropods and Annelid worms.

2. *Trilobita* Extinct marine animals with three-lobed bodies. Once the dominant form of life.

3. *Arachnida* A huge group in which the body is divided into two parts, the front part bearing four pairs of legs and two 'Chelicerae', or pincers. This group includes the spiders, mites, ticks, scorpions, the sea-spiders, the 'living fossil' King

crabs and the Eurypterids—giant extinct sea-scorpions, up to 9 ft. long.

4. *Crustacea* Another large group, in which the body bears three pairs of walking legs, one or two pairs of feelers, and has specialised mouth parts. It includes the crabs, lobsters, shrimps, woodlice, water fleas, copepods and barnacles.

5. *Myriapoda* A group with long, many-segmented bodies, each segment of which bears one or two pairs of legs. The millipedes and centipedes.

6. *Insecta* In these the body is divided into three parts—a head, thorax and abdomen—and there are three pairs of legs on the thorax, beside a pair of feelers on the head.

Hymenoptera: Bee

The insects form the largest of all animal groups in number of species, and apart from the mammals on land and the fishes in the sea, are the most successful. Many of them are of the greatest economic importance to man—as pests and disease carriers, on the one hand, but also as killers of pests, pollinators of crops, on the other. The chief subdivisions of insects are as follows:

Subclass 1 Apterygota. Primitive insects without wings, and with 9 pairs of appendages on the abdomen.

> Order Thysanura—Silverfish, small silvery insects living in cracks.
> Order Collembola—Springtails. Small insects with a jumping organ that live in damp leaves.

Subclass 2 Pterygota—insects with wings or vestiges of wings. Some forms go through a complete metamorphosis or radical change of form—from egg to caterpillar, to pupa, to adult—during their life cycles. Others pass more gradually through a series of larval forms, or 'nymphs', each becoming slightly more like the adult.

Order 1. Dictyoptera—Cockroaches and Mantids
    " 2. Phasmida—Stick Insects
    " 3. Saltatoria—Grasshoppers, Crickets
    " 4. Dermaptera—Earwigs
    " 5. Plecoptera—Stoneflies
    " 6. Ephemeroptera—Mayflies
    " 7. Odonata—Dragonflies
    " 8. Isoptera—Termites
    " 9. Psocoptera—Book Lice
    " 10. Mallophaga—Biting Lice, Bird Lice
    " 11. Anoplura—Sucking Lice
    " 12. Hemiptera—Bugs
    " 13. Thysanoptera—Thrips
    " 14. Neuroptera—Lacewing Flies, Ant Lions
    " 15. Trichoptera—Caddis Flies
    " 16. Lepidoptera—Butterflies and Moths
    " 17. Diptera—Flies
    " 18. Siphonaptera—Fleas
    " 19. Hymenoptera—Ants, Bees, Wasps, Sawflies
    " 20. Coleoptera—Beetles

Phylum—Mollusca These are soft-bodied animals covered by a layer, called the 'mantle', which usually secretes a hard lime shell. Most have a muscular locomotory 'foot', and many have a rasping 'tongue'.

There are six classes of molluscs:

1. *Monoplacophora* Extinct except for two deep-sea species.

2. *Amphineura* Chitons. Common animals on sea-shore rocks. Most have an oval, flat body with a shell of eight plates, and are firmly attached by their powerful 'foot'.

3. *Scaphopoda* The tubular-shelled burrowing tusk or tooth shells.

4. *Gastropoda* Crawling or swimming molluscs with a flattened foot, and usually a distinct head with eyes borne on tentacles. One group, the whelks and limpets, have the internal organs twisted spirally through 180°. The sea hares and sea slugs have 'unwound' themselves, and in some cases

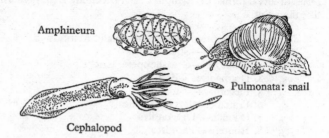

Amphineura

Pulmonata: snail

Cephalopod

have lost their shells. The air-breathing forms may have a shell (snails and some slugs) or none (some slugs).

5. *Lamellibranchiata* Bivalves. Aquatic molluscs with a shell in two hinged parts, enclosing the body, a muscular foot and no head. Some, like the scallops, swim by flapping their shells. Others burrow in sand and mud, like the mussels, or bore through rock or wood, like the shipworm (*Teredo*).

6. *Cephalopoda* Squids, Octopuses. Molluscs in which the foot is modified into several tentacles, equipped with suckers. The eyes have a single large lens, like the eyes of vertebrates, and the brain and nervous system are the best developed among invertebrates. Sometimes they inhabit a coiled shell, as does the nautilus; in cuttle fish the shell, reduced in size, lies inside the body (it is the 'cuttlebone' of bird-cages) and in octopuses there is no shell at all. The great groups of extinct animals called ammonites and belemnites belonged here.

Phylum—Chaetognatha Arrow worms. Small, transparent, dart-shaped animals with paired horizontal fins, common in marine plankton. They feed by means of grasping spines at the head end.

Phylum—Echinodermata These are all marine animals and have radially symmetrical bodies, usually with five arms or sections. They have no head, and possess an internal 'water-vascular' system, a form of organisation found in no other animal group. This is a series of water-filled tubes, extensions of which protrude outside in special grooves, in the form of 'tube-feet'. By adjusting water pressure these tube feet can be made to move, or to grasp by means of suction. Feeding is by

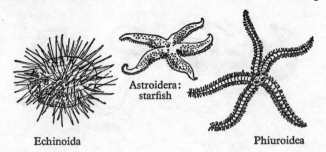

Echinoida   Astroidera: Phiuroidea
        starfish

protruding the stomach over the prey and digesting the prey and absorbing its juices. Most echinoderms have a warty or spiny surface (hence their name) and an internal lime skeleton. There are four extinct classes, and five living. These are:

1. *Crinoidea* Sea Lilies and Feather Stars. Live mostly in deep water. (*Antedon*, the Feather Star, is a common British shallow-water form.)

2. *Holothuroidea* Sea Cucumbers. Leathery and sausage-shaped creatures with a ring of tentacles round the mouth, which vomit up their internal organs when attacked, but soon grow another set. *Cucumaria Elongata* lives in mud, *C. Saxicola* in rocky crevices round the British coast.

3. *Echinoidea* Globular or disc-shaped animals covered with movable spines which are sometimes poisonous. The common sea urchin, *Echinus esculentus*, is abundant on rocky shores, and its curious mouth parts, which are known as Aristotle's Lantern, as well as its shell, may be found on the beach.

4. *Asteroidea* Starfish. Star-shaped animals with five flexible arms (as in our common *Asterias rubens*) or more, as in our sun star (*Solaster Papposus*), which has twelve or fifteen. Starfish are notorious pests of oyster beds, forcing the oysters open by continued slow pressure, and then eating them.

5. *Ophiuroidea* Brittle Stars. Starfish with a round central disc and long, flexible separate arms, not joined at the base. Brittle stars move rapidly by waving their arms, unlike true starfish, which glide on their hundreds of tiny tube-feet. *Ophiothrix fragilis* is a common British species.

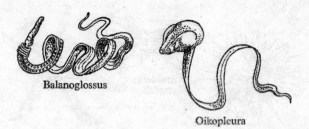

Balanoglossus

Oikopleura

Phylum—Chordata Bilaterally symmetrical animals with a 'notochord' (a primitive kind of skeletal rod), a hollow dorsal nerve cord and gill-slits at some stage of their development. This is the phylum to which the vertebrate animals, including man, belong. The main divisions are:

1. *Hemichordata* Soft-bodied, worm-shaped marine animals burrowing in sand and mud (*Balanoglossus*—the acorn worms) or in colonies of tubes (*Pterobrachia*). They have both dorsal and ventral nerve tissue.

2. *Urochordata* Marine animals enclosed in the adults by a sheath of cellulose, which feed by filtering water. *Oikopleura* is a floating, bulbous animal with a long tail. The sea-squirts, of which there are many British kinds, live fixed to rocks and stones, while the floating barrel-shaped salps often have a complicated life-cycle. All have a free-swimming tadpole-like larva which possesses a notochord, nerve cord and gill slits, although the adults do not.

3. *Cephalochordata* Small fish-like creatures that burrow in sand and filter food from water passing through their gill-slits. *Amphioxus lanceolatus* is found along the British coast.

4. *Vertebrata* These differ from the other chordata in having a skull, a well-developed brain and a skeleton of bone or cartilage. There are eight classes of vertebrates:

Class 1 Agnatha. Jawless vertebrates, fish-like in appearance. The first known vertebrates, called Ostracoderms, belonged to this group. Mostly extinct. The living kinds are the lampreys and hag-fish, which live by sucking the blood of fish. They are found in Britain.

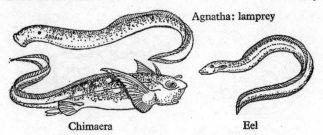

Agnatha: lamprey

Chimaera   Eel

Class 2 Placodermi. Extinct fish-like creatures with jaws, scales and paired fins.

Class 3 Selachii—cartilaginous fishes—the sharks, skates, rays, chimaeras. These have a skeleton of cartilage, their mouths on the undersides of their bodies and breathing holes or 'spiracles'. The males have 'claspers' with which they hold the female when mating. Nearly all are marine.

Class 4 Pisces—the bony fishes. These have bony skeletons, the mouth at the front end and slimy skins which are usually covered with scales. The two chief groups are:

A. *Paddle-finned Fish* Comprising the lung-fish (of which there are three living kinds, in Africa, South America and Australia) and the lobe-finned fish, from one group of which land vertebrates are believed to have evolved (and of which there is only one living example, the Coelacanth).

B. *Ray-finned Fish* Which comprise the primitive sturgeons and gar-pikes and the teleosts, the typical fish of modern times (mackerel, perch, carp, salmon, eel, pike, etc.).

Class 5 Amphibia. Air-breathing land animals with moist skin, four limbs (unless limbless), laying their eggs in water and having a fish-like larval stage (tadpoles). The chief orders include:

A. *Labyrinthodonts* Among these were the largest of all amphibians. Vanished now, they resembled the lobe-

Frog   Tortoise

finned fish, while others were transitional to reptiles, which evolved from them.

B. *Anura* Tail-less amphibians with hind legs adapted for jumping—frogs and toads. In Britain there are two toads—the common toad (not found in Ireland) and the natterjack; and two frogs, the common frog and the edible frog (found only in East Anglia). In warmer climates there is a vast number more, including the tree-frogs and leaf-toads.

C. *Urodela* Newts and salamanders—amphibians with four legs, a long body and a tail. Some live permanently in water, breathing with gills. There are three kinds of newt in Britain: the smooth newt, the crested newt and the palmate newt.

D. *Apoda* Small, limbless, worm-like burrowing amphibians, found in the tropics. Some have scales.

Class 6 Reptilia. Cold-blooded, dry-skinned and usually scaly air-breathing vertebrates, typically with four five-toed legs. Though many have returned to living in water, they are well adapted for life on land. Instead of being dependent on water for breeding, as are amphibians, the eggs are fertilised inside the female and are provided with plentiful yolk and enclosed in a protective skin containing liquid. The chief orders are:

A. *Ichthyopterygia* Ichthyosaurs. Extinct fish-shaped reptiles up to 40 ft. long.

B. *Saureopterygia* Plesiosaurs. Extinct water-dwelling

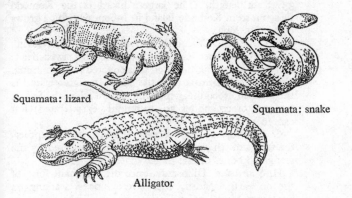

Squamata: lizard

Squamata: snake

Alligator

reptiles with long necks, short tails and paddle-shaped limbs. Up to 50 ft. long.

C. *Rhyncocephalia* Primitive lizard-like reptiles with beaked upper jaws, of which the only living example is the Tuatara of New Zealand.

D. *Chelonia* Turtles and tortoises. Water and land-dwelling animals encased in a hard shell of bone and horn. All lay their eggs on land.

E. *Squamata* Lizards and snakes. Horny-scaled reptiles, the snakes being distinguished by having their jaws joined by an elastic ligament which allows them to be stretched open widely. All snakes except the boas and pythons have lost all trace of limbs. So have certain lizards. This order contains the most widespread, numerous and successful of all living reptiles. In Britain there are three kinds of snake (there are no snakes in Ireland); the adder, the grass snake (not in Scotland) and the smooth snake, found only in the New Forest region. There are also three kinds of lizard: the common lizard, found almost everywhere, the sand lizard, found in Southern England, and the legless 'slow worm', common except in Ireland, where it does not occur. The longest snake is the royal python of Malaya, which grows up to

33 ft. in length. The largest lizard is the Komodo Dragon, from Komodo Island in Indonesia, which grows up to 7 ft. long.

F. *Crocodilia* Crocodiles and alligators. Water-loving reptiles with short legs, elongated, heavily jawed heads and long, powerful, flattened tails adapted for swimming. Confined to warm parts of the earth, the largest kind is the orinoco crocodile, which may attain a length of 23 ft. Lengths of crocodiles are commonly exaggerated; few exceed 15 ft.

G. *Pterosauria* Pterodactyls. Extinct flying reptiles, the wings of which were webs of skin supported by the elongated bones of one finger.

H. *Saurischia* Dinosaurs, once the dominant form of life on earth. Mostly these were bipeds, walking on enormous hind legs and using the fore limbs as hands. Brachiosaurus, the biggest, was 75 ft. long and weighed 50 tons. It was a swamp-dweller, where its weight was supported by the water. Tyrannosaurus, another kind, was probably the most ferocious of all known flesh-eaters.

I. *Ornithischia* Another extinct group of dinosaurs, chiefly four-legged; many of them, such as Stegosaurus, characterised by heavy protective bony plates.

J. *Synapsida* Extinct mammal-like reptiles. Some of these were probably partly warm-blooded, and a whole series of fossils show that mammals evolved from them. They were the chief reptile group before the appearance of the dinosaurs, and died out in Triassic times, some 175 million years ago.

Class 7 Aves—the birds. Warm-blooded vertebrates with feathers. The front limbs are modified into wings. The main groups are:

1. *Archaeornithes* Archaeopteryx. The earliest known birds (extinct) with teeth and jointed bony tails.

2. *Odontognathae* Hesperornis, Ichthyornis. Extinct water-birds with teeth, but with the tail bones fused as in all modern birds.

3. *Impennes* Penguins. Beaked birds with paddle-like wings, used for swimming and not for flying. Found only in the southern hemisphere.

Penguin   Kiwi

4. *Struthioniformes* Ostriches. Large, flightless two-toed birds found in Africa.

5. *Rheiformes* Rheas. Large, flightless three-toed birds with short wings and long soft feathers, found only in South America.

6. *Casuariiformes* Cassowaries and emus. Large, flightless three-toed birds with hair-like feathers. Found only in Australasia.

7. *Aepyornithiformes* Elephant birds. Enormous extinct flightless birds of Madagascar, their eggs up to 36 in. in circumference.

8. *Dinornithiformes* Moas. Huge flightless birds, up to 12 ft. tall, of New Zealand. Extinct only perhaps in the last four or five hundred years.

9. *Apterygiformes* Kiwis. Small, four-toed, flightless birds of New Zealand, with almost no trace of wings and fur-like feathers.

10. *Tinamiformes* Tinamous. Ground-dwelling birds of South America, with short rounded wings and tail and four toes.

11. *Gaviiformes* Loons and divers. Strongly flying diving birds with short, pointed wings and powerful webbed feet. Three kinds in Britain—the great northern diver, the red-throated diver and the black-throated diver.

12. *Colymbiformes* Grebes. Weak-flighted or flightless aquatic birds with short wings and lobed feet. In Britain, the great crested grebe and the dabchick or little grebe.

13. *Procelariiformes* Albatrosses, petrels. Aquatic birds with webbed feet, tubular nostrils and long wings. Strong fliers. In Britain, the Manx shearwater, fulmar and storm petrel.

14. *Pelecaniformes* Pelicans, gannets, cormorants. Aquatic birds with four webbed toes, vestigial or absent nostrils and often pouched throats. In Britain, the gannet, the black cormorant and the shag.

Stork

15. *Ciconiiformes* Herons, storks, spoonbills, flamingoes, ibises, bitterns. Long-necked, long-legged wading birds. Mostly tropical. In Britain, the common heron and the bittern.

16. *Anseriformes* Ducks, geese, swans. Web-footed water-birds with broad, skin-covered beaks having a harder tip and edges. In Britain, the greylag, the barnacle and brent goose, the mute and whooper swan, the shelduck, mallard, shoveller, pintail, teal, widgeon, pochard, tufted duck, golden eye, long-tailed duck, eider and scoter, goosander and merganser, among others.

17. *Falconiformes* Birds of prey—eagles, hawks, vultures. Strong fliers with hooked beaks and grasping, taloned feet. In Britain, the golden eagle, buzzard, kite, sparrow hawk, kestrel, peregrine, hobby, merlin and harrier.

18. *Galliformes* Grouse, pheasants, quail, etc. The

game birds. Plump, ground-dwelling birds with feet adapted for scratching. In Britain, the pheasant, partridge, French partridge, quail, ptarmigan, red (unique to these islands) and black grouse, capercaillie.

19. *Gruiformes* Cranes, rails, coots. Semi-aquatic birds with strong legs and unwebbed feet. Some are flightless. In Britain, the coot, moorhen, water-rail and corncrake.

20. *Charadriiformes* Waders, gulls, auks. Usually web-toed aquatic birds, with dense feathers and the legs set far back. In Britain, the razorbill, guillemot, little auk, puffin, Sandwich tern, Arctic tern, common tern, little tern, black-headed gull, herring gull, common gull, lesser and greater black-backed gulls, kittiwake, great and Arctic skuas, stone curlew, woodcock, snipe, dotterel, golden plover, lapwing, oystercatcher, dunlin, sandpiper, knot, redshank, godwit, curlew and whimbrel, among others.

21. *Columbiformes* Pigeons and doves. Slender-billed grain-eating birds with large crops. Secrete 'pigeon's milk' for feeding young. In Britain, wood pigeon, stock dove, rock dove, turtle dove.

22. *Psittaciformes* Parrots and macaws. Brightly coloured fruit-eating tropical and sub-tropical birds with strong hooked beaks and grasping feet with four toes, two in front, two behind.

23. *Cuculiformes* Cuckoos and road runners. Four-toed birds with feet adapted for running. Many are parasitic, laying their eggs in the nests of other birds. In Britain, the cuckoo.

24. *Strigiformes* Owls. Nocturnal birds with taloned feet, large round heads with staring, forward-directed eyes and soft feathers. Feed on small animals. In Britain, the barn owl, long-eared owl, short-eared owl, tawny owl and little owl.

25. *Caprimulgiformes* Nightjars. Nocturnal insect-eating birds with small, wide-gaping, fringed beaks. In Britain, the nightjar.

26. *Apodiformes* Swifts and hummingbirds. Insect- or nectar-eating birds with short legs and long, pointed wings, largely tropical. In Britain, the swift.

27. *Trogoniformes* Trogons. Mostly tropical forest birds, with long tails and short stout bills. Often brightly coloured.

28. *Coraciiformes* Kingfishers, motmots. Strong-beaked birds with the third and fourth toe basally fused. In Britain, the kingfisher.

29. *Piciformes* Woodpeckers, toucans. Stout-billed birds with stiff tail-feathers, grasping toes and roughened, protrudable tongues. In Britain, the green woodpecker, greater spotted woodpecker and lesser spotted wood-pecker.

30. *Passeriformes* Perching birds. Birds with three toes in front and one behind, adapted for perching. The largest order of birds, containing by far the greatest number of species. The families found in Britain are:

Alaudidae: larks—skylark and woodlark.

Hirundinidae: swallows—swallow, house martin, sand martin.

Corvidae: crows—raven, carrion crow, hooded crow, rook, jackdaw, magpie, jay, chough.

Paridae: tits—long-tailed tit, great tit, coal tit, marsh tit, willow tit, blue tit, crested tit, bearded tit.

Sittidae: nuthatches—nuthatch.

Certhiidae: creepers—tree-creeper.

Troglodytidae: wrens—wren.

Cinclidae: dippers—dipper.

Turdidae: thrushes and chats—mistle thrush, field-fare, songthrush, redwing, ring ouzel, blackbird, wheat-ear, stonechat, whinchat, redstart, nightingale, robin.

Sylviidae: warblers—whitethroat, lesser whitethroat, blackcap, chiffchaff, and garden, Dartford, willow, wood, reed, marsh, sedge and grasshopper warblers.

Regulidae: goldcrests—goldcrest.

Muscicapidae: flycatchers—spotted and pied fly-catchers.

Prunellidae: accentors—hedge sparrow.

Motacillidae: pipits and wagtails—tree, meadow and rock pipits and pied, white, grey and yellow wagtails.

Laniidae: shrikes—the butcher bird.

Sturnidae: starlings—starling.

Sparrow

Fringillidae: finches and buntings—greenfinch, haw-finch, chaffinch, brambling, goldfinch, siskin, lesser redpoll, mealy redpoll, twite, linnet, crossbill, bullfinch.

Passeridae: sparrows—house sparrow, tree sparrow.

Class 8 Mammalia. Warm-blooded animals with hair that suckle their young. The chief kinds of living mammals are:

Monotremata Egg-laying mammals. Very primitive, with a cloaca (common orifice for the intestine, bladder

Platypus

and reproductive organs), no external ears, a beak instead of teeth and milk glands without nipples. There are two living genera, *Ornithorhynchus*, the duck-billed platypus, found only in Australia, and *Echidna*, the spiny anteaters, found in Australia, Tasmania and New Guinea.

Marsupialia Pouched mammals. These have teeth, external ears, separate orifices for the intestine, bladder and reproductive organs, and mammary glands with nipples inside their pouches. Their young are in a very immature condition and finish their development inside the mother's pouch, attached to her nipples. Except for the opposums (which are found in America), marsupials

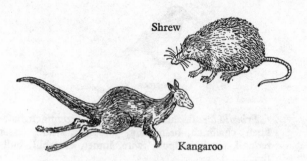

Shrew

Kangaroo

are found only in Australia, Tasmania, New Guinea and nearby islands. Typical kinds are kangaroos and wallabies, the marsupial mole, phalangers, wombats, rat-kangaroos, bandicoots, dasyures, Tasmanian Devil, Tasmanian wolf and pouched mice.

Eutheria Placental mammals in which the developing embryo is fed by the mother's blood through an organ known as the placenta. These include:

Insectivora Shrews, moles, hedgehogs. In Britain, the hedgehog, pigmy shrew, common shrew, watershrew and mole. (These last three not found in Ireland.)

Dermoptera Kobegos (flying lemurs).

Chiroptera Bats. In Britain, the greater and lesser horseshoe bats, the noctule, pipistrelle, long-eared and whiskered bats.

Primates Tree-shrews, lemurs, tarsiers, monkeys, apes, men.

Sloth

Rat

Pholidota: Scaly Anteater

Hare

Cetacea: dolphin

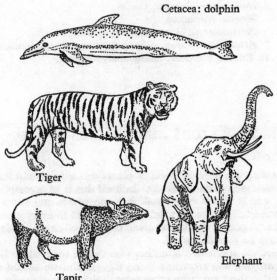

Tiger

Elephant

Tapir

Edentata Sloths, anteaters, armadillos—mostly in South America.

Pholidota Scaly anteaters, pangolins.

Lagomorpha Rabbits, hares, pikas. In Britain, the brown hare, the blue hare, the Irish hare (Ireland only) and the rabbit.

Rodentia Rats, squirrels, beaver, etc. In Britain, the red and grey squirrels, dormouse, long-tailed fieldmouse, harvest mouse (not Ireland), brown rat, black rat, bank vole, short-tailed and water voles (not in Ireland) and musk rat.

Cetacea Whales, dolphins, porpoises; mostly marine, and to be seen round our coasts at times.

Carnivora Dogs, cats, bears, seals, etc. In Britain, the wild cat (Scotland only), fox, otter, badger, stoat, weasel, marten, polecat, grey seal and common seal.

Tubulidentata Aardvark.

Proboscidea Elephants.

Hyracoidea Hyraxes, conies.

Sirenia Manatees.

Perissodactyla Horses, tapirs, rhinoceros.

Artiodactyla Cows, deer, pigs, camels, hippopotamus. In Britain, red deer, fallow deer, roe deer.

NATURE STUDY AND THE WEB OF LIFE

Nature Study

Knowing the different sorts of plants and animals and fungi is the first step in nature study. In itself this is an accomplishment, and it makes every walk into the woods and fields an adventure full of discovery, adding excitement to every journey we take. A person who knows about nature need never be bored, wherever he is in the world.

There are specialised scientists who devote their whole lives to identifying and recording living things. But we should not forget that there are many other sides to the study of nature. If we read a book like David Lack's *The Life of the Robin* (Pelican) we cannot help being amazed that there is so much to learn about one of our common birds, and which we could have learned for ourselves (had we been clever enough) just by watching what goes on in our back garden.

Animal Behaviour

No animal, however small, is without a life story, and many of these life stories are not known even to scientists. We can learn a great deal, and possibly even make scientific discoveries, if we are patient and careful in observing the birds and insects and other creatures around us. Even among professional naturalists there are very few who have ever seen the fabulous mating dances of the common snails and slugs.

When we see an animal we must try to discover what it is doing, and how this fits in with the rest of its behaviour. Watch an ant on a plant stem, and after a while we may see that it has reached a cluster of aphids, or greenflies, and is 'milking' them. For aphids are herded by ants just as we herd cows, and for similar reasons. Food-getting is a large part of most animals' lives. Some lie in wait and pounce. The kestrel hovers overhead, watching the waste land. The timid rabbit creeps out at night and eats a lettuce in the garden. The deer grazes watchfully in the wood, stripping the lower leaves from tree or munching grasses. The butterfly sips nectar, the spider weaves his snare and waits.

What happens when the pounce comes? Some creatures fight it out, others flee, running for their lives. The hedgehog curls up and offers a mouthful of sharp spines, the squid shoots out a 'smokescreen' of black ink into the water and dodges away, the moth or butterfly spreads its wings sharply and dazzles its attacker with a display of bright colour or a pair of alarming eye markings. The skunk emits an unbearable smell; the bombardier beetle releases a puff of explosive. Sometimes weak creatures band together in self-defence. We may often see a mob of tiny birds of different sorts harrying bigger birds.

Even when animals have nothing much to do, we can learn a lot. Have you ever observed the elaborate rituals with which a sparrow or a duck or a housefly cleans itself? And notice the ways in which animals settle down to rest or sleep, the places they choose, the postures they adopt. Where do the common birds in your neighbourhood sleep at night?

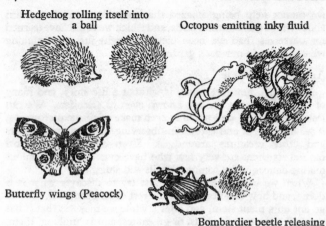

Hedgehog rolling itself into a ball

Octopus emitting inky fluid

Butterfly wings (Peacock)

Bombardier beetle releasing puff of explosive

The Breeding Season

Normally the lives of most animals centre round self-protection and food-getting. But during the breeding season an animal's whole behaviour may change. It may grow brilliant in colour and become suddenly aggressive, it may give up eating for the time being, it may even change its whole habitat—as when salmon swim up rivers from the sea to spawn. At breeding time we may observe fights between rival males, as with deer, or fights over territorial possessions, as among many birds. The robin stakes out its claim to a plot of land, in which its nest is built, and woe betide any other robin that crosses the boundary. If we watch we will see that even fighting is usually conducted to rules. A threat display may be enough to frighten the aggressor. If there is a fight, the loser may signal defeat: a losing jackdaw offers a grey patch on the back of its head to be pecked, a losing wolf the side of its neck to be bitten—but the victor does not take advantage, for its instincts immediately cause it to stop attacking.

Even courtship is often fraught with aggressiveness. Normally the male and the female may be rivals for food. Now the need to produce offspring brings them together. Courtship dances and ceremonies are often means whereby fear and mistrust are dispelled, so that the mating instinct can win. This is the case with birds, fish, many mammals, even many insects. In spiders, aggressiveness may return soon after mating, when the female often eats the male. In higher (and even some lower) creatures there may be long-continued co-operation—the building of a nest, the care of the young. All these are wonderful and rewarding things to observe.

Animal Language

It is not long before a nature observer discovers that nearly all animals have a *language*. This does not mean that they use words, or even sounds. But none the less they communicate with each other. The courtship displays of birds, in which the male quietens the fears of the female and attracts her, are an example. They consist, when analysed, of a series of signals and responses. Dogs often use smell to communicate. They sniff each other before wagging their tails and becoming friends. If they 'smell' fear, they bristle and attack. Among social animals there are often quite elaborate codes of signals—signals which summon the flock together, alarm signals, food signals, 'time-to-go-home' signals, signals that indicate rank (there may be quite an elaborate hierarchy). Sometimes very complicated messages can be conveyed. By dancing, bees can tell other bees in the hive the sort of flowers they have found, where they are and how far away. By watching closely and learning animal language, an observer can discover far more about what is going on in the lives of animals than he might at first believe possible.

The Web of Life

When we observe animals and plants we must try to think of them in their relationship to their surroundings. Why is the minnow slim, the perch fat, the eel snake-shaped? Why has the horse got long legs, the badger short? Each of these leads a very different kind of life, to which its shape is well adapted. Similarly with animal colouring. Sometimes this is for concealment, sometimes for conspicuousness, as with certain poisonous snakes or unpleasant-tasting insects which are quickly recognised and not attacked again. Some harmless or nice-tasting creatures even mimic others that are the opposite, for protection's sake.

But there is also a much wider relationship between living things and their environment. If we think of a British woodland, a desert, a savannah region in East Africa, the Arctic snows, a tropical rain forest, and what these call to mind, we will see that each has its climate, its typical soils (there will probably be many kinds) and its own peculiar populations of plants and animals, which will generally be tied pretty closely to the types of soil. Without exception (though the connection is sometimes quite difficult to trace) the animal depends upon the plant and the plant (here the connection is always evident) upon the soil and the climate. We would not expect to find grass growing in a desert because the climatic conditions, and therefore the soil, would be wholly unsuitable. And so we would not expect to find grazing animals, such as zebras, in deserts because there would be no food for them to eat. Because there are no grazing animals there are no lions in deserts. Lions prey upon grazing animals and so are themselves ultimately tied to grass. If we think about this we see that Nature has achieved a sort of rough balance and if we set about building and analysing food chains—grass, zebra, lion is an example of a very simple and straightforward food chain—we can learn a lot about how Nature works. Of course, food chains are not always as simple nor is distribution always as simple as in the examples given above. Nevertheless, it is possible to divide the world into broad floral and faunal regions, the controlling factor in each case being the climate.

Polar Region. Circling the top of the world, north of the arctic circle. Here the winters are very long, the winds tremendous and the snowfalls very heavy, and for weeks on end there is no daylight at all. The soils are often permanently frozen underground. No trees can survive such conditions. The plants are small, mostly mosses and lichens, but there are also many annuals which overwinter by seed and spring up and flower during the short summer when there is no true night. Not many animals are able to support life through the Polar winter. The mammals, as one would expect, are protected by thick fur and most of these either hibernate or migrate southward for the winter. Many species of birds migrate north of the arctic circle to breed during the short summer.

Palaearctic Region. Extending (in the Old World) roughly from the arctic circle to the Tropic of Cancer and including Europe, North Africa and most of Asia. Many species of mammals range almost unchanged from the British Isles to Japan. The cat family is well-represented by small and medium-sized species, but the typical carnivore is the wolf. There are more species of bears than anywhere else in the world and deer are common throughout the region.

Nearctic Region. The New World equivalent of the above, extending from the arctic circle to Central America. The mammals are so similar that it is evident that the two great land masses were joined until comparatively recently at the Bering Strait. For example, the elk of the Old World and the moose of the New, the reindeer of the Old World and the caribou of the New, the wolves, the foxes, the otters and the beavers are so alike that many authorities regard them as races of one species rather than as separate species.

Ethiopian Region. Including all Africa south of the Tropic of Cancer. The home of the world's largest land mammals (elephant, rhinoceros, hippopotamus, giraffe) and two man-like apes, the gorilla and the chimpanzee. The region is characterised particularly by the presence of large numbers of grazing animals, antelopes and zebras, and by the absence of deer. The typical carnivores are the lion and the leopard, the hyena and the jackal.

Oriental Region. That part of Asia lying south of the Himalayas. Many of the mammals are similar to those of the Ethiopian Region: elephant, rhinoceros, leopard, hyena, jackal. There is also one man-like ape, the orang-utan, and still a few lions. Bears, deer and tiger have spilled over from the Palaearctic Region.

Australasian Region. Separated from the Oriental Region by Wallace's Line, a deep oceanic trench. The region is the home of the most primitive mammals, the platypus and the echidna, and of the marsupials or pouched mammals (kangaroo, wombat, kaola bear, etc.), which are almost as primitive. None of the higher mammals, such as the dingo (a wild dog) is native to the region: all have been introduced by man.

Neotropical Region. Includes the whole of South and Central America. South America has some marsupials (opossum and small shrews) and edentates, mammals with few or no teeth (sloth, anteater, armadillo), which indicates that, like Australasia, it was for long cut off from the rest of the world. When the land bridge of Central America was formed, puma and jaguar, deer and llama and so on, penetrated from the north. The monkeys of South America, though resembling those of Africa and Asia, form a distinct sub-order. There are no man-like apes.

It must be remembered that within these broad regions there are many different types of habitat, both of land and water: desert, forest, steppe, marsh, bog, lake and so on. Each has its own peculiar flora and fauna, depending upon the soil and upon the climate. Desert plants, for example, have thick skins to conserve moisture, while most of the animals live underground and come out only at night when the temperature is much cooler. In the dense rain forests, such as those of the Amazon basin and western equatorial Africa, most of the animal life is confined to the tree tops and there is an abundance of insect life. In the northern parts of the Palaearctic and Nearctic regions insect life, save in summer, is comparatively scarce, so the resident birds are seed-eaters: in the warmer zones both seed-eaters and insect-eaters are resident. On the steppes and in savannah country (grassland with scattered trees, such as is to be found over much of East Africa) the plants are all drought-resistant and many are heavily armed with thorns as protection against animals. Such country supports great herds of grazing animals, many of them exceptionally fleet of foot as protection against predators. This 'habitat-link' is particularly well illustrated in the British Isles, for here within a very small compass we have a great variety of rock formations and many different types of soils.

Britain's Natural Habitats

It is true that many plants are tolerant of a variety of soils, but many are selective and many have strong preferences. For example, the foxglove is tolerant of many soils but avoids chalk and limestone, heaths and heathers grow only on acid soils, traveller's joy is a plant of the chalk, and so on. The dominant vegetation is, therefore, a good indication of the soil beneath. Here, listed by their dominant vegetation or by type, are Britain's chief natural habitats:

alder woods, ash woods, beech woods, birch woods, oak woods, conifer forests or plantations, chalk grassland (downland), acid grassland, heathland, water meadows, peat bogs, fens, marshes, salt marshes (saltings), lakes, rivers, coastal sand-dunes, shingle beaches, arctic-alpine mountain tops, sea cliffs.

In each of these the animal life will be slightly or completely different. The butterflies of downland are different from those of oak woods or mountain tops: the birds of deciduous woodland different from those of conifer plantations; and so on. And in each of these habitats the animal populations, particularly of birds and insects, will vary from season to season during the year.

And the habitats themselves change. Some are fairly stable. Others change fairly rapidly. Salt marshes and river banks may be building up and changing into dry land. As they do so, new species of animals and plants invade and colonise them. This sort of thing is always happening and elsewhere man interferes: new roads are built, valleys flooded to form reservoirs, hedgerows cut down. Each has its effect on animal and plant life. One of the ways in which scientists study this sort of thing is to make *population counts* of the different species (plants and animals) at intervals and to mark them on a large scale map. Even photographs of the same spot taken at different times of the year, and year by year at those times, can be of great interest and value.

Equipment

For most purposes sharp eyes and a note-book are all you need. If you are a bird-watcher, field-glasses or a telescope are a great help, and a camera adds permanence to your observations. If you want to make detailed maps or to study a small area of ground, a tape measure, a ruler and graph paper are needed. If you wish to study (and see all the beauty of) flowers and leaves, lichen or fungi, a fairly powerful pocket magnifying glass is essential. And you must never be without a notebook and a pencil to record in words (or, even better, in sketches) what you have found. Memories can be short in the excitement of discovery.

Good Books to Read

Reade & Stuttard: *A Handbook for Naturalists*
    (Evans Paperback)
R. S. R. Fitter: *Wildlife in Britain* (Pelican)
    Collins Guide to Bird Watching
John Hutchison: *British Wild Flowers* (Pelican)

Ernest Neal: *The Badger* (Pelican)
John Burton: *The Oxford Book of Insects*
Walter Shepherd: *The Living Landscape of Britain* (Faber
    Paperback)
Brian Vesey-FitzGerald: *The World of Fishes*

In addition any book in Warne's 'Observer' series or, for more
detailed but readable scientific treatment, any book in Collins'
'New Naturalist' series.

Useful Addresses

1. XYZ Club, Zoological Society, Regent's Park, London,
   N.W.1.
2. British Naturalists' Association. Branches all over the
   country. Address of local secretary obtainable from Council
   for Nature, 41 Queen's Gate, London, S.W.7.
3. Children's Centre, Natural History Museum, Cromwell
   Road, London, S.W.7.

Miscellany

HOWEVER you divide the contents of an encyclopaedia, there are always essential pieces of information left over that seem to go nowhere in particular. It is these that you will find in this final section of JUNIOR PEARS.

Time: Calendars and Clocks   2–5
British Flags   6–7
A Note on Heraldry   7–10
The New Decimal Coinage and Notes on Coins   11–13
Distance of the Horizon   14
The Seven Wonders of the Ancient World   14
Roman Numerals   15
Greek and Russian Alphabets   15–16
Deaf and Dumb Alphabet   17
Longest and Highest: Tunnels, Bridges, Buildings, Ship Canals   18–19
A Guide to some of the most important Museums in Great Britain   20–26

Lantern Clock 1688

Time: Calendars and Clocks

THE DAYS OF THE WEEK

The names of the days—Sunday, Monday, Tuesday (Tiw—the God of War), Wednesday (Woden or Odin), Thursday (Thor), Friday (Frig—wife of Odin) and Saturday come from Old English translations of the Roman names (Sol, Luna, Mars, Mercurius, Jupiter, Venus and Saturnius).

HOW THE MONTHS GOT THEIR NAMES

January From Janus, a Roman God. The Anglo-Saxons called it *wulf-monath*—the month of the wolves.

February From a Roman god, Februus. A.S.: *sprote-cal*—the month when the kale, a kind of cabbage, sprouted.

March Originally the first month in the Roman calendar. From Mars, the god of war. A.S.: *hreth-monath*—the rough month.

April From the Latin *Aprilis*. A.S.: *Easter-monath*—month of Easter.

May From Maia, a goddess. A.S.: *tri-milchi*—the month when the cows were milked three times a day.

June From Juno, mother of the gods. A.S.: *sere-monath*—the dry month.

July Named after Julius Caesar. A.S.: *maed-monath*—meadow-month.

August Named after Augustus Caesar. A.S.: *weod-monath*—the month of vegetation.

September The seventh Roman month. From the Latin word meaning *seven*. A.S.: *haerfest-monath*—harvest month.

October The eighth Roman month. From Latin word meaning *eight*. A.S.: *win-monath*—the month of wine.

November The ninth Roman month. From Latin word meaning *nine*. A.S.: *wind-monath*—month of wind.

December The tenth Roman month. From Latin word meaning *ten*. A.S.: *mid-winter-monath*—mid-winter month.

THE YEAR

The **Equinoctial** or **Tropical Year** is the time the earth takes to go round the sun: 365·422 solar days. The **Calendar Year** consists of 365 days, but a year of which the date can be divided by 4 without a remainder is called a **Leap Year**, with one day added to the month of February. The last year of a century is a Leap Year only if its number can be divided by 400 (e.g. 1900 was not a Leap Year, but 2000 will be one).

The **Longest and Shortest Days** The longest day is the day on which the Sun is at its greatest distance from the equator; this is called the **Summer Solstice**. It varies between June 21 and 22.

The shortest day is the day of the **Winter Solstice**, and in 1975 falls on December 22.

Dog Days These are the days about the rising of the Dog Star, the hottest period of the year in the Northern Hemisphere. Roughly they occur between July 3 and August 25.

St Luke's Summer is a warm period round about St Luke's Day (October 18).

St Martin's Summer is a warm period round about Martinmas (November 11).

The Christian Calendar Until 1582 the Calendar used in all Christian countries was the Julian Calendar, in which the last year of all centuries was a Leap Year. By the sixteenth century this had caused a difference between the tropical and calendar years (see **The Year**) of 10 days. In 1582 Pope Gregory ordered that October 5 should be called October 15, and that of the years at the end of centuries only every fourth one should be a Leap Year. This new calendar was called the Gregorian Calendar and was gradually adopted throughout the Christian world. In Great Britain and her Dominions it came into use in 1752; by then there was a difference of 11 days between tropical and calendar years, and September 3 of that year was reckoned as September 14.

Easter Day can be, at the earliest, March 22; at the latest, April 25.

Whit Sunday can be, at the earliest, May 10; at the latest, June 13.

The Jewish Calendar dates from October 7, 3761 B.C. In 1975 the Jewish New Year (5736) began on September 6.

The Moslem Calendar dates from the Hejira, or the flight of Mohammed from Mecca to Medina (July 16, A.D. 622 in the Gregorian Calendar). In 1975 the Moslem New Year (1395) fell on January 14.

SUMMER TIME

Summer time—the putting forward of the clock by one hour during the months of summer—was first introduced in the First World War. Its purpose then was to cut down on the use of power for lighting; but in peace-time it was continued so that people might enjoy longer summer evenings.

From February, 1968, summer time was established for a three-year trial period to conform with Central European time. The new title chosen for it was British Standard Time. This experiment was abandoned in October, 1971, when the United Kingdom reverted to Greenwich Mean Time.

Normally, British Summer Time is from the day following the third Saturday in March until the day following the fourth Saturday in October.

TIME ALL OVER THE WORLD

This table shows what the time is in the important cities of the world when it is 12 noon at Greenwich. Places in ordinary type are ahead of Greenwich; those in *italics* are behind Greenwich.

Accra, Ghana .	12 Noon	Baghdad, Iraq .	3.00 p.m.
Adelaide, Australia	9.30 p.m.	*Baltimore, U.S.A.*	7.00 a.m.
Algiers . .	1.00 p.m.	Bangkok, Thailand	7.00 p.m.
Amsterdam,		Belgrade, Yugo-	
Netherlands .	1.00 p.m.	slavia . .	1.00 p.m.
Ankara, Turkey .	2.00 p.m.	Berlin, Germany .	1.00 p.m.
Athens, Greece .	2.00 p.m.	Berne, Switzerland	1.00 p.m.

Bombay, India	.	5.30 p.m.	*Montevideo,*	
Boston, U.S.A.	.	7.00 a.m.	*Uruguay* . .	9.00 a.m.
Brisbane, Australia	10.00 p.m.	*Montreal, Canada* .	7.00 a.m.
Brussels, Belgium .	1.00 p.m.	Moscow, U.S.S.R.	3.00 p.m.
Budapest, Hungary	1.00 p.m.	Nairobi, Kenya	3.00 p.m.
Buenos Aires,		New Delhi, India .	5.30 p.m.
Argentina	.	9.00 a.m.	*New York* .	7.00 a.m.
Cairo, Egypt	.	2.00 p.m.	Nicosia, Cyprus .	2.00 p.m.
Calcutta, India	.	5.30 p.m.	Oslo, Norway	1.00 p.m.
Calgary, Canada	.	5.00 a.m.	*Ottawa, Canada* .	7.00 a.m.
Canberra,		*Panama* .	7.00 a.m.
Australia .	.	10.00 p.m.	Paris . . .	1.00 p.m.
Cape Town, South		Peking, China	8.00 p.m.
Africa	.	2.00 p.m.	Perth, Australia .	8.00 p.m.
Chicago, U.S.A. .	6.00 a.m.	*Port of Spain,*	
Colombo, Ceylon .	5.30 p.m.	*Trinidad* .	8.00 a.m.
Copenhagen,		Prague, Czecho-	
Denmark .	.	1.00 p.m.	slovakia .	1.00 p.m.
Darwin, Australia .	9.30 p.m.	*Quebec, Canada* .	7.00 a.m.
Detroit, U.S.A.	.	7.00 a.m.	*Quito, Ecuador* .	7.00 a.m.
Dublin, Ireland	.	12 Noon	*Reykjavik, Iceland*	11.00 a.m.
Freetown, Sierra		*Rio de Janeiro*	9.00 a.m.
Leone	.	12 Noon	Rome . .	1.00 p.m.
Gibraltar	.	1.00 p.m.	*St John's, New-*	
Halifax,		*foundland*	8.30 a.m.
Nova Scotia	.	8.00 a.m.	Salisbury, Southern	
Hamilton, Bermuda	8.00 a.m.	Rhodesia .	2.00 p.m.
Havana, Cuba	.	7.00 a.m.	*San Francisco,*	
Helsinki, Finland .	2.00 p.m.	*U.S.A.* .	4.00 a.m.
Hong Kong	.	8.00 p.m.	*Santiago, Chile*	8.00 a.m.
Honolulu, Hawaii .	2.00 a.m.	Seoul, Korea	8.30 a.m.
Jerusalem	.	2.00 p.m.	Singapore .	7.30 p.m.
Johannesburg,		Stalingrad,	
South Africa	.	2.00 p.m.	*U.S.S.R.* .	4.00 p.m.
Karachi, Pakistan .	5.00 p.m.	Stockholm,	
Kingston, Jamaica .	7.00 a.m.	Sweden .	1.00 p.m.
Kuala Lumpur,		Sofia, Bulgaria	2.00 p.m.
Malaya	.	7.30 p.m.	Suva, Fiji .	12 Midnight
Lagos, Nigeria	.	1.00 p.m.	Sydney, Australia .	10.00 p.m.
Leningrad,		Teheran, Iran	3.30 p.m.
U.S.S.R. .	.	3.00 p.m.	Tirana, Albania .	1.00 p.m.
Lima, Peru	.	7.00 a.m.	Tokyo, Japan	9.00 p.m.
Lisbon, Portugal	.	12 Noon	*Toronto, Canada* .	7.00 a.m.
Los Angeles, U.S.A.	4.00 a.m.	*Vancouver, Canada*	4.00 a.m.
Luxembourg	.	1.00 p.m.	Vienna, Austria .	1.00 p.m.
Madrid, Spain	.	1.00 p.m.	Warsaw, Poland .	1.00 p.m.
Mandalay, Burma .	6.30 p.m.	Wellington, New	
Melbourne,		Zealand .	12 Midnight
Australia .	.	10.00 p.m.	*Winnipeg, Canada* .	6.00 a.m.
Mexico City .	.	6.00 a.m.		

BRITISH FLAGS

The Union Jack* was adopted in 1606 following the Union of England and Scotland, and took its present form in 1801, when there was the further union with Ireland (see HISTORY). It consists of three heraldic crosses:

> the cross of St Andrew, which forms the blue and white basis;
> upon which lies the red and white cross of St Patrick;
> upon the whole rests the red and white cross of St George dividing the flag vertically and horizontally.

The Union Jack

The correct manner of flying the flag is with the larger strips of white next to the flagstaff uppermost.

* Although it has become usual to call this flag the Union Jack on all occasions, it is strictly correct to do so only when the flag is flown at the jackstaff of one of Her Majesty's ships. At all other times it should be called the Union Flag.

The Royal Standard is the sovereign's personal flag, only to be flown above a building when she is actually present. It is divided into quarters, the 1st and 4th containing the three lions *passant* of England, the 2nd quarter containing the lion *rampant* of Scotland and the 3rd quarter containing the harp of Ireland. (*Passant and rampant* are terms in heraldry, and are explained in the section on Heraldry that follows.)

The White Ensign, the flag of the Royal Navy, is a white flag bearing the cross of St George, with a small Union Jack in the top corner next to the flagstaff.

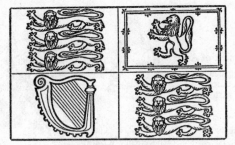

The Royal Standard

The Red Ensign (known as 'the red duster'), flag of the Mercantile Marine. It is a plain red flag with the Union Jack in the top corner next to the flagstaff.

The Blue Ensign (similar to the Red Ensign, but with blue background), flag of the Royal Naval Reserve (R.N.R.).

A NOTE ON HERALDRY

Man has always used symbols to decorate his armour; but heraldry as we know it started in Europe in the twelfth century. Knights began to wear helmets which completely covered their wearers' faces, making recognition difficult. So when they met together at tournaments or went on crusades it was necessary that each should have a personal badge. This became known as the knight's **coat-of-arms** because it was worn on his sur-coat over his armour. The most obvious place to put the arms was on the shield. On his helmet a knight sometimes bore another distinguishing badge—the **crest**—which rested on a band of twisted cloth—the **torse**. This held in place a **mantling** to protect the metal from the hot sun. When all these are brought together they form an **achievement of arms** (Fig. 1). Once you have seen them together you are unlikely to make the popular mistake of calling a coat-of-arms a crest.

Because heraldry was formulated so long ago, the language used is a mixture of Norman-French and Latin and English. At first this may seem difficult; but once a few terms are mastered it can be seen to be a very practical language. Describing arms in words is called **blazoning**, and the method is to name the colour or colours of the **field** (the background), then to describe the main **charge** and its colour, and finally to name the subsidiary

FIG. I

Achievement of Arms

Per pale gules and argent, a chief indented ermine

13th century Knight

charges with their colours. Only five **tinctures** are commonly used—red, called **gules**: blue, called **azure**: green, called **vert**: purple, called **purpure**: and black, called **sable**. There are two **metals**, gold (**or**) and silver (**argent**), and these are usually represented by yellow and white. In addition there are **furs—ermine, vair** and numerous variations. A basic rule of heraldry is that a coloured charge should not be placed on a colour nor a metal one on a metal.

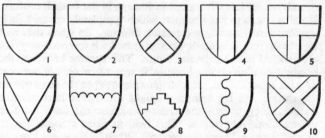

FIG. 2 SOME ORDINARIES AND LINES OF PARTITION

1 Chief: 2 Fess: 3 Chevron: 4 Pale: 5 Cross: 6 Pile: 7 per fess invected: 8 per chevron indented: 9 per pale wavy: 10 Saltire

All items on a shield are known as **charges** and can be anything and everything from ants to zebras. The main charges are known as **ordinaries**. Sometimes the field is divided into more than one colour (as in Fig. 1), and the ordinaries lend their names to these divisions. The dividing lines can be straight or wavy-shaped or angular; Fig. 2 shows some of these.

It is possible to tell from a coat of arms to which member of a

Eldest Son Label	2nd Son Crescent	3rd Son Mullet	4th Son Martlet
5th Son Annulet	6th Son Fleur-de-Lis	7th Son Rose	8th Son Cross Moline

FIG. 3

family it belongs. The head of the family bears plain arms, but his sons must carry a symbol to **difference** his arms from those of his father and his brothers (Fig. 3). Women bear their father's arms on a **lozenge** (a diamond shape), with no difference, and they cannot inherit arms if they have brothers. If a woman marries, her husband **impales** his wife's arms on the **sinister** side of his shield (Fig. 4). (In Latin **dexter** means right and **sinister** left, but in heraldry this refers to the left and right of the man carrying the shield.) If a lady has no brothers, she herself inherits the arms and her husband places them on his own arms on an **escutcheon of pretence**. Their children may **quarter** both parents' arms. Sometimes the quarterings may run into hundreds, but they are not all displayed.

FIG. 4

1 Per pale a chief indented impaling a bend: 2 Per pale a chief indented and on an escutcheon of pretence a bend: 3 Quarterly, 1st and 4th per pale a chief indented 2nd and 3rd a bend. (Note—Colours are omitted in these blazons.)

At first, no doubt, men chose their own symbols; but soon the monarch became the ultimate authority for granting arms. In England this authority is delegated to the Earl Marshal (at present the Duke of Norfolk), who is responsible for arranging great state occasions. To help him he has the College of Arms consisting of the Kings of Arms—Garter, Clarenceux and

Norroy and Ulster—six Heralds and four Pursuivants. In Scotland the principal officer is Lord Lyon, who has three Heralds and three Pursuivants.

Heraldry is a living part of our history. Not only is it found in old manuscripts and in churches and castles, but it can be seen on town halls, banks, company offices and advertisements. Look at your school badge and those of your friends. Some are real arms and have been granted to the school; but most are badges based on the arms of the town or a famous man (Fig. 5). Some, alas, may even have been invented by someone with no knowledge of heraldry.

B.B.C.
A gold band of
communication
surrounding the
Earth

National Coal Board
An heraldic
pictorial
representation of a
coal mine

U.K. Atomic
Energy Authority
Pictorial
representation of an
atomic pile

Barrow Grammar
School badge with
a bee and arrow
from the 'punning'
arms of Barrow
and the roses of
Lancashire

FIG. 5

This is no more than an introduction to the subject and you may want to read more about it. The books listed below are not dry but lively, well-illustrated and in one instance very amusing. Your library may have them. If you want to take your study further, write to the Secretary of the Heraldry Society, 59 Gordon Square, London, W.C.1, who will be pleased to send you information.

Simple Heraldry, by Iain Moncreiffe and Don Pottinger.
Boutell's Heraldry, revised by C. W. Scott-Giles and J. P. Brooke-Little.
Shield and Crest, by Julian Franklyn.
Discovering Heraldry, by R. H. Wilmott.

BRITAIN'S DECIMAL COINAGE

On Monday, February 15, 1971, Britain officially switched from its old coinage, based on pounds, shillings and pence, to decimal coinage.

There were two possibilities facing the Government when it had to make its choice of a form of decimal currency. One was to make ten shillings the major unit of the new coinage; and the argument in favour of this was, of course, that 10 is the basis of any decimal system. The second possibility was to make the pound the major unit; and that is what the Government decided to do. They gave many reasons for their choice: among them, that the pound was familiar to everyone, and so would form a bridge between the old system and the new; and that the pound was a known and respected unit of currency throughout the world.

The first decimal coins to be issued were the new five, ten and 50 penny coins: these could be released early because they corresponded exactly with the old shilling, florin and ten shilling note. The old halfpenny was demonetised (that is, it lost any value as money) on August 1, 1969, and the half-crown, another coin impossible to fit into a decimal system, on January 1, 1970. The three remaining bronze coins needed to complete the decimal coinage were put into circulation on the day of the changeover: they are the half new penny, the one new penny and the two new pence. These new coins are smaller and lighter than the old ones, and cost less to make. The old bronze coins cost rather more to produce than their face value (that is, an old penny as an object was actually worth more than an old penny)—largely because of the high price of copper. The new coins have as much copper in them as before, as a percentage of the total metal in the coin (97 per cent), but because the coins are smaller they have, as objects, rather less than their face value. The changeover has meant the loss of Britannia, for so long a feature of British coinage (she was originally modelled on the Duchess of Richmond, friend of Charles II). This was mainly because, to prevent confusion in the early days of the change, the figures indicating the value of the coins are very large, and this has left no room for

Britannia, her trident or even the distant lighthouse, which like the rest of the design reflected the importance to Britain of the sea that surrounds it.

The old sixpence was to be withdrawn, as another coin that would be merely confusing in a decimal system. (Like the old shilling, of course, it was part of a duodecimal system—that is, one based on 12.) It won a temporary reprieve, though the banks were unwilling to handle it, because at the time of the change-over it was still playing an important part in the tables of fares in many transport systems.

The old twelve-sided brass threepenny bit has been another casualty of the changeover. The new 50 penny coin is seven-sided—possibly the first coin in the world ever to have this shape, technically called an equilateral curve heptagon. It is estimated that each 50 penny piece will have a life of 50 years compared with the life of only five months that was usual with the ten-shilling note.

The symbols on the decimal coins are: on the halfpenny, the royal crown; on the penny, a portcullis with chains royally crowned; on the two penny piece, the badge of the Prince of Wales, three ostrich feathers enfiling a coronet of crosses pattée and fleurs de lys with the motto 'Ich dien'; on the five penny piece, the badge of Scotland, a thistle royally crowned; and on the ten penny piece, part of the crest of England, a lion passant royally crowned.

The changeover involved the conversion of some two and a half million slot machines, the same number of business machines, and all systems of accountancy. About 5,000 million new coins have been produced, most of them minted in the Royal Mint's new building in Wales.

Metrication Industry in Britain has changed over from the old imperial system of weights and measures to the metric system, and has adopted the International System of Units (SI). The year 1975 was set as the general deadline.

The Metrication Board (22 Kingsway, London WC2B 6LE) was set up in 1969 to supervise the changeover.

NOTES ON COINS

Coins as Weights and Measures A sixpence is $\frac{3}{4}$ in. in diameter. A penny weighs 3.564 grams, and has a diameter of 2.0320 cms.

British Coins Our **coppers** are really bronze (95 parts of copper, 4 parts of tin and 1 part of zinc). The **farthing** (then of silver) was first struck in 1279. Withdrawn at the end of 1960, when it was calculated that something like £250,000 worth farthings were lost or lying about unused. First **halfpenny** struck, in silver, in 1280: changed to bronze with penny and farthing in 1860: the old halfpenny ceased to exist on August 1, 1969. **Penny** introduced in 8th century: first copper pennies struck in 1797. **Threepence** struck as silver coin in 1551; replaced in 1937 by the twelve-sided brass coin that was demonetised in 1971.

Our **silver** in 1946 became cupro-nickel (75% copper, 25% nickel). The **shilling** (called then a testoon) was first struck as a silver coin by Henry VII. The **florin** appeared in 1849, the first step towards putting the English coinage on a decimal basis. (This earlier scheme was abandoned.) The **half-crown** was first struck in the reign of Edward VI: ceased to exist on January 1, 1970.

L.s.d. Librae, solidi, denarii—the Latin for 'pounds, shillings and pence'.

Legal Tender Bank of England notes and gold dated 1838 onwards are legal tender for any sum. Silver (cupro-nickel) coins with values up to and including 10p are legal tender up to £5; 50p coins up to £10, and bronze up to 20p.

American Coins The word **dime** comes from the French dixième, a tenth part, and is the name given to the silver 10 cent coin, which is a tenth part of a dollar. **Nickel** is the popular name for the five-cent American coin, made of copper and nickel. The probable origin of the **dollar sign** ($) is that it is an adaptation of the old Spanish method of recording the peseta or piece of eight as a figure eight between sloping lines (/8/).

DISTANCE OF THE HORIZON

The distance to which you can see depends on the height at which you are standing.

At a height of	You can see
5 ft.	2·9 miles
20 ft.	5·9 miles
50 ft.	9·3 miles
100 ft.	13·2 miles
500 ft.	29·5 miles
1,000 ft.	41·6 miles
2,000 ft.	58·9 miles
3,000 ft.	72·1 miles
4,000 ft.	83·3 miles
5,000 ft.	93·1 miles
20,000 ft.	186·2 miles

THE SEVEN WONDERS OF THE ANCIENT WORLD

1. **The Pyramids of Egypt** The oldest is that of Zoser, at Saggara, built about 3000 B.C. The Great Pyramid of Cheops covers more than 12 acres and was originally 481 ft. high and 756 ft. square at the base.
2. **The Hanging Gardens of Babylon** Adjoining Nebuchadnezzar's palace near Baghdad. Terraced gardens watered from storage tanks on the highest terrace.
3. **The Temple of Diana at Ephesus** A marble temple erected in honour of the goddess about 480 B.C.
4. **The Colossus of Rhodes** A bronze statue of Apollo (see A DICTIONARY OF MYTHOLOGY) with legs astride the harbour entrance of Rhodes. Set up about 280 B.C.
5. **The Tomb of Mausolus** At Halicarnassus, in Asia Minor. Built by the king's widow about 350 B.C. From it comes our word 'mausoleum'.
6. **The Statue of Olympian Zeus** At Olympia in Greece; made of marble inlaid with ivory and gold by the sculptor Phidias, about 430 B.C.
7. **The Pharos of Alexandria** Marble watch tower and lighthouse on the island of Pharos in Alexandria Harbour. Constructed about 250 B.C.

ROMAN NUMERALS

I					1	LX				60
II					2	LXX				70
III					3	LXXX				80
IV					4	XC				90
V					5	IC				99
VI					6	C				100
VII					7	CX				110
VIII					8	CXC				190
IX					9	CC				200
X					10	CCC				300
XI					11	CD				400
XII					12	D				500
XIII					13	DC				600
XIV					14	DCC				700
XV					15	DCCC				800
XVI					16	CM				900
XVII					17	XM				990
XVIII					18	M				1000
XIX					19	MLXVI				1066
XX					20	MD				1500
XXX					30	MDCCC				1800
XL					40	MCMLXXV				1975
L					50	MM				2000
LV					55					

SOME ALPHABETS

Greek

Name	Letter		English equivalent
Alpha	A	α	*a*
Beta	B	β	*b*
Gamma	Γ	γ	hard *g*
Delta	Δ	δ	*d*
Epsilon	E	ε	short *e* (as in 'egg')
Zeta	Z	ζ	*z, dz*
Eta	H	η	long *e* (as in 'bee')
Theta	Θ	θ	*th*
Iota	I	ι	*i*
Kappa	K	κ	*k* or hard *c*

Name	Letter		English equivalent
Lambda	Λ	λ	l
Mu	M	μ	m
Nu	N	ν	n
Xi	Ξ	ξ	x
Omicron	O	o	short o (as in 'box')
Pi	Π	π	p
Rho	P	ρ	r
Sigma	Σ	σ, s	s
Tau	T	τ	t
Upsilon	Υ	υ	u or y
Phi	Φ	φ	ph, f
Chi	X	χ	kh or hard ch
Psi	Ψ	ψ	ps
Omega	Ω	ω	long o (as in 'dome')

Russian

Letter	English eq	Letter	English eq
А а	a	Р р	r
Б б	b	С с	s
В в	v	Т т	t
Г г	g	У у	u
Д д	d	Ф ф	f, ph
Е е	yeh	Х х	kh as in 'loch'
Ж ж	zh	Ц ц	ts
З з	z	Ч ч	ch
И ий	e	Ш ш	sh
К к	k	Щ щ	shch
Л л	l	Ы ы	y as in 'did'
М м	m	Э э	e as in 'egg'
Н н	n	Ю ю	yu
О о	o	Я я	ya
П п	p		

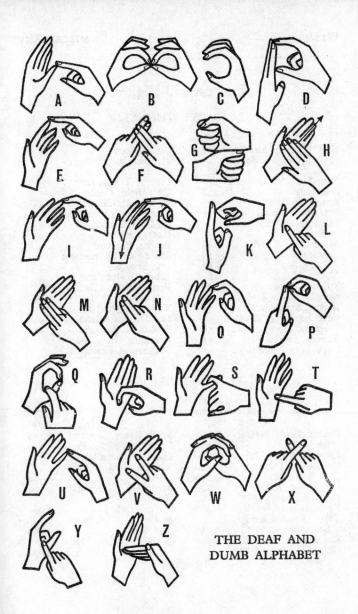

THE DEAF AND
DUMB ALPHABET

Longest and Highest

LONGEST TUNNELS

	Miles		Miles
East Finchley–Morden	17¼	Ronco, Italy . .	5
Golders Green to South		Hauenstein, Switzer-	
Wimbledon . .	16	land . . .	5
Simplon, Switzerland		Colle di Tenda, Italy .	5
to Italy . . .	12½	Connaught, Canada .	5
Appenine, Italy . .	11½	Hoosac, U.S.A. . .	4½
St Gothard, Switzerland	9¼	Sainte Marie-aux-	
Loetschberg, Switzer-		Mines, France .	4½
land . . .	9	Rove, France . .	4½
Mont Cenis, Italy .	8½	Severn, England .	4
Cascade, U.S.A. .	7¾	Mont d'Or, Switzerland	
Arlberg, Austria . .	6¼	to France . .	4
Moffat, U.S.A. . .	6	Albula, Switzerland .	4
Shimizu, Japan . .	6	Boughton to Cedera,	
Rimutaka, New Zealand	5½	S. Africa . .	3¾
Ricken, Switzerland .	5¼	Totley, England . .	3½
Grenchenberg, Swit-		Standedge, England .	3
zerland . . .	5¼	Woodhead, England .	3
Tauern, Austria . .	5¼	Puigcerda to Aix-les-	
Otira, New Zealand .	5	Thermes, France .	3

LONGEST BRIDGES

	Length of waterway in ft.		Length of waterway in ft.
Oosterscheide, Nether-		Forth Road, Scotland	6,156
lands . . .	16,476	Rio Dulce, Argentina .	5,860
Lower Zambesi, Africa	11,320	Hardinge, Bangladesh .	5,380
Storsstrom, Denmark .	10,500	Victoria Jubilee, Mon-	
Tay, Scotland . .	10,290	treal . . .	5,320
Upper Son, India .	9,840	Moerdijk, Netherlands	4,700
Godavari, India . .	8,880	Verazzano—Narrows,	
Forth Railway, Scotland	8,290	New York . .	4,260
Tay Road Bridge,		Sydney Harbour,	
Scotland . .	7,365	N.S.W. . . .	4,120
Rio Salado, Argentina	6,700	Jacques Cartier, Mon-	
Golden Gate, San		treal . . .	3,890
Francisco . .	6,200		

HIGHEST BUILDINGS AND OTHER STRUCTURES

	Feet		Feet
KTHI-TV mast, N. Dakota	2,063	G.P.O. Radio Tower London	580
TV Tower, Oklahoma City	1,572	Chicago Temple	569
Empire State, New York	1,472	Ulm Cathedral, Germany	529
ITA TV Masts, Emley Moor (Yorks), Belmont (Lincs)	1,265	Bank of State, São Paulo, Brazil	520
TV Tower, Tokyo	1,082	Blackpool Tower	518
Chrysler Building, N.Y.	1,046	Cologne Cathedral, Germany	512
ITA TV Mast, Winter Hill (Lancs)	1,015	St John the Divine, N.Y.	500
Eiffel Tower, Paris	984½	Strasbourg Cathedral	468
60 Wall Tower, N.Y.	950	The Pyramid of Cheops, Egypt	450
Bank of Manhattan, N.Y.	927	St Peter's, Rome	448
Rockefeller Centre, N.Y.	850	St Stephen's Cathedral, Vienna	441
Woolworth Building, N.Y.	792	St Joseph's Oratory, Montreal	414
Moscow State University	787	Salisbury Cathedral	404
Albert Hertzog Tower, Johannesburg	772	Antwerp Cathedral	397
City Bank, N.Y.	741	Torazzo of Cremona, Italy	397
Toronto-Dominion Bank Tower, Toronto	740	The Tower Block, Millbank Development, London	387
Terminal Tower, Cleveland	708	Freiburg Cathedral, Germany	385
Metropolitan Life, N.Y.	700	St Paul's Cathedral, London	365
TV Mast, Stuttgart	700		
500 Fifth Avenue, N.Y.	697	The Shell Centre, London	351
Chanin, N.Y.	680		
Lincoln, N.Y.	673	St Patrick's Cathedral, Melbourne	340
Husky Tower, Calgary, Canada	626		

LONGEST SHIP CANALS

	Miles		Miles
Gota, Sweden	115	Elbe–Trave, Germany	41
Suez	103	Manchester	35½
Volga–Moscow	80	Welland, Canada	27½
Albert (Antwerp–Liege)	80	Princess Juliana, Netherlands	20½
Kiel	61	Amsterdam	16½
Volga–Don, U.S.S.R.	60		
Panama	50		

A Guide to some of the most important Museums in Great Britain

NATIONAL MUSEUMS

The British Museum, Great Russell Street, London, W.C.1.
Victoria and Albert Museum, Cromwell Road, London, S.W.7.
Royal Scottish Museum, Chambers Street, Edinburgh, 1.
National Museum of Wales, Cathays Park, Cardiff.

PREHISTORY AND EARLY CIVILISATION

British Museum, Great Russell Street, London, W.C.1.
National Museum of Welsh Antiquities, University College of North Wales, College Road, Bangor.
National Museum of Antiquities of Scotland, Queen Street, Edinburgh, 2.
Pitt Rivers Museum, Parks Road, Oxford.
Ashmolean Museum, Beaumont Street, Oxford.
Fitzwilliam Museum, Cambridge.
Yorkshire Museum, Museum Street, York.
Wells Museum, Cathedral Green, Wells, Somerset.
Museum of the Glastonbury Antiquarian Society, Glastonbury.
Verulamium Museum and Roman City, St Albans, Hertfordshire.
Viroconium Museum, Wroxeter, Shropshire.
Reading Municipal Museum, Blagrave Street, Reading.
Bath Roman Museum, Abbey Churchyard, Bath.
Roman Site and Museum, Corbridge, Northumberland.
Legionary Museum, Caerlon, Wales.
Avebury Manor, Avebury, Wiltshire.
Segontium Roman Fort Museum, Beddgelert Road, Caernarvon.

NATURAL HISTORY AND GEOLOGY

British Museum (Natural History), Cromwell Road, London, S.W.7.
National Museum of Wales, Cathays Park, Cardiff.

Royal Scottish Museum (Natural History Dept.), Chambers Street, Edinburgh, 1.
Zoological Museum, British Museum, Natural History Dept., Akeman Street, Tring, Hertfordshire.
Oxford University Museum, Parks Road, Oxford.
Cambridge University Museum of Zoology, Downing Street, Cambridge.
Geological Museum, Exhibition Road, London, S.W.7.
Brooke Museum, Brighton, Sussex.
Robertson Museum and Aquarium, Marine Station, Keppel Pier, Millport, Scotland.
Hancock Museum, Barras Bridge, Newcastle-upon-Tyne, 2.
Marine Biological Station, Aquarium and Fish Hatchery, Port Erin, Isle of Man.
Cannon Hill Museum, Pershore Road, Birmingham.
Royal Botanic Gardens, Kew, London.
Botanic Gardens, Oxford.
University Botanic Gardens, Cambridge.
Zoological Gardens, Regent's Park, London: also in Edinburgh, Manchester and other big cities.

GEOGRAPHY

British Museum (Ethnographical Dept.), Great Russell Street, London, W.C.1.
Imperial Institute, South Kensington, London, S.W.7. (For the countries of the Commonwealth.)
Horniman Museum, London Road, London, S.E.23.
Royal Geographical Society Museum, 1 Kensington Gore, London, W.8.
Pitt Rivers Museum, Parks Road, Oxford.
Cambridge University Museum of Archaeology and Ethnology, Downing Street, Cambridge.
Pitt Rivers Museum, Farnham, Blandford, Dorset.

SCIENCE

Science Museum, Exhibition Road, South Kensington, London, S.W.7.
Museum of the History of Science, Broad Street, Oxford.
Whipple Museum of the History of Science, 14 Corn Exchange Street, Cambridge.

Science and Engineering Museum, Exhibition Park, Great North Road, Newcastle.

Wellcome Historical Medical Museum, 183 Euston Road, London, N.W.1. (Medical science.)

Anatomical Museum, University New Buildings, Teviot Row, Edinburgh, 8. (Medical science.)

Birmingham City Museum, Dept. of Science and Industry, Newhall Street, Birmingham, 3.

AGRICULTURE

Agricultural Museum, Wye College, Wye, Kent.

Rothamsted Experimental Agricultural Institute, Harpenden, Hertfordshire.

Reading University Dept. of Agriculture Museum, Reading, Berks.

Cambridge Agricultural Institute, Cambridge.

The Curtis Museum, High Street, Alton, Hampshire.

West Yorkshire Folk Museum, Shibden Hall, Halifax, Yorkshire.

TRANSPORT

The Museum of British Transport, Triangle Place, Clapham, London, S.W.4.

MOTOR CARS

Science Museum, Exhibition Road, South Kensington, London, S.W.7.

Museum of Carriages, Kent County Museum, Chillington, Manor House, Maidstone, Kent.

Museum of Motor Cars, Beaulieu Abbey, Brockenhurst, Hampshire.

SHIPS

Science Museum, Exhibition Road, London, S.W.7.

National Maritime Museum, Greenwich, London, S.E.10.

Royal United Service Museum, Whitehall, London, S.W.1.

Fisheries and Shipping Museum, Pickering Park, Hull.

RAILWAYS

Railway Museum, Queen Street, York.

AIRCRAFT

Science Museum, London, S.W.7.
Shuttleworth Collection, Old Warden Aerodrome, Old Warden, Bedfordshire.

PUBLIC SERVICES

Imperial War Museum, Lambeth Road, London, S.E.1.
Scottish United Service Museum, Crown Square, Edinburgh Castle, Edinburgh.
Royal Military Academy Sandhurst Museum, Camberley, Surrey.
The Armouries, Tower of London, E.C.3.
Wallace Collection, Hertford House, Manchester Square, London, W.1. (Armour.)
Glasgow Museum, Kelvingrove, Glasgow. (Armour.)
Airborne Forces Museum, Maida Barracks, Aldershot, Hampshire.
Chartered Insurance Institute Museum, 20, Aldermanbury, London, E.C.2. (Firefighting.)

SOCIAL AND DOMESTIC HISTORY

Victoria and Albert Museum, Cromwell Road, South Kensington, London, S.W.7.
London Museum, Kensington Palace, London, W.8.
Guildhall Museum, King Street, Cheapside, London, E.C.2.
Cambridge and County Folk Museum, Cambridge.
Welsh Folk Museum, St Fagan's, Glamorgan.
Stranger's Hall Folk Museum, Norwich.
York Castle Museum, Tower Street, York.
Bishop Hooper's Lodging Folk Museum, Gloucester.
Kent County Museum, Chillington Manor House, Maidstone, Kent.
Manx Village Folk Museum, Cregneash, Isle of Man.
Folk Museum, Kingussie, Inverness.

FURNITURE

Geffrye Museum, Kingsland Road, London, E.2.
Old House, High Town, Hereford.

Georgian House, Great George Street, Bristol.
Ham House, Petersham, Surrey.
Temple Newsam, Leeds.
The Pavilion, Brighton.
Iveagh Bequest, Ken Wood, London, N.W.3.

COSTUME

Victoria and Albert Museum, Cromwell Road, London, S.W.7.
Bethnal Green Museum, Cambridge Heath Road, London, E.2.
Gallery of English Costume, Platt Hall, Rusholme, Manchester, 14.
Museum of Costume, The Pavilion, Brighton, Sussex.
Canongate Tolbooth, Edinburgh, 8.
London Museum, Kensington Palace, Kensington Gardens.

CHILDREN'S MUSEUMS

Bethnal Green Museum, London, E.2. (Dolls and dolls' houses.)
Tollcross Museum, Tollcross Park, Glasgow.
Museum of Childhood, High Street, Edinburgh.

CRICKET

Imperial Cricket Memorial Gallery, Lord's Cricket Ground, London, N.W.8.

THE ARTS

National Gallery, Trafalgar Square, London, W.C.2.
National Portrait Gallery, Trafalgar Square, London, W.C.2,
Tate Gallery, Millbank, London, S.W.1. (Modern art.)
Victoria and Albert Museum, Cromwell Road, London, S.W.7.
Wallace Collection, Hereford House, Manchester Square, London, W.1.
Sir John Soane's Museum, 13 Lincoln's Inn Fields, London, W.C.2. (Architectural drawing.)
Dulwich College Picture Gallery, College Road, London, S.E.21. (Chiefly seventeenth and eighteenth centuries.)

National Gallery of Scotland, The Mound, Edinburgh, 1.
Scottish National Portrait Gallery, Queen Street, Edinburgh, 2.
National Museum of Wales, Cathays Park, Cardiff.
Fitzwilliam Museum, Cambridge.
Ashmolean Museum, Oxford.
Bowes Museum, Barnard Castle, County Durham.
Walker Art Gallery, Liverpool.
Whitworth Art Gallery, Oxford Road, Manchester.
Norwich Castle Museum, Norwich.
Barber Institute of Fine Arts, The University, Birmingham, 15.
Graves Art Gallery, Sheffield, 1.
Museum of Eastern Art, Broad Street, Oxford.
Royal College of Music, Donaldson Museum, London, S.W.7. (Musical instruments.)

MUSEUMS ILLUSTRATING THE LIVES OF FAMOUS PEOPLE

Jane Austen Jane Austen's House, Chawton, Hants.
J. M. Barrie The Birthplace, Kirriemuir, Angus, Scotland.
The Brontës Brontë Parsonage Museum, Haworth, nr. Keighley, Yorkshire.
John Bunyan Bedford Public Library, Bedford.
Robert Burns Alloway Cottage and Museum, Ayrshire.
Lord Byron Newstead Abbey, Nottinghamshire.
Sir Winston Churchill Chartwell, Westerham, Kent.
S. T. Coleridge Coleridge's Cottage, Lime Street, Nether Stowey, Somerset.
James Cook Museum of Literary and Philosophical Society, Whitby, Yorkshire.
Charles Darwin Downe House, Downe, Kent.
Charles Dickens Dickens' House, 48 Doughty Street, London, W.C.1.
Dickens' Birthplace, 393 Commercial Road, Portsmouth.
Bleak House, Broadstairs, Kent.
Francis Drake Buckland Abbey, Plymouth.
Thomas Hardy Dorset County Museum, Dorchester.
Samuel Johnson Dr Johnson's House, Breadmarket Street, Lichfield.

Dr Johnson's House, 17 Gough Square, Fleet Street, London, E.C.4.

John Keats Keats Memorial House, Wentworth Place, Keats Grove, London, N.W.3.

David Livingstone Scottish National Memorial to David Livingstone, Blantyre, Scotland.

John Milton Milton's Cottage, Chalfont St Giles, Buckinghamshire.

Horatio Nelson Nelson Museum, Glendower Street, Monmouth.

Isaac Newton The Museum, Grantham.

Cecil Rhodes Rhodes Memorial Museum, Bishop's Stortford.

Capt. Scott Polar Research Institute, Cambridge.

Walter Scott Huntley House Museum, Edinburgh, 8.

William Shakespeare Shakespeare Birthplace, Stratford-on-Avon.

New Place, Stratford-on-Avon.

Anne Hathaway's Cottage, Shottery, Warwickshire.

Mary Arden's House, Wilmcote, Warwickshire.

George Bernard Shaw Shaw's Corner, Ayot St Lawrence, Hertfordshire.

R. L. Stevenson Memorial House, Howard Place, Edinburgh.

James Watt Watt Institution, 15 Kelly Street, Greenock, Scotland.

Duke of Wellington Wellington Museum, Apsley House, Hyde Park Corner, London, W.1.

John Wesley Wesley's House, 47 City Road, London, E.C.1.

William Wilberforce Wilberforce House, Hull.

William Wordsworth Dove Cottage, Grasmere, Westmorland.

Wordsworth Museum, Grasmere, Westmorland.

Wordsworth's Birthplace, Cockermouth, Cumberland.